JAPAN'S FISCAL CRISIS

Japan's Fiscal Crisis

The Ministry of Finance and the Politics of Public Spending, 1975–2000

MAURICE WRIGHT

This book has been printed digitally and produced in a standard specification in order to ensure its continuing availability

OXFORD
UNIVERSITY PRESS

Great Clarendon Street, Oxford OX2 6DP

Oxford University Press is a department of the University of Oxford.
It furthers the University's objective of excellence in research, scholarship,
and education by publishing worldwide in

Oxford New York

Auckland Cape Town Dar es Salaam Hong Kong Karachi
Kuala Lumpur Madrid Melbourne Mexico City Nairobi
New Delhi Shanghai Taipei Toronto

With offices in

Argentina Austria Brazil Chile Czech Republic France Greece
Guatemala Hungary Italy Japan South Korea Poland Portugal
Singapore Switzerland Thailand Turkey Ukraine Vietnam

Oxford is a registered trade mark of Oxford University Press
in the UK and in certain other countries

Published in the United States
by Oxford University Press Inc., New York

© Maurice Wright, 2002

Not to be reprinted without permission
The moral rights of the author have been asserted
Database right Oxford University Press (maker)

Reprinted 2007

All rights reserved. No part of this publication may be reproduced,
stored in a retrieval system, or transmitted, in any form or by any means,
without the prior permission in writing of Oxford University Press,
or as expressly permitted by law, or under terms agreed with the appropriate
reprographics rights organization. Enquiries concerning reproduction
outside the scope of the above should be sent to the Rights Department,
Oxford University Press, at the address above

You must not circulate this book in any other binding or cover
And you must impose this same condition on any acquirer

ISBN 978-0-19-925053-0

Printed and bound by CPI Antony Rowe, Eastbourne

Preface

This is a book about Japan's Ministry of Finance, and its central budgetary system in the last quarter of the twentieth century. It is an account of its functions and roles, and its relationships with the Spending Ministries and Agencies, and the Liberal Democratic Party, in the performance of the core activity of government—deciding how much to spend and on what. It is based on research and field-work undertaken in the period 1992–2000, and is the second volume of a series of studies on budgetary systems and politics in G7 countries, a companion volume to that which dealt with the UK (Thain and Wright 1995).

I have been a frequent visitor to Japan for more than fifteen years. In the course of the research for this present book I have enjoyed the support, encouragement, and intellectual stimulation of many senior government officials, ministers, and members of political parties, and of course numerous academic colleagues as well. Most of the many intellectual debts I have incurred cannot be adequately repaid, although I hope that the publication of this book will be accepted by some of those who have contributed to its preparation as a down-payment.

At the outset of the research, I was indebted to Kogayu Masami, Administrative Vice-Minister of the Ministry of Finance 1990–1, Chairman of the Fair Trade Commission, and from 1998 Governor of the Development Bank of Japan. He arranged a visiting professorship for me at MOF in 1992–3. Matsushita Yasuo, then Governor of the Bank of Japan, and formerly Administrative Vice-Minister at MOF, 1982–4, arranged a visiting professorship for me at the Bank of Japan for 1993–4. These professorships provided unique opportunities to work inside two of the key institutions of the central executive.

Numerous other senior officials helped me to establish myself in Kasumigaseki, providing introductions to their colleagues, and 'opening doors' to other organizations. I am grateful to them all. My main debts are to Shiga Sakura, now Deputy Director-General of MOF's International Financial Bureau, formerly Deputy Commissioner at the Financial Services Agency, and earlier Budget Examiner in MOF's Budget Bureau; to Horié Masahiro, now Councillor in the Ministry of Public Management, formerly Deputy Director-General in the Management and Co-ordination Agency in the Prime Minister's Office; to Takatoshi Makato, Deputy Director-General in the Ministry of Land, Infrastructure, and Transport, formerly Director of Budget and Accounts in the Ministry of Construction, and later Director of the Co-ordination Division in the Minister's Secretariat; and to Sumi Chikahisa, Financial Counsellor at the Japanese Embassy in Washington, formerly Director of the Fiscal Investment and Loan Department in the Financial Bureau of the Ministry of Finance. All four have borne with patience and good humour my attempts to grasp the subtleties of the 'appearance and reality' of Japanese bureaucratic politics which they practise so skilfully. They have been invaluable guides through the labyrinthine processes. Yonezawa Junichirō, then an Executive Director of the Bank of Japan, formerly Director-General of MOF's Financial Bureau, was equally generous with his time and tuition. In the early stages Fujisaki Ichirō, formerly Director of Finance at the Ministry of Foreign Affairs, now Director-General of its North American Bureau, provided similar expert guidance and frank appraisal.

Numerous other senior officials in the Ministry of Finance, the Bank of Japan, and other ministries and agencies were equally generous with their time, patient with my inquiries and requests, and helpful in correcting errors and misunderstandings. Drafts of working papers, chapters, and the whole book were circulated widely among them, and, through endless hours of discussion and argument, they helped me to arrive at a fuller, if still incomplete, understanding of Japanese budgetary politics. Their comments and suggestions, together with those of my academic colleagues both here and in Japan, have helped to make the final product a more accurate and balanced account.

In the early stages of my research, Professor Itō Dai-ichi of Saitama University, and the National Graduate Institute of Policy Studies, provided invaluable help in effecting introductions to senior officials in many ministries and agencies through the medium of his own extensive network. Professor Noguchi Yukio of Tokyo University, Professor Ishi Hiromitsu, President of Hitotsubashi University, and Professor Muramatsu Michio of Kyoto University were helpful in discussions of particular facets of budget-making. In 1996–7 the Institute of Social Sciences at the University of Tokyo elected me to a visiting professorship, and I benefited greatly both from the facilities provided and from the encouragement and support of the then Director, Professor Wada Haruki, and Professors Kudō Akira and Shibuya Hiroshi.

Among the many ministers and politicians of the Liberal Democratic Party whom I interviewed, I should like to acknowledge the help provided by the late Prime Minister, Obuchi Keizō, and several ministers, former ministers, and members of the Diet, in particular Ochi Michio, formerly Minister of Financial Reconstruction; Hori Kōsuke, then Acting Chairman of the LDP's Policy Affairs Research Council, later Minister for Home Affairs; Hayashi Yoshirō, formerly Minister of Finance, then Chairman of the LDP's Tax System Research Council; and Koga Issei.

It is customary to absolve all of those who have helped with the research and preparation of a book from responsibility for its author's judgements, interpretations, and errors. I am happy of course to do so, while mindful that what appears under my name alone is a product of the contributions made in many different ways by a large number of people, of whom only a few have been mentioned above. To the larger number of unnamed officials, ministers, party members, and academics, and to the staff of the International House of Japan and its splendid library, I am grateful for their generosity, help, and encouragement, and for the unfailing friendliness they have shown towards me. Finally, my thanks to Kate Baker who, despite the continual provocation of barely legible and heavily amended text, remained cheerful throughout, deploying her consummate secretarial skills to the production of a ceaseless flow of clean drafts.

The research was supported at various times by the Economic and Social Research Council (R000/234125), the Leverhulme Trust, the Daiwa Anglo-Japan Foundation, Sheffield University's Japan Foundation Endowment Committee, and (in Japan) by the Japan Foundation and MOF. I am grateful to them all for their generous financial assistance, and for their patience.

M. W.

The Victoria University of Manchester
5 July 2001

Contents

List of Figures		ix
List of Tables		xii
Abbreviations		xiv
1	Introduction	1
2	The Origins of Japan's Fiscal Crisis	9

PART I: THE CONTEXT OF JAPANESE BUDGETING — 19

3	The Politico-Economic Context	21
4	Administrative Reform	53
5	Politicians and Bureaucrats in the Policy-Making Processes	75

PART II: INSTITUTIONS, STRUCTURES, AND ACTORS — 89

6	The Spending Ministries and Agencies	91
7	Ministerial Autonomy and Territorial Boundaries: Coordination, Competition, and Conflict in the Policy-Making Processes	114
8	The Ministry of Finance	137
9	MOF's Elite Administrators	159
10	The LDP's Policy-Making Structures	185
11	Budget Institutions and Structures	207
12	The 'Second Budget': The Fiscal Investment Loan Programme	215

PART III: INTERACTIONS — 237

13	Budget Objectives and Policies	239
14	Economic Forecasts and Fiscal Projections	264
15	Budget Strategy, Guidelines, and Ceilings	275
16	The Budget Processes in the Spending Ministries	291
17	The Budget Bureau's Hearings, Examination, and Negotiations	312
18	Rules-of-the-Game: Managing Relations with the Spending Ministries	340

19	Making the FILP Budget	346
20	The Role and Influence of the LDP in the Budgetary Processes	365

PART IV: THE OUTPUTS OF THE BUDGETARY PROCESSES — 375

21	Who Wins, Who Loses?	377
22	Cuts and Squeezes in the Bureaucracy	410
23	A 'Public Works State'	419
24	Winning and Losing in the FILP Budget	461

PART V: EFFECTS AND EFFECTIVENESS — 485

25	Fiscal Reconstruction: 'Smoke and Mirrors'	487
26	Deficits and Debt	522
27	Japan's Fiscal Performance in an International Context	537
28	FILP under Stress	551
29	Coping with Fiscal Stress	578
30	Budget Institutions, Deficits, and Debts	585

References	596
Glossary of Japanese Terms	610
Index	611

List of Figures

2.1	Underestimating economic growth, FY1955–FY1975	10
3.1	The Japanese economy, FY1947–FY2000	25
3.2	Main trends in the General Account Budget, FY1975–FY2000	49
6.1	The Organization of the functions of Central Government, 1869–1998	94
6.2	Internal organization of ministries	104
6.3	Hierarchy of 'career' officials	105
6.4	Organization of a Minister's Secretariat	106
8.1	Organization of the Ministry of Finance, 1975–2000	142
8.2	The Budget Bureau, 1975–2000	147
10.1	Organization of the LDP, 1999	186
10.2	LDP's policy-making bodies, 1975–2000	189
11.1	The central budgetary system, 1975–2000	208
12.1	Financing the road programme, FY2000	217
12.2	The FILP system, 1975–2000	219
12.3	FILP capital management operations: the postal savings financial liberalization fund, FY1987–FY2000	226
12.4	FILP capital management operations: pension fund consolidating activities, FY1987–FY2000	227
12.5	FILP interest rate system, April 1995	229
17.1	The Budget Bureau's formal hearings, 1975–2000	313
19.1	FILP policy community, 1975–2000	347
21.1	Planned and real changes in the General Account Budget, FY1975–FY2000	380
21.2	Outcome of MOF's negotiations with Spending Ministries and Agencies: delivery of the budget ceiling, FY1975–FY1998	382
21.3	Ratio of current to capital expenditures in the General Account Budget, FY1980–FY2000	383
21.4	The Defence budget: size and share of general expenditures, FY1975–FY2000	392
21.5	'Winners and losers': policy groups, FY1975–FY2000	393
21.6	Planned and real changes in the budget for the small businesses programme, FY1976–FY2000	395
21.7	'Unequal misery': changes in the budget allocations for Social Security Programmes in the Period of Fiscal Reconstruction, FY1980–FY1987	397
21.8	'Swings and roundabouts': changes in the budget allocations for Education and Science Sub-programmes in a Period of Fiscal Expansion, FY1988–FY2000	399
21.9	Changes in the Budget Shares of the Science and Technology Sub-programmes, FY1975–FY2000	400
21.10	Ministerial shares of the Budget for the Small Businesses Programme, FY1975–FY2000	402

List of Figures

23.1	Budget guidelines and planned allocations of public works expenditure, FY1975–FY2000	424
23.2	Planned and real changes in the public works' budget, FY1975–FY2000	426
23.3	Planned and real changes in public works' share of the budget, FY1975–FY2000	427
23.4	Budget and 'Off-Budget' public works' spending, FY1976–FY2000	433
23.5	Changing allocations to public works' programmes in the General Account Budget, FY1946–FY1999	438
23.6	Changing composition of the public works' budget, FY1965–FY1999	439
24.1	The growth of FILP and the General Account Budget, FY1975–FY2000	462
24.2	FILP and the General Account Budget: proportions of GDP, FY1975–FY2000	463
24.3	Planned and real changes in the FILP Budget, FY1975–FY2000	464
24.4	The squeeze on the Investment and Loan Programme in the FILP Budget, FY1975–FY2000	465
24.5	Planned and real changes in the Investment and Loan Programme in the FILP Budget, FY1987–FY1999	466
24.6	FILP agencies: Winners and Losers in FY1976 compared with FY1996	469
24.7	Annual allocations to FILP Agencies: 'Winners and Losers', FY1976–FY1996	470
24.8	FILP policy areas: 'Winners and Losers' in FY1975 compared with FY1996	472
24.9	Annual allocations to FILP policy areas: 'Winners and Losers', FY1975–FY1996	473
25.1	Revenue and expenditure in the period of fiscal reconstruction, FY1980–FY1987	488
25.2	Tax burden in Japan and G7 countries, FY1996–FY2000	495
25.3	Tax revenues: shortages and surpluses, FY1965–FY1999	497
25.4	Ratio of central government bonds issued to planned and actual budget totals, FY1975–FY2000	499
25.5	Central government bonds outstanding, FY1975–FY2000	500
25.6	Servicing central government debt, FY1975–FY2000	501
25.7	Fiscal rigidity: the squeeze on general expenditures in the General Account Budget, FY1965–FY2000	502
26.1	General Government expenditure FY1975–FY1998	523
26.2	Central and local shares of General Government expenditure, FY1975–FY1998	524
26.3	General Government fiscal balance, FY1975–FY1998	527
26.4	Composition of the fiscal balance of General Government, FY1975–FY1998	528
26.5	Profiles of fiscal balances of General Government, FY1975–FY1998	530
26.6	General Government gross debt, FY1975–FY1998	531

List of Figures

26.7	Profiles of General Government gross and net debt, FY1969–FY2000	532
26.8	Composition of General Government gross debt, FY1975–FY1998	534
27.1	Cumulative economic growth: Japan and G7, FY1989–FY1998	538
27.2	General government expenditure in G7, CY1975–CY1999	539
27.3	General government fiscal balances in G7, CY1990–CY2000	541
27.4	General Government Gross Financial Liabilities in G7, CY1975–CY2000	542
27.5	Fiscal balances of central/federal governments in G7, CY1990–CY1999	544
27.6	Ratio of fiscal deficits to budget expenditures in central/federal governments in G7, FY1973–FY1997	545
27.7	Government bonds outstanding in G7, FY1973–FY1996	546
27.8	Ratio of interest payments to Budget expenditures in central/federal governments in G7, FY1973–FY1997	547
28.1	The structure of FILP, April 2001	571

List of Tables

2.1	Growth of public spending, FY1965–FY1974	14
2.2	Tax revenues and expenditures, FY1971–FY1982	16
2.3	The fiscal deficit, FY1971–FY1982	16
2.4	Central Government borrowing, FY1971–FY1982	17
2.5	Rising costs of Government borrowing, FY1971–FY1982	18
3.1	Prime Ministers and Governments, 1975–2000	38
4.1	Regulations issued by ministries and agencies, FY1986–FY1996	63
6.1	Ministries, commissions, and agencies, FY1975–FY2000	92
6.2	The organizational jurisdiction and patronage of spending ministries and agencies, 1996–1997	102
6.3	Ministries, commissions, and agencies, 2001	111
8.1	MOF officials, FY1997 and FY1999	140
8.2	Public banks and finance corporations within MOF's jurisdiction, 1975–1997	154
9.1	MOF's elite intake: university and faculty, 1975–1997	161
9.2	Undergraduate recruitment to Tokyo University for 1998	162
9.3	Career progression of MOF's administrative vice-ministers, 1975–2000	171
9.4	MOF *amakudari kanryō* on boards of private banks, 1975–1993	177
9.5	MOF's patronage: public banks and finance corporations, 1997	180
9.6	The MOF 'family' of former administrative vice-ministers, 1994	181
9.7	MOF bureaucrats in the Diet, 1966–1997	183
10.1	The making of a welfare *zoku* boss: the career of Hashimoto Ryūtarō	195
10.2	The role and influence of *zoku-giin* on sectoral policy-making, 1975–1993	196
10.3	Reciprocal obligations of Spending Ministries, *zoku-giin* and interest groups	199
10.4	The 'profit-inspired' nexus: a typology of *zoku-giin*	200
12.1	Trust Fund Bureau Fund: balance of accumulated deposits, March 1999	224
12.2	Composition of FILP Budget funds, March 1999	225
12.3	Organizations in receipt of FILP funds, FY1998, and their sponsoring ministries and agencies	231
12.4	Local bond plan for FY1997	235
13.1	Programme 'caps' in the general account initial budget, FY1998–FY2000	261
14.1	The credibility gap: estimates and out-turns of GDP, tax revenues, and borrowing, FY1992–FY2000	273
15.1	Summary of the main budget guidelines, FY1961–FY2000	279
15.2	Guidelines for the budget requests for FY1996	284

List of Tables

17.1	The stages and main players in the Revival Theatricals, 1975–2000	337
18.1	The behavioural norms of Budget Bureau officials	342
22.1	Public-sector employment, March 1998	410
22.2	Central government employees, March 1998	411
22.3	Squeezing the central government, FY1967–FY1997	414
22.4	Spending ministries and agencies: staff numbers, FY1967–FY1997	416
22.5	Administrative core of the central executive, FY1967–FY1995	418
23.1	Gross domestic investment in the public and private sectors, FY1990–FY1997	419
23.2	Ministries' long-term sectoral plans and investments, 1996–2006	423
23.3	Public works planned spending in countercyclical fiscal packages, 1992–2000	428
23.4	Allocation of public works spending among ministries and agencies, FY1965–FY1999	435
23.5	Functional composition of the ministry of construction's public works budget, FY1980–FY1999	441
23.6	Functional composition of the ministry of transport's public works budget, FY1980–FY1998	442
23.7	Functional composition of MAFF's public works budget, FY1980–FY1998	443
24.1	Functional classification of the allocation of FILP funds by policy area, FY1975–FY2000	471
24.2	Changing priorities of the FILP Budget: budget outputs by policy areas, FY1955–FY2000	473
24.3	Social and industrial investment in the FILP Budget, FY1955–FY2000	475
24.4	Japan Development Bank: planned allocations, FY1994	477
24.5	Composition of the FILP Budget by allocation to agencies, FY1994	479
24.6	Functional balance of outstanding loans and investments among FILP Agencies, 31 March 1998	481
25.1	Increasing burden of taxation in the period of fiscal reconstruction, FY1980–FY1987	489
25.2	Ratio of direct and indirect tax revenues in the General Account Budget, FY1980–FY1989	491
25.3	Composition of central government tax revenues, FY1988 and FY1990	492
25.4	National consumption tax, FY1989–FY1999	492
25.5	Planned and actual changes in general expenditures in the General Account Budget, FY1981–FY1988	505
25.6	Deferred liquidation of the national debt, FY1982–FY1998	514
26.1	Changing composition of General Government expenditure, FY1975–FY1998	525
28.1	Direct subsidies to FILP agencies from the General Account Budget, FY1977–FY1996	558
28.2	Over-funding the investment and loan programme, FY1975–FY1997	560

Abbreviations

AFFFC	Agriculture, Forestry, and Fisheries Finance Corporation
AMA	Administrative Management Agency
ARC	Administrative Reform Council
BAD	Budget and Accounts Division
BE	Budget examiner
BOJ	Bank of Japan
CD	Coordination Division
CY	Calendar year
DA	Defence Agency
DBE	Deputy budget examiner
DBJ	Development Bank of Japan
DDG	Deputy director-general (of a Bureau)
D-G	Director-general (of a Bureau)
EA	Environment Agency
EMU	European Monetary Union
EPA	Economic Planning Agency
EXIM	Export–Import Bank
FILP	Fiscal Investment and Loan Programme
FSA	Financial Services Agency
FSRC	Fiscal System Research Council
FTC	Fair Trade Commission
FY	Fiscal Year
G7	Group of Seven (industrial countries)
GATT	General Agreement on Tariffs and Trade
GDP	Gross domestic product
GG	General Government
GGE	General government expenditure
GHLC	Government Housing Loan Corporation
HC	House of Councillors
HDA	Hokkaido Development Agency
HR	House of Representatives
HUDC	Housing and Urban Development Corporation
IAM	Institute of Administrative Management
IMF	International Monetary Fund
JBIC	Japan Bank for International Cooperation
JDB	Japan Development Bank
JEI	Japanese Economic Institute
JFCME	Japan Finance Corporation for Municipal Enterprises
JICA	Japan International Cooperation Agency
JNR	Japan National Railways
JSP	Japan Socialist Party
LDP	Liberal Democratic Party
MAFF	Ministry of Agriculture, Food, and Fisheries
MCA	Management and Coordination Agency

Abbreviations

MHA	Ministry of Home Affairs
MHW	Ministry of Health and Welfare
MITI	Ministry of International Trade and Industry
MOC	Ministry of Construction
MOE	Ministry of Education
MOF	Ministry of Finance
MOFA	Ministry of Foreign Affairs
MOJ	Ministry of Justice
MOL	Ministry of Labour
MOT	Ministry of Transport
MPT	Ministry of Posts and Telecommunications
NLA	National Land Agency
NPA	National Personnel Agency
NTAA	National Tax Administration Agency
NTT	Nippon Telephone and Telegraph
ODA	Overseas Development Aid
OECD	Organization for Economic Cooperation and Development
OECF	Overseas Economic Cooperation Fund
OkDA	Okinawa Development Agency
OTCA	Overseas Technical Cooperation Agency
PARC	Policy Affairs Research Council (of the LDP)
PC	Public Corporation
PCA	Policy Cost Analysis (MOF)
PCC	Policy Coordinating Council
PCPAR	Provisional Council for the Promotion of Administrative Reform
PFC	Public Finance Corporation
Rinchō	Rinji Gyōsei Chōsakai [Second Provisional Commission on Administrative Reform]
RPD	Research and planning division
SCAP	Supreme Commander Allied Powers
SDF	Self-Defence Force
SDP	Social Democratic Party (*until 1996, Japan Socialist Party*)
SII	Structural Impediments Initiative
SMEs	Small and medium-sized enterprises
SNA	System of National Accounts
SNTV	Single Non-Transferable Vote
STA	Science and Technology Agency
TFBF	Trust Fund Bureau Fund
VANs	Value Added Networks

1

Introduction

Japan, the world's second economic power and its largest creditor nation, has been in crisis for more than a decade. Its economy has been depressed or in recession for most of that time, its banking sector in a chronically critical state, and its public sector burdened by recurring fiscal deficits and mounting debt. The collapse of the *economic bubble* at the end of 1990 triggered the longest recession in Japan's post-war history, and precipitated the most serious financial and fiscal crisis since the 1930s. After the briefest of respites, the economy plunged into a still steeper decline in 1997, from which it was emerging only falteringly in 2000, and to which it returned a year later. A decade earlier, such was the apparently unstoppable progress of its economy, the strength of its currency, and the breadth of its commercial and trade imperialism through direct investment in the USA, Europe, and the emerging markets of China and East Asia, that Japan's capacity to play the hegemonic role in global trade and financial markets assumed by the USA since the Second World War, and a possible future Pax Japonica, was seriously debated.

The reversal in Japan's economic fortunes, combined with the (temporary) end of the LDP's thirty-eight years of rule in 1993, and the political turbulence that ensued raised, and continues to provoke, questions about the continuing effectiveness of Japanese institutions, and about the relationships between politicians, bureaucrats, and businessmen in organizations that underpinned many of those institutions. This book addresses and questions the effectiveness of one of them, the central government's budgetary system, in the last quarter of the twentieth century.

Any adequate explanation must include an assessment of the processes through which expenditure policies were made and carried out, processes historically dominated by the country's Ministry of Finance (MOF) wielding a formidable array of economic, financial, and fiscal powers. By the end of the twentieth century, however, MOF was no longer the dominant and dominating force at the heart of the central executive that it had been in the era of high growth in the 1960s and early 1970s. Sclerotic, frequently paralysed in its response to events, it was obliged in the 1990s to surrender to other bodies some of its formal powers. The declared intention of the reform of the central executive enacted in 1998 was to reduce MOF's role in central government still further, to that of a ministry of the budget. By 6 January 2001, the **Ōkurashō** had become the **Zaimshō**.

At one level, this book can be read as an historical account of the fiscal factors that contributed to MOF's decline and fall, if such it proves to be when viewed from the detachment of a still longer perspective. But that is not its prime purpose. Its main aim is to provide a comprehensive account of Japan's central budgetary system: to show how budgets were made, and by whom, situated within the historical contexts of the evolution and development of the economy, the polity, and the administration during the last quarter of the twentieth century. It focuses on the institutions of central government, the roles and contributions of the participants in formal organizations, and the policy and behavioural rules-of-the-game by which their interactions were regulated. It also assesses who or what won and lost in the budgetary game, and why.

MOF's structure, organization, and role in policy-making, its relationships with the Spending Ministries and Agencies, and the processes through which decisions were made about how much to spend and on what are the central concerns of this book. It deals mainly with the two central government budgets: the General Account Budget, and the Fiscal Investment and Loan Programme (FILP), the so-called 'second budget'. It does not deal with local government finance, apart from the determination centrally of the aggregates of local governments' current and capital spending, and borrowing. Nor does it deal with the quality of provision in health, welfare, education, defence, and other services financed through the central budgets, nor with the dynamics of change in those services. Its main concern is with the processes that determined the amount and distribution of public spending, and with the consequential budget deficits and debts to which they gave rise. The book focuses on the pre-Diet stages of budget planning, formulation, and allocation. The Diet's main contribution was made after the Cabinet had approved MOF's draft budgets following the conclusion of the negotiations between MOF and the Spending Ministries in the autumn. The issue of the accountability of MOF and the Spending Ministries and Agencies to the Diet is therefore dealt with only indirectly.

The broad theoretical stance on budgeting adopted here comes closest to that of Aaron Wildavsky in his last books and articles, where he argued a cultural theory of government growth: that the kind of organizations, the processes of decision-making in them, and the norms of the budgetary behaviour of ministers and officials determine policy preferences and hence outputs (Wildavsky 1988). That general theoretical perspective is informed by the methods of historico-analysis which I have developed and employed in other studies of public policy (Wilks and Wright 1987, 1991; Wright 1988*a*,*b*; 1991), and in particular in the study of the UK's Treasury and its planning and control of public spending (Thain and Wright 1995). I have argued and demonstrated that the study of the processes of a particular policy sector such as education or health or, as here, a meta policy sector such as budgeting requires the simultaneous contextualization provided by the macro-level analysis of the development of that sector, for example the historical role of the state through institutions such as the economy, the polity, the bureaucracy in that sector, and the relationships between the principal participants in its constituent organizations, and the macroeconomic and political objectives and policies of successive governments. 'Institutions connect the past with the present and the future so that history is a largely incremental story of institutional evolution in which the historical performance of economies can only be understood as part of a sequential story' (North 1990: 12). The 'story' of the institution of budgeting (and of MOF, its core organization) vividly demonstrates the connectedness of past and present, and of 'path-dependent' incremental policy-making.

Introduction

Of the three main variants of institutionalism identified by Hall and Taylor (1996), the approach here combines the methods and insights of the 'historical institutionalists' rather than 'rat-choicers' or those who prefer a sociological perspective. It is concerned with the origins and evolution of institutions, with how and why they change, and with the consequences of those changes for the dynamics of policy changes and policy outputs. Institutions have rules, procedures, and systems of authority; they allocate roles, impose obligations and duties, and place expectations on the behaviour of members of their constituent organizations. They

> regulate the use of authority and power and provide actors with resources, legitimacy, standards of evaluation, perceptions, identities and a set of meanings. They provide a set of rules, compliance procedures, and moral and ethical behavioural norms, which buffer environmental influence, modify individual motives, regulate self-interest behaviour and create order and meaning. (Olsen 1988: 6)

The book begins by tracing the origins of the fiscal crisis that emerged in the mid-1970s, and describes the symptoms and characteristics that persisted for the rest of the century. The fiscal *problematique* confronting MOF during that period can be briefly stated: fast-rising expenditure; inadequate revenue-growth; burgeoning fiscal deficits; heavy and continuous government borrowing; and accumulating debt. As the costs of servicing that debt absorbed an increasing proportion of total spending, the amount available to finance both mandatory and discretionary expenditures, themselves subjected to the pressure of the new 'welfare politics' inaugurated in 1973, was progressively squeezed. To those difficulties were added the imminent prospect of an increasing ratio of the elderly to the working population, imposing an additional burden of costs for expanded and new social security, pensions, health, and welfare programmes; and fewer wage-earners and tax-payers to generate additional revenues.

Part I provides the politico-economic, administrative, and bureaucratic contexts for the analysis in later chapters of the formal and informal budget institutions, structures, and processes within which MOF's policies were evolved, formulated, and implemented as it responded to the condition of continuing fiscal stress. Chapter 3 provides a general overview of the evolution of the political economy over the twenty-five-year period, from the emergence of that crisis in the mid-1970s, and identifies some of the main changes in the structures of the economy and the polity. Chapter 4 assesses the extent to which the administrative reform movement in the 1980s changed the administrative context within which the budgetary system was operated. Chapter 5 examines the roles and interactions of bureaucrats and politicians in a review of competing and conflicting explanations of policy-making in the Japanese policy processes, and argues that the more nuanced analysis of policy-making adopted in this book allows us to observe and assess the impact on fiscal policies of the role of the state, including its transnational dimension, its institutional structures, and their embedded 'collective identities'.

Within the historical 'setting' of those institutional structures, the remainder of the book focuses on organizations, actors, interactions, and outputs, combining and integrating the approaches and insights of the historical institutionalists. Part II examines the formal organizations, their authority, powers, and roles, and the processes through which fiscal policies were initiated, formulated, 'succeeded', changed, and carried out. Besides the formal processes, there is also the observance of policy and behavioural rules-of-the-game which structure the informal processes through which those organizations operate, and their members interact within the formal contours that prescribe their constitutional and statutory functions and roles. The rules-of-the-game, and their interpretation and application to the particularity of events and circumstances, are shaped by the values, norms, and collective identities that at one level characterize individual institutions, such as the economy or the bureaucracy, and that at another level have evolved and developed within particular organizations, such as *a* ministry or *a* political party, or *a* part of an organization—the Ministry of Finance's Budget Bureau rather than its Financial Bureau, for example.

Part III uses the historical and contextual setting of institutions, structures, and organizations established in the first two parts to situate the exposition and analysis of the budget processes of planning and controlling public spending in both MOF and the Spending Ministries and Agencies in the compilation of both the General Account Budget and Fiscal Investment and Loan Programme (FILP). The role and influence of the Liberal Democratic Party (LDP) in those processes are examined in each chapter, and assessed overall in Chapter 20. The outputs of the budget processes are examined in Part IV. Chapters 21 and 22 assess which ministries and agencies and what programmes gained or lost over the twenty-five-year period, and accounts for their success and failure. Because of the special place of public works in Japan's political economy, the outputs of those programmes are dealt with separately in Chapter 23, which provides evidence of the growth and maintenance of a 'a public works state', and shows how MOF and the LDP continued to finance it by the adroit manipulation of 'off-budget' sources. Chapter 24 examines FILP's outputs.

The concluding part of the book brings together the analysis and arguments of the previous chapters in a wide-ranging assessment of the effects and effectiveness of the budgetary system. First, it assesses the extent to which MOF achieved its short- and medium-term fiscal objectives, and contrasts the appearance of growing fiscal discipline from the early 1980s with the reality of the deteriorating state of the public finances. Secondly, it sets MOF's performance with central government finances in the wider national context, comparing the profiles of outlays, fiscal deficits, and debts of central government with those of other parts of the public sector. Next, the national context is broadened by comparing the fiscal performance of Japan's central government with that of other G7 countries. The final three chapters examine the origins, evolution, and implications of tensions in the fiscal system. The expansion of FILP, and its exploitation as an instrument of general financial management, contributed to its crisis of identity and function, as financial markets were progressively deregulated and liberalized, precipitating a review of its fiscal role and functions in 1997–8 and the decision to sever the historic statutory link between FILP and its main source of funds, postal savings and pension fund reserves. As budget deficits and public debt burgeoned at the end of the millennium, the penultimate chapter explains the main reasons for MOF's difficulty in dealing effectively with the causes of continuing fiscal stress throughout the previous twenty-five years. It also explains why the organization and roles of Japan's public sector were little changed in the 1980s and 1990s compared with experience in other G7 and OECD countries, and why conditions of continuous fiscal crisis did not serve, as they did there, as a catalyst for radical administrative and economic reform. The book concludes with a brief discussion of the relationships between budget institutions and fiscal performance, and considers whether a reconfiguration of Japan's budget institutions and structures would be conducive to the more favourable fiscal outcomes found in other G7 countries.

The conventional explanation of MOF's performance in response to the fiscal crisis that emerged in the mid-1970s is that through, first, policies of 'fiscal reconstruction' and then 'consolidation', it gradually regained control of public spending in the 1980s, successfully reasserted and re-established the principles of fiscal discipline relaxed in the years of Tanaka Kakuei's dominant and dominating leadership of the LDP, and, in consequence, presided over a decade of declining deficits and debts (see e.g. Pempel and Muramatsu 1995; Miyajima 1988). The culmination of that apparently successful period of budget retrenchment was the elimination (temporarily) of special deficit-financing bonds in 1990, an event mistakenly perceived by some academic writers as the achievement of MOF's main fiscal objective, the restoration of a balanced budget (Brown 1999; Suzuki 1999).

This book challenges and contradicts that view. Its central argument is that MOF failed to achieve not only the restoration of a balanced budget, but, other than briefly, both its short-term and medium-term objectives for public spending throughout the whole of the period 1975–2000 as well. It demonstrates that its policies for fiscal reconstruction in the 1980s failed to restrain the growth of both the General Account Budget and FILP, and to restore balance to the former. The appearance and rhetoric of control and fiscal discipline were belied by the reality of a continuing and deepening fiscal crisis which persisted throughout the whole of the 1980s and 1990s. The critical state of the central government's finances was obscured by the opacity and complexity of the budgetary system, by MOF's expedient exploitation of available off-budget sources of finance, and its adroit manipulation of cash flow transactions between the General Account Budget and Supplementary Budgets, some of the 38 Special Accounts, and FILP. By such means, MOF was able to obtain temporary relief for the symptoms of the stressed main budget. It was not, however, able to remedy the fundamental causes of the chronic crisis. Towards the end of the 1980s the critical underlying state of the public finances was exacerbated first by the fiscal implications of the 'bubble economy' and then in the 1990s by recessionary conditions which dogged the economy for almost the whole of the decade.

The causes of that failure were however only partly conjunctural—the business cycle, and international events, pressures, and stimuli. They were mainly the result of inherent constitutional and practical limitations to the exercise of MOF's control, and to the institutionalization of the role and influence of the LDP in the policy processes. MOF was unable, unwilling, or frustrated in its attempts to dictate to Spending Ministries and Agencies, or to impose its strategies upon them. Their relationships were interdependent; their room for discretionary manoeuvre mutually constrained. The paradigm of the politics of public spending at the heart of Japanese central government in the last quarter of the twentieth century was negotiated discretion, as it had been in the UK for most of the same period of time (Thain and Wright 1995).

There is no recent comprehensive and authoritative account in either Japanese or English of the Japanese central budgetary system, and spending policies and politics, for the period covered by this book. Some studies in Japanese deal with parts of the system, and with particular budgetary and fiscal issues (see e.g. Ishi 2000). The present book aims to fill that gap, complementing Katō Junko's (1994) account of taxation policies and politics, while seeking to provide an historical account of central budgeting comparable to that which Campbell (1977) produced for an earlier era. Repeated references to the latter in contemporary literature, especially by American scholars of public policy, attest to the continuing lack of a more up-to-date account. While much of what is said there remains relevant to the principles, less so to the practice of budgeting 25 years on, the economic and administrative contexts have inevitably changed profoundly. In the early 1970s there were few symptoms of fiscal stress, none of the impending crisis in the national finances that was to dog MOF after the first oil crisis; the central budget had become unbalanced only recently (1965), and modestly; the 'welfare era' and the rapid growth of public spending to which it contributed had scarcely begun.

This book can be read, then, in conjunction with Campbell's account as an historical record of Japan's post-war budgeting, although his approach and focus were narrower than that adopted here, most obviously in his treatment of FILP. As I shall explain, FILP was even then, and more so subsequently, a 'second budget', crucial to the operation of the whole budgetary system.

FILP is better served than the General Account Budget in contemporary secondary literature, mainly by Japanese scholars, but their focus has been mainly on the economic effects of FILP's contribution to economic growth, the development of particular industrial sectors, and assessments of the significance of steered funds on the success of the post-war Japanese economy. Its political and fiscal roles as a 'second budget' have attracted less attention. There is no comprehensive account in English. The book aims to fill that gap by providing an analysis of the purpose, role, and significance of FILP in central government budgeting. In particular, it focuses on the relationship between the General Account and FILP budgets after the adoption of the policies of fiscal reconstruction in 1980. Here there are three main issues: first, the extent to which the rapid growth of FILP, and the reorientation of its funding to the financing of social, welfare, and environmental programmes consistent with changing national goals, enabled MOF to relieve pressure on the General Account Budget, and to reduce the level of government borrowing, and progress towards the prime budgetary objective of reducing the fiscal deficit and GDP–debt ratio. A second set of issues is concerned with the use of FILP as an alternative to the General Account Budget, and the extent to which transfers between the two (and some Special Accounts) also enabled MOF to relieve short-term fiscal pressure. Thirdly, the book explains the sources and symptoms of growing tensions in the operation of FILP as a 'second budget', as it was progressively integrated into a general public fiscal system, precipitating the review of its purpose and role and reform implemented from 2001.

Japanese scholars of the central budgetary system have little to say about the budget processes through which budgets are evolved, formulated, negotiated, and carried out, concerned as they are more with the formal institutions and organizations, and their constitutional and legal powers, duties, and roles (see e.g. Ishi 2000; Shibata 1993; and Masujima and O'uchi 1995). While those provide the basic framework, and hence an essential starting point for an analysis of the budgetary system, they are an incomplete guide to the policy processes and the relationships between those who participate in them. My main sources for those were the evidence, triangulated wherever possible, of first-hand interviews with senior bureaucrats, politicians, and Diet officials. In the Budget, Tax, and Financial Bureaux of MOF and its Secretariat I interviewed at all levels, from the deputy director of a division to director-general of a bureau and administrative vice-minister. Among several former senior officials of MOF whom I interviewed were five former administrative vice-ministers, all of whom had served as director-general of the Budget Bureau. Data on budget-making in the (then) 22 Spending Ministries and Agencies was obtained mainly through interviews with those senior officials responsible for the coordination of budgeting in their Budget and Accounts divisions. They helped me to construct a picture of budget compilation from a different and complementary perspective to that of MOF, and provided a necessary corrective to a MOF-centric account. It helped to reduce the risk that I had become too closely identified with the perspective of the Budget Bureau examiners. I also interviewed senior officials in the Prime Minister's Office, in the Management and Coordination Agency, and in the Economic and Planning Agency (EPA), and ministers and former ministers in the LDP, and some senior politicians and officials in other parties as well. In all, I interviewed and re-interviewed more than 150 bureaucrats and politicians between 1992 and 2000. In all but a handful of cases, the interviews were conducted in English. Most senior officials have acquired proficiency in the language from time abroad in academic study as part of their earlier formal training, and through career postings to Japanese embassies or international organizations such as IMF and the World Bank. This was less true of ministers and party officials, and I am grateful to MOF for providing the services of various officials as interpreters on those and some other occasions. Interviewing in English had the additional advantage that it was normally unconstrained by those social conventions and contexts customarily observed in Japanese discourse.

My preferred method, tried and tested in the study of the UK's Treasury, was the open-ended interview, undertaken after I had informed myself as fully as possible from the materials available in the public domain. Each interview was conducted as a continuous seminar discussion keyed to an agenda of identified issues. Most took the form of a continuous, informal, progressive, and flexible dialogue lasting some one and a half to two hours; some lasted even longer. Subsequently I made a detailed record of the discussion, structured and organized around the themes and issues discussed in the interview. In this way I accumulated a rich source of material comprising documents of some 2,000–4,500 words in length which were drawn upon in the preparation of working papers. Interviewing and re-interviewing in MOF and the Spending Ministries enabled me to construct, verify, and refine the analysis and interpretation of events and issues as the research and writing progressed. Some of the principal interviewees were invited to comment on revised drafts of those working papers and, later, chapters of the book based on them. In all, I wrote and circulated more than forty.

Throughout the text, Japanese family names appear before given names. Macron marks are used where relevant, apart from words that have become anglicized. Technical terms are explained where necessary at appropriate places. Two used throughout the book require some brief explanation here. Japan's fiscal year runs from 1 April to 31 March, the same as the UK's; that of the USA runs from 1 October to 30 September. Unless otherwise indicated, budget data for Japan are presented and analysed on a fiscal year (FY) rather than a calendar year (CY) basis. Data in Japan's *National Accounts* are collected and presented in both forms, but most of MOF's time-series budget data are collected only on a FY basis; OECD and IMF data are normally published on a CY basis. The difference between FY and CY values for the same economic variable—GDP or general government outlays, deficits and debts, for example—can be substantial. Monetary values are given in yen, and for convenience normally in trillions. One trillion is equal to a thousand billion; a billion equals a thousand million; thus, the planned expenditure for the central government's General Account Budget for FY 2000 was 84.987 trillion or 84,987 billion, or 84,987,000 million. At May 2001 exchange rates that was roughly £475 billion (more than twice the UK's central budget) or $685 billion (approximately a third the size of the US Federal Budget).

There are three key guides for the reader. First, Figure 3.2 summarizes the major trends in the politico-economy from 1975 to 2000. Second, Table 3.1 lists prime ministers, their governments, and the results of the general elections for the House of Representatives. Finally, Figure 6.3 presents the nomenclature of Japan's hierarchy of elite officials, whose roles are briefly explained in Chapter 6.

2

The Origins of Japan's Fiscal Crisis

Both the cause and the chronic nature of Japan's fiscal crisis in the period 1975–2000 were due to a fundamental imbalance in the politico-economic forces which determined the size and composition of the annual General Account and FILP Budgets. Simply stated, there was an elasticity of demand for public spending, and a relative inelasticity of the supply of tax revenues to finance it. Over the whole period, revenues from taxation generally grew more slowly than the expenditures of central and local government financed through the General Account Budget. The resulting deficits were covered by government borrowing through the issue of government bonds, the annual servicing of which absorbed progressively more of the total of the General Account Budget, and squeezed the residual amount available for mandatory and discretionary expenditures.

This chapter traces the origins of the fiscal crisis, and describes its symptoms and enduring characteristics. Later chapters examine the aims and objectives of policies to treat those symptoms and to remedy its underlying causes. Here I begin with a brief review of the post-war period up to 1965, when the main budgetary aim was to achieve a balance between revenue and expenditure in the General Account Budget. I then explain how and why the budget became unbalanced as Japan entered the 'welfare era', at the beginning of the 1970s, examining both its long-term underlying causes—a combination of rising public spending, a 'decelerating economy', and revenue shortage—and the short-term, proximate causes which precipitated urgent action by MOF in 1975.

FISCAL BALANCE, 1949–1965

From 1949 onwards, the main policy objective for public spending of MOF and successive LDP governments was to balance the budget. The principle was introduced along with other recommendations for reconstructing the budgetary system by Joseph Dodge—the so-called 'Dodge Line'—at the time of the Allied Occupation in 1949. Such action had become necessary as a result of the growing burden of public debt, as post-war governments borrowed to cover the deficit on their spending programmes. For the next 16 years the objective of a balanced budget was achieved—indeed, over-fulfilled, as measured by the 'natural increases' of revenues accruing from the difference between the planned and out-turn yields of direct and indirect taxation.

Throughout the high-growth era, tax policy was regulated by the informal rule-of-the-game that the tax burden should not exceed 20% of national income. The means to implement it were provided by 'natural tax increases'. In almost every year prior to 1975, MOF was able to deliver tax reductions financed by such growth. The 'natural increase' was created intentionally by underestimating the amount of tax revenues appropriated for government spending at the time of compiling the General Account Budget. During the course of the fiscal year, 'natural increases' beyond that amount emerged as GDP grew at a faster rate than that also intentionally underestimated. Figure 2.1 shows the difference between the forecasted and out-turn levels of GDP in the high-growth area.

Although there were years of slower growth, the trend rate of growth of GDP was comfortably in double figures, boosted from 1960 by Prime Minister Ikeda's 'Income Doubling Plan', which envisaged a doubling of Japan's GDP within ten years. High rates of economic growth provided the means not only to finance large annual increases in public spending from buoyant tax revenues, but simultaneously to allow cuts in taxation. Other capital spending and loans were financed through the 'second budget', the Fiscal Investment and Loans Programme (FILP), and through numerous mainly self-financing Special Accounts. FILP's funds were drawn mainly from postal savings accounts and national pension funds, and helped to absorb the huge surplus of domestic household savings. In the 1950s FILP's budget was a third of the size of the General Account Budget, and absorbed about 4% of GDP. By 1965 it had grown to two-fifths the size of the General Account.

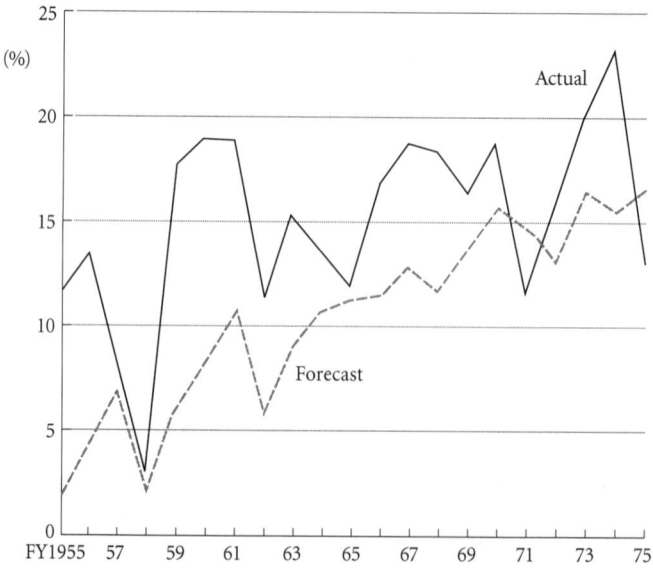

Figure 2.1   *Underestimating economic growth, FY1955–FY1975*
Nominal GDP; annual percentage change

Source: *Annual Report on National Accounts* (annually), EPA; *Zaisei Tōkei*, (annually), Budget Bureau, MOF.

The growth of public spending financed through taxation and savings enabled LDP governments from 1955 onwards to reward and compensate their supporters, drawn at that time mainly from the rural areas. Political support for the national goal of economic growth could be mobilized and maintained by the manipulation of public spending programmes, as LDP politicians became progressively more involved in the budgetary process. Pursuing a 'policy of positive-sum politics in a high-growth economy ... the LDP [responded] to public demand without making many hard choices about priorities' (Curtis 1988:46). Spending on public works, mainly in the regions and rural areas, on small businesses, and on agricultural support and subsidies increased substantially year by year. But even that growth occurred within a total expenditure that was low relative to GDP, and in comparison with other industrialized countries.

As with industrialization in the nineteenth century, Japan was a latecomer to social and welfare spending. Whereas welfare states 'took off' in the UK, France, Holland, and Western Germany in the 1940s and 1950s, a comparable process of transformation did not begin in Japan until the 1970s. Social security spending, which grew rapidly in those and other industrialized countries, and which was to become a key issue of spending policy in Japan in later decades, was not perceived as a burden in Japan. Social security transfer payments in 1955–7 were no more than 3.7% of GDP, half the average for other OECD countries, while the UK spent some 6%, and France and Germany 12%–13% of its GDP (OECD 1978, 1980). Defence spending, which resumed in the West with the onset of the Korean War, and the intensification of the Cold War, was significantly lower as a proportion of GDP in Japan. From the mid-1950s it declined steadily.

In such favourable circumstances, controlling public spending to achieve the objective of a balanced budget was in most years a relatively simple task for MOF. Annual increases in public spending were justified because of the need to rebuild infrastructure, and provide support for industry; they could be paid for out of expanding tax revenues (and FILP), and had the additional benefit of providing a painless means for the LDP to mobilize and maintain popular support, and provide the essential prerequisite for the single-minded pursuit of rapid re-industrialization and high economic growth—political stability.

THE TRANSITION TO SLOWER ECONOMIC GROWTH, 1965–1973

From 1950 to 1973 the annual real rate of growth of GDP averaged 10%. Although unrecognized at the time, the potential to sustain that rate was contracting. The transition to a period of slower growth proved a painful one.

The continued growth of public spending, despite the slowing down of economic growth, had both economic and political causes. But first I must explain why the principle of balancing the budget was abandoned in 1965. Prime Minister Ikeda's expansionary budget policies of the early 1960s had provoked discussion of the advantages and disadvantages of deficit-financing, but traditional MOF opposition had prevailed.

The decision to abandon the principle was caused by a slow-down in the economy in 1965 as the Budget was being prepared, and the expectation that the revenues from taxation would be insufficient to finance the level of expenditure felt necessary to provide a stimulus to the economy. Thus, 1966 became the first year of the 'new era of public finance', when deficit-financing would be used as a policy tool to try to correct cyclical fluctuation in the economy. Authority to do so was provided under Article 4 of the 1947 Finance Law, but the issue of government bonds, and direct government borrowing, was limited to the financing of those capital expenditures in the General Account Budget devoted to public works, investment, and loans, hence so-called ordinary or 'construction bonds'. This rule was to provide both the guidelines and a control mechanism for deficit-financing until 1975. By 1967 the emergency that had precipitated the abandonment of the principle of balanced budgets was over, but by now deficit-financing was accepted *faute de mieux*. Thereafter, and for the next 14 years, the debate turned on how much expenditure in the General Account Budget should be financed in that way. A new budgetary principle or performance indicator, the 'bond–dependency ratio', replaced the balancing rule. It measured the proportion of the General Account Budget covered by the annual issue of new government bonds to finance capital spending. From the start, targets to reduce the ratio were fixed for five and ten years ahead, but in the event neither was achieved—a failure that was to be repeated on many subsequent occasions in the 1980s and 1990s.

Alarmed at the continued expansion of public spending through the 1960s, as budget growth exceeded the growth of GDP in response to the expansion led by Prime Minister Ikeda, MOF launched a counter-offensive to regain control of public spending in 1968 (for details see Campbell 1977). MOF was worried that the expectations of continuing rising expenditure, nourished and sustained by the high-growth era of the 1950s and early 1960s, would continue into a period of predicted slower growth and less buoyant revenues. As the element of fixed costs in the Budget continued to expand at a faster rate than revenues, the flexibility to alter the composition of public expenditure—the element of discretionary spending—declined. While MOF secured some temporary advantage in the 1968 budget, its 'break fiscal rigidification movement' (zaisei kōchokuka dakai undō) from 1968 to 1972 was overtaken and ultimately lost in the longer term as the economy recovered strongly and revenues became available to finance higher levels of spending. In retrospect, the significance of MOF's campaign lay in the identification of a problem that was to become a central issue of budgetary policy throughout the 1980s and 1990s.

The first signs of the predicted transition to a slower-growing economy became apparent towards the end of the decade; in 1971 the real growth of GDP fell to 6.6%. Public spending continued to rise under political pressure from LDP politicians now becoming more involved in the budgetary process. In 1972 the demand for yet more spending threatened to remove the brake provided by the conditions of Article 4. For the time being, MOF was able to avoid an amendment to the statute to allow the deficit-financing of *current* spending by manipulating forecasted GDP growth rates and, contingently, the projected yield from taxation, a stratagem to which it had constant recourse in the following decades.

Spending money to make itself popular with the voters that kept it in power was not a difficult task for the LDP in the 1950s and 1960s when the economy was growing so strongly. But towards the end of the 1960s there were domestic pressures from an increasingly urbanized electorate hungry for more social and welfare spending, and for policies to deal with the social and environmental consequences of the ruthless industrialization of the previous two decades. Concern about pollution and environmental degradation became national issues. The threat to the party's continued dominance of the national political system became apparent with the electoral success of progressive movements in metropolitan and urban areas. By 1973 there were progressive mayors in all five of the largest cities, and in those and other local authorities popular programmes of welfare spending and pollution control had been initiated in the late 1960s. In 1972 the LDP won fewer seats than ever before in the House of Representatives, its average share of the urban vote falling from 52% in 1960 to 37.5% (Nakano 1997*a*). Both the Japan Communist Party and the Japan Socialist Party increased their representation.

'BIG GOVERNMENT' AND DEFICIT SPENDING

Throughout its history, the LDP has been a flexible and pragmatic party, responsive to changes in the demands of the wider electorate as well as the needs of its traditional supporters. In the 1970s it was to demonstrate its capacity for adaptation by reorienting its formal national policy goals away from producers and towards consumers and clients, and by widening the base of its electoral support to embrace urban as well as rural interests. Both policy changes had profound effects upon the size, composition, and distribution of public spending. The LDP's embrace of big government coincided with the slow-down of economic growth noted earlier, which with the first oil crisis of 1973 turned into a worldwide recession. The economic need to stimulate the economy in the harsher international environment of the 1970s coincided with the political imperative to respond to the growing domestic threat to the LDP's hegemony.

The LDP's conversion to big government and deficit-spending was signalled by the rise to power of Tanaka Kakuei and the publication in 1972 of his book *Nihon Rettō Kaizōron* (A Plan for Remodelling the Japanese Archipelago), which became his manifesto for his successful bid for the presidency of the party a year later. In it he argued:

We should free ourselves from the idea of annually balanced budgets and place more importance on balanced public finance over the long run. While it seems a kindly gesture to leave no debts behind, debts are not in themselves inherently evil. ... A fair distribution of costs among generations is necessary if we are to build a beautiful and pleasant nation to live in. (Tanaka 1973:70)

The framework for the new national priorities, and the basis for constructing a consensus on improving the quality of life, was provided in a new five-year plan drawn up by the Economic Planning Agency (EPA). The year 1973 has been called 'the first year of the Welfare Era', *fukushi gannen*—literally, 'welfare's birth year'.

No country has moved more quickly or with more gusto to embrace so broad a range of new and expanded government-sponsored social welfare programs than did Japan in the early seventies. (Curtis 1988:64)

Table 2.1 Growth of public spending, FY1965–FY1974[a]

FY	General Account Budget Total (tr. yen)	Annual increase (%)	GDP (nominal) Total (tr. yen)	Annual increase (%)	General Account–GDP ratio
1965	3.7	12.4	33.8	11.2	11.0
1966	4.5	19.8	39.7	17.4	11.2
1967	5.1	14.7	46.4	16.9	11.0
1968	5.9	16.1	54.9	18.3	10.8
1969	6.9	16.5	65.1	18.6	10.6
1970	8.2	18.4	75.3	15.7	10.9
1971	9.6	16.8	82.9	10.1	11.5
1972	11.9	24.8	96.5	15.3	12.4
1973	14.8	23.8	116.7	20.9	12.7
1974	19.1	29.2	138.5	18.7	13.8

[a]General Account Settled budget.

Source: *Zaisei Tōkei*, 1997, Budget Bureau, MOF.

The costs quickly became apparent. As Table 2.1 shows, public spending in the General Account Budget increased threefold between 1969 and 1974. Unlike the trend in the earlier era of high economic growth, this expansion outstripped the growth of GDP from 1970 onwards, and by substantial amounts. In each of the three years from 1972 to 1974, the annual increase of spending averaged some 25%, almost 10% more than in the second half of the 1960s. As a result, the General Account Budget's share of GDP rose by more than 3%.

Not only did public spending increase very substantially in the early 1970s, but the composition of the budget changed to reflect the greater emphasis on social security, transfer payments to local governments to provide social welfare programmes, and public works; most other programmes, such as education and overseas development aid (ODA), grew more slowly or, like defence, declined.

THE ORIGINS OF THE 1975 FISCAL CRISIS

The fiscal crisis that emerged full-blown in FY1975 had both long and short-term causes. With the transition to slower economic growth, it had been apparent for some time that large annual increases in public expenditures could no longer be financed wholly from the revenues generated by economic growth, as they had been in the era of high growth in the 1950s and 1960s. Secondly, the structure of the taxation system inherited from the US Shoup Mission after the Second World War relied excessively on revenues from direct rather than indirect taxation, which were more affected by cyclical fluctuations than the latter. As well, two shorter-term factors contributed to the emergence of the crisis in the middle of the 1970s. First, the ratcheting up of public spending at the beginning of the decade, as Japan entered upon its welfare era, encouraged the expectations of LDP politicians, Spending Ministries, special interest groups, and the electorate about its continued growth in the future. The other immediate and proximate cause of the crisis in FY1975 was the fiscal consequences of the first oil crisis in 1973. The impact on the Japanese economy, almost wholly dependent on imported energy, was especially severe. A slow-down in 1971–2 had precipitated an expansion of fiscal policy to try to stimulate demand, but had served mainly to fuel rising inflation which increased still further in 1973 and 1974 as the economy moved into recession, despite further stimulation. The end of the high-growth era was formally marked by the negative (in real terms) economic growth recorded in 1974, the first in Japan's postwar history. Japan was now experiencing the unfamiliar conditions of rising public spending, declining or stable economic growth, and inflation.

During the preparation of the FY1975 Budget, it became apparent that the estimated yield of both direct and indirect taxes would not be achieved. The fiscal deficit estimated initially at less than 10% was raised in a Supplementary Budget to more than 25% to provide for a large anticipated shortfall in revenue of 3.9 trillion.

The fiscal significance of the rapid growth of public spending in the 1970s was much less the growth of government and its absorption of GDP, which was still growing, albeit more slowly than in previous decades: rather, it was the financing of that growth of public spending that caused MOF anxiety, and was to create difficulties for the next twenty years. By 1975 the rapid increase in *current* spending could no longer be financed solely out of taxation and other revenues, and it became necessary to issue special deficit-financing bonds under special legislation to finance the deficit, in addition to the 'ordinary' construction bonds for capital investment. This proved to be a decisive turning-point in the history of Japan's national finances from the imposition of the 'Dodge Line'. Thereafter, deficit-financing became the norm.

The growing imbalance of tax revenues and expenditure that occurred between 1972 and the beginning of policies of 'fiscal reconstruction' in 1979 is shown in Table 2.2. The massive buildup of expenditures in the three fiscal years 1972–4 temporarily slowed with the decline in economic growth in 1975 following the first oil crisis. While tax revenues grew substantially, the rate of growth was nevertheless insufficient to match huge amounts of additional spending. The loss of revenues in FY1975, down almost 10% on the previous year, simultaneously with an increase of expenditure of almost the same magnitude, combined to produce a deficit on the General Account Budget of 5.28 trillion, which prompted the issue of the special deficit-financing bonds mentioned earlier. Thereafter, expenditure continued to rise annually by ever larger amounts, and, although there was a resumption in the annual growth of revenues, it was rarely enough in volume terms to match the much faster growth of expenditures. The critical and deteriorating state of the national finances in the second half of the decade was not so much a lack of revenue growth: rather, it was that revenues did not grow fast enough to sustain the still faster growth of expenditure. The resulting deficit on the revenues and expenditures of the General Account Budget rose sharply in the early 1970s, and by the end of the decade was averaging more than 30%, and more than 5% of GDP, as Table 2.3 shows.

Table 2.2 Tax revenues and expenditures, FY1971–FY1982[a]

FY	Revenues growth/decline tr. yen	%	Expenditures growth/decline tr. yen	%
1971	0.63	8.7	1.37	16.8
1972	1.84	23.2	2.37	24.8
1973	3.59	36.8	2.84	23.8
1974	1.67	12.5	4.32	29.2
1975	−1.28	−8.5	1.76	9.2
1976	1.90	13.9	3.60	17.2
1977	1.67	10.7	4.59	18.8
1978	4.59	26.5	5.03	17.3
1979	1.80	8.3	4.69	13.8
1980	3.14	13.2	4.61	11.8
1981	2.08	7.7	3.51	8.1
1982	1.56	5.4	0.32	0.7

[a]General Account Settled Budget.

Source: *Zaisei Tōkei*, 1997, Budget Bureau, MOF.

Table 2.3 The fiscal deficit, FY1971–FY1982 (%)[a]

FY	Budget deficit	Deficit/GDP
1971	12.4	1.4
1972	16.8	2.0
1973	12.0	1.5
1974	11.3	1.5
1975	25.3	3.5
1976	29.4	4.2
1977	32.9	5.0
1978	31.3	5.1
1979	34.7	6.0
1980	32.6	5.7
1981	27.5	4.9
1982	29.7	5.1

[a]General Account Settled Budget.

Source: *Zaisei Tōkei*, 1997, Budget Bureau, MOF.

As deficits widened, the government was forced to borrow ever larger amounts of money through the issue of bonds, as Table 2.4 shows. In FY1971 the value of new bond issues was 1.2 trillion; less than a decade later it was more than 14 trillion. The issue of ordinary and special deficit-financing bonds together in FY1975 more than doubled the bond–dependency ratio, that is the ratio of new issues to total budget expenditure, which rose from 11.3% in FY1974 to 26.3% a year later (third column). Thereafter the ratio continued to rise annually, to reach a peak of 37.7% in 1980. This meant that more than a third of current and capital expenditure in the General Account Budget

Origins of Fiscal Crisis

Table 2.4 Central Government borrowing, FY1971–FY1982[a]

FY	Bonds issued			Bonds outstanding[b]		
	Total (tr. yen)	Annual % increase	Ratio to total budget expenditure	Total (tr. yen)	Annual % increase	Ratio to GDP
1971	1.20	221.0	12.6	3.952	40.6	4.8
1972	2.30	89.3	19.1	5.818	47.2	6.0
1973	1.80	−21.6	11.9	7.550	29.8	6.5
1974	2.160	19.3	11.3	9.658	27.9	7.0
1975	5.580	153.7	26.3	14.973	55.0	9.8
1976	7.375	34.5	29.9	22.076	47.4	12.9
1977	9.985	35.3	34.0	31.902	44.5	16.8
1978	11.285	13.0	32.8	42.615	33.6	20.4
1979	14.050	24.5	35.4	56.251	32.0	25.0
1980	14.270	1.56	37.7	70.509	25.3	28.7
1981	12.900	−9.6	27.4	82.273	16.7	31.5
1982	14.345	11.2	30.2	96.482	17.3	35.3

[a]General Account Revised Budget.
[b]Figures are actual.
Source: *Yosan Jimu Hikkei*, 1998, Budget Bureau, MOF.

was now financed through government borrowing. The accumulated debt increased tenfold between 1974 and 1982 (fourth column), absorbing more than a third of GDP at the latter date compared with 7% in 1974 (sixth column).

The annual costs of servicing government borrowing and the costs of the accumulated debt rose steeply in the middle of the 1970s, from 0.32 trillion in 1971 to 1.04 trillion four years later, accounting for almost 5% of the total General Account Budget expenditures (Table 2.5). By 1982 annual payments had reached 7.8 trillion, and pre-empted over 15% of the total budget. Those costs comprised both the annual payments of interest on the bonds issued, and the cost of redeeming the principal of the mainly long-term bonds as they matured. The latter costs were still small, as relatively few bonds were issued between 1965 and 1974. As we shall see in later chapters, however, the problems of financing government borrowing in the mid-1980s were compounded by the maturing of the large numbers of ten-year bonds issued a decade earlier.

By 1975, then, the symptoms of a major crisis in the national finances were fully exposed: rapidly rising expenditure, inadequate revenue growth, burgeoning fiscal deficits, heavy and continuing government borrowing, accumulating debt, and increasing budget rigidity as the costs of servicing that debt absorbed an increasing proportion of total spending. The latter was especially worrying for MOF. The anxiety expressed in the 1960s about the prospect of 'fiscal rigidification' was now fully realized, as the fixed costs of servicing the debt increasingly squeezed the amount available in the budget to finance mandatory and discretionary expenditures, themselves subjected to the pressures of the new 'welfare politics' inaugurated in 1973. To those difficulties was

Table 2.5 *Rising costs of Government borrowing, FY1971–FY1982*[a]

FY	Debt service payment (tr. yen)	Ratio to General Account budget (%)
1971	0.32	3.4
1972	0.45	4.0
1973	0.70	4.9
1974	0.86	5.0
1975	1.04	4.9
1976	1.66	6.9
1977	2.35	8.2
1978	3.22	9.4
1979	4.08	10.6
1980	5.31	12.5
1981	6.65	14.2
1982	7.83	15.8

[a]General Account Initial Budget.

Source: *Yosan Jimu Hikkei*, 1998, Budget Bureau, MOF.

added the prospect of an increase in the number of elderly people in the population, threatening an additional burden on budgetary expenditures to provide for the costs of their care through the expansion of the new social security, pension, health, and welfare programmes introduced in the early 1970s. Contingently, the amount available to finance them would be increasingly constrained by the burden of the fixed costs of servicing the accumulated debt. Finally, the increasing ratio of the elderly to the working population meant that there would be fewer wage-earners and taxpayers to generate the additional revenues needed to cover the rising costs of both debt and programme expenditures.

This in outline was the fiscal *problematique* confronting MOF throughout the last quarter of the twentieth century. In later chapters I explain and analyse the aims and objectives of successive policies to 'reconstruct', then 'consolidate' and, briefly, to 'reform' central government finances to reduce deficits and debts, with the long-term aspiration of restoring a balanced budget. But first, in the next three we look at the politico-economic, administrative, and bureaucratic contexts within which the budgetary institutions, structures, and processes were situated, and the fiscal policies were formulated and implemented.

PART I

THE CONTEXT OF JAPANESE BUDGETING

3

The Politico-Economic Context

The unparalleled success of the Japanese economy for most of the post-war period, and the uninterrupted period of dominance of the political process by the Liberal Democratic Party (LDP) from its formation in 1955 to the Lower House election of 1993, testify to the strength and stability of both the economy and the polity during that period. By contrast, the 1990s were characterized by conditions of acute instability and uncertainty in both. A paralysis of government followed the (temporary) end of the LDP's one-party domination, as political parties fragmented, dissolved, and realigned in a succession of short-lived and unstable coalitions. The 'economic miracle' of the post-war years collapsed into the longest and deepest recession since the 1930s, while the very foundations of the financial system were shaken by the insolvency of banks, credit unions, securities firms, and housing loan companies, symptoms of the critical condition of most financial institutions burdened by the huge overhang of debts and non-performing loans inherited from the profligate bubble economy of the 1980s.

Paradoxically, the key dynamic in the spectacularly successful political economy of the post-war period was self-perceived economic insecurity, and political vulnerability. The former provided the motivating force for rapid re-industrialization after 1945: 'catching up with the West' was once again the prime objective of economic and industrial policy and policy-making, as it had been from the second half of the nineteenth century. The main condition for achieving and sustaining that economic security was perceived to be a stable political system which avoided the disruptive politics of the alternation of power of parties of the left and right. After a period of political turmoil, stability was achieved with the merger of the centre and right parties under the umbrella of the LDP in 1955.

The dominance of the LDP in the national political process thereafter tended to obscure the institutionalized insecurity that characterizes Japanese politics. Competition among and within the factions of the LDP proved more significant in the recent history of Japan's political economy than competition among rival political parties. Until 1994, the electoral system of the single non-transferable vote (SNTV) in multi-member constituencies obliged members of the same party to compete in many constituencies with each other rather than with opposition parties; factions provided additional sources of electoral funds and organizational support. Secondly, in the absence of significant ideological, class, religious, or ethnic cleavages, national parties mobilized and maintained their electoral support mainly through the distribution of benefits to local constituencies and special interest groups, making Japanese politicians especially vulnerable to grass-roots pressure. To these endemic pressures were added from time to time those that arose from periods of acute domestic political turbulence and crisis. Three such domestic crises occurred in the period 1949–86. They proved to be a major source of policy innovation, as the LDP responded flexibly and pragmatically with the politics of material compensation to maintain itself in power. However, it was an internal party crisis that led in 1993 to the LDP's loss of power, and to the end of its 38 years of uninterrupted rule. That was the proximate cause of the destabilization of the Japanese political system, a symptom of deeper-rooted tensions in the political economy that were exposed by the collapse of the 'bubble economy' after 1990.

This chapter provides a general guide to that political economy, and signals some of the main changes from the emergence of the fiscal crisis in FY1975, described in the previous chapter, to the beginning of the new millennium. Its purpose is to contextualize the analysis in later chapters of the formal and informal budget institutions, the processes and policies with which MOF and successive LDP governments responded to that crisis, and the conditions of continuing fiscal stress in the following two decades. It begins with the broad outline of the main economic trends: in summary, a period that began with the recognition of fiscal crisis, followed by years of proclaimed fiscal austerity in the early 1980s. Thereafter, from about 1986, there was a period of economic expansion fuelled by looser fiscal and monetary policy in the wake of the 1985 Plaza Accord. The 'bubble economy', as it came to be called, burst in late 1990, and collapsed into a decade of deep and prolonged recession. The second part of the chapter describes the main trends in the political system, focusing particularly on the role and significance of the LDP. The interdependence of the economy and the polity is briefly reviewed in the third section, and attention is drawn to five structural changes that have affected the stability of the politico-economic system, challenged the basic assumptions underlying the 'developmental state', and contributed to what Pempel (1998) has called the 'regime shift' that took place in the last three decades of the twentieth century.

THE ECONOMIC CONTEXT

Initial agreement on the national goal of rapid economic growth united politicians, bureaucrats, and businessmen after 1945, and was sustained after 1955 by the mobilization of electoral support for the newly merged parties under the LDP. Other, social, objectives were largely subordinated to the drive for economic security. Demands for the expansion of social and welfare services were muted, and where pressures arose, as in 1958–60, they were accommodated with compensatory politics.

In the achievement of the goal of rapid growth in the 1950s and 1960s, GDP grew for nearly twenty years at an average annual rate exceeding 10%, in conditions of full employment with average inflation of about 6%. With fixed exchange rates, macroeconomic policy was concerned mainly with controlling the money supply through interest rates to deal with periodic balance-of-payments crises, and to avoid a recurrence of the hyperinflation experienced in the immediate post-war period. The shift to floating exchange rates in 1971 following the collapse of the Bretton Woods agreement, and the shocks of the first oil crisis, precipitated Japan's first economic recession since the war, combined with very high inflation.

An excess of private-sector savings provided the means for the necessary private and public investment on which the high economic growth was based. While the flow and direction of much of that investment was controlled directly by government through the Fiscal Investment Loan Programme (FILP), and indirectly through influence on public and private institutions, government borrowing through the issue of government bonds was unnecessary: the General Account Budget was balanced. The alternating 'stop–go' conditions experienced by other industrialized countries in this period were unknown in Japan. Public spending was not used countercyclically to stimulate the economy until the slow-down of 1971–2.

Tax policy was more significant. The reform of the fiscal system undertaken by the Dodge and Shoup Missions during the Allied Occupation, when for a time inflation exceeded an annual average of more than 200%, eliminated traditional policies of support and protection for particular industrial sectors. After independence, the Shoup tax reforms were progressively dismantled, and the short-lived hostility to the preferential treatment of strategic industries was reversed. MOF and MITI (the Ministry of International Trade and Industry) combined to promote the growth and international competitiveness of particular industrial sectors, partly through the uninhibited use of tax exemptions, concessions, and breaks for businesses and corporations. The use of fiscal policy for the purpose of implementing a state-led industrial strategy was not new; it had occurred repeatedly in the process of modernizing the Japanese state, most notably in the late nineteenth century.

Japan's high-growth era was coming to an end even before the slow-down resulting from the first oil crisis began late in 1973. As it did so, the national consensus on the paramount objective of rapid growth was dissolving. The environmental and social consequences of unbridled growth were brought into sharp relief by the mercury-poisoning at Minamata, and led to the first serious attempts to control pollution. In the late 1960s the LDP lost control of many metropolitan and town councils to the socialist and communist parties, whose programmes of social spending excited further demands for their extension more widely through national policies. Increasing pressure for government spending on roads, houses, schools, health, and, above all, social security threatened the LDP's continuing dominance of the national political system. As explained in the previous chapter, within the LDP the most prominent advocate of change was Tanaka Kakuei, whose programme for 'Building a New Japan' gave greater emphasis to social objectives and the improvement of social overhead capital and social security. Following his appointment as prime minister in 1972, the 'policy switch' was signalled formally in the five-year National Economic Plan, *The Basic Economic and Social Plan for 1973–7*.

Before the implementation of those new social policies began in the FY1973 Budget, fiscal and monetary policy had been used to stimulate an economy depressed by the revaluation of the yen in 1971–2. The further stimulus provided by Tanaka's first budget added fuel to an inflationary fire that was beginning to take hold of the economy. Following the impact of the first oil crisis on the Japanese economy in late 1973, slow-down turned into recession the following year—the first occurrence of negative real growth in Japan since the end of the Second World War. Deeply rooted economic insecurity resurfaced as gloomy predictions were made about the long-term viability of an economy dependent on imported energy supplies, trading in the uncertain conditions of the new regime of floating exchange rates, and experiencing the appreciation of the yen following the abandonment of the Bretton Woods agreement.

In concert with other industrial countries, Japan attempted to increase the level of economic activity worldwide by using fiscal policy to stimulate its own economy in 1974 and 1975. After the immediate crisis of the first oil shock, high growth became an international priority, reflected in various OECD accords, the McCracken Report, and the acceptance of the so-called 'locomotive theory of growth', which held that the recovering economies of stronger countries pulled the weaker in their train.

The second oil crisis of 1979 brought a further wave of inflation, and macroeconomic policy was used once again, countercyclically, to deal with it. The process of recovery and adjustment to the conditions of a new era of slower growth, inflation, and rising public spending was a gradual one. The effect on GDP was remarkable. Whereas annual growth had averaged 9.1% in real terms from 1947 to 1973, in the following decade it declined to less than 4.0% (Figure 3.1). But this was slow-down, not stagnation or recession: the effect of long-term structural changes in the economy, such as the end of the process of technological catch-up, of lower rates of investment, and of a shift in national priorities towards social objectives. (For these and other contributory factors, see Lincoln 1988.) Nevertheless, it was to have a profound effect upon attitudes towards the role of public spending in the economy. The change was publicly acknowledged in MITI's 'Vision for the 1970s', which signalled the reorientation of national economic goals away from the narrow pursuit of high economic growth to the improvement of the quality of life through the improvement of social overhead capital, education facilities and opportunities, working conditions, the environment, and overseas development assistance. There was also to be a switch from heavy industries to knowledge-based industries.

As economic growth slowed in the early 1970s, the revenue from taxes grew less rapidly, and high and rising public spending had to be financed by government borrowing. More significantly, the lower rates of economic growth after 1973 brought about a fundamental shift in the balance between private-sector savings and private investment, which required a major reorientation of macroeconomic policy. Throughout the high-growth era, private-sector investment had been financed by household savings and surplus tax revenues. Borrowing from abroad was eschewed, and a current account deficit was avoided by strict control of imports and flows of capital.

In the 1970s the macroeconomic balance between savings and investment changed. The slow-down in economic growth was accompanied by a decline in investment, and an increase in net savings in the private sector. The latter surplus was accommodated in the period 1974–80 by the expansion of fiscal policy through government financing of public expenditure in response to the need to stimulate the economy, and to provide for the 'policy switch' to social objectives. The financing of the growing fiscal deficit by issuing large numbers of government bonds led directly to the gradual collapse in the tight control of interest rates, as the banks resisted the low, controlled rates at which the government tried to sell increasing amounts of debt. With hindsight, it is clear that the longer-term costs of fiscal expansion that took place in the 1970s, especially in the period 1976–9, were underestimated. The rising share of government debt was subsequently

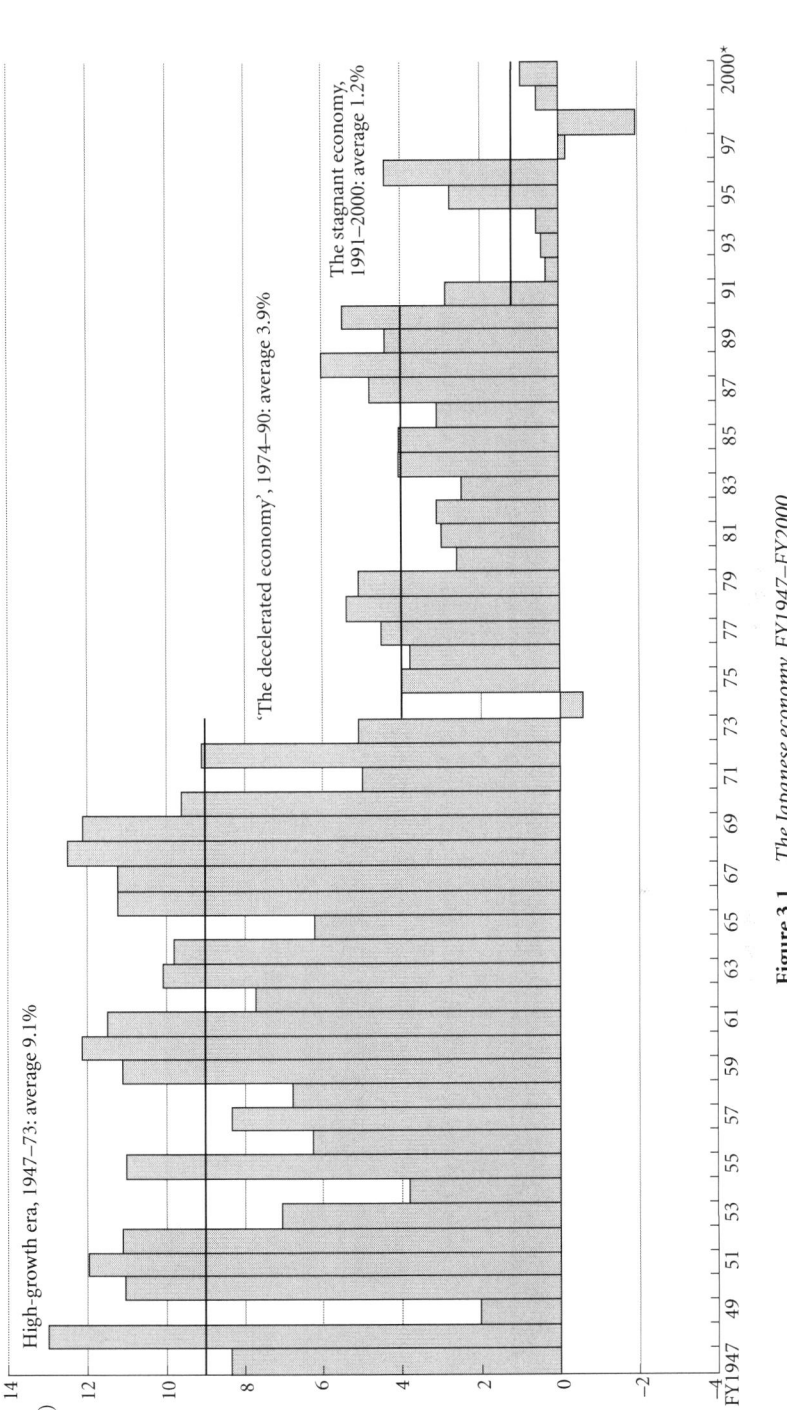

Figure 3.1 The Japanese economy, FY1947–FY2000
Real GDP growth, fiscal year: GDP at constant (1990) market prices

*Forecast

Source: Annual Report on National Accounts (annually), EPA; Main Economic Indicators (monthly), Planning and Research Division, Minister's Secretariat, MOF.

considered the unsustainable element of macroeconomic policy. The politico-economic context within which budgetary decisions were made was increasingly dominated by concern with the financing of public spending, and anxiety about the burden to a progressively ageing population of accumulating national debt. The decisive turning-point was not reached, however, until the end of the 1970s. From 1979 onwards the major objective became fiscal reconstruction and, subsequently, consolidation, in which both elements of fiscal policy—taxation and spending—were directed towards the reduction of the public-sector deficit.

With the appreciation of the yen in the mid-1980s following the Plaza Accord, export industries campaigned for policies to stimulate domestic demand. The ensuing debate was strengthened and then consumed in the bitter controversy with the USA and other industrialized countries over trade relations, and attempts to get Japan to open up markets to more foreign trade, and to stimulate domestic demand to help recovery from the world wide recession. The official response was contained in the Maekawa Advisory Commission Reports of 1986 and 1987, whose recommendations to the Prime Minister provided the focus for a continuing debate, but without committing the government to major changes in the tighter fiscal policy that had dominated macroeconomic policy since the adoption of MOF's policy of fiscal reconstruction at the end of the 1970s.

Nevertheless, 1987 proved to be a turning point in fiscal policy. Although the slowdown in world trade towards the end of the 1980s was felt less severely in Japan than in the USA or the UK, it was sufficiently worrying to induce a relaxation of fiscal and monetary policies. The political and economic imperatives of the domestic economy were always more important than obligations to the international economic community, but the latter, as so often, provided the rationale for the change of direction. MOF's enthusiasm for the Plaza Accord was rooted in its hope that it could exploit the emphasis on currency realignment to deflect pressures for expansionary fiscal policies. Yamaguchi Jirō, its administrative vice-minister, instructed his negotiators that the strategy should be 'first to realign the currencies, and second to reduce interest rates jointly, stressing the need to leave the "main castle" [fiscal policy] free from attack' (Funabashi 1988:40). Despite MOF's hostility, the austerity that had (ostensibly) characterized policy for the General Account Budget since 1982 was relaxed in May 1987 to provide a 6 trillion fiscal stimulus for the economy, to finance Prime Minister Nakasone's strong-yen (*endaka*) strategy, intended to accelerate the programme of economic reform through deregulation, and the liberalization of markets.

The Bubble Economy, 1986–1990

The four years from December 1986 to mid-1990 were years of uninterrupted economic growth. The 54 months following the appreciation of the yen under the Plaza Accord were the longest period of expansion since 1965–70. GDP averaged 4.7% p.a. in real terms. Growth rates for investment in plant and equipment between 1988 and 1990 matched those of the high-growth era. Inflation was low; unemployment fell; labour shortages appeared. As the yen appreciated in relation to the dollar, Japanese overseas investment grew rapidly. Japan displaced the UK as the world's largest creditor nation.

Despite the impressive performance of the Japanese economy, these years are now remembered more for the appearance and collapse of the 'bubble economy'. While coincident, the bubble economy was neither a cause nor a consequence of the growth of the Japanese economy at that time. They were, however, related. The two main elements of the 'bubble' were huge, speculative increases in land prices and stocks. Prices of the latter in 1989 were four times greater than in 1983; land prices three times their value in 1986–7. The prices of both were dissociated from 'fundamental prices', and hence were not a direct consequence of the changes in economic variables (EPA 1994*a*). The value of capital gains in stocks and land reached 489 trillion in 1987, more than 40% greater than Japan's nominal GDP. The rapid rise in the prices of stocks pushed the Nikkei Index to a record 38,915 in December 1989; urban land prices averaged for the six metropolitan areas were, at their height in mid-1990, nearly four times the level of 1986. Both the expansion and subsequent collapse exceeded anything in Japan's post-war economic history. It was arguably the greatest such 'bubble' in any OECD member country in the post-war era (OECD 1998).

There were three main causes of the 'bubble'. First, monetary policy was very loose. After the Plaza Accord of September 1985 and the appreciation of the yen, it was relaxed to provide for a continuance of the outflow of capital. The official discount rate was progressively reduced to 2.5%, (then) its lowest ever level. Secondly, the liberalization of domestic financial markets and interest rates meant that firms could earn increasing rates of return on their financial assets. Thirdly, tax revenues grew with an increase in capital gains, corporate profits, and land transactions, but were used less to finance increased expenditure than to reduce the budget deficit and the bond–dependency ratio in the General Account Budget, and hence the amount of national debt. As fewer government bonds were sold, and corporate borrowers turned increasingly to other domestic and international sources, banks and financial institutions had to look elsewhere for customers. Together, those three factors fuelled speculation in land, and encouraged large corporations to engage in *zai-tech*, or financial engineering. Capital raised through the issue of equity on the (rising) stock market was reinvested with banks and financial institutions competing aggressively for funds in liberalized markets, in which large corporations were much less dependent for investment capital than in the high-growth era. Financial institutions shifted the focus of their lending towards the booming real estate business and small businesses.

Loose monetary policy and fiscal reconstruction have been cited by some analysts as contributing factors to the bubble economy (Funabashi 1988; Hartcher 1998). On that argument, MOF was mainly responsible, because its macroeconomic policies were driven by concern for the defence of the 'castle'—fiscal austerity. While MOF undoubtedly influenced the Bank of Japan's monetary stance—low interest rates reduced the costs of government borrowing—tight fiscal policies were more apparent than real, as I shall show in later chapters. In practice, there was both loose money *and* fiscal expansion. As mentioned, the latter was initiated in the Supplementary Budget of 1987.

The collapse of both stocks and land prices was as dramatic as their rise. The Nikkei Index began to slide in February 1990 and continued downwards, bottoming out at 14,309 in August 1992; land prices declined for the first time in nearly twenty years. In the fallout, land purchased for speculative profits could not be resold, and property firms and small businesses were unable to maintain interest payments on money borrowed from financial institutions and banks. The number of non-performing loans grew alarmingly. Bankruptcies increased, and some small banks and credit institutions were saved from bankruptcy only by the concerted action of the larger banks under pressure from the Bank of Japan.

The Bank of Japan should have tightened monetary policy sooner than it did, as a former governor acknowledged on the tenth anniversary of the Plaza Accord. It was beginning to do so before the stock market crash in October 1987, but then relaxed its policy once again. It did not act to prick the speculative bubble because the main focus of its policy was broader: the movement in consumer prices, at or near zero throughout the bubble. With GDP growing at almost 5%, 'policies to achieve sustained price stability would probably have been desirable but must have been very hard to initiate', the Deputy Governor confessed in 1999 (Yamaguchi 1999). The bubble was in its third year before the government and the Bank of Japan began to deal effectively with its adverse consequences. The turning point came with the setting up in September 1989 of the US–Japan Structural Impediments Initiative, and American criticism of the lack of adequate land-tax policies to deal with the problem. The need for specific legislation had earlier been rejected by the Government Tax Commission, a statutory advisory council; but now, with the familiar prompting and pretext of 'foreign pressure' (*gaiatsu*), the Basic Land Act was passed in December 1989, and a Land Value Tax was eventually introduced in April 1992 (for details see Ishi 1992). Two measures were most effective. First, restrictions on the money supply were imposed through the raising of interest rates. In May 1989 the official discount rate was raised for the first time in nine years, followed by a succession of further sharp rises in 1990 to reach 6%. Secondly, in 1990 MOF restricted the proportion of total lending that financial institutions could make available to the real estate industry.

Recession, 1990–1995

Whether the collapse of the bubble was a major or a contributory cause of the contraction of the economy that began in 1990 is arguable. (For contrary views, see Noguchi 1994*a*,*b*; and OECD 1993.) It did however exacerbate its severity, and perhaps, through the consequential crisis in the financial system, prolonged the duration of what became not only the longest and deepest recession since the war, but the worst since the Showa depression in 1927–32. It lasted (officially) for 30 months, from May 1991 to October 1993. However, the 'mild recovery' had come to a standstill by the summer of 1995 (EPA 1995*a*), and by September was proclaimed as a 'prolonged standstill'. The recession was characterized by the '5Ds': deflation, debt, declining demand, de-industrialization, and default.

The remarkable growth of private investment that had taken place during the period of expansion in the late 1980s meant that the capital stock was now excessive, and investment in plant and equipment declined sharply in real terms. Unemployment rose beyond levels last seen in 1987, reaching 3.5% in May 1996. The real rate was estimated (EPA 1995*a*) to add at least another 3% of surplus employees. Defined more widely to include 'invisible unemployment'—those workers discouraged from seeking employment—and 'internal unemployment'—those workers receiving pay for little or no work—MCA's estimate of unemployment in 1994 was 8.9%; the comparable figure for the USA was 8.8% (Kishi 1995; but for a cautionary overview of the measurement of unemployment see Ostrom 1999). The continual employment of a further 2 million workers was subsidized through the government's adjustment programme. More worryingly, the job offers–applicants ratio, the indicator of labour market strength/weakness, fell to a level last experienced in 1987.

Banks were more cautious in their loan practices than in the late 1980s, reflecting the deterioration of their balance sheets resulting from non-performing loans accumulated earlier. The stock market remained stagnant, with the Nikkei Index rooted below 20,000. In covert 'price-keeping operations' (PKOs) between 1992 and 1995, the government pumped more than 12 trillion into the market through the purchase of equities using pension funds and postal savings (Smithers 1995). Despite those measures, the stock market continued to fall, reaching 14,813 in June 1995, its lowest point for three years, having lost more than 60% of its 1989 value. GDP growth was stagnant. Industrial production registered negative values in 1991 and 1992, with a sharp increase in unused capacity.

The appreciation of the yen against the dollar—the 'yen bubble'—created further problems. Earlier the accumulating surplus on the trade account had made it more difficult for Japanese exporters to compete in overseas markets, more necessary in conditions of depressed demand in domestic markets. Firms that had earlier moved production, assembly, and ancillary units 'off-shore' to Asia and Europe to take advantage of the economies of local labour supply and access to growing markets now began to move off-shore more sensitive corporate facilities, such as R&D, further contributing to the phenomenon of the 'hollowing out' (*kūdōka*) of Japanese manufacturing industry. Nearly 10% of total output had moved abroad to escape the costs of the high yen. Much of that production was sold back to Japan, and contributed to the high and rising level of imports. As a result, the current account surplus declined in both 1994 and 1995; a further fall of 31% in 1996 brought it to its lowest level since 1990.

The Japanese government's reluctance to take strong and decisive action to weaken the currency, in order to reverse the long-term appreciation of the yen since the Plaza Accord in 1985, was however ended with its agreement at the meeting of G7 central bankers and finance ministers in April 1995 that the dollar had fallen too far at 79.75 yen, and 'that an orderly reversal was desirable'. Hard on the heels of MOF's announcement of financial deregulation measures aimed to drive the yen down, concerted action by the Federal Reserve, the Bundesbank, and the Bank of Japan in August 1995 resulted in the biggest depreciation of the yen value of the dollar for three years. MOF was aiming at a dollar parity of 110 yen, at which level it was claimed exporters could compete in international markets.

Monetary policy was progressively eased; the official discount rate was brought down in a succession of steps, from a high point of 6% to 2.5% in 1993, and then to a lowest ever level of 0.5% in September 1995, where it remained for the next four years. From February 1999, the Bank of Japan set nominal short-term interest rates at zero. As the recession deepened, the government responded—at times reluctantly—to domestic and international pressures with fiscal policies to stimulate the economy. Fourteen packages of emergency fiscal and economic measures were introduced between August 1992 and October 2000, totalling more than 132 trillion of spending, loans, and tax cuts, equivalent to 25% of nominal GDP. The real stimulus to the economy however was considerably less than that 'headline' total, an issue I take up in later chapters.

Recession Returns, 1997–1999

As the countercyclical fiscal policies introduced in 1995 began to take effect, the economy began slowly to recover, GDP growing by 2.8% in real terms in FY1995. The following year Japan achieved the highest rate of growth of any G7 country: 3.2%. But despite almost boom-like conditions in the first quarter of 1997, the optimism that Japan was at last on the path to sustained recovery from the aftermath of the bubble economy proved false and short-lived. In the second quarter GDP declined by 2.8%, and by December 1997 EPA conceded that the economy was at a 'standstill'. Six months later, Japan was officially in recession once again after registering two successive quarters of negative real growth. By the end of 1998, there had been two further quarters of real decline, overall an unprecedented occurrence since 1955. A major contributory cause was the tightening of fiscal policy in FY1997. In April the national consumption tax was raised from 3% to 5%; the special income tax cuts of the previous two years came to an end; the traditional June and December tax rebates were cancelled; and the passage of the Fiscal Structural Reform Act in November paved the way for the implementation of Prime Minister Hashimoto's election pledge to reconstruct public finances by reducing the budget deficit and lowering the burden of public debt. FY1997 was designated the 'first year of fiscal structural reform', and the process of retrenching central government spending began with the General Account and FILP Budgets. Together, the effect of tax increases and public spending cuts tightened fiscal policy by an estimated 2.2% of GDP in FY1997. With little scope for offsetting that effect with the loosening of monetary policy—Bank rate was still 0.5%—and any further devaluation of the yen opposed by the USA, a return to economic recession was inevitable. The budget for FY1998 was tighter still, imposing statutory caps on most spending programmes, enabling MOF to claim a cut in programme expenditures for the first time in a decade, and the largest such reduction since the end of the Second World War.

As the signs of economic slow-down began to emerge in the summer of 1997, several East Asian countries with whom Japan had close trading relations began to experience difficulties with financial liquidity, leading to a sudden and dramatic collapse of their currencies and acute economic crisis. The Japanese government was slow to respond to those events, but, under continual pressure from members of the international economic community, purported to stimulate the level of domestic demand in its own economy with a series of monthly countercyclical fiscal measures from October 1997 to February 1998. They were widely perceived as inadequate.

The continuing procrastination and policy-paralysis of the Hashimoto government in the spring of 1998 reflected a fundamental dilemma. The Prime Minister was personally committed to, and publicly identified with, the reform of the fiscal system. He and the LDP planned to appeal to the electorate for the Upper House elections in July on the basis of the successful implementation in the budgets of FY1997 and FY1998 of the first stages of an ambitious programme of fiscal retrenchment and administrative reform. In those elections the LDP hoped to win enough additional seats to free it from dependence upon the support of its erstwhile Coalition partners, the SDP and Sakigake. A policy U-turn on fiscal reform—cutting taxes and increasing spending—would weaken the Prime Minister's position within the party, where his reform programme and his leadership were disputed by several senior politicians, some of whom were rivals for the presidency of the party, and would undermine his credibility as prime minister. The fiscal expansion demanded by Japan's East Asian neighbours, G7, and other international economic and financial organizations conflicted with the domestic imperative of fiscal restraint. The Japanese government was also mindful of the painful lesson taught by the experience of the 1980s when, acceding to US and G7 pressure for a weaker yen, looser monetary and fiscal policy contributed to the speculative excesses of the bubble economy. As the Hashimoto government agonized over the resolution of the dilemma, the slow-down in economic activity turned into recession, and the crisis in the financial system deepened. The value of shares on the Tokyo Stock Exchange (and on the Hong Kong and Singapore exchanges) continued to fall, the Nikkei Index sank to levels experienced in the aftermath of the collapse of the bubble economy; the yield on the benchmark Japanese government ten-year bond fell to a record low. More serious still, the rapid depreciation of the yen–dollar exchange rate threatened to further undermine the weaker, devalued currencies of its beleaguered trading neighbours, while contributing further to the massive buildup of its current account surplus. The Bank of Japan intervened massively in the currency markets in April 1997 to support the yen.

The abandonment of the policy of fiscal retrenchment began in December 1997 with the announcement of temporary cuts in national and local income taxes worth 2 trillion in FY1998. Hashimoto's conversion owed something to continuing pressure from the USA, and the leaders of those Asian countries facing severe economic recession. But it also reflected the need to rebalance intra-party forces, between the more conservative wing led by Kajiyama Seiroku, a former chief Cabinet secretary, urging tax cuts, and those led by Katō Kōichi, the secretary-general, espousing the cause of unbending fiscal rectitude. Under unremitting pressure from home and abroad to do still more, the Prime Minister announced on 26 March 1998 a fiscal stimulation package worth 16 trillion, albeit still without the substantial and permanent tax cuts that the USA and other foreign governments had urged upon him. The size of the package and its financing required an amendment to the recently passed Fiscal Structural Reform Act, and the rescheduling of the target dates for reducing the budget deficit and the burden of debt.

The irony of the policy U-turn was that, previous governments having avoided throughout the 1980s and early 1990s the political responsibilities of dealing effectively with the underlying causes of the chronic weakness of the national finances—the inexorable growth of public spending and the inadequate tax-base—Prime Minister Hashimoto and the LDP government prompted by MOF chose to cut spending and increase indirect taxes at a time when such policies were economically inappropriate. The budget for FY1997 proved disastrously inopportune; that for the succeeding year compounded the error, exacerbating a rapidly deteriorating situation. The fiscal reform programme was seriously holed, if not yet blown out of the water; that occurred a few months later in December 1998, when the new Obuchi government suspended the

Act indefinitely to allow it to finance a further fiscal stimulus of around 27 trillion, and to give the highest priority to economic recovery through countercyclical fiscal stimulus. It announced permanent cuts in national and local personal, income, and corporate taxes, totalling 9.3 trillion, and sharp rises in the planned General Account and FILP Budgets for FY1999, the former up 5.4% and FILP (net of portfolio investment) up 7.3% on the totals for FY1998. Relief for small and medium-sized companies was provided additionally by increased allocations to the Japan Finance Corporation for Small Business and the JDB, and an expansion of the programme for credit guarantee.

The recession, which began officially in April 1997, lasted for 25 months until April 1999. Growth in the next 12 months was modest, 1.4% in real terms. By the autumn of 2001 that had disappeared, as Japan stood on the brink of its fourth recession in a decade.

The Crisis in the Financial System

The dominant and dominating issue in Japan's political economy for the whole of the 1990s was the crisis in the banking sector. The collapse of the bubble left many banks, credit unions, and other financial institutions technically insolvent. Bad debts and non-performing loans for the purchase of land, house-building, and houses in the 1980s were estimated (in 1998) at 87 trillion, more than 17% of nominal GDP. The crisis penetrated to the heart of the financial system, involving Japan's largest banks, most of which had lent large sums of money to smaller financial institutions. It penetrated too the heart of the bureaucratic system, where the regime of inspection, supervision, and regulation of the banking and securities sectors was administered mainly by MOF and the Bank of Japan. The principle of 'regulatory forbearance', in which no bank, large or small, was permitted to fail, strong and weak treated 'like a convoy of ships sailing under their protection', was abandoned in 1997 after a sequence of events in 'Black November', when Hokkaido Takushoku Bank (the tenth largest commercial bank), a regional bank, and two leading securities firms collapsed in quick succession. Yamaichi Securities, one of the big four domestic brokers, was liquidated voluntarily with liabilities of 3.5 trillion, the largest corporate failure in Japanese history. Those events provided a shock to financial, political, and administrative systems, and marked a turning point in political attitudes towards the use of public money to deal with the crisis, and MOF's management of that crisis. Whereas earlier the proposed rescue of the failed housing loan associations (*jusen*) with 680 billion of taxpayers' money had provoked a political and public furore, the LDP's plan to provide up to 60 trillion to recapitalize weak banks, to protect investors, and to write off bad debts was accepted and enacted in October 1998 with little protest, despite the moral hazard entailed. Despite those measures, the crisis in the banking sector continued and, with the deterioration of the economy, worsened in mid-2001. As the Nikkei Index fell below 10,00 for the first time in 18 years, the FSA estimated that the total of 140.9 trillion of bad debts and non-performing loans outstanding (nearly a quarter of GDP) could not be liquidated by the target date of 2003.

MOF was relieved of responsibility for the inspection and supervision of banks and securities firms, which now passed to the newly created Financial Supervision Agency which began work in June 1998. In October MOF was stripped of its responsibilities for the management of the continuing crisis in the banking sector. A Financial Revitalization

Commission (FRC) headed by a (Cabinet) minister of state was set up in the PM's Office with funds of 60 trillion, and given powers to take ailing and collapsed financial institutions into public ownership, and to dispose of their assets, to inject capital to bolster the resources of both weak and strong banks, and (through the Deposit Insurance Corporation) to reassure investors and protect them from the consequences of any further bankruptcies. Before the end of the year, both the failed Long-Term Credit Bank and the Nippon Credit Bank had been taken into public ownership prior to the disposal of their assets. Early in 1999, the FRC approved the allocation of 7.5 trillion to recapitalize the base of 15 top-tier banks in exchange for the write-off of 9.3 trillion of bad debts, the restructuring of commercial operations, and cost-cutting measures. The origins of the crisis, the saga of failures, bankruptcies, and rescues, and the roles of MOF and the Bank of Japan are described in several accounts (e.g. Smithers 1995; Ostrom 1995; Hartcher 1998; Choy 1999).

In a broader context, the origins of the financial crisis, its (mis-)management during the 1990s, and the demonstrable failure of MOF and its policies to resolve it were both symptoms and contributing causes of the disintegration of Japan's post-war political economy, fuelling a growing mood of doubt about the viability and continued relevance of Japan's model of 'developmental capitalism': the role of the state, and the efficiency, effectiveness, transparency, and accountability of institutional structures such as the political system and the bureaucracy on which it depended. I return to those issues in the concluding section.

The loss of confidence in Japanese financial institutions contributed to the depressed and deteriorating status and trading performance of Tokyo as an international financial centre following the pricking of the bubble economy. Further financial deregulation was inevitable if Japan's financial markets were to compete in the international market for financial products and services. In November 1996 Prime Minister Hashimoto committed his new administration to a programme of reforms of financial markets and services, modelled on the Market Day reforms in the USA in 1975 and the Big Bang in the UK in 1986, designed to bring financial markets and institutions up to the standard of those in New York and London by 2001, making them 'free, fair, and global'. A year later the government committed itself to the removal of distortions in the markets for domestic household savings which arose from the historic privileges offered to small investors through postal savings. At the same time, the decision was taken to reform the principles and operation of FILP, and to sever the statutory link with postal savings and pension funds.

THE POLITY

Until the General Election for the House of Representatives in 1993, the LDP had been returned at 13 successive elections as the party with the largest number of seats. It had been continuously in government for 38 years, generally without the support of other parties although occasionally in coalition with small right-wing groups. The causes and consequences of its domination of the political system from 1955 to 1993, and the failure of other parties separately and combined to challenge it, are dealt with in several authoritative studies (e.g. Hrebenar 1992, 2000; Curtis 1988). My concern here is to draw attention to those features that shaped the politico-economic context within which the budgetary system was evolved and operated between 1975 and 2000. I focus mainly on the LDP, but have something to say about the role and effectiveness of other parties as they influenced and constrained the exercise of power by it. Relevant to the present discussion are: first, the frequency of general elections for the Diet; second, the electoral system before its reform in 1994—the SNTV and multi-member constituencies, and the over-representation of rural interests in the LDP, the Diet, and the Cabinet; third, the centralization of power within the LDP and its organs, and the incorporation of factions into the party apparatus in the 1970s and 1980s; fourth, the LDP's pragmatic electoral strategy of distributive politics, responding to periodic crises in its popular support, and challenges to its political hegemony, with 'compensation'; and, fifth, the checks, balances, and constraints on the LDP's exercise of political power. In conclusion, I provide a brief account of the turbulence and turmoil in the political system precipitated by the internal tensions within the LDP factions in the early 1990s which surfaced after the Recruit–Cosmos scandal of 1988.

Frequency of Elections

The LDP was constantly preoccupied with Diet (and of course local) elections, and electoral politics are an important factor in explaining the political salience of budgetary policies; public works budgets, agricultural subsidies, and help for small businesses, were all important elements of the distributive spending and tax policies of the LDP's local politics. Elections to the Lower House are held at least every four years, while a half of the members of the Upper House are elected every three years. The Lower House ran its full term on only three occasions, while on four occasions it was dissolved after three years. As a result, elections for one or both Houses took place in 14 of the 26 years from 1975. Twice, the gap between elections was only two years, while on four occasions it was a year or less. By contrast, the UK, with a similar unitary system of government (but with an unelected second chamber), had only six general elections for the House of Commons, roughly once every four years, in the period 1975–2000.

The LDP successfully broadened the basis of its electoral support in response to the challenge of the left in cities and urban areas, becoming less a party of rural interests, farmers, and small businessmen and more a 'catch-all' party incorporating new groups from urban constituencies. In 1960, 68% of its general election votes came from farmers, merchants, and the self-employed, with white- and blue-collared workers providing only 28%; by 1980 the latter two groups accounted for just over a half (Pempel 1987). Nevertheless it continued to draw almost a fifth of its support from farmers, and it continued to protect their interests, through policies of price-support and subsidies, and those of other long-time supporters, notably small businessmen. Limited electoral reform in 1986 did little to redress the malapportionment between rural and urban electoral districts, and rural constituencies continued to be over-represented in the House of Representatives up to 1993. Moreover, LDP members with such seats found them easier to defend than those in urban areas. One consequence of that was that rural interests were over-represented in the higher echelons of the party organization and the Cabinet, where a key rule-of-the-game was seniority calculated by the number of successive terms served in the Diet.

While the electoral appeal of the LDP became more broadly based in its public policies, reflecting for example urban demands for housing, a cleaner environment, and social and welfare programmes, its rural base remained significant throughout the period 1975–93 and exercised a disproportionate influence on the composition and allocation of budget expenditures.

The Pre-Reform Electoral System

The electoral system with its multi-member constituencies and SNTV, and the frequency of elections, was expensive to exploit successfully; the costs of embarking upon a political career, and maintaining it thereafter, rose sharply in the late 1970s and 1980s. In many constituencies elections were contests between LDP candidates from different factions. To win and retain a seat, a candidate needed to inherit or establish and sustain a personal local electoral network (*kōenkai*) to provide financial and organizational support. While the central party organization, and competing faction leaders, provided funds, more important sources were *kōenkai*, local corporations and small businesses, and individual donations and loans (Hrebenar 1992). After the restrictions on corporate donations in the 1980s, funds raised through *kōenkai* became more important still, the role of factions rather to support candidates' fund-raising efforts than to provide direct financial support. Debts incurred locally had to be 'repaid' with political favours, among which, in rural districts, agricultural subsidies, public works projects, and contracts and jobs continued to figure prominently.

The Centralization of Power

The number of competing factions within the LDP diminished from 12–14 between 1955 and 1971, to nine in 1972, and only five in 1980. The size of their membership increased, and they became institutionalized within the party apparatus (Satō and Matsuzaki 1986; for an overview and explanation of the changes, see Kohno 1992 and Katō Junko 1997). During the 1980s the LDP became bureaucratized, and its capacity to provide leadership diminished (Kitaoka 1993). First, the constituency support groups and local electoral networks established and nurtured by LDP Dietmen were institutionalized by the growing practice of choosing sons or relatives of retiring incumbents. Secondly, the freedom to join factions became more restricted because, increasingly, it was possible to get elected only by joining a faction not already represented in their electoral district. Thirdly, factions themselves became more bureaucratized. After Tanaka's arrest in the Lockheed scandal, the new faction post of administrative-director was created; by 1987 meetings of the administrative-directors of all the factions were a regular occurrence.

As a result of those changes, preferment within the party, and appointment and promotion to government posts, was increasingly linked to membership and seniority in factions, increasing the incentive for individual members to commit themselves long-term to particular factions. From the 1960s, most Cabinet and many party posts were allocated on the basis of factional affiliation. The share of offices allocated to each faction was proportional to its strength among LDP Diet members. While factions played a less direct role in funding their members after the revision of the law on political donations in 1976, they were still able to support their fund-raising activities indirectly in other ways. Controlling promotion and providing electoral and financial support, factions evolved into organizations able to discipline and control their members, checking or repressing incipient backbench revolts of LDP Dietmen, for example during the legislative processes of the new consumption tax in 1988 (Katō Junko, 1994). Through such means, they played a crucial role in building and maintaining a consensus across the party on particular policy issues.

That concentration of power within the LDP, and more generally in the political system at the end of the 1970s and the early 1980s, profoundly influenced the public policy processes, strengthening the ties between party leaders, Dietmen, and bureaucrats in the Spending Ministries. It was epitomized by the rise of the arch machine-politician Tanaka Kakuei to a position of unrivalled power and influence within the party, both during his tenure of the presidency, and subsequently as the leader of the most powerful faction (Johnson 1986). Even after his public disgrace in the Lockheed scandal in 1976, he continued to exert influence on party appointments, policies, and strategy. While prime minister, he led and extended the grip of the most powerful faction, and forged a personal political–bureaucratic network *within* the bureaucracy. As well, many former senior bureaucrats were recruited to the party and the Diet under his patronage, for example two administrative vice-ministers from MOF, the head of the National Police Agency, and administrative vice-ministers from MOC, MAFF, MOL, MPT, and MITI (Calder 1993). With the erosion of popular support for the party at the end of the decade, and in the more austere economic climate earlier in the 1980s, dominated by intra-party controversy over proposals for a consumption tax, competition between and within factions for the party presidency and other senior posts intensified, although the Takeshita–Tanaka faction (Keiseikai) continued to dominate the party. Centrifugal tendencies were exacerbated by secular trends in party recruitment and preferment. There were now fewer former bureaucrats in the Diet, and fewer of them became prime minister or chairman of the party's Policy Affairs Research Council (PARC) than in previous decades. Those recruited to the party and the Diet were younger, entering upon a political career in their thirties and forties rather than after the conclusion of a long, successful official life. The LDP was becoming a party of professional politicians, many with roots and experience in local and regional politics. A new breed of second-generation politicians began to emerge, the sons (and occasionally daughters) of former Diet members (known as *nisei* politicians), many of whom became frustrated with the strict seniority system which excluded them from the policy-making process. Among the older generation of LDP Dietmen, repeated electoral success had allowed them to progress through a variety of influential posts in Diet committees, party committees and councils, and Cabinet. In so doing, many had acquired specialist knowledge of particular policy areas, and developed close ties with bureaucrats in spending ministries. Informal groups of policy specialists (*zoku-giin*) began to make their influence felt in the making of policy in such fields as construction, agriculture, and transport.

Continued electoral success, and the repeated re-election of incumbents, produced large numbers of senior LDP Dietmen eligible for promotion to ministerial and Cabinet positions, and to posts within the party organization. Pressure of numbers contributed to a more rapid turnover of ministerial appointments, and to a lack of continuity. Cabinets lasted less than two years, and in the period 1955–93 '15 different Prime Ministers presided over 48 Cabinets whose duration never exceeded 18 months'. The average period of office of a Cabinet minister was nine months (Bouissou 1998). While progress through the lower ranks of the party, Diet, and government was predictable, the party leadership became more unstable. Competition between factional leaders and their supporters for the party presidency, and hence the premiership, became more intense. The greater sensitivity of faction leaders to public opinion, and the popularity of the Prime Minister and the party in relation to anticipated or actual electoral performance, made the tenure of office uncertain and, with the pressure of eligible candidates, short. After Satō Eisaku, who was prime minister from 1964 to 1972, no president of the party served more than two years as prime minister apart from Nakasone, who was re-elected for a second term following the LDP's unexpected success in the 1986 election. Hashimoto, who succeeded Murayama as prime minister of the Coalition government in January 1996, was re-elected president of the party in September that year, and held office as prime minister until the Upper House election of July 1998.

Electoral politics

Between 1975 and 1993, the LDP contested seven general elections for the House of Representatives. In none did it obtain a majority of the votes cast, but in all it emerged as the party with the largest number of seats because of its 'organisational prowess, its loyal supporters and its ability to exploit the advantages of a malapportioned legislature' (Allison 1993: 32). Its long-term electoral decline in the 1960s and 1970s was reversed in the 1980s. From the low point of the October 1979 election, when it won only 248 seats (out of 511) in the Lower House, it secured a spectacular victory nine months later, winning 56% (286) of the seats. In the period of fiscal austerity that followed in the 1980s its popularity declined, as is reflected in a loss of 36 seats at the 1983 general election. The setback proved temporary; the recovery dramatic. In July 1986 it secured 300 of the (now) 512 seats, largely at the expense of the JSP, which had seen its own representation decline from a high point in 1976 of 123 seats to a new low of 85. The fortunes of the two largest parties were reversed in the election of February 1990, when the JSP won nearly a quarter of the votes cast (141 seats); the LDP's majority was correspondingly reduced. The unpopular consumption tax had been introduced in 1989, and the LDP was embroiled in the Recruit–Cosmos scandal, and its aftermath, which precipitated the resignation of two prime ministers, Takeshita Noboru and Uno Sōsuke, and the selection of a little known, uncharismatic but 'clean' leader, Kaifu Toshiki. In elections for the House of Councillors in 1989 the LDP lost its overall majority for the first time since 1955. There was now a possibility that it would lose control of the Lower House as well. A loss of seats was anticipated in the 1990 election for the Lower House, and the retention of its overall majority was a surprise. Table 3.1 lists the appointments, terms of office of prime ministers and their governments for 1975–2000.

The LDP's electoral strategy began to change before the 1979 election. Earlier in the decade, responding to its declining popularity, the rise of the left in urban areas and

Context of Japanese Budgeting

Table 3.1 *Prime Ministers and Governments, 1975–2000*

Year	Prime minister (date appointed)	House of Representatives: seats won at General Election	Government
1975	Miki Takeo (9 Dec. 1974)		
1976	Miki	LDP 249; JSP 123	LDP
1977	Fukuda Takeo (24 Dec. 1976)		
1978	Fukuda		
1979	Ō'Hira Masayoshi (7 Dec. 1978)	LDP 248; JSP 107	LDP
1980	Ō'Hira/Suzuki Zenko (17 July 1980)	LDP 284; JSP 107	LDP
1981	Suzuki		
1982	Suzuki/Nakasone Yasuhiro (27 Nov. 1982)		
1983	Nakasone	LDP 250; JSP 112	LDP
1984	Nakasone		
1985	Nakasone		
1986	Nakasone	LDP 300; JSP 85; Kōmeitō 56	LDP
1987	Nakasone/Takeshita Noboru (6 Nov. 1987)		
1988	Takeshita		
1989	Uno Sōsuke (3 June 1989) Kaifu Toshiki (9 Aug. 1989)		
1990	Kaifu	LDP 286; JSP 141; Kōmeitō 46	LDP
1991	Kaifu/Miyazawa Kichi (5 Nov. 1991)		
1992	Miyazawa		
1993	Hosokawa Morihiro (9 Aug. 1993)	LDP 223; Coalition Parties 243 (JSP 70; Shinseitō 55; Kōmeitō 51; Japan New Party 35; DSP 15; Sakigake 13; SDL 4)	Coalition (non-LDP)
1994	Hata Tsutomu (28 Apr. 1994) Murayama Tomiichi (30 June 1994)		Coalition (LDP; JSP; Sakigake)
1995	Murayama		
1996	Hashimoto Ryūtarŏ (11 Jan. 1996)		
1996	Hashimoto (9 Nov. 1996)	LDP 239; SDP 15[a]; Sakigake 2; New Frontier Party 156; DPJ[b] 52; JCP 26; others 10	LDP

Table 3.1 (cont.)

Year	Prime minister (date appointed)	House of Representatives: seats won at General Election	Government
1998	Obuchi Keizō (30 July 1998)		LDP, Oct. 1998–Jan. 1999;
2000	Mori Yoshirō (5 Apr. 2000)		Coalition (LDP/Liberal Party), Jan.–Oct. 1999; Coalition (LDP, LP, New Kōmeitō) Oct. 1999–Apr. 2000; Coalition (LDP, New Kōmeitō) April 2000–

[a] At its Party Congress in January 1996, it changed its Japanese name from Shakaitō (Japanese Socialist Party) to Shakai Minshutō (Social Democratic Party).
[b] Democratic Party of Japan (Minshutō) formed from elements of SDP, Shinseito, and Sakigake.

rural prefectures, and the emergence of citizens' movements focused on 'issue politics', it had widened the basis of its appeal to embrace the new urban middle class. As in its response to previous crises since 1955, the LDP 'compensated' aggrieved and alienated voters with distributive public policies: new social, welfare and environmental programmes (Calder 1988). It became 'broad based, encompassing plural and often conflicting interests and emphasising pragmatic responses to concrete policy issues while downplaying ideology and a comprehensive world view' (Curtis 1988: 236). Changes in some policies were however only partly the result of top-down politico-electoral strategies to attract a new urban constituency. For example, the role of the media representing pressures from the grass-roots was more significant in the changes in policies for the elderly in the early 1970s (Campbell 1996).

Constraints on the LDP's Exercise of Power

The politics of 'crisis and compensation' is the fifth theme. Calder (1988) has demonstrated authoritatively the pragmatic, non-ideological response of the LDP from its formation to crises perceived as threatening its political domination of government. His analysis of the distributive politics practised by the LDP up to 1986 is supported by the evidence of the following decade. National and local budgets, especially public works programmes, grew in the years of the bubble economy. As well, the emphasis upon the continued improvement of living standards, especially housing but also environmental and leisure facilities, water supply and sewage facilities, and the extension of health and welfare programmes reflected the reorientation of national goals which the LDP had initiated earlier. With the onset of recession following the collapse of the bubble, the

LDP responded with a series of emergency packages centred upon public investment and public works programmes, referred to above.

The LDP's politico-electoral skills in exploiting the political system to translate a minority of the total votes into adequate majorities in the Lower House enabled it to dominate that system throughout the years 1975–93. But that dominance was precarious. The reluctance of its supporters to maintain it in power was tempered by the continual attractions of pork-barrel politics. The most important check to the use of the LDP's power was therefore the pragmatic, traditional one of a continuing flow of material benefits and favours: 'Voters prize local politicians who can "deliver the goods", not men of vision and reputation who are politically clean' (Allison 1993:39). Also, the modern Japanese political system has 'devised its own set of checks and balances, one in which Diet boycotts by the opposition, the mobilisation of press opinion and interest organisations to oppose LDP policy, and LDP fear of an electoral backlash act as powerful constraints on the ruling party' (Curtis 1988: 243). The most notable example before 1993 was Prime Minister Nakasone's failure to persuade the Diet in 1987 to pass his legislation for a consumption tax, despite the LDP's majorities in both houses.

While opposition parties remained weak, and unable to mount an effective challenge to the LDP at the polls, the rules-of-the-game observed by all parties in the conduct of Diet business, especially the procedures for scrutinizing government bills, imposed effective checks on the exercise of unconstrained power by the LDP. A cultural norm ensured that minority views were not only heard but accommodated, if possible by consensus. In contrast to previous decades, from 1976 to the middle of the 1980s the LDP was more disposed to consult and achieve accommodation with the opposition parties to smooth the operation of the legislative processes. In order to run the Lower House smoothly, a working majority of 17 seats more than an absolute majority was necessary. Without it, opposition parties could block legislation in the standing committees. For a total of six years, in the three Houses elected in 1976, 1979, and 1983, the LDP lacked such a majority (Bouissou 1998). It needed the cooperation and often tacit approval of the JSP to manage its legislative programme. The so-called 'Counter-measures' Committee was the forum for informal agreements and deals between the two parties. As the Diet is in session for a relatively short period of time, there is considerable pressure in the legislative timetable. To get its major legislation on the statute books before the session ended, the government was obliged to seek and reach accommodations and compromises with other parties. *Kokutai seiji*, the traditional practice of reaching decisions through behind-the-scenes deals among the various political parties, was 'typical of the way Japanese society operates, settling matters by groping for compromise and avoiding self-assertion' (Ozawa 1993: 21).

The blocking veto-power of opposition parties was used from time to time with considerable effect to obstruct the passage of legislation in order to win concessions from the government. In the period 1976–89, the even balance between the LDP and the opposition parties meant that on some legislative committees the latter had a majority where the non-voting chairman was selected from the governing party. This occurred in the Lower House Budget Committee in 1977. To pass the Budget before the end of the fiscal year, and thus avoid the need for a provisional budget, 'there were intense backstage negotiations between the governing and opposition parties' (Satō et al. 1990: 389–90). The result was a concession by the government of a larger tax reduction than originally planned. A similar concession was obtained as a result of opposition intransigence the following year. In 1979 the government and opposition parties failed to agree on revisions to the Budget, and the Budget was rejected in the Budget Committee for the first time since 1948. It was approved in the plenary session of the Lower House. By the time of the presentation of the government's draft budget for FY1980, the threatened use of veto powers by the opposition parties had become an annual ritual. On this occasion, their counter-proposals to revise budget expenditures upwards proved unacceptable to the government; negotiations broke down, and Diet proceedings came to a standstill. 'Complex negotiations, both open and secret, continued at several levels' (p. 515). Finally, after some additional expenditures were proposed, agreement was reached informally between the LDP and the main opposition parties. The Budget was again defeated in the Budget Committee, but was passed in plenary session. Thereafter, the LDP's majority improved and it became more independent.

The JSP and other opposition parties had still more influence on defence policy. Pressure for the maintenance of the ceiling of 1% of GDP was a major factor in restraining the increase of defence spending (Keddell 1993). The adoption of a special budget framework for defence expenditure to exclude it from budget cuts was postponed from 1980 to 1981 in anticipation of opposition from minority parties. Once established, Prime Minister Nakasone was prevented from removing the 1% ceiling because of pressure from the opposition. Its eventual breach in 1987 was due partly to the weakening of the electoral position of the opposition parties in the 1986 Lower House elections. With the subsequent decline of the LDP's own fortunes, and the loss of its majority in the Upper House in the 1989 election, the opposition parties reasserted their influence on governmental defence policy, particularly over the peacekeeping (PKO) legislation.

The De-alignment of the LDP

The breakup of the old political order dominated by the LDP's one-party rule began with the political fallout from the Recruit–Cosmos shares-for-favours scandal of 1988, implicating Prime Minister Takeshita, his finance minister, Miyazawa Kiichi, former prime minister Nakasone, and most of the other leading members of the party. In consequence, the party as a whole was obliged to give more serious consideration to the issue of political reform which hitherto had been largely the concern of younger, recently elected Dietmen calling for a new electoral system for the Lower House (Ōtake 1996). In 1989 the LDP lost its majority in the House of Councillors and concluded an alliance with Kōmeitō and the Democratic Socialist Party there. Stockwin (1999) argues that that arrangement, which gave them a say in policy-making, sowed the seeds of the LDP's subsequent split. Hitherto, the LDP's dominance had relied on the 'essential exclusivity' of its policy-making structures.

With Takeshita's resignation in June 1989, political reform became caught up in bitter disputes between and within factions over the succession to the leadership, and control of the dominant Tanaka–Takeshita faction. Kaifu Toshiki, who succeeded Uno

Sōsuke as prime minister in August 1989, after the latter's brief tenure, was the puppet of that faction, his Cabinet 'run as if Ozawa [the LDP's secretary-general] was the de facto prime minister' (Ōtake 1996: 283). Ozawa Ichirō advocated a broadly based programme of reform, and his support, together with that of Hata Tsutomu and the continuing campaign of the young reformers, led to numerous attempts to push it forward during the Kaifu administration and that of Prime Minister Miyazawa, who succeeded him after the 1990 Lower House elections. The LDP's surprise victory in those elections, following its loss of control of the Upper House a year earlier, reinforced the general reluctance within the party for political reform. The indifference and apathy of the following two years was dispelled with the arrest and disgrace of the party's 'godfather' Kanemaru Shin, vice-president and former secretary-general, for taking bribes from Sagawa Kyūbin, a haulage company. The process of the de-alignment of the LDP that followed in its wake owed very little to differences within the party over political reform, however. It was largely the result of a struggle for the leadership of the Takeshita faction, after Kanemaru's resignation as chairman. At the time of his disgrace, Ozawa was his senior deputy and was being groomed as heir-apparent to the leadership of the faction. His main rivals were Obuchi Keizō, Kajiyama Seiroku, and Hashimoto Ryūtarō, with whom he also bitterly disputed the issue of who should take responsibility for Kanemaru's fall. The Takeshita faction split into two, the main group led by Obuchi, the other (Ozawa's) led nominally by Hata Tsutomu, an ardent supporter of electoral reform. The split, together with the failure of Prime Minister Miyazawa to redeem his pledge on television to enact political reform in the June session of the Diet, sealed the government's fate. The Obuchi faction forced Hata's group to leave the party in June 1993. Hata, Ozawa, and 41 other dissidents from both Houses formed the Japan Renewal Party (Shinseitō). A smaller, more left-wing group of ten younger members of the LDP broke away under the leadership of Takemura Masayoshi, prominent in the earlier campaigns for political reform, to form the New Harbinger Party (Shintō Sakigake) after the Diet's vote of no confidence on 18 June brought down the Miyazawa government. The House of Representatives was dissolved, and in the election of 18 July 1993 the LDP government was defeated, its representation reduced from 286 seats (pre-defection) to 223.

Turbulence and Instability, 1993–1996

A coalition government of seven non-LDP parties took office in August 1993. This was led by Hosokawa Morihiro, leader of the Japan New Party (Nihon Shintō) which he had founded in mid-1992, and which had won 35 seats in the election. Hosokawa announced an ambitious programme of electoral reform, proposals for the deregulation of industry, the reform of the tax system, the decentralization of power to local governments, and political control of policy-making and bureaucrats. Proposals to replace the multi-member constituencies with 'British style' single-member constituencies, and the SNTV by a simple plurality system, were subsequently watered down after internal wrangling between the coalition partners, and by the price exacted by the LDP for ending its tactics of opposition and delay in the Diet, and to overcome rejection by the Upper House.

Proposals to restrict political fund-raising and to curtail political corruption were also amended. Progress with other reform measures was equally disappointing, as the time and energy of the partners were drained by their preoccupation with the main priority of electoral reform. In February 1994 the announcement of a new national welfare tax by Prime Minister Hosokawa, inspired by Ozawa in cooperation with senior MOF bureaucrats, was made without sufficient time for consultation with the coalition parties. Following their protests and those of the opposition parties it was immediately withdrawn, a humiliating climb-down for the Prime Minister. Thereafter a skilfully orchestrated campaign of critical scrutiny of his financial transactions while governor of Kumamoto Prefecture held up the progress of the Budget in the Diet. The paralysis of government that this threatened provided the pretext for his resignation in April, although the risk of further embarrassing disclosures about his personal finances, and his declining credibility, combined to make his position untenable (Takemura 1997; Shinoda 1994).

Deputy Prime Minister Hata Tsutomu, leader of the Japan Renewal Party, succeeded. The JSP had left the coalition before the formation of the new government, in protest at the manoeuvring of Ozawa to isolate it in a projected new parliamentary alliance of the non-socialist partners. Without a majority, the Hata government lasted a little over two months, its main task the passing of the Budget. Once that was enacted, the government was defeated on a no confidence motion by the combined votes of the LDP and the JSP. The third coalition government within twelve months took office on 30 June 1994.

Out of office for a year, the LDP returned to share power in an improbable alliance with the JSP under a socialist prime minister. This was no restoration. The political and numerical strength of the LDP had been eroded by the disaffection of many younger members, and subsequently by the defection of successive waves of dissident party members. Nor was its coalition partner, the JSP, the party of the *ancien régime*. It had lost even more heavily in the 1993 general election than the LDP, and faced further humiliation with the introduction of single-member constituencies following the enactment of electoral reform in 1994. Acceding to office for the first time since 1947, it jettisoned most of its long-held socialist principles, most notably its long-standing and rooted opposition to a standing army, disavowal of the Japan–US Mutual Security Treaty, and the involvement of the Self-Defence Forces in UN peacekeeping operations. It also dropped its opposition to nuclear power, and to the compulsory raising of the national flag and the singing of the national anthem in schools.

The alliance of the LDP, Sakigake, and the JSP was led by the chairman of the latter, Murayama Tomiichi, who became prime minister, with Kōno Yōhei, formerly chief secretary to the Cabinet in the Miyazawa government, now president of the LDP, as his deputy. The process of fragmentation, dissolution, and realignment of political parties continued throughout 1994–6. In September 1995 the LDP elected as its president Hashimoto Ryūtarō, minister of international trade and industry in the Coalition government, to replace Kōno, who had presided over the party since the defeat in the general election of 1993. A former minister of finance, Hashimoto had also held the key party posts of secretary-general and chairman of PARC.

Only the timing of Murayama's resignation on 5 January 1996 was unexpected. His credibility as a national and party leader had been all but eroded by his ineffectiveness in coordinating the government's lame and tardy response to the Great Hanshin–Awaji Earthquake on 17 January 1995, and its ambiguous public apology for Japan's war crimes on the occasion of the fiftieth anniversary of the end of the Second World War. Supported by the three coalition parties, Hashimoto defeated the New Frontier Party candidate, his arch-rival Ozawa, in the Diet election of the new prime minister, and reshuffled Cabinet posts to further strengthen the LDP's grip on government.

The LDP in Government, 1996–2000

In the election for the House of Representatives held on 20 October, the LDP gained 28 seats, 12 short of an overall majority. Both its former coalition partners fared badly; the JSP (now renamed the SDP) representation was halved to 15 seats, while Sakigake lost its leader and seven of its nine seats. They declined to join formally with the LDP in a new coalition government, but supported Hashimoto's re-election as prime minister, and offered his new all-LDP administration support on a case-by-case basis. Without a majority in either House, their support was crucial to ensure the passage of the government's ambitious legislative programme of fiscal, financial, economic, and administrative reforms.

The process of de-alignment and re-alignment of other political parties accelerated after the Lower House elections (see Laver and Katō 1998; Hrebenar 2000). Defections from other parties to the LDP continued and were sufficient to give it an overall majority in the Lower House by April 1998. In December 1997 Shinshintō was dissolved, largely on the initiative of its president, Ozawa Ichirō, into six separate parties, of which his new Liberal Party (Jiyūtō) had 41 seats.

Hashimoto was re-elected president of the LDP in September 1997, and the reshuffle of Cabinet posts that followed strengthened the representation of the main factions; Obuchi Keizō, heir to the Takeshita faction, was appointed minister of foreign affairs. The balance struck between the Obuchi, Miyazawa, and Mitsuzuka factions, and the reaffirmation of the seniority rule, both pointed to a revival of the factional politics which characterized the LDP's one-party rule prior to 1993; officially abandoned in December 1994, in reality they never ceased to exist. Such politics, for example, dictated the appointment of Satō Kōku to the post of director-general of the MCA, responsible for overseeing the programme of administrative reform. Convicted of bribe-taking in the Lockheed scandal in 1976, Prime Minister Hashimoto was obliged subsequently to remove him from the post in response to public criticism, and to apologize for the error of judgement in appointing him. In January 1998 Mitsuzuka, the minister of finance, resigned, taking formal responsibility for the illegal activities of senior officials involved in an unfolding bribery and corruption scandal within MOF. Both events contributed to a further weakening of the Prime Minister's own leadership both nationally and within the party. However, the lack of a credible alternative ensured his survival until the outcome of the July elections to the Upper House. The LDP, hoping to achieve an overall majority there, lost seats, and Hashimoto, accepting responsibility for the party's poor performance, promptly resigned. He was succeeded by Obuchi Keizō following an unprecedentedly public campaign for the party presidency, with a member of his own faction, Kajiyama Seiroku, formerly chief secretary to the Cabinet, a critic of Hashimoto's economic and fiscal policies, and Koizumi

Junichirō, the maverick minister for health and welfare. The elderly Miyazawa Kichi, a former prime minister, was appointed minister of finance.

Without a majority in the Upper House, the Obuchi government concluded a formal coalition compact with Ozawa's Liberal Party in January 1999, and an informal alliance with New Kōmeitō, partly to forestall attempts by opposition parties to mount a no-confidence campaign, and to ensure the passage there of the new legislative guidelines for US–Japan defence cooperation. In October 1999 the New Kōmeitō became a full partner with the Liberal Party in the LDP-led coalition. Each was allocated one ministerial portfolio in the Cabinet which Obuchi reshuffled after his successful re-election as president of the LDP. The coalition now controlled 357 of the 500 seats in the Lower House, and had a comfortable working majority in the House of Councillors, with 141 of the 250 seats. Ozawa's Liberal Party left the coalition on 1 April 2000, after long-running disputes with its partners over electoral reform and security-related matters. The next day Prime Minister Obuchi suffered a stroke, and lapsed into a coma. Mori Yoshirō, secretary-general, was elected president, and the Diet approved his appointment as prime minister on 5 April. The composition of the government remained unchanged.

Following Obuchi's death shortly afterwards, Mori called a general election for the Lower House on 25 June, timed to maximize sentiment for Obuchi, whose birthday fell on the same date. The LDP and its two partners all lost seats, but the weakened coalition retained an overall majority of the (now) 480 seats. In the second Mori Cabinet, formed on 4 July, the New Kōmeitō and New Conservative Parties were each given one portfolio. Deeply and increasingly unpopular with the public at large, Mori's position within the LDP was threatened by an attempted *putsch* led by Katō Kōichi in November. Its collapse amidst continuing interfactional feuding induced Mori to bring former Prime Minister Hashimoto, now the leader of the largest faction, within the Cabinet, which was reshuffled in December in anticipation of the reduction in the number of ministries and agencies which took effect from 6 January 2001.

THE CHANGING POLITICO-ECONOMY

The interdependence of the polity and the economy is deeply rooted in the evolution of the modern Japanese state, a characteristic of the process of its early industrialization and (after 1945) re-industrialization. From its formation in 1955, the LDP's political interests were closely identified with the economic interests of producer groups—mainly with agriculture, construction, and small businesses, traditionally strongly represented in the ranks of LDP Dietmen, but also with the manufacturing and financial sectors, dominated by large corporations. The electoral and financial support of both large and small business was essential for its continued dominance of the political system. The support of agriculture and small business was delivered in return for favourable tax policies, subsidies, public works projects, and protection from foreign competition in regulated local and regional markets. While the economic interests of big business later diverged from those of the protected and regulated sectors, they were generally consistent with those of the LDP in the era of high growth. The financial support of corporate institutions, through donations and gifts to the party and its factions, together with the support of small businessmen and *kōenkai* members to finance the personal local networks of LDP Dietmen, enabled the party to exploit an electoral system wherein interfactional campaigns in multi-member constituencies consumed increasing amounts of money. Big business benefited from the stability of one-party domination of the political system, and from supportive and protective macroeconomic, industrial, and trade policies.

Up until the early 1970s, harmonization of political and economic interests was achieved through a consensus on the priority accorded to the pursuit of growth, and through the incorporation of both small and big business interests into the policy-making process via networks comprising political patrons, clients, and bureaucrats. Threats to the stability of the political economy emerged towards the end of the 1960s and the end of the period of high growth, with a challenge to the LDP's political hegemony. Responding to the electoral success of opposition parties in local elections, the LDP adapted and expanded its policies for pensions, welfare, housing, and the environment. Clientelistic networks were expanded and consolidated to incorporate aggrieved interest groups now 'given the same treatment as agriculture and small business' (Inoguchi 1990: 216). The priorities of the previous decades were reordered as the LDP embraced the politics of a welfare society.

One consequence of all this was more competition and conflict among actors in the policy processes; policy-making became more complex, less coherent, and widely diffused with the 'unbundling of Japan Inc.' (Pempel 1987). As the LDP continued to practise the politics of compensation up until its fall from power in 1993, political power became still more widely dispersed and shared—among the LDP and its policy-making organs; with opposition parties, many of whose policies were incorporated into the LDP's strategy of policy adaptation; with bureaucrats, promoting and protecting their policy-jurisdictional interests in new and expanding policy areas; and with local governments, courts, and the organized interests of both producers and consumers. The resulting segmentation of policy processes increased the competition for policies and resources presided over by a largely immobilist LDP, whose leaders were preoccupied with interfactional competitions for succession to the post of prime minister, with career advancement in the party and government, and with control of the Tanaka–Takeshita faction.

A second source of tension in the political system was the continual flouting of the rules-of-the-game regulating the conduct of elections, corporate donations, and 'gifts' to political parties and politicians, and the behaviour of both politicians and bureaucrats. Marginal changes to the rules in the 1970s and 1980s—for example the reapportionment of a few electoral districts, the introduction of PR into the Upper House, and restrictions on fund-raising activities—were palliatives rather than remedies for the diseases of corruption and machine-politics that infected the body politic, rendering it increasingly incapable of dynamic policy-making.

Many of the elements of politico-economic interdependence, and the conditions that provided for the stability in the political economy, began to change. During the last three decades of the twentieth century, the economic and political institutions that underpinned the conservative regime, and provided the stability of Japan's political economy from the end of the Allied Occupation, were transformed. Pempel (1998) argues that a 'regime shift' occurred in those institutions, the consequence of four main changes: (1) the deconstruction of the stable system of government and opposition parties; (2) the gradual deterioration in Japan's hitherto unparalleled economic performance, marked by the slowing down of economic growth; (3) the realignment of the boundaries of the security relationships with the USA; and (4) the changes in the predominant socio-economic basis of the conservative alliance, for example the role and influence of organized labour, and the appearance of internal divisions within interest groups hitherto supportive of it, as positive-sum politics and economics became zero-sum after the collapse of the economic bubble. The causes of these and other changes are complex and the explanations, contestable. (Apart from that of Pempel himself, see e.g. Yamamura 1997, and, for a provocative and iconoclastic interpretation, Dore 1999.) Here, in a necessarily abbreviated and simplified account, I draw attention to some of those, and other, structural changes contributing to that regime shift, which have most relevance for the contextualization of the budgetary processes discussed in later chapters.

The Japanese economy was transformed from a high-growth industrial economy dominated by shipbuilding, iron and steel, textiles, and motor vehicles to one of much lower, less predictable, and more volatile growth, dependent upon high-tech industries such as consumer electronics, computers, and semi-conductors. Manufacturing plants for the new industries were only 20% as expensive per unit of production as the steel, shipbuilding, and petro-chemicals they replaced, and were less dependent upon government credit and capital investment traditionally channelled through FILP agencies, such as the Japan Development Bank and the EXIM Bank. The end of the high-growth era coincided with the end of the Bretton Woods system and the first oil crisis. As explained earlier, floating exchange rates, the progressive liberalization of financial services and products, and in particular the deregulation of interest rates all combined to loosen the grip of the Japanese government on the regulation of financial markets.

A second structural change occurred as a result of the gradual internationalization of markets, firms, and capital. This affected the role of large corporations and *keiretsu* in the Japanese economy, and their relationships with political and financial institutions. Large corporations became more international, less dependent upon national objectives and policies, and less dependent upon domestic sources of finance from 'main banks' in horizontal *keiretsu* (industrial groupings). Cross-shareholdings in the latter declined, as they became more 'open' in order to respond better to market forces. An identity of the aims and interests of national governments and big business could no longer be assumed. Tensions emerged in the historic reciprocal relationships, as government (and the LDP) was pulled in opposite directions. On the one hand, agriculture, construction, and small and medium-sized business (and manufacturing sectors in decline) continued to look to national government for protection, tight regulation of their local and regional markets, and tax breaks and subsidies; on the other hand, large corporations and their representative associations advocated more competition, the opening of domestic markets, lower consumer prices, and less government regulation of economic activity, and controversially the ending of restrictions on the formation of holding companies.

A third structural change in the political economy was the transformation of the role and size of the public sector, which resulted from the inauguration of the 'welfare era' in the early 1970s. The financing of new and expanded health, pensions, social welfare, education, and environmental programmes, and of the expansion of so-called 'social overhead' capital investment through public works programmes, led to a rapid and continuing growth of the General Account and FILP Budgets (and those of local government as well) in the following two decades. In conditions of decelerating economic growth and a shrinking tax base, the result was burgeoning public-sector deficits and debts. Government was obliged to borrow large and increasing amounts of money to finance both current and capital spending. As the recession persisted through the 1990s, repeated and ever-larger packages of countercyclical fiscal policies resulted in record amounts of borrowing and recurring budget deficits. The issue and sale of increasing numbers of long-term government bonds to finance them had consequences for financial products and markets, the money supply, and the regulation (and, later, deregulation) of short- and long-term interest rates. Figure 3.2 provides a summary and a reference-point of the main trends in spending, tax revenues, and borrowing in the General Account Budget, to be discussed in detail in later chapters.

A fourth structural change in the political economy was the transformation of the trading and security relationships with the USA in the 1980s and 1990s. With the end of the Cold War, the basis of the mutual dependence enshrined in the security treaty was eroding. The USA had less need of Japan as a base from which to counter the threat posed by the Soviet Union, North Korea, and China; Japan was less dependent upon American protection. The continued US occupation of Okinawa became a *cause célèbre* in 1996 following the rape of a young Japanese schoolgirl by US servicemen, contributing to the negotiation of new guidelines for defence cooperation. Unconstrained by common geo-political strategic interests, trade relations degenerated into a continuing saga of acrimonious mercantilist disputes institutionalized in the Market Oriented Sector Selective (MOSS) trade liberalization negotiations of 1985, the Structural Impediments Initiative (concluded in June 1990), the Semiconductor Trade Agreement of 1986–91 and the US–Japan Framework Talks on bilateral trade that succeeded it in 1993, and the Enhanced Initiative on Deregulation and Competition Policy of 1997 to improve access to Japanese domestic markets for foreign firms.

A fifth structural change is more problematic and contestable. The deregulation of economic activities, itself a symptom of the growing acceptance of the need for radical structural reform of the Japanese economy, was barely underway by the end of the LDP's one-party rule in 1993. A legacy of the high-growth era, when large and small companies were protected from 'excessive competition' in domestic markets all but closed to foreign companies, the momentum for change had gathered pace only slowly in the 1980s when the regulated but 'decelerated' economy was still able to deliver a respectable 4% p.a. GDP growth. That performance was not, and could not be, maintained once the 'bubble' had burst. Experience of the prolonged and deep recession convinced the leaders of big business, and then some (but not all) members of the economic bureaucracy, that the causes were structural rather than cyclical, and required more radical remedies than had been necessary in short-lived recessions of the past.

There were of course other pressures for deregulation. The global liberalization of markets that accompanied the rise of economic neo-liberalism in Europe and the USA exerted continual pressure on closed, regulated Japanese markets. External pressures

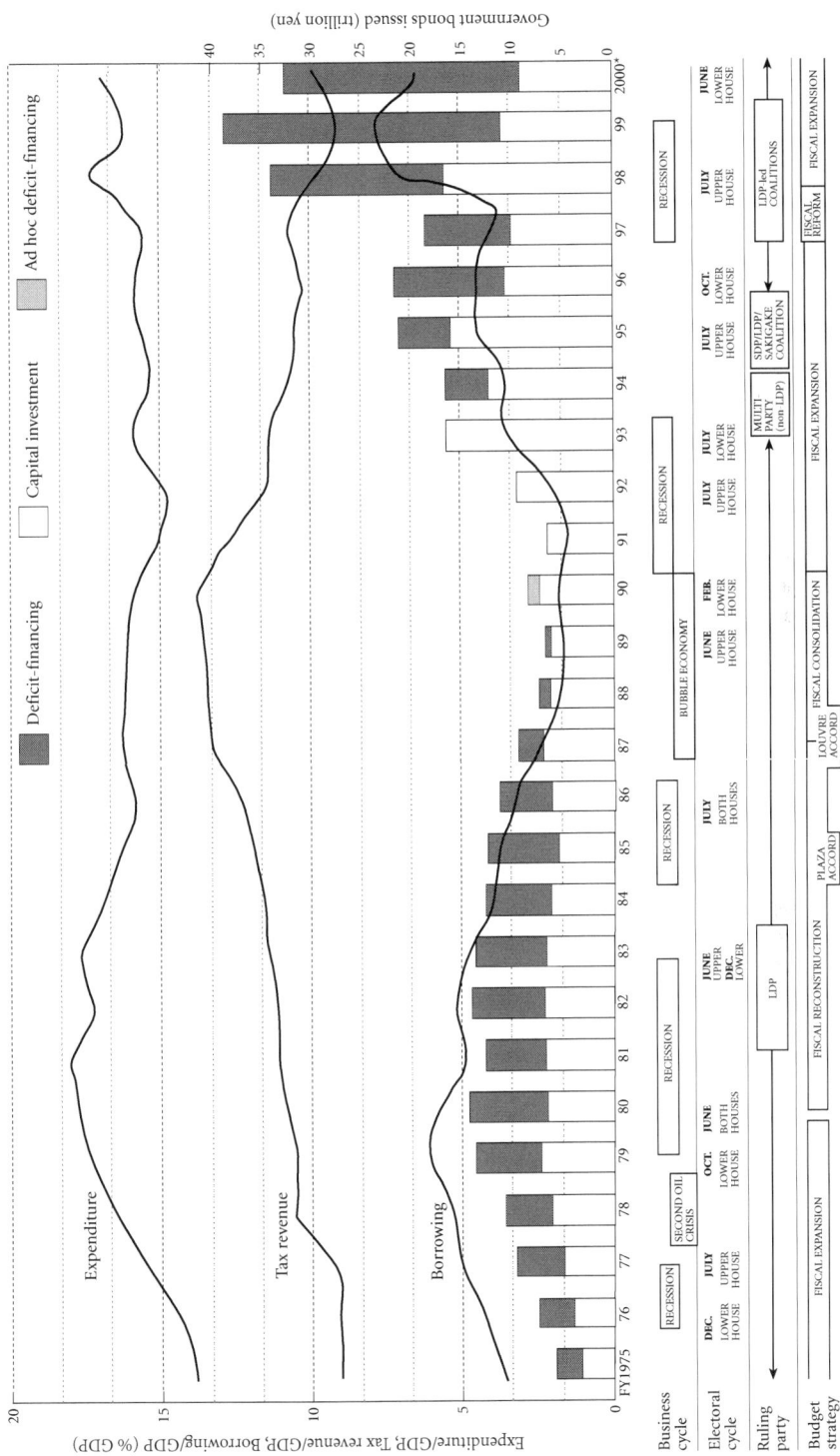

Figure 3.2 Main trends in the General Account Budget, FY1975–FY2000
General Account Settled Budget, nominal GDP

*Initial Budget

Source: Zaisei Tōkei (annually), Research Division, Budget Bureau, MOF.

from US–Japan bilateral trade negotiations throughout the 1980s were exacerbated by the progress of the GATT Uruguay Round and the response of other G7 governments to the deep global recession of late 1980s and early 1990s. The accumulated trade surplus from Japan's highly successful penetration of foreign markets—the USA and the EU, but also some of the old communist countries of Eastern Europe, and especially the new markets in China and SE Asia—led to an appreciation of the yen in the early 1990s which made exporting more difficult. Large exporting corporations wanted deregulation and an opening of markets to foreign firms to reduce the surplus and lower the yen–dollar exchange rate—by April 1995 it had reached 79.75 yen to the dollar, when a decade earlier it had stood at 238. The 'yen bubble' was the fourth in a series of major appreciations of the yen–dollar exchange rate since the floating of exchange rates in 1971, representing a marked shift in the stability of monetary and currency policies underpinning the political economy, and a loss of autonomy to determine them.

The spread of neo-individualism, and the resurgence of neo-classical economics in Western industrial countries, epitomized by the stunning performance of the US economy in the 1990s, prompted some reformers to campaign for the adoption of the Western capitalist model characterized by 'consumer/shareholder sovereignty' rather than the 'employee sovereignty' that had held sway. The commitment in principle to the deregulation of economic and financial activities and markets reflected a growing disillusionment among politicians, large corporations, and the public with the 'employee-sovereignty' firm, and with the efficiency of regulatory regimes administered by regulators with overlapping policy jurisdictions and divided responsibilities. To take but one of many examples, neither MITI nor MOF nor the Bank of Japan accepted responsibility for the failure to supervise and control the activities of the Sumitomo Corporation, one of the world's largest trading companies, which in June 1996 reported a loss of $1.8 billion in unauthorized copper trading.

The economic imperative driving these five structural changes in Japan's political economy was complemented by conjunctural factors in the late 1980s and 1990s, which combined to produce, simultaneously, economic insecurity, political turmoil, and a deterioration in civil order and public safety. As we have seen, the collapse of the bubble economy in 1990 exposed underlying weaknesses in the financial system. The recession that followed was the longest in Japan's post-war history, and raised fundamental questions about the continuing effectiveness of the unique Japanese institutions identified by 'revisionist' writers as responsible for the 'economic miracle', and of the relationships between politicians, bureaucrats, and businessmen that underpinned them. The so-called 'crown jewels' of lifetime employment, wage seniority, and enterprise-unions appeared to be disintegrating; the model 'developmental state' began to exhibit markedly anti-developmental tendencies. The USA had solved its problems of low economic growth, competitiveness, bad debt, and bank failures without the adoption of those strategies and industrial policies enjoined upon it by bedazzled observers of the performance of the Japanese economy in the febrile conditions of the late 1980s. By contrast, and with a rich irony, 'Japan's Strategic Structures' (Johnson 1990) now seemed incapable and ineffective in solving the deeply rooted economic and financial crisis that the bubble economy had temporarily obscured, or in restoring competitiveness to its manufacturing sector and reducing the growing burden of private and public debt.

The political events of 1993–6 ended the so-called '1955 system', in which the LDP, continuously in government, had presided over a politico-economic system managed by networks of LDP politicians, bureaucrats, and businessmen. The extent to which that system was responsible both for the successful transformation of the economy in the decades of high growth and for its collapse in the 1990s is arguable; the causes and consequences of the 'economic miracle' and its mythology continue to excite the passions of 'revisionists' and 'counter-revisionists' alike. (For the debate between them, see Wright 1999*d*.) A further dimension to that debate has been added by those who claim that the origins of the politico-economic malaise or crisis experienced in the 1990s are to be found not in the collapse of the '1955 system', but in the historical continuity of the unreconstructed '1940 system'; that in practice the SCAP reforms of the institutional structures of the economy—the financial system, the bureaucracy, and the political system—were more apparent than real (Noguchi 1995). Power had been transferred from politicians to bureaucrats, and the position of the bureaucracy strengthened, *before* the end of the war.

Whatever the underlying cause of Japan's politico-economic crisis in the 1990s, towards the end of the century a new political order was slowly emerging, displacing the old socio-economic coalition that had dominated the political economy from the end of the Allied Occupation. A new economic order was emerging too, albeit more slowly still. Thoroughgoing structural reform of the economy through deregulation and supply-side measures similar to those adopted in the USA, the UK, and other G7 countries in the 1980s appeared inevitable, and was almost certainly a necessary element of a medium-term strategy to restore competitiveness to many parts of Japanese industry.

The changes in the structures of the politico-economy underway from the end of the high-growth era discussed here, together with those that arose conjuncturally in the business and electoral cycles after the collapse of the bubble economy, have a broader significance for the continuing debate about models of capitalism, which I touch on briefly here by way of conclusion. As we shall see in Chapter 5, 'revisionist' writers have argued that the Japanese model was different from that of other industrialized countries, principally the USA and the UK. Japan and its political economy were 'divergent', the institutional structures, the economic strategy, and the behaviour of policy-makers, uniquely defining characteristics of a 'developmental state'. If however policy-making was determined by similar 'rational choices' in the USA, Japan, and elsewhere, as the new institutionalists argued, then Japan and its economy were less divergent. Support for that hypothesis is provided by several recent econometric analyses of data of more than 46 variables which influence economic and government behaviour in more than 150 countries (Alexander 1999*a*, 2000). Japan's capitalism is not much different from that of other advanced countries, the wealthiest of which develop a rough similarity of institutions (Gwartney *et al.* 1996; Alexander 2000).

Japan fits in the cluster of nations usually considered to subscribe to Anglo-Saxon capitalist norms. Far from being an outlier or significantly different, Japan comes as close to the behaviour patterns of experience of the United States, Canada and the United Kingdom as any other country. (Alexander 1999*b*: 10–11)

Other evidence is more ambiguous, and has been interpreted and used equally to support theories of both 'convergence' and 'divergence'. On the one hand, it is argued that Japan's political economy is converging towards the Anglo-American model of capitalism, as government, firms, trade associations, unions, and the bureaucracy respond to market forces, and the preferences and demands of consumers, in the interests of making its economy more efficient and competitive, and its government more transparent and accountable to the people. Alternatively, the same events and evidence can be seen as 'reactive measures to the slowed post-bubble economic performance and projected or promised changes that are more likely to change [the] appearance than [the] substance, [of] the fundamental character of Japanese political economy that has become deeply embedded in its institutions' (Yamamura 1997: 321). Further discussion, leading directly into a wider debate still about the existence and causes of national diversity and global capitalism, is beyond the scope of this book.

4

Administrative Reform

The administrative context within which the governments of G7 and OECD countries planned and managed their public spending was radically reshaped in the 1980s. A combination of increasing public spending and a shrinking tax base produced a rising level of government borrowing and outstanding debt. With the collapse of Keynesianism and the rise of economic liberalism, rolling back the frontiers of the public sector became both an ideological commitment and, with the burden of increasing deficits and debts, a fiscal imperative. More broadly, the pursuit of economy, efficiency, effectiveness, excellence, and above all enterprise in the design and delivery of public services provoked a radical re-think of the principles on which the public sector was organized and managed. A wave of administrative reforms swept over central (and local) government systems. The 'New Public Management' (Hood 1991) was embraced by most western industrialised countries.

Similar conditions of fiscal crisis were experienced in Japan from the mid-1970s, giving rise to a broadly based campaign of administrative reform associated with the work of the Second Provisional Commission for Administrative Reform (Rinji Gyosei Chōsakai: Rinchō for short), launched in 1981. This chapter begins with a brief review of its work, and assesses the extent to which it changed the administrative context within which the central budgetary system was operated in the 1980s. The second part examines the re-emergence in the 1990s of administrative reform as a political issue on the agenda of successive coalition governments. The broadening of the reform agenda in Prime Minister Hashimoto's six 'visions' is the subject of the third part. The chapter concludes that the conditions of persistent fiscal crisis in the 1980s did not act as a catalyst for a radical re-conceptualization of the role and purpose of the public sector in the Japanese state comparable to that which occurred elsewhere in other G7 countries at that time, and explains why its structure and organization remained relatively unchanged throughout the last quarter of the twentieth century.

ADMINISTRATIVE REFORM AND FISCAL RECONSTRUCTION IN THE 1980s

The administrative context within which the budgetary system was operated throughout the 1980s was dominated by a policy agenda of issues focused ostensibly on administrative reform. In practice, the real issue for MOF was the reconstruction of public finances in order to reduce the burden of government borrowing and accumulating debt. The agent of intended change was the Second Provisional Commission on

Administrative Reform set up in March 1981. The membership of the Commission, the status and influence of the expert members attached to it, the involvement of bureaucrats from almost all ministries and agencies in numerous working groups, the proceedings and the recommendations—all these, and related issues, have been exhaustively examined and discussed, and need no elaborate rehearsal here. Explanations and interpretations of the causes, the events, and the consequences are many and various (among which, see Elliot 1983; Itō 1988; Masujima 1993; Iio 1993; Katō Junko 1994; Ōtake 1994; Campbell 1999; Suzuki 1999). My concern is narrower: to establish why the Commission was set up at that time; to distinguish the real from the ostensible aims of both it and MOF; and to assess its effects on the administrative context within which the budgetary system operated.

'The Declaration of Fiscal Crisis' was officially proclaimed by Ō'Hira Masayoshi, Minister of Finance, on 15 April 1975, as he introduced the issue of special deficit-financing bonds to cover the budget deficit. Their elimination became a major personal objective of his ministerial career at MOF, later as secretary-general of the LDP, and subsequently as prime minister. To emphasize and publicize the critical state of the national public finances, MOF decided in 1976 to publish annually the implications for revenue and borrowing of continuing levels of high expenditure; implicit in those projections was the need to expand the revenue base if deficit bonds were to be eliminated, and more flexibility restored in the balance between fixed and discretionary expenditures. This became the annual *Medium Term Fiscal Projection* (see Chapter 14), and marked the beginning of MOF's long campaign to introduce a broadly based consumption tax to expand the revenue base. Its abortive attempt to do so in 1979 precipitated the setting up of Rinchō.

MOF's failure had, however, brought the fiscal crisis to the centre of the political agenda, and effectively politicized discussion of how it should be dealt with. While MOF wanted to combat the fiscal crisis with both expenditure cuts *and* revenue increases, it had now to abandon the latter and to promote the former until time and opportunity combined to make the contemplation of the latter practical politics once more. Among the opponents of the abandoned tax, there now existed a broad consensus among businessmen, politicians, and bureaucrats to deal with the crisis by reforming the administrative system, principally by cutting its costs. Suzuki Zenkō succeeded Ō'Hira as prime minister, endorsed the strategy, and initiated the reform movement. In anticipation, MOF's Budget Bureau exploited the opportunity to reiterate the urgency of dealing with the crisis, and outlined proposed reforms to Spending Ministries' expenditure programmes in an Encyclopaedia of Public Expenditure (*Saishutsu Hyakka*) published in July 1980. However, the membership and terms of reference given to the Commission appointed a year later implied a much broader inquiry than that envisaged in MOF's initial concern with achieving short-term expenditure cuts to deal with the immediate fiscal crisis. Responsibility for that shift lies partly with the Administration Management Agency (AMA) and its influence on its new minister, Director-General Nakasone Yasuhiro, and partly with Nakasone's own broader agenda for the reform of government and the administrative system; more widely still, he was concerned with the future orientation of the Japanese state. As well, ambitious to succeed Suzuki, he stood to gain political kudos from a high-profile, broadly based reform movement. AMA officials were keen to exploit a long awaited opportunity to implement reforms in the central administrative system. Legislation for the establishment of Rinchō was approved on 20 November 1980.

Dokō Toshio, chairman of Keidanren (Federation of Economic Organizations) an influential, prominent, and elderly businessman committed to the implementation of politically feasible reforms, was appointed chairman of Rinchō. He decisively influenced the direction it took, and reassured the business community by emphasizing 'fiscal reconstruction without tax increase'. The terms of reference nowhere mentioned that principle, but Dokō had secured the prior commitment of Prime Minister Suzuki and senior LDP leaders to it (Suzuki 1999). Thereafter the Commission interpreted its remit more broadly still to include not only issues of organizational and managerial change, the main thrust for example of the 'new public management' in other G7 countries, but also the policy implications of the transition from the era of high growth, the internationalization of the Japan economy, and the progressive ageing of Japanese society.

The Commission under Dokō was bent on comprehensive reform of administrative and fiscal structures. Specifically, it wanted to change the relationship between Spending Ministries and MOF in the determination of the aggregate of the General Account Budget, and its allocation among them. The intention was to create a policy system for the determination of the priorities of spending between programmes of expenditure within a capped aggregate, and to curtail and cut those expenditures accorded lower priority. That amounted to a radical reform of the budgetary system, entailed a change in MOF's traditional role *vis à vis* the Spending Ministries, and implicitly threatened its authority. The agenda was acceptable to MOF only in two respects: first, concerned to eliminate the issue of special deficit-financing bonds, it was not opposed to imposing a top-down limit on the annual General Account Budget; indeed, it had formally prescribed an upper limit each year since 1961, although in practice, through political intervention, it was generous and flexibly administered. What was new was the proposal to impose zero and negative ceilings on each ministry's allocation. Secondly, MOF was obviously supportive of the aim to cut expenditures.

Working within the grain of the Commission's initiative, MOF succeeded in the implementation of both those objectives. The Commission's aim of imposing an order of priority on the whole range of spending programmes precipitated a public expenditure review led and dominated by MOF's agenda, set by its earlier Encyclopaedia. The proposals for expenditure cuts and squeezes—in national health insurance, child care, public pensions, education, public works, and agricultural subsidies—that emerged in the Commission's recommendations in its first 'urgent' report to the Prime Minister in July 1981 were largely inspired by that report, and demonstrated that a programme of continuing fiscal austerity was an integral part of the broader administrative reform movement.

The threat to MOF's authority to compile the Budget, and the traditional 'primacy of the Budget' in determining policy, was more serious. In the event, the Commission's aim to reform the budgetary process to provide for the determination of the relative priorities of public expenditure programmes amounted to no more than the exemption of defence spending and ODA programmes from the general freeze on spending. Both reflected the initial aims of the Commission to recast the administrative and fiscal system to reflect Japan's changing international role and responsibilities, but owed as much to political expediency, the need to be seen to be responding to US and international pressures.

The Commission's first 'urgent' report, a mere four months after it had begun work, was at MOF's request in order that an austerity budget could be compiled for FY1982. The recommendations in it set the tone for the work and reports of the Commission subsequently. They emphasized the need to eliminate the issue of special deficit-financing bonds, and the fact that that required financial reconstruction, the first stage of which was the radical retrenchment of public expenditure for FY1982 to ensure that the Budget did not exceed the level of the preceding year. Those policy aims corresponded closely with those in MOF's Encyclopaedia. Reference was made to the imposition of a zero ceiling for the aggregate for the General Account Budget, but in any case MOF had already agreed to that and had announced it a month earlier.

The initiative for a zero ceiling originated with its Budget Bureau, and pre-dated the setting up of Rinchō. At the time of the 1980 summer review of budget expenditures for the up-coming FY1981 Budget, MOF indicated that expenditure would have to be frozen if a 2 trillion reduction in government bonds was to be achieved. The effects of zero-growth on all major expenditure programmes was demonstrated by MOF in a paper published in October 1980. The intention was not only to underline the gravity of the financial situation, but to urge the need for an order of priority in cutting spending programmes. The initiative for both the zero ceiling and the adoption of categories of priority for expenditure programmes lay with MOF. However, other senior and influential officials were canvassing similar reforms, among them Hayashi Shūzō, a highly respected former director-general of the Cabinet Legislation Bureau. The time was ripe for their introduction, and the powerful and influential Commission provided the opportunity. Its proposals in the first urgent report to the Prime Minister in July 1981 thus represented a public endorsement of the initiative, and served to politicize what MOF had argued a year earlier.

The Budget Bureau had been anxious that the Commission's inquiries and recommendations might pose a threat to its management of the budgetary system, and its control of FILP. Through a Subcommittee on the Budgetary System, it was able to manage an agenda of reform and to frustrate attempts to make radical changes. It was already apparent by the Commission's first Report that MOF had succeeded in influencing the agenda of reform, ensuring that its work and proposals would be oriented towards retrenchment and austerity rather than the transformation of the budgetary system. Over the next two years, the Commission proposed various measures related to deregulation, the central coordination of policy-making, and the enhancement of the role of the Cabinet Secretariat, more flexible arrangements for the internal reorganization of ministries and agencies, central–local relations, and the privatization of public corporations. The latter attracted most public attention. The AMA acquired some new responsibilities, and was redesignated as the Management and Coordination Agency. Rinchō was succeeded by a Provisional Council for the Promotion of Administrative Reform.

The effects of the administrative reform movement in the short term were more symbolic than substantive. The significance of the Commission lay more in what it represented than in what it accomplished in reforming the central administrative system. Its appointment, membership, terms of reference, and commitment all served to emphasize and politicize the fiscal crisis and the need to reconstruct public finances to deal with it. It brought the issue to the forefront of the public's attention, and kept it there for the following two years. The campaign informed the public of the critical state of public finances, and helped to mobilize political and public support for the aim of fiscal reconstruction without tax increase. It did not, however, succeed in restoring balance to the budget—Prime Minister Suzuki's resignation in 1982 was seen as acknowledgement of his formal responsibility for the failure to do so.

Whether the short-term retrenchment of expenditure achieved through the cuts and squeezes brokered by outside experts and officials drawn from the Spending Ministries and Agencies within the review procedures of Rinchō's Working Groups would have been accomplished without the administrative reform campaign is arguable. But the cuts were not deep, and the context was shaped by MOF's own agenda foreshadowed in its 1980 Encyclopaedia. Nevertheless, MOF needed Rinchō to provide the political legitimacy, and to mobilize support for cutting expenditure at that time.

In a longer perspective, the Commission's campaign for 'fiscal reconstruction without tax increase' proved of greater significance. While political and business support for the principle kept taxation reform off the agenda temporarily, it thereby paradoxically paved the way for its introduction in the late 1980s, because the work of the Commission demonstrated that the fiscal crisis could not be solved by expenditure cuts alone. In any case, it was not to be expected that the Spending Ministries and Agencies would agree to cuts in their programmes deep enough to eliminate the deficit. A *modus vivendi* agreed between them and MOF allowed them to write their own tickets of cuts and squeezes (Itō 1988).

Secondly, the introduction of budget guidelines with ceilings for ministerial allocations threatened political vested interests in the maintenance of spending in programmes such as agriculture and public works. 'The proposal to cut expenditure by a uniform rule of ceiling actually transferred public criticism of waste and inefficiency in the administration into apprehension about the possible reduction or elimination of specific programmes' (Katō Junko 1994: 149). The imposition of annual ceilings of minus 5% on public works programmes from FY1984 to FY1987 was especially worrying to LDP politicians. Increasingly, they began to appreciate that limits imposed upon the General Account Budget aggregate, and on ministerial allocations within it, had profound implications for their politico-electoral interests.

Thirdly, although MOF ostensibly acquiesced in 'fiscal reconstruction without tax increase', in practice it continued to raise tax thresholds and to increase corporate and community taxes from FY1982 onwards, on the singular interpretation that 'without tax increase' meant no *new* taxes. MOF's broader campaign to increase the burden of indirect taxes began to win support among LDP politicians, who wanted the restoration of the ritualistic annual cuts in direct taxes, suspended in 1977, and among corporate business associations. The latter, which had enthusiastically endorsed the administrative reform campaign to cut the costs of government and so avoid the possibility of corporate and indirect tax increases, began in 1984 to react publicly to the growing burden of tax borne by their members.

The administrative reform campaign and the work of the Commission did not significantly change the administrative context within which the budgetary system operated. The structure and organization of the central administration and the policy-making system remained largely undisturbed. Rather, it was change to the budgetary system through the formal prescription of more tightly drawn budget guidelines, and the prioritization of categories of expenditure and policy, that changed the administrative context in which budgets were made. MOF was not displaced from its central position in the budget-making process by substituting for the 'primacy of the budget' an alternative system for making policies and determining the priorities of spending. It survived the short-lived challenge to its authority, emerging with its control of both the aggregate and its allocation enhanced, and in a position to dictate the policy agenda for the reform of the tax base in order to eliminate the special deficit-financing bonds in progressing towards its ultimate goal of the restoration of a balanced budget. However as we shall see in later chapters, the real position of the public finances through the 1980s was more serious than MOF's presentation of the trends in expenditure growth suggested.

Administrative Reform after Rinchō

The Commission was formally dissolved in 1983. Thereafter administrative reform was relegated to a lower place on the political agenda, revived only with the de-alignment of political parties which began in 1993. The main focus of the inquiries and reports of the Provisional Councils for the Promotion of Administrative Reform (PCPAR) shifted from fiscal reconstruction to issues of deregulation and decentralization. Nevertheless, the continuing concern with the shortage of revenue, the elimination of special deficit-financing bonds, proposals for a consumption tax, the control of the growth of the General Account Budget—all issues that Rinchō had brought within the banner of 'fiscal reconstruction without tax increase'—continued to be discussed within the Councils, and outside in a continuing dialogue between MOF and LDP ministers and officials.

The formal responsibility of the Councils through the 1980s was to keep the roles and responsibilities of the national government under continuous review. In theory, their work was premissed on two principles of the 'new public management': first, that public services that could be efficiently provided through competition in the market should be transferred to the private sector; and, secondly, that both individuals and companies in the private sector should be freed from regulation by central government. Progress was made in the implementation of the first principle at the central level with the sale of shares in Nippon Telegraph and Telephone (NTT), Japan National Railways (JNR), and the Japan Tobacco and Salt Company, and the disposal of assets in several public companies, among them Japan Air Lines (JAL), the Japan Automobile

Terminal Company, the Tōhoku Development Corporation, and the Okinawa Electricity Company. However, the reduction in the number of public corporations from 99 in 1981 to 92 at the end of the decade was achieved largely through the merger and integration of existing functions rather than abolition.

The numerous measures of deregulation that were recommended by successive Councils and, independently of their work, by agreement between the MCA and individual ministries and agencies, resulted in incremental and gradual changes rather than radical reforms. While economic deregulation was a major policy issue in trade disputes and negotiations with the USA throughout the 1980s and early 1990s, the relaxation or abolition of regulations that restricted entry to, and competition in, domestic markets occurred piecemeal in response to particular pressures and incentives from the USA and the international economic community rather than as part of a concerted, comprehensive programme of reform. The issues of deregulation and improved access to Japanese domestic markets were highlighted in the so-called Maekawa Reports of 1986 and 1987, as the Japanese government responded to growing foreign criticism of its chronic and large current account surpluses. However, there were few specific proposals, and few changes resulted. In retrospect, the reports and the reaction to them were more significant in establishing an agenda of reform issues helping to educate and prepare business and political elites for change; more immediately, they paved the way for the Market Oriented Sector Selective (MOSS) trade liberalization negotiations with the USA, and the Structural Impediments Initiative.

The limited impact of the work of the Provisional Councils in the 1980s is due to several factors. First, until the arrival of the Hosokawa coalition government in 1993 there was little political support—especially little prime ministerial support, after Takeshita's resignation in 1989—for a programme of comprehensive administrative reform. Secondly, the power of ministries and agencies to make economic and social regulations under their laws of establishment defined and delimited their jurisdictional authority *vis à vis* each other. The scope and use of their regulatory power was jealously protected. Thirdly, and relatedly, bureaucrats and politicians had a shared interest in maintaining ministerial regulatory powers as a valuable resource of authority to exchange with special interest groups, many of whom were direct financial beneficiaries of regulatory regimes of licences, permits, and authorizations that had served hitherto to restrict entry to markets, or limit competition. MOT regulations for car inspection sustained an estimated work-force of half a million in the private sector; the restrictive provisions of the Large-Scale Retail Store Law benefited large numbers of small shopkeepers, traditional supporters of the LDP. 'Easements', 'abatements', and regulatory dispensations were equally useful as tradable resources exchanged by bureaucrats for political support, specialist information and advice from politicians and interest groups, and by politicians for donations to their personal campaign funds and LDP factional funds.

Fourthly, the inherent conservatism and caution of the central administration, combined with the fear of the unknown among special interest groups, inhibited radical deregulation throughout the 1980s, and ensured that reform where it occurred would be piecemeal and the pace gradual. Finally, the implementation of agreed reforms required the cooperation and willingness of each ministry and agency. A typical tactic was 'to convey gestures of agreement in principle, but to disagree with the particulars' (*sōron-sansei, kakuron-hantai*).

ADMINISTRATIVE REFORM IN THE 1990s

Administrative reform re-emerged as a major political issue in the realignment of political parties that followed the breakaway of dissident members of the LDP in 1993. The partners of the coalition government of Prime Minister Hosokawa had earlier campaigned (some within the LDP) to reform the political and administrative systems. A *Blueprint for a New Japan* and an agenda was provided by Ozawa Ichirō (1994), secretary-general of the newly formed Shinseitō, which combined with six other parties to form the coalition government in August 1993. The three main elements in the administrative reform movement at that time were: the deregulation of economic and social activities; the decentralization of functions from central to local government; and the reduction and rationalization of public corporations.

Deregulation

The Hosokawa, Murayuma, Hashimoto, and Obuchi coalition governments all endorsed, with varying degrees of enthusiasm, the principle of more competition in more open domestic markets, and the relaxation of the bureaucratic control of economic activities of firms in those markets. But proposals for the abolition of ministerial regulations in a succession of reports and action programmes were more limited in scope and substance than those urged by Keidanren, Nikkeiren (Japanese Federation of Employer's Association), and their large corporate members, and inevitably by the US government. Representing the interests of large corporations, Keidanren lobbied for the opening of domestic markets to foreign competition, and for more and faster deregulation of a wide range of economic activities and markets. With the rapid appreciation of the yen in the early 1990s making it difficult for its corporate members to sustain the competitiveness of exports, it argued that increased competition in domestic markets would help to reduce the surplus on the balance of trade, reduce the yen–dollar exchange rate, and make exporting easier.

The Deregulation Action Programme agreed by Prime Minister Murayama's Cabinet in March 1995 had three main aims: to improve consumer choice and reduce price differentials between foreign and domestic goods; to promote imports and expand domestic demand and business opportunities; and to simplify administrative regulations and controls. The guiding principle, first enunciated in the Maekawa Report in 1986, was 'freedom from regulation in principle, with regulation as the exception' (*Deregulation Action Programme*, 31 March 1995). The programme initially comprised 1,091 measures to be implemented over a three-year period, 1995–7. Greater emphasis was attached to the disclosure of administrative information and transparency in the process of implementation. A new three-year programme to promote deregulation, to run from 1998 to 2000, was approved by Cabinet in March 1998. Its principles and objectives were largely restatements of those in earlier programmes: the abolition of economic regulations, and the simplification, speeding up, and transparency of regulatory procedures. Action consisted mainly of a series of comprehensive reviews of existing procedures in 16 sectors, for example barriers to entry, approval and notification requirements, international standards and specifications. Measures for promoting fair and free competition were mainly cast in the subjunctive mood—'strict and vigorous measure will be taken against price cartels'; 'prompt action will be taken against unfair trade practices'; 'the FTC shall take strict measures against violations of the Anti-Monopoly Law' (MOF 1998*d*). Of the 1,268 measures proposed in the programme, some 90% had been partially or fully implemented by October 2000 (MCA 2000). A further three-year programme of deregulation began in April 2000, and included an agenda of 234 proposals from the government's own Committee at the Administrative Reform Promotion Headquarters in the Cabinet.

The Implementation of Deregulation

The process of the implementation of regulatory reform in Japan, as elsewhere, is complex, the appearance of deregulation frequently belied by the substance. 'In too many instances in the recent past ... we have learned that what was to occur after deregulation and what did in fact occur were frequently different' (Yamamura 1997: 316)

All new regulations in the form of Laws or Cabinet Ordinances were scrutinized by the Cabinet Legislation Bureau, the Administrative Management Bureau of the MCA, and by MOF's Budget Bureau to ensure that they were necessary and appropriate. Existing regulations were subject to formal review every five years, and were inspected by MCA's Administrative Inspection Bureau as part of its programme of continuous review of ministerial activities. It could and did make recommendations for the reform of regulatory practices, but their implementation was conditional on the willingness and agreement of the ministry or agency concerned. The MCA could require them to report on measures taken in response to recommendations made by it; both recommendations and responses were published. It also monitored the process of implementation through the use of administrative inspection, and required ministries and agencies to report on progress. Nevertheless, neither the MCA, nor the PCPARs through which it frequently operated, nor the Administrative Reform Committee and its Working Groups set up in the Prime Minister's Office in December 1994 could impose reforms on unwilling, reluctant, or obstructive ministries and agencies which had final responsibility for their own internal structure and organization. That they proved a formidable obstacle to the achievement of significant reforms in the past was evident in the *cri de coeur* of the Director-General of the MCA's Administrative Inspection Bureau, and the Director of the Administrative Reform Division of its Administrative Management Bureau. Without strong and committed political leadership,

Ministries and agencies ... are inclined to stick to the existing systems and policies and are unwilling to make efforts to reform on their own initiatives particularly when various interests are intertwined in a complicated manner ... Especially, to [an] issue such as de-regulation which might affect their power and authority, ministries and agencies show negative attitudes, unless other ministries and agencies are required to make the same efforts. (Tanaka and Horié 1993: 220)

More than 70% of the total regulations were issued by five ministries: MOF, MAFF, MHW, MITI, and MOT (Table 4.1). Only in the latter two was there a reduction between 1986 and 1995. After seven years of continuous growth, the number of permits, licences, notifications, and approvals in force in 1993 stood at a record 11,402, 460 more than the previous year, and about 1,000 more since the Provisional Council's Report in 1985 on the need for deregulation; however, numbers declined in the next two years.

The evaluation of the implementation of deregulation by reference to such quantitative data presents a misleading and oversimplified picture. First, ministries had different standards for counting regulations, narrow for some (such as MOT) and broader for others (e.g. MOL and MITI). Secondly, many *de facto* regulations were imposed by administrative guidance, lacked an explicit legal basis, and thus were not counted by MCA. Thirdly, the number of regulations did not distinguish qualitatively between either the types or the strength of regulations, for example between permits (*kyoka*) and licences (*menkyo*) on the one hand, and the much weaker requirement to notify (*todokede*) or to submit information (*teishutsu*) on the other. In many cases the latter had replaced the former—a weakening of regulatory discretionary authority—without altering the number of regulations, and in some cases actually increasing it. A section of an Act might contain one or several 'permissions', and one permission might be much stronger than the collective force of several. Fresh regulations might also be necessary where an activity previously illegal or restricted was now permitted, subject to certain conditions, resulting in the relaxation of regulation but an increase in the number of permissions. In 1996 there were 314 cases of new regulations attributable directly to the implementation of the Deregulation Action Programme (IAM 1999). Fourthly, the 'headline' total was the net result of both increases and decreases. In 1995–6 there were 176 increases and 127 decreases, contributing a net increase of 49 to the total of 11,032. The liberalization of markets and the privatization of public corporations had in many cases (as in other G7 countries) led to re-regulation, partly because competition in markets among large private companies required both a regulatory regime and a regulatory authority to administer it. Until 1998 and the creation of the Financial Supervision Agency, the latter role was played in Japan mainly by ministries and ministerial agencies rather than being yielded up to independent regulatory agencies which characterized re-regulation in the UK, the USA, and elsewhere. At the same time, the process of deregulation in Japan was characterized by paradoxical 'expansionary re-regulation' as Spending Ministries and Agencies sought to protect existing policy jurisdictions and to establish claims to exercise discretionary authority in new policy areas.

Nearly a decade of deregulation yielded only modest gains to GDP, little more than 10% in the period 1990–8, according to an official government estimate (EPA 1999). Commitment to deregulation did not in itself provide the conditions for the revival of long-term growth. What was required was regulatory reform of institutions, processes, transparency, and regulators. If such reform was undertaken and addressed the key issues of the barriers to market entry and price restrictions, a real boost to the economy could occur (OECD 1999*a*).

Table 4.1 Regulations issued by ministries and agencies, FY1986–FY1996 (at 31 March each year)

	1986	1987	1988	1989	1990	1991	1992	1993	1994	1995	1996
Prime Minister's Office	27	27	29	32	32	32	33	33	32	32	32
Fair Trade Commission	26	26	26	28	28	26	26	26	26	26	26
National Public Safety Commission	81	95	97	100	100	99	114	134	144	141	149
Management and Coordination Agency	29	29	29	34	34	34	34	37	35	35	35
Hokkaido Development Agency	26	26	28	31	31	31	31	31	31	31	31
Japan Defence Agency	26	26	28	31	31	31	31	31	31	31	31
Economic Planning Agency	26	26	26	31	31	31	31	31	31	31	31
Science and Technology Agency	218	260	263	291	291	298	298	303	301	297	307
Environment Agency	149	149	156	159	162	164	165	188	194	199	204
Okinawa Development Agency	27	27	27	32	32	32	32	32	32	32	32
National Land Agency	81	81	81	86	86	86	89	89	88	87	87
Ministry of Justice	146	146	148	149	153	154	166	172	172	168	176
Ministry of Foreign Affairs	37	37	39	42	46	46	50	53	50	50	48
Ministry of Finance	1,116	1,134	1,143	1,173	1,195	1,210	1,236	1,387	1,391	1,374	1,460
Ministry of Education	310	308	317	314	315	312	322	333	327	327	328
Ministry of Health and Welfare	936	945	985	1,015	1,033	1,106	1,170	1,221	1,246	1,221	1,262
Ministry of Agriculture, Forestry, and Fisheries	1,263	1,256	1,270	1,270	1,299	1,315	1,357	1,427	1,419	1,400	1,394
Ministry of International Trade and Industry	1,870	1,886	1,883	1,900	1,908	1,916	1,915	1,986	1,769	1,780	1,841
Ministry of Transport	2,017	1,976	1,977	1,962	1,988	1,966	1,966	1,893	1,700	1,607	1,573
Ministry of Posts and Telecommunications	265	273	279	284	306	308	313	319	291	292	303
Ministry of Labor	532	559	563	560	559	565	579	631	629	633	605
Ministry of Construction	742	770	776	804	808	842	870	910	879	841	863
Ministry of Home Affairs	104	107	108	113	113	113	114	134	127	125	125
TOTAL	10,054	10,169	10,278	10,441	10,581	10,717	10,942	11,402	10,945	10,760	10,983

Source: MCA (1998*a*).

Decentralization

The issue of more autonomy for local government through the decentralization of authority from central government was less one of needing to respond to grass-roots pressures, more an administrative issue of freeing prefectures and municipalities from the close supervision and tight control of central government ministries and agencies. The principle of local autonomy was a key element in the reform agenda of Rinchō and its successors throughout the 1980s and into the 1990s, but attempts to decentralize were 'lukewarm', and implementation proved 'unsuccessful owing to the bureaucracy's stubborn resistance', in the words of the former deputy director-general of MCA, the senior official with overall responsibility for administrative reform during the period 1981–93. Proposals to curtail national intervention in local government, to transfer functions from the centre in order to rationalize the practice of agency delegation, and to eliminate grants-in-aid were either 'inadequate' or 'insufficient'. There were no proposals to increase citizens' participation in local government, or to curb the practice of seconding officials from central government ministries (Masujima 1998).

The year 1993 proved a turning point, as politicians seized the initiative on administrative reform. The reports of a Commission for Promoting Decentralization, set up within the Prime Minister's Office, paved the way for the Decentralization Action Programme approved by Cabinet in May 1998. Legislation passed by the Diet in 1999, implemented from April 2000, was based largely on its proposals to clarify the roles of central and local government, to increase the independence of the latter, and to decentralize power and devolve functions and responsibilities down the hierarchy. The measures are more extensive and stronger than any proposed in the 1980s. First, they provide for the abolition of agency delegation functions (*kikan-inin-jimu*), whereby statutory functions are delegated to and carried out by prefectural governors and municipal mayors as agents of the national government, supervised and directed by the responsible ministries and agencies. Principal–agent relations are replaced by 'equal partnership' between the central and subnational governments, with the jurisdiction, functions, and responsibilities of each hierarchical level prescribed by statute. Secondly, the standards and procedures whereby central government intervenes formally and informally in the activities of prefectural governors, and at both levels in those of the municipalities, are restricted and regulated by statute. Thirdly, intergovernmental disputes are referred to a commission set up in the Prime Minister's Office. Fourthly, grants-in-aid and subsidies are to be rationalized.

The abolition of agency-delegated functions is potentially a far-reaching reform, removing a major source of the tension in the relationships between the centre and prefectural governors. But the enhanced discretionary authority of the latter will provoke municipalities to seek greater autonomy through the transfer of functions and responsibilities. The effectiveness of the implementation of the statutory-based policies for the decentralization of power and authority will depend crucially on the willingness of central government to make sufficient financial resources available to enable local governments to discharge their new functions. Local governments are to enjoy more freedom to issue their own bonds, and to institute their own taxes without the permission of the minister. However, prior consultation will be necessary in both cases.

Public Corporations

The number, role, and functions of public corporations, the third element of administrative reform, had, like decentralization and deregulation, been the subject of continuing attention from both Rinchō and the PCPARs. Reform began with the adoption of the principle of 'scrap and build' in 1965 as part of a concerted government initiative to reduce the size and cost of the public sector, as the burgeoning fiscal deficit unbalanced the national finances for the first time since the adoption of the 'Dodge Line'. The process of the 'consolidation and rationalization' of the 113 public corporations made little headway until after 1975 and the emergence of the fiscal crisis, although within that total there had been a number of mergers and abolitions. As noted above, the inquiries and recommendations of Rinchō in the early 1980s led to a gradual reduction in their number, and to a rationalization of the functions of several other smaller public corporations.

Under the Hosokawa government's initiative on administrative reform, each ministry and agency was required to conduct a review of the *raison d'être*, functions, employment, and efficiency of those public corporations within its jurisdiction. The Murayama Coalition endorsed that review, but radical proposals were shelved or deferred for later consideration, the Cabinet finally agreeing to only a modest reduction in the number of public corporations, from 92 to 84, achieved through the merger of the functions of 12 pairs of mainly minor organizations and the abolition and privatization of two further small public corporations. A fresh impetus was provided by the LDP's Administrative Reform Headquarters, which prepared a more radical agenda for Prime Minister Hashimoto's electoral campaign in the summer of 1996, proposing the abolition of a further five corporations and the privatization of another. By 31 March 1998 the number had been reduced to 81. Legislation passed the previous year provided the framework for securing the disclosure of more management and financial information in order to improve public accountability of their performance.

The Structural Reform of the Economy

The deregulation of economic (and social) activities, increasingly advocated and urged upon the government by business leaders, was itself a symptom of the growing acceptance of the need for radical reform of the structure of the economy. The momentum for change had gathered pace only slowly in the 1980s when the regulated but 'decelerated' economy was still able to deliver a respectable average of 4% p.a. GDP growth. That performance was not and could not be maintained once the 'bubble' had burst. Nevertheless, the response of both government and business to the continuing downturn of the economy was slow and hesitant. There was a persistent and pervasive perception that the causes of slow growth in the 1990s were cyclical and conjunctural rather than structural, and that a resumption of historical rates of growth would occur by 'sitting out' the downturn. The delay in dealing effectively with the crisis in the banking sector was due partly to the same belief that the restoration of growth would remedy the problems of bad debts and non-performing loans.

The tardy response was also due to the LDP's investment in the maintenance of the existing politico-economic structures: it needed to protect its clients and supporters from the consequences of the collapse of the bubble economy they had helped to create. Construction companies, among the largest contributors to LDP funds, were heavily indebted to banks and credit companies; agricultural cooperatives were substantial creditors of the bankrupt housing loan associations (*jusen*); small businesses were threatened by any further restriction of credit lines if financial institutions were obliged to liquidate their debts quickly. Thirdly, business policies and practices appropriate to the conditions of a developing economy pursuing growth and market-share were not changed easily or quickly to respond to the different demands of a mature economy in which the sovereignty of producer and employee was replaced by that of the consumer and shareholder.

Within the economic bureaucracy, the process of constructing a consensus on the need for (but not the policies for achieving) structural change began with the publication of MITI's annual White Paper on Trade in the summer of 1995. It urged recognition 'that Japan's economic system, which has supported our past economic growth, is no longer able to adapt to the changing international environment'. The uncompetitiveness of much of industry, it argued, was due to government regulations and special business practices which maintained domestic prices at higher levels than in other countries. The high cost structure had forced many leading companies to move production and corporate functions abroad, and had discouraged inward investment. Unless the economic structure was changed, Japan would be 'left behind in the global business scene'. It 'must undertake immediate reform in order to build an affluent and vibrant economic society'. Deregulation, the correction of price differentials, and an increase in domestic investment opportunities were all necessary ingredients.

Neither the diagnosis nor the prescription was novel; discounting the inevitable element of rhetoric to appease international critics, the public endorsement of both by an influential part of the economic bureaucracy, one with more interests invested in the regulatory regime than most other economic ministries, was nevertheless significant. However, MITI's advocacy was driven by its search for a new role, and its enthusiasm for deregulation was partly, perhaps mainly, influenced by its own bureaucratic agenda to establish a jurisdictional claim *vis à vis* its competitors.

The Economic Planning Agency's (EPA) annual White Paper, *Toward the Revival of a Dynamic Economy*, published in July 1995 was, if anything, a franker recognition of the economic crisis than MITI's. It was consistent with the general direction and thrust of the Interim Report on the new National Economic Plan produced the same month by the Economic Council; EPA was responsible for servicing the Council. To continue the 'closed policies', because of the fear of the short-term social and financial consequences of opening domestic markets to competition, was to risk long-term economic stagnation. The reference here was to the estimate that deregulation would increase unemployment by upwards of three million in the short-term, and would increase public spending. EPA called for the removal of barriers to entry and competition in large parts of the service sector, including transport, telecommunications, medical services, health, housing, and leisure. But those general prescriptions were not followed up with concrete policy proposals, and the Cabinet was comfortably able to approve the EPA White Paper, as it had earlier that of MITI.

MOF influenced EPA policy-making through strategic secondment of senior officials—the permanent head of the Agency, the deputy-director general, was normally a senior official on secondment from MOF. On this occasion, shortly after the publication of the White Paper, Komura Takeshi returned to MOF to become deputy vice-minister in the Minister's Secretariat (and later director general of the Budget Bureau and, in July 1997, administrative vice-minister). EPA's call for structural reform thus had at least MOF's tacit approval, and as mentioned was consistent with the thrust of the new National Economic Plan submitted by the Economic Council to the Cabinet in December 1995. It was now frankly admitted that the existing social and economic structure was unable any longer to cope with the progress of globalization and the transition to an advanced, mature economy and society. The title of the National Economic Plan, *Social and Economic Plan for Structural Reforms*, and its main theme both emphasized the need for structural reform. Graphic public testimony was provided by the senior EPA official (on secondment from MOF) responsible for the formulation of the Plan, which reads like an epitaph to the developmental state. Many of the myths held dear by the Japanese had completely collapsed:

All of our long-cherished assumptions—that the Japanese economy will always grow, that asset prices always rise, that full employment is virtually guaranteed, that financial institutions are invulnerable, that Japan has the safest society in the world—are now being overturned. People in Japan are losing self-confidence and wondering what has gone wrong. In short, we are aware that we are in crisis for the first time in these fifty years of post-war prosperity, and we know we have to revamp our society and economy. (Shiga 1995: 1)

HASHIMOTO'S SIX 'VISIONS'

The momentum for structural reform of the economy, or, more accurately, for recognition of the need for reform, was given a further and substantial boost during and after the LDP's campaign for the general election to the House of Representatives in October 1996, part of a broader electoral platform of change and reform 'envisioned' by Prime Minister Hashimoto in five key areas: the economy, the financial system, the fiscal system, the administration, and social security; a sixth, education, was added later.

The Economy

In swift succession, the Economic Council, MITI, and the Prime Minister's new Administrative Reform Committee independently produced proposals for the acceleration of the action programme for the deregulation of economic activities, the further liberalization of markets, and reforms of key economic structures. The promptings of EPA's earlier White Paper, consistent with the National Economic Plan, were echoed in the Economic Council's recommendations to the Prime Minister for urgent structural reform in six strategic sectors—advanced telecommunications, the distribution of industry, the financial system, land and housing, employment and labour, and medical care and welfare—all highlighted in the National Plan. MITI, in its continuing search for a new policy role, similarly followed up its own earlier White Paper with a policy framework for deregulation designed (by its Industrial Policy Bureau) to create 7.4 million jobs in 15 strategic sectors by 2010. This was approved by Cabinet in December 1996, and MITI was awarded the task of coordinating its implementation. At the centre, the Administrative Reform Committee in the Prime Minister's Office produced its own independent report urging faster progress in the reform of economic structures in 15 areas. For the most part, the rehearsal and reiteration of familiar aims and objectives in those and other initiatives lacked the details of policies, or the means to implement them. (For a summary and assessment of progress to 1999, see OECD 1999*a* and MCA 2000.)

The Financial System

The second envisioned reform, of the financial system, was to be achieved mainly through the deregulation of financial markets, products, and services initiated by a 'Big Bang' in April 1998 comparable to that which had occurred in the USA in 1975 and in the UK financial markets a decade later. Changes included the liberalization of cross-national capital transactions, relaxation of controls on financial products, easier access to financial markets, and improved financial disclosure and reporting (MOF 1997*a*; 1998*b*). The substance of those and other changes, their effects, and the commitment of MOF and the LDP to radical reform were greeted with reactions varying from outright scepticism to cautious optimism that a process had begun leading inexorably to the creation of those 'free, fair and global financial markets' envisaged by Prime Minister Hashimoto, although few believed that this would be achieved by 2001. Nevertheless, a former sceptic conceded in 2000 that the reforms were being largely implemented as announced in 1997 (Lincoln 2000). More immediately, the constitutional status and powers of the Bank of Japan were changed by legislation in 1997 to give it greater independence and more control over monetary policy. Both MOF and EPA were deprived of their membership of its Policy Board, but were allowed to attend without voting rights. In June 1998 the Financial Supervision Agency, within the jurisdiction of the Prime Minister's Office, assumed responsibility for those functions of inspection and supervision of private institutions previously undertaken by MOF's Banking and Securities Bureaux.

The Fiscal System

In Hashimoto's third vision, budget deficits and public-sector debt were to be tackled in a wide-ranging reform of the fiscal system. By 2003 the deficit was to be reduced to no more than 3% of GDP, and the issue of special deficit-financing bonds eliminated. Public spending in the General Account Budget was to be reduced in real terms in FY1998 and FY1999, the budget for public works programmes cut by 10%, and long-term plans for both capital and current expenditure programmes reviewed. As an integral part of the fiscal system, the agenda for reform was widened to include consideration of the future size, funding, and role of FILP. Apart from the latter, most of those proposals were enacted in the Fiscal Structural Reform Act in November 1997, and a start made on their implementation in the budget for FY1998. However, the rapid deterioration of the economy in the last quarter of 1997, and the decline into recession in 1998 forced a policy U-turn on a reluctant Hashimoto. The Act was revised in June to enable the government to borrow above the prescribed limits to finance a package of countercyclical measures of spending and tax reductions, but it constrained the issue of deficit bonds. The target date for the achievement of the policy objectives was extended to FY2005, but as the economic situation worsened his successor Prime Minister Obuchi Keizō announced a three-year suspension of the whole fiscal reform programme in December 1998 as he introduced yet another countercyclical package.

Whereas fiscal and administrative reform had been at the centre of Prime Minister Hashimoto's change programme, his successor Obuchi had pledged, in his campaign for the presidency of the party, to make the revival of the economy his first priority. On the demand side, tax cuts of 9.3 trillion and additional spending of 17 trillion were announced in November 1998; but, those and other earlier pump-priming measures having yielded only modest results slowly, the focus of government attention switched to the supply side. For the first time, there was government acknowledgement that the elimination of excess plant and employment capacity in the manufacturing sector was a prerequisite of economic recovery. In March 1999 an Industry Competitiveness Council of senior Cabinet ministers and businessmen was appointed and chaired by the Prime Minister. Modelled on the US Commission on Industrial Competitiveness set up by President Reagan in the 1980s, its task was to make proposals for the reduction of production capacity in such industries as steel, motor vehicles, and chemicals, for job retraining, and, contingently, for the revision of corporate taxation and the laws on mergers/acquisitions and bankruptcy.

The strategic context for the Council's deliberations was set by the reports of the Economic Strategy Council which the Prime Minister established on his accession to office in August 1998. Chaired by Higuchi Hirotarō, chairman of Asahi Breweries, it proposed a ten-year plan to be implemented in three stages designed, first, to dispose of the debts and loans problems of the financial sector, then to achieve an economic growth rate of 2% by 2001, and finally to rebuild public-sector finances with the aim of restoring a balanced budget by 2008. Among more than 200 radical proposals was the judgement that an increase in the consumption tax was inevitable, that a radical review of FILP might lead to its abolition, and that the salary-linked welfare pension system could be privatized. However, those and other proposals were subsequently diluted by bureaucrats, whose influence permeated the final report. The themes of competitiveness and further deregulation were taken up in the new National Economic Plan endorsed by the Cabinet in July 1999. However, the LDP was far from united in the belief that a radical restructuring of the economy was either necessary or inevitable. Opposition within the party became more apparent as legislation was drafted. The threat to the heavily protected and subsidized small business sector from the implementation of retail deregulation and anti-trust policies was opposed by a powerful informal group of 165 LDP Dietmen, which in 1999 succeeded in diluting legislation to decontrol the taxi-cab sector.

The Administrative Reform Programme

Prime Minister Hashimoto committed himself personally to an ambitious programme of administrative reform, responding to the public mood of dissatisfaction and distrust with the role and behaviour of bureaucrats, and outrage at a succession of corruption scandals involving senior officials in MOF, MHW, MITI, and (later) the Bank of Japan and the Defence Agency. Criticism of a general deterioration in standards of honesty, fairness, and integrity added to the public perception of administrative incompetence. Bureaucrats were blamed for a succession of policy failures and mismanagement. Reforming the central executive was then both electorally popular, and part of the general strategy of the LDP and its coalition partners to take more control of policy-making and to reduce the power and influence of bureaucrats, cutting the bureaucrats down to size, literally and metaphorically. MOF was a particular target, blamed for its failure to foresee and prevent the consequences of the 'bubble economy', to rescue the economy from the recession of the 1990s, and to handle the crisis in the banking sector. In September 1996 Prime Minister Hashimoto floated a plan to reduce the number of ministries and agencies from 22 to 14 (later reduced to 13 in the legislation); to cut the power and authority of MOF by transferring its responsibilities for the supervision and regulation of the financial sector to a newly created and independent body, and to make the Bank of Japan more independent. More radical still was the proposal to relocate the whole apparatus of central government outside Tokyo by 2010.

After the general election, and the formation of his second administration in November 1996, Hashimoto's 'vision' of a reformed and reconstructed central executive was incorporated into a broader, more ambitious Administrative Reform Programme, which the Cabinet approved on 25 December for implementation between FY1997 and FY2000. The guiding principle was 'to restructure "*kono-kuni no katachi*" [the shape of this country] by aspiring to form a society that is free and fair, composed of autonomous individuals' (ARC 1997: 1). It had four main objectives: (1) to create a simpler, more efficient, and responsive system of public administration; (2) to provide more opportunities for the exercise of personal initiative by individual citizens through greater private-sector involvement; (3) to provide greater openness and transparency in decision-making; and (4) to improve the quality of public services. To achieve them, the size and role of the public sector was to be further reduced by continuing the programmes of privatization and deregulation, by reducing the number of public corporations and rationalizing their functions, and by transferring functions from central to local governments. While those proposals for the most part reaffirmed earlier policy initiatives, that for the reform of the machinery of the central executive was new and was given the highest priority. The proposals and their implications are discussed in Chapter 6. Access to government information was established in principle through legislation passed in May 1999. The extent to which the right to request the disclosure of government documents will improve the transparency of decision-making will not become apparent until the Act comes into force after 2001. A Code of Ethics regulating the conduct of government officials was also enacted in May 1999. All gifts and entertainment above 5,000 yen have to be declared by officials above the rank of deputy director. Bureau heads and administrative vice-ministers are required additionally to submit annual reports of their financial assets. An Ethics Review Board in the National Personnel Authority is responsible for overseeing compliance with the new regulations.

Assessments of the impact of the fresh impetus given to the administrative reform movement by the Hashimoto government of 1996–8, and that of his successor, Prime Minister Obuchi, must await the implementation of the various action programmes, many of which, like those for the reorganization of the machinery of the central executive, fiscal structural reform, FILP, and the reform of financial markets, stretch well beyond the year 2000. Understandably, the reform agendas and the process of implementation have been invested with a great deal of political rhetoric, partly to help foster and sustain the political momentum for change, and partly to contribute to the education of public opinion generally, and that of specialized interest groups in particular. But the rhetoric has also often served to obscure the reality of what was intended, and what has been accomplished. However, while doubts and scepticism have been voiced by both domestic and foreign critics—for example about the scale of the ambition of the broad reform programme for restructuring the economy, the commitment of politicians and bureaucrats to it, and the feasibility of carrying it out (e.g. Yamamura 1997)—the outcome is neither entirely predictable nor controllable. There might be unintended consequences arising from the acceptance and implementation of reform in one policy area. For example, the liberalization of money markets in the first stage of Big Bang in 1998 made it more difficult to resist the logic of privatizing postal savings, and removing the market advantages accruing to public finance corporations such as the Japan Development Bank and EXIM Bank in providing financial services and products at cut rates. The momentous decision in 1997 to decouple the statutory link between postal savings, pensions, and FILP might eventually make the argument for privatizing postal savings irresistible. As I shall argue in Chapter 28, it made the reform of FILP both more necessary and inevitable. In turn, that gave a much-needed boost to the administrative reform action programme to reduce the number of public corporations and rationalize their functions, as many of the former FILP agencies were now forced to compete for funding in the market place.

Social Security and Education Policy

The fifth and sixth envisaged reforms in social security and education policy were, at first, little more than restatements of various policy proposals and prescriptions in train. The reform of education had been an explicit commitment since 1987, when Prime Minister Nakasone established the National Council on Educational Reform. However, Hashimoto's education vision contributed to the emerging consensus among bureaucrats in central government that reform was needed if the labour force was to be equipped with the new skills to meet the challenge of global capitalism. A succession of reports and proposals flowed from MOE's advisory councils on primary and elementary education, curriculum development, national textbooks, and higher education.

Concern about the increasing costs of the national system of medical care insurance, pensions, and the care of the elderly had produced a number of cost-containment measures and new schemes, such as the 'Ten Year Gold Plan' for the welfare of the elderly over the previous decade. An insurance system for the long-term care of the elderly, providing both institutional and in-home services, was introduced in 1997, while the occasion of the statutory revaluation of the benefits and contributions of the national pension system in 1999 provided the rationale for the debate on radical reform of the whole structure which began shortly after Hashimoto's announcement.

CONCLUSION

Japan's public sector was little changed in the 1980s and 1990s compared with the experience of other G7 and OECD countries. Whereas in the UK, France, Germany, Italy, and Canada there occurred in the 1980s a radical re-conceptualization of the size, role, and purpose of the public sector, in Japan the principles of the new public management resonated only weakly. Public services provided by central (and local) government were not 'marketized' according to the dictates of the doctrines of neo-liberal economics espoused by the 'new right' regimes of those and other countries. Where in those countries the conditions of burgeoning public-sector deficits and debts served as a catalyst for the reconstruction of the institutions and structures of the public sector, and government's role in the economy, in Japan the turning point, if such it proves to be, occurred much later. A consensus among influential elite groups of businessmen, politicians, and bureaucrats that radical change in the institutions and structures of the Japanese state was necessary, above all in the economic and financial systems, was emerging only slowly toward the end of the century.

In other G7 and OECD countries, the fiscal imperative (deficits and debt) continued to drive administrative reform in the late 1980s and the first half of the following decade, Canada and the UK being two notable examples. There was a logical progression from the decentralization of public financial management systems to the privatization of public utilities and services, the creation of Executive Agencies, the widespread contracting-out of activities and functions to private-sector firms, 'marketization', and the introduction of resource and contract budgeting; here the UK was a prime example (Thain and Wright 1995). The occurrence of a fiscal crisis comparable to, or greater than, that experienced in those countries did not serve as a catalyst for radical administrative reform in Japan, at least not before 1997. After Rinchō was established in 1981, the campaign was skilfully orchestrated by MOF to transform an initial political agenda of comprehensive reform of the policy-making system into a more limited set of issues concerned with financial reconstruction, focused on short-term expenditure cuts and changes to the budgetary system, which served its longer-term interests in controlling the aggregate and allocation of the General Account Budget. The response to continuing fiscal crisis in Japan focused more narrowly on the reform of the tax structure. The switch in the burden of taxation from income to consumption had taken place earlier in other G7 countries, and by comparison Japan's over-reliance on direct taxation was increasingly anomalous. After 1983 the time and energies of MOF bureaucrats, senior LDP politicians, and business associations were preoccupied with successive attempts to introduce (and frustrate) a consumption tax.

Why then was the public sector so little changed between 1975 and 2000? Why did the principles of the 'New Public Management' apparently resonate so weakly in Japanese central government? Why did the conditions of chronic weakness in the fiscal system, exposed and exacerbated by the economic recessions of the 1990s, not serve as a catalyst for radical administrative (and economic) reform in Japan as they had elsewhere?

First, the dissolution or collapse of the Keynesian consensus in Western industrialized countries towards the end of the 1970s, provoking a reassessment of the role of the public sector, did not occur in Japan because Keynesianism had never provided the intellectual basis for the politico-economic management of the economy, although from time to time—as in 1983 and 1987, and repeatedly in the 1990s—fiscal policy was employed pragmatically to stimulate domestic demand in the economy. (For the argument that the implementation of macroeconomic policy had been consistently more Keynesian, see Asako *et al.* 1991.)

Secondly, there was no political disjuncture between left and right, and especially 'new right' governments, as occurred in the UK, the USA, Canada, France, and Italy: one-party rule continued uninterruptedly and (electorally) successfully until the onset of the deep economic recession in 1991, and the fragmentation of the LDP two years later.

Thirdly, and relatedly, until the general election for the House of Representatives in 1993, the mutual interests of politicians, bureaucrats, and special interest groups were served by a political system that allowed them to exchange money, votes, authority, and information. The preservation of the status quo was a *sine qua non* of that system. It was reflected in, and reinforced by, a central administrative structure characterized by autonomous verticalized ministries, simultaneously protecting their independent jurisdictional authority, promoting their territorial claims and ambitions, and influencing and controlling the activities and senior posts in the public corporations and government enterprises they supervised. Ministers and bureaucrats were ill-disposed to relinquish voluntarily key elements of their discretionary authority. Many private-sector groups and clients whose activities fell within the jurisdiction of a ministry also had an interest in maintaining a regulatory regime of licenses, permits, and authorizations which conferred financial and other benefits denied to their potential competitors.

An alternative explanation for the lack of radical change in the central administrative system was provided by senior MOF and MCA officials (in interviews). They argued that it was due partly to the size, role, and significance of the public sector in Japan, and partly to the traditional and inherently cautious approach to processes of change characteristic of the Japanese political system. In brief, they argued, there was much less to change, because the size, scope, and cost of the public sector in Japan was much smaller than in other G7 countries. They emphasized that the ratio of public-sector employees (central and local governments and government enterprises) to the size of population, at some 4% was considerably lower than in France, where it was three times as high, or in the UK, the USA, and Germany, where it was double; and that its cost in terms of the ratio of general government expenditure to GDP was much smaller.

They argued also that there had been more change in the public sector than was apparent, but that that change had taken place over a longer period of time, and had been piecemeal, gradual, and step-by-step rather than comprehensive and radical. That process began in 1967, a full decade or more before most other G7 countries. As I shall describe in Chapter 22, the size of the national government work-force was reduced gradually but modestly over a 30-year period, but also flexibly, to accommodate to the changing needs and demands of existing and new government functions. Comparable changes in other countries were more dramatic, abrupt, and implemented over a shorter period of time, based on the principles of the 'New Public Management'. By contrast, Japanese governments and officials were more sceptical about the widespread introduction of private-sector concepts of management and their associated techniques, for example rejecting the abrupt, convulsive, and costly Anglo-American approach to deregulating markets, preferring instead to spend more then 15 years dismantling controls over interest rates to prevent sudden dislocations to the system (Hartcher, 1998).

While there is some force in those bureaucratic arguments, they only partially qualify the explanation offered earlier which emphasizes the feasibility and practical difficulties in achieving the necessary broadly based consensus for change among the political, economic, and bureaucratic interests vested in the '1955 system'.

The slow pace of the reform process in the 1980s and the 1990s, despite conditions of acute economic, financial, and fiscal crisis, was characteristic of the Japanese politico-administrative system and can be variously interpreted, virtuously as a symptom of the gradual, step-by-step approach traditionally favoured by bureaucrats and politicians, the result of long, painstaking, and extensive consultation and *nemawashi* designed to achieve a broad and acceptable consensus among all interested parties, and to avoid commitment to a change which might have uncertain or unintended consequences. Before Hashimoto's visions for the six policy areas could be translated into concrete proposals leading to the formulation of explicit government policies and the drafting of appropriate legislation, it was necessary to involve the relevant statutory advisory councils and committees in an elaborate formal process of consultation, apart from the informal processes involving politicians and bureaucrats. For example, three of MOF's statutory advisory councils—the Financial System Research Committee, the Securities and Exchange Council, and the Insurance Council—were formally charged with the discussion of Hashimoto's Big Bang vision, each producing separate reform agendas and timetables as the basis for government policy and legislation. At the same time, an informal process of consultation and negotiation within the LDP, and between it and the SDP and Sakigake, was necessary to build a consensus and ensure a smooth passage for the legislation in both houses of the Diet.

An alternative interpretation of the gradual, complex, and time-consuming process of constructing a broad consensus before commitment to policy change is that the reluctance on the part of unwilling bureaucrats was supported by the reluctance of the vested interests of discrete networks of politicians and interest groups to exchange the certain benefits of the status quo for the uncertainty of the consequences of radical reforms. Undoubtedly, such a construction can be placed on the events surrounding the formulation and carrying out of successive 'action' plans to deregulate economic activities, and to reduce and rationalize the number and functions of public corporations, between 1993 and 1998. The initiative taken by the LDP's own reform committee and the ruling parties' working party after the 1996 election was partly an impatient response to the slow pace of reform hitherto.

5

Politicians and Bureaucrats in the Policy-Making Processes

The reversal in Japan's economic fortunes after the collapse of the bubble economy, combined with the end of the LDP's 38 years of rule in 1993 and the political turbulence that ensued, raised, and continues to raise, questions about the continuing effectiveness of Japanese institutions, and about the relationships between politicians, bureaucrats, and businessmen in the organizations that underpinned those institutions. This chapter provides a broad overview of the continuing academic debate about the policy-making processes, in order to provide a general frame of reference within which to locate discussion in later chapters about the role and influence of bureaucrats and politicians (and other participants) specifically in the budget-making processes.

I begin with the concept of the 'developmental state', in which bureaucrats are accorded the pre-eminent role in policy-making, Chalmers Johnson's (1982) trail-blazer, and the inspiration or provocation for much that followed. I then look briefly at the qualification to theories of bureaucratic dominance to accommodate the evidence of competition and conflict in the policy-making processes provided by the neo-pluralists. The work of area and sector specialists is briefly reviewed in the general context of the thrust of a 'counter-revisionist' challenge, emphasizing the interdependence of relationships of politicians, bureaucrats, and societal interest groups in sub-governments or networks. This leads on to a more detailed and critical review of the recent work of the 'new institutionalists'. Adopting and adapting theories of rational choice, they have attacked both revisionists and counter-revisionists, arguing that the relationship between politicians and bureaucrats is one of principal and agent, bureaucrats acting merely as the instruments of politicians. In conclusion, the chapter urges the essential complementarity of the different approaches, and seeks a more nuanced analysis of budget policies and processes which captures the dynamics of institutional structures and their historical 'settings'.

BUREAUCRATIC DOMINANCE IN THE 'DEVELOPMENTAL STATE'

Revisionists argued that Japan's capitalist system is different from Anglo-American models; that its institutions, the role of the state, and its mercantilist economic policies are (or were) fundamentally different, even unique. Hence those who pointed out those differences were 'revisionists'. Central to the argument was the role of the state, in which the dominant role was played by elite bureaucrats; by implication, the ruling Liberal Democrat Party was accorded a subordinate role.

The thesis was set out most challengingly by Chalmers Johnson (1975), the 'godfather of revisionism'. In his later magisterial historical study of the role of the Ministry of International Trade and Industry (MITI) in industrial policy-making, he explained the origins and causes of the 'economic miracle' that occurred in Japan, roughly from the mid-1920s to the mid-1970s. (Johnson 1982). The centrepiece of his model of the 'developmental state' was the bureaucracy, accorded a crucial and explicitly instrumental role in the Japanese political system. Although influenced by interest groups, 'the elite bureaucracy of Japan makes most decisions, drafts virtually all legislation, controls the national budget, and is the source of all major policy innovations in the system' (pp. 20–1). But power within the developmental state was not exercised by a bureaucratic monolith. There were many competing sources among the different ministries, and conflict between them occurred within the policy-making processes. Nevertheless, Johnson argued that 'the centre that exerts the greatest *positive* influence is the one that creates and executes industrial policy.' That centre was dominated by the economic bureaucracy, principally MITI and EPA. Johnson's conclusion from his analysis of the empirical evidence of the fifty-year period, is explicit: 'Japan's is a system of bureaucratic rule' (p. 320).

That phrase has been used by other writers to characterize (and criticize) Johnson's explanation of the role of the bureaucracy in policy-making. His account became the benchmark by which to judge those who offered alternative explanations. Later, as empirical evidence of policy-making in other sectors accumulated, Johnson modified his position. He conceded that the LDP had begun to play a more prominent and influential role in policy-making from the early 1970s onwards, dating roughly from the accession to the post of prime minister of Tanaka Kakuei, a proto-typical machine politician. But he repeated his earlier claim that, until about 1975, there was no question of who governed Japan: it was the official state bureaucracy.

However, during the 1970s a subtle combination of events started an apparent decline in the power of the bureaucracy, and a concurrent rise in the power of the LDP ... It seems wise to speak of an *apparent* trend because none of the evidence about it is conclusive. There are still powerful ideological pressures in Japan to pretend that the LDP is more influential than it actually is; and the relationship between the bureaucracy and the politicians has historically been cyclical rather than linear, with the bureaucracy regaining power during times of crisis. (Johnson 1986: 206–7)

Nevertheless, Johnson concluded that the trend away from a 'bureaucratic leadership structure' (*kanryō shudō taisei*) towards a 'party leadership structure' (*tō shudō taisei*) was real. Although the bureaucracy's monopoly of policy-making powers remained 'virtually complete', political rather than bureaucratic interests prevailed in some domestic, non-industrial sectors such as education, defence policy, and agricultural subsidies. 'Most important policies still originate within a ministry or agency, not within the political or private sectors' (Johnson *et al.* 1989: 182).

THE NEO-PLURALISTS: COMPETITION AND CONFLICT IN THE POLICY-MAKING PROCESSES

The first challenge to theories of a dominant bureaucracy was mounted by a number of (mainly Japanese) scholars arguing from a variety of pluralist and neo-pluralist perspectives. While still biased towards a 'strong bureaucracy', they identified and incorporated into their explanations the countervailing pressures exercised by other social groups: the LDP and its organizations, both formal and informal; sectional interest groups clustered around fragmented policy areas; and opposition parties in the Diet. 'Patterned pluralism' qualified the assumption of a normally dominant and monolithic bureaucracy with two institutional characteristics of Japanese policy-making: jurisdictional competition and conflict within the bureaucracy, and the incorporation of minority opinion (mainly the opposition parties in the Diet) into decision-making, either directly by negotiation or indirectly through anticipated reaction.

The LDP made [the] final decision on political competition between groups and the bureaucracy or between agency-group coalitions. Patterned pluralism promotes competition among ministry bureaucracies to push forward new projects that appeal to their constituents. Ministerial bureaucracies propose, and the LDP decides. (Muramatsu and Krauss 1987: 60)

Subsequently, Muramatsu (1993) argued that the bureaucracy became more defensive in the 1980s in response to the impact of administrative reform and American pressures to open the economy and expand domestic demand, and as individual ministries struggled to maintain their jurisdictional boundaries and their policy-making authority. Other major neo-pluralist accounts of policy-making were constructed along similar lines, and acknowledged the polycentric character of Japanese bureaucracy, with its inherent and endemic jurisdictional competition and conflict (Inoguchi 1983; Murakami 1983; Satō and Matsuzaki 1986). This became more evident and intractable, it was argued, as policy-making became less orientated to national goals associated with the high-growth era, and as ministries and agencies competed for jurisdictional authority to control policy-making in new areas associated with social and welfare objectives, the environment, and the development of new technologies.

The analysis of patterns of conflict and methods of conflict resolution became an issue of central concern for some analysts of policy-making within the emerging critique of theories of dominant bureaucracy. Thus, while Pempel (1989) continued to emphasize 'consensual and bureaucratic policy-making' within the conservative coalition of the bureaucracy, LDP, and business, he conceded that conflict could arise—but only from the intervention of foreign actors and/or the opposition parties. Campbell (1984) argued the now more familiar proposition that conflict could and did occur within the conservative coalition itself, in those circumstances where policy issues transcended the boundaries of ministerial jurisdiction, or where jurisdiction was disputed between 'sub-governments' founded on policy areas. Later Samuels (1994) went further still, arguing that a permanent state of conflict and contestation might be the natural order of Japanese politics, paradoxically serving to stabilize the system and to reinforce the values to which all participants must appeal. Through confrontation and political struggle, they constructed 'ever denser networks of obligation and reciprocity—tacit compacts and protocols of reciprocal consent' (p. 334).

The increasing influence of the LDP in the policy-making processes in the two decades before 1993 was partly a reaction to excessive sectionalism and jurisdictional in-fighting within the bureaucracy, which presented politicians with opportunities to support one ministry against another, or to assume a leadership role when policy-making became stalled or deadlocked; and partly the result of the growth of policy expertise among senior LDP politicians. A third factor was the shift in the recruitment and preferment of LDP leaders away from former bureaucrats towards long-serving politicians from rural constituencies. Through its formal organs, most notably the Policy Affairs Research Council (PARC) and its divisions, special committees, and research societies, and informally through the emergence of powerful policy tribes (*zoku-giin*), but also through attempts to influence particular policies by more active and interventionist prime ministers, such as Tanaka and Nakasone, the LDP played a more active role in policy-making. Most accounts date this greater influence to the early 1970s, when the accession of Tanaka led to a spate of policies in the new era of welfare and compensatory policies, as the LDP responded to the challenge to its political hegemony. Thus the argument runs: the subordinate or acquiescent role of the LDP in the era of national consensus on the goals of high growth in the 1950s and 1960s contrasts with its more pro-active stance in setting policy agendas subsequently, and in the choice of policy options.

That conventional wisdom has in turn been challenged from a wide-ranging historical perspective of several policy areas by, among others, Kent Calder (1988), who demonstrated that the occurrence of politico-electoral crises *before* the early 1970s provoked the LDP to respond with compensatory policies. Other more narrowly focused studies of individual policy sectors have found comparable evidence of LDP influence earlier still, in the 1950s and 1960s, to deny or qualify theories of bureaucratic-led or dominant policy-making (Yasutomo 1986; Campbell 1993; Calder 1993). In his study of policy-making in the industrial-credit area, Calder concluded that the role of politics since 1945 had 'been more than simply static approval of bureaucratic dictates. It became more systematically important during the 1970s and 1980s but had significant impact in complicating state industrial strategy long before that' (Calder 1993: 230).

Silberman (1996) roots LDP influence more explicitly in the historical development of the state in the early part of the twentieth century. Political decisions were constrained by the adoption of Weberian specialized and scientific rules of administration, and political parties were subordinated to the bureaucracy. Attempts to establish long-term majoritarian control over the Lower House, forcing the bureaucracy to come to terms with the political parties, were vitiated by inter-party strife over control of the Diet. The conditions in which political parties might re-establish and maintain control of the legislature, and make the bureaucracy accountable, were spelled out by Prime Minister Hara (1918–21): majoritarian politics in the Diet, and a combination of distributive politics and economic development designed to produce an appearance of an economically rational strategy for development which neither the bureaucracy nor private interests could resist. Those conditions proved impossible of fulfilment in the inter-war period.

Nevertheless, Silberman argues, that earlier vision was implicit in the reconstruction of party politics after the Second World War. The LDP became the ruling majoritarian party, and achieved and sustained a dominant position for 38 years by a combination of distributive politics and economic development. The LDP's continuing monopoly of legislative power obliged the bureaucracy to work with the party in the pursuit of economic development goals. As the LDP successfully maintained itself in power, the bureaucracy became increasingly politicized. In short, Silberman argues that the relationships between bureaucrats and politicians were embedded in the long-term historical evolution of the institutional structures of party politics, the bureaucracy, and the role of the state in economic development; the appearance of bureaucratic domination belied by the reality of the LDP's structural power. That conclusion, but not the premises from which it derived, is similar to the arguments of 'historical institutionalists', who believe that rationality is a product of institutional circumstances. We look at their work below, but first we examine the challenge of the 'counter-revisionists'.

THE 'COUNTER-REVISIONISTS': THE SECTORAL CHALLENGE TO THE THEORIES OF BUREAUCRATIC DOMINANCE

A more sustained attack upon the characterization of Japan as a 'strong state', according a pre-eminent role in policy-making to the bureaucracy, was mounted by the growing number of scholars who argued that, whatever might have been the case in the period of high growth, the political system had (before the end of the LDP's rule in 1993) changed, and that the role and influence of politicians in the policy-making processes had increased. In 'The Unbundling of Japan Inc', Pempel (1987) concluded that Japanese policy-making was far more complex and less coherent than two decades earlier, with 'a relative decrease in the hegemonic powers of bureaucratic agencies, and a rise in the influence of the LDP and its parliamentary members' (p. 152). More emphatically, Haley (1987) declared that 'the dominance of the Japanese bureaucracy in the political process has been grossly exaggerated. Not only has bureaucratic influence rarely been as significant as generally perceived, but also what powers the bureaucracy has exercised have declined steadily during the post-war period.' The capacity of government officials to determine and implement policy was constrained by a variety of institutional factors. Any assessment of their influence 'must be particularised to specific issues and programs, requiring careful analysis of the circumstances of each case' (p. 178).

More narrowly, Johnson's theory of the 'developmental state', with its centrepiece of economic and industrial policy-making dominated by the bureaucracy, has been confronted by the accumulating evidence of empirical analysis of individual industrial sectors, policies, and processes. Like Johnson, the 'counter-revisionists' too emphasized the historical context or 'setting', but, whereas his approach and model of the 'developmental state' was top-down, they proceeded 'bottom up'. Collectively, their work comprises a powerful and persuasive critique of Johnson's thesis of bureaucratic dominance. From different perspectives, using different analytical frameworks, they arrive at similar conclusions about the constraints on the exercise of bureaucratic power. (For a discussion, see Wilks and Wright 1991: 39–45.)

Several recent empirical studies of sectoral industrial policies provide further support. Writing as an unabashed 'counter-revisionist', Callon (1995) argues that MITI's industrial policy regime collapsed as the Japanese economy was transformed from that of a 'catch-up' follower to a 'caught-up' economic superpower in the period 1975–85. The paradigm of coherence and cooperation that formerly marked the relationships between MITI, private companies, and other bureaucratic actors, was replaced by one of competition and conflict. MITI's industrial policy for micro-electronics was neither cooperative nor successful. The dominant position achieved by its companies occurred despite, not because of, MITI.

Callon's claim that the whole basis for Japan's post-war industrial policy has disintegrated since the 1970s is contestable. While it is true that a significant disjuncture apparently occurred in the making and carrying out of industrial policy between 1975 and 1985, it is still unclear what role MITI and the other institutions of the economic bureaucracy really played before that. The explanation of the economic miracle of the high-growth era now appears to be more complex than Johnson and the 'revisionists' once argued. Other institutions in both the public and private sectors, and other processes such as the formation of industrial credit, might have contributed as much or more to it than MITI bureaucrats and their industrial policies. The assumption that the Japanese state automatically acted strategically and purposefully has been increasingly questioned. Empirical findings of research at the sectoral level have revealed the structural complexity and fragmentation of state institutions and processes, and the difficulty in moving the Japanese state to purposeful action.

Johnson earlier argued that credit allocation had been one of the state's most important instruments for achieving the strategic transformation of the industrial structure. Zysman (1983) had gone further, arguing that the financial system centred on credit relationships was 'the eyes and hands of the state's industrial brain' (p. 308). Calder's (1993) study of government credit and industrial capital, which questions the respective roles of the public and private sectors in bankrolling the economic miracle in the 1950s and 1960s, is therefore a critical test of the concept of the 'development state'. 'Strategic capitalism' is a 'hybrid public–private system, driven pre-eminently by market-created private-sector calculations, but with active public-sector involvement to encourage public spiritedness and long-range vision' (p. 6). The implications of the detailed analysis of that system for the discussion of policy-making here are fourfold. First, it casts yet more doubt on the dominant role of the bureaucracy, even in the era of high growth. 'Japanese bureaucrats had more difficulty attaining their sector-specific objectives than commonly thought', other than in the provision of industrial infrastructure. Private-sector actors—here, banks, trading companies, industrial associations, and firms—were more influential. Secondly, while state structures matter, they are not undifferentiated, as implied in Johnson's MITI-centric account. State institutions and structures vary sectorally, and the amount of regulatory authority that they possess and dispose affects the coherence of policy outcomes. Thirdly, the complexity and fragmentation of state structures at the sectoral level (here) undermined the possibility of achieving broad-gauge, cross-sectoral targeting of the kind conventionally ascribed to the Japanese state. Fragmentation and decentralization provided the means of access, and of the opportunity for influence, of private-sector actors. As a result, fourthly, there was a pluralist bias to the allocative processes. Relationships between public and private actors with shared interests in the financial policy area were institutionalized within the policy processes in 'circles of compensation', through which the Japanese state allocated benefits.

In a similar vein, Tilton (1996) argues that 'to understand the true scope of industrial policy, one must look beyond official state-sponsored policies to unofficial policies initiated and implemented by trade associations' (p. 205). Their role in four basic but declining industries reflected a paradigmatic system of private-interest governance of Japan's political economy. Bureaucrats did not usually attempt to impose their will on business: they worked with it to solve common industrial policies in ways that served national policy goals. Typically, MITI provided the encouragement, and sometimes the initiative, for the organization of cartels which the firms wanted but were unable to coordinate on their own. But its aim was neither forward-looking nor efficiency-oriented. It did not try to ease companies out of inefficient declining industries, but rather, sought to maintain self-sufficiency in those vital for national security. Schaede (2000) explores these and other themes in greater depth in her study of the role and influence of trade associations in the Japanese economy.

By contrast with those and some other recent studies (e.g. Vestal 1994; Weinstein 1995; Uriu 1996), Vogel's comparative study of the transformation of the relationships between governments and markets in Japan, the USA, and Western Europe is a compelling restatement of the thesis of bureaucratic dominance. It challenges the conventional wisdom that the processes of globalization, privatization, and above all deregulation have led to less government intervention and control. In the Japanese case (as in the UK) more competition meant more government control, as markets were 're-regulated'. In the policy-making processes, state actors not only held autonomous preferences; they 'acted upon those preferences, and influenced outcomes in ways that we can not understand by focusing on private interests alone'. But private interests also helped shape policy outcomes: 'both state and societal actors matter' (Vogel 1996: 268). Vogel demonstrates the leading role played by bureaucrats in policy-making, arguing that the state is relatively autonomous of societal interests. Competition and conflict between different interest groups leave state actors as the interpreters and arbiters of those interests. To that task they bring their own specific ideological biases and institutional capabilities. How state actors define and interpret the public interest and how they pursue it is shaped by the 'ideological and institutional context' in which they operate.

'GOVERNANCE BY NEGOTIATION'

While the high-ground of strategic industrial policy-making has been claimed (mainly) by the counter-revisionists, the challenge to theories of a dominant bureaucracy has continued to advance on a broader front, encompassing a variety of both domestic and international policy sectors, institutions, and processes; there is now a long list and it continues to grow.[1] Most such studies accept the need 'to engage in extensive historical analysis to determine concrete instruments, institutions and processes of national goal setting' in order to understand 'how actual public and private organizations operate at the micro-level' (Calder 1993: 8). They provide explanations of particular policy outputs, or changes in policy outputs, and show why attempts to change them succeed or fail, as for example in Campbell's (1993) study of health policy. Using different methods, and developing different frameworks for analysis, their characterization of the policy-making processes is nevertheless remarkably similar.

Horne's (1985) masterly study of Japanese financial markets, an exemplar of the genre, analyses the interaction between the LDP, MOF, public and private financial institutions, and other corporate and non-corporate bodies with an interest in the development and implementation of regulatory policy for Japanese financial markets in the 1970s and early 1980s. It shows, first, that public policy-making for the regulation of financial markets is complex, rich, and varied. Disaggregation of the sector revealed five different but related policy areas, for each of which the number and the range of participants, and the nature of their interaction in the policy processes, differed. In four of them the LDP had little or no direct involvement: policy was dominated by MOF. In postal savings, however, where there were important electoral implications, the LDP's view prevailed: MOF was 'relatively helpless in the face of effective political alliances built within the LDP' (p. 212). Secondly, Horne shows that the role and influence of the participants varied with the nature of the policy-making activity. Thus, the LDP was uninterested in the *implementation* of regulations within settled policy.

Thirdly, the LDP could and did influence the general context of policy-making—without explicit intervention, like Adam Smith's 'invisible hand' or the 'ghost in the machine'—by establishing the parameters within which policy options could be initiated and discussed by MOF. Thus, in the development of the government bond market, the intransigent position of the LDP to tax increases ruled out certain policy options. 'The MOF was bound by the parameters set by the LDP. It was unable to lift taxes or cut expenditures. Instead its responsibility was that of implementing the policy of the LDP' (p. 58). By preventing the restoration of the revenue–expenditure equilibrium in the late 1970s and early 1980s, the LDP defined the range of options available in the regulation of the government bond market. Thus, the LDP determined the general contours of the policy-making framework by exercising an implicit veto power. MOF had to work within them.

Fourthly, the influence of the LDP in shaping policy and its implementation was also evident, but not visible, in its support for the aims of particular interest groups. Fifthly, the institutional structures of political party, bureaucracy, and private sector were complex, polycentric, and differentiated. For example, within MOF there were different

---

[1] It includes financial markets and services (Horne 1985; Rosenbluth 1989, 1993; Calder 1993; Vogel 1994, 1996); education (Schoppa 1991*a*); social policy (Anderson 1993; Campbell 1993); agriculture (George 1981; Donnelly 1984; Mulgan 2000); overseas development aid (Rix 1980, 1993; Orr 1990; Ensign 1992; Koppell and Orr 1993; Yasutomo 1986; 1995; Arase 1994; 1995) tax policy (Katō Junko 1994); defence and national security (Chinworth 1992; Keddell 1993; Katzenstein and Okawara 1993; Katzenstein 1996*a*,*b*).

interests and objectives among competing bureaux, with different jurisdictions, appealing to different constituencies of interest groups.

RATIONAL CHOICE: 'POLITICIANS REIGN AND RULE'

There is little support in the work of 'counter-revisionists' for a general interpretation of policy-making that accords a consistently dominant role to politicians, although from time to time in different policy sectors the evidence shows that the LDP's influence could be decisive, and in a few policy areas, such as agriculture, public works, defence, and some education issues with ideological overtones, the policy-making process has been traditionally politicized. Beyond that, most sectorally based accounts agree only that the LDP's influence relative to the bureaucracy has increased since the early 1970s, although as we have seen even that generalization is qualified by some authors.

The most provocative and full-blooded attack on the dominant-bureaucracy thesis has come from those schooled in rational choice approaches and the methodology of individual determinism, the advocates of the 'new institutionalism'. Ramseyer and Rosenbluth's (1993) claim that the LDP dominates policy-making, and did so even before the 1970s, is a singular and, as presented, deliberately iconoclastic interpretation of Japanese policy-making, which, if tenable, not only subverts Johnson's thesis but runs counter to the general thrust of most of the sectoral and area studies. Their 'choice-theoretic' approach prescribes political actors as principals and agents competing in a political market, manipulating the institutional framework of government to their private advantage. Sets of actors behave rationally to maximize their self-interests. The dominance of the LDP (principal), it is claimed, is secured through its control of the bureaucracy (agent). The leadership delegates power to bureaucrats who make and carry out policies consistent with the aims and strategies of the party. Bureaucrats predict or anticipate the policy preferences of the party and act accordingly. Their apparent dominance occurs because of the acquiescence of the leadership in their assumption of the initiative, for example in drafting legislation. In practice, they are allowed to do so because the leadership has the means to monitor and control their actions, and where necessary punish them if they act inconsistently with the leadership's politico-electoral interests. Because bureaucrats know more than their principals about the work they have been 'contracted' to do, information is asymmetrical. It is vital then for principals to monitor and sanction agents to ensure that they comply with the conditions of the contract. Unless this is done effectively, agents can pursue interests other than those specified by their principals. Thus, they can veto bureaucrats' policy proposals, legislation, and actions; control their careers through promotions and postings; and their post-retirement careers through the practice of *amakudari*, the 'descent from heaven' into lucrative and prestigious private (and public)-sector jobs. Thus, bureaucrats acting in their own self-interest provide the LDP with those policies aimed to maximize their self-interest in holding on to power. In brief, Japanese bureaucrats are nothing more than the agents of LDP politicians; bureaucratic dominance is an illusion.

However, Ramseyer and Rosenbluth agree with the 'counter-revisionists' on the need for rigorous empirical testing of their model, and draw upon a wide range of secondary material in support of their argument. While it provides some support independently for each of the building-blocks used in the construction of the argument, it fails as a coherent explanation of policy-making when tested against the empirical evidence of different policy sectors and issues. Like all successful political parties, the LDP's conduct in office is shaped by both short- and longer-term electoral considerations. Until electoral reform in 1994, the SNTV in multi-member constituencies obliged LDP Dietmen in different factions to compete for votes and build and maintain local personal networks in which votes and organizations for the mobilization of those votes were traded for tangible community and personal benefits—jobs, infrastructure, environmental amenities, business opportunities, and contracts.

Bureaucrats understand the need to take such considerations into account. But it is only one factor, whose significance varies between policy sectors, and within them from one issue to another, and over time. To assert that all policy-making is driven by such a politico-electoral imperative is not supported by the empirical evidence of the sectoral studies reviewed above. Nor does it follow that the behaviour of *all* LDP Dietmen is governed all of the time by such self-interest. Indeed, Ramseyer and Rosenbluth acknowledge the tension between the self-interest of rank-and-file LDP Dietmen, and the collective interest of the party as a whole represented by the leadership, which they argue may dictate restraint or policies that contradict or vitiate those immediate local interests.

The application of principal–agent theory to Japanese politics is modelled closely on earlier applications to congressional politics in the USA, which revealed a 'dominant legislature'. The critique of that model applies equally to Ramseyer and Rosenbluth's interpretation of Japanese policy-making, in which the Diet is accorded a similarly dominant role: for example the failure to identify and explain the preferences of bureaucrats themselves, or the underestimation of 'agency slack' available to bureaucrats, especially in the implementation of policies.

Two further comments may be made briefly. First, the policy-making that the LDP supposedly dominates is treated by Ramseyer and Rosenbluth as an undifferentiated activity. No distinction is drawn between initiation, formulation, legitimation, and implementation—all identifiable activities undertaken in policy processes, involving different mixes of public and private organizations and players interacting in different 'arenas', such as the ministry, the Diet, local and prefectural governments, and the courts. Sectoral studies of social policy, education, overseas development aid, and defence, for example, reveal the complexity of the process of initiating and formulating policy options to which many different societal groups contribute. Studies of policy-making of industrial capital and credit, and the regulation of financial markets, point to the lack of interest of the LDP in some policy-making activities, and its minor role in others. In many policy areas where the LDP is active, it is interested and involved mainly or wholly at the stage of implementing policy, for example overseas development aid, or public works, and takes little or no part in the earlier stages of initiating or revising policy. Thus, the second criticism is that an interpretation of policy-making that postulates a relationship of principal and agent does not allow for a plurality of interests other than those of the LDP and the bureaucracy, whose interests may conflict with either or both. The potential to exercise power, defined as the possession of resources of authority, information, expertise, and money (Thain and Wright 1995), is distributed more widely than Ramseyer and Rosenbluth allow, and includes a variety of private-sector actors, intermediary structures, and quasi-governmental bodies. It differs between policy sectors, and changes over time. It is deployed differently, and with different outcomes within policy sectors, according to issue, circumstance, and context.

Ramseyer and Rosenbluth's explanation of policy-making drew heavily upon work then in progress of a number of historical institutionalists (Cowhey and McCubbins 1995). McCubbins and Noble (1995*b*) use two key institutional variables—electoral system and regime type—to explore and explain differences in policy-making in the USA and Japan, drawing a sharp distinction between the 'abdication' of authority by politicians to bureaucrats and 'managed delegation'. Central to the abdication thesis (for which read 'dominant bureaucracy') is the possession of 'hidden knowledge' of information and expertise by bureaucrats, and their control of the agenda. The appearance of bureaucratic power is however belied by the reality of policy-making in which, by contrast to abdication, politicians delegate authority and manage it so that in 'equilibrium' there is a balance between what legislators expect of their bureaucratic agents, and what those agents deliver.

The model applied to Japanese policy-making and the relations between politicians and bureaucrats allows little qualification: either there is abdication or there is delegation; bureaucrats have 'hidden knowledge' or they do not; they control the agenda or not; the legislature is important or not; ministers and cabinets are ineffectual or not. In rejecting dominant bureaucracy *tout court*, an unqualified thesis of delegation from principals to agents ascribes all policy-making authority to politicians. In practice, as the empirical evidence of sectoral studies demonstrates, for some kinds of policy issues in some kinds of policy-making activity, ministers may or do abdicate authority, may be or are willing to leave bureaucrats with discretionary authority; in others, they may themselves prescribe specific policy options.

As an explanation of how policy is or was made in Japan, Ramseyer and Rosenbluth's (1993) choice-theoretic model is reductionist, oversimplified, and misleading. Nevertheless 'rat-choicers' have provided a welcome stimulus to the perennial debate, forcing others to re-examine their own methodological positions and the interpretation of their data, if only to provide more persuasive proof of the validity of their own approaches. At the very least, their model provides a set of alternative hypotheses to those of the revisionists and sectoral and area specialists. Much of the empirical underpinning of the Ramseyer–Rosenbluth explanation of the dominant role of politicians in the policy-making process is provided by McCubbins and Noble's (1995*b*) application of rational choice theories to Japanese budgeting. I discuss their work and conclusions in Chapter 25, drawing upon my own empirical evidence of the LDP's role and influence in the budgetary processes presented in the chapters in the next part of the book.

CONCLUSION

With the challenge of the new institutionalists, the explanatory wheel has turned almost full circle, from policy processes dominated by a 'conservative coalition' of politicians, bureaucrats, and businessmen, to dominant bureaucrats, through neo-pluralist modifiers—'politicians stronger, bureaucrats weaker'—to 'politicians both reign and rule'. The theories generating those hypotheses were constructed, tested, and refined largely when both the political and economic systems were stable. The volatile conditions of the continuing 'regime shift' since the end of the high-growth era will provide a searching test of their robustness and parsimony. The longer-term consequences of that volatility for the roles and relationships of politicians and bureaucrats in the new political and, less certainly, economic and administrative orders slowly emerging at the end of the twentieth century will not be apparent for some time to come.

While the uncertainty, complexity, and delay that characterized the policy-making processes in the period of multi-party governments (described in Chapter 10) proved to be temporary, the return of the LDP to (mainly) one-party rule after October 1996 was no restoration of the *status quo ante*. There was no resumption of 'business as usual'; 'normal relations' in the policy-making process were not restored. Relationships between politicians and bureaucrats had deteriorated and continued to do so, partly the result of a deliberate and sustained campaign of criticism and denigration waged by the LDP (and other parties) against the bureaucracy in general and MOF in particular. The LDP's earlier call for more political control of policy-making was strengthened by the mounting evidence of bureaucratic incompetence and helplessness in several policy areas, above all in MOF's perceived mismanagement of the economy, and its demonstrably inept handling of the banking crisis. The electorate had long believed that, 'even if the political system becomes paralysed, the country's superlative bureaucrats will see to it that nothing major goes amiss' (Sakaiya 1994). But when the bubble burst, so did the myth of able and trustworthy bureaucrats. While the general public traditionally held politicians in low esteem as self-serving, corruptible, and dishonest, bureaucrats were thought to be efficient, and generally honest and fair. In the 1990s there was a growing mood of cynicism and distrust of a bureaucracy, many of whose senior officials—including four administrative vice-ministers—were implicated in a succession of highly publicized episodes of improper behaviour, bribery, and corruption.

Back in government, the LDP seized the policy initiative on particular issues in several policy areas—or rather, was seen publicly to be claiming the initiative from a defensive, beleaguered, and demoralized bureaucracy. It claimed to be the inspiration of the programmes of reform in the administrative, economic, financial, fiscal, and welfare systems between 1996 and 2000. How and by whom they are implemented in the first decade of the twenty-first century will determine whether that assertion of political power and influence in the policy-making processes is matched by the reality.

TOWARDS ANALYTIC CONVERGENCE

Revisionists, counter-revisionists, and rat-choicers share some important explanatory ground in their reaction against theories of neo-classical economics, and their rejection of culturally determined explanations of Japanese policy-making. Each differs in the 'one big idea', but both the macro-level approach favoured by most revisionists and rat-choicers and the meso-level approach of the policy area and sector specialists are necessary to a fuller understanding of how and why policy is made, and by whom; they are essentially complementary. The common ground provides the basis of the analytical framework employed in this book, which emphasizes the importance of institutional structures and of the historical 'setting' or context in which the dynamics of both institutional and policy changes are captured longitudinally. A more nuanced analysis of policy-making allows us to observe the impact on budgetary policies and processes of the role of the state, including its transnational dimension, and of its institutional structures and their embedded 'collective identities'; and to distinguish the 'appearance' of power from the 'reality' of its use. It is to those institutional structures that we now turn in Part II.

PART II

INSTITUTIONS, STRUCTURES, AND ACTORS

6

The Spending Ministries and Agencies

Japan's public sector is multi-layered. The first layer comprises the central government proper with three branches: the executive, the legislative, and the judicial. The second layer comprises the local governments of the 47 prefectures and the 3,229 municipalities of (671) cities and (2,558) towns and villages. The third layer comprises a variety of public corporations, banks, and finance corporations, established, supervised, and financed partly or wholly by organizations of the central government. In addition, there are the public corporations (*chihō kōsha*) set up by local governments, and local public enterprises (*chihō kōei kigyō*) such as public utilities, railways, hospitals, and so on operated by local governments. The fourth layer is a grey area intermediate between the public and private sectors, with organizations established as joint stock companies or as quasi-governmental organizations (*kōeki hōjin*) set up in principle by private initiative but approved by ministries, agencies, and prefectures. Non-profit-making in principle, some of them earn profits and pay corporate taxes (Komiya 1999).

The organizations and structures with which the book is mainly concerned include the executive branch of the central government, comprising the Cabinet, ministries, agencies, and commissions, and those public corporations (*tokushu hōjin*) subject to the supervision and control of ministers, but exclude the local governments of prefectures and municipalities. In 2000, and for most of the previous twenty-five years, the executive branch consisted of the Prime Minister's Office, 12 ministries, eight agencies, and one commission, each with a Cabinet minister, and 24 non-ministerial agencies and commissions headed by government officials. Table 6.1 lists the ministries hierarchically in order of their historical establishment, together with the commissions and agencies that fall within their jurisdiction. That total of 46 organizations defines the Spending Ministries and Agencies with which the book is mainly concerned, together with government enterprises, public corporations, and companies that fall within the legal supervisory jurisdiction of ministers, and whose activities are also financed wholly or partly through the General Account Budget or FILP, or one of the 38 Special Accounts.

This chapter provides an organizational map of the terrain inhabited by them before the implementation in January 2001 of the reforms to the central government enacted in 1998–9. It begins with a brief historical review of the origins and development of ministries and agencies from the foundation of the modern state to the present day, to illustrate and emphasize the importance of stability, continuity, and evolutionary change in the structure of Japan's central government. The second section examines their hierarchical status, and identifies the government enterprises and public corporations that they supervised; the third section looks inside the ministries and agencies,

Table 6.1 *Ministries, commissions, and agencies, FY1975–FY2000*

Ministry	Commission	Agency
Prime Minister's Office	Fair Trade Commission National Public Safety Commission (and National Police Agency) Environmental Disputes Coordination Commission Financial Reconstruction Commission	*Ministerial agencies* Management and Coordination Agency Hokkaido Development Agency Defence Agency Economic Planning Agency Science and Technology Agency Environment Agency Okinawa Development Agency National Land Agency *Non-Ministerial Agencies* Imperial Household Agency Defence Facilities Agency[a] Financial Supervision Agency
Ministry of Justice	National Bar Examination Administration Commission Public Security Examination Commission	Public Security Investigation Agency
Ministry of Foreign Affairs		
Ministry of Finance		National Tax Administration Agency
Ministry of Education		Agency for Cultural Affairs
Ministry of Health and Welfare		Social Insurance Agency
Ministry of Agriculture, Forestry, and Fisheries		Food Agency Forestry Agency Fisheries Agency
Ministry of International Trade and Industry[b]		Agency of Natural Resources and Energy Patent Office Small and Medium Enterprise Agency
Ministry of Transport	Central Labour Relations Commission for Seafarers	Maritime Safety Agency Marine Accident Inquiry Agency Meteorological Agency
Ministry of Posts and Telecommunications		
Ministry of Labour	Central Labour Relations Commission	
Ministry of Construction		
Ministry of Home Affairs		Fire Defence Agency

[a]The Defence Facilities Administration Agency was a part of the Defence Agency.
[b]The Agency of Industrial Science and Technology did not have formal status as an agency as defined in the National Organization Law, but MITI translated its title thus.
Source: Organization of the Government of Japan, 1999, Appendix 1, p. 128 (MCA 1999).

Spending Ministries and Agencies 93

and draws attention to the key role there of the Minister's Secretariat generally in the policy-making processes, and to its Budget and Accounts Division more narrowly in the budgetary processes. The concluding section explains and assesses the proposals for the reconstruction of the central government in the legislation enacted by the second Hashimoto government in 1998, and that of Prime Minister Obuchi in the following year, implemented on 6 January 2001.

Two organizational issues material to the budgetary processes—the scope and use of the jurisdictional authority conferred upon each ministry and agency by its law of establishment, and inter-ministerial coordination competition and conflict—are dealt with in the next chapter.

CONTINUITY AND EVOLUTIONARY CHANGE IN THE MACHINERY OF CENTRAL GOVERNMENT, 1869–2000

The machinery of central government in Japan has evolved gradually and incrementally over more than a hundred years. MOF and MOFA were both established in 1869. Together with Ministries for Criminal Justice, the Imperial Household, and Civil Affairs (which became the Ministry of Internal or Domestic Affairs (Naimu-shō) four years later), they provided the central core from which new ministries, agencies, and commissions gradually evolved. The Ministry of Home Affairs has a more chequered history, but in its former guise as the Ministry of the Interior (1873) provided the root stock from which were grown and transplanted separate ministries and agencies, as responsibilities for a range of domestic public services and welfare functions became important enough or sufficiently burdensome to warrant a separate organizational identity. For example, a Railway Board evolved from its responsibility for railways in 1908, leading to the creation of a separate ministry in 1920, the forerunner of MOT. Agriculture and commerce were hived off in 1881, separated in 1925, and progressively evolved into MITI and MAFF. Health and welfare were hived off in 1938; MOL (1947) and MOC (1948) were hived off after the breakup of the Ministry of the Interior in the SCAP reforms of 1947. The post of prime minister, together with the Cabinet Secretary's Office, was created in 1885. The latter became formally institutionalized as a Secretariat in 1924, but the Prime Minister's Office was not set up until 1949, two years after its designation as the Prime Minister's Agency. Subsequently it has provided a supervisory home for new agencies and commissions charged with coordinating or regulatory functions, or which, because of their political sensitivity, required that they be brought formally within the prime minister's jurisdiction. Figure 6.1 shows the organizational evolution of the functions of central government from 1869 to 1998.

The increasing importance of the promotion and regulation of industry, an integral part of the creation of the 'developmental state', provided a major source of organizational evolution from the original central core. MITI's origins can be traced directly to the creation of a Ministry of Agriculture and Commerce, hived off from the Ministry of the Interior in 1881. Those two functions were subsequently separated, and commerce combined with industry in a new Ministry of Commerce and Industry in 1925,

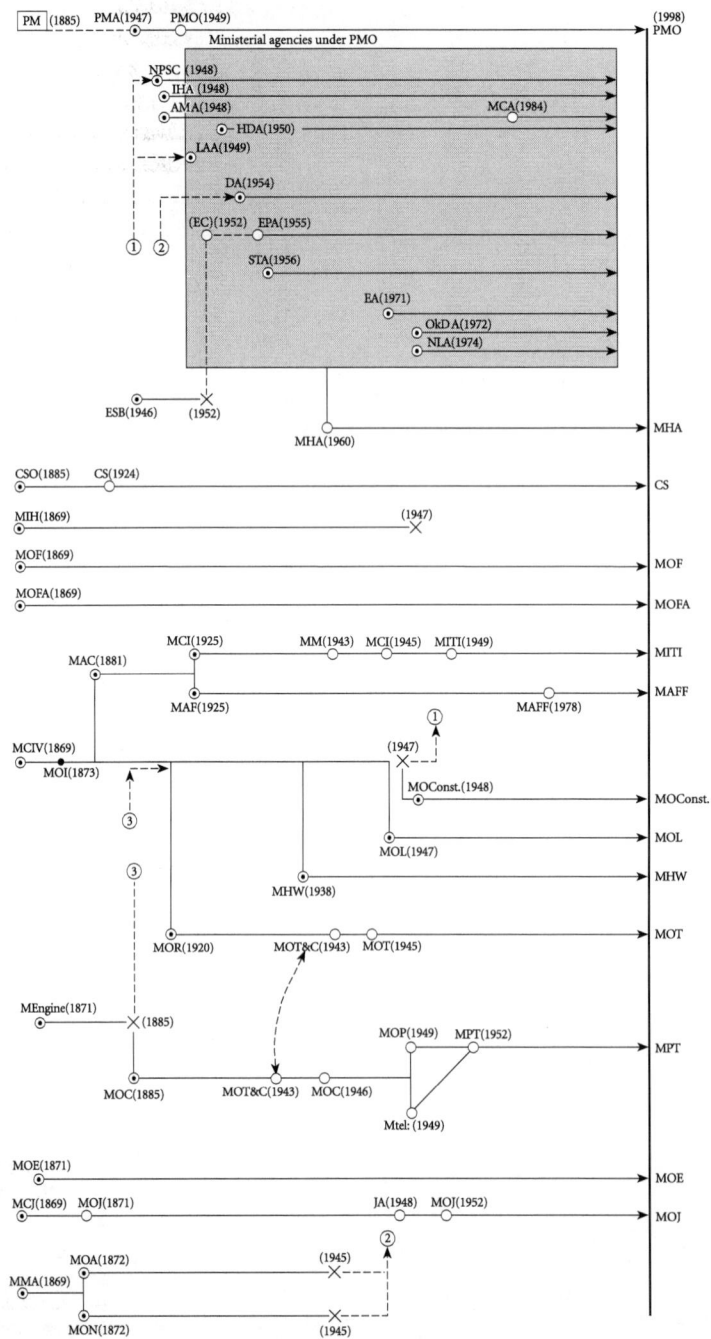

Figure 6.1 *The organization of the functions of central government, 1869–1998*

at which time MAF(F) acquired its separate identity; Fisheries was added to its title in 1978, to emphasize its responsibility for that industry after the international agreement on the 200-mile fishing limits. The Ministry of Commerce and Industry was briefly transformed into a Ministry of Munitions during the Second World War, but resumed its old title and responsibilities in 1945 until replaced by MITI four years later.

The telecommunications function was provided in a separate Ministry of Communications created in 1885 on the abolition of the original Ministry of Engineering (1871). Separate ministries for Postal Services and Telecommunications were established in 1949, but the latter was abolished in 1952, and the two functions recombined in MPT. At the same time, Nippon Telegraph and Telephone (NTT) was set up as a public corporation, drawing most of its technical and specialist staff from the old Ministry of Telecommunications.

The most significant organizational developments after the end of the Second World War derived from the SCAP reforms of 1947. The Ministry of the Interior had been from its creation responsible for internal security, and for the supervision and control of both local governments and prefectures. The two functions combined to forge a powerful instrument of control and coercion, exploited and abused by governments both before and during the Second World War. It was quickly stripped of much of its power. Responsibility for internal security was removed to a new National Police Agency under the supervision of a National Public Safety Commission brought within the jurisdiction of the Prime Minister's Office. The newly created Local Affairs Agency achieved independent ministerial status in 1960, its main responsibilities those of the

---

Figure 6.1 *The organization of the functions of central government, 1869–1998*

Key ⊙: established; ○: change of name (and jurisdiction); X: abolished.

AMA, Administrative Management Agency; CS, Cabinet Secretariat; CSO, Cabinet Secretary's Office; DA, Defence Agency; EA, Environment Agency; (EC), Economic Council; EPA, Economic Planning Agency; ESB, Economic Stabilization Board; HAD, Hokkaido Development Agency; IHA, Imperial Household Agency; JA, Justice Agency; LAA, Local Autonomy Agency; MAC, Ministry of Agriculture and Commerce; MAF, Ministry of Agriculture and Forestry; MCA, Management and Coordination Agency; MCI, Ministry of Commerce and Industry; MCIV, Ministry of Civil Affairs; MCJ, Ministry of Criminal Justice; MEngine, Ministry of Engineering; MFA, Ministry of Foreign Affairs; MHW, Ministry of Health and Welfare; MIH, Ministry of Imperial Household; MITI, Ministry of International Trade and Industry; MM, Ministry of Munitions; MMA, Ministry of Military Affairs; MOA, Ministry of Army; MOC, Ministry of Communication; MOConst, Ministry of Construction; MOE, Ministry of Education; MOF, Ministry of Finance; MOI, Ministry of Interior; MOJ, Ministry of Justice; MOL, Ministry of Labour; MON, Ministry of Navy; MOP, Ministry of Post; MOR, Ministry of Railway; MOT, Ministry of Transport; MOT&C, Ministry of Transport and Communication; MPT, Ministry of Post and Telecommunications; MTel, Ministry of Telecommunications; NLA, National Land Agency; NPSC, National Public Safety Commission; OkDA, Okinawa Development Agency; PM, Prime Minister; PMA, Prime Minister's Agency; PMO, Prime Minister's Office; STA, Science and Technology Agency.

Sources: *Naikaku Seido Kyūjūnenshi Shiryōshū*, [Ninety-year History of the Cabinet System] edited by Cabinet Secretariat, (Tokyo: Government Printing Bureau, MOF, 1975); *Naikaku Hyakunen No Ayumi* [One Hundred Years of the Cabinet], Editorial Committee of the One Hundred Year History of the Cabinet-System, Cabinet Secretariat (Tokyo: Government Printing Bureau, MOF, 1975); *Kokka Gyōsei Soshiki Hōsei Sanjūnen-shi* [Thirty Years History of the National Administrative Organization System], ed. Administrative Management Bureau, MCA, 1980.

supervision and regulation of local governments and prefectures, reflected in its new Japanese title Jichi-shō, literally the Ministry of Autonomy or Local Autonomy.

The armed forces occupied a central place in government from the outset. A Ministry of Military Affairs was established in 1869, divided into separate ministries for the Army and Navy in 1872. Together they played a central, often decisive, role in the formation and maintenance of national governments, culminating in the imperialist expansion from the late 1920s to 1945. Each had its own air force; no separate Air Ministry was ever established. The new constitution permitted only self-defence forces, and the (now) three arms were brought within the new Defence Agency set up in 1954 within the Prime Minister's Office.

The conclusions to be drawn from this brief historical review are threefold. First, the machinery of central government has strong roots in the arrangements made at the time of the Meiji Restoration. MOF, MOFA MOJ, MOE and the Cabinet Secretariat have an unbroken organizational line from the last quarter of the nineteenth century to the end of the twentieth. Secondly, the stability and continuity of those organizational arrangements have resulted in the 'collective identities' of individual ministries and agencies becoming deeply embedded. That embeddedness has reinforced organizational inertia by strengthening the 'verticalization' of Japanese bureaucracy, as ministries and agencies sought to protect long-established jurisdictional boundaries. Thirdly, change has taken place only gradually: new functions were grafted on to existing responsibilities, or transferred to organizations evolved from existing structures. The one major reorganization of functions and responsibilities after 1869 was imposed externally. The creation of the Prime Minister's Agency in 1947 was to provide mainly for the new arrangements for internal security following the abolition of the Ministry of the Interior. Its expansion to accommodate new agencies whose coordinating functions transcended the interests and jurisdictions of competing ministries, or, those, like defence, that were politically sensitive did little to enhance the authority of the prime minister, or make it much easier for him to play a coordinating role in policy-making.

HIERARCHICAL AND ORGANIZATIONAL STATUS

The central government comprises four main organizational types: offices (*fu*) on the ministerial level (in 2000 there was only one, the Prime Minister's Office), ministries (*shō*), agencies (*chō*), and commissions (*iinkai*). The formal legal status of agencies is inferior to that of ministries. They are set up when an area of work or activity dealt with by one of the ministries or the Prime Minister's Office is sufficiently large and different in character from its other work or activities that it is deemed appropriate to separate and manage it independently (MCA 1999). While that reason explains the creation of some of the agencies under the jurisdiction of particular ministries, for example the Maritime Safety Agency under MOT, the Food Agency under MAFF, the Social Insurance Agency under MHW, the boundary-politics of different ministries with competing interests, seeking to control areas of policy-making, has meant that many of the agencies created since the end of Allied Occupation have been brought within the jurisdiction of the Prime Minister's Office. In addition to the Defence Agency, created in 1954, there were within its sphere of responsibility in 2000: the Economic Planning Agency (1955), the Science and Technology Agency (1956), the Environment Agency (1971), the National Land Agency (1974), the Hokkaido (1950) and Okinawa (1972) Development Agencies, and the Management and Coordination Agency (1984), all of which had functions that transcended those of one or more of the 12 ministries. Ostensibly, they were 'administrative organs specializing in coordination', but ministries competed to influence their policy-making and coordinating activities through the secondment of their senior staff. On the abolition of the Banking and Securities Bureaux in MOF, the Financial Supervision Agency was established within the Prime Minister's Office in June 1998 and inherited the Bureaux' investigatory and supervisory functions.

Commissions are more independent of their supervising ministries than agencies, and are set up when it is felt that supervision and direct control by a minister is likely to thwart the achievement of the objectives of a discrete government function (MCA 1999: 110). Their functions are variously supervisory or regulatory, or to provide arbitration in disputes between contending parties, employing quasi-judicial or quasi-legislative procedures. The National Public Safety Commission within the Prime Minister's Office supervises the work of the National Police Agency to ensure its political neutrality in sensitive issues of civil liberties and rights. The Financial Revitalization Commission, with a minister of state, was established within the Prime Minister's Office in 1998 to oversee the recapitalization of the banking sector, and to deal with failed and failing financial institutions.

The formal and constitutionally prescribed distinction between ministries and agencies with ministerial status, and those agencies and commissions without it, defines their scope for the exercise of independent discretionary behaviour in legislative matters, personnel, and the preparation and submission of budgetary requests to MOF. Ministries and ministerial agencies have discretion to prepare and submit their own draft bills and ordinances to Cabinet, where their ministers as members can speak directly in support of them; formally, those of ministerial agencies are submitted to the Cabinet in the name of the prime minister. Other agencies, and all commissions, do so only with the prior approval of their sponsor ministry; in practice, they also need the authority and support of the Cabinet Secretariat and the Prime Minister's Office. Secondly, ministers—but not the heads of non-ministerial agencies—can propose to the Cabinet the issue of Cabinet Orders on matters falling within their jurisdiction. Thirdly, ministers can issue on their own authority ordinances regulating the implementation of existing laws or Cabinet Orders; the heads of non-ministerial agencies and commissions have to submit drafts of proposed ordinances to, and seek the approval of, their sponsor minister before they can do so. All ministries, agencies, and commissions can issue on their own authority formal notices concerning affairs that fall within their prescribed jurisdictions. These are published in the official government gazette (*kanpō*). Finally, all ministries, agencies, and commissions are empowered to issue directions (*tsūtastsu*) in the form of 'instructions or circular notices' to those organizations and personnel that fall within their jurisdiction.

Organizational longevity partly determines the hierarchical status of ministries and agencies, but functions and jurisdictional authority are more significant factors. Johnson (1989: 183) claims that policy ministries (*seisaku kanchō*), such as MOF, MOFA and MITI, comprise an elite, an 'ultra first class bureaucracy' (*chō-ichiryū kanchō*), ranked higher than regulatory ministries (*kisei kanchō*) or operational ministries (*jigyō kanchō*), such as MOE, MOC, MOL, MOT, MOJ, and MHW, or business ministries (*gengyō kanchō*) such as MPT. Both of the latter, it is argued (Johnson 1989; Muramatsu 1991) aspired to a higher status, and MPT claimed recognition for its promotion of telecommunications policy in contests with MITI in the 1980s. Less convincingly, MOT declared that it had changed from a regulatory to a policy ministry following an internal reorganization of its bureaus in 1984.

The distinction between policy and regulation/business is oversimplified, and a less accurate guide to both the status and function of ministries and agencies than was perhaps the case at an earlier stage in Japanese history. A similar criticism can be levelled at attempts to differentiate ministries by 'clientalization' (Calder 1993) or their subscription to 'big/small' government. (Muramatsu 1993) All three so-called elite policy ministries had substantial and important regulatory functions; while so-called regulatory and business ministries made policy as well as carried it out. MPT was both a policy ministry and a business ministry, responsible for the government's largest business, the postal services. (For a discussion of the historical evolution of its functions and status, see Nakano 1998.) It may be true that some policy ministries were generally less clientelized, but even there, some bureaus had mature clientelistic relations, as was the case with MOF's Banking Bureau until 1998.

A more relevant distinction is perhaps between those ministries and agencies with organizational responsibilities for the core policy-making activities of government—financial and economic policy, diplomacy, trade and industry, and defence—and the rest. But even that broad categorization may exaggerate the status and prestige of those ministries, as the politico-economic context within which policy was made and carried out changed over time. Thus, MITI's status relative to other ministries declined with the end of the high-growth era and the reorientation of national goals towards social, welfare, and environmental issues. In the 1990s MOF's pre-eminent status was damaged by a succession of policy failures in the wake of the collapse of the bubble economy, and by the corrupt behaviour of some of its senior officials, discussed in Chapter 8. MHW's prestige and authority was damaged by its incompetence in the handling of HIV-contaminated blood supplies, and by the resignation of its administrative vice-minister, Okamitsu Nobuharu, in 1996 for allegedly receiving bribes. Conversely, the political salience of the issues of decentralization and devolution in the reformist manifestos of successive coalition governments provided opportunities for MHA to exploit its formal responsibility for local government so as to influence the direction, content, and pace of the policy agenda, and to enhance its relatively modest status.

The status and significance of ministries and agencies also varied with their perceived utility as instruments of the LDP's politico-electoral strategy, through the distribution of budget benefits and regulatory favours. The three core ministries MOF, MOFA, and MITI scored relatively modestly on the rough index provided by membership of the LDP's PARC divisions, which monitored the activities of ministries and agencies; indeed, there was no dedicated division shadowing MOF. Pre-eminent were those divisions that marked MOC, MAFF, and MOT, where LDP Dietmen competed for membership. The size, competition and influence of *zoku* provide similar evidence of the relative political importance and salience of ministries and agencies. Among the largest policy tribes are those for agriculture, telecommunications, and construction; the weakest, those for justice, science and technology, and the Cabinet Office. I have more to say about that in Chapter 10.

The Cabinet and Cabinet Ministers

The size of the Cabinet is fixed by law: it comprises the prime minister and a maximum of 20 ministers. All 12 ministries were invariably represented there throughout the period 1975–2000, together with ministers of state from eight of the agencies within the Prime Minister's Office; neither the Imperial Household Agency nor the Defence Facilities Administration Agency was normally accorded ministerial status. The inclusion of the chief secretary to the Cabinet, who presides over the Cabinet Secretariat and is in day-to-day charge of the Prime Minister's Office, meant that in practice two of the eight agencies were normally represented by the same minister of state, or that one was excluded.

Each ministry and ministerial agency had one parliamentary vice-minister, and MOF, MAFF, and MITI had two. Formally, their role was to assist the minister in the formulation of plans, policies, and programmes within the ministry, and in Diet and party business outside it. In practice, the political role was more important than the administrative. The overall size of the government was under 50, less than half the size of that of the UK. After 2001 the increase in the number, role, and status of parliamentary vice-ministers will add a further 20 or so posts to that number.

Appointment to ministerial office in LDP governments, and the time spent in post, was regulated by three rules-of-the-game, which applied equally to preferment in the LDP's organization with which ministerial appointments were inseparably linked. First, a condition of ministerial preferment was progressive advancement through the ranks of the party organization and its factions. This was partly a function of 'biological age', but not wholly so, because some (but fewer in recent years) Dietmen came late in life to politics, from the bureaucracy and business for example, and were middle-aged or even elderly. Here the second criterion for promotion was more important: 'political age', or the number of times a Dietman had been re-elected. The rules were well defined and scrupulously observed. A member of the Lower House re-elected five or six times, and nominated by his faction, might expect to obtain a first Cabinet post as a minister of state in charge of an agency or even a ministry such as Education, Posts and Telecommunications, or Labour (but not MOF, MOFA or MITI), provided that he or she met the minimum requirements of performance, i.e. proven political ability and skills demonstrated in the party organization, and in the work of the Diet, for example as chair or vice-chair of a specialist committee.

To provide for the promotion of all eligible candidates, and to avoid a blockage, each ministerial appointment was necessarily of short duration, the third rule-of-the-game. Between 1972 and 1986 there were 17 major Cabinet reshuffles. The average length of appointment of a Cabinet minister before the coalition governments of 1993–6 was

278 days. There were several consequences of such rapid turnover for the Japanese political system, but here I note only that there was little time to acquire knowledge and experience of the business of a ministry or agency; it was therefore difficult for ministers to impose their personal stamp upon its policy-making, thereby increasing their dependence upon bureaucrats (who of course as generalists rotated through posts on a one- or two-year cycle).

Each ministry and ministerial agency, together with the Imperial Household Agency and Commissions in the Prime Minister's Office, submitted its budget request directly to the Ministry of Finance and negotiated directly with the Budget Bureau officials. The remaining agencies and commissions did so indirectly through their supervisory or sponsor ministry, although they explained their requests to, and were examined directly by, Budget Examiners. In practice, they were subject to the guidance and direction of their ministry's secretariat and staff, and their budget proposals were set within the framework of its policies, priorities, and strategies. Two other categories of spending agency obtained funds from the General Account or FILP, but dealt with the Ministry of Finance through the intermediation of their sponsor ministries: government enterprises and public corporations.

Government Enterprises

Government enterprises comprise an intermediate organizational category between, on the one hand, ministries and agencies fully funded through the General Account, and (nominally) self-financing, public corporations, on the other. In 2000 there were four, each within the jurisdiction of a ministry: the postal service (MPT), the national forestry service (MAFF), the Mint, and the Government Printing Agency (MOF); a fifth, the Alcohol Monopoly, was previously administered by MITI until 1982, but was then absorbed within the New Energy and Industrial Technology Development Corporation within that ministry's jurisdiction. Like those in ministries and agencies, the employees of enterprises were subject to the Public Service Law; their Special Accounts were submitted by their parent ministries concurrently with the budget requests under the General Account.

Public Corporations

In 1999 there were 81 public corporations (*tokushu-hōjin*), which fell solely or jointly within the supervisory and controlling jurisdiction of particular ministries and agencies. They were set up

> when particular government activities are better managed in the form of a profit-making enterprise, when efficiency in performance is more likely to be achieved than under direct operation by the national government agencies, or when more flexibility in financial or personnel management is required than is normally possible under the laws and regulations pertaining to government agencies. (MCA 1999: 100)

Most public corporations were established in the high-growth period between 1955 and 1965. From about 30, the number had reached 113 by the time of the introduction of the consolidation and rationalization policy in FY1967. As we saw in Chapter 4, the Administrative Reform Movement of the 1980s led to a reduction in their number, to 87, with the notable privatization of Japan National Railways, NTT, and the Japan Tobacco and Salt Company, but thereafter it rose again to 92, where it remained until 1995. For the next three years the reduction in the number of public corporations, and the consolidation and rationalization of functions among the survivors, became an important objective of the programme of administrative reform followed by successive coalition governments. By 1 April 1999 the number had been reduced to 81, as a result of the abolition and merger of several public corporations.

As part of a ministry's 'bailiwick', the activities of each public corporation are subject to its supervision and control, and can be steered and guided to contribute to the policy aims of the parent ministry. The appointment of senior staff to the executive boards of public corporations—president, chairman, directors, and members—comprises an important part of each ministry's patronage, and is jealously protected. Such posts provide a major source of *amakudari* for those ministry and agency officials who retire or resign before the age of 60. In this respect, MOF, MITI, MAFF, MOC, and MPT had numerically more public corporations within their sole or shared jurisdiction, or more powerful corporations, or both, than other ministries and agencies. Table 6.2 shows the extent of the organizational jurisdiction of the Spending Ministries and Agencies, and the number of Executive Board appointments which each controlled solely or jointly in 1996–7. As of 1 January 1997, there were 1,373 posts at board level in the then 92 public corporations, of which 1,091 were full-time. In those corporations where control and supervision was shared, patronage was regulated by informal agreement between the co-sponsors. Besides the patronage of appointments to the boards of public corporations, through their sponsorship ministries and agencies also influenced appointments to more junior posts. With some 520,000 employees (January 1997), public corporations provided an important source of *amakudari* for those who retired at or below the career-grade of director of a division, and for technical and specialist staff. I discuss those issues in more detail in Chapter 9.

The budgetary significance of public corporations in the period up to 2000 lay mainly in the eligibility of most of them as FILP agencies for the allocation of investment and loan capital through FILP. Those that qualified, submitted their budget requests through their sponsor ministries to the First Fund Division of MOF's Financial Bureau (see Chapter 19). Pre-eminent in this respect were the then 12 public finance organizations, comprising three banks (*ginkō*) and nine public finance corporations (*kōko*). MOF had sole jurisdiction of the Japan Development Bank and the EXIM Bank, and shared jurisdiction of the Shōkō Chūkin Bank with MITI. It had sole jurisdiction of the People's Finance Corporation, but shared jurisdiction with various other ministries and agencies for the other eight, for example the Government Housing Loan Corporation, which it co-sponsored with MOC, the Japan Financial Corporation for Small Businesses, co-sponsored with MITI. They are listed in Table 8.2.

Ministries and agencies reviewed and, where necessary, revised the substantive policy plans and expenditure programmes prepared by the boards of the corporations which they sponsored. MOF was of course directly involved in the scrutiny of their budgets

Table 6.2 *The organizational jurisdiction and patronage of spending ministries and agencies, 1996–1997*

	Jurisdiction of public corporations[a]			Executive board directorships[b]		
	Sole	Shared	Total	(FT)	(PT)	Total
Ministries						
MOF	4	10	14	123	19	142
MITI	10	8	18	152	15	167
MAFF	7	5	12	82	42	124
MOT	14	7	21	276	58	334
MOC	4	7	11	94	12	106
MHW	5	4	9	44	30	74
MPT	4	2	6	92	15	107
MOL	5	1	6	34	6	40
MHA	1	2	3	18	15	33
MOFA	1	1	2	17	4	21
MOE	7	1	8	42	32	74
Agencies						
MCA	0	2	2	10	11	21
NLA	0	4	4	31	2	33
HDA	0	1	1	7	1	8
STA	4	2	6	45	12	57
EPA	2	0	2	11	5	16
EA	0	2	2	8	2	10
OkDA	0	1	1	5	1	6
TOTAL				1091	282	1373

[a] 1 January 1996.
[b] 1 January 1997.
Source: derived from data provided by MCA (1998*b*).

when requests were made for the allocation of FILP funds. Secondly, many public corporations were significant in the budgetary process because any deficits on their trading accounts required subsidy from the General Account or FILP. For example, the Japan National Railway Debt Settlement Corporation (sponsors: MOT, MOL, MHA, and MCA) ran a continuing and mounting deficit from 1987. Having inherited a debt of 30 trillion (almost a half of the size of the annual General Account Budget at that time) from JNR prior to its division and privatization in 1987, it received annual subsidies from the General Account and FILP to cover payment of interest on the sum outstanding. As an instrument of government housing policy, the Government Housing Loan Corporation (MOF and MOC) also received annual subsidies from both the General Account and FILP to enable it to provide loans for house purchase and building at preferential rates. Those and other subsidies are discussed in Chapter 28.

The number but not the main functions of the public finance corporations was reduced from 12 to nine as a result of the implementation in 1999 of the policies for rationalization and consolidation pursued by successive governments over the previous five years. The changes were more cosmetic and titular than a substantive reorganization of structures and functions. The Development Bank of Japan was created from a merger of the Japan Development Bank (sponsored by MOF) and the Hokkaido–Tōhoku Development Corporation (MOF/HDA/NLA); the National Life Finance Corporation brought together the People's Finance Corporation (MOF) and the Environmental Sanitation Business Finance Corporation (MOF/MHW); the Small Business Credit Insurance Corporation (MOF/MITI) was merged with the Japan Finance Corporation for Small Businesses (MOF/MITI); and the EXIM Bank (MOF) merged with OECF (EPA) to form the new Japan Bank for International Cooperation. Among other changes, the Housing and Urban Development Corporation (MOF/MOC) became the Urban Development Corporation on the loss of its housing functions; the Japan National Railway Debt Settlement Corporation was abolished and its debts transferred mainly to the General Account Budget.

THE INTERNAL ORGANIZATION OF SPENDING MINISTRIES AND AGENCIES

Common principles and standards for structuring the organizations comprising the central government are prescribed in the National Government Organization Law. While the effect of this is to provide for uniformity, each ministry's jurisdiction and functions are prescribed separately in an Establishment Law. Organizational principles and operational standards for each ministry, agency, and commission are prescribed separately by a Cabinet (organizational) Ordinance. Figure 6.2 provides a stereotypical organizational map of a Japanese ministry in the last quarter of the twentieth century.

Agencies differ organizationally according to their ministerial status. Ministerial agencies—those with a minister of state, such as the Environment Agency or the Defence Agency—had a similar organization to ministries; non-ministerial agencies, headed normally by a career official as director-general, were forbidden by law to establish bureaux. Instead, they had a Director-General's Secretariat, and a number of departments with constituent divisions. In ministries the senior official was the administrative vice-minister. MOF, MITI, MAFF, and MOT had a second post, sometimes described as administrative vice-minister, for certain policy areas or aspects of administration such as international affairs.[1] In MOC this post was held, unusually, by a specialist, an engineer. In recent years there was a tendency for other ministries to use the title of deputy vice-minister for some senior officials. In ministerial agencies the senior official was deputy director-general. Many ministries and agencies had branches and offices at the regional, prefectural, and local levels; some had research and training institutes. Advisory councils and commissions, set up to provide institutional expert advice, were attached to each ministry and agency. More is said about them in the next two chapters.

---

[1] Their titles in Japanese do not include the words meaning 'vice-minister'.

Institutions, Structures, and Actors

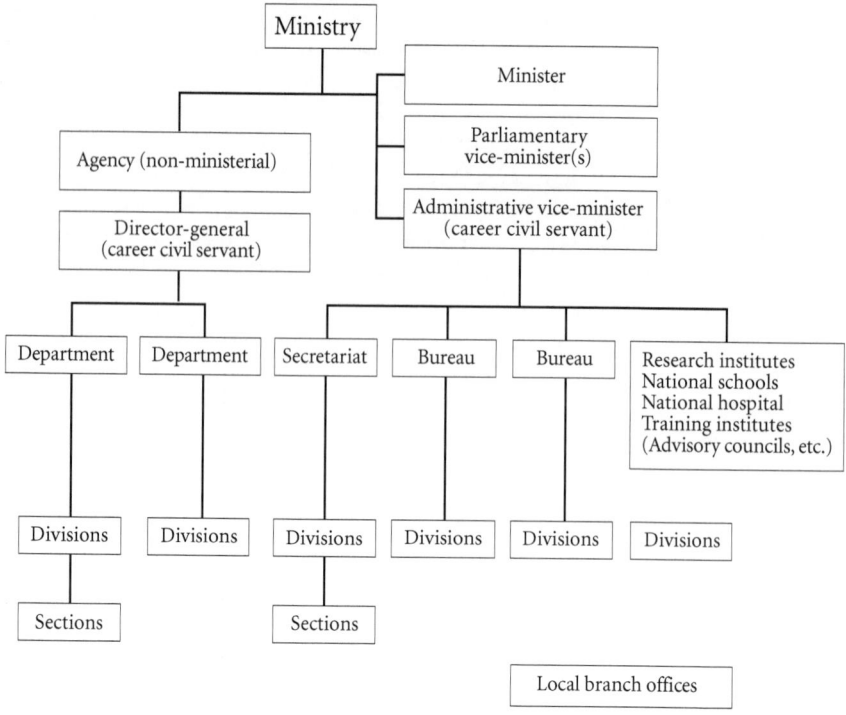

Figure 6.2 *Internal organization of ministries*

The functions, tasks, and activities within each ministry and agency were divided between bureaux (or departments) organized functionally or geographically, and a central coordinating secretariat. Bureaux (*kyoku*) were internally divided into divisions (*ka*), and subdivided into sections (*kakari*). Figure 6.3 shows the general hierarchy of posts held by 'career' officials, although there were some local variations and practices in particular ministries.

The key posts in the policy-making processes within and between bureaux were those of a director of division (*kachō*), and his principal deputy directors (*kachō-hosa*). At MOFA, for example, they were at the hub of all activities, prepared 'talking points and speeches for their superiors, including the prime minister, [made] up answers for Diet interpellations, brief politicians and business leaders, and attend[ed] ministry-wide liaison meetings' (Ahn 1998: 6). Informal communications among *kachō*, and between them and their superiors, had 'more substantive significance in policy-making than formal meetings or the formal chains of communication'. They also played crucial roles in the processes of coordinating the making and carrying out of policy between ministries and agencies. Elsewhere, the post of assistant director of a division (*han-chō*) was sometimes ranked with other deputy directors, sometimes as *primus inter pares* of the section chiefs, again depending on duties and seniority.

Spending Ministries and Agencies

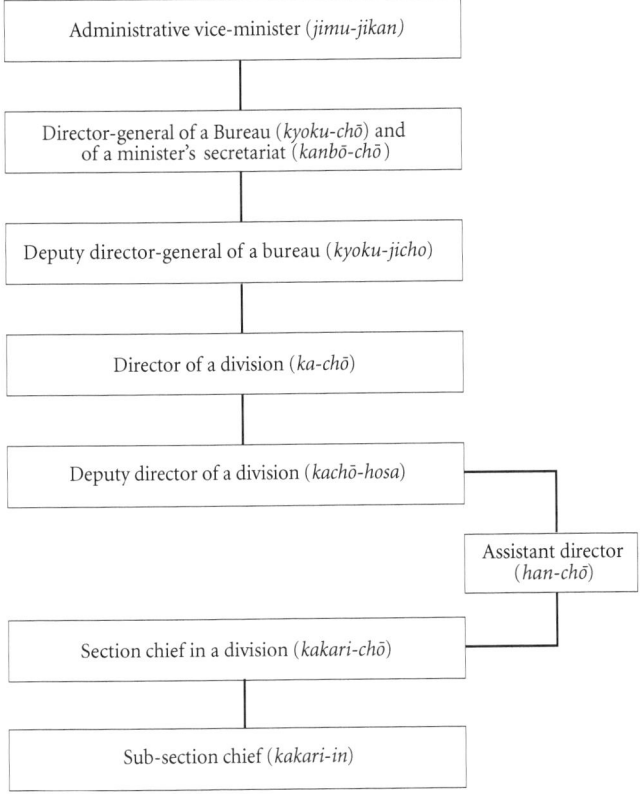

Figure 6.3 *Hierarchy of 'career' officials*

Those were all 'line' posts. There were two positions, one senior and one junior, whose incumbents performed a variety of 'staff' functions and services, such as coordination and advice, or who were employed on specialized tasks, sometimes transcending the responsibilities of several bureaux. Their precise hierarchical status varied, but generally councillors (*shingi-kan*) were ranked at or around the level of a deputy director-general, sometimes above, sometimes below, depending upon the local circumstances and customs, and the specification of the duties. *Sanji-kan*, comparable in rank to a deputy director of a division, was referred to in English, confusingly, as 'counsellor' (*sic*). Some large ministries and agencies had departments (*bu*) within bureaux, normally headed by a councillor (*shingi-kan*) who might be accorded the courtesy title of director-general (*bu-chō*). In MOF's Budget Bureau, a budget examiner (*shukei-kan*) was comparable in rank to a director of a division. His deputy (*shusa*) had a status similar to a deputy director of division. He had the discretion to make cuts in budget requests, a legal authority not possessed by assistant budget examiners (*shukei-kan-hosa*), whose hierarchical status might in other respects be comparable to deputy budget examiners.

With the acquisition and growth of new functions and responsibilities in the era of high economic growth, the numbers of bureaux and secretariats increased rapidly. To curb organizational expansion, it was decided in 1968 that each ministry and agency would abolish one bureau. Thereafter some slight increase occurred as a result of the creation of new agencies, but the total number of bureaux and secretariats remained at 128 from 1979. The principle of 'scrap and build' adopted in the late 1960s was rigorously enforced, and additional bureaux had to be compensated by the abolition of equivalents. The principle applied also to public corporations.

Minister's Secretariat

At the heart of each ministry, the Minister's Secretariat (*kanbō*), is normally headed by a director-general; in a non-ministerial agency a councillor (*shingi-kan*) is in charge of a Director-General's Secretariat. Within the Secretariat there are typically divisions with responsibility for central functions such as policy planning and the coordination of the activities of the ministry's bureaux; research and intelligence; the coordination of budgeting and accounts; parliamentary and public relations, and political liaison activities; legal drafting and advice, and counsel on the issue of ministerial orders and regulations, and the control of recruitment, promotion, postings, retirement, and the pay and conditions of personnel. These include the most important activities of the ministry, central to the work of all its bureaux and to the careers of all its staff. Figure 6.4 shows the structure of a typical Secretariat.

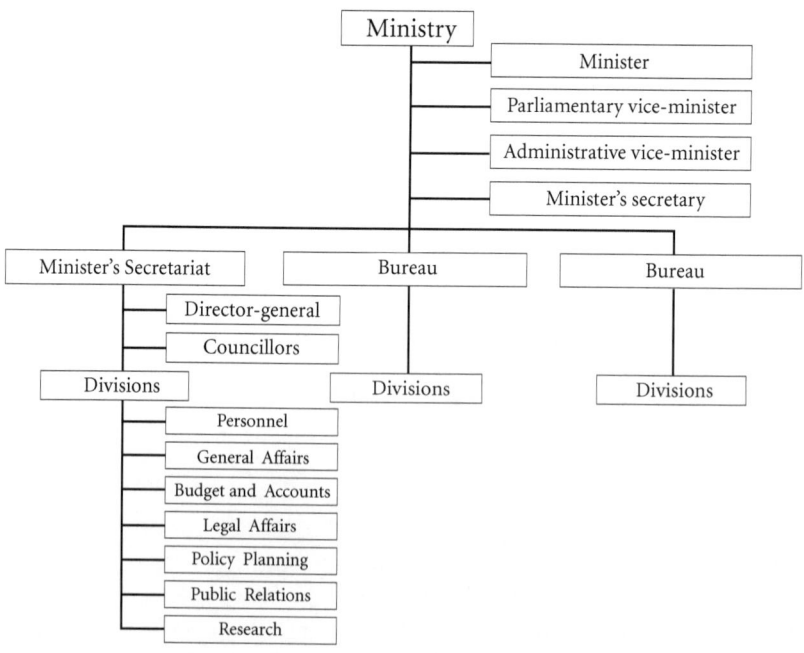

Figure 6.4 *Organization of a Minister's Secretariat*

In addition, the Secretariat provides service and support facilities for the minister. It is thus well equipped to play the coordinating role ascribed to it. But the extent to which it is able to achieve greater coherence and comprehensiveness in the making and carrying out of policy for the whole ministry varies with the extent of the *de facto* independence and autonomy of the vertically organized functional bureaux, and the extent of rivalry between them; the hierarchical status of the Secretariat in relation to them, and the number and ability of the staff; and organizational culture and practice. In a few ministries where there was a 'grand secretariat' (*dai kanbōchō sei*), such as MOFA, MOC, and the National Land Agency, the director-general of the Secretariat outranked bureau directors-general. In others, the Secretariat ranked no higher than a middle-level bureau, while at MPT its status was lower still.

BUDGET AND ACCOUNTS DIVISION

Ministerial and agency budgets and budget requests are compiled by policy divisions within each bureau, coordinated by its General Affairs Division. The latter is the main channel of communication with the ministry's Budget and Accounts Division, located in the Minister's Secretariat. The function of the Budget and Accounts Division (BAD) is to compile the ministry's budget, consistently with the objectives and policies prescribed for the ministry as a whole. The process of preparing the budget, and the role played by BAD within the ministry and between it and the Budget Bureau, is described in greater detail in Chapter 16. The director of BAD and one or more deputy directors are among the handful of key staff in the Secretariat; the others are the directors and deputy directors of the Legal Division, the Personnel Division, and the General Affairs (Coordination) Division, together with one or more staff posts of the rank of councillor. They represent the ministry externally in negotiation with bureaucrats in other ministries and agencies, senior politicians in the LDP and its policy-making organs, senior members of the Diet, special interest groups, and the media; internally, they provide the central focus and perspective for the disparate activities of the functional bureaux. These key posts in the Secretariat provide both an opportunity for young, able administrators to broaden their experience and develop their networks, and a test of their political and administrative skills. Those who acquit themselves well are destined for the highest offices in the ministry.

The organization of the Prime Minister's Office and the Cabinet Office and Secretariat differed in some important respects from those of other ministries and agencies, and this is discussed in the next chapter.

THE REORGANIZATION OF THE CENTRAL EXECUTIVE

The structure and organization of the central executive described in this chapter changed very little in the last quarter of the twentieth century. There were four main reasons for this. First, major changes required amendments of existing law, or new legislation, time-consuming and difficult processes for which careful planning and preparation were necessary to achieve a sufficient consensus among the political and bureaucratic interests affected. It had been rarely accomplished in the past without strong and committed political leadership, with the prime minister playing a key role, as Hashimoto was to do in 1996–7. Until 1993 neither politicians nor bureaucrats were much disposed to disturb the status quo of the politico-administrative arrangements based on the 1955 political realignment, from which both benefited. Nearly forty years of uninterrupted rule by the LDP meant that organizational changes inspired by the alternation of parties of the left and right, characteristic of other G7 countries, were entirely lacking in Japan.

Secondly, there were strong vested interests within ministries and agencies supporting the maintenance of the organizational status quo. Bureaucrats were recruited to individual ministries or agencies, to which they owed and expressed a strong personal loyalty rather than to the public service as a whole. Until resignation or retirement and a 'soft landing' in other parts of the public-sector or private-sector organizations, senior officials spent the whole of their professional careers in one ministry or agency. Planned, patterned, and strategic secondments to other ministries and agencies paradoxically served to reinforce those organizational loyalties.

Thirdly, the verticalized administrative structure both reflected and reinforced the independence and autonomy of Spending Ministries and Agencies to supervise and control policy areas within their formal jurisdictional authority. Each provided the principal organizational node of a discrete policy network, focusing the policy interests of representatives of special interest groups, the members of the formal organizational party structures of the LDP's PARC divisions, research commissions and study groups, and both senior LDP officials and rank-and-file Dietmen. All shared with bureaucrats a common interest in the maintenance of the existing organizational structures and their policy domains.

Fourthly, 'machinery of government' issues have traditionally excited little party-political or ministerial interest. There was little political interest or will among the LDP leadership to promote such changes after Nakasone's resignation in 1987, and such apathy continued until the second Hashimoto government took office in November 1996. Nakasone's commitment of time, energy, and political capital to issues of administrative reform when director-general of the Administrative Management Agency in 1979 was unusual, and partly inspired by longer-term political ambitions. While Prime Minister Takeshita showed some enthusiasm initially, neither of his weaker successors, Kaifu and Miyazawa, evinced any interest. In the absence of political commitment, such as that which had inspired the setting up of Rinchō and supported its work in the 1980s, the provisional commissions and the MCA could accomplish only modest and largely ad hoc, piecemeal reforms. In power, the LDP had little to gain from changes to a machine that continued to deliver and distribute the benefits and services that it believed were crucial to its continuing electoral success. Basic assumptions about the politico-administrative arrangements of the so-called '1955 system' were not seriously challenged within the LDP before its de-alignment in 1992–3.

On 12 June 1998 legislation was passed by the Diet to reconstruct the organization of the central executive. It provided a blueprint, an enabling act paving the way towards the eventual reduction of the number of ministries and ministerial agencies from 23 to 13.

Spending Ministries and Agencies

The laws of establishment of each ministry and agency were revised and amended in June 1999.

The immediate origins of that reform were discussed in Chapter 4. They derived from a personal initiative of Prime Minister Hashimoto in the runup to the election for the Lower House in September 1996, subsequently developed as one of his six 'envisioned' reforms. On forming his second government after that election, he committed himself personally to the reform of the central executive, setting up and chairing a new body, the Administrative Reform Council, charged specially with producing proposals within a year. Its Final Report, submitted on 3 December 1997, was less radical than an earlier Interim Report, the result of deals and compromises worked out within the LDP, and between it, the SDP and Sakigake, both of whom were supporting the government in the Diet on a case-by-case basis.

The reform had four main objectives. The first was to enable the Cabinet to play a larger role in policy-making, to become the principal instrument of a 'top down approach to the formation and execution of policy' (ARC 1997: 1). The second was to strengthen the authority of the prime minister to allow him to provide both leadership and the initiative in the formulation of policy, and to provide him with the necessary support through an enhanced Cabinet Secretariat. Thirdly, because it had grown 'excessively large and rigid', the central government organization was to be streamlined and made more efficient, and the processes of decision-making were to be made more open and transparent. Finally, the implementation of policy was to be made more efficient, by adopting the principles of the UK's Executive Agencies.

The guiding principles of the reform, and the reconstruction of the machinery of the central government designed to achieve them, entailed a reduced role for the public sector through continued deregulation and privatization, the transfer of functions from central to local governments, and the separation of the functions of policy-making from those of implementation. The latter principle was new, the first two a reiteration of those that had underpinned the administrative reform initiative since 1993 (discussed in Chapter 4). By 2001 the core of the central government comprised one office, the Cabinet Office (Naikaku-fu), ten ministries, and three ministerial agencies: the Defence Agency, the Financial Services Agency, and the National Public Safety Commission (raised to ministerial status). The reduction was achieved by the merger and amalgamation of existing functions in larger organizational units. Here we distinguish four analytical categories. The first comprises those ministries and agencies whose names and functions were largely unchanged: MOFA, MAFF, the Defence Agency, MOJ, and the National Public Safety Commission. In the second category are those ministries and agencies whose status and title were changed, but whose functions remained essentially the same: MITI was retitled the Ministry of Economy, Trade and Industry (METI); the Environment Agency upgraded to a full ministry. The third category comprises four new ministries created by the merger and amalgamation of the functions of 11 of the existing ministries and agencies:

1. Ministry of Health, Labour, and Welfare (MHW; MOL)
2. Ministry of Education, Culture, Sports, Science, and Technology (MOE; STA)

3. Ministry of Land, Infrastructure, and Transport (MOC; MOT; Land Agency; Hokkaido Development Agency)
4. Ministry of Public Management, Home Affairs, Posts, and Telecommunications (MHA; MPT; MCA)

Finally, both MOF and the Prime Minister's Office lost functions and responsibilities, but for contrasting reasons; the one intended to reduce the power and authority of the ministry, the other to strengthen and enhance the authority and leadership of the prime minister in strategic policy-making, and to provide him and the Cabinet with a central planning and coordinating capability through an enhanced and strengthened Cabinet Office and Secretariat. MOF was a prime target of the reforms, its dismemberment canvassed by some but not all LDP ministers and Dietmen, and various coalition partners. The details of the proposed changes in its functions and organization and their implications are discussed in Chapter 8.

Potentially the most far-reaching reforms of the central executive were those of the Prime Minister's Office and the Cabinet Office. The authority of the latter has been increased and its functions focused more on strategic policy-making. To assist it, there are four new statutory advisory councils: for Science and Technology, Central Disaster Prevention, Gender Issues, and Economic and Fiscal Policy. In the new structure EPA was abolished, and its functions for coordinating economic and fiscal policy transferred to the Cabinet Office, advised by the enlarged and retitled Council.

With ministerial members, as well as those drawn from non-governmental groups, the four councils are more akin to those of Cabinet committees than conventional advisory councils. Ministers of state are appointed as required for special issues, one of whom is in charge of Okinawa and Northern Territories Affairs. The Cabinet Secretariat has also been strengthened to provide more direct assistance for the prime minister and the Cabinet in the planning and coordinating of 'basic policies'. The enlarged Cabinet Office has inherited the formal jurisdictional responsibility of the Prime Minister's Office for the Imperial Household Agency, the Defence Agency, and the National Public Safety Commission, and has acquired that of the new Financial Services Agency. No changes were made in the number of commissions and non-ministerial agencies. Table 6.3 shows the ministries, agencies and commissions after the implementation of the reorganization on 6 January 2001.

Compromises and deals struck among politicians and bureaucrats in the period preceding the drafting of the enabling act in 1998 meant that the campaign for the privatization of the postal services was unsuccessful. Led by Koizumi Junichirō, minister of health and welfare in Hashimoto's second administration, formerly minister for posts and telecommunications, and supported by Keidanren, it was defeated by the combined pressure of MPT bureaucrats, postmasters, and LDP politicians. MPT disappeared into the new Ministry of Public Management, and postal services are to be provided by an agency until the establishment of a new public corporation some time after 31 March 2003. The attempt to transfer the powerful River Bureau from MOC to MAFF also failed. Arguably, the merger of MOC, MOT, and the Land Agency created an even stronger organizational unit for the promotion of public works, with a budget

Table 6.3 *Ministries, commissions, and agencies, 2001*

Ministry	Commission	Agency
Cabinet Office	National Public Safety Commission	*Ministerial Agencies* Defence Agency Financial Services Agency *Non-ministerial agencies* Imperial Household Agency Defence Facilities Administration Agency
Ministry of Justice	National Bar Examination Administration Commission Public Security Examination Commission	Public Security Investigation Agency
Ministry of Foreign Affairs		
Ministry of Finance		National Tax Administration Agency
Ministry of Education, Culture, Sports, and Science		Agency for Cultural Affairs
Ministry of Health, Labour, and Welfare	Central Labour Relations Commission	Social Insurance Agency
Ministry of Agriculture, Forestry, and Fisheries		Food Agency Forestry Agency Fisheries Agency
Ministry of Economy, Trade, and Industry		Agency of Natural Resources and Energy Patent Office Small and Medium Enterprise Agency
Ministry of Land Infrastructure, and Transport	Central Labour Relations Commission for Seafarers	Maritime Safety Agency Marine Accident Inquiry Agency Meteorological Agency
Ministry of Public Management, Home Affairs, Posts, and Telecommunications	Fair Trade Commission Environmental Disputes Coordination Commission	Postal Services Agency Fire Defence Agency
Ministry of the Environment		

of more than 7 trillion. MOT fought off the attempt by the National Public Safety Commission to add the Marine Safety Agency, responsible for policing coastal waters, to its general responsibilities for traffic safety. Other proposals abandoned in the period between the Interim and Final Reports of the Administrative Reform Council in 1997 included the merger of the Environment Agency with MHW, the integration of MITI and MPT, and the creation of separate ministries for land preservation and development. MITI survived with almost all its functions intact, albeit with a reordering of the priorities of its industrial responsibilities. MAFF too retained its separate identity, successfully resisting the earlier proposal to incorporate it in a Ministry for Land Preservation. Along with MOFA and MOE, both emerged with their status, organizational identity, functions, and jurisdiction virtually intact.

Assessment

The reorganization was implemented on 6 January 2001. What actually happens on the ground after that date may prove to be quite different from the proposed changes, but even at face value they are less radical than claimed. The functions of the central government are less changed than rearranged in different larger boxes. Secondly, many of those changes (of title, for example) are cosmetic, 'changing colours' (*oironaoshi*). Thirdly, the attempt to create a smaller Cabinet, better able to discuss and formulate general strategy, assumes that its members are willing and able to play that role. Besides the support and services of an enhanced Cabinet Secretariat, they will need a substructure of Cabinet committees with the authority to coordinate and settle issues of ministerial policy, leaving the Cabinet free to concentrate on broader strategic issues across the whole of government. The management and political control of larger departments will make greater demands on the time and energy of ministers. Partly in recognition of this, each ministry will have two parliamentary vice-ministers who are intended to relieve the minister of some of the burden of policy-making. Nevertheless, the Cabinet minister of a large ministry will face a larger number of bureaucrats, responsible for a wider range of functions. The new Ministry of Land, Infrastructure, and Transport will have some 70,000 officials.

Paradoxically, the attempt to impose more political control 'top-down' on policy-making might strengthen the power of bureaucrats through the institutionalization of traditional 'verticalization' in large conglomerate ministries. At least in the short term, there is a risk that large ministries will become loose federations of autonomous states with their own (old) embedded identities and loyalties. Past precedents are not encouraging. For example, within the MCA, the separate identities of the old AMA, merged with the Personnel Bureau of the Prime Minister's Office in 1984, were still apparent at the end of the century. The directors-general of the Administrative Management Bureau and the Personnel Bureau were (with a single exception) in each case appointed from within the ranks of the old organizations. Moreover, many of the overlapping jurisdictions and responsibilities of ministries and agencies in the old administrative structure remain. For example, MOF's residual regulatory functions for the financial sector overlaps with those of the new FSA; its budgetary functions, with the new Council on Economic and Fiscal Policy.

A smaller Cabinet of some 14 (including the chief Cabinet secretary) plus one or more of the four ministers of state (for special issues) will also reduce the prime minister's patronage. There will be fewer opportunities for political preferment, and the task of balancing the representation of party factions within the Cabinet will be made more difficult. (In his reshuffled cabinet in December 2000, Prime Minister Mori created a special post for former Prime Minister Hashimoto, leader of the largest faction, to strengthen his position in the government.) The rapid turnover of Cabinet posts under the old system was criticized because it denied ministers sufficient time in a post to acquire the necessary knowledge and expertise to get on top of their ministries. Smaller Cabinets would increase the pressure on prime ministers to reshuffle as least as often, perhaps more frequently. To play the strategic role in Cabinet envisaged for them, ministers would need to be more experienced, not less, in managing their ministries, and to spend more time in post, not less. The UK's experiment with 'giant departments' in the 1970s proved to be too great a burden for a single Cabinet minister to carry alone; 'double banking' of Cabinet ministers became common, and the smaller Cabinet was soon returned to its previous size.

One of the stated objectives of the reorganization was to reduce the size of the civil service by a quarter by 2010. The number of secretariats and bureaux is to be reduced from 128 to 'wherever possible as close as 90', and the number of divisions, from about 1,200 to 'in the neighbourhood of 1,000' at the time of the reorganization and to about 900 by 2006 (IAM 1999). The Administrative Reform Council had recommended that 'even for large ministries, the number of internal bureaux should not exceed 10' (ARC 1997: 7). The implementation of those proposals will pose formidably difficult problems of integrating the bureaux of the ministries to be merged. For example, the Ministry of Construction had six bureaux; MOT had nine. Together with those of the Land Agency and the Hokkaido Development Agency, some 20 bureaux had to be reduced to 'less than 10' in the Ministry of Land, Infrastructure and Transport. In the past, faced with much less restrictive covenants on the number of bureaux and directors-general, ministries responded creatively with organizational solutions of 'departments' and 'councillors'; they might do so once again.

The 1998 legislation aimed to weaken bureaucratic influence and control of policy-making by reducing the number of statutory advisory councils, through abolition, consolidation, and rationalization. A year later the government announced that the 212 councils would be reduced to 93, and the number of members from 5,300 to 1,800. Council membership was limited to 30 (some had more than 100 members; MITI's Industrial Structure Council, 130), and Cabinet ministers and bureaucrats were banned from serving on them. Earlier, a Cabinet decision of September 1995 had provided for a review of the selection procedures, and for greater transparency by opening meetings to the public, and publication of minutes and proceedings. Finally, to separate policy-making functions from those of implementation, independent administrative institutions (IAIs) 'with an independent legal status outside the state's normal organizational framework' were proposed for the delivery of certain services, similar to the Executive Agencies set up under the 'Next Steps' initiative in the UK in the 1980s (ARC 1997: 9). In 1999, 89 of these organizations, mainly research institutes, testing laboratories, inspection and accreditation bodies, and a variety of health and safety bodies, altogether employing some 67,000 civil servants, were integrated into 59 IAIs.

7

Ministerial Autonomy and Territorial Boundaries: Coordination, Competition, and Conflict in the Policy-Making Processes

The most difficult problem of governmental organization since the restoration of the Meiji, according to Ōkōchi Shigeo, has been the need to coordinate the sectional interests of the central ministries (Johnson 1980). Throughout the last quarter of the twentieth century, Japan's ministries and agencies were often deeply divided over the making and carrying out of many policies that were related or inter-departmental. Jurisdictional competition, derived from and fostered by the verticalized structure of the central administration, was the principal cause of that division. Other factors were the historical continuity, stability, and conservatism of organizational structures, and their individual recruitment, socialization, and lifetime employment systems. Prime loyalty to the group or faction was more important than loyalty to a more abstract concept such as 'the public service', 'the government', or 'the national interest'. 'Bureaucrats are officials of the various ministries first and only second are they bureaucrats to the nation' (Johnson 1989: 74). Bureaucratic insularity was reflected and reinforced by the particularistic interest of politicians focused more on discrete policy issues than comprehensive policy or collective good government.

This chapter examines the governmental and party structures through which attempts were made to coordinate the interests, functions, and responsibilities of ministries and agencies, and the informal processes, procedures, and behavioural rules-of-the-game that supported them. It is argued that the latter provided more coordination in practice than an inspection of formal structures suggests.

JURISDICTIONAL AUTONOMY

The jurisdiction of each ministry was separately prescribed in an establishment law. Some, like those of MOF and MITI, were couched in general, often vague, terms, conferring upon their bureaucrats considerable discretion to decide the extent of ministerial authority, to interpret its application to policy issues and to groups, and to regulate the behaviour of those falling within its jurisdiction. Thus,

Many Japanese bureaucrats appear to view their enabling legislation not merely as establishing substantive areas over which they are to exercise regulatory control, but rather as descriptions of the various groups in society over which they have charge. (Young 1984: 936)

For example, MAFF's establishing law vested it with responsibility for agricultural development. 'Yet the Ministry generally interprets this legislation as placing under its purview all farmers and their families for any conceivable purpose' (Young 1984: 937). Clients and groups often asked for interpretation, or to be brought within the ambit of a ministry's jurisdiction, by requesting the regulation of their activities, whereby certain benefits or privileges were conferred. Bureaucratic interpretation of the exercise of jurisdictional authority was rarely tested and decided through the courts, or subject to review and control by dedicated regulatory agencies. MOC's public announcement that it had decided 'to penetrate the new telecommunications industry after its deregulation' had no legal basis in its law of establishment. Despite that, MOC bureaucrats 'perceived that the telecommunications sector was a newly created world open to any party and thus they were free from existing restrictive provisions'. Emulating MITI's principle of discretionary interpretation and behaviour, it entered a 'turf that belonged to nobody' (Takahashi 1988: 21). It was searching for new ideas in order to maintain and, if possible, expand its jurisdictional authority in policy-making for highways, partly to resist encroachment by MITI as it developed policies for the 'information society'.

The formal, legal powers of ministries, agencies, and commissions were complemented by 'extra-legal processes', through which they sought to explain how laws, ordinances, and regulations were to be interpreted, and thereby to regulate the activities of organizations and clientele within their jurisdiction. The definition and use of so-called 'administrative guidance', and its effects and effectiveness in different policy areas, but especially industrial policy, has generated a considerable literature in its own right.[1] It is not necessary to rehearse it here, but it is worth emphasizing that 'administrative guidance', however defined and used, was practised as a 'rule-of-the-game' by which the relationships between the members of various policy networks were regulated. In some circumstances, ministries preferred to devolve responsibility for the regulation of a policy area for which they had policy jurisdiction to other members of a network. Private ordering of the market without direct regulation by a ministry was common, according to Upham (1993), obviating the need for bureaucrats to investigate and evaluate applications. Members of the network could thus create the framework within which private regulation of their activities took place, by voluntary agreement. For example, during the 1980s MITI did not exercise the jurisdictional authority conferred on it by the Large-Scale Retail Stores Law to regulate the number of new shops: instead, it granted local merchants a veto power over the opening of new

---

[1] For a discussion see Haley(1991); Rixtel (1997) provides an overview and summary of the debate, mainly concerned with industrial policy, and discusses the operation and significance of administrative guidance in MOF's supervision and regulation of banking.

stores in their district. In effect, it created an informal framework within which private parties worked out their own accommodations.

COMPETITION AND CONFLICT

Both formal legal powers and extra-legal processes helped to define the boundaries of the jurisdictional territory of each ministry, agency, and commission, and hence the extent of their autonomy. However, policy issues rarely arose, or achieved recognition as agenda items requiring attention, wholly within the separate domains thus defined. Less likely still was it that the formulation of an appropriate, acceptable, and funded response, or its implementation, would involve a single ministry or agency. Policy issues were 'messy' and inchoate; they spilled over and transcended ministerial jurisdictional boundaries. Many were interdependent and required a coordinated organizational response. At the same time, each ministry sought to maintain its autonomy, ceaselessly and vigilantly patrolling the boundaries of its territory to forestall and resist the encroachment of others. Competition and conflict between ministries could and did occur in such circumstances. It occurred also where the formulation of policies and/or their implementation required the cooperation or collaboration of several different ministries and agencies. To take an obvious and well documented example, jurisdiction for both the formulation and implementation of policy for overseas development aid (ODA) was fragmented and dispersed through 18 central ministries and agencies, with interrelated, sometimes overlapping, responsibilities. Thus, responsibility for multilateral aid was divided between MOFA and MOF; MOFA was responsible for UN-related aid; MOF, for contributions to multilateral development banks; MITI, for yen loans; JICA and OECF, for implementation. A whole host of other ministries, among them MAFF, MOC, and MHW, had related policy interests. The division and overlapping responsibilities of MOF, BOJ, MITI, and MAFF in the supervision and regulation of banking and financial services contributed in the 1990s to the failure to take, first, appropriate preventive and, later, corrective action in the collapse and rescue of the housing loan associations (*jusen*).

Competition and conflict between ministries and agencies occurred also in circumstances of the emergence of a new policy area or policy responsibility. 'Everywhere it turns, MITI seems to confront other major ministries with regulatory jurisdiction and powers over new policy areas' (Callon 1995: 205). It competed with MOF over the financing of new businesses and the provision of venture capital, and disputed access to Japan's universities with MOE in a struggle for control of government R&D policies. Both were disdainful of and largely ignored the STA as it tried to play a formal coordinating role. Hi-tech projects and policies did 'not fit easily or wholly into traditional categories within government organizations. This fragmentation tends to cause jurisdictional disputes within ministries and intensifies inter-ministerial conflicts' (Tanaka 1991: 111). One effect of that competition was to increase the importance of a ministry's collaboration with its clients or groups, in a bid to hold on to its territory. Ministries and state agencies fought over which should take the lead in formulating a policy to promote biotechnology. The 'turf' of MHW was threatened by the incursion of MITI and, to a lesser extent, STA, MAFF, and MOE. MITI wanted to incorporate its concept of biotechnology policy into a 'vision' of high-tech Japan; both STA and MOE, with responsibility for the promotion of science, devised 'life-science/biotechnology projects'. MAFF's interest derived from its responsibility for controlling the agriculture industry, and regulating rice prices. Each of the four ministries created a separate research programme related to its territory, 'even though most of the research activities in each ministry's programme were almost the same' (Tanaka 1991). A ministry with a close relationship with a firm was often reluctant to have it participate in another ministry's programme, and hence contribute to the expansion of the latter's jurisdictional authority to regulate through the extra-legal processes described above.

The turf fights between MITI and MPT to control policies for telecommunications in the 1980s, the so-called 'telecom wars', are well known (Johnson 1989). Technological innovation created a policy vacuum between the territorial domains of the two ministries and competition for the expansion of their own jurisdictions. One of those involved policy for teletopias or 'new media communities'. With MITI's announcement of plans to establish 11 of these, the Director-General of MPT's Telecommunications Bureau 'scurried to the postal *zoku* to complain that MITI was infringing on its turf', and was counselled to accelerate its own policy announcement. MPT announced plans for 20 teletopias. Subsequently it and MITI produced separate draft bills which the LDP rejected on the grounds of cost. MOC then decided that both MITI and MPT were encroaching on its turf and produced its own 'teleway' legislation, provoking MOT to bring forward its own proposals for optical fibre cables. MOF declined to fund all four sets of proposals; the LDP hedged, and then negotiated a compromise, temporarily solving 'inter-ministerial conflict through an omnibus pork barrel bill that gives something to everybody' (Johnson 1989: 227).

Competition and conflict occurred also when a new agency was set up whose jurisdiction infringed that of existing ministries. The extent of its authority, and crucially which ministry would supervise its activities, were contested. In 1974 competing bureaucratic interests prevented the creation of a separate Ministry of Overseas Development. Several ministries were at that time seeking to expand their influence in an emerging policy field. MAFF and MITI wanted to set up their own agencies; EPA opposed their proposals because of the threat to its own OECF, supported by MOFA because of potential conflict with its own Overseas Technical Cooperation Agency (OTCA). The Japan International Cooperation Agency (JICA) was a compromise incorporating OTCA (Orr 1990).

Competition among ministries to control the direction of policy-making in those agencies whose responsibilities overlapped with their own was often claimed to be at its fiercest in the battles for control for those attached to the Prime Minister's Office. Ministries competed to obtain a share of supervisory control, and the right to appoint their own officials or nominees to senior and influential positions. Besides the potential for influence and control in areas of policy-making of related interest, each ministry benefited from the acquisition of more placements for its retired officials, and added to its 'assets' (*kabu*) spread throughout the administration.

Competition between ministries to establish jurisdictional authority for new or expanding policy areas, and to supervise and control new agencies, commissions, and quasi-governmental organization, centred on three issues: influence and control in the policy process, money, and patronage. Any diminution in the scope of a ministry's jurisdictional authority was a potential threat to its share of the Budget. Conversely, a ministry able to extend its territorial boundaries could argue for an increase in its budget to reflect additional responsibilities. The extent and quality of a ministry's jurisdictional authority over other governmental and quasi-governmental organizations were important for two other reasons. First, the regulatory and supervisory activities of a ministry's satellites, together with the ministry's own issue of regulations, provided an instrument of influence, leverage and control over clients and special interest groups. Secondly, supervision and control over senior appointments to ministerial satellites provided a major source of 'soft landings' for senior ministerial and agency staff who retired or resigned before the age of 60. I return to that issue in Chapter 9.

INTER-MINISTERIAL COORDINATION

There were at least three prerequisites of coherent and coordinated policy-making and policy implementation in Japanese central government. First, there was the need to integrate the different policy interests represented by the ministries and agencies, and, indirectly through them, to reconcile their clients' overlapping, competing, and often conflicting special interests. In short, there was a need within the central government system of a capability to aggregate and integrate diverse interests. Secondly, there was the need to ensure that the different knowledge, expertise, skills, and information possessed by each ministry and agency were brought to bear on particular policy issues at the appropriate time. Thirdly, there was the need to provide for a mutually acceptable means of resolving conflicts which arose from competing claims of jurisdictional authority. Those three needs were provided through institutional structures: formally through dedicated organizations and processes, and also through informal processes and rules-of-the-game.

Formal Organizational Coordination

The institutional structures for coordinating policy in Japanese central government in the period 1975–2000 were, first, the Cabinet, supported by the Cabinet Secretariat and Office. Both were closely linked to the Prime Minister's Office and the prime minister personally, a second potential source of formal (and informal) coordination. Thirdly, there were formal bureaucratic structures for inter-ministerial consultation, ground-clearing, and negotiation. Finally, there were organizations, mainly agencies and commissions, with dedicated functions of coordination within a number of policy areas.

Inherent in the procedures for bringing business to Cabinet for its formal approval was an inescapable element of coordination, both formally, through the procedures managed by the Cabinet Secretariat, and informally, through processes of consultation and discussion between the affected parties before a submission was made. Entering the Cabinet domain was itself a guarantee of some prior minimal level of coordination.

Generally, the Cabinet's role was passive, reacting to business that came before it: legitimating, through formal approval, agreements and decisions reached elsewhere in the bureaucracy, and, also formally, by the LDP's Executive Council and the Deliberation Council of PARC. Cabinet rarely provided a forum for substantive discussion of strategic or comprehensive policy-making, or sought to coordinate the different policy interests represented by its members. Nor did it act as a final court of appeal in those very few cases where inter-ministerial conflict had proved irreconcilable at lower levels in the hierarchy. More commonly, that role was played by the most senior members of the LDP *qua* party officials.

Coordination through formal Cabinet meetings and, where necessary, Cabinet committees was underpinned by the twice-weekly meetings (on Mondays and Thursdays) of the administrative vice ministers of all the Spending Ministries and Agencies. Of the non-ministerial agencies and commissions, only the National Police Agency was represented. Supporting staff from the ministries and agencies attended, together with the deputy director-general of the Cabinet Legislation Bureau, the deputy director-general of administrative affairs in the Prime Minister's Office, and the relevant Cabinet Secretariat counsellors as assistants.

The meetings in the form of 'working lunches' chaired by the deputy chief secretary to the Cabinet for administrative affairs were brief and formal. The main purpose was to prepare for the meetings of Cabinet held the following day: to consider and discuss particular agenda items. Unresolved differences of opinion between ministries or agencies occasionally surfaced. It was also possible, although very rare, for a substantive decision to be made: the meeting could exercise its authority to oppose the further progress of a bill, for example. More likely, it would be agreed that the matter had not yet been sufficiently coordinated, and referred back.

Meetings of administrative vice-ministers were in turn preceded by formal and informal inter-ministerial consultations between officials at different hierarchical levels, held as progress was made towards a Cabinet submission. Within ministries, preparation for the inter-ministerial administrative vice-ministers meetings was undertaken by formal meetings of bureaux directors-general, which in turn were preceded by less formal meetings at the divisional director level, to consider papers and proposals referred to them by earlier meetings of the deputy directors of the General Affairs Division of each bureau. The latter was normally chaired by the deputy director of the Coordination and Legal Affairs Division (Bunsho-ka) or General Affairs Division (Sōmu-ka) of the minister's Secretariat, reflecting the importance of that division, and his status in the issue of ministerial ordinances, notices, and directions.[2] Two other key personnel from the minister's Secretariat attended as well: the deputy director of the Budget and Accounts Division, and the deputy director of the Personnel Division.

---

[2] The nomenclature varies: bunsho-ka literally Documents, or Archives Division, was translated variously: in MOF, the Overall Coordination Division; MOT, the Administration and Legal Affairs Division; MAFF, the Legal Affairs Division; MOC, the Administrative Coordination Division. Sōmu-ka literally General Affairs Division, was translated as General Affairs Division in MOE; and General Coordination Division in MITI, MOL, and elsewhere.

The Prime Minister's Office

The Prime Minister's Office comprised his secretary for political affairs and attendant staff, and four private secretaries on secondment from MOF, MOFA, MITI, and the National Police Agency. The official from MOF had the widest and most general responsibility, including the economy and financial policy; the MOFA secretary had responsibility for diplomatic and foreign policy, while the NPA official had a general responsibility for all security matters internationally and domestically (including natural disasters), and local government matters. While representation at the heart of government was recognition of the centrality of the activities of those ministries, and undoubtedly enhanced their claim to recognition as 'primus inter pares', the selection of particular officials was often dictated as much or more by the preferences of prime ministers. MITI's representation began only with the accession of Tanaka Kakuei in 1972, when he appointed his former secretary at MITI as the fourth private secretary.

Until the implementation of administrative reforms in 2001 designed to strengthen his authority in Cabinet, the prime minister did not have legal powers under the Constitution to impose his will on his colleagues, for example by taking an initiative in Cabinet to secure an integrated or coordinated response to a policy issue. His role and leadership in policy-making was normally passive or reactive. The flow of information, advice, proposals, and recommendations to the prime minister was controlled by the 'gate-keepers' in his Office, i.e. the senior officials on secondment from MOF, MOFA, MITI, and the National Police Agency, and those in the Cabinet Secretariat. One senior MOF official described it thus: 'If we need a decision by the Prime Minister, even on a simple either–or proposition we always make a judgement first and then submit it for approval... If we don't we're told to arrive at a decision ourselves and come back with what we've decided. [Prime Minister] Miyazawa is no different' (Tase 1993: 43).

When unresolved issues, disagreements, and conflicts rose to the prime minister's level, the principle of non-intervention was normally observed; to decide between conflicting policy proposals of two or more ministries was to risk degrading the status of those ruled against. Nevertheless, there were examples of prime ministerial initiatives and interventions, although the constraints of time and energy, the countervailing resources of other players, and particularly the strength of sub-governments focused on particular ministries combined to limit his capacity to involve himself in only a handful of disputes and conflicts (Hayao 1993; Shinoda 1994). When he did so, he could draw upon both positional and personal resources: the formal status of his office; sometimes, but not invariably, factional seniority in the party; and the information and intelligence that flowed through his party and private office networks.

Yasutomo (1995) shows how prime ministers focused attention on the importance of both bilateral and multilateral aid, and helped to define the broader policy context of specific policies for multilateral development banks. They 'raised multilateral aid above the immediate, technical, and standard operating procedure level to a longer-term, political and national priority status... transforming bureaucratic politics into national priorities and ordering measures into policy initiatives' (p. 141).

Untypically, Nakasone favoured a more presidential style of leadership. Through large-scale plans formulated by various advisory councils and prime ministerial commissions, he attempted to implement broad policies top-down rather than bottom-up through ministerial bureaux. To free himself from the constraints of PARC and the Diet, where he was weak factionally, he created and used private councils and advisory commissions modelled on Rinchō (which he had initiated while minister at the (then) Administrative Management Agency in 1981) to try to influence public opinion over the heads of both party and Diet, and indirectly to bring pressure to bear on both. 'His advisory-body politics were, in essence, an attempt to assert the predominance of a prime-minister-centred executive branch' (Schwartz 1993: 239). While he enjoyed some success with administrative reform, notably the privatization of the *san kosha*, and in defence and foreign policy, where he took the initiative on the Plaza strategy for the yen–dollar currency realignment in 1985 (Funabashi 1988), the radical reform of education was largely frustrated by MOE's protection of its jurisdictional authority. Likewise, attempts to deregulate land use policy were deflected by MOC officials who were able to exploit the low level of expertise in land use policy among members of the advisory commission appointed to make proposals for reform (Ōtake 1993). Other parts of his agenda were frustrated by the preference of his own party for the continued distribution of benefits to traditional clients and supporters. From time to time, his successors established ad hoc commissions and committees to report on specific issues that transcended the policy interests and jurisdictions of several or all ministries and agencies. Prime Minister Hashimoto set up and chaired an Administrative Reform Council in 1996 to make recommendations to him for the reorganization of the functions of central government. Prime Minister Obuchi's style of 'council politics', incorporating both special and general interests to achieve a broad consensus for his policies, led to the establishment of seven advisory councils, including a Council on Economic Strategy which reported to him personally, and a Commission on Industrial Competitiveness, which he chaired himself.

The Cabinet was collectively responsible to the Diet for the exercise of executive power. That constitutional requirement has been interpreted as requiring the unanimous consent of the Cabinet to any policy, or Cabinet Order. Objection by a minister was a rare and singular occurrence. To uphold the principles of collective responsibility and unanimity in Cabinet meetings of the coalition governments of the LDP, SDP, and Sakigake in 1994–6, the ministers of the three parties first discussed formally and agreed consensually the official agenda of Cabinet business, for which the preparatory groundwork had been undertaken at the inter-ministerial levels, and through the Cabinet Secretariat. At the conclusion of the official agenda, the Cabinet then engaged in an informal 'free discussion', where differences of opinion on policy issues, strategic and tactical, between the members of the three parties were aired. There was no official, pre-determined agenda, but the Cabinet's deputy chief secretary for administrative affairs 'took note of' the discussions and alerted ministries 'where appropriate action was deemed necessary' (MCA 1997*a*). In practice, the principle of collective Cabinet responsibility was (and is) more often honoured in the breach, as ministers on returning to their departments held press conferences, and briefed journalists on who said what and why.

Together, the prime minister and Cabinet could, if they had the will and were in broad agreement, sometimes provide invaluable collective support for particular policies. The Ōhira, Suzuki, and Nakasone Cabinets either initiated or endorsed the use of overseas aid as a diplomatic tool. Together, the prime minister and Cabinet provided the one consistent source of support for the concept of strategic aid, set the framework for policy, and created the momentum within the bureaucracy. Without that support, MOFA's policy of comprehensive security would have been weaker. But even here, the involvement of the prime minister and Cabinet was sporadic rather than continuous (Yasumoto 1986).

The Cabinet Office

The Cabinet Office was headed by a minister, the chief secretary to the Cabinet, a Cabinet post. He was the official spokesman for the government as a whole, acting head of the Prime Minister's Office responsible for the day-to-day business. His secretarial assistance paralleled that of the prime minister. With experience, expertise, and special knowledge of the central activities of finance, foreign affairs, industry, and security, his officials were by definition (and selection) well connected, and provided conduits for the two-way transmission of information and intelligence between the prime minister and his private office, the Cabinet Secretariat, and the 12 ministries and their agencies. The Cabinet's deputy chief secretary for political affairs was a political appointee.

The Cabinet Secretariat

At a more routine level, formal coordination of policy issues and legislation that rose to the level of Cabinet was provided by the Secretariat headed by the deputy chief secretary to the Cabinet for administrative affairs. His staff (in 1998) of 175 officials provided services and support for both the Cabinet and the prime minister, for example the preparation and arrangement of agendas, and the supervision and control of business entering into the Cabinet domain. More broadly, the deputy chief secretary, his right-hand man, the chief councillor, and their staff were primarily responsible for high-level coordination of policy throughout the government: formally through the status and responsibilities of the Secretariat, and informally through his and their access to, and nodal position in, the networks that joined the prime minister, ministers, party officials, and bureaucrats in the ministries and agencies.

Appointed by the prime minister, the Cabinet's deputy chief secretary for administrative affairs was normally chosen from the ranks of recently retired administrative vice-ministers from MHW, MOL, or the National Police Agency. Those were, allegedly, more 'neutral' ministries, and thereby enhanced his status as an impartial mediator. At a time of political turbulence, which saw ten different prime ministers come and go in 13 years, the post also provided for essential administrative continuity. Between 1987 and 2000 there were only two incumbents: Furukawa Teijiro, who by the latter date had been in office for almost six years, had previously been administrative vice-minister at MHW; his predecessor had served even longer.

The extent to which they and others before them were able to play the role of an impartial mediator, helping to coordinate the overlapping or competing policy interests of different ministries, varied with the politicization of each issue, and the extent to which the interests of organized groups were mobilized and brought to bear by the ministries. When the latter occurred, the intervention of LDP senior officials, the chief secretary to the Cabinet, and senior *zoku* was both inevitable and necessary to resolve disagreements, according to one former deputy chief secretary to the cabinet (Ahn 1998). The mediating and coordinating roles of the deputy chief became more important in the period of the short-lived multi-party governments between 1993 and 1996, when coalition partners were unable to agree on the resolution of policy issues, and bureaucrats in the Spending Ministries were forced to be more pro-active.

In 1998 the Secretariat had five offices—Internal Affairs, External Affairs, Security and Crisis Management, Public Relations, and Information and Research—each headed by a Cabinet councillor, with a rank, status, and salary intermediate between that of a bureau director-general and an administrative vice-minister. They were appointed from the relevant ministries, MOF, MOFA, and the Defence Agency. The Prime Minister's Office provided the councillor for public relations, and the National Police Agency the councillor for information and research, whose work was concerned mainly with civil security matters. For most councillors it was normally their last posting before retirement, although the councillor for external affairs could expect appointment to an ambassadorial post. Exceptionally, in January 1998 the councillor for internal affairs, Tanami Koiji, was brought back to MOF as administrative vice-minister following the enforced resignation of Komura Takeshi, who was obliged to take formal responsibility for charges of corruption brought against senior officials in the Banking Inspection Department of the minister's Secretariat. Tanami had been director-general of the Finance Bureau before his appointment to the Cabinet Office, and was not in the line of succession to MOF's top post (See Chapter 9). There was also a Cabinet counsellor's (*sic*) Office, whose staff provided advice and services for the Cabinet directly, and performed coordinating functions across the range of the Cabinet's business.

Besides the Cabinet Secretariat, there was also the Cabinet Legislation Bureau, with a staff of 74 headed by a director-general, supported by a deputy director-general, an Administration Office, and four departments. The responsibility for the initiation of new legislation, and the provision and amendment of existing law, rested with individual ministries and ministerial agencies. The role of the Cabinet Legislation Bureau was passive, reacting to the proposals that were submitted to it. Its scrutiny was concerned to establish the need for such legislation or amendment, and its appropriateness to the issue; to assess the consistency of the proposal with existing legislation; to consider and declare on its constitutionality; and to provide technical assistance with the legal drafting (MCA 1998*a*). Its functions included the examination of drafts of bills and Cabinet Orders proposed by ministries and agencies; advice to the prime minister, Cabinet, and ministers on legal issues; and research and data collection on domestic and international laws. When bills were discussed in the Diet, the director-general of the Bureau was required to attend, and to respond to questions in committee hearings. The Security Council of Japan was also a part of the Cabinet Office, whose officials provided secretarial services for it, and oversaw the implementation of its decisions. The headquarters of the Administrative Reform of the Central Government was also a part of the Cabinet Office after the enactment of the 1998 reform legislation. Its secretariat was responsible for the smooth transition to the new structure, the drafting of contingent laws and orders, and the implementation of the proposals to reduce the size of the central executive.

By the time that most policy issues entered the Cabinet domain, whether or not they required changes in the law or Cabinet Orders, all those ministries and agencies with a legitimate interest had been consulted, and the necessary 'adjustments' made to accommodate them, even if those adjustments represented a minimal level of consensus rather than a coherent and integrated response. In a few cases differences were irreconcilable, and the Cabinet/party leadership had to determine how the matter was to be handled. There were Cabinet committees, or more accurately a number of prescribed subject areas where 'ministerial conferences' took place prior to Cabinet meetings, where 'adjustments' were occasionally made. In October 1992 there were 27 of these, some concerned with broad policy areas or issues (education reform, the ageing of society, economic policy, defence, environmental protection), others with more specific problems or issues (land subsidence, foreign workers, AIDs, Kansai International Airport) (Masujima and O'uchi 1993). The number of such 'ministerial conferences' varied with each new government or, from 1993, change of regime, to accord with different styles of collective discussion and the political salience and priority of particular themes and issues. As in full Cabinet, ministerial conferences were occasions mainly for registering formal agreement, and legitimating decisions arrived at elsewhere in the policy process (Ozawa 1994).

The slow and ill-coordinated response of the Japanese government to the immediate consequences of the Great Hanshin–Awaji earthquake in January 1995 provided graphic evidence of the lack of capacity for leadership and command in the Prime Minister's office. The prime minister had no formal constitutional power to declare a state of national emergency and assume command of the relief services, as in the USA, the UK, Germany, or France, for example. Nor did he have legal authority to issue instructions to ministries and agencies, even in a crisis situation. Nor was the Cabinet Secretariat empowered, or possessed of the organizational capacity, to provide for a swift and coordinated response to a national emergency. Responsibility for providing relief services was divided among several ministries and agencies, and neither the prime minister nor the Cabinet Secretariat was able to mobilize, command, and deploy them decisively in the crucial hours after the first tremors were felt in Kobe.

At that time, the Basic Law on Disaster Countermeasures fell within the jurisdiction of the National Land Agency; responsibility for the management of national disasters was shared between its Disaster Prevention Bureau and the Cabinet Secretariat; relief services were the responsibility of the Self-Defence Forces (Defence Agency) and the police (National Police Agency), while fire and emergency services were provided by local governments under the general supervision of MHA. In a fiercely critical attack on the mismanagement of the crisis, a former director-general of the Cabinet Security Affairs Office commented: 'Our government officials waited passively on a formal request from the governor [of Hyōgo Prefecture] before mobilising the SDF' (Sasa 1995). That such action was strictly in accordance with the Self-Defence Forces Law served only to underline the inability of the centre — Prime Minister, Cabinet, Cabinet Secretariat — to take action that was appropriate to the circumstances, rather than that which accorded strictly with the law. While not condoning or excusing the failure of crisis management, it is necessary to understand the historical context within which organizational responsibilities have been distributed. This includes a number of controversial and sensitive issues centred on the role of the state in providing internal security, public safety, and civil order, for example long-standing anxiety about the constitutional role of the SDF and their deployment in national emergencies, the protection of civil liberties under the constitution, and the spectre of a revival of the control and coercion exercised by the old Ministry of the Interior. Despite jurisdictional and organization changes made as a consequence of the failure of an integrated governmental response to the earthquake disaster, the central government's slow and hesitant response to the plutonium leak at Tōkai-mura in September 1999 revealed continuing weaknesses in coordinated policy-making and implementation.

Coordinating Agencies
Formal organizational coordination through agencies such as the National Land Agency, the MCA, EPA, STA, and the Environment Agency, ostensibly created to achieve coordinated policy-making and implementation in areas that involved several different interests, proved difficult to achieve in major policy issues, where one or more ministries had a legitimate interest, and a claim to exercise some jurisdictional authority over the initiation of new policies and the financing and carrying-out of existing policies, and where, traditionally, they appointed their own officials to certain key posts. Thus, EPA was unable to provide an independent, integrated response to major issues of economic policy, the forecasted rate of GDP for example, without the agreement of at least two other major players, MOF and MITI. In practice, both had considerable and, occasionally decisive, influence on what the EPA did and said through their control of several senior appointments, and because of EPA's lack of executive authority (discussed in Chapter 14). Similarly, the policy coordination functions of STA were constrained by the major interests of MITI, MOE, MAFF, and MOF in the initiation of new policies, the prioritization of new and old, the size and distribution of budget allocations, and the responsibility for carrying out policies. MAFF had a critical resource: the largest corps of research staff in its affiliated research institutes.

The Management and Coordination Agency had coordinating functions for both policy and organization. The scope of its formal policy coordinating functions was limited, but included several important programmes to which different ministries contributed across government, for example for youth education, training and employment; for the elderly, and for traffic safety. Such functions were intended originally to strengthen the MCA's position in discharging its main role of coordinating the personnel and management programmes of all ministries, agencies, and commissions throughout central government. It was also responsible for the planning and implementation of administrative reform. Where its activities were supported by law or Cabinet Order, as for example in the control of staff numbers and organizational structures, it could, through precept, persuasion, and the encouragement of local initiatives, be effective in achieving broad policy objectives set for the whole national government. Even on matters that were not specifically provided for by law or Cabinet Order, MCA's Administrative Management Bureau had informal powers of influence and persuasion derived from its formal authority to examine and approve or reject bids for staff, and requests for organizational changes.

Nevertheless, the autonomy of individual ministries was jealously protected, and they were reluctant to surrender jurisdiction over the organizations and staff they controlled or influenced, as became evident in their response to MCA's initiative on the privatization of public corporations in the 1990s, perceived as a threat to their jurisdictional autonomy.

As trade and industrial issues began to dominate foreign policy with the progressive internationalization of the Japanese economy in the 1980s, a multiplicity of new players entered the policy-making processes to challenge MOFA's jurisdictional authority, for example MPT in communications policies, MOT in international civil aviation, MOC in the liberalization of Japan's construction market. Inter-ministerial coordination was both more necessary and more difficult. The ineffectiveness of the formal organizations charged with achieving an integrated governmental response led to criticism by the Provisional Council for the Promotion of Administrative Reform in its 1985 report. Acknowledging the growing interdependence of external and domestic policies, the report concluded with characteristic understatement:

> There has been a one-sided tendency to self-righteous handling of external affairs by individual ministries owing to the technical and complex nature of individual problems. As a result, it is difficult to say that an all-out response by the Ministry of Foreign Affairs and the ministries concerned has always been made from a total-government point of view.
>
> The management of external relations deeply linked with the domestic policy must more often than not deal with a broad range of related administrative jurisdictions. The exercise of coordination in such areas is not necessarily easy. (Masujima and O'uchi 1993: 21)

The report went on to note as well that newly emerging problems did not always reflect or correspond to the existing divisions of ministry and agency responsibilities. It was an 'urgent task' to strengthen the means of achieving effective inter-ministerial coordination. Immediate action resulted in a reorganization of the Cabinet Secretariat in 1986 in which the Cabinet Councillor's Office was divided into Internal and External Affairs, the latter created to deal with the increase in business relating to international affairs. However, as domestic and international policy issues were often interrelated, in practice the Cabinet Councillor's Office on Internal Affairs continued to be responsible for most of the business dealt with at Cabinet level. An Office for Security Affairs was also created. The aim of the reorganization was 'to narrow down policy options for the Prime Minister by co-ordinating and synthesising diverse policy recommendations originating from individual ministers' under the purviews of the three newly created offices' (Ahn 1998: 43). Their coordinating activities were largely ineffective, partly because the staff, drawn from various ministries, represented the policy stance and interests of their parent ministries rather than a concern with the coordination of the different policy interests (Hayao 1993; Shinoda 1994). Moreover, ministries in dispute were often unwilling to accept their legal authority to mediate. However, on a personal basis, the director of a Cabinet Councillor's Office, with sufficient status, knowledge, and professional skills could be 'a factor in effective co-ordination' (Ahn-1998: 54).

The Provisional Council for the Promotion of Administrative Reform returned to the problem of inter-ministerial coordination in 1990, and reported in 1993. As a result, the status and salary of the directors of (the now six) Cabinet Offices were enhanced in an attempt to increase their influence over ministries and agencies. The Council also recommended, as had its predecessors, the appointment from outside of government advisers or senior assistants to the prime minister. The Cabinet Law was amended to allow him to appoint up to three, from among members of the Diet or from outside.

Advisory Councils
Advisory councils were an important constituent element of the organizational apparatus of each ministry and agency for the making and carrying out of policy. In 1996 there were 217 councils (*shingi-kai*), the five oldest of which had origins traceable to 1900. Their formal role and purpose were 'to obtain information from experts in various fields, to secure fairness of administration, to adjust the conflicting interests or to coordinate various fields of administration' (MCA 1997*d*: 111). While some advisory councils played a role in the formal coordination of inter-ministerial policy, for example the Council on Economic Policy in the Prime Minister's Office, which was formally responsible for the formulation of the five-yearly National Economic Plan, most advisory councils served the narrower interests of their parent ministry or agency; at best, they helped to coordinate private-sector interests with the public interest and policy objectives of the ministry.

Advisory councils were statutory bodies, whose functions and membership were defined precisely, set up by law or Cabinet Ordinance at the ministry or agency level to advise the prime minister or a minister. In practice, officials asked outside groups to nominate a list of candidates from which a choice was made. Apart from *ex officio* members, all advisory councils were required to appoint persons of 'learning and experience'; journalism, law, business, labour unions, research institutes, and academia provided most members. The Advisory Council for the Prevention of Prostitution stipulated only that its members be 'persons of learning'. The potential for bureaucratic influence was partly a function of their composition. In the mid-1980s, bureaucrats and ex-bureaucrats provided more than 40% of the membership (Sone 1985). In 1995 more than a third of the chairmen were recruited from the ranks of former bureaucrats. However, after a Cabinet decision of September 1995, in principle retired bureaucrats were excluded from membership, although there were some exceptions. Former officials were de-barred from the chairmanship of advisory councils established by their own ministries, but again, in practice, exceptions were made and justified.

The agenda, draft policy statements and explanations, information and data, minutes, and draft reports were normally prepared by the secretariat. Katō Hiroshi, chairman of the Government's Tax Research Council, admitted that 'it was normal for panels of this sort to use documents drawn up by ministries and agencies as the basis of their own proposals' (Katō 1995: 26). 'Thus, through the selection of members, the assignment of a council's task, the provision of reference materials, and the drafting of the final report, the government has ample, sometimes excessive, opportunity to have its views reflected in consultative councils' (Schwartz 1993: 229). The formal, ceremonial character of the proceedings of most councils frequently obscured the discussions, even negotiations that took place *sub rosa* between members and bureaucrats. 'Ministries use councils to designate those actors whose views they were willing to consider and to provide a framework for both the official and unofficial consultation of those views. The formal talks and the substantive talks advance in parallel; they were like two wheels of a cart' (p. 232). The Foreign Economic Cooperation Advisory Council, for example, 'tends to ratify a consensus position worked out by staff and other less formal deliberation mechanisms such as ad hoc study groups' (Arase 1994: 181). More recently, the influence and control traditionally exercised by officials on the proceedings and recommendations of advisory councils were tempered by the practice of expert members conducting their own hearings, preparing reports, and making recommendations independently of bureaucrats, as happened with the Administrative Reform Committee set up in 1994 and the Provisional Council for Decentralization in 1995 (MCA 1998*b*).

Statutory advisory councils performed a number of functions in the making and carrying out of policy. First, they provided a means of incorporating into those processes outside advice, especially of a specialist and technical kind which generalist bureaucrats frequently lacked. Advisory councils could be exploited by bureaucrats to develop or acquire knowledge about a new policy field or issues that arose within it. Ministries and agencies faced with the need to provide funds for risky, pre-competitive research in the development of biotechnology policy used advisory councils 'to identify those branches of research which will meet [future social and economic] needs and to explore their technological potential ... to generate new ideas for policy ... establish consensus on concrete measures among concerned parties ... and to define research fields' (Tanaka 1991: 114). Secondly, councils provided for the participation of a wide range of non-governmental interests, groups, and independent individuals, necessary in a consensual model of policy-making. Thirdly, they provided support for their parent ministry or agency, for example by supporting or defending particular policies or actions, or defending the status quo, and by protecting the 'turf' of a ministry or agency from the encroachment of another in an established policy area or in a dispute over an emergent one.

Fourthly, advisory councils were managed and exploited by skilful bureaucrats to legitimize the ministry's policy-making activities. 'Outside experts' served to 'highlight both the *neutrality* and *rationality* of the MOE's point of view' (Schoppa 1991*a*: 112). Experts with different views apparently agreed independently of the ministry on a policy recommendation or course of action, which could be used as a basis for the construction of a wider public consensus. A ministry could use a council to set and manage an agenda of proposals to focus and delimit a policy debate; equally, it could keep other proposals off the agenda. By influencing council recommendations at an early stage in the policy-making process, before politicians and other ministries formally entered the debate, a ministry tried to have its point of view reflected in 'neutral' and 'objective' policy proposals which provided the focus for subsequent discussion.

Most importantly, perhaps, as the burden of interest adjustment increased, councils provided a means of adjusting conflicting interests. They were a public demonstration of the reconciliation of the ministry's representation of the public interest with those of the private interests represented by the council's members. While the ideal of achieving mutually acceptable policies was not always or mainly achieved, 'council deliberations accurately reflect contending points of view and oblige participants to clarify and justify their respective positions' (Schwartz 1993: 231). They served as useful listening posts, where ministries and agencies could sound out the interested parties, and learn of their plans, and those of other groups, before embarking on new policy initiatives, or gauge the appropriate response to an event or policy issue. Finally, consultations with affected interests and groups helped to ensure their commitment to the carrying out of policies with which they had formally and publicly expressed agreement.

Those functions, and the councils' relationships with the bureaucrats in parent ministries and agencies, complemented the function of interest group intermediation performed politically by the LDP's leadership, PARC and its subordinate bodies, and *zoku*, helping to defuse potential confrontations, and to provide mediation where they were unavoidable.

Rules and regulations that had to be observed in the establishment, composition, and procedure of statutory advisory councils did not apply to private, unofficial committees, commissions, and study groups. They were set up at the instigation of the prime minister, or a minister or an administrative vice-minister or director-general of a bureau. Their number, use, and prominence increased from 1980, attributable in large part to the style, personality, and reformist zeal of Prime Minister Nakasone. As Schwartz notes, bureaucrats had increasing need of such committees to collect information, to provide specialist intelligence, opinion and knowledge, and even to draft policies. More contentiously, he argues that, as bureaucrats' autonomy was threatened by the greater involvement of LDP politicians in policy-making, and by the erosion through deregulation of traditional bureaucratic powers to issue and interpret ministerial orders and decrees, bureaucrats turned to private councils and study groups, in an attempt to regain the initiative in policy-making.

Formal Processes of Coordination

While most but not all formal organizations charged with responsibility for coordination were generally weak and ineffective, the integration of interrelated policies and policy areas was achieved as much or more through formal *processes* of making and carrying out policy. The most notable of these was the budget process, which at various levels confronted issues of the prioritization of policies competing for scarce resources, within the broad context of agreed politico-economic objectives. Budgeting was inherently a coordinating activity; MOF was, through the Budget Bureau, quintessentially a coordinating ministry. At the margins, it had to determine priorities between programmes, and between ministries, and to take into account party-political as well as bureaucratic claims and interests. On a few issues of substance, the LDP leadership was required to resolve an irreconcilable difference between MOF and a Spending Ministry. The perception of budgeting, and MOF's role in it, as low-level coordination, where ministries competed, and trade-offs, bargains, and compromises were inevitable, is not inaccurate but incomplete. Most policy-making had budgetary implications. Discussions of issues during the budget cycle, especially at the early stage of programme review, often highlighted the need for a new policy initiative or a policy change. At the stages of initiation and formulation, or earlier still when manifest problems, for example of an ageing society, stimulated discussion of long-term policy change, MOF might play a major role in achieving a more coherent, if rarely a fully integrated, response from the sectional interests and responsibilities of several ministries and agencies. While this should not be exaggerated, nevertheless, the centrality of the budget function in Japanese policy-making provided a process that MOF exploited formally and informally to achieve some better integration of related policies, to confront competing interests and priorities, and to force consideration of the costs of overlapping and duplicating policies, as in the example of the competition between ministries and agencies for jurisdiction in the development of policy in telecommunications, described above.

The Ministry of Home Affairs had cross-cutting responsibilities for the coordination of the interest of several ministries and agencies with responsibility for national policies implemented by prefectures and local governments—education and hospitals, for example. But it had no formal powers of coordination; it was obliged to consult and negotiate. When another ministry or agency prepared a bill or proposed a policy development, MHA considered how the proposal affected the interests of prefectures and local governments; whether what was proposed was feasible and practicable; the amount and distribution of any additional financial burden, and whether it could and should be borne in part or as a whole by local or central government. But where the current or proposed policies of central ministries and agencies had financial implications for local governments, the relevant ministry or agency dealt directly with MOF, which largely determined the appropriate means of financing the policy—through direct, categorical grant, through subsidies, or through national taxation—and decided what contribution local government should make through its own sources of revenue.

Formal Coordination through the Political Process
Through its policy-making organs, the LDP formally provided some element of coordination, although it was concerned more with conflict resolution than with the achievement of better integrated policies directed towards an agreed overall governmental objective. Indeed, the specialization of LDP members through PARC divisions and commissions reinforced bureaucratic verticalization, and contributed to the strength of subgovernments focused on the jurisdictional territory of individual ministries or policy areas. In turn, the organization and procedure of the Diet reinforced that specialization, the spheres of responsibility of legislative and scrutiny committees mirroring those of the party organizations, and the bureaucracy. Disputes over jurisdictional autonomy between ministries, especially where there was overlap or ambiguity, often were carried over deliberately into the parallel party policy-making organizations. A former deputy vice-minister at MITI explained in 1995: 'When each ministry insisted on its own position and would not yield to other ministries, the LDP would make the final decision on the basis of the appeals made by affected ministries' (quoted in Ahn 1998: 56).

The PARC itself, through its chairman, but more particularly the acting chairman, was centrally involved in the coordination process—helping to defuse disputes, securing compromises, and achieving consensus. Substantive policy issues, or those where the competition and conflict between ministries was acute, protracted, or widespread, drew in the senior LDP leaders, and influential *zoku*, as for example in the dispute over tax reform in the 1980s. More will be said about PARC's role, and that of its acting chairman, in Chapter 10. From time to time, the LDP set up special ad hoc committees to oversee a particular policy area, or to try to make the party's policy stance more coherent. Such bodies sometimes played a coordinating role, as for example the Headquarters Committee for the Promotion of Administrative Reform did in the initiation and development of policies in the Hashimoto governments of 1996–8. Such party committees were additional to research commissions and study groups set up under the aegis of PARC and its divisions, although the subject matter was often similar.

The capacity and willingness of the LDP to play a formal coordinating role through such party organs, especially where there was jurisdictional competition among ministries and agencies, was limited. Both the potential for coordination and its limitations were revealed in the development of biotechnology policy in the 1980s, referred to earlier in the chapter. The four ministries—MHW, MITI, MAFF, and MOE—and the STA had no formal links or liaison to coordinate the promotion of their different policy interests until the LDP set up a Survey Committee on Bioscience in 1985 comprising party members, academics, and officials from the ministries. The intention was to establish and coordinate 'a co-operative system among the machinery of state to overcome fragmented administrative boundaries of government agencies', and it 'dedicated its activities to securing the necessary research funds and to act as liaison between government agencies' (Tanaka 1991: 127). The bold rhetoric was belied by the Committee's preference for the continuance of rivalry and inter-ministerial competition for new policy initiatives because of the prospect of increased public expenditure, and hence the possibility of more benefits and favours to distribute to supporters. As explained earlier, in the end, the LDP supported all five policy initiatives.

Informal Processes of Coordination

In practice, the weakness of formal coordination was partly compensated by various informal bureaucratic processes and procedures, by 'standard *informal* operation procedures' (Keehn 1990), and by rules-of-the-game which guided or regulated the behaviour of bureaucrats (and other participants) in the policy processes. 'Functional unanimity' arose from the formal requirement under the National Government Organization Law (Article 2) that ministries and agencies 'shall maintain liaison with one another'. This meant in practice that ministries and agencies with interests in, or affected by, proposed legislation were obliged to consult and agree before bills were proposed to Cabinet. Usually they were drafted in general, even vague, terms, partly because of the difficulty of obtaining such agreement, but also to provide for a flexible and varied response to different circumstances, and to retain the powers of interpretation of those laws in the hands of bureaucrats, exploited subsequently through the issue of ministerial ordinances, directions, and administrative guidance—a crucial element in the clientelistic relationships with interest groups. The interpretation of law might represent agreement between ministries and their competing interests and views, and might be made public or known to those organizations and clients affected by it. But in practice, some of the formal agreements of ministries and agencies to proposed legislation were underpinned and conditioned by 'secret covenants' between them, which mutually bound them to agreed specific interpretations and use in the implementation of the broad legislative provisions (Keehn 1990).

The key actors in those informal processes of policy coordination among ministries and agencies were the directors of divisions (*kachō*) and their principal deputy directors. The source of their influence was partly the authority that derived from the legally established 'jurisdiction of each division,' and the acceptance by the bureau of their expertise in the areas that fell within their competence. Their influence was also partly positional, at the nodal point of ministerial and inter-ministerial networks of governmental, political, and private-sector actors; and partly personal, borne of well-honed bureaucratic and political skills practised in a variety of posts in a career of some twenty years.

A second bureaucratic behavioural rule-of-the-game that contributed to informal coordination was the practice of strategic secondments or cross-postings between ministries and agencies. These occurred at all levels of posts held by 'career' officials, and about four-fifths of all bureau directors-general had had experience in one or more ministries before appointment (Keehn 1990). Some, like MOF and MITI, had long-standing arrangements whereby certain posts were reserved for their nominees in key divisions and bureaux in certain agencies. In 1994 Cabinet instructed all ministries and agencies to increase the level of secondment to help improve coordination. At that time there were 1,742 secondments among 'career' officials; two years later the number had increased by more than 12%, when nearly 2,000 such arrangements were made. More than a third were officials of the rank of director or above; MOF had 91 officials on secondment, of whom 69 were of the rank of director or above (MCA 1997*b*). The process was managed and controlled by bureaucrats without political involvement, and was subject to neither the approval nor the review of the LDP, Diet or even the Prime Minister's Office. Strategic cross-posting

> helps blur organisational boundaries among ministries, between ministries and agencies, and between the public and private sector. It results in the extensive exchange of elites and information, and helps ensure that developments in one ministry were quickly and efficiently telegraphed throughout the bureaucracy and through other groups plugged into these informal networks. (Keehn 1990: 1034)

Keehn perhaps exaggerates the purpose and achievement of strategic cross-postings as an informal means of coordination, claiming that the informal networks 'provide the crucial inter-organisational links'. The purpose of such postings was as much or more to enable a ministry to obtain and maintain influence and, where possible, control over the direction and substance of the policy-making activities of satellite organizations, and to try to ensure consistency with its own policy objectives. At the same time, rising officials broadened their experience and gained insight of cognate policy areas. Thus, over time, MOF and MITI each established a traditional claim to appoint, on secondment, their own officials to senior posts in EPA and the Defence Agency.

In the latter, a MOF official was normally head of the Finance Bureau, while the post of director-general of the Facilities and Equipment Bureau was normally filled by a MITI official. The administrative vice-minister in 1998, a former director-general of its Finance Bureau, was a MOF official on secondment. Until 1987 MOF and MITI rotated appointments to the post of deputy director-general in EPA, but MOF monopolized secondments to it for the next ten years. The practice was widespread in other arrangements between ministries and those agencies, commissions, public enterprises, and corporations that fell within their jurisdictional authority. Even where there was no such formal supervisory relationship, ministries and agencies quite commonly contracted informal mutual exchanges, to provide a valuable broadening of administrative experience for potential 'high flyers', while simultaneously helping them to extend and develop contacts, and networks of relationships in the bureaucracy necessary for the roles they would play subsequently in the most senior posts.

There was also a strong tradition of the exchange of staff between central ministries and local and prefectural governments, and local public enterprises. In 1996 over a thousand officials from ministries and agencies were on secondment to local authorities, while the latter provided more than 600 to the centre (MCA 1997b). MHA seconded the more senior of its own staff to positions of influence in prefectures, allegedly to extend its influence and exercise control over the implementation of policy (see Samuels 1983; Reed 1986).

Arase (1994) adds a further dimension to the informal processes of coordination achieved through secondments and strategic postings, suggesting that public corporations as 'intermediary structures' played a role in the coordination of the carrying out of policy where many ministries had an interest and coordination at that level would be difficult to achieve. Bodies such as OECF and JICA had a large number of staff on secondment from the private sector as well as ministries and organizations, a phenomenon also observable in MOFA's Economic Cooperation Bureau, with which they were closely associated in the implementation of overseas aid policy. In 1987 the Bureau employed 120 temporary staff from private-sector organizations, while a further 50 officials were on secondment from other ministries and agencies. Arase argues that these employees compensated for the lack of technical expertise in MOFA; helped to break down the barriers to the flow of information horizontally between the 18 ministries and agencies involved in the implementation of ODA policy; promoted the exchange of information between the public and private sectors; and provided an element of inter-ministerial coordination by ensuring that 'informal rules governing the referral of project requests were being honoured' (Arase 1994: 185). However, staff on secondment from the private sector, and from other ministries and agencies, were employed mainly in subordinate positions, for example the processing of applications for aid; policy-making and diplomatic relations were handled by MOFA's elite staff.

Secondment from ministries and agencies to the 'intermediary structures' of OECF and JICA was more extensive still. It served some of the same purposes of inter-organizational coordination of the implementation of overseas aid policy, but secured and maintained the influence and control of main line ministries over their activities. Thus, the senior and supervisory posts in both tended to be held by officials or former officials rather than those on secondment from the private sector. OECF presidents were recruited from former senior officials of MOF. In 1996 the post was held by Nishigaki Akira, formerly administrative vice-minister at MOF. The vice-president was a former EPA official; the board of directors comprised former officials from MOF, MITI, and MOFA, and only one internal appointee. However, apart from the General Affairs Department headed by a MOF official, the Budget and Accounting, the Credit Management and all the Business Operations Departments were headed by OECF staff. The presidency of JICA was monopolized by former MOFA officials. Its senior staff were recruited from six ministries who between them controlled 11 of its 18 departments. EPA's Coordination Bureau, one of whose two divisions was responsible for OECF, was always headed by a MITI official. Such exchanges of officials between the public and private sector and 'intermediary structures' also helped to cross-fertilize ideas and perspectives on common issues, and to expose bureaucrats to the 'real world'. However, relationships between the regulators and the regulated could become too comfortable and cosy, with the risk of collusive behaviour or structural corruption such as that which developed between banks, securities companies, and MOF's Banking and Securities Bureaux in the 1980s and 1990s, and that between the Defence Agency's procurement divisions and industrial suppliers, exposed in 1997–8.

Providing a necessary dimension of informal coordination through behavioural rules-of-the-game such as secret covenants and strategic cross-postings also constrained the potential ability of politicians to manage and control bureaucrats. Politicians who became specialists, even experts in policy areas, lacked the time, energy, and skills to 'manipulate the minutiae of bureaucratic negotiation and informal organization' to achieve the accommodation of different public and private interests which was a necessary pre-condition of the making and carrying out of policy (Keehn 1990: 1035). That there were a very few important exceptions among senior politicians, such as Tanaka and Takeshita, testifies to the difficulty most politicians found in penetrating bureaucratic networks; both spent years and money building networks they could use and exploit within the bureaucracy.

CONCLUSION

Jurisdictional autonomy and inter-ministerial coordination were relevant in two main ways to the budget processes, and the outputs of those processes, discussed in later chapters. First, the scope of each ministry and agency's autonomy was a constituent element in the determination of its budget allocation. Secondly, the processes of making and carrying out the budget were a principal medium of the coordination of policy-making, obliging ministries and agencies to confront and attempt to reconcile their over-lapping, competing, and conflicting interests in particular policy areas.

Jurisdictional autonomy was also important because it provided ministries and (to a lesser extent) agencies with the formal discretionary authority to regulate the activities and interests of clients and special interest groups. The issue of ministerial ordinances, notices, and directions, and the granting of dispensations, were key elements in the money–votes–favours nexus of politicians, bureaucrats, and groups. Jurisdictional autonomy also conferred powers of patronage. Through 'strategic postings' of serving officials to satellite organizations, whose activities and senior posts they supervised and controlled, and through the placement of retired officials in key positions in public corporations, ministries and agencies had the opportunity to enhance their influence and control over the making and carrying out of policy; and of course provided congenial 'landing places' for retiring officials. For such reasons, ministries and agencies sought simultaneously both to protect their jurisdictional boundaries from incursions and raids, and to expand them. Consequential and endemic competition and conflict between them were exacerbated by two other factors: the budgetary constraints imposed by the ceiling system, and the changing political agenda. The redrawing of the budget guidelines in 1982, with restrictive top-down limits imposed by MOF on ministerial allocations, intensified the competition between ministries for a share of scarce 'new money', i.e. the additional increments allocated to identified priority areas each year. To establish a prima facie claim, for example for a budget to fund R&D costs in a new technology, or for a share of the ODA budget, ministries had first to demonstrate jurisdictional authority.

The reorientation of national goals in the 1970s and 1980s produced a policy agenda of issues that emphasized the growing interdependence of domestic and international policy in such areas as competition, trade, and financial regulation, and gave greater weight to social, welfare, and environmental issues. The coordination of policy-making and implementation became more necessary but more difficult to achieve as verticalized, functionally differentiated ministries and agencies competed to control items on the new agenda. Little was done to strengthen the formal organizational mechanisms of coordination before the reform proposals of 1997 (discussed in the previous chapter). The Second Provisional Council for Administrative Reform had discussed the merger of EPA, NLA, and the Hokkaido and Okinawa Development Agencies to create a Comprehensive Planning Agency, but bureaucratic resistance forced them to abandon the idea. The 'primacy of the Budget' in policy-making, challenged in the early 1980s by the advocates of radical administrative reform, survived as the main forum for the discussion and confrontation of competing programmes.

Informal processes of coordination through the observance of standard operating procedures, and behavioural rules-of-the-game such as consultation and *nemawashi* (behind-the-scenes manoeuvring), strategic cross-postings, secret covenants, and the exploitation of advisory councils, research committees, and study groups, contributed more in practice to the achievement of a sufficient cohesiveness to prevent the paralysis of the policy process, at least until the coalition governments of 1993–6. But consensual policy-making through such mechanisms was not optimally coordinated policy-making, and provided no guarantee that the different values, aims, and interests represented by the ministries and agencies were integrated in coherent and comprehensive policies and programmes. The perceived weakness of strategic policy-making through the Cabinet, and the ineffectiveness of the Prime Minister's Office and its agencies, such as STA and the Environmental Agency, and that of the Cabinet Secretariat, to provide formal coordination of the processes of making and carrying out policy in contested areas where the jurisdiction of several ministries overlapped, partly explains Prime Minister Hashimoto's 'visionary' aim to reconstruct the central executive, in order to achieve more top-down strategic direction and control, discussed in the previous chapter.

The pathological weakness of the Japanese political system to provide for interministerial coordination should not be exaggerated. In practice, the informal processes, procedures, and behavioural rules-of-the-game provided more coordination than an inspection of the formal organizational structures suggests. Nor was Japan's central government unique in its difficulty in achieving the effective integration of different interests, objectives, and values through its verticalized, functional differentiation of ministries and agencies. With similar Cabinet systems and central executives, and even longer traditions of administrative continuity, the UK and France experienced similar difficulties. Even in 1999, a former permanent secretary of the UK's Cabinet Office lamented 'the difficulty of getting departments with cross-cutting links and overlapping agendas to talk to one another. The old vertical fiefdoms find horizontal thinking and policy-making inordinately difficult' (Kemp 1999). Hence the emphasis throughout the 1990s on so called 'joined-up government'.

8

The Ministry of Finance

The Ministry of Finance (Ōkurashō) is located geographically at the heart of Kasumigaseki, Japan's Whitehall, a manifest symbol of the core position it occupied as the 'ministry of ministries' in the administrative structure of the Japanese political system, from its establishment in 1869 until the end of the twentieth century. No other ministry could match its commanding and dominating position in fiscal, financial, and economic policy-making, or lay claim to the status that its officials traditionally enjoyed, derived historically from the ministry's position in the ancient Imperial Court, dating at least to AD 678 (new recruits were told). The Court comprised an inner shrine for the gods, an outer shrine for the Emperor, and the treasure-store or Ōkura—hence 'Ōkurashō', literally, the great storehouse ministry. However, by the end of the twentieth century MOF's formal powers were being eroded, the reputation of its elite administrators for honest and effective management of the economy tarnished by scandal and ineptitude, and its authority and influence in central government challenged by other organizations.

This chapter outlines the structure, functions, and organization of MOF, its constituent bureaux, and its advisory councils. Particular attention is drawn to the central role of the Budget Bureau and the Minister's Secretariat, and to the processes for the coordination of budgetary and other policy-making through them and other mechanisms. It describes the boundaries of the ministry's supervisory jurisdiction, within which were to be found several of the most important public banks and finance corporations. The conclusion argues that in the 1990s MOF suffered a crisis of confidence and authority, and traces the origins of the erosion of its formal powers in the reorganization of the central executive in January 2001.

MOF emerged from the SCAP reforms with its powers undiminished, and its authority guaranteed in the new constitution. Its jurisdiction, responsibilities, and functions were conferred formally by the Establishment Law of 31 May 1949. For the next fifty years it was 'responsible for the overall control and management of all the affairs pertaining to the administration of national finances and monetary, fiscal, foreign exchange, and securities transactions, as well as the mint and printing operations' (Article 3). It was responsible for the planning, management, and control of public expenditure, the compilation and implementation of annual and supplementary budgets, and the management of cash flow and accounts. Its second main function was the raising and collection of revenue, mainly through direct and indirect taxation, the management of assets and debts, and the issuing of government bonds. Its third responsibility was for the management of public funds collected under national systems of trust, and deposited in Special Accounts for postal savings, welfare insurances, and national pensions. Those accounts were used to finance a part of public investment, for example through FILP, and were also controlled by MOF. Fourthly, it had responsibility for overall policy-making for all foreign exchange matters, and for Japan's participation in the international monetary system. It was also responsible for policy-making and the management of the financial system as a whole. Until 1998 that included the supervision and regulation of financial institutions such as banks, insurance companies, and securities companies, to protect depositors and investors and to ensure appropriate provision of capital.

MOF's responsibility for economic policy-making was not formally prescribed, but its core role was ensured by the centrality of its fiscal, monetary, and financial policy-making functions. Two other institutions, the Economic Planning Agency (EPA) and the Bank of Japan, had formal responsibility for economic forecasting and analysis, and for setting the framework for the conduct of monetary policy through the management of the money supply, the regulation of interest rates, and the formal and informal regulation of banking and credit practices. In practice, MOF sought, through the control of key appointments to both, and through its formal and informal networks, to steer the direction of the inputs to macroeconomic policy-making made by both bodies. Appointments to the posts of governor and deputy governor of the Bank of Japan were until 1998 traditionally made in rotation from within the Bank, and by MOF from among its senior, retired officials, discussed in the next chapter. The exercise of such patronage directly, or through indirect influence in the choice of non-MOF officials, did not automatically ensure that MOF and Bank policy were always in accord; there were occasions of important and public differences of opinion about interest rate policy, the issue and purchase of long-term government bonds, and the money supply, increasingly so in the 1990s. In 1997 the Bank was given a greater measure of formal independence over monetary policy and the determination of interest rates.

THE MINISTER OF FINANCE

Appointments to the post of minister of finance were normally made from among the most senior of the LDP leaders. Standing, experience, and authority in the party reinforced the unrivalled positional power that a minister commanded through the wide-ranging economic, financial, and fiscal functions discharged by MOF. As with other Cabinet posts, ministers served normally for only one or two years. Their short tenure made it difficult for individuals to put a personal stamp on policy-making, and tended to make them still more dependent on their officials. Several ministers, however, came to office with previous experience as bureaucrats in the ministry—Ikeda, Fukada, Ueki, and Aichi from an earlier era, Fuji and Miyazawa more recently. Miyazawa was recruited to MOF in 1942. Before resigning to enter politics ten years later, he served for three years in the minister's private office. Both Ikeda and Fukada had held the post of administrative vice-minister, and on their return as minister exercised considerable influence over policy and senior appointments through extensive networks constructed earlier. By contrast, Takemura Masayoshi, minister of finance in Murayama's coalition government in 1994–6, had had no such previous experience in MOF (although he was a former MHA official), nor any allies. His approach was more confrontational, partly the result of his earlier experience when, as leader of Sakigake in the Hosokawa Coalition, he and his party were excluded from the discussion preceding the announcement of the abortive national welfare tax. With scores to settle, he interfered in internal promotions, and lent his weight to the campaign to oust as administrative vice-minister Saito Jirō, held formally responsible for a scandal involving senior MOF officials (discussed in the next chapter).

The post of minister of finance could be a stepping-stone to that of prime minister, but there was no automatic progression; it was more common in the 1960s and 1970s. Of Prime Minister Miyazawa's immediate predecessors—Kaifu, Uno, Takeshita, Suzuki, Nakasone—only Takeshita had held that office, although Ō'Hira was a notable earlier exception. Subsequently, of the four prime ministers of the coalition period 1993–6, Hata and Hashimoto had both served as minister of finance. Neither Prime Minister Obuchi Keizō (1998–2000) nor his successor Mori Yasuhiro had held that office.

The extent to which individual ministers of finance contributed to policy-making varied with experience, expertise, predisposition, and (to some extent) tenure. But even the most active minister was heavily dependent on the assessments made by officials, and on the advice and recommendations tendered by the administrative vice-minister(s) and the heads of the Secretariat and the Bureaux. There was clearly a political input into macroeconomic policy-making, for example in setting the medium-term objectives and designing the overall policy framework for taxation, expenditure, bond issues, interest rates, and the supply of money. But in practice it was not easy to distinguish the contribution of an individual minister of finance from that of either the LDP leadership as a whole or the ministry's officials. In the annual budgetary cycle, the minister was involved first at the crucial early stage of deciding the budget target in the light of the general economic assessment and policy objectives for the economy, and then, publicly and prominently, at the time of the 'revival negotiations'. Those roles are examined in more detail in later chapters.

Equally important was his role as representative of the ministry to the outside world, for example in international meetings of G7 finance ministries, the IMF, and the World Bank. Domestically, he was seen publicly to be engaged in high-level discussions or negotiations with other ministries, financial institutions, and the leaders of major interest groups. He presented the Budget to the Diet and, with the assistance of his officials from the Budget Bureau and the Secretariat, steered it through the hearings and examination of its Committees. His Private Office was small—a personal political secretary, and two secretaries appointed from among the ministry's officials, normally with the rank of deputy (division) director. Two parliamentary vice-ministers assisted with the political business outside the ministry, taking responsibility for liaison with the House of Representatives and the House of Councillors, respectively. They were rarely assigned specific administrative duties within the ministry, nor did they answer for the ministry in the Diet.

THE MINISTRY

In 1999 there were 79,211 MOF officials, more than two-thirds of whom were employed in the assessment and collection of taxes in the National Tax Administration Agency (NTAA). Excluding the latter, MOF 'Proper' employed 22,111, of whom most worked in local and branch offices, and custom houses, or in its two government enterprises, the Mint, and the Government Printing Office. Less than 2,000 were employed on the 'central core' functions of fiscal, financial, and economic policy-making at its headquarters in Kasumigaseki. Of those, only about a quarter, some 560, were so-called 'career' officials, the elite bureaucrats. The most senior was the administrative vice-minister, with overall charge of the ministry; the director-general of the Budget Bureau ranked second. The next most senior official was the deputy vice-minister in charge of the Minister's Secretariat. At the same level, but designated director-general, were the heads of the functional bureaux. Some, like the Budget Bureau, had deputy directors-general. A second administrative vice-minister had responsibility for International Financial Affairs. Table 8.1 shows the distribution of staff before and after the reorganization of 1998. The reduction in the size of the central core staff was mainly the result of the abolition of the Banking and Securities Bureaux, and the transfer of their functions to the new Financial Supervision Agency. The causes and consequences of those and other changes are discussed later in the chapter.

Until the reorganization of 1998, the internal structure of MOF 'Proper' had remained virtually unchanged for more than thirty years. After the creation of a separate Securities Bureau in 1964, the only change of any note occurred in the early 1990s, in the wake of a series of scandals associated with the illegal activities of several securities companies, most notably Normura. The Securities Bureau was implicated, and the ministry reacted to criticism by removing the director-general, who along with the administrative vice-minister was penalized with a 10% pay cut. The Minister, Hashimoto Ryūtarō, accepted formal responsibility and resigned. The inspection of securities firms and stock exchanges was removed from the Bureau, and given to a new advisory council, the Securities and Exchange Surveillance Commission, albeit still attached to MOF. The inspection of banks and financial authorities was transferred from the Bureau to a Financial Inspection Department within the Minister's Secretariat.

Table 8.1 *MOF officials, FY1997 and FY1999*

	1997	1999
(1) MOF Central Core	1,965	1,700
(2) MOF HQ (Central Core, Mint, Printing Office, and training and research staff)	9,680	9,199
(3) MOF's local/branch offices	12,927	12,912
(4) MOF 'Proper' (2)+(3)	22,607	22,111
(5) NTAA	57,202	57,100
TOTAL	79,809	79,211

Source: Minister's Secretariat, 1999, MOF.

During the whole of the period 1975–97 there were seven bureaux and the Minister's Secretariat. In terms of its status, authority, and influence, the Budget Bureau outranked all the others. Together with the Tax Bureau, ranked second, the Financial Bureau, and the Customs and Tariff Bureau, it was a part of the Public Finance Group, complemented by the Banking Bureau, the Securities Bureau, and the International Finance Bureau, which dealt with financial institutions in the private sector. Figure 8.1 shows MOF's organizational structure between 1975 and 2000, and the main changes made in the reorganization of 1998.

The Minister's Secretariat

The Secretariat was the hub of the ministry. It was responsible for the overall coordination of policy across the bureaux, and was the main source of advice for the minister and his two parliamentary deputies. It was also responsible for all the ministry's personnel matters, handling its relations with the Diet, and its budget and accounts. More broadly, it had the task of 'preserving harmony and integration within and among the Ministry's organizations ... by integrating and coordinating the entire spectrum of the operations performed by its other bureaux and agencies' (MOF 1996a: 16–17).

That task was more difficult, but also more necessary in the Japanese bureaucratic context because of inter-bureau competition and rivalry, and the fervour with which each bureau promoted and protected its interests. Achieving a unified and coherent ministerial position on an issue that involved more than one bureau was a task calling for skills of negotiation, patient argument, and persuasion. The Secretariat also provided the 'window' through which each bureau conducted its formal relations with other ministries and agencies, and represented the ministry and its policies to the outside world, and to politicians, the Diet, and organized interests. The elite course (*erīto kōsu*) for the high-flying MOF bureaucrat included time spent in posts in either its Secretarial or Policy Coordination Divisions.

The Secretariat was headed by a deputy vice-minister; a second deputy vice-minister had charge of the Policy Coordination Division. Beneath them were a number of councillors (*shingi-kan*), an intermediate rank between deputy director-general and director of division, responsible for the day-to-day coordination of the work of each bureau (apart from the Budget and the Financial Bureaux), and linked directly to the relevant deputy directors-general and their senior staff. Other councillors, together with more junior counsellors (*sanji-kan*), were employed within the Secretarial Division, on matters of public relations, natural disasters, pensions, administrative reform, and other special tasks as events and circumstances dictated.

The Minister's Secretariat had five divisions, the most important of which were the *Policy Coordination Division* and the *Secretarial Division*. The latter was responsible for all the Ministry's personnel matters: recruitment, education, training, postings, promotion and retirement, and discipline, pay, pensions, and conditions of work. Here was held the 'secret information' about MOF's staff. Personnel decisions relating to the three most senior levels of director-general, deputy director-general, and councillor were made after discussions between the administrative vice-minister and the deputy

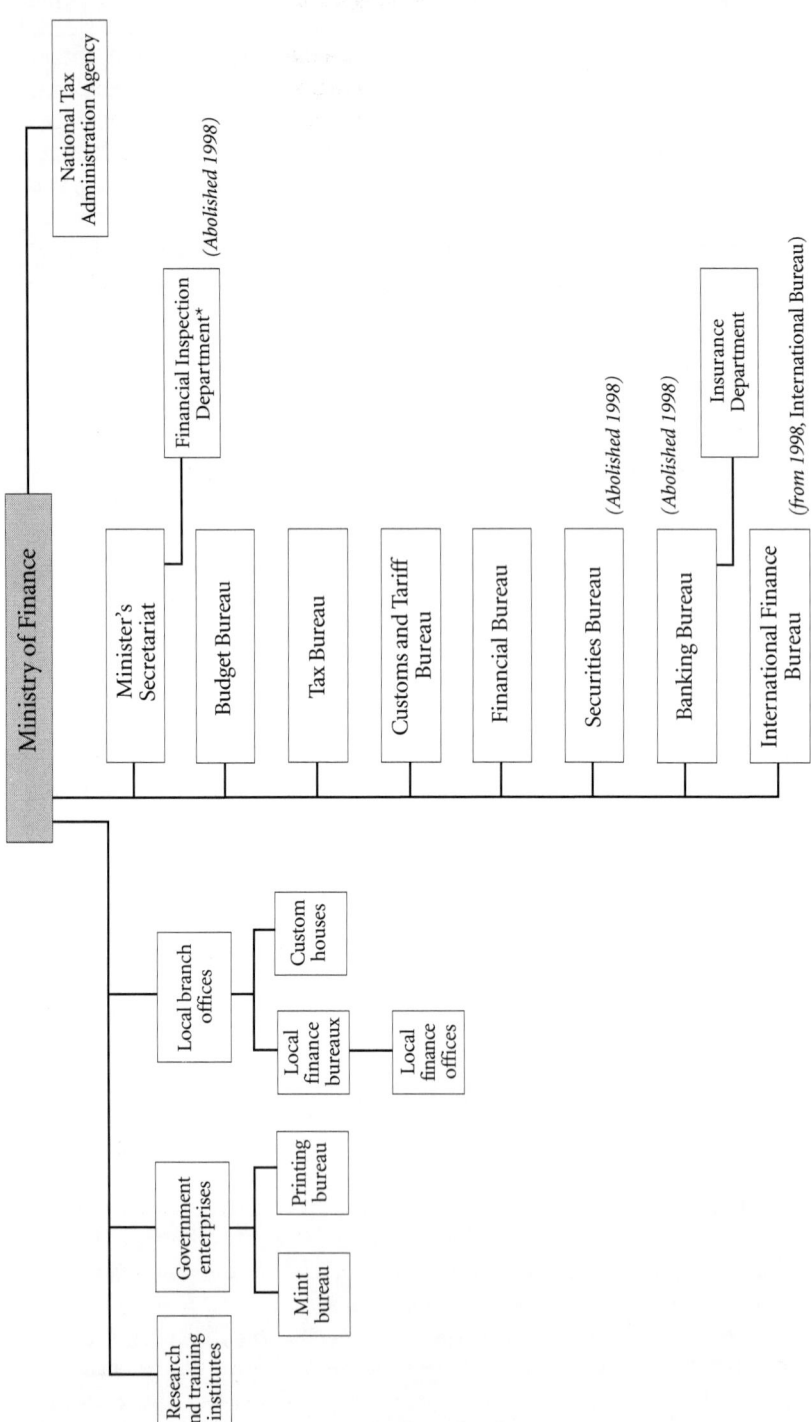

Figure 8.1 *Organization of the Ministry of Finance, 1975–2000*

*Established 1992

Source: adapted from MOF (1996a).

vice-minister of the Secretariat, in consultation with the minister and senior members of the LDP. Appointments, postings, promotions, and so on of staff at the level of divisional director and below were made by the director of the Secretarial Division in consultation with the deputy vice-minister and the administrative vice-minister. Those decisions were crucial to the career progression of young officials, and the post of director of the Secretarial Division was a key one in the Ministry, whose incumbents were themselves already marked for advancement on the '*erīto kōsu*'. An important part of the Division's work was the placement, through *amakudari*, of officials retiring from the ministry (discussed in the next chapter). The Secretarial Division also housed the office of the administrative vice-minister for international affairs.

The *Policy Coordination Division* was headed by the second deputy vice-minister, and was responsible for the coordination of the information and policy of the Ministry as a whole. It monitored all the changes to statute proposed by the functional bureaux, and collected and collated information for the minister and the administrative vice-minister. Through its Public Relations Office, it conducted the ministry's relations with the media, and formally with all other ministries, agencies, and external organizations. The Division maintained and serviced MOF's Government Committee Office located in the Diet, and through it coordinated the Ministry's parliamentary business. Where some issue or aspect of the work of a bureau attracted the attention of a Dietman, or was the subject of inquiry or discussion by a legislative committee, the Division coordinated the response, where necessary within a broader context shaped by the interests of the minister and/or the advice of the administrative vice-minister and deputy vice-minister. Formal meetings of the LDP and its PARC divisions at which MOF policies were discussed or questioned normally required the attendance of officials from the appropriate bureau. The Coordination Division arranged for their attendance, and for that of one of its own senior officials. More generally, as the focal point for the receipt and analysis of all kinds of written and verbal political information from the LDP and the Opposition parties, the Division transmitted assimilated data, perhaps with its own 'spin', to appropriate parts of the Ministry. It also transmitted to the relevant bureaux data and interpretative analysis arising from its monitoring of the formal proceedings of the Diet, and that acquired informally through contact with individual Dietmen. For the deliberations of the Diet's Budget and Finance Committees, it ensured that junior 'career' officials attended to provide assistance with the business and to transmit questions to the appropriate bureaux. It also coordinated the attendance of budget examiners and deputy budget examiners at Budget Committee hearings. At a more senior level still, the deputy vice-minister of the Secretariat, together with the deputy vice-minister of the Policy Coordination Division, liased informally with members of the government, and senior members of the LDP and its PARC divisions. Until the Bank of Japan was given more independence in 1997, one of the Division's most important tasks was the coordination of interests and views on the determination of the official discount rate. Nominally the responsibility of the Bank of Japan, the direct interests of the Ministry's Budget Bureau, Financial Bureau, and Banking Bureau meant that the views of their directors-general, together with those of the minister of finance (and the most senior of his Cabinet and LDP colleagues), had to be coordinated. Its work here overlapped with that of the Research and Planning Division.

The *Research and Planning Division* (RPD), supervised by the deputy vice-minister for policy coordination, had several important coordinating functions. Formally, it was responsible for the collection and analysis of information relating to the domestic economy, and its interaction with other economies internationally. In practice, it played a key role in the determination of budget strategy as well. The politico-economic context within which that evolved required the coordination of the different, often conflicting, values, aims, and interests of MOF's bureaux, concerned with the estimates and implications of GDP growth, the contingent estimated yield of tax and other revenues, the amount, sale, and issue of government bonds to cover the fiscal deficit, the costs of servicing the outstanding debt, and the aggregates of both the General Account Budget and FILP.

The Division had two special officers for research and planning, with the status of director and a staff of about 50. The two special officers worked directly under the deputy vice-minister and shared the work between them, the more senior with responsibility for domestic policy issues and the general coordination of MOF policy, the other with a more limited and specialized responsibility for the provision of research and analysis of international economic issues. The Division had five main functions relating to the general coordination of MOF policy. First, under the senior special officer, it took the initiative on the preparation of the forecasts for the GDP growth rate. Formally, EPA had responsibility for the technical production of this (and other economic analysis), but (in the words of a Special Officer) 'as its analysis and assessment tends to be economistic it had to be supplemented with consideration of wider interests' (MOF 1993). The latter was a euphemism for political interests. The estimate of GDP growth was a critical decision in Japan's politico-economic policy-making, and in practice often reflected greater concern with issues of broader strategy than cool, detached economic analysis. Domestically, it had implications for the level of 'affordable' (i.e. politically desirable) expenditure, and hence was integral to the formulation of the overall budget strategy in the Budget Bureau, for the projections of tax yields (which involved the Tax Bureau), estimates of the money supply (involving the Financial Bureau and (formerly) the Banking Bureau), and the level of 'affordable' capital investment financed through FILP (Financial Bureau). Externally, the estimated GDP growth rate had implications for business confidence, investment decisions, and estimates of output, with all of which MITI was closely associated. Internationally, the announcement of the estimated growth rate sent signals to G7 and other industrialized countries about Japan's intentions, for example to increase domestic consumption through increased expenditure, lower taxes, increased government borrowing, and so on. The process of estimating the annual GDP growth rate is discussed in Chapter 14.

RPD's second main coordinating function was the preparation of Supplementary Budgets to adjust estimates of revenue yields, to provide for contingent expenditures after the preparation of the main budget, and to finance emergency packages of economic and fiscal measures to counter cyclical fluctuations in the domestic economy. The decision to introduce a Supplementary Budget, its size and contents, and the timing of the announcement were all key decisions involving the interests of several ministries besides MOF; apart from MITI, the expenditure programmes of MOC, MOT,

MAFF, and MOL were almost always involved. EPA, through its Coordination Division, was once again a major player. Within MOF, the interests of several bureaux had also to be incorporated.

The coordination of monetary policy, RPD's third function, was primarily the responsibility of the Bank of Japan, but changes in the money supply, the official discount rate, and the selling of government stock were normally made in close consultation with MOF, its minister and the prime minister, before the Bank was given a more independent role in 1997. The Division acted as the liaison office between the Bank and MOF, and consulted where necessary with the Minister's Office and the Prime Minister's Office. MOF's Financial Bureau and Budget Bureau both had a direct interest in the outcome of all of those issues. The views of their directors-general had to be reconciled and incorporated.

The Division's fourth function was to provide a general information service for the Minister's Office, providing answers to questions and issues with an economic, fiscal, or financial content which had a contemporary political salience, for example the analysis of the extent of concealed and 'in-house' unemployment in Japanese companies during the recessions of the 1990s.

RPD's fifth function was to provide a general coordinating mechanism, where the need arose from the routine of day-to-day business. Normally inter-bureau differences were settled by discussion and agreement between their respective Coordination Divisions. Where this proved difficult or impossible, then RPD and the deputy vice-minister might be drawn in, to negotiate a settlement. Where issues that involved the interests of several bureaux were sufficiently important politically, or difficult to resolve, and reached the level of administrative vice-minister or the minister, then the deputy vice-minister and the Division were drawn in. It set out the issues, the evidence, and the arguments, and perhaps proposed options for resolving differences. Its capacity to act neutrally and independently was, however, constrained in practice by the dominance of the Budget Bureau, whose views carried greater weight than other MOF bureaux, and whose preferred option was that normally adopted.

RPD and its two special officers for research and planning had close relations with the directors and the staff of each bureau's Coordination Division, particularly those of the Budget Bureau and the Tax Bureau. Through the deputy vice-minister, and their access to the private office network that linked ministries and agencies throughout Kasumigaseki, they were well placed to assess both the party political and ministerial interests, in addition to the different bureaucratic interests of the MOF bureaux and other ministries.

The *Accounts Division* was responsible for the formal compilation of the Ministry's budget, and kept the accounts for the whole of its financial activities. Unlike comparable divisions in other ministries and agencies, it did not occupy a critical central position *vis à vis* the other bureaux in the internal negotiation and allocation of the Ministry's budget.

The fifth division in the Minister's Secretariat, the *Local Finance Division*, was responsible for controlling the work of MOF's ten local finance bureaux. From 1992 to 1998 the Secretariat also housed the Financial Inspection Department responsible for the inspection and supervision of banks and financial institutions.

The Budget Bureau

The main task of the Budget Bureau was to prepare the draft General Account Budget and (with the Financial Bureau) the FILP budget for approval by the Cabinet before submission to the Diet. It took the lead in the design of the overall budget strategy, prescribed budget guidelines, negotiated spending limits with each ministry and agency, and examined their budget requests. These and related functions are examined in detail in later chapters. It also prepared the budget legislation for submission to the Diet, monitored and controlled spending and revenue collection in-year, and supervised the preparation and presentation of ministerial accounts for public audit.

The formal structure of the Budget Bureau remained unchanged throughout the period 1975–97. With both 'line' and 'staff' divisions, it was similar to other MOF bureaux. In March 1999 it had 344 officials, of whom about 90 were 'career officials'. Most of the latter (69) were direct entrants; the remainder were on secondment from other ministries. Beneath the director-general there were three deputy directors, the senior of whom had responsibility for general budget policy and coordination, besides responsibility for three line divisions. Each of the other two deputies had responsibility for three line divisions and two staff divisions. Figure 8.2 shows the structure and distribution of functions and staff.

Each line division was headed by a budget examiner (*shukei-kan*), with between four and seven deputy budget examiners (*shusa*) and assistant budget examiners (*shukei-kan-hosa*), each of whom shadowed or 'marked' one or more of the (then) 12 Spending Ministries and seven Agencies, and/or major government activities. Two senior budget examiners worked with the director of the Coordination Division and the senior deputy director-general in the evolution of the budgetary strategy and the general coordination of the budget processes of allocation.

The *Coordination Division* occupied a central position, not only within the Budget Bureau, but in the Ministry as a whole. Its role and influence, together with that of the bureau's *Research Division*, are discussed separately later in the chapter. The *Fiscal Division* was responsible mainly for the oversight and administration of the processes of the settlement of accounts at the end of the fiscal year, and for the control in-year of the expenditure of the Spending Ministries and Agencies, to ensure that money spent was consistent with principles of propriety and regularity, and with reference to the rules of appropriation, delegation, virement, and audit. One of the two senior budget examiners had a seat in the Fiscal Division. The twelfth budget examiner had responsibility for all the legal aspects of budget-making, and liased closely with the bureau's *Legal Division* responsible for the preparation and coordination of budget legislation. It ensured that the budget of each ministry and agency was consistent with the draft MOF budget approved by Cabinet, and presented in the appropriate form to the Diet. The *Allowance Control Division* was responsible for the policy and administration of the payment of allowances to all public-sector employees. The *Mutual Assistance Insurance Division* administered the public-sector compulsory pension scheme, and the voluntary health care system. All six divisions provided support and technical services for the nine line divisions which dealt with budget requests from the Spending Ministries and Agencies.

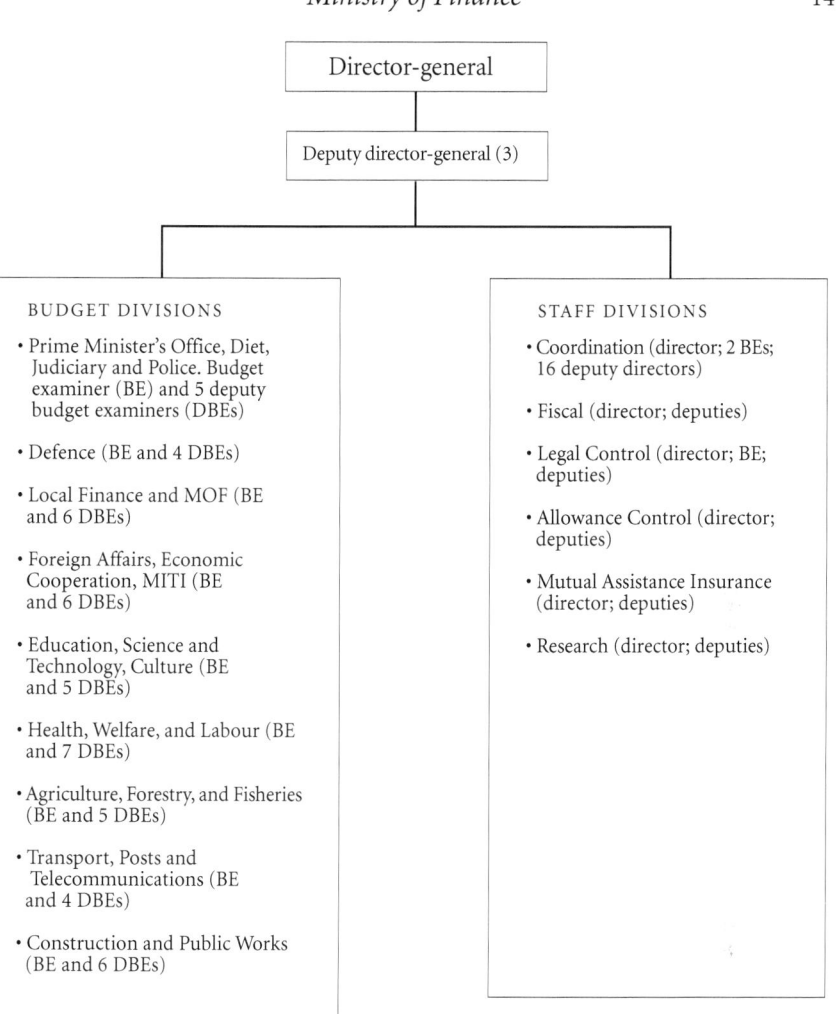

Figure 8.2 *The Budget Bureau, 1975–2000*
Staff numbers at 1998

Source: Budget Bureau, 2000, MOF.

MOF'S Other Bureaux

The *Tax Bureau* had four functional tax divisions, together with a Coordination Division and a Research and Planning Division, responsible for the formulation of tax policy, legislation, and matters relating to the tax system; the assessment of tax revenue; the licensing of tax accountants; and local authority revenue. The implementation and enforcement of tax laws, and the collection of taxes, was the responsibility of MOF's agency, the National Tax Administration Agency (NTAA): it had 11 regional tax bureaux and 524 district tax offices, with a combined staff of 55,630 (1999). The post of director of the NTAA was a grade higher than those of other non-ministerial agencies, and in MOF was senior to all directors-general, other than that of the Budget Bureau. It was frequently a final pre-retirement posting for a director-general of the Tax or Financial Bureau.

The *Financial Bureau* had 13 divisions and its director-general was supported by two deputy directors-general and a councillor for the Japan Tobacco and Salt Corporation. With a staff of 371 (1999), it was second in size only to the Secretariat. That was due mainly to the incorporation of the National Property Bureau in 1968. In practice, the work of its six divisions managing, controlling, and disposing of state property was separate from the Bureau's other functions. The status of the Financial Bureau, ranking third behind the Budget and Tax Bureaux, derived mainly from its responsibility for FILP, 'the second budget'. It managed the Trust Fund Bureau Fund, the main source of FILP funding, prepared the annual Fiscal Investment and Loan Programme, and allocated funds to the FILP agencies. The divisions worked closely with their opposite numbers in the Budget Bureau. The Financial Bureau also managed the Industrial Investment Special Account. Its second main function was the management of the government's monetary business, which included the control and monitoring of the provision and flow of currency (Treasury Division), and the issue and administration of government bonds, and their servicing and redemption (Government Debt Division). The amount of government bonds to be issued to finance budget deficits, and the terms of issues, were essential elements of the overall budget strategy, and decisions were taken in close consultation with the Budget Bureau.

The *Customs and Tariff Bureau* became a separate entity only in 1961, before which time it was a part of the Tax Bureau. It was an executive rather than policy-making bureau, responsible mainly for the tariffs and quotas on imported goods, and the administration of export procedures. The three remaining bureaux, comprised the private finance group. The *Securities Bureau* evolved from the former Securities Department of the Financial Bureau in 1964, at the end of the first post-war stock market boom, with Japan's membership of the IMF and OECD. Before its abolition in 1998, it was responsible for the supervision, regulation, and guidance of both domestic and international securities companies, investment trust companies and securities' exchanges. The *Banking Bureau* was established as an independent bureau in 1881. It lost, regained, and again lost that independence during the next fifty years, but was self-standing from 1949 until its abolition in 1998, and the transfer of most of its functions to the Financial Supervision Agency within the Prime Minister's Office. During that period it was in charge of general policy for private financial institutions, regulating interest rates, supervising the Bank of Japan, disseminating investment trading information, and controlling the traders of financial futures and the Financial Futures Exchange. Apart from the postal savings programme (Financial Bureau), it supervised and guided the whole of the private-sector financial sector—city banks, regional banks, long-term credit banks, trust banks, and foreign banks operating in Japan—and supervised government-controlled financial institutions, such as the Export–Import Bank of Japan, the Japan Development Bank, and the Government Housing Loan Corporation, and the financial institutions of agricultural, fisheries, and forestry cooperatives.

The *International Finance Bureau* had its origins in the Foreign Exchange Administration Division set up in 1933. After several changes of name and function, it was re-established in 1952 as the Exchange Bureau. Its name was changed to that of International Finance Bureau in 1964, the year Japan joined the OECD and accepted member status of the IMF, which prohibited currency exchange controls to protect the balance of payments. Its main responsibility until 1998, when it was retitled the International Bureau, was with the formulation and coordination of overall international financial policy and foreign exchange; and, with the work of international finance institutions, in Japan and abroad, in fields such as the international monetary system, the internationalization of the Japanese yen, the international balance of payments, the foreign exchange rate, the foreign exchange control, the introduction of foreign capital, overseas investments, and economic cooperation.

THE COORDINATION OF MINISTERIAL POLICY-MAKING

MOF is commonly characterized—or, more accurately, caricatured—as 'all bureaux, no ministry'. The implication is that policy-making is often inchoate, lacking cohesiveness, the result of a failure to integrate adequately and consistently the disparate aims, interests, and values of its several bureaux. Three factors are commonly cited to explain that perceived failure. First is the traditional independent discretionary authority exercised by each of them, but especially the Budget Bureau, and to a lesser extent the Tax and Financial Bureaux, (and the Banking and Securities Bureaux before their abolition in 1998), each supported by different constituencies of public and private sector interests with whom they were closely linked in complex socio-economic relationships, and to whom they appealed when their mutual interests were threatened. Second is the intrinsic weakness of institutions, mechanisms, and processes intended to provide transcending horizontal coordination of those vertically structured bureaux, principally the minister *qua* minister and his Secretariat. The third factor is the dominance of the Budget Bureau, reflecting the primacy of the functions of planning and controlling the raising of revenue and the spending of money: 'the Budget Bureau *is* the Ministry,' or 'No Budget Bureau, no ministry' (*Shukei-kyoku atte shō nashi*). Thus, the argument runs, where the interests of the Budget Bureau were involved, the coordination of policy-making might be less the agreed reconciliation of competing, conflicting interests of the bureaux and the achievement of a negotiated integrated outcome than the imposition of the Budget Bureau's preferred option.

Undeniably, on some occasions those three factors did prove dysfunctional in several major policy areas, where overlapping responsibilities and disputed jurisdictions contributed to a slow, hesitant, or incomplete response, inadequately integrating the policy aims of the bureaux into a robust, ministry policy. One such example occurred in the flotation of shares in NTT and the Japan Tobacco and Salt Company, where the interests of the Budget Bureau in raising revenue to offset government borrowing prevailed, to the detriment of the wider issues of protecting the investor, represented by the Securities Bureau. Another example was the precipitate and ill-prepared proposals for a national welfare tax in April 1994, brought forward despite the strong reservations of the Tax Bureau. In those and other examples, the difficulties of achieving an integrated and coherent policy were exacerbated by the need to accommodate the political interests of the LDP *qua* political party.

The dominant role often played by the Budget Bureau occurred annually in the formulation of the ODA budget, which involved it, the Financial Bureau, and the International Financial Bureau, alongside the overlapping interests of some eighteen other ministries and agencies. On one occasion, the Budget Bureau attempted to remove the 1:1 ratio of borrowing to capital prescribed in the law regulating the Overseas Economic Cooperation Fund, because it wished to reduce the impact of its spending on the General Account Budget. An increase in permitted borrowing, by allocating more resources from the Trust Fund Bureau Fund controlled by the Financial Bureau, would enable it to reduce the size of the allocation made from the General Account Budget. OECF's sponsor, the EPA, opposed the Budget Bureau's proposal, along with MOFA, who feared an adverse effect on the rates of interest that OECF charged borrowers. MOF's Financial Bureau, responsible for the administration of the Trust Fund Bureau Fund, was opposed also because of the additional burden on the FILP Budget. Nevertheless, the Budget Bureau prevailed, and the law was revised in 1979, to permit a borrowing ratio of 3:1 (Rix 1980).

MOF's Secretariat has been criticized for providing less coordination than comparable institutions in other ministries. With 'the smallest secretariat of any major government organization in Japan, relative to overall personnel levels', representing only 2.1% of MOF's total staff in 1992, compared for example with MITI's 25%, it was capable of only weak coordination of the disparate functions performed by its bureaux (Calder 1993: 96). Calder's total of 22,396 MOF officials in 1992 includes MOF's regional and local branch offices, and the Mint and Government Printing Office, whose staff performed executive, not policy-making, functions. Policy-making in MOF was centralized in a small core comprising the staff of the Secretariat and the (then seven) bureaux, in 1992 a total of 1,893 officials. It was their policy-making activities that the Secretariat sought to coordinate. With 470 staff, the Secretariat represented a quarter of the total, rather than the 2.1% claimed by Calder.

The extent to which the Secretariat was able to coordinate those policy-making activities efficiently and effectively is a separate issue, but clearly, size was not a factor, at least compared with other ministries. Calder is on surer ground when he emphasizes the historical continuity and traditions of the Budget, Tax, and Banking Bureaux, all of which date from the establishment of the Ministry in 1869. Together with the Financial Bureau, established a decade later, they created their own distinctive constituencies in the private (and public) sector, to which they looked for support in inter-bureau and inter-ministerial disputes. Clientelism, practised and fostered independently by each, undoubtedly made the task of achieving central coordination through the Secretariat more difficult. How difficult is a matter of investigation of particular issues in discrete policy areas.

Formal coordination was provided at several levels. At the highest, the Ministry's senior officials met weekly as an Executive Council. Here the two administrative vice-ministers met with the bureaux directors-general, the director-general of the NTAA, members of the board of the bank of Japan, and the two deputy vice-ministers in the Minister's Secretariat, the senior of whom took the chair. Each was accompanied by senior members of his staff. The Secretariat was represented by three of its councillors, together with the directors of the Secretarial, Coordination, Accounts, Local Finance, and Research and Planning Divisions, the two special officers from the latter, and officials from the Public Relations Office.

The Council received formal reports on the work of the Ministry, and notice of those issues that were causing difficulty among the bureaux. However, it was not a forum for the detailed discussion and negotiation of such issues, or the reconciliation of conflicting aims and interests. Lower-level meetings involving divisional directors and deputy directors, and the intermediation of bureaux Coordination Divisions, attempted to settle differences, and achieve a consensus prior to the Executive Council. The Council however provided a focus for that prior exploration of issues, and a stimulus to clear and agree as much of the ground as possible informally, and then by formal ratification, before it met.

Most of MOF's bureaux were involved at some stage or other in the processes of compiling and implementing the General Account and FILP Budgets. Besides the Budget Bureau itself, the Tax Bureau and the Financial Bureau had major inputs through their responsibilities for tax policy and raising revenue and (until 2000) the collection and use of postal savings to finance FILP through the Trust Fund Bureau Fund, and the management of government debt. The International Finance Bureau had a role to play as well, for example in the preparation of the ODA budget requests. These disparate budget interests and activities were coordinated mainly by the Budget Bureau's Coordination Division.

The Coordination Division of the Budget Bureau

The Coordination Division (CD) was the focal point for the preparation of the whole budget, overseeing and managing the process within the Budget Bureau, coordinating the aims, interests, and inputs of other bureaux, and liasing with the Minister's Secretariat, and his Private Office. It had a staff (in 1999) of 38. Its director was treated as senior to other divisional directors. In addition, there were two senior budget examiners, one of whom had responsibility for general budget issues and the coordination of the budget processes, and oversaw the collection and analysis of statistical data. The other had responsibility for the formulation of the budget strategy, and for non-tax revenues.

At the heart of the Budget Bureau, CD initiated, prepared, and coordinated the overall budget strategy, which determined the size of the General Account and its allocation among the Spending Ministries and Agencies. It oversaw and monitored the progress of the Budget Bureau's negotiations with them, and tried to ensure that the outcomes were consistent with the politico-economic strategy as it evolved and was refined through the updating of economic forecasts, estimated yields of tax revenue, and consequential adjustments to the political stance of the government. CD took the lead in the initiation and coordination of the policies that framed the three key strategic decisions determining the annual budget: the size of the overall budget; the criteria and guidelines for the preparation of budget requests, and the prescription of ceilings for the budget of each Spending Ministry and Agency.

As the eyes and ears of the director-general, it served as the general staff for the whole of the Budget Bureau, providing strategic analysis, advice, and guidance on tactics to the 'shock troops' in the nine line divisions dealing with the Spending Ministries. Occupying the nodal position in the policy network that connected the principal players in MOF with those in the Spending Ministries, it received, processed, and transmitted formally and informally a variety of written and verbal information. It connected those who contributed from within the nine line divisions to other MOF bureaux and divisions, and to the Minister's Secretariat; and, through the latter, to the minister and his colleagues in the Spending Ministries.

Coordination by the Research Division of the Budget Bureau

The Research Division worked closely with the Coordination Division of the Minister's Secretariat. Its main responsibility was the collection and analysis of statistical and other data related to budget issues. Two deputy directors divided the management of the work between them, one for domestic issues and the other for international affairs, paralleling the division of responsibility between the two special officers for research and planning in the Minister's Secretariat, and with whom they shared some of the general coordinating functions. Research was concerned mainly with medium- and long-term issues, with broad politico-economic contextual assessments, such as the impact on budget expenditure of the sales of government bonds, and with international comparisons, for example the effects of fiscal constraint in other G7 countries. The Research Division was also responsible for the preparation of all published and promotional material relating to the annual budgets and budgeting.

Its second major responsibility was to provide support and service for one of MOF's most important advisory councils, the Fiscal System Council and its subcommittees, which met about twenty times a year. The most significant parts of the Council's work were the published *Chairman's Comment* on the annual Budget Guidelines, and ad hoc reports on matters concerning the fiscal system as a whole. It was also nominally responsible for the production of the annual Medium Term Fiscal Projection. In practice, the latter was prepared by one of the two special officers for research and planning in the Minister's Secretariat, supported by the Research Division, which collected and analysed the technical data required. The Council also made and published recommendations on the compilation of the draft Budget in December. With a membership of about twenty drawn from business, industry, and the universities, supported and serviced by the Research Division and one of the special officers for research and planning, its public pronouncements were normally consistent with the general tenor of the Budget Bureau's budget strategy and policies, although it could sometimes appear to challenge them, as in 1992 when it called for a resumption of the issue of special deficit-financing bonds to meet a part of the deficit between revenue and expenditure, a view that had some support among the leadership of the LDP. In reality, the Budget Bureau was using the medium of the Council to put down a marker to which it could refer to legitimize the resumption of the issue of bonds should that prove necessary at a future date. Two years later, it quoted the Council's recommendation as authority for its *volte face*.

The Research Division was the main source of statistical and analytical support for the director-general and the three deputy directors-general of the Budget Bureau, whose responsibilities were broader than the immediate issues of the current budget, and included for example the review of expenditure policies and programmes, the medium and long-term implications of particular budget issues, such as the future costs of pensions and social welfare, and the long-term effects of government debt. On a day-to-day basis, the Research Division routinely responded to requests for information, analysis, and assessment from budget examiners and their deputies in the line divisions as the annual budget process proceeded. While the latter relied mainly on their ministries and agencies for factual and technical information, they also needed data and analysis to confront and challenge some of the arguments and evidence presented to them.

By providing statistical information, data analysis, and technical support services throughout the Bureau, the Research Division contributed to the coordination of policy functionally. A wider coordination still was achieved through its organizational links to the Coordination Division of the Minister's Secretariat, partly through one of the two special officers for research and planning, and more generally through its service and support for ministers and Budget Bureau officials at meetings of IMF, G7 and the World Bank when budget issues were part of their agendas.

MOF'S ADVISORY COUNCILS

The most important of MOF's Advisory Councils was the Fiscal System Council, whose work was described above. The Government Tax System Research Council had the formal role of studying the existing tax system, and making policy proposals at the prime minister's request. Formally, it was within the jurisdiction of his Office, with the MCA providing the secretariat, but in practice MOF's Tax Bureau (and to a lesser extent the Tax Bureau of MHA) controlled its agenda, proceedings, and recommendations. MOF's Tax Bureau prepared papers and technical data and research for it, and drafted the Council's annual report for its members to discuss, and agree, prior to submission to the prime minister in December (see Ishi 1989; Katō Junko 1994). In practice, it was much less influential in the formulation of tax policy than the LDP's Tax System Research Council. MOF's thirteen other advisory councils and research committees included: the Financial System Council, the Securities and Exchange Council, and the Insurance Council, which were merged in 1998 into a Financial Council; the Banking System Research Committee, the Customs Tariff Council, and the National Property Council. The NTAA had three advisory councils.

MOF'S PUBLIC BANKS AND CORPORATIONS

MOF had formal jurisdictional control of several important organizations in the public sector, and informal influence though patronage and secondment (*shukkō*) in others in which formal jurisdiction belonged to other ministries and agencies. First, it had direct control of the National Tax Administration Agency. Separated from the central policy-making core of the *honshō* (headquarters) office, it was an executive agency implementing government policy determined in the Tax and Budget Bureaux.

Secondly, until 1998 MOF had sole jurisdiction and supervisory powers of two public banks, plus the People's Finance Corporation, and the Japan Tobacco and Salt Company. In addition, it shared jointly with other ministries and agencies jurisdiction and supervisory powers over eight other public finance corporations, and the Shōkō Chūkin bank shown in Table 8.2. In principle, the public banks and finance corporations and companies were profit-making enterprises, intended to be largely independent of central government's control. In practice, their activities were closely tied to government policies, their plans, policies, and budgets closely supervised and, where necessary, controlled by MOF and its co-supervisory ministries. Unlike other public corporations, they were fully capitalized by government, and their budgets required the approval of the Diet; those of other public corporations were merely submitted for consideration. They provided MOF with an important source of influence and control of a wide range of economic and financial policies and of patronage, providing resting places at all levels for its retired bureaucrats.

From 1999, the Japan Development Bank and the Hokkaido–Tōhoku Development Corporation were merged to form the Development Bank of Japan; the Japan Bank for

Table 8.2 *Public banks and finance corporations within MOF's jurisdiction, 1975–1997*

Banks
Japan Development Bank
Export–Import Bank
Central Bank for Commercial and Industrial Cooperation (Shōkō Chūkin)(shared with MITI)

Public finance corporations
People's Finance Corporation
Housing Loan Corporation (MOC)
Agriculture, Forestry, and Fisheries Finance Corporation (MAFF)
Small Business Credit Insurance Corporation (MITI)
Japan Finance Corporation for Small Business (MITI)
Environmental Sanitation Business Finance Corporation (MHW)
Japan Finance Corporation for Municipal Enterprises (MHA)
Hokkaido–Tōhoku Development Corporation (NLA and HDA)
Okinawa Development Finance Corporation (OkDA)

Other finance corporations
Japan Tobacco and Salt, Inc.
Fund for the Promotion and Development of the Amami Islands

Source: Budget Bureau, MOF.

International Cooperation was formed from the EXIM Bank and the OECF; the National Life Corporation, from the merger of the People's Finance Corporation and the Environmental Sanitation Business Corporation. The salt sales business of the Japan Tobacco and Salt Corporation was privatized.

Thirdly, MOF exercised informal influence and control over a wide range of economic, industrial, and financial policy-making, through the practice of *shukko*, i.e. arrangements for the secondment or appointment of MOF career officials to key posts in other ministries and agencies. These and MOF's patronage of appointments in public corporations are discussed in the next chapter.

A CRISIS OF CONFIDENCE AND AUTHORITY

By the end of the twentieth century, MOF's traditional dominance of economic, financial, monetary, and fiscal policy-making at the heart of central government appeared to be waning. The erosion of its formal authority, and its declining status at the centre of government, were marked symbolically by the decision to change its title. In the reconstruction of the central executive, the Ōkurashō became from January 2001 the Zaim-shō, literally the Ministry of the Treasury, with the intention of making it mainly a ministry for the implementation of budget plans and policies decided politically.

Until 1997, MOF's size, structure, organization, and functions had remained virtually unchanged from 1975; indeed, in all those essentials, the Ministry was recognizably that which had been re-established at the end of the Second World War. However, the political–economic context within which it was operating became increasingly turbulent after the collapse of the bubble economy in 1990. Its aims and policies, its functions and organization, its competence, and its omnipotence were all the subject of continual public criticism, led, fermented, and often orchestrated by an alienated and increasingly hostile LDP.

Responsibility for the performance of the Japanese economy was shared among a large number of actors in both the public and private sectors. However, the public perception accorded MOF, and to a lesser extent the BOJ, key central roles in the management of the economy through their responsibility for monetary and fiscal policy. MOF's elite administrators were publicly accused, and held responsible for, policy failures in the management of the economy since the 'bubble' of the late 1980s—indeed, for the failure to foresee and prevent the speculative activity in land and real estate which contributed to that phenomenon, and for their failure to foresee and limit the impact of the economic decline that followed. Some have argued that MOF's obsession with fiscal reconstruction in the 1980s contributed to the 'bubble' phenomenon by its reliance on monetary rather than fiscal expansion (Funabashi 1988; Hartcher 1998).

The collapse and bankruptcy of housing loan associations (*jusen*), credit associations, several second-tier regional banks, and securities firms—the direct result of the pricking of the 'bubble'—were widely perceived by the public as MOF's responsibility: it had encouraged the setting up of the housing loan associations, and their financing by city banks and agricultural cooperatives, and had indulged many of their dubious borrowing and lending practices during the 'bubble'. The regulation and supervision of banks and financial institutions, the responsibility of its Banking and Securities Bureaux, were criticized as poorly coordinated, and its 'convoy' policy (to prevent the capsize of any bank, large or small), as inefficient and ineffective, criticisms that acquired greater salience with the revelation of corrupt practices in the New York branch of Daiwa Bank in 1995 and the collapse of several second-tier regional banks. MOF's proposals for the use of public money to rescue housing loan associations not only represented a *volte face* of its policy, but proved widely unpopular, and were exploited by Opposition parties to delay the passage of the budget for FY1996. The expectation that examination of the Budget in the Diet would provide the opportunity to expose the responsibility of the (then) new prime minister, Hashimoto, who, as minister of finance, had earlier been formally responsible for the financing of the *jusen*, together with the involvement of other senior LDP politicians, provided further embarrassment for MOF. The poisoned chalice of the second most important Cabinet post was rejected by all the leading LDP candidates. The appointment of Takemura Mayoshi, the leader of Sakigake, as minister of finance was politically expedient, but seen as further evidence of the Ministry's loss of status.

Earlier, MOF's unsuccessful attempt through the mouthpiece of Prime Minister Hosokawa to raise more revenue through a national welfare tax represented a humiliating climb-down, and a personal rebuff for Saitō Jirō, its administrative vice-minister, credited with a leading role in an initiative masterminded by Ozawa Ichirō. Criticism of MOF's role in that ill-fated initiative was a major factor in the deterioration of its relationships with the LDP, when the latter returned to power in the Murayama Coalition shortly after.

Historically, MOF's close relationship with LDP ministers, senior party officials, and influential backbenchers was grounded in a compact of mutual interests. That compact was broken, at least temporarily, as the LDP surrendered the role of governing party for one of opposition. It was now openly critical of MOF's senior officials, held to be too closely identified with the policies of the Hosokawa and Hata Coalition governments, and in particular with its chief strategist, Ozawa Ichirō. There is a nice irony in this complaint from a party that enjoyed an even closer symbiotic relationship with MOF and other ministries for 38 years, and in the personal hostility of the LDP leadership towards Ozawa, who had broken with the party in 1993 in the wake of the Kanemaru affair and the struggle for succession. More significantly, and worryingly for MOF, the orchestrated public campaign of denigration which the LDP conducted in its brief period in opposition in 1993–4 continued after its return to office in the Murayama Coalition. Here again, the politics of the power struggle within the coalition was a factor; like Ozawa, the Minister of Finance, Takemura, the leader of Sakigake, had broken away from the LDP. Criticism of MOF was partly intended to embarrass Takemura, and tactically was an element in the LDP's continuing struggle to dominate its coalition partners. Nevertheless, the LDP's criticisms, direct and indirect, of MOF were a new factor, and contributed to a perceptible deterioration in its traditional relationships with the party.

Public confidence in MOF's ability to regulate the behaviour and activities of the securities industry, and to resolve the long-running crisis in the banking sector, already at a low ebb, was further undermined by the evidence of improper and corrupt behaviour by several senior officials in the Banking and Securities Bureaux, revealed in the highly publicized raids on MOF by the Tokyo Prosecutor's Office in January 1998; earlier, in

1995, two senior officials, one a former deputy director-general in the Budget Bureau, the other chief of the Tokyo Customs House, had been reprimanded for improper behaviour in accepting gifts and entertainment. In the political fallout of the more extensive 'wining and dining' scandal in 1998, both the Minister of Finance and administrative vice-minister resigned, obliged to accept formal responsibility. An internal inquiry led to severe reprimands for 44 officials, reprimands for 58 others, and an official warning to the administrative vice-minister for international affairs, the so-called 'Mr Yen', Sakakibara Eisuke. Two officials about to be questioned by the Tokyo Prosecutor committed suicide; two others resigned, including the director-general of the Securities Bureau. The orderly and predictable line of succession to the top posts in the Ministry was broken, as erstwhile candidates were obliged to accept formal responsibility for the conduct of their subordinates and were passed over for promotion.

It is the fate of all ministries of finance to be condemned both for their acts of commission and for their sins of omission. Those responsible for raising and collecting taxes and for spending the taxpayers' money can expect little sympathy, and become inured to public criticism and denigration. MOF officials had few friends or supporters outside the central government, and within it the performance of its fiscal functions bred a 'siege mentality', with the beleaguered few surrounded by the larger, hostile battalions of Spending Ministries and their clients. There was therefore nothing novel or unexpected in the chorus of public disapproval and criticism of MOF's role and performance in the 1990s, or even in the demands of politicians, media analysts, and commentators for the dismemberment of a ministry with an historic concentration of power and authority. The 'longest continuing struggle in the Japanese Government, dating from well before the war, has been on the attempt to take control of the budget away from the Ministry of Finance in order to lodge it in the cabinet or some supra-ministerial coordinating agency' (Johnson 1982: 75). Successive attempts to relieve the Ministry of Finance of its budgetary function in 1947, 1955, 1963, and 1970, and to diminish its power and authority, all failed. But this time round, demoralized and humiliated by the events of the 1990s, and with its prestige and reputation tarnished, MOF was much less well placed to resist the growing pressures for its dismemberment.

The lead was taken by the MOF Reform Study Group, set up by the coalition parties in the Hashimoto government early in 1996. In the biggest shakeup of the Ministry since 1945, it was subsequently obliged to surrender functions and jurisdictions to other bodies, while the boundaries of its supervisory jurisdiction of public finance and other corporations were nominally redrawn more narrowly. In 1997 it was forced to surrender to the Bank of Japan authority to determine interest rates and domestic monetary policy. In June 1998, the functions of inspection, supervision, and regulation of all private financial institutions were transferred to the newly created Financial Supervision Agency brought within the jurisdiction of the Prime Minister's Office; the Banking and Securities Bureaux were abolished, their residual policy-making functions incorporated for a brief period in a new bureau, Financial System Planning. The re-capitalization of the banking sector passed to the Financial Revitalization Commission, established in the Prime Minister's Office in December 1998 as part of a package of measures to give legislative effect to Prime Minister Obuchi's pledge to resolve the banking crisis. The International Finance Bureau lost some of its financial responsibilities to the FSA, and was renamed the International Bureau. Three of MOF's long-standing advisory councils were merged into a new Financial Council.

Not only had MOF lost supervisory and regulatory functions to the Financial Supervision Agency, and responsibility for dealing with failed and bankrupt institutions to the Financial Revitalization Commission: its remaining financial policy-making powers were also threatened. The failure to win a majority in the Upper House elections in July 1998 meant that the LDP needed the support of other parties to ensure the passage there of its bills for administrative reform and the new US–Japan defence operational guidelines. In protracted discussions and negotiations with the Liberal Party, with whom it concluded a formal coalition compact in January 1999, and with New Kōmeitō brought into the coalition in October 1999, the main issue of contention in the proposed reorganization of the machinery of central government was the extent of MOF's powers. Earlier in the autumn of 1998, the LDP agreed with them that there should be a complete separation of its fiscal and financial powers, but the interpretation of the agreement was subsequently disputed, the LDP arguing that MOF should retain a general oversight of the financial system and responsibility for policy planning. A compromise arrangement in April 1999 provided for an indeterminate sharing of authority between MOF and the proposed Financial Services Agency.

The Financial System Planning Bureau, set up after the abolition of its Securities and Banking Bureaux, was abolished and its functions transferred in July 2000 to the new agency which incorporated both the Financial Supervision Agency and the Financial Revitalization Commission. This now had responsibility for the whole of the domestic financial system, including the drafting of legislation, coordinating cooperation among banks, security companies, and insurers, and overseeing corporate accounting systems, and for the international operations of private financial institutions. With MOF, it was jointly responsible for risk management when the failure of financial institutions caused excessive credit problems for lenders, disagreements between them mediated by a Financial Security Council chaired by the prime minister.

The extent to which MOF will continue to influence policy for the private financial system is uncertain, but it will continue to supervise the *public* financial system and financial policy planning, the international financial system, and the stability of foreign exchange relations; and it will continue to be responsible for the Bank of Japan, the Bank for International Cooperation, and the reconstructed FILP.

MOF's future role in the formulation of macroeconomic policy was equally uncertain. In the reorganization of central government implemented in January 2001, EPA was abolished and its functions transferred to the Cabinet Office and incorporated within a new Council for Economic and Fiscal Policy, given a general responsibility for the coordination of both economic and fiscal policy. However, MOF, with continuing responsibility for taxation and expenditure, customs and excise, FILP, and international finance, would obviously continue to play a key role in the formulation and coordination of macroeconomic policy. Less certain was its future role in the formulation of the Budget, as the Obuchi and Mori governments sought to wrest control from MOF, and enhance political influence through the new Council. We return to that issue in Chapter 30.

9

MOF's Elite Administrators

Japan's elite bureaucrats have five defining characteristics. First, their recruitment is open and competitive, but those appointed are drawn predominantly from among the graduates of Tokyo University's Law Faculty. Secondly, those recruited are generalists, rather than specialists with pre-entry technical or professional qualifications, and they dominate the elite bureaucracy in headquarters (*honshō*) ministries. Thirdly, bureau and ministry interests are stronger than national, centralizing tendencies; most bureaucrats serve the whole of their official life in the same ministry or agency, although secondment is common and increasing. Fourthly, behavioural norms of seniority, and rotation of posts, provide for the strictly regulated progression of class-cohorts with broadly based experience, mainly within ministries, up to the level of deputy director of division. Fifthly, officials passed over for promotion at more senior levels in *honshō* ministries resign; most, together with some other retirees, seek (with the assistance of their ministry) 'second careers' elsewhere in the public and private sectors, and in the Diet.

MOF's administrative elite is proto-typical, exhibiting all of those general characteristics, but in a more pronounced and marked fashion than found in other ministries and agencies. In this chapter we look at its recruitment, socialization, career progression, and retirement, within the context of those five broad characteristics.

RECRUITMENT

Japan's elite bureaucrats, so-called 'career officials' (*honshō kyaria*), are recruited through open competitive examinations, among those successful in the Administrative Service Level 1 examination.[1] In FY1994 there were 41,433 candidates, 20% of whom were women. Of the 1,863 successful candidates, fewer still were women—about 12%. Only about half of all successful candidates obtained posts in ministries and agencies, and less than 10% of these were women (NPA 1995).

Each year MOF recruits about 20–25 graduates, between 22 and 24 years of age. Formally, it requests from the National Personnel Authority the list of eligible candidates in rank order, and the hiring process nominally begins in November. Informally, it gets underway after the completion of the second stage of the examination, before the results of the competition are known. Candidates hoping to obtain an appointment in MOF

---

[1] So-called 'non-career' officials comprise both graduates and non-graduates, and are recruited by a variety of other examinations to posts in local branch and headquarters offices. The most successful can reach the level of deputy director of a division by the end of their career.

must normally pass in the top 50 of successful candidates in the Civil Service Examination (Kuribayashi 1986). In a series of informal interviews, candidate and ministry sound each other out. Formal interviews follow the publication of the examination results.

The process of informal and formal interviews is important. Appointments to MOF (and other ministries and agencies) are made for life, or more accurately until enforced resignation in the mid-fifties or, rarely, until retirement at the statutory age of 60. There is no probationary period of service. Careers are made almost entirely within the ministry or agency of first appointment. Both candidate and ministry take great care, therefore, that they are mutually suited. New recruits join a 'family', and the members of the family want to be sure that a new member will fit in and get on well with the others. The criterion for employment in MOF is said (by the Secretariat) to be 'character and ability rather than academic record', although the applicant's university track record and ranking in the public service examination are taken into account as well (Kawakita 1991: 21). MOF's self-proclaimed yardstick in screening candidates is 'First and foremost the candidates as individuals. We are not sticklers about exam scores . . . . Solid bright young people who will become acclimated to the ministry and bring with them a balanced perspective' (*Tokyo Business Today*, July 1992: 58).

National universities provide between 80% and 90% of those successful candidates hired by Spending Ministries and Agencies each year. Tokyo graduates provide the great majority of them, on average between 35% and 40%, followed by graduates from Kyoto and Hokkaido. The traditional dominance of Japan's elite bureaucracy by graduates of Tokyo University is of long standing. The university was founded in 1877, and its Law School was granted special status to supply bureaucrats for the new state. Private universities, such as Keio and Waseda, and national universities other than Tokyo, are steadily increasing their small shares. In 1991 Tokyo provided just over a half of all successful candidates, Waseda 11.8%, and Kyoto 7% (Kim *et al.* 1995). A similar trend was observable in MOF's graduate intake, but the dominance of Tokyo graduates was much more marked for the period 1975–97, as Table 9.1 shows. On average, some 80%–90% of recruits were from Tokyo, with only a handful from Kyoto and Hitotsubashi; very few entered from the private universities. The LDP government of Prime Minister Miyazawa (a former minister of finance, and MOF official) pledged in 1992 to reduce the proportion of Tokyo graduates there and in other ministries to a maximum of 50% within five years. At first the directive was largely ignored in MOF, but, called to account for the slow progress in implementation by the Chairman of PARC, Katō Kōichi, the Minister's Secretariat set a target figure of 70%. Even that was not quite achieved in the entries for 1996 and 1997.

The traditional dominance of law graduates in the Japanese bureaucracy continued throughout the last quarter of the twentieth century. Seventy per cent of successful candidates in the Level 1 examination had specialized in law at university. Of those subsequently appointed, about a quarter of all those hired annually had specialized in law. MOF recruits were not only predominantly from Tokyo University: they were overwhelmingly Law Faculty graduates (Table 9.1). Throughout the period 1975–97, in most years more than two-thirds had studied law; most of the other entrants graduated from faculties of economics.

The elite of the Japanese bureaucracy is heavily male-dominated, reflecting the small proportion of successful women candidates in the Level 1 examination, mentioned

Table 9.1 MOF's elite intake: university and faculty, 1975–1997

Entry year	Total	University Tokyo No.	%	Kyoto	Hitotsubashi	Other	Faculty Law No.	%	Economics No.	%	Other
1997	19	14	73.7	1	—	4	11	57.9	6	31.6	2
1996	22	17	77.2	3	1	1	17	77.3	4	18.2	1
1995	20	18	90.7	1	1	—	12	60.0	6	30.0	2
1994	21	18	85.7	1	—	2	17	80.9	4	19.0	—
1993	23	19	82.6	—	3	—	13	56.5	9	39.0	—
1992	24	22	91.7	2	—	—	17	70.8	6	25.0	1
1991	24	21	87.5	1	1	1	16	66.6	7	29.2	1
1990	26	23	88.5	2	—	—	18	69.2	6	23.0	2
1989	24	21	87.5	—	2	—	15	62.5	9	37.5	—
1988	24	21	87.5	1	—	2	16	66.6	7	29.2	1
1987	25	19	76.0	2	3	1	16	64.0	8	32.0	1
1986	25	22	88.0	2	—	1	18	72.0	7	28.0	—
1985	25	22	88.0	1	1	1	15	60.0	6	24.0	4
1984	26	21	80.8	—	2	3	16	61.5	7	27.0	3
1983	25	20	80.0	3	1	1	17	68.0	4	16.0	4
1982	27	22	81.5	1	1	3	19	70.4	8	30.0	—
1981	24	22	91.7	1	1	—	16	66.6	8	33.3	—
1980	23	19	82.6	2	2	—	14	60.9	8	34.8	1
1979	28	26	92.9	1	1	—	20	71.4	7	25.0	1
1978	26	22	84.6	—	3	—	16	61.5	9	34.6	1
1977	23	19	82.6	1	2	1	n/a		n/a		n/a
1976	25	19	76.0	3	3	—	n/a		n/a		n/a
1975	27	21	77.8	3	3	—	n/a		n/a		n/a

Source: compiled from data supplied by Minister's Secretariat, MOF, 1997.

earlier. In the early 1980s there were no more than 20–24 women entrants out of a total of about 800 for Level 1 posts; by the late 1990s that number had risen to about 100. In April 1996 there were only 1,190 women in 'career' posts throughout the bureaucracy, about 6% of the total (Kataoka 1996; Kaneko 1998). Moreover, post-entry progress for women was slow and modest compared with male entrants. In 1987 only 12 women, in six ministries, had attained the level of director of a division in *honshō*. In MOF, 'on average one woman is hired every two or three years' (Kawakita 1989 edn: 21). In 1996 there were six women 'career' officials in MOF out of a total of 559, the most senior of whom held the post of director of a division in the (then) Securities Bureau.

SOCIALIZATION

Tokyo University students tend to come from relatively affluent families, mainly the professional and managerial classes (Koh 1989). This is partly accounted for by the success of a small number of private high schools in obtaining entry for their pupils. In

1997, 16.5% of the total intake for the following year was provided by five private schools (Table 9.2). Enrolment there is more expensive than at public high schools, entrance is highly competitive, and preparation is both lengthy and costly. No firm conclusions about the effect of social origins, behaviour, and experience on future bureaucrats can be drawn from this or other survey evidence about their political and social orientation, but some senior officials in MOF emphasized, in interviews with the author, the greater significance of common school experiences than of the Tokyo Law Faculty connection in the establishment and nurturing of crucial social networks among the elite bureaucracy and politicians.

By the time of their arrival at Tokyo University's Law Faculty, future bureaucrats will have overcome a succession of hurdles, and become innured to trial by examination. All undergraduates undergo a 'general education' on the Komaba campus before entering their specialized faculties to complete their four-year degrees. The intending bureaucrat must secure a place in Humanities Group 1, one of six groups into which all entering students are divided. It alone guarantees entry to the Law Faculty for a prescribed quota of students. Very few places are available for those students admitted to other groups.

Successful candidates for the Law Faculty choose to specialize in one of three departments, the second of which (public law) is that normally chosen by those aiming for the bureaucracy. The courses and instruction provided are not vocational: formal training leading to careers in the legal profession is provided separately in another department. Those destined for the bureaucracy take a wide range of courses in constitutional law, civil law, administrative law, and international law, as well as the law of foreign countries, and courses in political science, economics, and finance. 'They not only receive varying doses of legal training but also become exposed to the historical, theoretical, and institutional underpinnings of the Japanese and foreign political and economic systems' (Koh 1989: 165). Criticism of the quality of the general and specialist education provided by the Tokyo Law Faculty—that it produces 'narrow-minded technicians, well versed in the fine points of legal theories and interpretation and supremely adept at taking examinations' (pp.168–70)—can be directed equally at successful candidates in the entrance examination who come from other elite universities. Whether

Table 9.2 *Undergraduate recruitment to Tokyo University for 1998*

High school	No. (%)
Kaisei High School (Tokyo)	186
Tōin High School (Yokohama)	85
Azabu High School (Tokyo)	82
Nada High School (Kobe)	82
Kyūshū High School	71
	506 (16.5)
Others	2,667 (83.5)
TOTAL	3,073

Source: Administrative Management Bureau, MCA, 1998.

the qualities tested in those and earlier examinations put a premium on memory and problem-solving ability, rather than independent thinking and the development of critical modes of analysis, raises much wider questions about the quality of Japanese higher (and secondary) education which fall outside the scope of this chapter.

Tokyo University has a general rather than a particular mission to produce Japan's future leaders in a wide range of professional occupations, most of which are in the private rather than the public sector, although its original mission when established in the Meiji period was to train Japan's administrative elite. The historical continuity is similar to that which has marked Oxford's (and to a lesser extent Cambridge's) dominance of the graduate entry to the UK administrative elite since the educational and Civil Service reforms in the mid-nineteenth century. Whereas Tokyo Law graduates have strengthened their position since the Second World War, in recent years the grip of Oxbridge has become progressively weaker, under challenge from the graduates of other, newer universities.

It is difficult to decide whether Tokyo Law Faculty graduates do well in the public service because of the quality of their pre-entry education, social origins, and experience, or because they are Tokyo Law Faculty graduates. Their numerical domination of those successful at the public service entry examinations and, subsequently, among those offered posts alone ensures that, other things being equal, they will dominate positions in the ministries and agencies later on. But as I shall explain later, they become more dominant still with progression to the most senior posts.

The making of an elite bureaucrat thus begins with success in a series of progressively more difficult and competitive examinations, which equips men and women with the will to succeed, and the ability to work hard for long hours under pressure, and to compete.

Post-entry socialization comprises both formal and informal training, most of it on-the-job in a ministry or agency, but some of it through formal courses provided by the National Personnel Office and the Bureau of Personnel of the (then) Management and Coordination Agency. Apart from induction courses, the main formal training programmes are for section chiefs, deputy directors, and directors of divisions. While those and other courses do something to instil a national, service-wide perspective, and help to provide for better communication horizontally between ministries as a result of informal networks, it is the formal and informal training provided within each ministry that is more significant in the career of a bureaucrat. In addition to formal in-house training, in the course of their early careers promising bureaucrats are seconded for short periods to other ministries or agencies, or posted abroad to embassies or international organizations. Arrangements exist for some middle-rank officials to be seconded for a year to the University of Saitama's Graduate School of Policy Sciences, and from 1997 to the newly established National Graduate Institute of Policy Studies.

The importance of post-entry socialization in Japanese ministries and agencies is even more pronounced in the Ministry of Finance, noted for its commitment to the idea of a 'finance ministry family' (ōkurai-ikka). There is a prolonged and intense period of formal and informal socialization into the culture and mores of the ministry, to develop personal responsibility and self-confidence, and to engender a sense of loyalty and dedication to the ministry. An important part of this is the formal and standardized five- to six-year training programme, and the particular importance paid to the periods of *en stage* training to develop leadership and management qualities.

Socialization into the culture, traditions, standard operating procedures, and policy predispositions of each bureau is part of the more general family socialization. Budget Bureau officials have been called the 'samurai of the Japanese government' and the 'elite of the elite', and their status and prestige are assiduously cultivated and jealously guarded. I have more to say about behavioural and policy rules-of-the-game regulating the conduct of budget examiners in Chapter 18.

Informal socialization occurs through class cohorts and study groups, while the common educational experience at schools and the Tokyo Law Faculty provides the basis for particularly close social relationships within the Ministry. A fifth of the career officials recruited are the sons of former MOF officials. Arranged marriages are common in Japanese society, and new entrants to MOF might ask their division directors to help, and seek the assistance of the Secretarial Division of the Minister's Secretariat, which maintains a register of recommendations made to the Ministry. Marriage-broking is a routine part of its work, and on average it arranges about two marriages a year. There is something of a tradition of MOF officials marrying into the families of prominent politicians; in the last forty years there have been 41 documented cases, including eight marriages into the families of prime ministers. In 1980 alone, nine serving MOF officials were married to daughters of politicians. There is also some evidence of young officials marrying into the families of MOF administrative vice-ministers; the daughters of three of them married MOF officials serving in the Budget Bureau in the 1990s (Hartcher 1998).

In MOF, and elsewhere, socio-cultural characteristics are reinforced and strengthened by the physical conditions of the work-place, and the cultural norms that underpin the transaction of routine business there. Elite bureaucrats below the rank of deputy director-general and councillor share large open-plan offices with their junior colleagues and non-career officials. Only the most senior career officials in MOF have their own rooms, and a personal secretary. Apart from the directors and deputy directors of divisions who sit at separate desks, officials sit cheek-by-jowl with their neighbours, according to a hierarchy of their seniority, exchanging seats and moving upward towards the director's 'top tables' as they are promoted.

By Western standards, MOF's offices are dingy, harshly lit, and overcrowded; and officials' desks and tables contiguous, cluttered and overburdened with PCs, files, documents, and books. Such close physical proximity both fosters the sense of family togetherness and commonality of purpose, and provides for ease of supervision. Most offices have TV sets, and these often play throughout the day as background, especially when important baseball or golf matches are screened. Throughout the day there are tannoy broadcasts of stern injunctions to pause for a period of collective keep-fit and relaxation exercises. On arrival, many officials change into flip-flops, as they would before entering their own homes. Informality is enhanced by the discarding of suit jackets, although the universal short-sleeved white shirt and discreet tie is in fact a *de rigueur* uniform. The office works together, eats together—sections, even whole divisions, take lunch together in the MOF canteen—and, after hours, drinks together.

Hours of work are long, far exceeding the nominal five-day week and the annual permitted overtime of 360 hours. In 1992 MOF bureaucrats worked on average an extra 5.4 hours each working day, with many senior officials working more than nine hours a day of unrecorded overtime. 'Let's go home while it's still dark', MOF bureaucrats say (Hartcher 1998). At busy times of the year, in December for example, at the climax of the budget process, officials often sleep overnight in beds provided in MOF's basement, or at their desks, for many a preferable alternative to the prospect of a journey of up to two hours to a distant suburb, late at night or very early in the morning.

CAREER PROGRESSION

The closed system of recruitment and promotion engenders feelings of loyalty and commitment to a ministry or agency, and reliance upon it. It encourages solidarity, but also competition among its members; only exceptionally are outsiders appointed, other than temporary secondments. It provides an expectation of job security, normally at least until the mid-fifties; and offers post-retirement rewards for ministerial loyalty and (comparatively) modest levels of pay.

Advancement to the level of deputy director of a division, which is the normal expectation of all career officials in the public service, follows a predictable formula. There are two general norms: strict adherence to rules of seniority, and frequent rotation between posts. Seniority determines the rate at which new recruits move through career stages. Thus, all those recruited in a particular year ('the class of 1992') move upwards as a cohort at roughly the same time until they reach the level of deputy director of a division (*kachō-hosa*). However, not all posts are equally demanding or prestigious. Those identified as the brightest and best of their intake are posted to those bureaux, and divisions within them, earmarked for the high-flyers with perceived (or ascribed) potential to rise to the top of the ministry. Thereafter the best posts go to those who have demonstrated their potential in previous key appointments. As qualification for the key posts is, for most young officials, previous experience in other key posts, advancement on the 'fast track' is to a large extent preordained for the elite within each class cohort. After the completion of the training period, progression upwards is almost a self-fulfilling process. Given the better-quality work that characterizes posts in the central policy-making divisions of a ministry's major bureaux, there is a greater opportunity for the chosen few to demonstrate those qualities and qualifications necessary for further advancement: intellectual ability, capacity for hard work, judgement, and political sensitivity. As well, key posts in a minister's private office, the Minister's Secretariat, and in the Coordination divisions of ministerial bureaux provide opportunities to develop and nurture networks, through exposure to politicians and the leaders of elite business and professional groups.

Career progression in MOF follows very similar lines. New recruits in MOF are inducted into the 'life of the family' in their first year, guided by a second-year mentor. The first assignment within a bureau is normally to a division dealing with general or coordinating business or research, or, for the potential high-flyers, a posting to the

Coordination Division of the Budget Bureau, or the Minister's Secretariat. Recruits become familiar with the broad range of the Ministry's work; they learn the standard operating procedures, help to prepare documents, gather and process statistical data, and accompany senior officers in meetings within the Ministry and in negotiations with other ministries. Unusually, MOF uses its new recruits as 'question-takers' in the Diet, a task performed by more senior bureaucrats in other ministries. This exposure to parliamentary politics provides an early learning process.

In their second year, MOF recruits go *en stage* for a year to local and regional finance or tax branches to serve as 'inspectors', serving under (non-career) mentors, the chiefs of tax bureaux. In their third year all return to Tokyo, and until 1992 they then underwent a year-long formal in-house training in economics, equivalent to a master's programme. Now, all career officials are sent abroad for two years to study economics or business administration, mainly in the USA but also in Germany, France, and the UK. Thereafter, training on the job through frequent rotation in a succession of posts takes precedence for the next two years, as a recruit moves upwards from a senior member of a sub-section (*shunin*) to chief of a section (*kakari-chō*). In the final fifth or sixth year of training, the recruit is sent out once again to the field for a year, but this time as the head of a local tax office. There he has the opportunity to display qualities of leadership and management, develop self-confidence, and demonstrate an ability to establish and maintain relationships with the leaders of local organizations, businessmen, politicians, and local government officials.

The training, and the thinking behind it, is similar to that of the French *inspecteur des finances*. For an official still in his twenties, it represents an exciting and formidable challenge, and an important part of the process of conferring and reinforcing elite status. Great care is taken in the selection of suitable local tax offices, where there are no major problems of tax collection, and where there are experienced and reliable deputy directors and chiefs of general affairs sections to hand who are suited to act as 'minders' (*omamori yaku*), normally senior non-career officials. Not all trainees are appointed head of a local tax office; others may serve for two years. Their performance is closely monitored by MOF back in Tokyo, and provides further evidence of future potential for progress on the fast track.

Some trainees are appointed to the level of deputy director of a division (*kachō-hosa*) immediately upon completion of their training, in the sixth or seventh year. A succession of mainly two-year postings in a variety of divisions throughout the ministry follows for the next ten years, roughly between the ages of 30 and 40. An official will now be 'expected to develop his general administrative ability, his capacity to respond promptly to a new situation, to negotiate effectively, to take leadership in reaching a consensus among those concerned, and to be knowledgeable—or to appear knowledgeable—about the matters within his jurisdiction' (Komiya 1990: 372).

The level of deputy director of a division is a key one in policy-making. It is here that much or most of the initial preparatory work is done on a policy issue—the background, the collection, collation, and analysis of statistical and other data, the legal and financial aspects, the arguments for and against different policy options, and possible changes to policy. Horne's (1985) study of Japan's financial markets showed that a

MOF official at this level 'participated in debate on policy matters within his own bureau, and between the bureau and the public sector' (p. 195). A deputy director in the Small Banks Division of the (then) Banking Bureau might hold discussions with general managers of mutual banks and credit associations, 'assume responsibility for keeping the LDP's Finance Sub-Committee abreast of relevant policy issues, as well as keeping himself abreast of policy matters within the bureau more generally'. Apart from the initiation and development of new policy, his other main function would be the implementation of existing policy, 'which involved discussions with all groups within the finance industry, interaction with other bureaux also involved in administering the policy and, sometimes, contacts with other ministries'.

Changes in regulations, and reforms of policy, are considered as a matter of course by deputy directors, but controversial initiatives normally originate higher up, from the divisional director or the director-general of the Bureau, or one of his deputy directors-general. While the deputy director initiates and drafts many of the basic policy documents, he is constrained by the general policy stance of both his division and the bureau as a whole. Directors are involved informally in discussions, and comment on drafts. The more sensitive issues involve both the directors and the director-general. Draft proposals for which he has responsibility are frequently presented to meetings (*kyokugi*) of senior bureau officials, including the director-general, deputy director-general, division directors, and officials from other bureaux. There he will have to argue and defend his policy proposal if it is to become the policy position of the Bureau as a whole.

After ten years' or so experience at the level of deputy director, promotion to the post of director of a division usually follows. As deputy director, he will already have developed and demonstrated skills in research, negotiation, and legislative draughtsmanship. Now he will be expected to show powers of coordination, leadership, and man-management, to manage a defined policy area, and to attend to the problems that arise in it. There is keen competition and rivalry between members of a class cohort for the posts of division director and above, and especially for those on the *erīto kōsu*, in the Minister's Secretariat, the Coordination Divisions of the bureaux, and key posts in the Budget Bureau. A director-general of the Customs Bureau explained:

In each intake year, there is a strong sense of belonging and also a strong sense of competition. After you have spent ten years in the ministry together with the same group of colleagues, you know yourself how competitive you are, and it is already clear what you will be able to achieve ultimately, and others know too. It is a judgement by peers, and it is an extremely harsh system. (Kubota Isaro; quoted in Hartcher 1998)

The kind and quality of postings as director, and one's performance in them, are crucial to further advancement. The influence of the Secretarial Division of the Minister's Secretariat in deciding who gets what job, and when and how officials are promoted, is crucial, and in turn enhances the powerful position occupied by the Secretariat within MOF. Careers can be promoted through the influence of senior officials, through paternalistic relationships (*senpai-kōhai*) with their juniors.

Rotation between different posts and bureaux is an essential part of the training and learning process, subjecting high-flyers to a variety of different experiences, including periods of secondment to other ministries and agencies. In 1996, 160 MOF officials were on secondment in other ministries and agencies, of whom 69 held the rank of director or above (MCA 1997*b*). As well, in any one year some twenty high flyers, at or around the level of deputy director or director, are posted abroad to Japanese embassies and international organizations such as IMF, the World Bank, and OECD. Rotation reflects the behavioural norm of general rather than specialist administration, and is very similar to that of the British civil service generally, and the Treasury in particular. 'Going round the track' (*sotomawari*) is an essential part of the training and education of the MOF bureaucrat, as it is for the UK Treasury official (see Thain and Wright 1995). Movement takes place in an annual ritual each May or June. Most career officials spend on average two years in each post. Appointments in one or more of the key divisions of the Minister's Secretariat, and/or as a budget examiner, will mark out the director for further promotion. In 1986 all eight officials who held the position of director-general of a bureau, or deputy vice-minister of the Minister's Secretariat, had served previously either as director of one of the core divisions in the Minister's Secretariat—Secretarial, Policy and Coordination, Research and Planning—or in the Coordination Division of a bureau (Directory of the Finance Ministry 1986). Service in the Budget Bureau, as deputy budget examiner or budget examiner, is a prerequisite of progression to the top jobs there.

Solidarity and identification with the Ministry are promoted through a variety of informal internal groups whose membership is defined according to common experience of school, university, and entry-cohort, and a variety of clubs and study-groups based on common interests. Most classes evince an *ésprit de classe* (*dōkō no ishiki*). The solidarity of the MOF 'class of 1947' was expressed and fostered organizationally in a club that continued in amity for 31 years until its only surviving member became director-general of the Tax Bureau (Johnson 1982: 65). Similar clubs or regular informal meetings of class cohorts existed in MOF in the 1990s:

We do everything together, so eventually we become friends. Later on, we still meet, talk to each other, exchange experiences and ideas. The whole group is very smart to begin with, and then receives very good training, and we add to this *dōkō no ishiki* [same-class-consciousness]. We identify ourselves through this group.

After retirement, they form a *dōkō no kaigō* [same-class get-together] (interview with MOF official in 1993; quoted in Schaede 1995). Other informal groups of former MOF officials include the quarterly meetings of the Society of the Friends of the MOF (Ōkura Dōyū Kai), for those retired officials of the rank of *kachō* or above, and the Karuta Kai, a small group of some 40–50 senior ex-officials which meets annually (Brown 1999).

The size of the initial class-cohort (*nenji*) thins progressively as promoted members advance beyond the career grade of deputy division director. Before the reorganization of 1998 reduced the number of MOF bureaux, only eight members of a class of 20–25 could hope to be appointed director-general or deputy vice-minister of the Secretariat; only two of those could reach the top posts of administrative vice-minister and administrative vice-minister for international affairs, or perhaps director-general of the NTAA. The remainder would be obliged to resign. The seniority rule is not inviolate, but there is a very strong presumption that those whose ambitions are disappointed will resign to avoid embarrassment as relationships of equality are transcended by those of organizational hierarchy. Resignation also clears the way for the advancement of juniors, and refreshes the elite. There are however occasional exceptions to the rule. Between 1945 and 1983 there were five, but in most of those cases classmates who remained were in charge of external agencies, or were appointed to them, and thus were outside the direct chain of command of the *honshō* ministry under the administrative vice-minister.

Profile of the High Flyer on the Erīto Kōsu

Once identified and marked out as destined to reach the top positions in MOF, career progression for the high-flying young official is inevitable and predictable. A succession of postings to a handful of the most central, critical, and important jobs ensures that he has the opportunity to demonstrate his potential. There are four stages. First, after the completion of the initial training period, a succession of one- or two-year appointments at the deputy director level will include, typically, service in the Coordination Division of one of the leading bureaux, ideally Budget or Tax or in the Minister's Secretariat; or an appointment to the post of deputy budget examiner, with the most prized posts in those key divisions dealing with public works or agriculture.

The second stage occurs in mid-career, after about twenty-five years of service, between the ages of 46 and 48, when high-flyers can expect promotion to the rank of director of a division. Here, again, there are a handful of key divisions and posts. More than 80% of those who reach the top-level of administrative vice minister have served as director of a division in the Minister's Secretariat or the Coordination Division of a key bureau, normally the Budget Bureau, the Tax Bureau, or the Financial Bureau. Among the key posts in the Secretariat and in the Budget Bureau are the following:

- Director, Secretarial Division, Minister's Secretariat
- Special Officer for Research and Planning in the Minister's Secretariat
- Councillor in Minister's Secretariat
- Budget examiner (pre-eminently, with responsibility for coordination; and/or in the public works division)
- Director, Coordination Division, Budget Bureau
- Director of Legal Division, Budget Bureau
- Financial Counsellor in US/UK embassies, World Bank, IMF
- Personal secretary to the PM or minister of finance

The third stage occurs in late career, from about the age of 50. The high-flyers can now expect promotion to senior bureau positions, at the level of councillor or deputy director-general, or director-general of a less prestigious bureau. Those destined for the very top will have served a year or two as director of the Coordination Division in the Minister's Secretariat or the Budget Bureau; from there, a final year *en stage* at MOF's most important branch office at Osaka. Promotion then follows to the junior of the three posts of deputy director-general of the Budget Bureau. After a year in each, the senior deputy director-general might then return to the Policy Coordination Division of the Minister's Secretariat, but this time in charge as deputy vice-minister.

Not all will proceed to the fourth and final stage, which leads to the top position of administrative vice-minister. The stepping-stones are clearly marked, and the progression predictable, regulated by informal rules-of-the-game. By tradition, the outgoing vice-minister nominates his successor from among the eligible candidates in the class year below, after informal consultation with former vice-ministers. The top post is always filled from within MOF, normally but not invariably from those holding the position of director-general of the Budget Bureau. There is a formal, token consultation with the minister of finance, confirming the appointment. But it can happen, as in 1974, that ministerial intervention proves decisive. On that occasion the Prime Minister, Tanaka, ensured the promotion of the director-general of the Tax Bureau, rather than the more obvious candidate from the Budget Bureau. Thereafter no director-general of the Budget Bureau failed to be appointed subsequently to the post of administrative vice-minister until Wakui Yoji in 1998 (discussed below). Most serve for a year, a few for a further year, depending upon the availability of the 'heir apparent'. All 39 administrative vice-ministers appointed between 1945 and 1997 had graduated from Tokyo University's Law Faculty. Between 1975 and 1997, all but three had followed a predictable route to the top, progressing through the senior posts of deputy director-general (i.e. the senior official under the minister) in EPA (on secondment), deputy vice-minister of the Minister's Secretariat in MOF, and director-general of the Budget Bureau (Table 9.3).

The career profile of Saitō Jirō, administrative vice-minister 1993–5, is prototypical. After ten years of training and rotating posts at the level of deputy director and director of division, he was appointed a budget examiner with responsibility for construction and public works. Thereafter he became successively director of the Budget Bureau's Coordination Division; director of the Policy Coordination Division of the Minister's Secretariat; and deputy director-general of the Budget Bureau. He then made the classic move to deputy director-general at the EPA, before returning to MOF as deputy vice-minister in the Minister's Secretariat. From there he was appointed director-general of the Budget Bureau, and finally administrative vice-minister.

The pattern of predictable, orderly, and predetermined succession to the top post came to an end in the mid-1990s. Three of the four administrative vice-ministers appointed after Ozaki in 1992–3 resigned or retired early. Saitō's retirement a month early was perhaps no more than a token appeasement of political pressures on him to so do, but Shinozawa, who succeeded, served only seven months before resigning, accepting personal responsibility for 'several incidents which evoked criticism' of the Ministry. Earlier his pay had been cut by 20% for failure to supervise senior officials charged with bribery, the first time such an action had been taken against a MOF administrative vice-minister in 16 years. Komura Takahashi, his successor, served only six months before his enforced resignation in January 1998, compelled to accept formal responsibility for the inadequate supervision of senior officials in the Financial Inspection Department of the Minister's Secretariat, arrested on suspicion of taking bribes from banks. The preordained succession was broken with the appointment to the top post of Tanami Kōji

Table 9.3 *Career progression of MOF's administrative vice-ministers, 1975–2000*

	MOF			EPA
	Administrative vice-minister	Director-general, Budget Bureau	Deputy vice-minister Minister's Secretariat	Deputy director-general Minister's Secretariat
Takeuchi	1975–77	1974–75	1971–73	—
Yoshise	1977–78	1975–77	—	1973–74
Ōkura[a]	1978–79	—	—	—
Nagaoka	1979–80	1977–79	1975–77	1974–75
Tanaka	1980–81	1979–80	—	1976–77
Takahashi[a]	1981–82	—	—	1977–78
Matsushita	1982–84	1980–82	1978–80	—
Yamaguchi	1984–86	1982–84	1980–82	1978–80
Yoshino	1986–88	1984–86	1982–84	1981–82
Nishigaki	1988–89	1986–88	1984–86	1982–83
Hirasawa[b]	1989–90	—	—	1985–86
Kogayu	1990–91	1988–90	1986–88	—
Yasuda	1991–92	1990–91	1988–90	1986–88
Ozaki[a]	1992–93	—	—	—
Saitō	1993–95	1991–93	1990–91	1988–90
Shinozawa	1995–96	1993–95	1991–93	—
Ogawa[c]	1996–97	—	—	—
Komura	1997–98	1995–97	1993–95	1992–93
Tanami[d]	1998–99	—	—	—
Usui[c]	1999–2000	—	—	—
Mutō	2000–	1999–2000	1995–97	—

[a] Previously D-G, Tax Bureau.
[b] Previously D-G, Banking Bureau.
[c] Previously commissioner of the National Tax Administration Agency and D-G, Tax Bureau.
[d] Previously councillor, Cabinet Office and D-G, Financial Bureau.
Source: Minister's Secretariat, MOF.

(MOF, class of 1964) head of the Councillor's Office on Internal Affairs in the Cabinet Office. He was brought back to MOF, where he had been director-general of the Financial Bureau, on the personal initiative of Prime Minister Hashimoto, with whom he had worked closely on the resolution of the issue of American bases in Okinawa. Tanami had no previous experience in the Budget Bureau, but in a difficult period for MOF this was a clean, safe appointment which commanded respect. Komura's (MOF, class of 1963) heir apparent was intended to be Wakui Yoji from the class below (MOF, class of 1964), director-general of the Budget Bureau, groomed for the top post through a predictable succession of senior posts in MOF and EPA. However, he was deputy vice-minister in the Minister's Secretariat at the time of the alleged bribery of officials in its Financial

Inspection Department, and was disciplined for a failure of supervision, together with Mutō Toshirō, who succeeded him in that post. Mutō (MOF, class of 1966) was destined to succeed Wakui as director-general of the Budget Bureau, and then as administrative vice-minister. Mutō's successor (in 2001) was intended to be Taya Hiroaki. Taya had been reprimanded and removed from his post as director-general of the Tokyo Customs House in 1995 for accepting a free flight to Hong Kong, and entertainment from a businessman, Takahashi Harunori, former president of the defunct Tokyo Kyōwa Savings and Loans Association. Mutō was 'demoted' to councillor, but his career and the orderly progression was restored with his appointment first as director-general of the Budget Bureau in 1999, and then a year later as administrative vice-minister in succession to Usui Nobuaki (MOF, class of 1965), whose appointment from the National Tax Administration Agency had filled a 'gap' in the class cohorts.

The post of administrative vice-minister for International Finance is more specialist, and those who are eventually appointed to it have normally progressed through key positions in the Financial Bureau and (formerly) the Banking Bureau, and have served overseas on secondment to international financial organizations. One of the most renowned of recent incumbents was Gyōten Tōyō, whose career profile is typical. After graduating from the Economics Faculty of Tokyo University, he entered MOF in 1955 and was posted to the Tax Bureau. He spent a year at Princeton in his training period, and was seconded successively to IMF, and the Asian Development Bank. In 1975, after twenty years' service, he was appointed director of the Second Fund Division (responsible for FILP) in the Financial Bureau and, five years later, to one of the key posts in the Minister's Secretariat as councillor with responsibility for the International Finance Bureau. In 1983 he was appointed deputy director-general of the Banking Bureau, and the year after, director-general. He became administrative vice-minister for International Finance in 1986, a post that he held for three years.

Officials normally serve no more than one or two years in the most senior posts, depending upon the circumstances of who is next in line and 'available', and their seniority relative to younger competitors in other class cohorts. The short incumbency and possession of the prize for which they have competed for thirty years is to avoid blocking the promotion prospects of those queuing below.

The dominance of Tokyo University graduates generally among elite bureaucrats in the national public service noted earlier is still more apparent among senior posts above the level of division director. Together with Kyoto, Tokyo University graduates filled 70% of the senior posts in the public service as a whole in the 1980s and 1990s, rising to 89% at the level of director-general, while 95% of all administrative vice-ministers graduated from Tokyo University. The dominance of Tokyo University, and more especially its Law Faculty, among senior officials of MOF is more striking still. As we have seen, all administrative vice-ministers and all directors-general of the Budget Bureau who held office between 1975 and 1997 were graduates of Tokyo's Law Faculty. Within the Budget Bureau, of the 57 officials who reached the level of budget examiner between 1972 and 1992, 90% had been educated at Tokyo University; all but three of those had also graduated from its Law Faculty (84% of the total). Only two budget examiners had been educated elsewhere, at Kyoto University; while four had entered MOF as non-graduates via local tax offices.

RETIREMENT

As explained above, a deeply embedded behavioural norm was that those career officials passed over for promotion would resign to avoid embarrassing their more successful classmates, as superior–subordinate relationships replaced those of equality. Pressures to resign, both from superiors 'encouraging retirement' (*taishoku kanshō*), and unofficially, via informal pressures of 'a the tap on the shoulder' (*kata tataki*), reinforced that expectation. The average age of those appointed to head a bureau was about 55, and for those appointed administrative vice-minister, 56 (Koh 1989). Thus, those of the original class-cohort who were passed over for the handful of the most senior posts normally retired in their mid-50s. Retirement was compulsory for all officials at the age of 60. Compared with levels of salary in analogous positions in the private sector, senior officials were modestly paid, and pension provision often inadequate. The need to enhance future, post-retirement, income therefore reinforced the cultural expectation of early retirement for most senior bureaucrats in the public service passed over for promotion to the post of director-general of a bureau, or even deputy director-general.

There were three main re-employment options: to seek employment within the private sector; to obtain a post with a public corporation or government enterprise; or to seek election to the Diet. *Amakudari*, 'the descent from heaven' into private or public-sector organizations, is a practice closely related to employment customs such as lifetime commitment or long-term employment (*shūshin-koyō*) and promotion by seniority (*nenkō-joretsu*). After a lifetime in a ministry or agency, the career official retired at the age of 55 or 60 into an *amakudari* post or posts arranged by its Secretariat. The initiative might be taken by a company 'scouting' for a person with particular experience and skills, or by the official as a result of contact formally or informally with a company or public corporation at an earlier stage of his career. There were obvious dangers from 'structural corruption', as those passed over for promotion or approaching the end of their careers might look to safeguard their future, and risk compromising their integrity and neutrality in dealing with prospective private firms and public corporations.

In MOF, placements for retiring officials below the rank of administrative vice-minister and director-general were arranged by the Secretarial Division of the Minister's Secretariat, under the guidance and ultimate control of its deputy vice-minister and the administrative vice-minister, both of whom played an active part in the placement of the most senior of their colleagues. An informal association of former senior MOF officials, the Fourth Wednesday Club (*Yon Sui Kai*), helped to negotiate and allocate *amakudari* posts for its members, and for those about to retire. As the most prestigious ministry, it conferred upon its officials a status and cachet that (at least until the taint of the corruption scandals in 1996–8) enhanced their marketable value, although with the declining prestige of MOF from the mid-1980s that value had become a depreciating asset. It was particularly well placed to secure appointments in the public and private sectors for its retiring career and non-career officials, both from its headquarters and from local branch offices. Its responsibilities, particularly (until 1998) those of the regulation and licensing of banks, insurance companies, securities companies, and credit associations, but also the implementation of corporate taxation and, from 1989, the national consumption tax, were central to the work of all public and most private-sector financial organizations. Qualified by experience, inside knowledge, and expertize, MOF officials from the Tax, Customs, and (until 1998) Banking and Securities Bureaux could contribute in an executive or advisory capacity to that work.

It was however harder to place officials from the Budget Bureau or Financial Bureau in private-sector organizations (director of Secretarial Division, MOF 1995; quoted in Hartcher 1998). Senior officials recruited predominantly from the Tokyo Law Faculty, whose penetration and dominance of other business, commercial, political, and academic elites, together with common educational experiences at a handful of private high schools, were supremely well connected to both public and private policy-making and policy-implementing networks in Tokyo and the prefectures. With time and experience, they had become adept in the exploitation of such networks to acquire and use influence. In the 1980s it was estimated that, for every five career officials in MOF, there was one retired MOF official in a public or private financial institution (Horne 1985). For example, 29 MOF bureaucrats with the rank of divisional director or above retired in 1984. Only one—a former administrative vice-minister—did not seek immediate re-employment; six went to MOF's controlled public banks and financial corporations; nine, to other public corporations; two, to private banks; eight, to private companies; and three became licensed tax accountants. Sixteen of the 29 were appointed as board directors, and five became advisers.

Retirement into Private-Sector Organizations

Re-employment within two years of retirement, in a private (for-profit) organization, is prohibited in principle by the National Public Service Law. Officials in central government are also prevented from taking jobs 'closely connected' with posts held within five years of retirement. Legal restriction is designed to avoid potential conflicts of interest, and the use of public knowledge for private advantage.

In practice, exemptions from the two-year rule are common. The number of bureaucrats permitted by the National Personnel Authority to take such posts averaged some 200 each year throughout the 1980s, peaking in 1985 at 318; thereafter there was a trend of continuous decline. In 1997, of the 118 approved by the NPA, 21 were from MOF, most of whom were re-employed in credit unions and securities' firms; 17 from MITI, 16 from MOC, and 11 from MPT. Some ministers imposed restrictions on the re-employment of their officials following several well publicized scandals in the 1990s. In 1993 the Minister of Construction refused all requests for exemptions from bureaucrats above the rank of deputy director, until the conclusion of the investigations into the conduct of ministers, officials, and LDP politicians in the Sagawa Kyūbin corruption case. The Minister of Health and Welfare took similar action in 1996, after the implication of some of his most senior officials in the sale of HIV-tainted blood products to haemophiliacs. Those and other cases of incompetence and misconduct contributed to a more general loss of public esteem for bureaucrats, and made their employment less attractive to private-sector firms.

Both before and after that decline, MOF retirees into the private sector easily outnumbered those from other ministries, at an average of 45–60 in the period 1975–95, or about a quarter of the total for the public service as a whole. But less than half that number found employment in private-sector firms in 1996, while in 1999 only 12 did so. Most of the *amakudari* retirees from MOF and other ministries (mainly MITI, MOC, MAFF, and MOT) were former technical bureaucrats whose work was closely connected with the regulation or supervision of various economic activities, and were drawn mainly from branch or local offices or from subordinate agencies. Retirement into the associations (*kyōkai*) responsible for the administration of regulations, such as the Electronics Communications Terminal Equipment Testing Association, was common.

Less than half of the total retirees entering private employment each year were elite career officials, and of those only a handful had served at headquarters (*honshō*); fewer still had achieved the rank of director-general or administrative vice-minister. In MOF, they were mainly non-'career' officials from the National Tax Administration Agency seeking re-employment in credit associations. A much larger number of MOF career officials were re-employed in the private sector after the two-year formal delay.

Amakudari
There are three main interpretations of the role of *amakudari* in the private sector. First, there are those who argue that *amakudari* is an instrument for government control of private industry, and an important means of enhancing the effectiveness of ministerial administrative guidance (e.g. Johnson 1974). Secondly, there is the 'equalizing school', which claims *amakudari* as an equalizing mechanism of differences in access to information between small and large companies. 'Smaller firms in Japan have stronger incentives for wanting ex-bureaucrats and are willing to pay relatively more [because] economically strategic information is much more frequently unavailable from public sources in Japan than in Europe and the US' (Calder 1989: 395). The adherents of the third interpretation emphasize the importance of *amakudari* as a mechanism for informal consultation and consensus-building between the public and private sectors. The continuing debate between the protagonists of the three schools is summarized and discussed by Rixtel (1997: 65–71).

Those interpretations are not mutually exclusive, and the *raison d'être* of *amakudari* might vary with the circumstances of each case, and with the particular motives of the ministry and private-sector organization at that time. Extending the debate, Schaede (1995) argues that *amakudari* is a means of managing the uncertainty that arises from bureaucratic regulation through administrative guidance. Retirees act as intermediaries, lobbying on behalf of their firms for changes in ministerial regulatory frameworks, and acting on behalf of their former ministries to monitor the implementation of existing regulations by their firms. Concurring, Nakano (1998) adds a further dimension to her 'management of regulation' model in a wide-ranging historical study of MPT and the telecommunications industry. As the scope of MPT's regulatory jurisdiction expanded in the 1980s, retirees were placed 'in every corner of the telecomms. industry', not because they possessed technical expertize valuable to firms, nor because *amakudari* provided a means to control them. *Amakudari* was a product of bureaucratic control, not a means to it, a 'spoils system' in which officials were rewarded with prominent and well-paid posts according to MPT's internal rules of personnel management (p.113).

Retirement of senior MOF officials into the private banking industry was one of the ministry's prime sources of *amakudari*, and provides an empirical test of the hypotheses of the various schools. Those who obtained senior executive positions on management boards, or posts as 'auditors' or 'advisers', tended to be drawn from the highest echelons of MOF bureaucracy. The number of former MOF officials holding senior positions on the boards of all private banks averaged between 130 and 150 throughout the period 1975–93 (Table 9.4). But less than 10% were employed in the largest and most important financial institutions—city banks, long-term credit banks, and trust banks—and none in any of the seven leading city banks, apart from Sakura. The major banks of Sumitomo, Dai-ichi Kangyo, Mitsui, Fuji, and Mitsubishi appointed no senior MOF bureaucrats to their boards on retirement in the whole of the period 1975–93. Where *amakudari* occurred, it was among the smaller, weaker city banks. The vast majority (90%) of the *amakudari* appointments of MOF officials was made to the boards of regional banks, and second-tier regional banks, with the latter predominating. On a broader definition of board membership to include advisers, auditors, and councillors, the small number of former MOF officials employed by the city banks and long-term banks was roughly doubled, and the totals for all private banks marginally increased. But it is the narrower definition, which excludes such posts, that is used in the annual data published by the National Personnel Authority. (For a discussion of definition, see Rixtel 1997.) Rixtel's historical analysis was confirmed by MOF's own data for 164 former MOF officials holding executive posts in 1998 in 128 financial institutions, banks, and insurance companies. Of the 117 employed in banks, only one was at a city bank, three at long-term credit banks, and two at trust banks; the remainder were all employed in regional and second-tier regional banks (MOF 1998*b*).

MOF *amakudari* to private banks in the period 1975–2000 had two main characteristics. First, MOF had a monopoly of retirement appointments in particular banks; for example, it monopolized appointments in the Sakura Bank among the smaller city banks, the Industrial Bank of Japan among the long-term credit banks, several regional banks, and a large number of second-tier regional banks. Secondly, within those banks where MOF had a monopoly, there were high succession rates. For example, continuously from 1971 former administrative vice-ministers held the position of 'auditor' at the Industrial Bank of Japan. A similar continuity of MOF bureaucrats was evident in the Saitama Bank, the Bank of Tokyo, and the Nippon Trust Bank. Former administrative vice-ministers held the highest executive position at the leading regional bank, the Bank of Yokohama, continuously from 1977. Former administrative vice-ministers for international financial affairs were consistently appointed to the highest positions on the board of the (then) Bank of Tokyo, at the level of deputy-president, president, or chairman. Gyōten Tōyō, vice-minister for international financial affairs in 1986–8, was appointed chairman in 1992, succeeding Kashiwagi Yūsuke who had held the same vice-ministerial appointment. In addition, Miyazaki Tomoo, a former director-general of the International Finance Bureau, had served previously as its managing director and vice-chairman. In the Kyūshū Bank, a medium-sized second-tier regional bank,

Table 9.4 MOF amakudari kanryō on boards[a] of private banks, 1975–1993

	1975	1979	1984	1988	1989	1990	1991	1992	1993
City banks (11)[b]	9	9	10	8	8	9	7	5	5
Long-term credit banks (3)	8	2	5	3	3	3	3	3	4
Trust banks (7)	2	2	3	1	1	2	2	2	2
TOTAL (% of all private banks)	19	13 (9.2)	18 (11.5)	12 (8.5)	12 (8.6)	14 (9.8)	12 (9.2)	10 (7.6)	11 (8.0)
Regional banks (64)	32	44	47	51	50	50	47	47	47
Second-tier regional banks (65)	N/A	84	92	79	78	79	72	74	79
TOTAL (% of all private banks)	—	128 (90.7)	139 (88.5)	130 (91.5)	128 (91.4)	129 (90.2)	119 (90.8)	121 (92.4)	126 (92)
All private banks[c]	—	141 (100)	157 (100)	142 (100)	140 (100)	143 (100)	131 (100)	131 (100)	137 (100)

[a]For definition and composition of see Rixtel (1997: ch. 8).
[b]( ) Numbers of banks in each category, as at 1993.
[c]Totals marginally increased by adopting a broader definition of 'board' to include positions of 'adviser' and 'auditor'.

Source: derived from Rixtel (1997: tables 8.3–8.7).

senior ex-bureaucrats from MOF held the position of president continuously from 1973, a characteristic found in several other similar banks.

There is little doubt that MOF consistently exploited *amakudari* to manage the careers of its elite administrators, by providing both an incentive and a reward for those who aspired to and achieved the most senior positions in the Ministry. But, while it monopolized *amakudari* appointments in specific banks, and ensured a continuous succession of its own retirees to them, it did not do so in the largest and most influential city financial institutions, where the striking absence of MOF (or Bank of Japan) *amakudari* throughout the period 1975–98 suggests that it was unable or unwilling to use it more generally as an instrument of bureaucratic influence and control, or as an important means of exercising administrative guidance, as some have argued (e.g. Johnson 1974, 1975, 1978). The big banks were reluctant to appoint MOF *amakudari* whom they did not need and whose employment was seen as 'bureaucratic interference and meddling with company policy', and as disturbing or threatening to internal career structures (Rixtel 1997: 252). That conclusion is confirmed in a wider study of *amakudari* in a sample of the largest stockholding corporations (Schaede 1995), which found little evidence of *amakudari*, not only in the banking sector, but also in the securities and insurance industries.

Secondly, the evidence of MOF *amakudari* in private banks provides little support for those who have argued that its purpose and effect is to achieve and reinforce consensual policy-making between the public and private sectors (e.g. Okimoto 1989; Upham 1987). The largest and most influential banks, whose presidents traditionally provide the chairmen of the influential banking associations, had few or no MOF *amakudari*.

Thirdly, MOF's practice provides only qualified support for those who have argued that it is intended primarily as a mechanism to equalize differential access to information among competing interest groups. While the appointment of former MOF (and BOJ) officials to the boards of the smaller city banks, long-term credit banks, and trusts suggests that equalization might have been a factor, there is no comparable pattern among the regional banks, where a significant number of the smaller institutions had few or none, compared with their larger rivals. But that pattern is reversed among the second-tier regional banks, where the smaller, weaker institutions had large numbers of MOF *amakudari*. However Rixtel (1997) argues that this 'pattern equalization' is the result of *ad hominem* decisions taken by specific banks, rather than the implementation of a policy of deliberate equalization by MOF (or BOJ).

Nevertheless, such was MOF's influence in small and medium-sized financial institutions in the 1980s that it served to constrain the implementation of the policy of financial deregulation promoted by its own bureaux (Horne 1985). The resistance of those institutions to proposals for radical change through merger and amalgamation was supported by the LDP, and increased as a result of the interest of retiring MOF officials in obtaining posts in those institutions. The financial deregulation of financial markets that took place at that time occurred mainly in the sector dominated by the large banks and securities companies, where MOF's influence through its retired officials was much weaker.

The difficulties experienced by many regional banks, and especially second-tier regional banks after the collapse of the 'bubble economy', induced MOF to be more interventionist, appointing both former and serving MOF bureaucrats to the boards of those banks most at risk of failure in order to strengthen their management, in some cases to oversee the implementation of reconstruction measures, and to monitor performance. The rescue of Hyōgō Regional Bank in 1992 was accompanied by MOF's insistence on the appointment as president of a former director-general of its Banking Bureau, who, after its collapse and liquidation three years later, nevertheless continued as managing director of the new bank which assumed responsibilities for its debts; a former director-general of the NTAA became president of the ailing Nippon Credit Bank. Here and in similar cases MOF's use of *amakudari* is to be explained more as an instrument of 'crisis management' and control than as a reward for its retiring elite administrators.

Retirement into Public-Sector Organizations

'Side-slip' (*yokosuberi*) into public corporations and companies is not subject to legal restriction, and some retirees constructed lucrative careers moving from one to another in a succession of appointments, each with a lump-sum separation allowance. More than a quarter of all *amakudari* officials, and 40% of MOF *amakudari* moved twice or more. The options open to the retiring official varied with status and seniority and with the number of such corporations and companies that fell within the jurisdiction of the ministry or agency, which is one of the reasons why they competed for and jealously protected jurisdictional control. Appointments to posts on the boards of public-sector organizations were supervised by the secretariat of each ministry. In 1997 there were 820 full-time and 229 part-time executive directors, and 519,639 other staff employed (in the then) 88 corporations (MCA 1998c). One estimate is that some 60% of directors had been appointed from among retired bureaucrats, and more than a half of the middle managers had been transferred from supervisory ministries (Inoki 1995: 217).

Public-sector banks and financial corporations, supervised and controlled mainly by MOF, provided a prime source for the placement of retired career and non-career officials. Table 9.5 shows the extent of its patronage in those organizations where it had sole jurisdiction, or shared supervision and control (and hence appointments) with other ministries. Banks and finance corporations employed 90 full-time and 14 part-time executive directors, and 16,721 other staff. In addition, the Japan Tobacco and Salt Company had 30 full-time and three part-time executive directors and a staff of 22,648.

Placements in all those banks and finance corporations, and in other public corporations and companies that were within its jurisdiction, were arranged through its Secretariat, the deputy vice-minister and administrative vice-minister assuming personal responsibility for the placement of retiring directors-general and other senior staff. Taking 1991 as an example, there were 28 *amakudari* officials from MOF holding directors' posts in public corporations. Such appointments were normally made from among headquarters staff, with the rank of director of division or above. In the People's Finance Corporation, MOF *amakudari* held four of the eight directorships, the other four being filled by internal promotion. The president was a former MOF administrative

Table 9.5 *MOF's patronage: public banks and finance corporations, 1997*

	Directorships full-time/ (part-time)	Employees
Public banks and finance corporations		
Sole jurisdiction		
Japan Development Bank	10 (7)	1,102
EXIM Bank	8	560
People's Finance Corporation	8	4,715
TOTAL	26 (7)	6,377
Shared jurisdiction		
Housing Loan Corporation (MOC)	9	1,146
Agriculture, Fisheries, Forestry Finance Corp. (MAFF)	8	926
Small & Medium-Sized Business Credit Corp. (MITI)	6 (1)	405
Japan Finance Corp. for Municipal Enterprises (MHA)	5	74
Hokkaido Development Corporation (HDA)	7 (1)	288
Environmental Sanitation Finance Corp. (MHW)	4 (1)	56
Japan Finance Corp. for Small Businesses (MITI)	8 (1)	1,707
Okinawa Development Finance Corp. (OkDA)	5 (1)	220
Shōkō Chūkin (MITI)	12 (2)	5,522
TOTAL	64 (7)	10,344
TOTAL	90 (14)	16,721
Other public corporations		
Japan Tobacco Inc.	30 (3)	22,648
Amami Islands Fund (NLA)	3 (2)	26
TOTAL	33 (5)	22,674
TOTAL BANKS, PUBLIC FINANCE, AND OTHER CORPORATIONS	123 (19)	39,395

Source: MCA (1998c).

vice-minister; the vice-president, a former senior official of MOF's NTAA, and one of the four directors, formerly the director-general of the Tokyo Tax Bureau. In 1993, 40% of the directorships at the Japan Development Bank and all of those at the Finance Corporation for Municipal Enterprises were held by former MOF bureaucrats. The average for all the public finance corporations was more than 50% (Seirōren 1993).

MOF's patronage extended to other public-sector organizations. For example, from 1977 it monopolized appointments to the post of chairman of the Fair Trade Commission, and for longer still to the presidency of the Tokyo International Financial Futures Exchange. The most senior and prestigious posts in the public sector were 'reserved seats' (*shitei-seki*) for the small, exclusive, and powerful 'family' of former administrative vice-ministers. By negotiation and agreement among themselves, and with the current incumbent, they controlled the succession to the post of president in several leading public organizations. Yamaguchi retired from MOF as administrative vice-minister in 1986, and 'waited' as president of the Japan Centre for International

Finance, a sinecure in a MOF-controlled organization, for his appointment as president of the Export–Import Bank in 1990. Four years later he succeeded to the presidency of the Tokyo Stock Exchange, a post MOF had monopolized from 1967. Until 2000 all such incumbents were former administrative vice-ministers; the appointment in May of that year of Tsuchida Masaaki broke that line of succession, although MOF retained its grip on the presidency: Tsuchida had been Commissioner of the National Tax Administration Agency. Table 9.6 shows the hierarchy of the 'family' posts, and the incumbents with their MOF class dates, at December 1994, the eve of the succession of Matsushita Yasuo (MOF, class of 1950) to the governorship of the Bank of Japan.

Until 1998, appointments to the BOJ governorship were decided by informal agreement between the Bank and MOF, who rotated the nomination. A governor appointed after nomination by the Bank, normally from within its own staff, was followed by a MOF nominee. Thus, at the end of Governor Mieno's tenure in 1994, the MOF 'family' and the Bank of Japan agreed and nominated a MOF candidate acceptable to the Bank. There were four candidates: Yamaguchi, the front-runner; Hirasawa; Yoshino; and Matsushita, then president of the Sakura Bank, brought in to oversee the merger of Mitsui Bank and Taiyo–Kobe Bank in 1990, which two years later became Sakura. After a great deal of politicking, in which Saitō Jirō, MOF's administrative vice-minister, and Mieno, the Bank's governor, played leading roles, Matsushita emerged as a compromise candidate. The Minister of Finance, Takemura Masayoshi, was allegedly strictly neutral, and was persuaded without too much difficulty to agree to his nomination. Yamaguchi was rewarded with the presidency of the Tokyo Stock Exchange; Yoshino stayed on at the JDB, and Hirasawa succeeded to the presidency of the Bank of Yokohama, replacing Tanaka Takashi, MOF administrative vice-minister in 1980–1. Hirasawa's post at the People's Finance Corporation went to Ozaki Mamoru (MOF, class of 1958), administrative vice-minister, 1992–3, and the outstanding candidate from the ranks of the MOF's *rōnin*, those retirees 'on hold', awaiting placement. Yamaguchi's election to the Tokyo Stock Exchange created a vacancy at the EXIM Bank which was filled by another *rōnin*, Yasuda Hiroshi (class of 1957), administrative vice-minister, 1991–2.

MOF's control of those top posts was weakened with the resignation of Governor Matsushita in March 1998, who was obliged to accept formal responsibility for the corrupt behaviour of one of the Bank's senior officials, the head of the Capital Markets Division of the Bank's Credit and Market Management Department. Charged with accepting bribes from commercial banks, the arrest was the first since the Bank's establishment

Table 9.6 *The MOF 'family' of former administrative vice-ministers, 1994*

Bank/public corporation	Former administrative vice-minister
Bank of Japan (governor)	Mieno Yasushi (BOJ)
Tokyo Stock Exchange (president)	Nagaoka Minoru (1947)
EXIM Bank (president)	Yamaguchi Mitsuhide (1951)
Japan Development Bank (president)	Yoshino Yoshihiko (1953)
OECF (president)	Nishigaki Akira (1953)
People's Finance Corporation (president)	Hirasawa Sadaaki (1955)

in 1882. In the inquiry that followed, the Bank revealed the close links between its supervision of banks and financial institutions, and the employment of its retired officials: 72 of 146 retirees were employed in financial institutions, 11 of whom had been offered posts either a year before or a year after the Bank's Supervision Department had conducted a formal contractual inspection; 36 former officials in that department were employed in credit banks. With the damning evidence of conflict of interest, the LDP and Opposition parties publicly opposed the appointment as governor of any candidate who had served as an official in either the Bank or MOF. The government intervened decisively to block the appointment of the deputy-governor, next in line through the practice of rotation. The new governor was an outsider, Hayami Masaru, president of Nisshō Iwai Corporation, who had served on the Bank's board of governors from 1978 to 1981. The vacant deputy-governorship was filled by another outsider, Fujiwara Sakuya, a writer and journalist.

MOF's own *amakudari* practice was similarly subjected to exposure and public scrutiny with the arrest in January 1998 of one of its former officials, director of finance at the Japan Highway Public Corporation, charged with accepting bribes from the Industrial Bank of Japan and Normura Securities. MOF announced a 'drastic review' of the practice of *amakudari*, involving both the MCA and the National Personnel Authority.

Retirement into Politics

The third main employment option open to those senior officials retiring from the public service was to seek election to one of the Diet's two houses. The number of ex-bureaucrats elected as LDP Dietmen since the Second World War has been significant. On average, they have accounted for nearly a quarter of LDP members in the House of Representatives, and a third of all LDP councillors in the Upper House. Most of them had been re-elected several times. In 1986, 26 ran for the first time for the House of Representatives and 11 were successful. However, those included two former administrative vice-ministers, a director-general, and four division directors. Retired bureaucrats elected to the House of Representatives tended to be very senior, and drawn mainly from MOF, MITI, and MAFF. According to one MITI official, sheer numbers were not so important. 'As long as there are about five who will back the ministry after being elected, that's enough' (*Nikkei Weekly*, 27 January 1997). In the House of Councillors, successful candidates from among retired bureaucrats were older and more senior still. Table 9.7 shows the total numbers, and those for MOF bureaucrats.

From the 1960s, MOF had consistently the largest number of ex-bureaucrats in the House of Representatives, twice as many as any other ministry. From 1979 it provided almost 40% of the total number. Almost all of them were elected for the LDP. In the 1990 election more than a quarter of the LDP's 281 seats were held by former bureaucrats, with former MOF bureaucrats taking 10% of the total. In the Upper House the distribution of ex-bureaucrats was more evenly shared between MOF, MOC, MHA, and MAFF.

Close links with senior officials in the LDP were often established well before retirement, providing regular opportunities for both formal and informal contact. The

Table 9.7 MOF bureaucrats in the Diet, 1966–1997

	House of Representatives					House of Councillors					Diet totals				
	1966	1979	1986	1992	1997	1966	1979	1986	1992	1997	1966	1979	1986	1992	1997
MOF	14	20	26	27	24	6	7	8	1	2	20	27	34	28	26
(All bureaucrats)	(71)	(53)	(74)	(69)	(67)	(45)	(37)	(42)	(41)	(40)	(116)	(90)	(116)	(110)	(107)
% of total	20	38	35	39	36	13	19	15	2.5	5	17.1	30	29	25	24.3

Source: Secretarial Division, Minister's Secretariat, MOF, 1997.

legislative and scrutiny work of the Diet and its committees provided further occasions, as did MOF's formal involvement with the LDP's PARC divisions and, informally, with leading and influential members of the latter, and *zoku*. During the formulation of the Budget, and before its submission to the Diet, contact between Budget Bureau officials and senior party officials was institutionalized. Also, some young officials had links with the LDP through (often arranged) marriages to the daughters of Dietmen; and sometimes officials inherited or were bequeathed the seats of their fathers-in-law on death or retirement, and retired from the Ministry to enter the Diet. Most had held prominent positions in the Budget Bureau or the Tax Bureau, evidence of the importance the LDP attached to those policy areas. Many went on to hold key positions within the party and government. Murayama Tatsuo, formerly director-general of the Tax Bureau in 1950–3, left to enter politics, and in the 1980s became chairman of the LDP's powerful Tax System Research Council. Between 1960 and 1980, three out of eight prime ministers, and six out of eleven ministers of finance began their careers in MOF. More recently, Prime Minister Miyazawa (1991–3) had been a MOF bureaucrat before entering the Diet, as had Fuji Hirosha, minister of finance in the Hosokawa Coalition.

A 1983 survey found that 60% of bureaucrats in the national public service who had graduated from Tokyo University supported the LDP, compared with 37% in the population at large (Koh 1989). The consistent and persistent trend of movement between MOF and LDP was evidence of broadly shared political values, at least up until 1993. It ensured that most MOF bureaucrats worked within established guidelines of which they generally approved.

The strong flow of MOF officers into the LDP did much to prevent the erosion of the power of the MOF in its attempts to deregulate financial markets in the 1970s ... It established a trust, within a broad set of political values or a broad ideological framework, which enabled the MOF to go about much of its business unhindered by overt political interference. Communication channels between the MOF and LDP were strengthened by the entry of former MOF personnel, and sympathetic hearings were guaranteed. (Horne 1985: 203)

After 1993, however, shared values and common interests were strained by the LDP's sustained critical attack on MOF's purpose, functions, and organization, and its management of economic and financial policy-making, discussed in the previous chapter. The causes and consequences of the changing relationships between them, and MOF's declining power and prestige, are examined in later chapters.

10

The LDP's Policy-Making Structures

The LDP's Constitution prescribes that all proposed legislation and policies adopted by the party must first be examined and approved by the party before submission to the Cabinet and the Diet. The Policy Affairs Research Council (Seimu Chōsakai) is charged with 'studying, researching and planning party policies' (Article 39, LDP Party Rules). The Council was the party's central policy-making body throughout the last quarter of the twentieth century. Its chairman was one of the party's five senior leaders—the president (and prime minister when the LDP is the ruling party), the vice-president, the chairman of the Executive Council, and the secretary-general were the others. Their positions in the party hierarchy, and that of the Policy Affairs Research Council in relation to the LDP's other organizational structures in the 1990s, are shown in Figure 10.1.

Appointments to both senior and junior party posts were normally made by agreement between the leaders of the various formal party factions, and broadly reflected their numerical strength. Cabinet and other ministerial posts were distributed similarly, with seniority measured by the number of successive re-elections to the Diet. As the turnover of both party and government posts was high, there was a large group of party elders, some of whom were also leaders of factions or, like Takeshita in the 1990s, remained influential within them. Elders and senior party leaders provided initiative, guidance, management, coordination, and control in the party's policy-making. This chapter examines their role and influence in the LDP's formal policy-making structures, together with the contribution made by the rank-and-file Dietmen, and the role played outside those structures by informal policy-tribes (*zoku-giin*). It provides the general context for the discussion in later chapters of the LDP's role and influence specifically in those policy-making processes through which budgets were made and carried out. The focus is mainly on the LDP in the period 1975–93, and again in 1996–2000. The changes in the policy-making structures and processes that occurred during the period of multi-party governments are discussed briefly towards the end of the chapter.

THE POLICY AFFAIRS RESEARCH COUNCIL (PARC)

PARC had a Policy Deliberation Commission (Seisaku Shingi-kai), and beneath it 17 divisions (*bukai*), corresponding roughly to the number and policy areas of the principal ministries and agencies. Divisions had numerous specialist sub-committees. There were also regional development committees, research commissions, special committees, and research societies, and numerous study groups set up ad hoc to study and report on particular policy issues. Membership of PARC divisions was determined

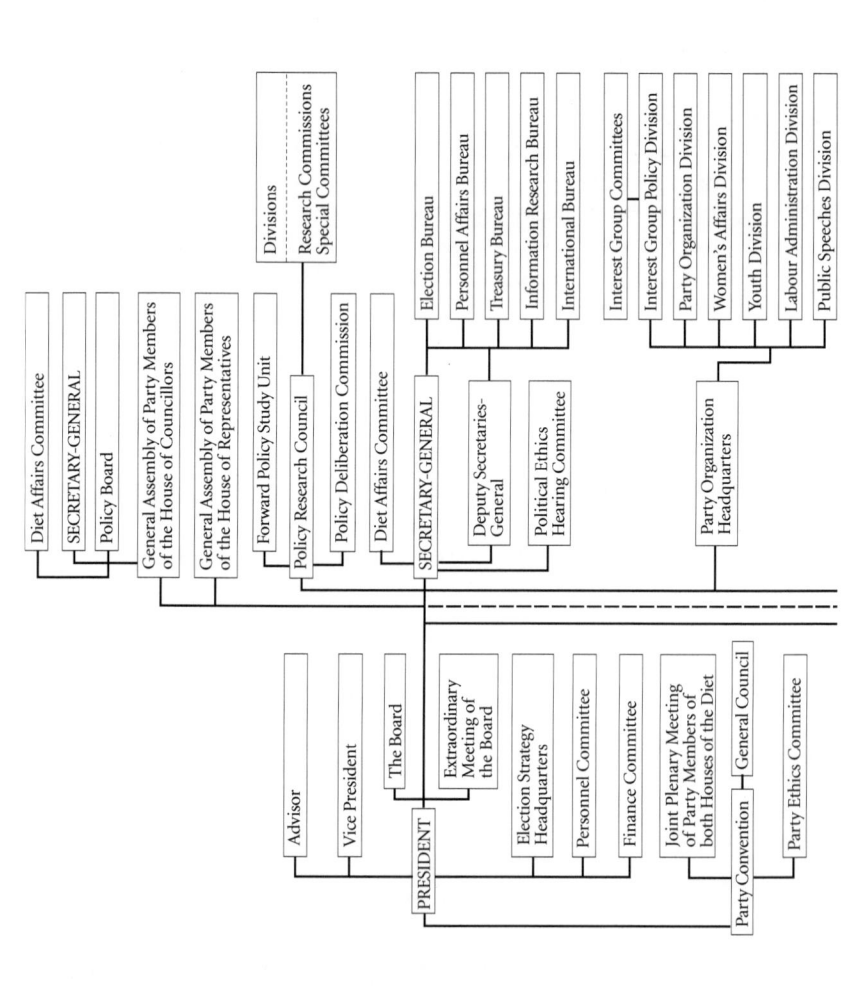

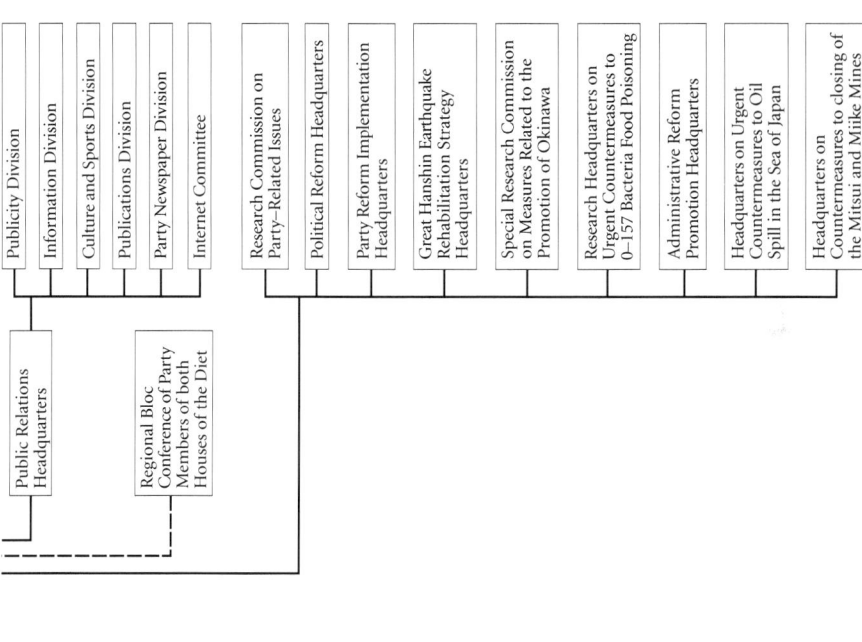

Figure 10.1 *Organization of the LDP, 1999*

Source: LDP headquarters, 1999.

partly by the interests of individual Dietmen, and partly by the control exercised by the leadership. After serving at least one completed term, LDP Dietmen normally belonged to four divisions, two of which reflected their membership of parallel Diet standing committees, also controlled by the leadership. LDP members normally also joined PARC research committees and other special party committees, societies, and leagues, and tended to specialize in areas related to those of their PARC divisions. Figure 10.2 shows the LDP's policy-making bodies in 1999.

Membership of PARC divisions can be co-related with policy outputs measured in terms of the regulations, licenses, and permits issued by ministries and agencies, and with budget benefits. The two most popular divisions were Agriculture and Construction; MAFF and MOC were both responsible for large numbers of ministerial regulations (see Table 4.1) and were a traditional source of budget benefits through agricultural subsidies, and local and regional public works projects. The PARC Division on Agriculture and Fisheries had over 200 members in 1985. The least popular divisions shadowed those ministries with the smallest budgets, and which issued fewest regulations, for example the Prime Minister's Office, MCA, EPA. PARC divisions such as Agriculture, Construction, and Commerce and Industry, together with Social Affairs, Transport, and Communications, were attractive to LDP Dietmen concerned with the local interests of their constituencies, the promotion of the local interests of special interest groups, and the maintenance of personal electoral networks. Such was the popularity of the Construction Division, and the PARC Research Commission for Roads, that Dietmen could not join them in their first term of office. Membership of other research commissions and special committees was discretionary. In the 1980s nearly two-thirds of LDP Dietmen from both Houses were members of the Research Commission on Comprehensive Agriculture Policy.

The activities of PARC divisions were coordinated and, where necessary, controlled by the party leadership. Formally, the draft legislation and policy proposals prepared in the ministries and agencies, including those for annual budgetary allocations, were submitted to the relevant divisions, and after consideration by them to the Policy Deliberation Commission, which gave final approval before submission to PARC itself, and then the Executive Council of the party. The Commission had 20 members, 15 from the House of Representatives and 5 from the House of Councillors; most were veteran Dietmen with experience in the Cabinet, and as PARC divisional chairmen. At its twice-weekly meetings, the chairman and vice-chairman of each division explained the purpose and context of their policy proposals. Officials from the Spending Ministries attended when draft legislation was brought forward. Normally meetings went 'very smoothly', according to one acting chairman of PARC. Decoded, that means that business was conducted and decided formally and briefly, the substantive issues having been discussed and agreements concluded earlier through *nemawashi* (Hori 1995). Revised, amended, or confirmed proposals were then forwarded to PARC, and from there to the Executive Council for formal approval. PARC's chairman attended its twice-weekly meetings. Occasionally the Executive Council intervened decisively in a policy issue. For example, it overruled proposals from the party's welfare specialists, preferring a politically expedient free system of medical care for the elderly to that of limited subsidization, which had been

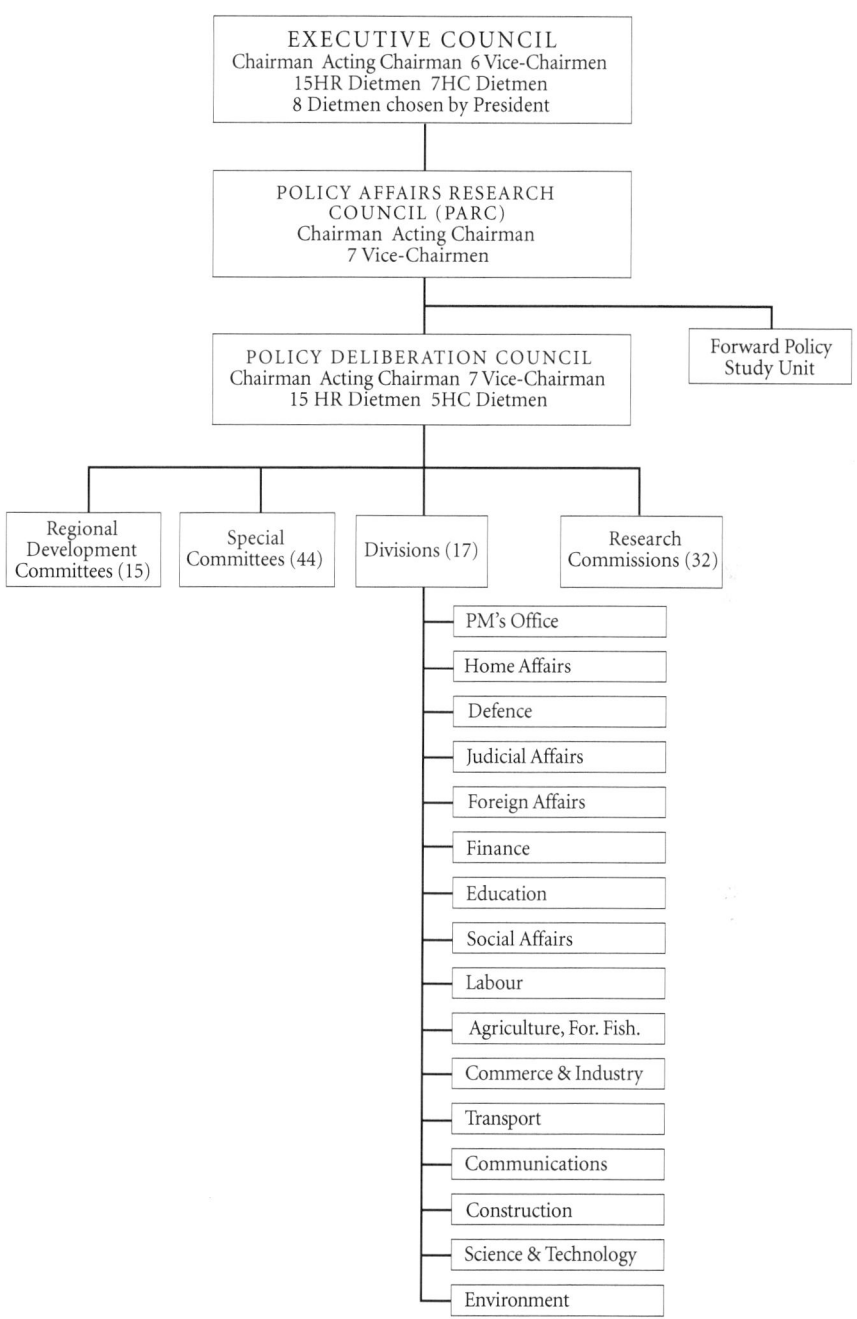

Figure 10.2 *LDP's policy-making bodies, 1975–2000*
Source: LDP headquarters, 2000.

recommended on the grounds of cost (Campbell 1993). More normally, the Executive Council gave its seal of party approval without substantive discussion.

As one of the five most important party posts, the chairmanship of PARC was a stepping-stone to the presidency, and hence to the post of prime minister. Of the prime ministers who held office up to Kaifu, only Kishi had not been chairman of either PARC or the Executive Council; Prime Minister Hashimoto (1996–8) was chairman of PARC during the Hata Coalition in 1994 (see Table 10.1 for details of his other party posts). Prime Minister Obuchi, however, never held the post, although he had been secretary-general, like his successor Mori Yasuhiro.

The key official of PARC, however, was not the chairman, but the acting chairman, the senior of the numerous vice-chairmen. He presided in the absence of the chairman, but more crucially played the central role in the coordination of all PARC's policy-making, presiding over meetings of the Deliberation Commission. In his hands were gathered the threads of all the policies discussed, and recommendations made, by each division, research commission, and special committee. He was the main source of policy advice and guidance for the bureaucrats from all ministries and agencies, and for his ministerial colleagues in the Spending Ministries. Familiar with the whole range of PARC activities, he could steer the course to be taken to best promote and protect the party's interests in the light of its current objectives and strategy, taking into account the pressures from rank-and-file members, and from major interest groups, many of whom contributed to party funds (Hori 1995).

The position of acting chairman normally led to the chairmanship and membership of the party's top leadership, a post for a rising, experienced, politician able to move easily in and between the worlds of politics and bureaucracy. He needed not only the authority of his office, but the skills of persuasion and cajolery to effect agreements and secure compromises between PARC divisions, commissions, and committees whose policy jurisdictions overlapped and frequently conflicted, mirroring those of the ministries and agencies they shadowed. Close, frequent contact with ministers was essential, to keep them apprised of policy discussions within PARC, to alert them to potential difficulties, and to secure their support for compromise agreements.

PARC was a private party organization, but became formally integrated into the public policy-making processes. (Fukui, 1987, provides a general account of its earlier policy-making role.) Although not legally required to do so, officials from the ministries and agencies attended meetings of divisions and their sub-committees to explain and discuss their policy proposals and draft legislation. Meetings of divisions, and of the numerous commissions, committees, study groups, and working parties, fulfilled an educative role in briefing party members about policy issues, and provided opportunities for the development of relationships between LDP members and bureaucrats that were of mutual benefit to both. Participation also helped LDP Dietmen to be better prepared for the defence of the party's policy, and its bills in parallel standing committees in the Diet. Through appointments to chairs, they also provided opportunities for LDP Dietmen to progress through the party, acquiring experience, status, and the potential for formal and informal influence in policy-making.

The chairman and vice-chairman of each PARC division were chosen by the chairman of PARC from among those who had served at least three terms in the Lower

LDP's Policy-Making Structures

House, or two terms in the House of Councillors. Division chairmen normally served *ex officio* as the Whips of the corresponding Diet standing committees. The most important role of the chairman of a PARC division was to reconcile the interests of his members with those of the bureaucrats in the relevant Spending Ministry, and to achieve a consensus, consistent with the broader policy interests of the party. There was necessarily a great deal of informal discussion, consultation, and ground-clearing at various different levels within the party and the bureaucracy (Hori 1995; Obuchi 1995; Kondō 1994). As the party publicly admitted,

> in many cases ministry staff will meet with individual members of the division in an attempt to build a consensus before official deliberation of the division. Because of this custom, little dispute on policy matters surfaces within the division's meetings. (LDP 1993)

Increasingly from the 1970s onwards, many divisions began to play a more proactive role, instead of merely reacting to proposals initiated by a ministry's policy divisions. Some, like the PARC Education Division, began to take the initiative in policy-making, forming small 'project teams' and sub-committees to develop party positions on key issues. Their stream of reports 'gave the [education] *zoku* the policy-making initiative for virtually the whole period' of the 1970s and 1980s (Schoppa 1991*b*: 94). Similar project teams to develop policy proposals were set up by most other PARC divisions (Yamazaki 1986).

Some of the party's research commissions and committees became increasingly powerful. The LDP Tax Policy Research Committee was perhaps the most influential (even more so than the government's Tax Policy Research Council), with a membership of more than half of the LDP's total Dietmen. The chairman, acting chairman, 14 vice-chairmen, and 7 secretaries comprised an 'inner group' responsible for 'all the substantial decisions on tax policy made inside the LDP' (Katō Junko 1994: 96). Among its routine tasks were the coordination and balancing of backbench requests, mostly made on behalf of various interest groups and constituents—for tax-breaks within the framework of the anticipated need for additional revenues. Each December it discussed tax policy for the following financial year. More importantly, it played a leading role in the various attempts in the 1980s to introduce a consumption tax (Katō Junko 1994).

Formal and informal links between bureaucrats and politicians through the mechanism of PARC were an integral, customary, and crucial component of policy-making. The difficulty is knowing how to weight them; the empirical evidence is remarkably thin. Most studies of the party system describe the formal mechanisms of PARC, but are silent on the influence that the party exercised through them in particular policy areas (see e.g. Curtis 1988; Hrebenar 1992). Ramseyer and Rosenbluth (1993) assert that PARC division 'members use their committee positions to induce the bureaucracy to modify policy to promote their individual electoral needs' (p. 32). That and similar generalizations need qualifying to take account of the differential strength and influence of particular PARC divisions, commissions, and committees, the stage in the policy cycle at which the attempt to influence is exercised, and the particularity of policy issues. For example, in the formulation of policy to regulate the banks in the 1980s, PARC's Public Finance Committee and the Financial Issues Study Group combined to defeat MOF's proposals on disclosure requirements, on lending limits, and on bank management. Much of the proposed bill was re-drafted by the two committees in joint sessions. This represented an LDP *volte face*. Having initially supported MOF against the banks, it now changed sides. 'For favourable revisions in the MOF's banking bill, banks allegedly paid to individual influential LDP politicians 500 million yen in unreported gifts over the usual contributions' (Rosenbluth 1989: 131).

Not all PARC divisions were motivated by consideration of personal electoral advantage, or such favours. For example, Schoppa (1991*a*) found the PARC Education Division in the mid-1980s composed of politicians with secure electoral bases, unconcerned with 'money' and 'votes'. They did not intervene with ministry officials on behalf of sectional interest groups. Instead, with 'burning convictions', they pushed for the adoption of LDP policies. Secondly, while division members might attempt to persuade bureaucrats to modify policy, success varied with the stage of the policy cycle: they were more likely to succeed at the stage of implementation, when projects were being allocated by individual bureaux in a Spending Ministry, than earlier when policy was being formulated. For example, there was little evidence that either senior or junior LDP politicians paid sustained attention to the formulation of ODA policy. Their attention and influence were directed more to the allocation of contracts at the implementation stage. Generally their interventions were 'more in the nature of rent seeking than serious deliberations over substantive policy principles' (Arase 1994: 194).

Thirdly, the LDP often had no unified policy in a particular sector, responding to policy issues ad hoc on a case-by-case basis. Of the sixty or so members of the PARC Special Committee on Overseas Economic Cooperation, only a handful were really active. 'Meetings at which high ranking bureaucrats must appear are irregular and consequently there appears to be no systematised oversight. When officials are invited, it is usually during times of scandal.' A MITI official admitted: 'We get very little interference' (Orr 1990: 22). Even after the Committee initiated a number of research projects in the 1980s to examine the amount and distribution of aid to third world countries, MOFA continued to enjoy a free hand in ODA policy-making. 'It does what it wants. It hasn't reached a stage yet where Foreign Ministry people are called in and the Committee tells them what it wants. It is more a report after the fact that aid was given to country X' (Yasutomo 1986: 67). The Committee's principal role was to serve as an information window for the LDP on current policy debates between the bureaucracy and the private sector (Arase 1994). Fourthly, the LDP was often content to maintain a bureaucratic-regulated system in some policy sectors, or for some policy functions within them, e.g. the initiation of new policy, the canvassing of options. For example, the PARC Commerce and Industry Division was wide-ranging, with numerous research and special committees. Even so, there were in MITI policy divisions, even whole bureaux, which excited little interest or attention from LDP politicians. One example is the Quality of Life and Culture Division of MITI's Industries Bureau, set up as the result of a MITI policy initiative in 1993 (Seki 1994); another, the Standards Bureau of the Agency for Science and Technology (Tanaka Masami 1994). However, a general lack of political interest, or indifference, could change over time, depending upon the particularity of circumstance and issue. More broadly, the interests and involvement of PARC divisions in policy-making varied with the politico-electoral salience of a policy area.

LDP's Policy-Making Structures

Relationships between bureaucrats and PARC division were both formal and informal. Formally, each division received drafts of proposed legislation, and new or revised policy initiatives from a Spending Ministry, but it also had informal meetings with those directors of divisions, and their superiors, the bureau director-general and deputy directors-general, to hear explanations, discuss details, and consider implications. Subsequently, in the Diet the same officials would be examined in committee on the substance and details of each bill.

Informal links with individual members of PARC divisions were more important than presentations at formal meetings of divisions. At early stages of the initiation of new policy proposals or legislation, divisional directors and their bureau directors-general met informally with the chairmen, vice-chairmen, and other senior, influential members of the PARC division to outline and discuss policy options, and explain bureau positions and preferences. Pre-notification and consultation provided opportunities for an exchange of views to ensure that what was sent formally to PARC had at least been aired, perhaps even pre-negotiated. Those ground-clearing consultations might or might not have resulted in substantial revision to policy proposals; the evidence is hard to come by. But the opportunity existed for bureaucrats to argue the case for their policies, and for politicians to express concern or reservations if they doubted their acceptability to the party as a whole, or the narrower interests represented on a PARC division. In framing their proposals, bureaucrats had already considered and perhaps taken into account the probable reaction of those PARC politicians with whom they habitually dealt, and the acceptability to them of what they were proposing.

Informal networks of politicians, bureaucrats, and private-sector interests ensured that embryonic ideas, options, and firmed-up proposals were tested informally against the probable or anticipated reaction of individual politicians and others affected. As well, bureaucrats brought forward their proposals knowing the general stance of the government/party on an issue or policy area. What they proposed was informed and constrained by the contours of the general policy framework laid down by it or, where there was no such explicit framework, by the attitudes, preferences, and predilections articulated by senior party officials, or simply their unspoken but known assumptions and premises. Of course, bureaucrats might have had some/much influence on the design of such a policy framework, where for example a new policy initiative or change of direction had been signalled by the report of a ministry's advisory council, and accepted by the Cabinet, or where a report of an LDP research committee had led to the adoption of new policy guidelines by the party, the initiative for which might have originated with one or more of the Spending Ministries.

The extent to which frequent interaction through informal links, complemented by the formal hearings and meetings, contributed to an 'alliance' between a PARC division and its ministry or agency is a matter of empirical investigation. It varied between divisions, at different stages of the policy cycle, and over particular issues. They were, however, allied in maximizing the allocation of budget resources, albeit for some-times different reasons. I say more about that, and the other issues touched on here, in Chapter 20.

Informal links between bureaucrats in the policy divisions of Spending Ministries and Agencies and those individual, rank-and-file PARC division Dietmen representing the interests of particular organized groups or clients were only one of several mechanisms for such groups seeking to influence policy outputs from particular ministerial policy divisions. For example, there is evidence that LDP politicians attempted to influence the allocation of contracts in the implementation of policy for public works, construction, and ODA. Success varied, depending on the intimacy and regularity of their relationships with individual bureaucrats and the mutual benefits, i.e. what the Dietmen could contribute through expertise and special knowledge, for example rank-and-file opinion, local circumstances, and so on; their status and seniority in the party; and the degree of respect and weight the bureaucrat had to give to the views expressed. Arase (1994: 182) contends that 'in some cases, a politician has been able to shepherd a project request through the entire process' of an ODA contract.

THE LDP'S POLICY TRIBES (*ZOKU-GIIN*)

The argument that the role and influence of the LDP in policy-making had increased from the early 1970s is invariably supported by reference to the emergence of so-called policy tribes, *zoku-giin*, although opinion differs on whether they were a contributory cause or a symptom (Nihon Keizai Shinbun Seijibu 1983; Satō and Matsuzaki 1986; Yusasa 1986; Inoguchi and Iwai 1987; Itagaki 1987; Schoppa, 1991*b*). There is evidence of *zoku* influence in some areas of policy-making in the 1960s, or even earlier (Muramatsu 1993; Campbell 1993).

A *zoku* comprised a number of LDP Diet members 'who have a considerable amount of expertise and practical experience about a particular area of government policy and enough seniority in the party to have influence on a continuing basis with the ministry responsible for that policy area' (Curtis 1988: 114). *Zoku* were not formal LDP organizations with formal memberships. Although there was a close identify of interests, and overlapping membership, *zoku* were distinguishable from PARC and its divisions. *Zoku* status was earned or attributed to those senior LDP members who had 'acquired significant influence in a specific policy area through service in numerous party and Cabinet positions related to that area' (Schoppa 1991*b*: 82). Progression through a series of senior posts in PARC divisions, and corresponding Diet committees, and appointments at junior and senior ministerial level, was characteristic of those LDP Diet members with *zoku* status. Inoguchi and Iwai (1987) identified 21 members of the education *zoku*, all but two of whom had held office as vice-chairman and chairman of the PARC Education Division; most had served as director or chairman of the Diet Education Committee, and a few had been both. Most had served as parliamentary vice ministers in the Ministry of Education; eight had held Cabinet office as minister of education. However, it was the length of tenure on party or Diet committees in a specific policy area, rather than the number of such posts held, that was a better indicator of policy expertise, according to Richardson (1997).

The career progression of Hashimoto Ryūtarō, elected to the House of Representatives in 1963 and re-elected 11 times up to 1996, shows the key stages in the making of a prominent member of the welfare *zoku* (Table 10.1).

The role and influence of a *zoku* were related to its numerical strength relative to the LDP as a whole; its composition—whether it represented one, some, or several

Table 10.1 The making of a welfare zoku boss: the career of Hashimoto Kyutaro

	LDP policy posts	Diet posts	Ministerial posts
1970			Parliamentary vice-minister, Health and Welfare (1970–1)
1972	Director, PARC Social Affairs Division (1972–4)		
1974	*Deputy-chairman, LDP Ad Hoc Committee on Pensions		
	*Deputy-chairman, PARC Welfare Division		
	*Deputy-chairman, PARC (1974–6)		
1976		*Chairman, Social Affairs Standing Committee (1976–8), House of Representatives	
1978	*Chairman, Pharmaceuticals Subcommittee, PARC Social Affairs Division		*Minister of Health and Welfare (1978–9)
1979	*Acting chairman, LDP Research Commission on Fundamental Policies for Medical Care		
1980	Chairman, LDP Research Commission on Public Administration and Finance, PARC (1980–6)		
1980	*Deputy-chairman, LDP Research Commission on Social Security		
1984	*Chairman, LDP Research Commission on Fundamental Policies for Medical Care (1984–6)		
1986			Minister of Transport (1986–7)
1987	*Acting secretary-general (1987–9)		
1988			
1989	Secretary-general		
1989			Minister of Finance (1989–91)
1993	Chairman, LDP Research Commission on Environment		
1993	Chairman, PARC (1993–4)		
1994			Minister of International Trade and Industry (Murayama Coalition) (1994–6)
1995	President, LDP (1995–8)		Deputy PM (1995–6)
1996			Prime Minister (1996–8)
2000			Minister for Administrative Reform (Mori Government)

*Key post for zoku status.

factions; the seniority and status of its members; access to the LDP leadership; special knowledge and expertise, and the extent and quality of relationships with senior policy officials in the relevant ministry.

Zoku were identifiable for each of the 17 policy areas shadowed by PARC divisions. Their size, and their role and influence in the policy-making process, varied. In the 1980s the agriculture *zoku*, for example, represented

> the LDP's inner party Cabinet on agricultural matters. They act as a direct channel for MAFF proposals into the party and engage in extensive behind-the-scenes negotiations with all major participants in the agricultural policy process. They are prime movers in moulding the party consensus on agricultural policy, working hard to obtain agreement amongst members of agricultural committees before they actually sit. (George 1988: 120)

Table 10.2 presents a classification of the relative strengths of *zoku* in different policy sectors from 1975 to 1993, based on assessments by bureaucrats and senior politicians interviewed by the author. There was no budget *zoku* as such, but there was a 'public finance tribe' (*zaisei zoku*), and a 'tax tribe' (*zeisei zoku*).

Zoku had both formal and informal roles and opportunities for influence in the policy processes. As members or office-holders of PARC divisions, they had the opportunity formally and informally to influence policy proposals brought forward by the policy divisions of Spending Ministries, as described earlier. Some more senior *zoku* members also chaired and convened PARC research commissions and special committees, to design party policy in a particular area. Informally, *zoku* members developed and exploited relationships with senior bureaucrats in their policy area, and sought to influence the determination of policy options both before and after formal positions were taken up at PARC division meetings, and in proceedings of Diet committees.

Zoku played several different roles in the policy-making processes, mostly within their policy area, but also from time to time more broadly across policy areas. Within the jurisdiction of a ministry, acting as sympathetic 'guard dogs', they promoted policy proposals emerging from the bureaucracy, and cooperated with officials to protect its turf from the encroachment of other ministries (Inoguchi and Iwai 1987). Here support, and the promotion and protection of the ministry's interests, might conflict more broadly with the

Table 10.2 *The role and influence of zoku-giin on sectoral policy-making, 1975–1993*

Very strong	Strong	Medium	Weak/embryonic	Non-existent
Agriculture	Welfare	ODA	Science and Technology	Economic Planning
Telecommunications (*tsūshin zoku; nyū media zoku*)	Education Defence Transport	Labour	Environment Finance	Justice PM's Office
Construction			Public Service Industry	Public Service Management
	Commerce and Industry			
Postal (*yūsei zoku*)			Foreign Affairs	Home Affairs

LDP's Policy-Making Structures

interests of the LDP leadership in promoting policy change, or attempts to reconcile the overlapping and competing interests of several ministries. In the 1980s the postal *zoku*, especially its 'don' Kanemaru Shin, played a prominent role in protecting MPT's turf from encroachment by a MOF intent on ending the system of multiple postal deposits.

Where policy issues transcended the jurisdiction of several ministries, *zoku* often played a similar role, seeking to influence the outcome most favourable to its ministry's interests. In the 1980s, MAFF's interest in protecting the agricultural production of raw silk from foreign imports was supported by vigorous lobbying by the agriculture *zoku*, against MITI's interest in providing its clientele of small and medium-sized manufacturers of silk products with cheaper imports backed by the industry and commerce *zoku*, and against MOFA's concern to avoid a damaging trade dispute following import control (Zhao 1993).

Zoku played a very different role as 'hunting dogs', using their influence both formally and informally in attempts to modify, change, or nullify policy proposals sponsored by their ministry's officials (Inoguchi and Iwai 1987). Normally, when they did so they represented or acted on behalf of the interests of sectional groups. For example, four *zoku* leaders of the 'social labour' specialists among LDP Dietmen had close ties and frequent contact with 21 interest groups representing a broad range of managers, practitioners, clients, and parents of the needy (Anderson 1993: 99). At the height of the battles over Value Added Networks (VANs) and the privatization of NTT in the 'Telecom Wars', representatives of domestic computer manufacturers made almost daily calls on the leading postal *zoku*; most were substantial contributors to LDP funds (Johnson 1989). The influence of the powerful agricultural *zoku* was evident in the Cabinet's approval in 1994 of a large ad hoc subsidy to rice growers, much greater than that reluctantly agreed by MOF with MAFF as a *quid pro quo* for the opening of the rice market under the GATT Uruguay Round.

A third role played by some senior *zoku* members was that of mediator, seeking to reconcile the different interests of bureaucrats in their ministry, factions in the LDP, rank-and-file members, and sectional interest groups. Here their role was not that of a neutral umpire or arbitrator: rather, they tried to build consensus and support for a compromise, hopefully most favourable to the policy position of their ministry, or an interest group. The defence *zoku* became more influential in the 1980s, partly because of changes in its composition and size, which facilitated access to and contacts with faction leaders and the top leadership. It was also more influential because of the greater politico-economic salience of defence issues, as the USA put greater pressure on Japan to increase defence spending after the Soviet Union invaded Afghanistan in 1979. One consequence of that pressure was more tension in the policy-making processes, as other political parties opposed an increase in defence spending, and as MOF sought budgetary restraints following the adoption of the policy of fiscal reconstruction. To influence policies for increased defence spending, access to the top LDP leadership was crucial. In alliance with the Defence Agency, defence *zoku* canvassed their support; but in 1980 the leadership was concerned more with longer-term party and electoral interests, and acted to restrain pressures from *zoku* and rank-and-file Dietmen for increased defence spending, which it feared would lose it seats at general elections.

Defence issues throughout the 1980s were determined largely through the budgetary processes, and *zoku* were normally in alliance or supportive of the policy stance taken up by the Defence Agency, rather than seeking to change bureaucrats' policy preferences. Because of the multiplicity of players and interests in defence policies—both MOF and MITI had direct interests, and some control through their appointees in the Defence Agency—and the political salience and sensitivity of the defence issue in Japanese politics, consensus was necessary but difficult to achieve. *Zoku* helped both to shape the consensus and to articulate it, consulting widely among the interests, and mediating among contending groups within LDP factions, and among the rank-and-file membership (Keddell 1993). In 1982 it supported the Defence Agency's successful bid to obtain from MOF a 'special framework' and priority status for defence spending, conducting extensive consultations throughout the party, the bureaucracy, and interest groups (see Chapter 15).

The extent to which a policy-tribe influenced policy-making within its policy sphere has two dimensions: first, its influence relative to that of the bureaucracy, the extent to which it rather than the bureaucracy shaped the policy output; and secondly, its influence relative to the LDP as a whole. From his study of the influence of the education *zoku* on the reform policies of the 1970s and 1980s, Schoppa (1991*b*) concluded that its main role was as the Ministry's guard-dog, limiting the attempts of Prime Minister Nakasone to assert his leadership in the education sphere. But, at the same time, the policy of fiscal restraint embraced by the LDP leadership constrained the ability of the education *zoku* to develop and implement many of its own reform proposals. 'The result was a set of reform policies that represented the least common denominator,' i.e. was acceptable to both sets of protagonists (p. 101).

In practice, the two main roles of *zoku* were inseparable—indeed, often indistinguishable. Seeking to change the policy preferences of bureaucrats, *zoku* might act simultaneously to protect the interests of sectional groups, where those conflicted with those preferences. The role of *zoku* was primarily the promotion and protection of the interests of such groups, on whom over the years the party had come to rely for electoral campaign funds and votes.

Zoku, however powerful and however independent of their ministries, are essentially sectional. They contribute to the influence of the LDP in the policy process *within their sector*, but— whether they are 'guard dog' *zoku* or 'hunting dog' *zoku*—serve sectional interests and therefore reduce the ability of LDP leaders to mediate between competing priorities and establish a central direction for the nation's policy. (Schoppa 1991*b*: 103)

'The Profit-Inspired' Nexus: Zoku, Spending Ministries, and Interest Groups

Zoku, Spending Ministries, and special interest groups were bound together in triangular sets of interdependent exchange relationships: the currency of the exchange was 'profit-inspired', benefits of money, votes, and favours. There were five main elements: (1) budget benefits, such as contracts, subsidies, grants, tax reliefs; (2) political donations to LDP factions; (3) the acquisition of political and policy information; (4) the mobilization of electoral support; and (5) relief of dispensation from legislative regulations and decrees. The reciprocal obligations of the three sets of players are shown in Table 10.3.

Table 10.3 *Reciprocal obligations of Spending Ministries, zoku-giin and interest groups*

Need	Supply
Spending Ministries	
Support for policy and legislation in the Diet	Legislative benefits for special interests
Specialist information and policy expertise	Relief from legislative regulations, decrees, and ordinances
Political information	Budget benefits; tax reliefs
Support for policy and legislation among special interest groups	Recognition and conferment of favoured status on specific interest groups, clients
Zoku	
Political donations (personal and factional).	Specialist policy and political information and expertise
Votes	Influence and support for ministries in the passing of legislation
Policy benefits, favours	
Recognition and status by Spending Ministries	Support and protection for ministries in jurisdictional competition and conflict
	Mediation and 'brokerage' between interest groups and Spending Ministries
	Representation for special interest groups, constituents
Special interest groups	
Favourable legislation	Political donations
Relief and benefits from legislative regulations	Employment
Financial benefits: subsidies, grants, tax breaks	Information
	Mobilized political support
Protection and promotion of special interests	
Recognition and status	

The 'profit-inspired' nexus of the triangular relationships became stronger as the economy grew in the 1960s. Annual and sustained double-digit economic growth provided simultaneously for increasing tax revenues, tax reductions, and increased spending. Spending Ministries competed in a positive-sum game for shares of the expanding budgets of both the General Account and FILP, and called upon *zoku* (and PARC divisions), many of whom at that time were ex-bureaucrats, for support in their budget requests. Concurrently, LDP faction-leaders, especially Tanaka Kakuei, were building formidable electoral machines in the constituencies, the costs of expensive personal support groups (*kōenkai*) financed by political donations from national and international companies and businesses on the one hand, and local businesses on the other. Factions competed to raise money, their ability to do so an indication of the power and esteem of their leaders, and a determinant of career progression to the second Cabinet

Table 10.4 *The 'profit-inspired' nexus: a typology of zoku-giin*

Benefits	Votes	Altruism	Hybrid
Construction	Posts	Education	Defence (benefits
Welfare	Agriculture	Foreign Affairs	and patriotism)
ODA	Industry	(Diplomatic)	Welfare (benefits
Transport	and Commerce	Environmental	and altruism)
	(SMEs)	Justice	
		Science and Technology	

post. Table 10.4 shows a broad classification of *zoku* by the strength of the benefits–votes nexus in the period up to 1993. Categories overlap; for example, the construction of agricultural roads, or flood prevention measures, provided benefits for public works contractors, and at the same time helped in the mobilization of local political support through job creation and improvements in infrastructure; subsidies for rice-farmers provided both benefits and electoral inducements in local communities; the votes and electoral support of small businessmen (SMEs) were 'exchanged' for benefits of loans, subsidies, and tax breaks.

Zoku in policy areas such as education, foreign affairs, and environmental protection were less 'profit-inspired'. Their motivation, and hence their roles, were more altruistic, concerned to promote effective and efficient policies, or to protect the jurisdiction and policy interests of a Spending Ministry. In so doing they might also directly or indirectly represent the interests of particular special interest groups, but without the prime motive of obtaining tangible benefits for those groups, or expecting political donations to factional war-chests.

Where neither money nor legislation nor votes was involved, *zoku* tended to be less interested in a policy issue, or to ignore it. The discretionary room for manoeuvre by bureaucrats was correspondingly greater, as they were able to proceed by administrative guidance, or by securing the agreement/consensus of the affected parties, unless one or more of the latter wanted to involve or appeal to the LDP. Apart from medical care, there was 'not as much interest or expertise at the specialized *zoku* level in social welfare as in several other policy areas in which the LDP has played a real sponsorship role' (Campbell 1993: 368). The creation of Japan Teleway in 1985 showed the lack of involvement in a major policy issue of one of the strongest *zoku*, the Kensetsu–*Zoku*, with close ties to the Ministry of Construction. Its members had no specialist knowledge or expertise in telecommunications technology; there were no budgetary implications; and the formal cooperation of Dietmen was not needed, because the policy was effected by MOC through administrative guidance, and not legislation. In such an area of high-tech policy, 'the traditional Kensetsu–*Zoku* member does not offer meaningful support or a serious threat to the conduct of the Department' (Takahashi 1988: 23).

Most studies of *zoku* assert rather than demonstrate their influence on policy-making. Inoguchi and Iwai (1987) uniquely present a series of case-studies of *zoku* influence on actual policies, from which they distil a number of generalizations about the LDP's role in policy-making; but even here, there is more detail on those policy issues that achieved public visibility than on the day-by-day, routine exchange of information and views between *zoku* and bureaucrats in the policy divisions of Spending Ministries and Agencies. Little is known about the extent to which *zoku* interest was focused on particular bureaux and the constituent policy divisions within them. In most accounts, 'the Ministry' is treated as a monolithic, undifferentiated organization, despite the variation in politico-economic and electoral salience among bureaux, and within them between policy divisions. Not all bureaux, and not all of their policy divisions, engaged the attention or engendered the same degree of interest of *zoku* or sectional groups; some were insulated from such pressures. I have more to say about that issue in the particular context of the interactions in the budgetary processes in Part III.

POLICY-MAKING IN COALITION GOVERNMENTS, 1993–1996

When several parties shared responsibility for policy-making in coalition governments after 1993, each party separately had to take a view about policy issues as they emerged on the agenda in the light of its policy preferences, general politico-electoral strategy, and tactical manoeuvring, while at the same time responding to the pressure of events and circumstances. Collectively, the parties had then to achieve a consensus about the direction and content of government policy. Coalition government placed a premium on inter-party liaison and coordination. The fusion of party policy and government, characteristic of the LDP's one-party rule, was replaced by a separation between the policy of each party and government policy; the latter might or might not reflect the position of one or more parties to the coalition: what emerged as government policy might be the minimum to which all could agree. In a multi-party coalition it was more difficult for senior party politicians, even as ministers, to commit and deliver their rank-and-file to a policy position, as previously senior LDP ministers and party officials had been almost always able to do.

Policy-making was a novel experience for most of the seven parties comprising the Hosokawa Coalition, only a few of whose former members of the LDP had had experience of ministerial office, or had contributed through PARC to the policy and budgetary processes. A *modus vivendi* between politicians of the seven parties, the bureaucrats in the Spending Ministries, and MOF's Budget Bureau evolved only slowly and gradually. Inexperienced, cautious, and often in conflict with each other, the representatives of the coalition partners were often reluctant to commit themselves in formal policy coordinating bodies without reference back. For bureaucrats, making policy without the institutionalized incorporation of the LDP into formal and informal processes of consultation, discussion, and negotiation was a wholly novel experience. To whom were they to turn for their political information, advice, and guidance? They had to deal directly with the representatives of each of the seven parties, then with the coalition partners collectively, in inchoate coordinating structures. No party had a formal policy-making apparatus to compare with that of the LDP's PARC, with its established routines and points of access to enable bureaucrats to explain, consult, and defend their policy positions, preferences, and, importantly, budget requests; to acquire insight into party attitudes; to obtain guidance on preferred party options; and to enlist political support, for example to resist MOF's cuts and squeezes. No coalition party had senior party officials with the experience, authority, and confidence to commit it, resolve difficult policy issues, and coordinate competing and overlapping ministerial jurisdictions. No coalition party had the equivalent of the LDP's policy-tribes of long-serving, experienced, and knowledgeable policy specialists to act as entrepreneurs, or as brokers, or mediators in inter-ministerial disputes.

Relationships of mutual obligation and trust between bureaucrats and LDP politicians were abruptly terminated by the enforced withdrawal of the latter from the policy-making processes (although some officials continued discreetly to consult and take advice from senior LDP Dietmen). The political vacuum thereby created was not, in the short term, crucial. Apart from electoral reform and legislation to regulate political donations to political parties, there were few urgent issues on the political agenda, other than the opening of the domestic rice market to implement the GATT treaty. The time and energy of all the parties was consumed by the issue of electoral reform, and the tortuous and contested passage of the draft bill through both houses of the Diet.

Below the Cabinet, ministers and members of the coalition parties met as a Chief Executives Committee to discuss the management of the government, but it lacked both the authority of a formal government body and the political clout of a formal party body. In practice, the most influential body was the Council of the Ruling Parties (Yotō Daihyōsha Kaigi), on which each of the five largest parties was represented by its secretary-general. A Policy Adjustment Council responsible for the coordination of policy, on which each of the five parties was represented by its chairman/director of policy affairs, reported to it. A number of project teams reported to it on specific policy issues. The appearance of new, more open, and transparent organizational structures was belied by the *realpolitik* practised informally by influential politicians, for example the group led by Ozawa Ichirō (Shinseitō) and Ichikawa Yuichi (Kōmeitō), the so-called Ichi–Ichi line. Ozawa was the power behind Hosokawa's throne, and his top-down, dictatorial style was at odds both with his own professed commitment to more open government and the formal structures set up by the government. 'Politics behind closed doors' (*misshitsu seiji*) remained as characteristic of coalition government as it was of the one-party governments of the so-called '1955 system'.

The LDP's return to government as the senior partner in the Murayama Coalition formed in July 1994 was not a return to the *status quo ante*. Power-sharing meant that coalition policy-making had to be shared too. New tripartite consultative and decision-making bodies were superimposed upon each of the three coalition parties' formal policy-making structures: PARC and its divisions and committees, and parallel bodies in the other two, smaller parties, the SDP and Sakigake.[1] There were now two

---

[1] The following account of the structures, organizations, and processes is based on materials from the LDP headquarters, and on interviews with Obuchi Keizō, then vice-president of the LDP, 27 April 1995; Hori Kōsuke, then acting chairman of PARC, 26 April 1995; and Hayashi Yoshirō, member of LDP and former minister of finance, 26 April 1995; and with senior officials in MOF and the Spending Ministries in 1994–5. Corroboration is provided by Shinoda's (1998) analysis and interpretation, drawing upon secondary sources and interviews with former Prime Minister Murayama.

policy-making ladders, one separately for each party, and one for all three parties collectively. The top rung of the latter was the Cabinet and its committees. Immediately beneath it was the Coalition Consultation Council, comprising the three party leaders and the three major ministries. It was in effect an inner-Cabinet, receiving, digesting, and discussing major policy issues to be brought before Cabinet. The formal ratification of policies agreed elsewhere was the function of the General Affairs Council of the Coalition, which received reports and recommendations from a tripartite Policy Coordinating Council (Seisaku Chōsei Kaigi) and a Diet Affairs Council, the latter coordinating the coalition's strategy and tactics in the Diet. Immediately beneath it was the Diet Council of Whips.

Like the LDP's PARC, the day-to-day policy-making functions of the Policy Coordination Council were performed by subordinate bodies which reported to it. Nineteen divisions shadowed the ministries and agencies; and 18 ad hoc project teams coordinated policy-making for particular policy issues.

The tripartite super-structure was imposed upon the policy-making apparatus of each of the three coalition partners. That for the LDP was described earlier in the chapter; there were no significant changes of organization or process. Parallel but simpler organizational structures existed in the other two coalition parties. With fewer Diet members, neither could match the complex of divisions and research committees through which the LDP involved its senior party officials and backbench Diet members in formulating party policy, and monitoring the work of ministries and agencies. In practice, the LDP's superior organization and experience of policy-making in government, its numerical superiority, and its (re-)established relationships with bureaucrats gave it an advantage over its coalition partners. In turn, bureaucrats tended to turn to the LDP representatives on tripartite bodies as more knowledgeable, informed, and (often) able or more willing to commit their coalition colleagues.

The contribution of the three coalition parties to policy and budget-making was partly a function of size, but mainly one of experience and expertise. Numerically, the LDP was the largest party, with 211 seats in the Lower House, prior to the 1996 election. In Cabinet and in other tripartite consultative and decision-making bodies, the LDP had more representatives than either of the other two parties. More important than its numerical predominance was its much greater ministerial experience, and its tenure of all the key ministries apart from MOF: none of the SDP and Sakigake ministers had held office, other than briefly in the Hosokawa and Hata Coalitions; nor did they possess a tried and tested organization for making party policy whose members were accustomed to participating in the initiation, formulation, and legitimizing of national government policy.

The LDP and its policy-making apparatus increasingly dominated the Murayama Coalition. While bureaucrats prudently and tactically gave greater weight to the policy positions and preferences of the LDP, they could not ignore those of the other two parties. The dilemma was nowhere more evident than at MOF, where its budget officials dealt formally and informally with mainly LDP-controlled ministries, while its own minister was the leader of Sakigake.

The effects of the structure of tripartite policy-making bodies were fourfold. First, it superimposed an additional level of complexity on to the policy-making process.

Secondly, in consequence, achieving consensus through the interaction of party structures and coalition bodies took much longer, and the resulting agreements tended to be more general than before 1993. Thirdly, bureaucrats had to deal with four sets of organizations, rather than one. Even formal explanations necessarily took more time, as bureaucrats met separately with the representatives of each party; the necessary informal processes of consultation and *nemawashi* that preceded them took even longer. Fourthly, there was more uncertainly, and a greater element of unpredictability, with the views, anticipated reactions and policy positions of *three* parties to be taken into account in the preparation of official papers.

The role and influence of LDP *zoku* and (in the management of the Diet) *jitsuryokusha* (capable people) declined sharply during the brief period of the Hosokawa and Hata governments. Out of office, long established lines of communication with bureaucrats were cut, or could be maintained only discreetly. In the lifetime of both LDP politicians and bureaucrats, the severing of the bonds of mutual obligation and trust that had underpinned their interdependence in the policy processes was a wholly novel experience. Bureaucrats had to look elsewhere for policy guidance, political information and advice, and support. Policy areas previously characterized by the interaction among senior bureaucrats, LDP leaders, *zoku*, and the representatives of special interest groups were now more open as new alliances were sought and tentatively forged. Both bureaucrats and interest groups had now to take into account the policy preferences, strategies, and tactics of several parties rather than one. On the one hand, that added a further dimension of complexity and time to the processes of discussion, consultation, and negotiation, and to the proliferation of decision-points and the potential for the exercise of veto-powers; on the other, there were now more opportunities for the exercise of influence, as the points of access and the number of decision-making routes multiplied.

The exploitation of those opportunities for influence in the policy-making processes had barely began before the LDP was once again a part of government in the Murayama Coalition. This did not, however, signal an immediate resumption of those roles previously played by *zoku*, or of their informal relationships with bureaucrats. First, the breakup of the LDP in 1993 had removed from its ranks some senior members, although generally it was the younger, less experienced party members who followed Ozawa into Shinseitō and Takemura Masayoshi into Sakigake. Secondly, there was now suspicion and mistrust of bureaucrats on the part of many senior LDP members. Thirdly, bureaucrats were both defensive and uncertain about how to operate in the conditions of continuing political turbulence and unpredictability, and in any case they had to take into account the preferences and positions of the other two parties besides the LDP. Fourthly, the greater openness and competitiveness of the policy-making processes arising from multi-party politics had encouraged interest groups to seek support from, and tactical alliances with, influentials other than *zoku*. Nevertheless, there was a resurgence of *zoku* activity and influence. For example, in concert with emergent SDP *zoku*, the LDPs powerful agricultural *zoku* won important concessions on rice prices, and then forced the government to increase MOF's proposed 3.5 trillion compensation to farmers for the opening of the rice market to 6.1 trillion.

POLICY-MAKING, 1996–2000

After their losses in the October 1996 election, the SDP and Sakigake declined to participate in a formal coalition with the LDP, but agreed to support it in the Diet. The policy-making structures inherited from the Murayama government were progressively dismantled. The LDP's policy-making bodies assumed the initiative, and, together with resurgent LDP *zoku*, resumed those roles in the policy-making processes described earlier in the chapter. There was however a crucial difference. Relationships between politicians and bureaucrats in the policy-making processes had deteriorated sharply in the period of the Murayama and Hashimoto governments, partly as a result of a deliberate and sustained campaign of criticism and denigration aimed at the bureaucracy in general, and MOF in particular, orchestrated by the LDP and SDP from within the coalition, and conducted openly in the Diet and the media.

More generally, it was also a reflection of the recognition by all political parties that politicians should have more control of policy-making, and that the priorities of spending programmes, and the budget ceilings prescribed for ministries, should be decided after Cabinet discussion, rather than formally approved by it after proposals negotiated by Budget Bureau officials with their opposite numbers in the Spending Ministries. During the Hosokawa Coalition, Ozawa had proposed to limit the power of bureaucrats by reducing the number of those who would be allowed to answer questions in the Diet; by upgrading the status of parliamentary vice-ministers, and by appointing politicians to posts of political counsellor within the ministries and agencies. The latter proposal came to nothing, but there was some reduction in the numbers of answers given by bureaucrats in the Diet budget committees, which in the period 1993–5 fell by about a half in both the Upper and Lower Houses (Nakano 1997a). In July 1999 the Obuchi government statutorily abolished the practice of bureaucrats answering for their ministers in Diet committees. Increasingly, that role was assigned to parliamentary vice-ministers, whose numbers were increased partly for that purpose, and partly to enable them to make a greater contribution to policy-making within ministries.

CONCLUSIONS

In the period 1975–1993, and again from 1996, both PARC divisions formally, and PARC senior officials and *zoku* informally, had the potential to influence the policy-making process, and played several different roles: sponsor, guardian, mediator, consensus-builder, and promoter and protector of the interests of sectional groups. Those roles became progressively institutionalized in the processes of initiating, formulating, and implementing policies. Bureaucrats in Spending Ministries and Agencies consulted, listened to, and discussed policy proposals informally with the members of PARC divisions and commissions, and especially with their senior members and *zoku*, at different stages of policy development. The extent to which PARC initiated and developed policy proposals independently of the bureaucracy, or merely endorsed and legitimized proposals sponsored by the latter, or did not seek to influence either the making or carrying out of policies, varied between policy areas and within them over particular issues. In any assessment, it is necessary to distinguish the apparent influence of the LDP, and its policy-making organs and *zoku*, from the reality. It was in the interests of the ruling party collectively, and Dietmen individually, to demonstrate publicly to their supporters, clients, and interest groups that they, rather than the bureaucracy, controlled policy-making. The need to be seen to be taking formal and explicit responsibility for a policy or its implementation often masked the reality of who in the policy process had exercised discretionary authority. That issue is taken up and examined in more detail in the particular context of budget-making and the budget process in Chapter 20.

11

Budget Institutions and Structures

The formal institutions and structures of Japan's budgetary system are complex; the processes of making budgets through them labyrinthine and opaque. The proliferation of the number and different types of budgets and accounts is partly an historical legacy of the creation of the modern state after the Meiji Restoration, when many of them were established, and used explicitly as instruments of national economic development. At that time, the main central government budget was already separated from various special accounts, and from the budgets of public and financial corporations and state enterprises, while the antecedents of a separate capital investment budget, the forerunner of FILP, was evident in the creation of the Deposit Bureau Fund in 1885 to purchase government bonds and finance industrial development.

There are two main central government budgets: the General Account Budget (Ippan Kaikei Yosan) and the so-called 'second budget', the Fiscal Investment and Loan Programme, dealt with separately in the next chapter. Both budgets are revised in-year, and revisions are incorporated in one or more Supplementary Budgets (Hosei Yosan). There are, besides, the budgets of public banks and finance corporations, compiled under the sole or shared supervisory jurisdiction of MOF, and those of other public corporations and special companies, supervised by various Spending Ministries and Agencies. Finally, there are 38 Special Accounts (Tokubetsu Kaikei Yosan), established by law to manage the revenues and expenditures of specific government activities or special projects. Figure 11.1 shows the main structures of the central budgetary system, and their relationships through the transmission of loans and investments, transfer payments, grants and subsidies, and the underwriting of bonds issued by central and local government.

THE GENERAL ACCOUNT BUDGET

The General Account Budget is an annual cash-based budget with a time-horizon (normally) of one year, the fiscal year running from 1 April to 31 March. Although compiled within the broader medium-term contexts provided by five-year national economic plans, and three-year medium-term fiscal projections, discussed in Chapter 14, there is no multi-year budgeting. Revenues (including borrowing) and expenditures are balanced in each single-year budget, and spending on individual programmes, even public investment, is planned and allocated only for the year ahead. The General Account Budget provides the main source of finance for the current and

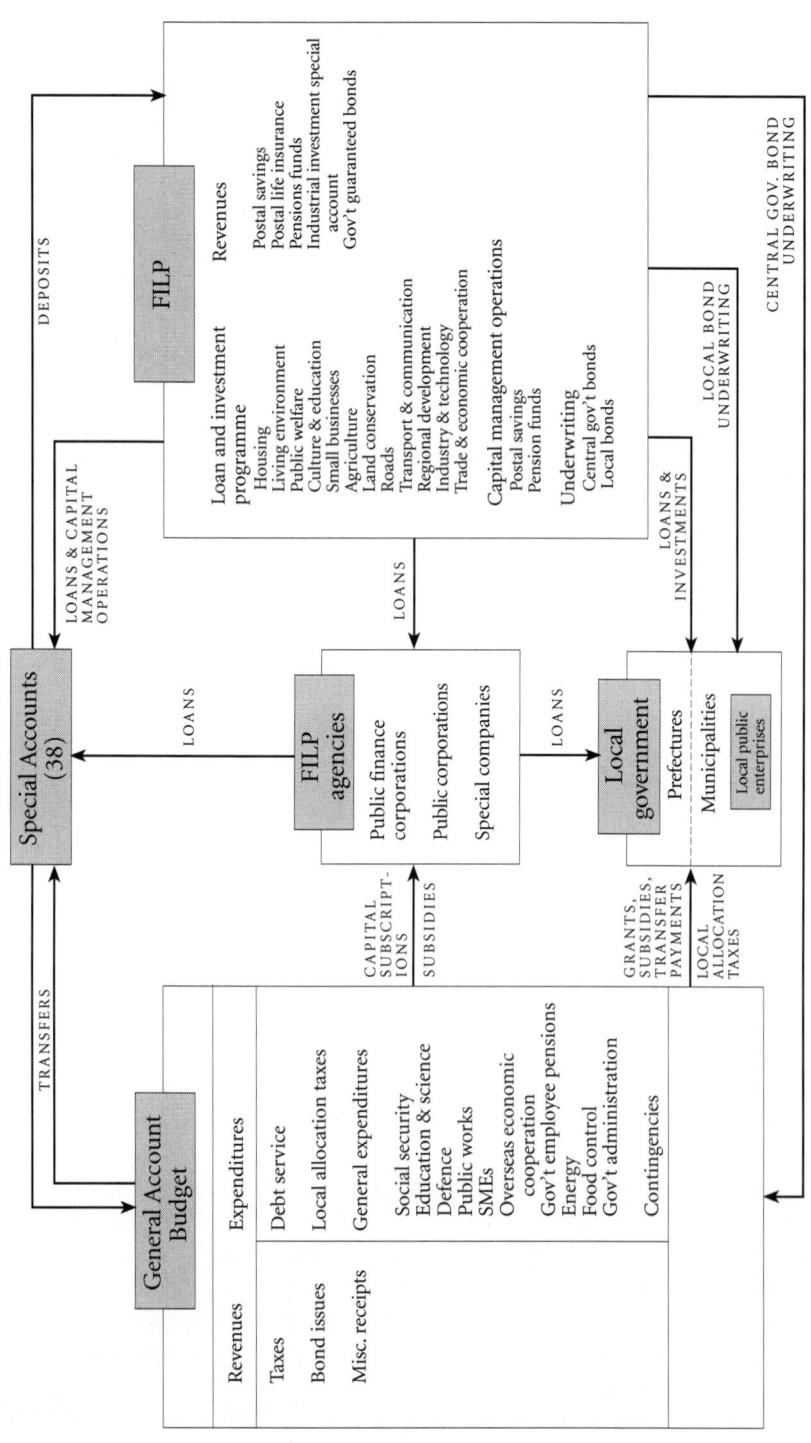

Figure 11.1 *The central budgetary system, 1975–2000*

capital expenditure programmes of the Spending Ministries and Agencies, and, through statutorily assigned revenues, grants, subsidies, and other transfer payments, about 40% of the finance for local governments. Revenues to finance expenditures are raised mainly from national taxes. Direct taxes on income, corporations, and inheritance account for about 40% of the total, indirect taxes on consumption, liquor/alcohol, tobacco, gasoline, and motor-vehicles about 20%. The remaining 40% is provided (in the late 1990s) by government borrowing.

Expenditures in the General Account Budget are divided roughly into two categories. So-called 'fixed expenditures' comprise the costs of servicing debt, and the proportions of some nationally collected taxes assigned statutorily to local government. The remainder are the 'general expenditures' (*ippan saishutsu*) on programmes within ten broad policy areas, such as social security, education, and defence.

Government bonds are issued to finance some of the capital and current expenditures in the General Account Budget. There are two main types: so-called 'ordinary' or construction bonds (*kensetsu kokusai*), to finance capital spending, and so-called 'special deficit-financing bonds' (*akaji kokusai*), to finance budget deficits. The conditions and terms of issue for both are governed by public finance legislation.

Budget Guidelines

Decisions on the size and broad composition of the General Account Budget in the period 1975–2000 were taken in June–July when the Cabinet approved MOF's proposed budget strategy, and the budget guidelines to be followed by ministries and agencies in the preparation of their budget requests. The guidelines prescribed the overall limit for the budget, limits for current and capital expenditure, and the broad allocation of monies to individual programmes. The main guidelines and their development, and the processes of prescription and implementation, are discussed in Chapter 15.

SUPPLEMENTARY BUDGETS

Over the last quarter of the twentieth century, in-year revisions to the General Account Budget and FILP became an institutionalized, regular, and customary part of the annual budget process. In the period from December 1990 to the end of March 2000 there were 19 Supplementary Budgets. In some years, as in FY1993 and FY1995, the General Account Budget was revised formally three times. The purpose of Supplementary Budgets was twofold. First, it enabled the aggregates of planned revenue, expenditure, and borrowing in the period after the compilation of the draft initial General Account Budget in December to be adjusted and controlled, as more accurate estimates became available and some additional expenditure and/or revenue was deemed necessary. In other G7 countries borrowing limits are not prescribed in the Budget, and can be adjusted without changing budget aggregates. In Japan, the level of borrowing was included in the initial General Account Budget; hence any adjustment in-year, upwards or downwards, required a Supplementary Budget.

Secondly, Supplementary Budgets were used to finance changes to fiscal policy in-year, for example to implement ad hoc countercyclical macroeconomic measures.

Apart from size, the main difference between the annual General Account Budget and Supplementary Budgets was that the latter were not subject to the annual budget guidelines. In principle, there were no limits on the amount of supplementary expenditure or its distribution between the categories of expenditure or programmes, or ministries and agencies. Any such additional expenditure was not incorporated into the base-line for the calculation of next year's main budget. This had two effects. First, those Spending Ministries and Agencies whose programmes benefited (or suffered) from in-year changes could not count on permanent additions (or cuts) to their budgets. Secondly, while the total of planned expenditure in the General Account Budget was revised and published accordingly, the main performance indicator of fiscal performance was the measurement of changes in *planned* expenditure from one fiscal year to the next. With frequent in-year revisions, the initial planned budget was therefore an inaccurate predictor or guide to how much was spent in total and on what. I return to the issue of measurement in Chapter 21.

Supplementary Budgets provided the means to adjust the estimated yield of taxation revenues and, contingently, the amount of government borrowing, but also to finance extra spending. In almost every Supplementary Budget, additional resources were made available for public works programmes, the ostensible justification for which was the occurrence of 'natural disasters', such as floods and typhoons, causing damage to the infrastructure of roads, railways, ports and harbours, coastal defences and so on. Such additional expenditures and/or reductions in the yield of estimated tax revenues were frequently partly offset by savings in planned budget expenditures. In the examination and negotiation of the initial budget requests with Spending Ministries and Agencies in the autumn, budget examiners normally required some or all of them to plan for possible further cuts, of up to 10%, to provide for anticipated or possible adjustment in-year. For example, in the first Supplementary Budget for FY1994, the costs of an estimated shortfall in revenue of 2.247 trillion, *and* additional expenditures of 1.331 trillion for public works and agricultural subsidies, were partly offset by further savings on planned budget expenditures of 1.086 trillion. As in FY1994, where cuts proved insufficient to balance the anticipated shortfall of revenue, and the necessary additional expenditures, the level of borrowing planned in the initial budget was adjusted accordingly. In all but four years of the period 1975–2000, the level of planned government borrowing in the initial budget was revised upwards in-year, sometimes hugely, as in FY1993 and FY1995, and again in FY1998, to cover the deficit caused by the shortfall of revenue and/or additional spending.

SETTLEMENT AND 'CARRY FORWARD'

At the end of each financial year, the Spending Ministries and Agencies accounted for their spending to MOF by 31 July. MOF then produced an account of the final out-turn or settlement (*kessansho*) of the revenues and expenditures of the General Account

Budget. After formal approval by the Cabinet, it was sent to the Board of Audit for scrutiny and certification. In December the Cabinet submitted the audited accounts, together with the Board's report, for the Diet's consideration.

Until the onset of the fiscal crisis in the mid-1970s, the normal expectation was that the settlement of the General Account Budget, which included all the in-year revisions made through Supplementary Budgets, would generate a surplus of revenues over expenditures, as a result of 'natural revenue growth', the difference between revenues collected and those estimated yields in the initial budget, and systemic underspending. In the era of high economic growth, 'natural revenue growth' had generated large surpluses, as explained in Chapter 2. Under the 1947 Public Finance Law, at least 50% of any such surplus had to be transferred to the Special Account for National Debt Consolidation to redeem the national debt. However, the persistence of revenue shortfall from the mid-1970s led to the occurrence of a deficit rather than a surplus on the settled accounts. To cope with the 'unforeseeable decline in tax revenue', a Settlement Adjustment Fund was set up in 1977 with an initial capital of 200 billion. The intention was that future deficits on the settled accounts would be covered by payments from the Fund, which would be replenished by payments in years when there were surpluses, after the statutory transfers to redeem the national debt, at the discretion of MOF. In fact, very little was paid into the Fund, and the deficits on the settled budget accounts that occurred in the 1980s were almost wholly covered by transfers from the Special Account for National Debt Consolidation Fund.

THE REDEMPTION OF THE NATIONAL DEBT

Government bonds issued to cover deficits on the General Account Budget were redeemed in two ways: by purchase on maturity, and by issuing refunding bonds. MOF operated a 60-year redemption rule, whereby one-sixth of bonds issued were redeemed in each ten-year period, the remaining five-sixths being refunded five times before the real redemption. Sixty years was taken as the average economic depreciation period of the assets purchased by those bonds. Redemption payments were made through the Special Account for National Debt Consolidation in three ways: first, statutorily by a fixed-rate appropriation from the annual General Account Budget of one-sixth of the value of bonds outstanding at the beginning of the previous fiscal year; secondly, and again statutorily, by the transfer of not less than half of the surplus on the settlement of the General Account Budget; and, thirdly, by discretionary transfers from the General Account Budget. Chapter 25 shows how MOF manipulated those transfers, and deferred liquidation of the national debt, to relieve pressure on the stressed General Account Budget.

SPECIAL ACCOUNTS

Since the establishment of the modern state in the nineteenth century, the central government has from time to time set up legally constituted special accounts to manage the financial operations of particular government activities or special projects. During the period 1975–2000 there were 38 Special Accounts, each of which was managed by a designated ministry or agency; some were administered separately by dedicated agencies, for example the Food Agency, but remained within the jurisdiction of the sponsoring ministry (MAFF).

Special Accounts were budgetary mechanisms to manage dedicated revenues collected or deposited from fees, charges, and some hypothecated taxes, and to control outlays on specific activities or projects. They provided finance for a variety of functions, projects, and services—for example the management of government enterprises such as the Mint, the Government Printing Bureau, and the postal services, and for handling the contributions and benefits of various national insurance schemes. Others provided a convenient administrative device for financing particular government activities, such as national schools and hospitals. Some accounts, like those of the Trust Fund Bureau Fund (for FILP) and the National Debt Consolidation Fund, provided the means for managing funds collected for a special purpose. Six Special Accounts provided specifically for the financing of the costs of public works projects: ports and harbours, roads, flood control, airport development, land improvement, and national forests and fields projects. Deposited revenues in the accounts for roads and airports included a portion of some hypothecated taxes, e.g. petrol, motor vehicle tonnage, aviation fuel. Almost two-thirds of all public works projects were financed mainly by those six and the Special Accounts for industrial investment and urban development.

Special Accounts were similar to trading accounts: outgoings as designated expenditures were in principle balanced or exceeded by the revenues collected, together with the accumulated balances of assets and liabilities. In practice, some of them (e.g., among public works, those for harbours, flood control, land improvement, national forests and fields projects, and the JNR Debt Settlement Corporation) had both negative assets and net worth. Recurring deficits, in a few cases heavy and persistent, were subsidized by payments from one or other of the two main budgets. For example, the Foodstuff Control Special Account ran a substantial annual deficit for several years, the difference between the costs of the government's purchase of rice produced domestically and the proceeds of its sale. As we shall see in later chapters, there were numerous cash-flow transactions between some of the Special Accounts and the two main budgets, partly to relieve pressure on the General Account Budget.

GOVERNMENT-AFFILIATED ORGANIZATIONS

The 11 (1998) public banks and finance corporations had a special legal status, independently of the central government. However, as 'policy-based' financial institutions, their functions were closely aligned with the objectives and policies of the ministries and agencies that sponsored them. Their capital funds were provided mainly by subscriptions from the central government, and annual loans from FILP through the Trust Fund Bureau Fund. For that reason, their budgets and accounts were submitted for the Diet's approval at the same time as the two main budgets. Their revenue and expenditure accounts, with transfers to and from the General Account Budget netted off, were counted as 'General Government' consistently with the conventions of the System of National Accounts.

The requirement to obtain formal Diet approval of their budgets distinguished these banks and finance corporations from other public corporations and special companies. Formally, the latter two were not part of the central government's budgetary institutions and structures, and their accounts were excluded from the calculation of general government expenditures. (But see Chapters 26 and 30 for a discussion of this issue.) In practice, the distinction was much less clear-cut. First, the capital investment programmes of public corporations and companies were subject to the approval of their sponsoring ministries and agencies, and were generally consistent with their overall policy objectives. Secondly, in some cases, for example road construction, capital investment programmes could be and were financed partly through the main budget, partly through loans to public corporations through FILP, and partly through hypothecated revenues in the Special Account for Road Improvement (see Figure 12.1). Those public corporations and companies engaged in road building were therefore an integral part of the central (and local) government's overall budget strategy for the road programme. Thirdly, public corporations and companies seeking loans from FILP to finance their activities were dependent on the approval and support of their ministries and agencies in bidding and negotiating with MOF. Fourthly, those with trading losses or debts might be dependent on FILP and/or the General Account Budget for subsidies, for example to service the costs of previous borrowing. I have more to say about the status of both government-affiliated organizations and public corporations in the next chapter.

LOCAL GOVERNMENT FINANCE

Many of the functions undertaken by the 47 prefectures and 3,279 municipal governments were 'agency-delegated' functions, and as agencies they carried them out as directed by the relevant Spending Ministries and Agencies. In addition, for almost all activities of local government, those ministries and agencies set standards, regulations, and guidelines, compliance with which was ensured through various financial controls and inducements.

At a general level, MOF (with MHA) exercised a comprehensive and detailed control of the aggregates of revenues and expenditures of local government as a whole. It had a number of instruments with which to influence and control them. First, there was the Local Government Finance Plan drawn up by MOF, an annual official estimate of standard targets for the aggregates of revenues and expenditures based on formal criteria. Its aims were to guarantee sufficient financial resources to local government, to coordinate national and local public finances in the context of the national economy, and, to provide guidelines for local government's own financial management. In estimating total revenues, MOF prescribed the aggregate amounts to be contributed locally through taxes on individuals, businesses, land and property, and some specific goods and services.

Central government contributed about a third of local government revenues as transfer payments from the General Account and Supplementary Budgets, and some Special Accounts; the remaining two-thirds was financed mainly through the issue of local bonds, and revenue income from local governments' own tax-based 'Ordinary Accounts'. Transfer payments (*kokko shishutsu-kin*) comprised statutory contributions to the costs of providing certain national services, mainly education, welfare benefits, and nationally determined public works projects; discretionary grants-in-aid for certain current expenditures; and subsidies for agency-delegated services (e.g. managing national elections).

MOF also contributed through the General Account Budget a proportion of certain nationally collected taxes: 32% of the personal income tax, 35.8% of the corporate income tax, 32% of the alcohol tax, 29.5% of the consumption tax, and 25% of the yield of the tobacco tax. The resulting aggregate, the Local Allocation Tax (Chihō Kōfuzei Kōfu-kin), was distributed as general grants to local authorities according to a formula that reflected needs and resources, and was intended to maintain a minimum uniform standard of local services. The Local Transfer Tax (LTT) was an aggregate of various nationally collected taxes, on local roads, motor vehicles, petrol, and aviation fuel. Unlike the Local Allocation Tax, the LTT aggregate was not included in the revenues and expenditures of the General Account Budget. It was deposited in and distributed to local governments from the Special Account of Local Allocation Tax and Local Transfer Tax.

The second source of MOF's influence and control of local finance was the requirement that individual local governments had to obtain 'loan permits' from the MHA. Funds for those approved loans were provided mainly from the Trust Fund Bureau Fund managed by MOF's Financial Bureau, and from the Finance Corporation for Municipal Enterprises which it co-sponsored with MHA. Larger, mainly city, local authorities were allowed to issue local bonds on the open market, and to borrow long-term from the private sector. The number and size of loans from all these sources were controlled in aggregate through the Local Loans Programme, MOF's third instrument of influence and control.

12

The 'Second Budget': The Fiscal Investment Loan Programme

The Fiscal Investment Loan Programme, which the Japanese call 'Zaitō' (*Zaisei Tōyūshi Keikaku*), was established in 1953 when the Japanese government regained independent control of its own budget, but its origins and principal characteristics are much older, derived from the Meiji era. As with much of the budgetary system, and other structures of central government, the continuity of its institutions and processes is striking and important for an understanding of how the system operates in the contemporary Japanese political economy. (For brief historical accounts, see Rosenbluth 1989; Calder 1990.)

FILP (until 2001) was a policy-based public finance system through which traditionally the national government transmitted the accumulated savings of small investors to dedicated governmental and quasi-governmental organizations for investment in projects and programmes designed to achieve prescribed national economic and social (and party political) objectives. Since its inception, it has been characterized, first, by the unique source of its funds, and the control of their allocation by MOF for the development of economic, industrial, and social infrastructure; secondly, by the methods of financing capital projects and programmes through investments, loans, and the underwriting of bonds issued by a number of eligible national, regional, and local organizations; and, thirdly, by the provision of loans and subsidies to some Special Accounts, and the General Account Budget itself. Those institutional and structural characteristics were recognizably present in the transition of the Japanese state which began with the Meiji Restoration, and the industrialization that followed in the Taishō period. In 1872 the Meiji government established the 'Reserve Fund System' to finance the construction of railways and other communications' infrastructure, to provide investment for the Bank of Japan and some other government-affiliated agencies, and to help finance private-sector industrial development.

The main source of funds for FILP in the period 1975–2000 was domestic personal savings deposited with the postal savings system operated through more than 24,000 local post offices. The system was set up in 1875, and modelled on the UK's Post Office Savings Bank. As with many other institutional transplants, it was adapted for the purposes of national development. Managed and controlled initially by the Postal Bureau of the Ministry of the Interior, jurisdictional authority passed to the Ministry of Agriculture and Commerce in 1881, then to the newly created Ministry of Communications in 1885, and after the Second World War to its successor, the Ministry of Posts, and finally to

MPT. From the outset, funds from accumulated postal savings were transferred to Special Accounts controlled by MOF. A Deposit Bureau (Fund) was set up and managed by it under legislative authority in 1885. Soon after, it began to use the Fund to purchase government bonds, a characteristic of the modern FILP. A second function, also characteristic of the contemporary FILP, was soon added: the financing through loans and underwriting of the activities of specially created financial institutions to stimulate financial and industrial growth. The Industrial Bank of Japan, the forerunner of the Japan Development Bank set up in 1951, was created in 1902. Loans to the Special Accounts of some public financial and industrial corporations, the third characteristic, began in 1909, along with the fourth, the underwriting of bonds issued by local governments.

By that time, all the main elements of the modern FILP were recognizable. Postal savings accumulated in a Special Account provided the bulk of the money, channelled through loans and bonds, to finance industrial development, supervised and controlled by MOF. Thereafter, the size and scope of the funds increased; the number of eligible organizations burgeoned, and the management of the deposits in the postal savings system drew in other government bodies, principally the Ministry of Communications. Subsequent changes reflected the response to the increasing size of the accumulated aggregate of the deposits in the inter-war period, the increase in the use of government bonds to finance development, and, later, the industrial base to support the imperialist expansion and the war economy.

Until the implementation of reform in FY2001, the FILP system was based on the Trust Fund Bureau Fund Law of 1951 (amended in 1987; see below) which transformed the Deposit Bureau system set up in the nineteenth century. With the agreement of SCAP, the Fund was used to supply the growing demand for long-term capital investment which, until the implementation of the Dodge Line to control inflation, had been supplied by the Reconversion Bank. At the same time, the Postal Savings Fund and the reserves of several dedicated Special Accounts were integrated within a single fund, the Trust Fund Bureau Fund, and its uses statutorily prescribed.

Independent control of the whole budgetary system was regained in 1953. With the suspension of US aid—a major source of long-term investment funds in the immediate post-war period—the government responded to pressure for the financing of capital investment by issuing government bonds. Until that time, in accordance with the Dodge Line, the government had been required to balance the whole Budget—the General Account, and the separate Special Accounts of various government-related financial and industrial organizations. Thereafter, the General Account Budget was distinguished conceptually, and for accounting and control purposes, from those Accounts and from FILP. The long-term objective of balancing the Budget, to which MOF re-dedicated itself in the policy of fiscal reconstruction in the 1980s, referred to the General Account Budget alone.

Both the General Account Budget and FILP were compiled, managed, controlled, and closely coordinated by MOF. Judgements about their size and composition, and the allocation of expenditures, were interrelated, and set within the politico-economic context of MOF's assessment of the prospects for the economy for the coming year, shaped by national economic and social objectives, and by consideration of the LDP's narrower party political interests.

In principle, the methods of financing capital projects through the two budgets were not interchangeable: those where there was no expectation of profits being earned to repay principal and interest charges on loans could be financed only through the General Account Budget (or that of local governments). But there were projects—roads, transport, and communications for example—where capital investment could be financed wholly through either the General Account or FILP (and other private-sector funds). For example, road construction could be undertaken by public bodies wholly as a non-profit-making undertaking financed by the General Account and/or the Special Account for Road Improvement, or by private-sector organizations or public corporations earning revenue through tolls and charges to repay loans and interest charges made available through FILP. Figure 12.1 shows the contributions of different budget organizations to the overall road programme in FY2000.

Some capital projects were financed partly through the General Account and partly through FILP, for example some toll roads financed through the Japan Highway Public Corporation; housing loans through the Government Housing Loan Corporation; loans through the ODA programme, and some special loans to SMEs through the National Life (formerly People's) Finance Corporation and the Japan Finance Corporation for Small Businesses. FILP also played a part in the financing of public–private capital ventures in the 1990s. The construction of Kansai International Airport was co-financed by subsidy from the General Account, from FILP funds allocated to the Special Account for Airport Construction, and from finance provided by

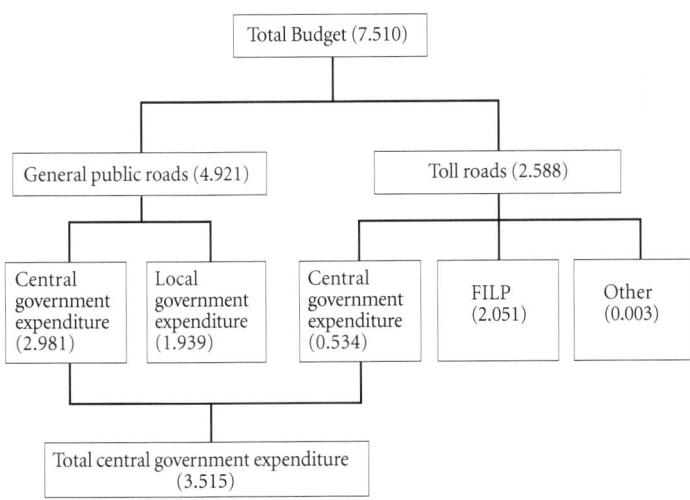

Figure 12.1 *Financing the road programme, FY2000* (trillion yen)
Source: *FILP Report 2000*, Financial Bureau, MOF.

a consortium of private banks. A similar co-financing arrangement provided the capital investment for the Tokyo Bay Express Highway.

Formally, the size of the FILP budget until FY2000 was determined by the availability of funds in the Trust Fund Bureau Fund managed and controlled by MOF. The annual allocation to eligible public organizations—the FILP agencies—was ostensibly governed by the criterion of the future profitability of the investments and loans financed by them, and the need to pay interest charges and repay the principal. In practice, as I shall show in later chapters, FILP decision-making was more complex, and more politicized, than the application of that commercial criterion suggests.

As with most institutions of Japanese society, in characterizing FILP it is necessary to distinguish principle from practice; the appearance from the reality. What actually happens was often different from what was said to happen. This chapter outlines the structure, purposes, main principles, and characteristics upon which the FILP system was founded, and which ostensibly governed its operation; examines the sources of its funding; and identifies and categorizes the recipients of those funds, briefly contrasting principles with practice, thereby foreshadowing the argument of the detailed analysis and assessment in Chapters 19 and 24.

The account given here refers to the period 1975–2000. In 1997 the Hashimoto government initiated an inquiry into the role of FILP in the economy. As a result, it was decided, *inter alia*, to break the historic statutory links between FILP and the compulsory use of postal savings and pension reserves as the main source of finance. That, and other changes to the system implemented from April 2001, are discussed in Chapter 28.

THE FILP SYSTEM IN OUTLINE

Figure 12.2 outlines the structure of the FILP system from 1975 to 2000. (The reformed structure implemented from April 2001 is shown in Figure 28.1.) It shows the accumulation of funds—through savings, insurance premiums, and pension contributions, and their transmission through the two main sources of FILP funding—the Trust Fund Bureau Fund and the Postal Life Insurance Funds—to the FILP agencies that carried out the investment and loan programme. The latter programme was one of three elements of the FILP Budget: the others were the funds used to finance some of the central government's borrowing requirements through underwriting government bonds, and (from 1987) funds allocated specifically to finance capital market operations designed to generate capital growth for the postal savings and pensions reserves. Those operations are not shown in the diagram, but are explained later in the chapter, and illustrated in Figures 12.3 and 12.4. The FILP Budget, comprising all three elements, was self-evidently larger than that for the constituent investment and loan programme. As I shall explain in later chapters, the distinction is important in the analysis and assessment of the role of FILP in the fiscal system as a whole.

The 'Second Budget': FILP

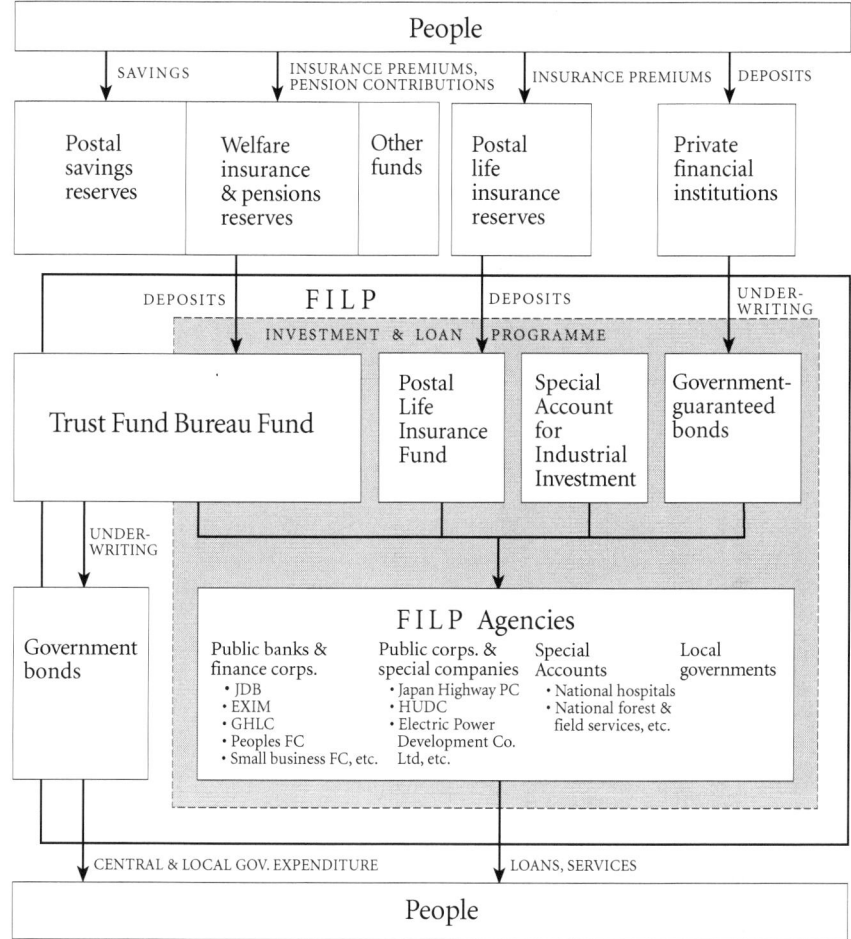

Figure 12.2 *The FILP system, 1975–2000*
Source: *FILP Report 1999*, Financial Bureau, MOF.

PRINCIPLES AND CHARACTERISTICS OF THE FILP SYSTEM, 1975–2000

FILP was an integral part of the formal institutions and structures of the central government's budgetary system, providing funds for the creation and improvement of industrial, social, and environmental capital through the agency of public banks and finance corporations, and public corporations and special companies. By the end of FY1998, the FILP Budget had reached a record level of 65.6 trillion, four-fifths the size of the General Account Budget, and much larger than the sum allocated for all the current and capital expenditure programmes. It was an instrument (with the General Account Budget) of fiscal policies designed to achieve three declared purposes: first, to allocate resources in order to provide benefits and services that would not be provided adequately, or at all, if left to competition in the market; secondly, to redistribute income through progressive taxation and welfare spending in order to remove gross inequalities; and, thirdly, to help smooth functions in the economic cycle by increasing and decreasing the amount and direction of public spending and taxation (FILP 1998). FILP's distinctive functions 'reduce policy costs in terms of the tax burden on the public', and help to achieve the purposes of resource allocation and adjustment to economic cycles (p. 4).

The FILP system was based on four main principles, three of which were prescribed statutorily in the Trust Fund Bureau Laws. First, the integrated management and allocation of FILP funds was intended to provide a system of 'effective fund management and fund procurement which simplifies administrative organisation and reduces administrative costs' (FILP 1998: 24). Unified administration enabled funds to be allocated in a way compatible with nationally determined fiscal and monetary policies, in particular with central government budgetary policies. As well, through integrated management and allocation, the Trust Fund Bureau Fund administered by MOF was able to absorb interest rate risks arising from fund procurement and management.

The second principle was 'safe and secure allocation'. Public funds 'were provided only to public institutions to ensure that the principal and interest of the loans can be collected' (FILP 1998: 25). One advantage, it was claimed, was that 'FILP–financial institutions can pay off their debts over a long period of time'; another, was that 'because FILP funds were not subsidies...they give fund recipients a great incentive for self-discipline and business improvement'. While FILP funds borrowed from the public were undoubtedly safe and secure because they were backed by the central government, as we shall see in later chapters, some recipients of those funds were unable to repay the principal and interest, while others received straight subsidies.

Thirdly, in principle, the interest rates prescribed for deposits with the Trust Fund Bureau Fund, and for loans to the FILP agencies, were 'determined in accordance with market interest rates'. Here again, I shall show later on that practice differed from principle. Until 1987 MOF controlled official discount rates, and hence the coupon rate on ten-year government bonds; at different times FILP agencies set interest rates both lower and higher than long-term prime rates charged by private financial institutions in the market.

The fourth FILP principle, not prescribed statutorily, was that the allocation of funds was continually reviewed to respond to changing social and economic conditions. MOF claimed that from 1955 onwards there were four main shifts in the sectoral allocation of FILP funds: (1) until 1960 the focus was on establishing the industrial and economic base; (2) from 1961 to 1970 it was on achieving a balanced economic development with priority for small and medium-sized businesses, and the improvement of roads and social infrastructure; (3) from 1971 to 1980 the focus was on the improvement of social and welfare infrastructure, especially housing; and (4) from 1981 it was 'on active responses to economic issues', while continuing to give priority to housing, local infrastructure, and small and medium-sized businesses. As a result, it was claimed, the target for FILP funds switched from industry and technology to social, welfare, and environmental projects designed to 'help improve people's lives' (FILP 1999). The validity of that claim is examined in Chapter 24.

Characteristics

FILP funds accrued 'passively'. Postal savings, and the accumulated premiums and payments paid into pension and welfare funds, were not collected 'actively' and expressly for the purpose of financing FILP activities. While this was formally the case, in practice there was an operating assumption that they would be so used, and that assumption was predicated upon the propensity to save of householders and small businesses, and their continuing preference for postal savings rather than other alternative outlets available in the financial markets. As we shall see in Chapter 19, the continued accumulation of funds to finance FILP was not left to the chance of competition in the market: historically, postal savings were accorded a special status and certain privileges denied to comparable financial products offered by private financial institutions. Up to 1987, MOF and MPT shared an interest (but had different objectives) in attracting a continuous flow of new deposits by offering tax-exemption status, preferential rates of interest, and exceptional conditions for long-term depositors.

It was true of course that in principle the size of the annual FILP Budget was determined by the level of passively collected and accumulated postal savings and pensions and welfare contributions—or, rather, by the proportion of the balance of accumulated and new deposits which it was thought prudent to invest with the Trust Fund Bureau Fund each year (and by the demand for FILP investments and loans). But this was the case only in a narrow, formal sense. Unlike taxes, the level of which was determined actively, and the revenues collected compulsorily, for specific purposes of financing general expenditure, postal and other savings were voluntary deposits. In theory, investors could decline to deposit, and/or withdraw their savings, and opt for alternative financial products, sufficiently to threaten the viability of FILP. While, from time to time, they did indeed do so, causing a temporary crisis of accumulation, in practice MPT and MOF (supported by the LDP) ensured that postal savings remained attractive enough to provide a continued flow of funds. Chapter 19 will argue that in practice the growth of FILP was not constrained by the apparent 'passivity' of collection; in fact, there was evidence that the size of the accumulated funds available to the Trust Fund Bureau Fund drove the FILP budget.

The second principal characteristic of FILP was that it was 'self-financing'. Unlike expenditure (including investment) financed through the General Account Budget, which was funded from taxation (and borrowing), FILP loans had to be repaid. In principle, fiscal investments and loans were made only where the capital investment was recoverable through project income, and where repayment of both principal and interest was guaranteed. There was then an assumption and expectation of profitability in the allocation of FILP funds to FILP agencies, and through them to capital projects and programmes. Provided on a 'low cost' basis in the national interest, those loans and investments were expected to generate profits sufficient to cover operating costs, and to service the debts incurred. In practice, as we shall see, some investments and loans were made where the expectation of profit was low or very long-term, and in some cases non-existent; and, increasingly, FILP funds were used in the period 1975–2000 as an alternative to the General Account Budget to finance some expenditure where there was no expectation of profit, and as explicit subsidies to programmes, projects, Special Accounts, and FILP agencies. Relief for the General Account Budget was provided also by the use of FILP funds to finance a (growing) proportion of the central government's borrowing requirement to finance the deficit on the balance between expenditure and revenue. As we shall see, the sharp conceptual distinction between the sourcing and purposes of the General Account and FILP Budgets became blurred in practice. Such a distinction proved impossible to maintain in the conditions of fiscal stress that obtained from the late 1970s. The two budgets, together with those for the 38 Special Accounts, became integrated in a general public financial system.

The third general characteristic was that FILP funds were derived from national institutions, based on national credit, and used to achieve national objectives. In practice, that linear relationship was by no means clear-cut. The principle that national funds must be used for the benefit of the national interest had underpinned the financing of industrial development by the state since the Meiji Restoration. The underlying and unstated premiss was that such funds could be used only in that way: by using them for 'public benefit', the government protected the collective interests of the depositors. In practice, their use provided a rationale for continuing state control of the amount and direction of large amounts of capital investment in the private sector. In the immediate post-war period, arguably, the reconstruction of basic industries such as steel, coal, shipbuilding, and electricity, the promotion and development of new technologies, and the provision of industrial infrastructure—roads, transport, and communications—all required state funding and the control and direction that accompanied it. (But see Calder, 1993, for an alternative explanation of the role and effectiveness of government credit in the high-growth era.) In the changed economic conditions that followed the end of the high-growth era, with the West having been 'caught up' and all save the US economy surpassed, that rationale for FILP was more difficult to sustain. Moreover, there was no longer a shortage of funds available in both domestic and international financial markets for capital investment. The continued expansion of FILP through the 1980s and 1990s raised questions of need, purpose, and viability: whether the central government (MOF) was able to determine, more efficiently and effectively than private financial institutions subject to market forces, the amount and allocation of capital investment in the economy; whether the creation and improvement of social, welfare, and environmental capital should more properly be a charge on general expenditures financed out of taxation and borrowing, and subject to public control and accountability through the political process; and whether the expansion of FILP to finance those and other purposes of general expenditure purposes threatened the viability of the FILP system. Those and other issues raised by the operation of FILP from the end of the 1970s are examined in detail in Chapter 28.

The operation of the FILP system, from the point of entry of the accumulation of postal savings and pension funds to the point of exit of loans and investments made by the FILP agencies, was intensely politicized, the fourth general characteristic. I have more to say about that in Chapter 19, which deals with the budget-making process.

THE SOURCE OF FILP FUNDS

MOF was able to finance annually a large and increasing FILP Budget. This was first and foremost because of the status and popularity of national postal savings, and the availability of substantial surpluses in national pensions' funds. Throughout the period 1975–2000, postal savings accounted for about a fifth of all personal savings, and by the 1990s for more than a third of all deposits and savings in the private sector. Secondly, both MPT and MHW, responsible for the collection and management of postal savings and pensions' funds, preferred (until 1987) the safety and security provided by the government-guaranteed Trust Fund Bureau Fund. This, the first and most important of the four main sources of FILP funds, provided annually about 80% of the annual FILP Budget in the 1990s; when FILP was established in 1953, it had provided less than half, with the Special Account for Industrial Investment providing a third.

The Trust Fund Bureau Fund was an administrative device established by law in 1951 to provide for the unified management of postal savings, the surplus funds of the government's Special Accounts, principally those for welfare insurance and national pensions, and other small deposit funds. Its purpose was 'to contribute to the promotion of the public good' through: (1) the central government; (2) government-related institutions with budgets requiring the approval of the Diet, including the public finance corporations and the Special Accounts of some public corporations, enterprises and companies; (3) local authorities; (4) other public corporations (Articles 1 and 7, Trust Fund Bureau Fund Act, 1951). In addition, the TFBF could be used to purchase bank debentures and foreign bonds.

The second source of FILP funding was the Postal Life Insurance Fund, managed independently (and exceptionally) from the Trust Fund Bureau Fund by the MPT. Its income derived from insurance premiums and instalments, and from the revenues generated from the operation of its reserve funds. The surplus remaining after deductions of insurance and pension payments and administration expenses was also deposited with the Trust Fund Bureau Fund.

The accumulated balance of the deposits in the Trust Fund Bureau Fund from those two major sources totalled 433 trillion in March 1999, larger than any commercial or state bank in the world. Postal savings contributed the largest share, 58% of the total. Table 12.1 shows the composition at the end of March 1999.

The third source of FILP funding was the Industrial Investment Special Account, set up after the end of Occupation. It derived its funds from transfers from the General Account Budget, where expenditures were specially earmarked for long-term industrial investment, in addition to those provided in various investment programmes in that Budget; and from the operating income derived from its loans and investments to FILP organizations such as the Japan Development Bank and the Export–Import Bank. In 1953 the Special Account provided a third of FILP funding, but thereafter the proportion declined. By 1980 it provided less than 1% of the total. No transfers from the

Table 12.1 *Trust Fund Bureau Fund: balance of accumulated deposits, March 1999*

	tr. yen	%
Postal savings deposits	250.967	57.9
Welfare insurance deposits	129.116	29.8
National pension deposits	10.381	2.4
Postal life insurance and postal annuity deposits	5.291	1.2
Other deposits[a]	35.571	8.3
Other	1.943	0.4
TOTAL	433.273	100

[a] Special Accounts for labour insurance, foreign exchange, postal savings, motor liability insurance, and earthquake insurance; the mutual aid cooperative, the special health and welfare programme fund, the Small and Medium-Sized Credit Insurance Corporation.

Source: First Fund Division, Financial Bureau, 1999, MOF.

General Account Budget were made after 1981. From 1985 dividend income from the sale of some of the stock of the privatized NTT provided the main source of that part of the Industrial Investment Special Account earmarked for FILP (discussed in Chapter 23).

The fourth source was the issue of bonds, and the borrowings made by the recipients of FILP, the principal of which together with interest payments were guaranteed by the government.

Each year MOF had to decide how much of the accumulated balance of the deposits in the Trust Fund Bureau Fund was to be made available to finance FILP activities, together with the contribution from the Industrial Investment Special Account, and the issue of government-guaranteed bonds and borrowings. Estimates were made of the probable cash flow into and out of the deposits, and included new deposits and redemption payments (both of principal and of interest on previous loans), withdrawals, payments of insurance, pensions, and so on. Table 12.2 shows the contributions from the four main sources to the FILP Budget at the end of FY1998–9. Trust Fund Bureau Funds, comprising postal savings and pensions' premiums, together with redemption payments, contributed 85% of the 65.6 trillion, with interest receipts and loan repayments accounting for more than half of that total. Postal savings (mainly in the form of new deposits) contributed less than a fifth. The increasing reliance on redemption payments raised an issue of the continuing viability of FILP funding, to which we return in Chapter 28.

CAPITAL MANAGEMENT OPERATIONS

Apart from the projects and programmes funded by FILP, a proportion of the deposits made to the Trust Fund Bureau Fund was invested to provide for the future capital

Table 12.2 *Composition of the FILP Budget funds, March 1999*

	tr. yen	%	tr. yen	%
Trust Fund Bureau Fund			55.8	85.1
Postal savings	12.2	18.6		
Welfare and national pensions	5.7	8.7		
Funds repaid: interest receipts and loan repayments	37.9	57.8		
Postal Life Insurance Fund			6.7	10.2
Industrial Investment Special Account			0.4	0.6
Government-guaranteed bonds and borrowings			2.6	4.0
TOTAL			65.6	100.0

Source: FILP Report 1999, Financial Bureau, October 1999, MOF.

growth of the Postal Savings Special Account, and the Special Accounts of the Employees Pension Fund and the National Pension Fund. Portfolio investment began in 1987, and continued annually to absorb between 10% and 20% of the overall FILP Budget thereafter until the implementation of the reforms began in FY1999.

There were two main capital operations managed by the First Fund Division of MOF's Financial Bureau. The first of those provided for a proportion of the Trust Fund Bureau Fund derived from postal savings to be managed through a Fund for Financial Liberalization. The aim was to 'contribute to the sound management of the postal savings business' through the management of money-market operations (FILP 1998: 18). The sum set aside was loaned to the Postal Savings Special Account, and a proportion was used to purchase government bonds, debentures, foreign bonds, and the like. Profits on those 'in-house operations' were returned and retained by the Fund for Financial Liberalization, within the Postal Savings Special Account. Figure 12.3 shows the flow of funds and market operations. In addition, capital management operations involved the investment of some funds from the Postal Life Insurance Fund, managed by the Postal Life Insurance Welfare Corporation. Profits on those operations were credited to the Postal Life Insurance Special Account.

The second capital management operation, the Pension Fund Consolidating Activities, provided for the transfer of funds from the Trust Fund Bureau Fund to the specially created Pension Welfare Services Public Corporation supervised by the Ministry of Health and Welfare. Funds were managed through trust banks, insurance companies, MOF's own in-house operations in the purchase of debentures, and so on (Figure 12.4). The aim was to generate a higher rate of return than would be available through loans from the Public Pension Fund, made available to FILP through the Trust

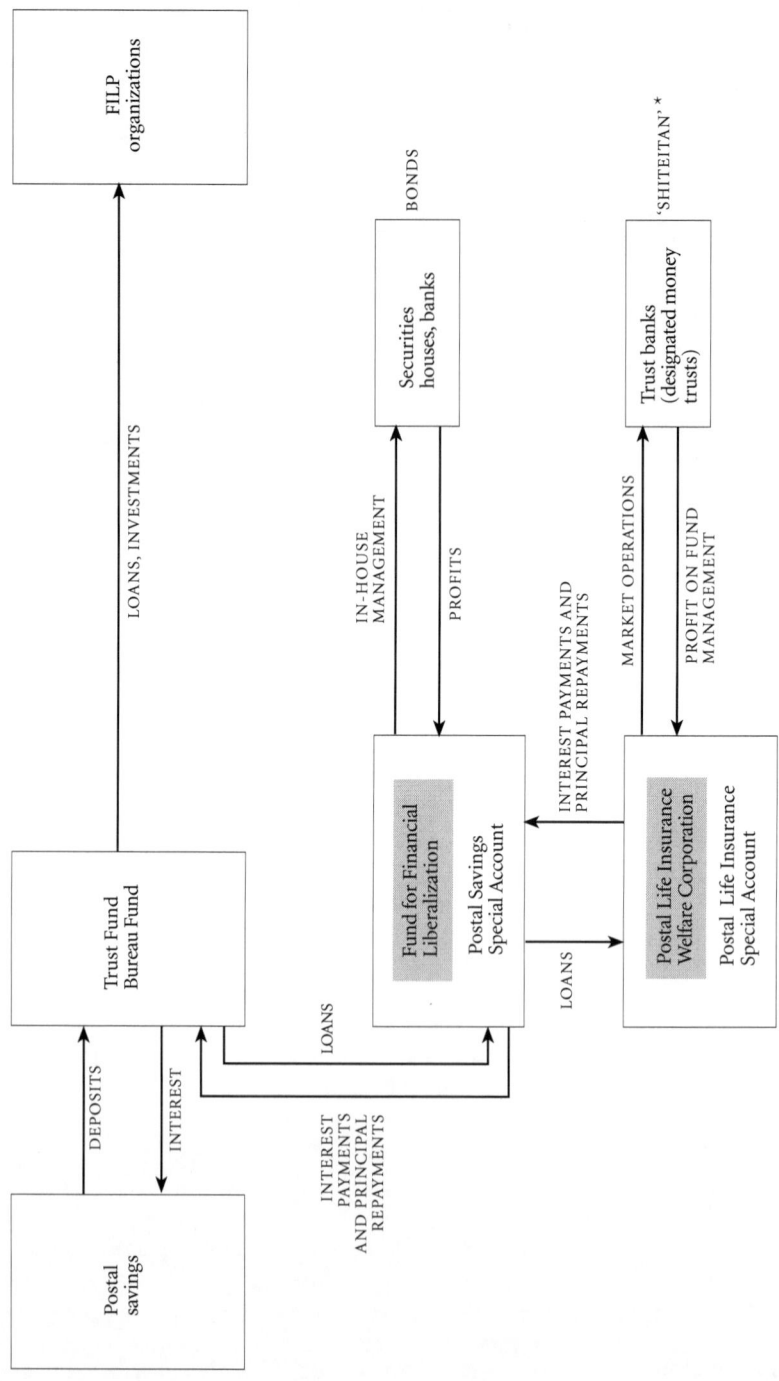

Figure 12.3 *FILP capital management operations: the postal savings financial liberalization fund, FY1987–FY2000*

* Individually operated designated money trusts at trust banks.

Source: Asset and Liability Management Office 1999, Financial Bureau, MOF.

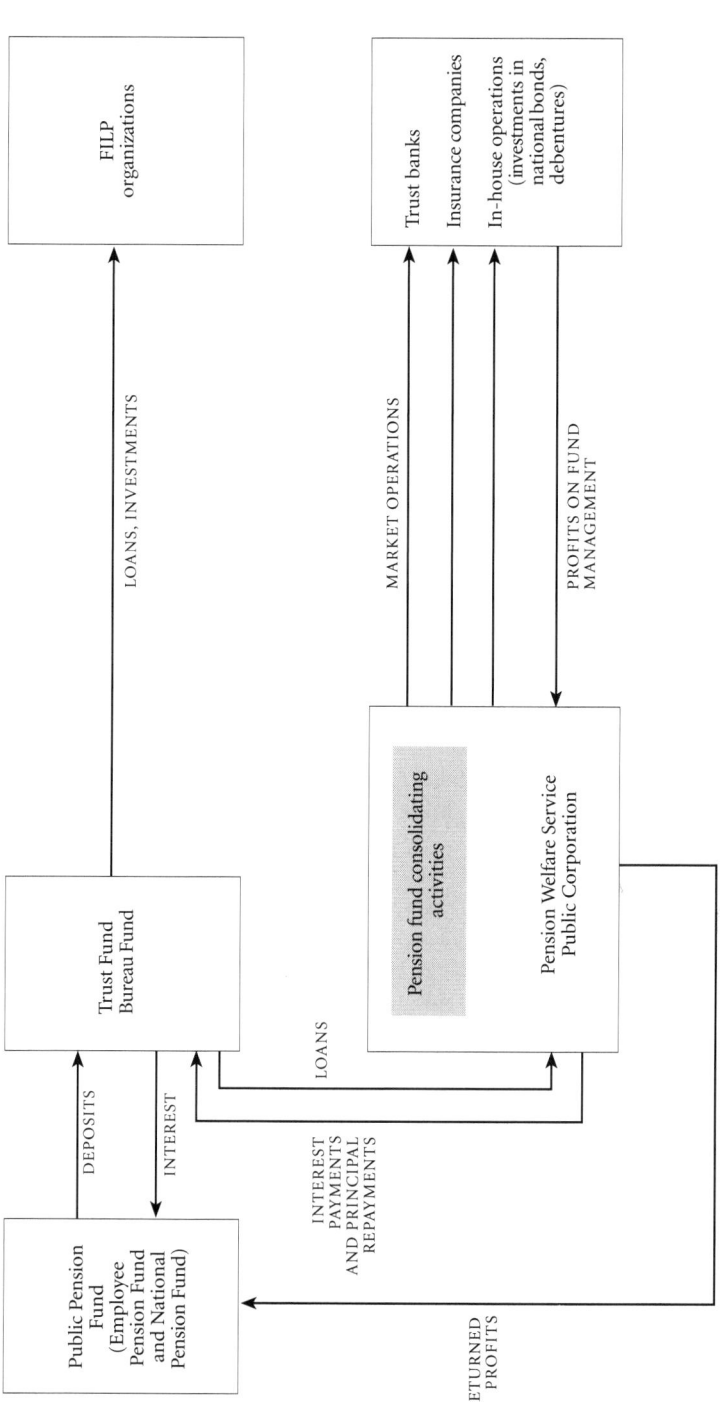

Figure 12.4 *FILP capital management operations: pension fund consolidating activities, FY1987–FY2000*

Source: Asset and Liability Management Office, 1999, Financial Bureau, MOF.

Fund Bureau Fund. The additional income generated in that way accrued to the Special Accounts for Employees' Insurance, and National Pensions. The management of postal savings and pension reserves through capital market operations became a major issue in the reform of FILP in 1997, and is discussed in Chapter 28.

THE PRESCRIPTION OF INTEREST RATES

The accumulation of savings, and their flow through the Trust Fund Bureau Fund to the FILP agencies, and thence to capital projects and programmes, was regulated by a series of interconnected decisions about rates of interest, determined in relation to market rates. At the point of entry, these had to be high enough to attract a continuous supply of savings into the postal savings system, although security and accessibility became as important factors in the 1990s with the failure of several regional banks. At the other (exit) end, the rates of interest charged on loans and investments by the FILP agencies to clients had to be at least competitive with private market rates for comparable long-term investments, and normally marginally more attractive. There were four sets of linked decisions. The first decision concerned the interest rates, terms and conditions of deposits with the postal savings system, the postal life insurance fund, and the interest earned on payments into the Welfare Insurance Fund. Those rates were determined after discussion and negotiation between MOF, MPT, and MHW, whose recommendations to the Fund Operation Council were invariably approved by the Cabinet. After financial liberalization in the mid-1980s, they were set in relation to rates of interest charged on similar types of three-year deposits by private-sector banks, or the coupon rate of ten-year national bonds.

The second decision was that of the rate of interest on deposits with the Trust Fund Bureau Fund from postal savings, postal life insurance, and welfare and pensions accounts. This was normally set higher than that paid investors in postal savings deposits, and was based on the coupon rate on ten-year government bonds. The third interest rate was that paid by FILP agencies and local governments for their loans from the Trust Fund Bureau Fund. As the TFBF was a non-profit, government institution, there was no spread between the main, long-term rate at which it borrowed and that at which it lent. Until 1987 that rate was fixed by law. Thereafter it was determined by the Cabinet on the recommendation of the Fund Operation Council, which normally approved the rate informally agreed between its three most influential members: MOF, MPT, and MHW.

The final and most critical interest rate decision for FILP was that to be charged by the FILP agencies on their loans and investments to their clients—private and public-sector firms and corporations, and local governments. As they had to pay interest on their borrowings from the Trust Fund Bureau Fund, they had in turn to seek a higher return on most, if not all, of their loans and investments in projects and programmes. Those FILP agencies such as the public banks and finance corporations (PFCs), which lent capital to other organizations, normally had two rates of interest: the standard FILP rate, which was set higher than the Trust Fund Bureau Fund rate, reflecting the

The 'Second Budget': FILP

long-term prime rate set by private-sector financial institutions, and a 'most preferred lending rate', normally set at a lower level. Some PFCs, notably the Government Housing Loan Corporation, but also the Agriculture, Fisheries and Forestry Finance Corporation, which charged a lower rate than the Trust Fund Bureau Fund rate in the 1990s, had the costs of the difference financed by a direct subsidy from the General Account Budget. Figure 12.5 shows in a simplified form the interconnection between interest rates and institutions, with the prevailing rates of interest at April 1995, when there was a positive spread between the rates at which the FILP agencies borrowed from the Trust Fund Bureau Fund and the rates it charged its clients for loans and investments. The lower rates in 1997 show the negative spread.

The deregulation of financial services, the liberalization of interest rates, and looser monetary policy combined to narrow the differential between public and private-sector interest rates. Whereas in the 1950s and 1960s the standard FILP rate was some 1% to 2% lower than comparable long-term prime rates, and the 'most preferred rate' as much as 2.5% lower still, by the end of the 1970s, the 'spreads' had become much thinner, with brief periods in the 1980s, and again in 1993 and 1996–7, when the FILP rate was higher than the private-sector long-term prime rate. As well, interest rates became more volatile after financial liberalization and deregulation, and fluctuations

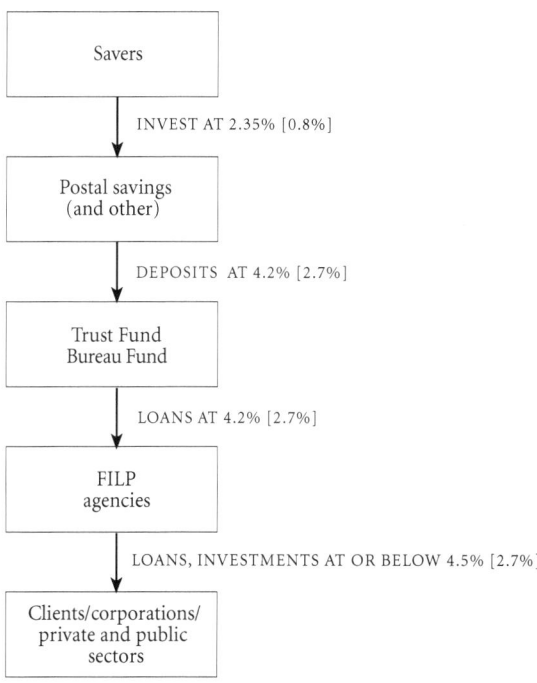

Figure 12.5 *FILP interest rate system, April 1995*
1997 rates given in square brackets

caused problems in the management of assets and liabilities for the Postal Savings Special Account, the Trust Fund Bureau Fund, and the FILP agencies. 'Negative spread' became more common, with the narrowing of the differential between public and private-sector interest rates.

THE RECIPIENTS OF FILP FUNDS: THE FILP AGENCIES

FILP's remit ran wide in the last quarter of the twentieth century, very much wider than when it was relaunched in its contemporary mode in 1953, when only 14 organizations were eligible for funding, and the greater part of those funds was directed to projects and programmes through the aegis of the Japan Development Bank, and the Export–Import Bank, for the development of basic industrial sectors and the promotion and diffusion of new technologies. In 1998 public banks, finance corporations, and public corporations and companies in receipt of FILP funds extended into every part of the public and private sectors. Directly and indirectly, with FILP funds, they supported agriculture, land acquisition, communication, and transport; social and environmental infrastructure—housing, hospitals, nursing homes, schools, water, and sewage facilities; leisure, recreational, and environmental projects; small and medium-sized businesses; industrial, scientific, and technological development; urban and regional development; and international economic aid and cooperation.

FILP funds for those purposes were provided in three main ways: by direct loans made on a long-term (over five years), low-interest basis to finance capital projects or programmes, or to fill a specific 'credit-gap' where borrowers lacked collateral or credit-worthiness; by government-guaranteed loans; and by loan insurance. Direct loans were the most important and common method of finance.

At the end of March 1999 FILP assets totalled 436 trillion, the balance of loans and investments outstanding to public organizations, among which were 68 public finance and other corporations, ten Special Accounts, the General Account Budget, and a number of local public enterprises. FILP's overall liabilities totalled 434 trillion, leaving a surplus of 1.6 trillion (FILP 1999). The number of FILP agencies in receipt of FILP funds varied marginally year by year, depending upon needs, priority, and the availability of resources. In the 1990s, before the implementation of policies of reduction and consolidation of public corporations, about 60 received some funding each year. In FY1998, 54 public organizations were allocated FILP funds, in five broad categories, differentiated by legal status, function, and their relationship with central government. They are shown in Table 12.3.

The growth of the number of public corporations and special companies in the 1950s and 1960s reflected the changing role of FILP in the economy. Many of those provided finance for the creation, improvement, or maintenance of 'social capital', where the expectation of earning profits on capital employed sufficient to repay the interest and redeem the principal was low and/or very long-term. For some agencies that was acknowledged explicitly by the receipt of annual subsidies from the central government budget; other agencies, with inherited or accumulated debt, were

Table 12.3 *Organizations in receipt of FILP funds, FY1998, and their sponsoring ministries and agencies*

Organizations in receipt of funds	Sponsoring ministries/agencies
Public finance corporations and banks (Kōko, Ginkō, etc.) (11)	
Government Housing Loan Corporation (1950)	MOC and MOF
People's Finance Corporation (1949)	MOF
Small Business Finance Corporation (1953)	MITI and MOF
Environmental Sanitation Business Finance Corporation (1967)	MHW and MOF
Agriculture, Forestry, and Fisheries Finance Corporation (1953)	MAFF and MOF
Finance Corporation for Municipal Enterprises (1957)	MHA and MOF
Hokkaido–Tōhoku Development Finance Corporation (1956)	HDA, NLA, and MOF
Okinawa Development Finance Corporation (1972)	OkDA and MOF
Japan Development Bank (1951)	MOF
Export–Import Bank of Japan (1950)	MOF
Small Business Credit Insurance Corporation (1958)	MITI and MOF
Public corporations (Kōdan, Jigyōdan, Eidan, etc.) (31)	
Housing and Urban Development Corporation	MOC/MOT
Pension Welfare Service Public Corporation	MHW
Employment Promotion Projects Corporation	MOL
Japan Environment Corporation	MITI/MOC/MHW/MOT/EA
Teito Rapid Transit Authority	MOT/MOC
Japan Regional Development Corporation	NLA/MOC/MITI
* Japan Sewerage Works Agency	MOC
Social Welfare and Medical Service Corporation	MHW
* Organization for Adverse Drug Reaction Relief and Drug Research Promotion and Product Review	MHW
Japan Private School Promotion Foundation	MOE
Japan Scholarship Foundation	MOE
Agricultural Land Development Agency	MAFF
Forest Development Corporation	MAFF
* Bio-oriented Technology Research Advancement Institution	MAFF
Japan Highways Public Corporation	MOC
Metropolitan Expressway Public Corporation	MOC
Hanshin Expressway Public Corporation	MOC
Honshu–Shikoku Bridge Authority	MOC/MOT
Japan Railway Construction Public Corporation	MOT
New Tokyo International Airport Authority	MOT
* Telecommunications Satellite Corporation of Japan	MPT
Water Resources Development Corporation	MAFF/NLA/MITI/MHW/MOC
Amami Gunto Promotion and Development Credit Fund	NLA and MOF

Table 12.3 *(cont.)*

Organizations in receipt of funds	Sponsoring ministries/agencies
Metal Mining Agency of Japan	MITI
Japan National Oil Corporation	MITI
Japan Science and Technology Corporation	STA
*Information Technology Promotion Agency	MITI
*Japan Key-Technology Centre	MITI/MPT
Overseas Economic Cooperation Fund	EPA
Post Office Life Insurance Welfare Corporation	MPT
Corporation for Advanced Transport and Technology	MOT
New Energy and Industrial Technology Development Organization	MITI
Special companies, banks (5)	
Central Bank for Commercial and Industrial Cooperatives (Shōkō Chūkin Bank)	MOF/MITI
Kansai International Airport Co. Ltd	MOT
*Organization for Promotion of Urban Development	MOC
Electric Power Development Co. Ltd	MITI
Central Japan International Airport Co. Ltd	MOT
Special Accounts (9)	
Financing for Urban Development Funds	MOC
National Property Consolidation Fund	MOF
National hospitals	MHW
National schools	MOE
National land improvement project	MAFF
National forest and field services	MAFF
Postal services	MPT
Airport development	MOT
Postal savings	MPT
Local governments and local public enterprises	

Note: *were not public corporations in the strict sense used in official definitions of the term (*tokushu-hōjin*).

Source: Asset and Liability Management Office, First Fund Division, Financial Bureau, MOF, 1998.

subsidized implicitly through FILP by the continuation of loans and rollover and recycling arrangements, for which there was little expectation of repayment. A few agencies, for example OECF, continued to receive annual capital subscriptions from the central government, as well as government grants, i.e. subsidies, without which they would have been unable to balance annual income and expenditure.

FILP agencies were differentiated by status and function. First, there were the 11 public banks and finance corporations established originally to fill a need for capital investment which private-sector institutions could not or would not meet. They borrowed money to finance the activities of private and public organizations. The two banks, the (then) Japan Development Bank and the (then) Export–Import Bank of

Japan, were special corporations wholly capitalized by the government; they had legally guaranteed autonomy from the government, and held substantial capital of their own. The government was heavily involved in the activities of the other nine finance corporations, which had more circumscribed policy objectives. Ministerial approval was required quarterly for their projects, and funding programmes; most of their funds were provided by FILP loans.

The public banks and finance corporations were at the heart of the FILP system, and between them accounted annually for about 40% of the total FILP Budget, and 35% of the outstanding balance of the Trust Fund Bureau Fund. A quarter of the FILP Budget went to other public corporations and companies, while Special Accounts and local government each attracted about 16%. In addition to FILP funds, and any subsidy from the General Account Budget, the FILP agencies drew upon their own funds to finance a part of their operations, or to supplement those allocated from FILP for particular projects. These included loan repayments from client firms and companies, and accumulated internal reserves. In addition, FILP agencies raised money from the private sector through the issue of bonds not guaranteed by the government, and the issue of bonds overseas (with government guarantees), a method used actively by the Japan Development Bank and the Export–Import Bank in the 1980s.

The Japan Development Bank and the Export–Import Bank were established in the early 1950s and, as the engines of the strategy for industrial reconstruction, were then the principal recipients of FILP funds. Thereafter, new public finance corporations were established, partly to meet the sectoral diversification of public investment, but also as a result of pressure from special interest groups, particularly those representing farmers and small businessmen, both traditional supporters of the LDP, seeking access to privileged sources of finance. The Agriculture, Forestry and Fishery Finance Corporation was set up in 1953 on the initiative of the Diet to ensure that agriculture would not have to compete for scarce funds with basic industries supported by the JDB. Similarly, the Small Business Finance Corporation was set up (1953) to insulate small firms from competition for funds with large corporations. The special needs of doctors, small hospitals, and clinics were recognized with the creation in 1962 of the Medical Care Facilities Finance Corporation, abolished in 1985. Credit for small businesses at the grass-roots level crucial to the LDP was provided also through the Environmental Sanitation Businesses Finance Corporation set up in 1967, allegedly at the instigation of the then secretary-general of the LDP, Tanaka Kakuei (Calder 1993).

The second category of FILP agencies comprised (in 1998) 31 public corporations, established by law to undertake on their own account specific profitable capital investment projects which contributed to public welfare, such as road-and house-building, urban and regional development; the development and improvement of airports, docks, and harbours; education, social, welfare, and environmental facilities; and industrial and technological development. They were wholly dependent on FILP funds for their capital, and repaid their loans and interest payments from the accruing revenues over the lifetime of the projects. Their number and diversity (*kōdan, jigyōdan, eidan*, etc.) grew rapidly in the 1960s, from eight to 25, complemented by the addition of a number of public–private enterprises (*tokushu gaisha*) in the industrial and communications sectors. Most, but not all, received FILP funds subsequently. From 1995, coalition and LDP governments were committed in principle to the reduction and consolidation of their number and functions, as discussed in Chapter 4.

The third group of FILP agencies comprised four Special Companies and the Shōkō Chūkin Bank, which provided credit facilities for the agricultural (and other) cooperatives. The fourth group comprised nine of the 38 Special Accounts, each with its own budget, part of whose capital requirements were provided through FILP. Finally, local authorities and their local public enterprises were also eligible for FILP funds.

FILP AND LOCAL GOVERNMENT

Local governments owned, operated, and managed some 3,500 legally constituted local public enterprises, which provided services such as water supply and sewage disposal, and also electricity and gas supply, some hospital services, and local transportation. In principle, the enterprises were financially self-sufficient, charging their customers for the services provided. Their current and capital revenues, and expenditures, were managed in Special Accounts by local governments, separate from their own tax-based 'Ordinary Accounts'. There were also some 1,700 local public corporations for housing, toll-road construction, the acquisition of land for public works projects, and so on. Finally, there were so-called 'third sector' companies, jointly established by the public and private sectors.

Most of the capital required by local governments for the construction of public facilities, such as hospitals and schools, was not expected to generate future profits, and was provided therefore through subsidies from the central government, local revenue income, and local borrowing, the costs of which were borne mainly on the 'Ordinary Account'. By contrast, the capital for the public works projects of local public enterprises was expected to generate sufficient returns to cover the costs of the annual interest, and repayment of the principal, of loans. It is here that FILP had a major role to play. Directly, FILP provided almost a half of their annual capital requirements; indirectly, through the financing of one of its agencies, the Japan Finance Corporation for Municipal Enterprises, it provided a further tranche of funds.

Two other sources provided most of the remaining capital: local bonds issued by local governments for sale to the public in the money markets, and guaranteed by central government; and loans raised through the placement of local bonds with private-sector financial institutions, mainly regional and city banks. The aggregates of the four main sources were decided centrally by MOF's Financial Bureau, which annually compiled the Local Bond Plan concurrently with the Local Finance Plan, both within the wider context of the overall budget for FILP and the General Account Budget. The composition of the Local Bond Plan for FY1997 is shown in Table 12.4.

The issue of local bonds for both the capital programmes of local governments and their local public enterprises was tightly controlled by the central government, through the Loan Permit system. Prefectures, designated major cities and some special wards in cities and towns required the permission of the MHA; other towns and cities required

Table 12.4 Local bond plan for FY1997

	tr. yen	tr. yen	%
FILP funds		8.6	49.5
Postal savings	5.4		
Pension funds	1.5		
Postal insurance	1.7		
Japan FC for Municipal Enterprises (government-guaranteed bonds and JME bonds)		2.2	12.8
Private sector			
Local government bonds offered to the public on the market		1.4	8.3
Loans from regional, city banks, etc.		5.1	29.4
TOTAL		17.4	100

Source: JFCME (1997a).

the permission of the prefectural governor. The purposes for which bonds might be issued were prescribed by law. In certain circumstances, shortfalls in the revenue from the national consumption tax (a proportion of which was allocated to local governments) could be covered by the issue of extraordinary bonds. In FY1997 about 10% of the total bonds planned for issue by local governments on their 'Ordinary Accounts' were for that purpose.

The issues raised in this chapter, in particular the contrast between principle and practice, and the exploitation of FILP to relieve pressure on the stressed General Account Budget, are taken up in Chapter 19, which deals with the processes of making the FILP Budget, in Chapter 24, which analyses the outputs of those processes, and in Chapter 28, which explores the tensions in the operation of the FILP system, which precipitated the review and reforms initiated in 1997–8 and implemented in 2001.

PART III

INTERACTIONS

13

Budget Objectives and Policies

MOF reacted to the emergence of the fiscal crisis in 1975 by prescribing three related policy aims: to devise and implement a strategy to change the structure of the tax system so as to provide a more stable and productive source of revenue; to constrain the growth of public spending; and to reduce and, if possible, eliminate the fiscal deficit, and with it the rising costs of government debt. Over the following 25 years those aims were translated into specific short- and medium-term policy objectives, refined and adjusted contingently to accord with conjunctural changes in the economy and the polity. This chapter explains the origins and evolution of those objectives, and describes the formulation of policies, and the process of 'policy succession', to achieve them. The effects and effectiveness of the implementation of those policies, and an assessment of the achievement of MOF's declared objectives, are dealt with in Chapter 25.

THE SEARCH FOR REVENUE

With the expansion of welfare programmes in the early 1970s, the rising costs of the sophisticated compensatory politics practised by the LDP to maintain itself in power, and the prospect of a progressively ageing Japanese population, it became imperative for MOF to search for additional sources of revenue. MOF had begun to prepare the ground for a reform of the tax structure before the onset of the crisis in FY1975. Observing the switch from direct to indirect taxes in other industrial countries with the introduction of general value added taxes, it had proposed in 1971, through the medium of the Government Tax System Research Council, the desirability of introducing a general consumption tax at some future date. By 1977 what had been merely desirable had become imperative and urgent, and the Council's proposals for the introduction of a new tax were endorsed by Prime Minister Ō'Hira and his government a year later. It failed, partly because of opposition within the LDP, but mainly because of its general unpopularity in the country. The poor showing of the LDP in the 1979 Lower House election was widely believed to have been attributable to the tax proposal, even though Ō'Hira had withdrawn it during the election campaign.

Opposition to a general consumption tax as a means of ameliorating the fiscal crisis inspired, and then energized, a more popular movement for eliminating waste and inefficiency in government, cutting public spending, and reforming administrative and budgetary structures. For the time being, MOF turned its attention away from new methods of revenue-raising to ways of cutting or slowing the growth of public expenditure, and managed and then exploited the political agenda for reform set by the Provisional Council on Administrative Reform to tighten its own expenditure control, as explained in Chapter 4. However, as Katō Junko (1994) argues, MOF's policies for controlling both expenditure and revenue-raising during the period 1980–6 paved the way for the second attempt to raise additional revenue through a consumption tax in 1987. This occurred because of its narrow and singular interpretation of 'fiscal reconstruction without tax increase' (adopted in 1982) to mean no tax increase in FY1982, and no reform of tax *structures* thereafter. MOF argued, and the Council accepted, that existing special tax measures could be rationalized, and existing rates of taxes could be adjusted marginally. From 1982 to 1984, MOF continued to abolish tax privileges for corporations, and to increase the rates for corporate taxation. These helped to raise additional revenue, and served to keep the issue of tax reform on the political agenda.

Attitudes towards a consumption tax began to change. In the first place, the increase of existing corporate and indirect taxes made big, but not small, business interests less hostile to the alternative of such a tax. Secondly, as policies of fiscal reconstruction were implemented by MOF, the squeeze on some politically popular, and electorally expedient, expenditure programmes helped to shift opinion among the LDP rank-and-file towards tax reform as a preferable alternative. Thirdly, and crucially, MOF was able to show that the fiscal crisis could not be solved simply by cutting public spending, as the Administrative Reform campaign proposed and then endorsed: the imposition of limits on the General Account Budget merely slowed the growth of the budget aggregate. MOF also proposed shifting the balance of taxation from direct to indirect taxes, thereby capitalizing on the popular and political mood to reduce the burden of income taxes.

The second attempt to introduce a new sales tax in the mid-1980s was no more successful than the first, but for different reasons. There was now more support for it within the LDP, and among the representative associations of big, but not small, businesses. However, Prime Minister Nakasone's public pledge that he would not introduce 'a large-scale indirect tax levied on every stage of transaction like a casting net' (Katō Junko 1994: 189), effectively ruled out a value added tax. But in any case, a radical income tax reduction similar to that introduced by President Reagan in the USA was a more important priority for him. In the face of popular hostility to a new sales tax, his pledge proved crucial in the July 1986 general election. MOF had hoped to combine in a tax reform package both Nakasone's income tax reductions and its own new sales tax, justified on the grounds of 'revenue neutrality'. In the end, the sales tax had to be withdrawn in order to pass the stalled FY1987 budget. A major difference between the failure of the second attempt from that of 1979 was that in 1987 the LDP leadership, and the leaders of the business community, were more supportive of MOF's attempt to introduce a sales tax. The former were worried by the further cuts in programme expenditures if additional revenue sources were not found, the latter by the concern to avoid increases in corporation taxation as an alternative to a new tax.

The significance of the second failed attempt was that it served to politicize the wider issue of the reform of taxation, and to move it higher up the political agenda. Within six months of the withdrawal of the doomed proposals, the Cabinet and the LDP had agreed to introduce a broadly based consumption tax. As before, it was linked to measures to reform tax inequalities designed to appeal broadly to the public, and to the special interests of business; but both MOF and the LDP had to pay a price. A consumption tax was not politically feasible without the inducement of cuts in income tax, and some concessions to business interests, through cuts in corporation tax, and excise duties. The compromise package devised by MOF and the LDP leadership was not intended to solve the fiscal deficit in the short term. MOF's aim was longer-term, to change the structure of taxation; securing the principle of a consumption tax was a necessary first step. The LDP could offer the electorate significant tax reductions to offset the unpopularity of the new tax, and to limit the electoral damage. Nevertheless, it was a high-risk strategy.

The new tax was unpopular not only with the general public: small businesses, a traditional source of electoral and financial support, were uniformly hostile. Following the enactment of the tax reforms in December 1988, the LDP lost its majority in the House of Councillors in July 1989, the first time this had occurred since 1955. However, soon after, public interest in the new tax began to wane, and without a credible alternative the opposition parties were unable to capitalize further on their electoral success. In the 1990 general election for the House of Representatives, despite the new tax and the political fallout from the Recruit–Cosmos scandal, the LDP unexpectedly retained control, albeit with a reduced majority.

MOF had begun to implement its long-term aim to reform the structure of the taxation system, but the shortfall in revenue remained. To make the new consumption tax politically acceptable, it had been obliged to provide the LDP with inducements, designed to remove tax inequalities, to offer a generally hostile public, and to compromise with special interest groups on the details of the new tax. The short-term effects of those necessary and politically expedient compromises added to the shortfall of revenue. MOF estimated the revenue from the new consumption tax at 5.4 trillion, outweighed by cuts in direct and indirect taxes totalling 8.3 trillion. But MOF had not compromised on the principle of a broadly based consumption tax, and its acceptance was a necessary first stage towards securing a more stable and productive source of revenue. Thereafter, MOF could seek opportunistically to exploit the potential of such a tax to raise further revenue.

The gravity of the continuing critical condition of the national finances was temporarily obscured by the economic expansion of the years of the bubble economy. The burst of economic activity generated sufficient revenues from direct and indirect taxes for MOF to reduce the amount of government borrowing, to eliminate the issue of special deficit-financing bonds, and to progress towards its target for the bond dependency ratio. After some minor revisions to the categories of products and businesses affected by the consumption tax, supported by all parties, the issue of revenue shortfall lay dormant. With the collapse of the bubble economy at the end of 1990, the 'windfall' revenues quickly disappeared.

The accession to office of a new multi-party government in 1993 provided an opportunity for MOF to launch a fresh initiative to raise more revenue through indirect taxes. Primed by MOF, the Government Tax Research Council reported in November 1993 on the urgent need for a radical reform of the tax system, which the Hosokawa

Coalition government promptly endorsed in principle. MOF's pre-emptive and maladroit attempt to launch the reform process as a personal initiative of the Prime Minister in April 1994, without consultation with the coalition partners, and without the customary ground-clearing, is explicable only in terms of a deliberate high-risk tactical strike prompted by alarm at the rapid deterioration of the state of the national finances. The revised estimates of expenditure and revenues during the course of FY1993 necessitated yet another massive increase in government borrowing, from a planned 8.1 trillion to 16.1 trillion. The political ground was so badly prepared that the Prime Minister was obliged to withdraw the proposal for a national welfare tax within 24 hours, as the SDP threatened to leave the coalition. The need for such a tax, and the merits of the proposal, were barely discussed, consumed by the politics of an unstable coalition, and the integrity and credibility of the Prime Minister. The immediate and humiliating withdrawal of the proposals contributed further to a weakening of MOF's prestige and authority, and precipitated the downfall of Hosokawa and the breakup of the coalition government.

More remarkable even than MOF's attempted *putsch* was the *volte face* of the SDP a few months later on returning to office in the coalition government led by Murayama Tomiichi. From a position of outright opposition to the principle of a consumption tax in all three previous attempts to introduce one, and its repudiation of Prime Minister Hosokawa six months earlier, the SDP now agreed to a package of tax reforms in September 1993 which included an increase in the consumption tax, albeit to be deferred until April 1997, and subject to review before final confirmation. On this occasion MOF had prepared the ground more carefully, but it had nevertheless been obliged to accept compromises over income tax reductions as the price of political agreement to prospective increases in the consumption tax. In July 1996, the Hashimoto Coalition government approved the deferred proposal, and the consumption tax was raised from 3% to 5% in April 1997. I shall consider the consequences of that decision later in the chapter, but first examine the aims and objectives of MOF's policies to 'reconstruct', and then 'consolidate', the national finances mainly through tighter control of the General Account Budget expenditures.

FISCAL RECONSTRUCTION, 1976–1987

Following the death of Prime Minister Ō'Hira, Suzuki Zenkō formed a new LDP administration in July 1980, and declared his Cabinet's mission to be the reconstruction of the national finances. In his budget speech to the Diet in January 1981, the Minister of Finance, Watanabe Michio, proclaimed FY1981 as the first year of that reconstruction. The announcement preceded the establishment of the first Provisional Council for Administrative Reform (Rinchō) a few months later, although that decision had already been taken. Fiscal reconstruction became the unifying theme of its inquiries and recommendations.

In practice, MOF had been committed to the reconstruction of the national finances for at least four or five years before the FY1981 budget. The aims and objectives, and the broad thrust of future fiscal policies to achieve them, were embryonically present in its ad hoc responses to the emergence of the fiscal crisis of the mid-1970s, in particular as the gravity of the fiscal situation was exposed in FY1974 and FY1975. The aim of eliminating the issue of special deficit-financing bonds was set in 1976; the Medium Term Fiscal Projection was inaugurated in 1978. The significance of the earlier date for the initiation of the policy of reconstruction is twofold: first, it makes clear that the initiative lay with MOF and not with Rinchō, as some have argued; and, secondly, it makes clear that the objectives and the agenda of fiscal policies to achieve them were evolved by the Ministry, and were already in place and approved by the LDP leadership before Rinchō began work. As explained in Chapter 4, MOF exploited the opportunity provided by its creation and work to reinforce the commitment of the LDP leadership, and to forge a broader and more public consensus among the other members of the LDP's ruling coalition of politicians and businessmen. Rinchō was seen by MOF as a medium through which to convey to the public the urgency of the need of fiscal reconstruction, and as an instrument to be played upon to further its own aims, objectives, and policies for public finance. While it is true, as Suzuki (1999) and others have argued, that the fiscal crisis required a new, broader budget consensus to support MOF's policies to cut expenditure, that consensus was more apparent than real. In Chapter 25 I show that in practice MOF's policies of fiscal reconstruction were frustrated and thwarted by pressures from the LDP and its clientelistic supporters for more public spending throughout the 1980s.

The Principles of 'Sound Management' of the National Finances

Before MOF could initiate policies to reconstruct the national finances, it had first to convince the LDP leadership of the gravity of the fiscal crisis, and that the causes were structural rather than cyclical. Prime Minister Ō'Hira took little convincing. Earlier in the 1970s, when minister of finance, he had been worried about the long-term fiscal consequences of the rapid expansion of welfare programmes. Now as prime minister he identified himself personally with MOF's response to the crisis (see Sato *et al.* 1990). Secondly, MOF had to convince the LDP leadership that fiscal reconstruction was a necessary and appropriate response to the underlying causes of the crisis, and, to prescribe a set of guidelines broadly acceptable to it, which crucially could be invoked subsequently to validate unpalatable fiscal policies and commit ministers to them.

The first basic principle of 'sound management' was a balanced budget, the dominant characteristic of MOF's orthodox fiscal policy in post-war Japan. In his budget speech for FY1977, the Minister of Finance announced the government's aim 'to restore fiscal balance at the earliest possible opportunity' (MOF 1977: 26). The other principles were all contingent on the symptoms of annual fiscal deficits that resulted from imbalance. Two related specifically to the management of the economy. First, it was argued that the expansion of the money supply through the sale of government bonds carried the risk of 'fiscally induced' inflation (a reminder of the hyperinflation of the 1940s, triggered by the Bank of Japan's willingness to purchase government bonds, action prohibited under the 1947 Constitution), and of 'crowding out' private-sector investment.

Secondly, 'sound management' of the national finances required that current expenditures should be financed by current revenues to avoid a burden on future generations of taxpayers, for example by the issue of government bonds to finance a deficit that arose from a shortfall of revenue to cover them. From the implementation of the Dodge Line onwards, government borrowing through the issue of bonds was strictly regulated by Finance Law. Finally, 'sound management' required that the budgetary system should be operated flexibly, and resources allocated efficiently. Fiscal deficits and the growth of 'fixed expenditures' associated with the servicing of contingent national debt (and the statutory allocation of a fixed proportion of nationally collected taxes to local government) led to 'fiscal rigidification', constraining the funding available for programme expenditures in the annual General Account Budget and obstructing the efficient and effective allocation of resources among them.

Policy Rules-of-the-Game

Two informal policy rules-of-the-game had governed the implementation of fiscal policy in the high-growth era. In the preparation of the budget plan, MOF deliberately underestimated the so-called 'natural increase' in tax revenues that accrued from the growth of the economy. It did so partly to dampen expectations about the resources available to finance spending programmes. MOF's estimate of GDP growth was almost always intentionally cautious. When, as normally happened up to 1974, the economy grew at a much faster rate, it generated a surplus of revenues by the time of settlement at the end of the fiscal year greater than the tax yield forecasted 18 months earlier. Carried forward to the next year, the surplus was used partly to enable the LDP to deliver annual tax reductions, an important element of its electoral politics. The expectation and regularity of the 'natural increases' provided the resources to implement MOF's second policy rule: to maintain the ratio of total taxation to national income at a constant 20%.

Both policy rules became more difficult to implement in the changed economic and fiscal climate from 1975. Annual tax reductions paid for out of the surplus were suspended as tax revenues shrank with the slow-down of the economy, and the phenomenon of 'natural increase' evaporated until the occurrence of the 'bubble' in 1986. The 20% rule was breached in 1980, and reformulated three years later to reflect the need to raise more revenue from tax changes. In 1983 MOF announced that it would be guided by the rule that the ratio of taxes *and* social security payments to national income would be less than 50% at the peak period of the ageing of the population. MOF's deliberate underestimating of the growth of the economy gave way to a more flexible and expedient rule dictated by the objective of reducing government borrowing. As I shall explain in the next chapter, the politics of the GDP forecasts became a contentious issue within the bureaucracy in the 1980s and the 1990s as MOF consistently argued, and urged upon EPA, unrealistically high growth rates, and hence unrealistically high estimates of revenues based upon them. Overestimation of GDP and revenue yields in the planned budget enabled MOF to reduce the planned (but not actual) borrowing requirement, and to avoid drastic cuts in expenditure.

Until the emergence of a fiscal deficit in 1965, the principles of 'sound management', and the informal budgetary rules-of-the-game, had provided the underlying basis of MOF's management of the national finances from the imposition of the Dodge Line onwards. Hitherto largely unstated or unemphasized, their public articulation, affirmation, and continual reiteration thereafter served three purposes essential to MOF's evolving strategy for dealing with the causes and consequences of the fiscal crisis. First, Cabinet ministers and senior LDP politicians could not easily repudiate the implications for fiscal policy which followed logically from their acceptance of those principles, viz. the reconstruction of the expenditure and tax system that MOF advocated. Secondly, in order to attempt fiscal reconstruction, MOF had to try to change political perceptions and expectations of the role of public spending in the economy. Here the principles and budgetary rules provided a set of guidelines to which MOF officials and ministers referred in the preparation, discussion, and presentation of the annual budgets, and reiterated in the official analyses and commentaries that accompanied economic forecasts and medium-term projections and plans. Repetition and reiteration helped in the process of 'educating' politicians, bureaucrats in the Spending Ministries, interest groups, the media, and the public to acknowledge and accept the fiscal consequences of changed and changing economic circumstances. Thirdly, the principles of sound management provided a set of broad contextual constraints within which bids for more spending, and demands for less taxation, from ministers, bureaucrats, local politicians, and special interest groups could be negotiated.

Political subscription to those principles did not of course guarantee that in practice participants in the budgetary processes would exercise self-restraint when their own interests, or those of their clients or supporters, were threatened by MOF's policies to cut spending or raise taxes. But by signing up publicly to them, the LDP legitimized MOF's reformulation of the fiscal agenda.

While all the principles were reiterated in successive budgetary cycles from 1977 onwards, two were given increasing weight as the size of annual fiscal deficits increased. MOF repeatedly drew attention to the accumulation of national debt, and its absorption of increasing amounts of GDP, and to the annual costs of servicing the total of the debt outstanding. Discretion to vary expenditures on programmes to reflect political priorities was being progressively eroded. The implication was clear. If LDP ministers and their backbench supporters could deliver less to their constituents and clients because of the inescapable costs of servicing the debt, they were more vulnerable politically. The LDP's electoral success, and its domination of the Diet, had been built, and then rebuilt (in the early 1970s), on the politics of the distribution of budget benefits to supporters and compensation for aggrieved or disaffected groups. Fears and anxieties about future prosperity were also exploited skilfully by MOF as it warned repeatedly of the fiscal consequences of an ageing population obliged to bear the burden of the mounting costs of the accumulating national debt, and its rising demands on public expenditure programmes such as pensions, social security, health care, and welfare.

Those longer-term implications of continuing fiscal deficits and consequential government borrowing were less persuasive arguments for LDP politicians than those where MOF was able to show that the short- and medium-term effects of fiscal rigidification limited their discretion to adjust the amount and distribution of expenditure on favoured programmes. Nevertheless, both arguments were deployed with increasing sophistication and emphasis through the 1980s to justify MOF's policies of fiscal reconstruction.

Aims and Objectives

The main objectives of fiscal reconstruction were outlined by MOF in the budget statements for FY1976 and FY1977, some five years before Rinchō began work in 1981. Thereafter they were progressively elaborated and refined, but remained in essence unchanged throughout the period to 2000. The main aim was to eliminate special deficit-financing bonds, first issued in response to the fiscal deficit that arose from the huge shortfall of revenue in 1975, described in Chapter 2. The second related objective of reducing the bond dependency ratio, was broader in its intent, including not only the elimination of those bonds but a reduction in the issue of 'ordinary' (construction) bonds as well to finance capital projects. 'Bond dependency' measures the proportion of the total General Account Budget financed by the issue of government bonds, both ordinary and special. Realistically, MOF accepted the economic argument for continuing to finance a proportion of capital investment by issuing ordinary bonds. Nevertheless, reduction in the issue of those bonds was implicit also in its third objective: to reduce the size and accumulating service costs of the total central government debt outstanding.

Policies for Reconstruction

Those three objectives, repeated in successive budget statements, drove fiscal policy for the next fifteen years until 1990, when the elimination of the issue of special deficit-financing bonds was briefly achieved. Alarmed by the huge revenue shortfall that occurred after the preparation of the initial budget for FY1975, MOF began simultaneously to search for ways to raise additional revenue, and to cut expenditures to plug the gap. For the moment, those were mainly ad hoc, short-term measures, marginal adjustments to existing patterns of expenditure growth and sources of revenue. Nevertheless, the General Account Budget for FY1976 marked the end of the era of rapid expansion of public spending begun under Prime Minister Tanaka Kakuei's tutelage. The expectation of rising public spending had been nurtured by the politics of welfare and compensation practised by LDP governments, and their supporters, for almost a decade. To those continuing pressures were added those of an economy in recession after the first oil shock in 1973, and the negative real-term GDP growth recorded in the following year. MOF's dilemma was that it was confronted simultaneously by a fiscal crisis which required the raising of more revenue, and less spending, to relieve it, and by an economic crisis which required countercyclical fiscal policies incorporating higher spending and lower taxes. Its response was cautious. It cut the rate of growth of the General Account Budget for FY1976. Again, the significance was less the size of the cut than what it symbolized. Reconstruction had begun: MOF (and the LDP) was committed in principle to reversing the trend of the inexorable growth of the Budget. The 14% increase in the initial budget was 'quite small compared with the average rate of increase of the last ten years', and represented 'a step towards the integration of public finances into the new pattern of economic growth' (MOF 1976: 26). MOF was unable to sustain even that modest momentum in FY1977, when, under pressure from the international economic community to expand domestic demand as a key 'locomotive' economy, it budgeted for an increase on the General Account of 17.4%. It was, however, able to claim some small success in reducing the number of bonds issued initially to cover the fiscal deficit, although in the event it was obliged subsequently to issue more after revised estimates of a lower yield of taxes became available.

FY1980 was targeted by MOF in January 1976 as the date for the elimination of the issue of special deficit-financing bonds, but continuing increases in expenditures, and depressed revenues, combined to produce a sharp increase in their number to cover the deficit, and the bond dependency ratio rose from 29.7% in FY1977 to 32% in FY1978 and 39.6% a year later. Short-term, ad hoc marginal adjustments to expenditures, tax rates, and thresholds had proved inadequate to deal with the rapid growth of the fiscal deficit, and had failed completely to address its root cause. In January 1979, MOF conceded that the aim of eliminating special deficit-financing bonds by the following year would not be achieved, and set a new target date of 1984. It also acknowledged publicly that the causes of the deficit were structural, and could not be remedied by 'natural increases' to revenue which would occur when higher economic growth was resumed. The structure of the tax system needed to be changed to increase the proportion and yield of indirect taxes compared with direct taxes, and MOF confidently committed itself to introducing a new general consumption tax in FY1980. This provided the context and the rationale for the launch of its first bid to introduce a national consumption tax, and annual incremental adjustments to the rates and scope of indirect taxes.

The failure to do so brought it back to a search to 'increase revenues *within* the basic framework of the existing tax system' (MOF 1981: 15; emphasis added). At the same time, there was growing recognition that reconstruction was a medium-term project: expenditures would have to be cut, and taxes raised, over a period of years. The transition from a short- to a medium-term horizon was signalled by MOF's public presentation of its new Medium-Term Fiscal Projection in 1978, revised and rolled forward annually thereafter. The purpose of the projection was to focus the attention of ministers, LDP backbenchers, and the electorate on the critical state of the national finances by presenting stylized projections of expenditure and revenue three years ahead, exposing the gap between them, and estimating the amount of borrowing that would be needed to finance the resulting deficits. The accuracy of the projections was less important than the demonstration that fiscal deficits were not a temporary phenomenon, and that tough action would be needed on both expenditure and taxation for several years to come. Indeed, the projections were deliberately biased to emphasize the borrowing implications of continually rising public spending and persistent revenue shortfall.

From FY1982, the projections were used to plan the path to achieve fiscal objectives over the medium term. FY1984 was targeted for the elimination of special deficit-financing bonds on stylized assumptions about cuts in expenditures, and projected revenue yields, in each of the previous three years, and hence about the achievement of annual targets for the reduction of their issue. In practice, MOF first set those targets, and then worked backwards to derive the policy implications for expenditures and revenues in the General Account Budget. Thus, political acceptance of the need to eliminate the issue of special deficit-financing bonds, and MOF's annual targets to achieve it, enabled the Ministry to demonstrate the implications of reducing or limiting the growth of expenditures. This was done explicitly for the first time in the preparation of the budget for FY1982. In the spring of 1981, MOF prepared a *Trial Estimate of the Fiscal Situation in Fiscal 1982*. In its published form, it showed that, if the issue of new government bonds was cut by the agreed target reduction of 1.830 trillion, and the assumptions about the yield of taxes and other revenues were accurate, then a sum of only 570 billion would be available to finance all budget requests for increased expenditure. In effect, this was tantamount to a declaration that no new money was available for the FY1982 budget. This paved the way for MOF's introduction of the 0% ceiling for general expenditures in the General Account Budget, the first occasion since the reform of the budgetary system under SCAP that a freeze on spending had been imposed across the board. Having agreed on the objective of eliminating special deficit-financing bonds, the government and the LDP were now obliged to accept the budgetary implications of making progress towards achieving it.

The available resources were now allocated more selectively in the General Account Budget, as recommended in the reports of the Provisional Council on Administrative Reform. Programmes for defence, energy, science and technology, and overseas economic cooperation were exempted from the freeze. Other programmes for which there were statutory entitlements, such as pensions and social security, were treated as 'exceptions' to the 0% norm. For FY1983, MOF tightened expenditure controls still further by setting a ceiling for budget requests of -5% for current spending; investment expenditures were frozen. The need for those deeper cuts, and a more restrictive stance on both priority programmes and those treated as exceptions, was legitimated by MOF's Fiscal System Research Council's report on the budget requests submitted by Spending Ministries and Agencies. Under MOF's guidance, it produced a 'hit list' of 32 items for reduction and rationalization. MOF invoked those ostensibly 'neutral' recommendations, together with the Provisional Council's endorsement of 'fiscal reconstruction without tax increase', to justify its new tougher policy, and to stiffen the resolve of ministers when the draft budget was submitted to Cabinet in December 1982.

Shocks to the fiscal system caused by the fallout from the 1979 oil crisis were minor by comparison with those experienced during the course of FY1983. The emergency economic measures of April and October 1983 to stimulate domestic demand added a further 6 trillion to public spending. Consequential adjustments to expenditure and revenue policies were necessary as, once again, MOF tried to reconcile the conflicting needs of economic expansion—increased public spending and reductions in personal and corporate taxation—with those of closing the widening fiscal gap through tighter control of spending, reducing the amount of borrowing, and restructuring the tax system to yield more revenues from indirect than direct taxes. MOF's second attempt to introduce a general consumption tax dates from this period, as explained above.

The adjustment of objectives and policies to the longer time-horizon was announced in the new five-year national economic plan prepared by EPA under MOF's guidance, and approved by the Cabinet on 12 August 1983. Annual targets for the progressive reduction of the issue of special deficit-financing bonds were adjusted to a seven-year period stretching from FY1983 to FY1990, the new (third) target date for their elimination. Expenditure policy was aimed at securing more radical reforms of some expenditure programmes to deliver cuts over several years ahead, for example medical insurance, pensions, and employment insurance. In the short term, the guidelines for budget requests for the coming fiscal year, 1984, were drawn more tightly still. Planned current expenditures were cut further by raising the limit from −5% to −10%. Investment expenditures were no longer excluded, but subject to a lower ceiling of −5%. Priority programmes—now overseas economic cooperation, energy, defence, government employee pensions, and personnel expenses—were excluded, while those for medical care insurance, subsidies to some FILP agencies for interest payments, and the reserve were treated as exceptions to the cutback rules. Income tax was reduced by 870 billion, but compensated by a rise in indirect taxes. As a result, the initial Budget for FY1984 was planned to rise by only 0.5% on FY1983, while within it the total of general expenditures was to be cut. Partly as a result, there was a reduction in the number of bonds issued, and the bond dependency ratio at 25% was the lowest since 1975.

Budget policy was now ostensibly tighter than at any time since the emergence of the fiscal crisis in the mid-1970s. The policy of fiscal austerity (but not its implementation, as I argue in later chapters) was maintained for three successive years, in each of which the guidelines for budget requests were maintained at the levels set in FY1984: −10% for current expenditures and −5% for investment expenditures. The guidelines, progressively elaborated and refined, applied only to general expenditures, nearly two-thirds of the total General Account Budget. The remaining third, comprising the costs of servicing the national debt and distributing the statutory Local Allocation Taxes to local government, was excluded.

On the revenue side, MOF turned its attention once more to the reform of the tax system. The Government Tax System Research Council, which in practice it controlled, in its *Report on the Tax Revisions for Fiscal Year 1985* in December 1984 criticized 'the patchwork amendments of the tax system' that had characterized fiscal reconstruction since the mid-1970s, and called for a 'full-fledged reform of the entire tax structure covering both direct and indirect taxes' (MOF 1985: 4). A similar view was taken by the LDP's Tax System Research Council, and the Minister of Finance called for a structural tax reform in his budget speech of January 1985. The next two years were spent in building a consensus for a general consumption tax through political–business–bureaucratic networks (see Katō Junko 1994 for details), and legitimizing the proposed reform through the reports of Government Tax System Research Commission.

FISCAL CONSOLIDATION, 1987–1991

The transition from the policy of fiscal reconstruction to the resumption of a more expansionary, looser fiscal policy, which MOF euphemistically dubbed 'fiscal consolidation', occurred in the course of FY1987. Following the Plaza Accord of 1985 and the appreciation of the value of the yen that followed, Japan came under increasing pressure from the international economic community to expand domestic demand to help generate more global economic activity. The Comprehensive Economic Measures introduced in September 1986 added 3 trillion to public spending; the Emergency Economic Measures of May 1987, a further 5 trillion of non-tax increases. There was pressure too on the revenue side, with 1 trillion tax reductions in the 1987 package.

These measures effectively marked the end of the period of fiscal reconstruction. The fiscal austerity associated with the objectives and policies of the ten years of reconstruction was abandoned, with MOF's administrative vice-minister, Yoshino, complaining that the Minister of Finance had undermined its campaign of fiscal discipline (Hartcher 1998). There was a nice irony in that MOF was forced to change tack at the time when its policies of tighter control of general expenditures in the Budget, and of government borrowing, were beginning to show progress towards the achievement of its main objectives of eliminating special deficit bonds, and reducing the bond dependency ratio. Nevertheless, those objectives had not yet been achieved when MOF was obliged to relax fiscal policy, while the broader objectives of restructuring the tax system and introducing more flexibility into the composition of the Budget remained unfulfilled. The costs of servicing the national debt continued on a rising trend to absorb a fifth of the General Account Budget, more than double the figure at the beginning of reconstruction a decade earlier. The total of debt outstanding continued to grow annually, and by 1987 was pre-empting nearly 44% of GDP, its highest ever level.

MOF's commitment to the restructuring of the tax system in the medium term now assumed a greater urgency, with the prospect of rising public spending, a widening of the fiscal deficit, and increasing government borrowing. In the autumn of 1987, with the concurrence of the Cabinet, MOF launched its third campaign to introduce a consumption tax.

Fiscal reconstruction evolved pragmatically, and at first cautiously, into fiscal expansion. The progress of the previous decade in reining back the growth of *planned* (but not actual) expenditure in the General Account Budget, and reducing the size of the fiscal deficit, was not however to be squandered in a frenzied burst of public spending; MOF had learned painfully the lessons of the LDP's spending spree of the 1970s, and of the fiscal consequences of its commitment to the 'locomotive' economic strategy. It was determined not to repeat those mistakes. 'We got burned in the late '70s,' confessed one very senior official (Funabashi 1988: 84). The dilemma that it now faced exactly paralleled that of the late 1970s: the need to stimulate domestic demand in the economy by countercyclical fiscal policies, while continuing to maintain firm control of public spending and borrowing to reduce fiscal deficits. It hoped to achieve the reconciliation of those conflicting purposes through policies designed to consolidate the gains made in the years of crisis and reconstruction.

Expenditure policies were gradually and cautiously relaxed. The guidelines for budget requests were loosened for the first time in six years, but only on the capital account, where the limit of −5% was replaced by standstill. No change was made in the limit for all other expenditures, which were still subject to 10% cuts, apart from those programmes exempted or treated exceptionally. The result was a 4.8% increase in the total of the planned General Account Budget, the largest since 1982.

This cautious, modest beginning was soon overtaken by a tide of public spending as the economy first entered the frenetic period of the 'bubble', and then collapsed into a deep and persistent recession. Revenues grew strongly throughout the period 1986–90, the direct consequence of the speculative appreciation of land and asset prices. The short-lived period of unstable, higher economic growth provided the means and the political rationale for a rapid increase of public spending. In such circumstances, and with a general election for the Lower House imminent, growth of the General Account Budget was irresistible. Nevertheless, the fiscal deficit narrowed sufficiently for MOF to achieve its long-held objective of eliminating the issue of special deficit-financing bonds in 1990, albeit through some fiscal sleight of hand (explained in detail in Chapter 25). It was also able to make steady progress in the reduction of the number of ordinary (construction) bonds issued. As a result the bond dependency ratio fell to 7.6% in the planned budget for FY1991, the lowest level for twenty years. Burgeoning revenues enabled MOF to repay some earlier 'borrowings' from various Special Accounts, and to resume the annual statutory obligation to redeem the national debt, payments for which had been 'suspended' from FY1982 to FY1989. Those and related issues are discussed in more detail when the effects of the implementation of MOF's policies are assessed in Chapter 25.

With the elimination of special deficit-financing bonds, MOF turned its attention to the 'second stage' of reconstructing the national finances. Under its guidance, the Fiscal System Research Council reported in March 1990 a new Medium Term Fiscal Policy, with objectives designed to constrain the growth of the massive national debt, and to restore flexibility in the allocation of expenditures within the General Account Budget. In effect, this was little more than a restatement of the existing objectives, although in the light of recent experience it was felt necessary to emphasize the need to make the Budget more flexible so that it could be used more easily and effectively to implement countercyclical fiscal policies without the need to resort to the issue of special deficit-financing bonds. Secondly, it was proposed to use any annual surplus on the settlement of the General Account Budget, together with the revenue of the sales of NTT stock deposited with the Special Account for National Debt Consolidation, to accelerate the redemption of those bonds.

The third objective was to constrain the growth of expenditures further in order to reduce future tax and social security burdens. The bond dependency ratio was to be progressively reduced to less than 5%, the first occasion that a target had been set by MOF since the emergence of the 1975 crisis. With the ratio set at 7.6% in the Budget about to be proposed for FY1991, that seemed a realistic target. FY1995 was set as the date for its achievement, with targeted annual reductions of 450 billion in the number of new bonds issued—another realistic target, given the much greater annual reductions that had been achieved during the previous six years.

Budget guidelines remained unchanged. However, with the slow-down of economic activity, the limit on public investment was relaxed, from 0% to +5% in 1988; and the resources available were further boosted in each of the next three years by using funds from the sale of NTT stock after privatization. This represented the first year of the implementation of the *Basic Plan for Public Investment* following the conclusion of the Structural Impediments Initiative with the USA, which provided initially 430 trillion over a ten-year period to improve living standards and the quality of life by investment in social overhead capital. In a wider context, it reflected the reorientation of national objectives set out in the five-year national economic plan for the period 1988–92, *Economic Management within the Global Context*.

FISCAL CRISIS RESURFACES, 1991–1996

MOF's public confidence that it would be able successfully to reconcile the competing demands of an expansionary economic policy to stimulate domestic demand with tight fiscal policy to consolidate the gains made in the period of reconstruction evaporated with the bursting of the bubble economy. The imperative of countercyclical economic policy quickly overrode the residual concern with the tight control of public spending, as the economy plunged into deep and prolonged recession.

The re-emergence of the symptoms of acute fiscal crisis was the result simultaneously of a large and sustained shortfall in revenue, and a rapid buildup of public spending. The sharp decline in revenues resulting from the slow-down in domestic economic activity once again exposed the underlying structural weakness of the tax system, to which MOF had repeatedly drawn attention during the previous decade. While it had achieved some rebalancing of direct and indirect taxes, most notably through the introduction of a general consumption tax in 1989, the shock to the tax system of the collapse of the economic bubble was severe. Tax revenues on an out-turn basis declined for five successive years from FY1991, and again in FY1997 and FY1998. As they fell, the need to stimulate demand in the economy led to political and business pressures for tax reductions, and threatened still further loss of revenues. Throughout the decade, tax and other revenues collected annually were between 5 and 8 trillion less than those of FY1990. Revenues of 49.4 trillion in FY1998 were the lowest for more than ten years.

As the means to finance additional public spending contracted, so the politico-economic pressures for expansionary budgets, and countercyclical packages of fiscal measures, intensified. Responding to them, MOF was powerless to prevent a sudden and dramatic widening of the fiscal deficit. The turning-point occurred during the course of FY1991. The estimate of revenues in the initial General Account Budget for that year proved unduly optimistic, and provision had to be made in a Supplementary Budget subsequently to cover a projected loss totalling 2.78 trillion. MOF was obliged to borrow an additional 1.387 trillion to finance the resulting fiscal deficit.

Despite that, for the moment budgetary policies were aimed to slow down the growth of the General Account Budget, from 6.2% in FY1991 to 2.7% in FY1992, rather than to impose widespread real cuts; the rates of growth of the main expenditure programmes were cut only marginally. By the following year, the full impact of the fiscal crisis was felt. The revised estimate for the yield of revenues in the Supplementary Budget for FY1992 showed a shortfall of more than 5 trillion above the estimate in the planned initial General Account Budget. The eventual yield proved even more disastrous: 8.1 trillion less than that planned. In his budget speech for FY1993, the Minister of Finance warned of 'the most severe revenue situation since fiscal 1983' (MOF 1994b: 90), and announced a cut in the growth rate of the General Account Budget from 2.7% to 0.2%, to be achieved mainly by postponing or deferring the costs of servicing the national debt, and the payment of the statutory local allocation tax grants to local governments. Again, only marginal reductions were made to the major spending programmes; this was still a slow-down of growth, not real cuts. With public spending continuing to grow while revenues declined sharply, MOF had no alternative but to resume heavy borrowing, but through the issue of ordinary rather than special government bonds to finance the deficit. The downward trend in the bond dependency rate was quickly reversed as the government planned for an issue of 3 trillion more bonds in FY1993 than were issued two years earlier. As the financial year proceeded, it became necessary to issue still more: an additional 8 trillion bonds to finance three separate mini-budgets of emergency economic measures. Within the space of two years, MOF had been obliged to resume borrowing at levels comparable to the worst years of fiscal crisis a decade earlier. The planned bond dependency rate rose from a low point of 7.6% in FY1991 to 18.7% in FY1994. The reality was far worse. The implementation of countercyclical fiscal policy through Supplementary Budgets *in-year* led to further borrowing still, and the actual bond dependency rate was more than 22%.

The rapid deterioration in national finances, and the prospect of little improvement without a radical adjustment in the structure of the economy to the changed conditions of international trade and marketing in the 1990s, caused MOF to warn in 1993 that it might become necessary to resume the issue of special deficit-financing bonds in the special circumstances of 'substantial decreases in tax revenues during a recession' (MOF 1993b: 10). But for the moment it was able to relieve pressure on the General Account Budget, and hence to limit the further growth of the fiscal deficit, by using various budgetary stratagems to postpone and defer payments, and manipulating cash-flow transactions (discussed in Chapter 25). Nevertheless, the longer-term implications of the three Supplementary Budgets in FY1993 added to the pressures on public spending in the General Account Budget and to its constituent programmes of general expenditure, both of which increased marginally over the FY1993 totals.

The Gulf War added further to MOF's fiscal difficulties. To finance Japan's contribution of 11.7 trillion to the cost of the UN action, it had to resort to the issue of 'ad hoc' special deficit-financing bonds. As this occurred simultaneously with their trumpeted elimination, MOF was at pains to emphasize that their re-issue did not signal a resumption of the practice of the previous 15 years. Nor were the costs to be added to the national debt. The bonds were to be redeemed by receipts from a special temporary tax. However, the return of special deficit-financing bonds on a more permanent basis was not long delayed. Having signalled in 1993 the intention to do so in certain exceptional circumstances, by the following year the pressures of increased spending, current as well as capital, and declining revenues proved irresistible, and MOF was forced to issue bonds totalling 3.133 trillion. In addition, 10.5 trillion of ordinary (construction) bonds had to be issued to fund public works expenditures in successive emergency economic packages, and to redeem earlier loans to finance capital projects under the NTT programme (discussed in Chapter 23).

With the resumption of the issue of special deficit-financing bonds in 1994, the fiscal wheel had turned full circle. But this time round the crisis was deeper, and MOF's authority to deal with it weakened by its failure to constrain the growth of the General Account Budget, by the paralysis of the policy-making process that followed the breakup of the old political order in 1993, and by the progressive erosion of its own authority as the banking crisis (and other contingent events) unfolded in the wake of the collapse of the bubble economy. The fiscal consequences of that collapse destroyed the credibility of MOF's medium-term strategy for achieving those fiscal objectives set out in the 1990 Medium Term Fiscal Policy to rebalance revenue and expenditure, reduce the size and burden of the accumulated national debt, and restore flexibility in the allocation of budgetary expenditures. The Budget was now less rather than more flexible, as the increase in the costs of borrowing and accumulated debt exerted a tighter squeeze on general expenditure programmes; moreover, it had proved impossible to implement countercyclical economic policy without resorting to the issue of special deficit-financing bonds, progress towards reducing the bond dependency ratio to less than 5% had been reversed, and the redemption of special deficit-financing bonds had been deferred as MOF sought to constrain the pressures on the General Account Budget.

Yet again, the vicissitudes of economic activity had exposed the underlying structural weakness of the tax system. In times of recession, revenue yields were unreliable and inadequate to cover the increasing costs of the major spending programmes. The general consumption tax was too little and too late to address the fundamental cause of that weakness.

Moreover, it soon became apparent that the recession that began officially in 1991 was different in kind and in duration from those that had preceded it in 1985–6, 1980–2, and 1974–5, which were largely consequential or contingent on global economic conditions. On this occasion, the Japanese economy proved stubbornly resistant to the improvement in international trade which helped deliver the USA and European economies from conditions of recession; moreover, the appreciation of the yen—the 'yen bubble'—and the large surplus on the current balance of trade made it more difficult than in earlier periods to stimulate the economy through the promotion of exports. Ever-larger packages of countercyclical economic and fiscal policies between 1992 and 1995, with a combined face value of 64.2 trillion, had little immediate effect on stimulating domestic demand (see Chapter 23 for an assessment).

The state of the national finances deteriorated rapidly throughout FY1995 and FY1996. MOF was forced to borrow 22.0 trillion to finance a deficit swollen by the large fiscal stimulus in September 1995, resulting in a bond dependency ratio of 28.2%, its highest level since 1980. In FY1996 the planned issue of 10.1 trillion of special deficit-financing bonds exceeded all previous experience. By the end of FY1995 the accumulated debt totalled 213 trillion, equal to 43% of GDP. The servicing of that debt absorbed a fifth of the total General Account Budget. The principles of 'sound management' were necessarily sacrificed to politico-economic expediency. The achievement of the three policy objectives was more distant in 1996 than when they were formulated twenty years earlier. MOF had however succeeded at the third attempt in implementing its long-term aim of changing the tax structure; more accurately, it had begun on the process of implementation. Once it had secured the principle of a consumption tax, it was able to exploit the circumstances of a continuing shortfall in revenue during the economic recession to persuade the coalition governments led by Murayama and then Hashimoto to agree to increase the rates levied. However, the benefits in the yield of gross revenues were offset in the short term by the costs of financing tax reductions in the recession; the longer-term significance would emerge only with the resumption of economic growth.

THE RISE AND FALL OF FISCAL REFORM, 1996–1998

The Fiscal Structural Reform Act of 1997 represented a concerted attempt by the Hashimoto government to remedy the underlying causes of the fiscal crisis. For the first time since its emergence in the mid-1970s, fiscal principles, objectives, and policies were backed by statute, and were set for several years ahead. Legislative controls were imposed on the growth of the total of general expenditures in the General Account Budget, and the budget allocations to specific programmes were capped. Quantitative targets for the overall budget deficit, government borrowing, and most major spending programmes were prescribed for the FY1998 budget, with rules for future allocations for two years ahead. The main aims were to reduce the deficit on the combined budgets of central and local government to no more than 3% of GDP in FY2003, i.e. by 31 March 2004, to end the issue of special deficit-financing bonds by the same date, and to reduce the bond dependency ratio in the General Account Budget.

The latter was a reaffirmation of a key objective of MOF's fiscal policy throughout the previous two decades. The explicit focus on the reduction of the fiscal deficit was wholly novel. While implicit in previous policies to control the growth of spending, and to raise more revenue, it had not been specifically targeted, nor had it included the aggregate local government budget. The legislative commitment to a quantitative target was bold, clearly influenced by the convergence criterion set for membership of the EMU; it was also risky. Success or failure would be transparent, measured precisely by the deficit–GDP ratio on the due date. No such target was set for the reduction of the overall level of government debt. While, earlier, Prime Minister Hashimoto had spoken of the need to reduce the ratio of gross government debt to GDP in line with the Maastricht criterion of 60%, this objective was omitted from both the five principles (see below) and the 1997 Act. Instead, a narrower, less ambitious target was set for central government borrowing alone.

The immediate and proximate cause of the reform of the fiscal system in 1997 was the response of the Hashimoto government to the rapid deterioration of the national finances in the aftermath of the severe economic recession of 1991–6. The overall fiscal deficit on central and local government spending combined had reached 6.6% of GDP in FY1996, the highest ratio among the G7 countries. Borrowing to finance the deficits at both central and local levels, measured by the gross debt of general government in the System of National Accounts, had risen from 61.1% of GDP in FY1992 to 82.6% in FY1996. Undoubtedly, the rapidly rising deficit, and the increasing burden of public debt, were key factors in the timing of the reform. With the recovery of the economy in 1995–6, MOF could return to the problem of the chronic weaknesses in the fiscal system with which it had grappled for more than twenty years, and endeavour to exploit the opportunity provided by a prime minister and coalition government publicly committed to a broad agenda of reform, and anxious to be seen as fiscally responsible, in the campaign for the elections to the Lower House in October 1996.

While the combination of economic factors and political circumstances explains why fiscal reform had arrived at the top of the agenda in both government and MOF in 1996, the longer-term origins are to be found in the underlying chronic weaknesses of the fiscal system which first became apparent in the mid-1970s. As will be shown in Chapter 25, the effects of the implementation of policies described above to 'reconstruct' and 'consolidate' the fiscal system in the 1980s never achieved more than an alleviation of the worst symptoms of deficit and debt, but failed to remedy the main causes—an inappropriate tax structure which generated inadequate and unstable revenues, and an ineffective budgetary system which failed to control the growth of spending. While both the size and the scale of the deficit and debt were exacerbated by the severity of the economic recession and the countercyclical measures to deal with it, they were only the most recent manifestations of the symptoms of a continuing crisis in the finances of central government.

As explained in Chapter 4, reforming the fiscal system was one of Prime Minister Hashimoto's six 'visions' in a broadly based programme of reform of the economic, financial, and administrative systems outlined in the election campaign for the Lower House in October 1996. In his first administration, both he and the Minister of Finance gave the highest priority to reforming the fiscal system. MOF had already turned its attention to the issue, having begun in 1995–6 the essential ground-clearing, and the process of building a consensus for its ideas through its advisory council, the Fiscal System Research Council (FSRC). Guided by MOF, the Council recommended to the Minister of Finance that fiscal consolidation should be implemented without delay. In 1996 it focused more narrowly on the roles and scope of future fiscal policies, and considered the setting of specific targets. Discussions took place against the backdrop of MOF's Medium Term Fiscal Projections, which showed the implications for government borrowing of continuing trends of expenditure and revenue, and the annual amount of reduction necessary to eliminate special deficit-financing bonds by 2003 or 2005. Worried by the 'nation's free-fall into a fiscal black hole of debt', the Council produced a list of specific recommendations in its final report of 12 December 1996, among which was that the deficit on central and local government spending should be less than 3% of GDP by FY2005, and that the issue of special deficit-financing bonds should be ended by the same date. The primary fiscal balance, i.e. excluding debt costs, should be restored 'within a few years' (FSRC 1996). Those and other recommendations—restricting the growth of the priority programmes of defence and overseas aid, cutting the costs of medical care and social security—anticipated the policies written into the November 1997 Act and implemented in the FY1998 Budget.

A month earlier, a still more alarming report was presented to the Prime Minister by his Economic Council, whose work and proceedings, guided and steered by EPA, warned that 'the current situation of state finances and social security is potentially unsustainable' (JEI 1996: 2). Without fiscal (and social security) reform, taxes, deficits, and social security transfers would exceed 73% of Japan's National Income in 2005, compared with 39.4% in FY1994 (Economic Council 1996).

The Cabinet approved both reports in December 1996, and in his budget speech on 20 January 1997 the Minister of Finance set out the broad objectives of future fiscal policy based on the Economic Council's recommendations. Local governments were requested to follow a similar budgetary discipline. FY1997 was declared (yet again) the 'first year of fiscal structural reform', as MOF publicly committed itself and the government to policies of fiscal austerity. However, compilation of the draft budget for FY1997 now before the Diet had begun in the early autumn of 1996 in the midst of the election campaign for the Lower House; it was hardly austere. While the temporary reductions of income tax and local inhabitants' tax were ended, and the national consumption tax set to rise in April from 3% to 5%, general expenditures were planned to rise also, albeit at a slower rate than in FY1996. The 1.5% increase was the lowest for nine years. The Minister warned of tougher times to come. MOF would take a fresh look at all expenditures in the early stages of the process of compiling the budget for FY1998, and impose stricter controls on ministerial and agency bids.

The initiative in fiscal reform now passed from MOF to politicians—or, rather, the public running was now seen to be made by them rather than bureaucrats. As I shall explain, the fiscal objectives formulated by the new Council on Fiscal Structural Reform were all anticipated in MOF's earlier long-term aims, while the principles and policies were derived almost wholly from those proposed by its Fiscal System Research Council, and were for obvious reasons consistent with MOF's own reform agenda. However, the work of the Council on Fiscal Structural Reform demonstrated to a public increasingly hostile to MOF that politicians had taken control of the key budget decisions, and was responsible for devising the strategy to rescue the country from deficits and debt. Secondly, the Prime Minister had personally committed himself to fiscal reform, and had pledged to cut spending across the board, 'allowing no sanctuaries'. The Council, which he set up in January 1997 with himself as chairman, provided the vehicle for him to demonstrate that commitment and redeem his pledge.

The Council comprised former prime ministers, Takeshita and Nakasone among them, former ministers of finance, serving members of the new Cabinet, including the Minister of Finance, together with the leaders and elder statesmen of the three ruling parties. Their status ensured that their recommendations would carry weight in the three parties, while their experience ensured that their proposals would have the necessary authority to command confidence and respect. Both were necessary to overcome the entrenched interests of Spending Ministries and their constituents in maintaining the status quo.

On 18 March 1997 the Prime Minister, reporting on the Council's progress, announced that the target date for the achievement of the main objectives of reducing the deficit and debt would be advanced from 2005 to 2003, and that the main efforts would be concentrated in the period FY1998–FY2000. He listed five principles of the reform programme agreed by the Council, which were to form the basis of the legislation to be brought forward in the autumn:

1. a reduction of the deficit on central and local budgets combined to 3% or less by FY2003;
2. a reduction of general expenditures in the FY1998 Budget below that of FY1997;
3. a review of spending programmes, 'with no sanctuaries', and the prescription of quantitative targets for three years ahead to cut or constrain their growth;
4. a reduction or postponement of spending in long-term public investment programmes, with no new commitments;
5. a ratio of combined taxes and social security payments to national income of not more than 50%.

Substantively, the principles were not new, being firmly grounded in MOF's agenda of long-term aims to restore fiscal balance, which it had tried to implement through the fiscal policies of reconstruction and consolidation in the 1980s. The first four were more detailed and explicit versions of the general recommendations made earlier by MOF's Fiscal System Research Council, trailed by the Minister of Finance in his budget statement in January. The fifth principle was a restatement of MOF's reformulation in 1983 of its long established informal policy rule-of-the-game, reaffirmed a decade later in the last report of the Third Provisional Council for the Promotion of Administrative Reform on 27 October 1993. The aim to reduce the bond dependency ratio in the General Account Budget was not explicitly targeted in the five principles, but was implicit in the commitment to eliminate the issue of special deficit-financing bonds by 2003. An explicit target was, however, later incorporated into the legislation. What *was* new, and was politically driven if not wholly politically inspired, was the prescription of quantitative targets and dates for their achievement. In particular, the setting of a precise target for the reduction of the deficit, and a date for its attainment, represented a radical departure in fiscal policy, although its origins can be traced to the Fiscal System Research Council, and to MOF's adroit steering of its deliberations. Implicitly, the time-frame of central budgeting had changed from a focus on the year ahead to planning the allocation over the medium term.

The translation of the five principles into specific objectives and concrete policies was the next task. The process was almost wholly dominated by the Council on Fiscal Structural Reform, and represented a shift in the balance of formal fiscal power between politicians and bureaucrats; MOF's role was subordinate, although, directly through the Minister of Finance and informally through other members, it had some input into the proceedings (MOF 1998*b*). Again, it was perhaps less necessary for MOF to try to steer and shape policies that it was reasonably confident would be consistent with its own agenda. The main work of drafting was done by the Council's Planning Committee. The sensitive issue of public works spending was handled separately by a subcommittee chaired by the LDP's secretary-general, Katō Kōichi. During the spring and early summer, it took evidence from the relevant Spending Ministries, all of which,

Budget Objectives and Policies

unsurprisingly, were opposed to the Council's proposals for cutting long-term programmes of public works, reducing the scale of the additional agricultural infrastructural support approved in FY1995 following the Uruguay Round of GATT, and abolishing certain hypothecated revenues, such as that from the motor vehicle tonnage tax, used to finance some public works.

Announcing the Cabinet's approval of the Council's report in June 1997, Prime Minister Hashimoto said:

> We were able to hammer out [a plan] worthy of being called a very definitive collection of fiscal reconstruction measures, and to set a strong and clear-cut direction which can be called a first milestone in the Cabinet's campaign to carry out thorough reform in six areas. (JEI 1997: 1)

Commentators were less enthusiastic. When the Prime Minister had set up the Council in January he had pledged to cut spending across the board, 'allowing no sanctuaries'. The Council's proposals left 'virtually the entire herd of sacred cows still grazing on the public purse', the *Nikkei Weekly* commented:

> While the draft [plan] is laudable as an unprecedented attempt by politicians to trim the budget, it nevertheless lacks the teeth needed to bite really deeply into the structural rot in Japan's fiscal policy... Real cuts in government spending require setting priorities... The panel just chipped away at the easiest budget targets and left untouched the many sacrosanct projects LDP zokugiin were prepared to fight tooth and nail to protect. (*Nikkei Weekly*, 19 May: 14)

Across-the-board cuts were never a realistic option for the LDP-dominated Council, which was scarcely likely to risk alienating its constituencies of local small businessmen, construction workers, and farmers by recommending deep real cuts in public works and agricultural subsidies. If they emerged virtually intact from the spending review, there was nevertheless a major change in government priorities, with the withdrawal of the most-favoured status which the ODA and defence programmes had enjoyed in the budget guidelines since the early 1980s.

The Council's final report on 3 June 1997 emphasized that the reform of the structure of the fiscal system was inseparable from the 'broader tide of reform' in other areas of government activity which Prime Minister Hashimoto had initiated in his other five 'visions'. As we have seen in Chapter 4, they intersected at several points with the proposals for reforming the fiscal system.

The Council set out in detail 'concrete measures and policies for reform and reduction of expenditure' (Council 1997: 2). The years FY1998–FY2000 were designated as 'an intensive reform period', for the first of which the Council proposed an overall cut of 0.5% in the total of general expenditures; no such similar cut had occurred for more than a decade. Quantitative targets or 'budget caps' were prescribed for all the main spending programmes for FY1998 and, in less detail, for two further years. The Cabinet adopted the *Report*, and all the recommendations were incorporated subsequently into the Fiscal Structural Reform Act passed in November 1997. (In anticipation, the targets and caps were implemented in the processes of setting the budget aggregate and programme totals for the FY1998 Budget which began in the summer of 1997. In effect, the Cabinet's approval of the Council's report provided the authority to impose them in the compilation of the budget.) The five principles were translated into specific and detailed objectives, with target dates for their attainment. The Council's proposals for the elimination of special deficit-financing bonds and the reduction of government borrowing were given greater specificity in the legislation, influenced by MOF's Medium Term Fiscal Projections. The bond dependency ratio in the General Account Budget was to be reduced by FY2003 to 21.6%, the level of that of FY1997. To achieve it, annual targets for the issue of government bonds were set beginning with FY1998. Targeting levels of government borrowing in this way, with progressive annual reductions, was not new; as we have seen, MOF had employed such means repeatedly and unsuccessfully in the 1980s. Giving them statutory force was unprecedented. It meant that any changes to increase borrowing through the issue of additional bonds in-year would require an amendment of the 1997 Act.

Some programmes—ODA, public investment, and transfer payments to local government—were cut in real terms; in others—education, defence, energy, small businesses, and food subsidies—spending was frozen at the levels of the FY1997 Budget; a few programmes were allowed to grow but at lower rates, constrained by estimates of GDP growth. Cuts were made to the ten-year Basic Plan for Public Investment by spreading annual allocations over a longer period of time. These translated into a 7% cut in FY1998 and 5% and 3% in the two following years. Similarly, the duration of the programme of public works infrastructure for farmers, compensation for the opening of domestic markets under the Uruguay Round of GATT, was extended by two years although the total, 6.1 trillion, remained unchanged. Finally, priority status was given to a special category of programmes cross-cutting ministerial and agency jurisdictional boundaries—environment, science, technology and telecommunications; distribution and transportation; social capital. Table 13.1 shows the budget 'caps' for FY1998, and the two succeeding years of the period of 'intensive reform'.

Statutory budgetary controls of expenditure have both advantages and disadvantages. The advantage for MOF, and for a government bent upon controlling both the aggregate and composition of the General Account Budget, was that Spending Ministries could not resist MOF's demands for specific quantitative cuts in their programmes; the loopholes afforded by the implementation of the old non-statutory budget guidelines were closed. The disadvantage was that MOF's discretion to respond flexibly to changing economic circumstances, and to the electoral imperatives of LDP politicians, was greatly reduced, circumscribed by the rules enshrined in the 1997 Act. It could not, as in the past, finance extra spending in Supplementary Budgets by issuing more government bonds without putting at risk the deficit and debt targets prescribed in the Act. While in the past MOF might have found it useful to have the backup of statutory obligations to resist the importunate demands of LDP politicians for extra spending, in the circumstances of an economy in deep recession this could be a handicap, as the unfolding events of 1997–8 soon proved.

The sharp and swift deterioration in the performance of the economy in the last quarter of 1997, exacerbated by the economic and financial instability of several Asian

Table 13.1 *Programme 'caps' in the general account initial budget, FY1998–FY2000[a]*

	FY1998	FY1999 and FY2000 (planned)
Programmes cut		
ODA	at least −10%	To be cut each year
Public investment	at least −7%	To be cut each year
Subsidies for local government		
Institutional/legal	—	Reduced and rationalized
Other	—	Cut by 10% for each ministry and agency
Programmes frozen		
Education (national schools)	0%	No more than FY1997 allocation
Defence	0%	Cuts of 92 bn, equivalent to 10% of equipment costs
Energy	0%	No more than FY1997 allocation
Small businesses	0%	No more than FY1997 allocation
Food	0%	No more than FY1997 allocation
Programmes with constrained growth		
Social Security	Growth below trend rate (less than 300 bn increase)	Restrained growth, below trend annual rate of 2%
Science and Technology	Growth limited to 5%	'Greatly restrained growth'
Priority programmes		
Measures of economic structural reform to promote environmental policies, science and technology, and telecomms (9 sub-programmes)	150 bn increase	Not prescribed
Measures of economic structural reform to promote greater distribution efficiency (international and regional airports, ports, harbours, and trunk roads; inner-city transport infrastructure rail facilities)	150 bn increase	Not prescribed
Social overhead infrastructure	250 bn increase	Not prescribed
Other programmes		
Pensions	No statutory control	No statutory control
Other minor programmes	'Strictly restricted'	Frozen

[a] Initial Budget.

Source: Cabinet, 3 March 1997; Budget Bureau, MOF, 1997.

countries with whom Japan had close trading links, brought renewed pressure from the USA and the governments of G7, the OECD, and other international organizations for the Japanese government to make permanent cuts in taxation and to increase public spending, especially investment. The dilemma was that any permanent reduction in taxes would frustrate earlier attempts to raise more revenue, for example through the economically ill-timed increase in the national consumption tax in April 1997; while any substantial increase in public spending would have to be financed through the issue of more special deficit-financing bonds, requiring an amendment to the 1997 Fiscal Structural Reform Act. Four successive packages of so-called countercyclical measures announced between October 1997 and February 1998, produced largely on the initiative of LDP committees, with MOF again playing (at least publicly) a subordinate role, were criticized both at home and abroad as inadequate and inappropriate to the critical condition of the Japanese economy. The last of these, on 20 February 1998, contained no new spending or tax cuts, which might have put at risk the achievement of the borrowing targets in the November legislation, and would certainly have breached some of the statutory controls incorporated in the draft budget then before the Diet.

After two successive quarters of negative growth, the economy was now technically once again in recession. Under pressure internationally and within parts of his own party, the Prime Minister was obliged to reconvene the Council on Fiscal Structural Reform. Again, the initiative rested with the LDP rather than MOF; the former was divided between those who argued for fiscal stimulus, and those who continued to support fiscal reform. The former eventually prevailed. A package of temporary tax cuts and increased spending totalling 16.65 trillion was announced in March 1998. Leaving aside arguments about how much 'clear water' (*mamizu*) or 'new money' was on offer, it nevertheless represented a humiliating reverse for a prime minister personally committed to the principles of fiscal reform. The Act was amended in May 1998, to authorize the issue of special deficit-financing bonds, and the target dates for the achievement of the deficit and debt objectives were extended by two years, to the end of FY2005. The agonizing reappraisal, prevarication, and delay that preceded the policy U-turn fuelled criticism of Prime Minister Hashimoto's handling of the crisis, and provoked calls for his resignation. The newly appointed Governor of the Bank of Japan in a public rebuke argued that stimulating the economy was more important than cutting the deficit, and called for permanent cuts in income and corporate taxes. More extraordinary still was the outburst from the President of Sony, Norio Ohga, who, claiming that the economy was on the verge of collapse, compared Hashimoto's indecisiveness with that of Herbert Hoover in the early years of the 1930s depression in the USA.

The policy U-turn of April 1998 fatally undermined the credibility of the fiscal reform programme, and of Prime Minister Hashimoto himself. Within the LDP, Cabinet ministers and senior party leaders continued to dispute the policy options for the economy, and for the resolution of the deepening crisis in the banking sector, and jockeyed to position themselves for the general election to the Upper House in July 1998 and a future challenge for leadership of the party. Fiscal reform was dead and buried, although officially the legislation was merely suspended in December 1998, cryonically awaiting the future discovery of a remedy for Japan's apparently incurable fiscal disease.

FISCAL EXPLOSION, 1998–2000

Prime Minister Obuchi Keizō, who succeeded Hashimoto following the LDP's loss of seats in the Upper House election, had promised in his campaign for the presidency of the party to provide a further substantial stimulus to the economy. In November 1998 he redeemed that pledge with the announcement of increased spending and tax cuts worth 24 trillion to be implemented in FY1999. Together with the April package, it represented some 8% of GDP and included tax cuts of 6 trillion, later raised to 9.3 trillion as part of a deal with Ozawa Ichirō to bring the Liberal Party into a coalition government; 37.4 trillion of special deficit-financing bonds were issued in three Supplementary Budgets to finance the April package and the revised estimates of shortfall in revenue on the FY1998 budget.

Economic recovery was now the main priority of the Obuchi government. Relegated to the back-burner of the policy agenda after Hashimoto's *volte face*, fiscal reconstruction was now removed from the stove. The expansionary momentum was sustained in the budgets for the next two years, and bolstered by yet more spending and tax cuts in-year. The planned budget for FY1999 of 81.8 trillion represented a 5.4% increase on 1998. With MOF's issue of 31 trillion of government bonds to finance the expansion, the fiscal deficit reached 38%. Servicing the total of outstanding debt now pre-empted a quarter of budget expenditures.

A further fiscal expansion was planned in the budget for FY2000. Expenditures totalling 85 trillion, up by 3.8% on 1999, increased the fiscal deficit to 43%. Worried at the slow-down of the economy in the second half of 1999, and with an eye to the general election of the House of Representatives due no later than July 2000, the Obuchi government announced in November 1999 yet another additional stimulus to economic activity with a package of increased spending and tax cuts with a face value of 18 trillion, the ninth in-year pump-priming package since 1992 (see Table 23.3 for details).

The accumulation and growth of deficits and debts in the 1990s is dealt with in detail in Chapters 26 and 27. The remaining chapters of this part of the book describe and analyse the processes through which the policies discussed here were planned and implemented, reserving until the concluding part an assessment of their effects and their effectiveness in achieving MOF's objectives in the 1980s.

14

Economic Forecasts and Fiscal Projections

The general context of budget-making, up to the Cabinet's approval of MOF's draft budgets for both the General Account Budget and FILP in December, was shaped by a combination of short-term and medium-term political and economic factors. The medium-term context was set by the five-year National Economic Plan, and the Medium Term Fiscal Projection. Revised and rolled forward each year, the latter provided stylized projections of aggregate expenditures and revenues for the upcoming fiscal year and three years ahead, based mainly on the (equally stylized) economic growth assumptions in the National Economic Plan. The shorter-term macroeconomic context was provided mainly by the annual estimates of GDP (and other key economic variables), and the consequential projections of revenue and borrowing.

THE NATIONAL ECONOMIC PLAN

The National Economic Plan set out the government's main economic and social objectives, and the general orientation of its domestic and international policy-making for the following five years. Its purpose was to provide general guidelines for government, business leaders, and consumers as an indication of the direction in which the government intended or hoped to move, and to summarize existing and contemplated policy initiatives. Some of the earlier plans in the period of re-industrialization and high growth in the 1950s and early 1960s had a strong 'indicative planning' element, as governments aimed to steer both public and private-sector organizations in preferred directions. This had long since disappeared. In the last quarter of the twentieth century, the Plan was less a plan of action, an instrument for achieving agreed policy objectives, than a declaration of aspiration for the nation as a whole. As such, it was an important symbol of national unity, a public manifestation of a sense of common purpose to achieve certain desirable goals for society as a whole.

Specific and explicit policy commitments in the plan were normally derived from initiatives either already taken or signalled in recent budgets or policy statements. For example, some of the commitments in the 1992–6 Plan to improve health and welfare facilities for elderly people were derived directly from the Ministry of Health and Welfare's 'Ten Year Strategy to Promote Health Care and Welfare for the Aged', the so-called Gold Plan. The 'Outline for Promoting Comprehensive Land Policies'; the ten-year Basic Plan for Public Investment from 1991 to 2000; the Fourth Medium Term Target for Official

Development Assistance (ODA)— these and similar plans reflected policy initiatives already decided upon and in some cases already in the process of implementation.

The 1992–6 National Plan, *Sharing a Better Quality of Life around the Globe* (EPA 1992), combined two themes: the need for a global perspective, and greater concern for the interests of consumers rather than producers. While there was a series of generalizations about how Japan would play a greater role in the international economic community, and expand its domestic demand in response to pressures from the IMF or G7 for example, there were also detailed policy objectives and commitments designed to improve the quality of life of the Japanese people: for example the reduction of working hours to provide for more leisure time, the improvement of adult education and public facilities for leisure activities, the promotion of health and welfare policies for elderly people, the expansion of facilities for sewerage and main drainage, the creation of more urban parks, the alleviation of traffic congestion, and the improvement of the regions. The creation or improvement of those and other 'social overhead projects' was linked directly to specific quantitative targets for some two dozen existing policies. For example, under the general head of 'Improving opportunities for learning and culture', there was an explicit performance indicator: the percentage of local public schools with specified facilities for supporting adult education activities, such as community centres with changing rooms, and so on. Such commitments had expenditure implications throughout the medium-term period of the Plan.

The Five Year Plan was produced until 2001 by the (then) Economic Council, a statutory advisory body that reported to the prime minister, composed of 26 leading businessmen, industrialists, bankers, academics, journalists, and economic commentators. Preparation of the Plan was divided among eight sub-committees whose 142 members were drawn from a wider spectrum still, including representatives of chambers of commerce, trade unions, the media, the professions, ex-government officials, the business world, media, and universities. Work for the Twelfth Plan began with the formal institution of an inquiry addressed by the Prime Minister to the Chairman in January 1992. The themes, discussed and agreed to beforehand, were spelled out directly:

What sort of long-term economic plan should Japan formulate in order to realise a better quality of life, to make Japan a country in which each and every person can appreciate a comfortable and leisurely life? How can we provide the infrastructure necessary for the development of our economy and society in the 21st century, and at the same time be considering global issues, make an active contribution to the world? (EPA 1992: 87)

The Council's Report was presented to the Prime Minister in June 1992, approved by the Cabinet later the same month, and published under the auspices of the EPA in September 1992. A similar timetable was followed in the preparation of the 1995–2000 Plan, *Social and Economic Plan for Structural Reforms towards a Vital Economy and Secure Life* (EPA 1996a). Prime Minister Murayama made a formal request to the Economic Council in January 1995. It produced an Interim Report in June summarizing the main themes, and a Final Report approved by Cabinet in December.

In implementing its terms of reference, the Economic Council and its sub-committees worked closely with EPA, MOF, and MITI, with MOF's Fiscal System Research Council and the Prime Minister's Tax System Council, and with other ministries and agencies whose interests were directly affected by the Plan's proposals, such as MHW, MOC, MHA, and the Science and Technology Agency. Through their participation, through the Secretariat provided by EPA, and informally through policy networks, MOF and individual ministries were able to steer and manage the overall direction and substance of the Council's deliberations in line with their own thinking, and to ensure the acceptability of its recommendations. That is not to say that the Council and its advisers had no influence, but that that influence was exercised informally in the discussions that preceded the formulation of the formal proposals that appeared in the final Report/Plan. Thus, the Cabinet (and the LDP and its coalition partners) was able to accept the Plan without reservation, because any doubts or misgivings it might have had were taken into account at an earlier stage, before the final Report was drawn up. As the Report was not merely a vague statement of general intentions, pious hopes and indications, but also included a number of explicit commitments (mentioned above), some of which had targets attached, it is evident that those ministries and agencies affected were involved, through formal and informal consultation, at earlier stages. The general orientation and thrust of the Plan was of course determined first by the tenor and wording of the Cabinet's remit to the Council, itself the result of prior agreement between senior party officials, MOF, MITI, and EPA, and subsequently by the influence of the prime minister, ministers, and the LDP policy-making organizations on its deliberations.

Whereas previous plans aimed to increase economic growth, or to distribute the benefits of that growth, to achieve social, welfare, and environmental objectives, that for 1995–2000 was preoccupied with the management of crisis. Prepared in 1995 at a time of economic stagnation, with the financial system in a critical condition and continuing instability in the political system, in place of the confidence of earlier plans, there was here a sense of foreboding, of impending economic and social disaster, unless radical changes were made to the structures of both the economy and society. Most of the policies designed for that purpose, for example re-invigorating the economy through deregulation and the opening of domestic markets, improving the quality of life, and implementing administrative and fiscal reform, were already in place and in the process of implementation, albeit with varying degrees of commitment and urgency.

The need for radical reform of the economy along those lines had been widely discussed before the adoption of the plan in December 1995. Earlier in the year, both EPA and MITI had warned in their Annual Reports of the critical condition of the economy, and had called for urgent structural reform, as explained in Chapter 4. Each of the first three coalition governments had been committed to the principles of deregulation and the liberalization of markets, and had brought forward proposals prepared by advisory committees, most notably the Hiraiwa Report in November 1993. Hiraiwa Gaishi, formerly president of Keidanren, was also chairman of the Economic Council, responsible for the preparation of the National Plan. To underline the urgency of the need for reform, the Plan outlined an alternative prospect of much lower economic growth, productivity, and employment should its recommendations be ignored or fail to be implemented. Nevertheless, a growing consensus on the principle of reform did not guarantee agreement on the policies to achieve it; still less did it ensure that those policies would be implemented.

As in previous plans, that for 1995–2000 provided no detailed quantitative analysis and assessment of the main economic variables, but there were 'general indicators' for the plan period of the average annual rates of real and nominal economic growth, inflation, and the level of unemployment by 2000. No great weight was attached to the reliability of those figures, but that for economic growth was important in shaping the medium-term context of budget-making because it was used as the key assumption in the preparation of the Medium Term Fiscal Projection.

Unlike its 13 post-war predecessors, *The Ideal Socio-Economy and Policies for Economic Rebirth* (Economic Council 1999), covered a ten- rather than five-year period, from 1999 to 2010. Consistently with the initiatives and reports of Prime Minister Obuchi's Economic Strategy Council, and Industry Competitiveness Council, it emphasized the breakdown of the post-war economic system and its main structures, and echoed their calls for more freedom from government regulations, greater emphasis on individual creativity and initiative, and the sovereignty of consumers, as the economy shifted to a new knowledge-based industrial era. The time-horizon, the title—a guideline (*hōshin*) rather than a plan (*keikaku*)—and the tenor of the Report represented a departure from previous plans, largely as a result of the personal initiative of the minister, the director-general of the Agency, Sakaiya Taichi, who attended meetings of the Council, led the discussions, and wrote much of the final report himself. However, while the plan outlined the kind of economic structure that might deliver the 2% p.a. growth forecast over the period 1999–2010, like most of its predecessors, it was short on concrete policies and commitments to achieve the envisioned new framework of economic management.

The general orientation of each national plan—especially that of 1992–6, with its emphasis on the need to improve the quality of life by improving social overhead capital—provided an important context for fiscal policy during the following five years, and was reflected most obviously in the priority given in subsequent budgets to certain types of spending. According to circumstances, those priorities might change during the plan period, as governments reacted to changes in the international and domestic politico-economic context: shorter-term considerations might take precedence as the government conducted its annual economic assessment at the time of the formulation of the Budget. In that as well, it had the advice of the Economic Council, which each year reviewed the foreign and domestic economic situation, and the state of the government's progress in the implementation of the proposals made in the Plan. The Council reported to government on the policies needed to manage the economy in the light of prevailing circumstances; but that advice was again the formal product of informal discussions and soundings between Economic Council members, and ministers and officials of EPA, MOF, MITI, and those other ministries and agencies whose interests were affected. Where the need arose, as in the case of abrupt changes in the international or domestic economies, the Council was convened specially to advise government.

THE MEDIUM TERM FISCAL PROJECTION

The focus in the preparation of the General Account (and FILP) Budget was mainly the next fiscal year. There was no medium-term expenditure planning with allocations to spending programmes two, three, or more years ahead, such as that found in the UK and some other G7 countries. While there were multi-year sectoral plans for investment (discussed in Chapter 23), defence, and ODA, allocations were decided annually. There was an attempt, in the Fiscal Structure Reform Act of 1997, to introduce longer-term expenditure plans for spending programmes, but, as explained in the previous chapter it was soon abandoned.

From 1978, when it presaged the initiation of the policy of fiscal reconstruction, MOF produced and published annually projections of expenditure, revenue, and borrowing for three years ahead, together with figures for the past year's budget, and for the one upcoming. The Medium Term Fiscal Projection provided the medium-term context for the annual decisions of the size of the expenditure and revenue aggregates, and the amount of government borrowing. The figures for three years ahead were calculated using stylized policy assumptions: tax revenues, on the basis of the fixed nominal GDP growth rate in the National Economic Plan, multiplied by a fixed elasticity ratio (1.1), plus or minus the estimated effects of any tax reforms in the pipeline. Projections of expenditures were based on similarly stylized policy assumptions about the continuing costs of servicing the debt, and of financing the aggregates of current and capital spending programmes. Projections of the costs of additional government borrowing reflected given policy assumptions and targets to achieve the main fiscal objectives of eliminating the issue of special deficit-financing bonds, and reducing the bond dependency ratio.

Comparisons of projected expenditures with those for revenues plus targeted borrowing produced a 'bottom-line' fiscal adjustment for each forward-year, the amount by which expenditure had to be cut and/or tax revenues increased. In practice, the adjustment necessary to cover the difference between planned expenditures and revenues plus borrowing in the annual Budget was almost always made by increasing the amount of borrowing above the levels projected, normally resulting in the deferral of the target dates for the progressive reduction in government borrowing, and for the elimination of special deficit-financing bonds.

Before 1981, MOF used annually estimated changes in nominal GDP rather than the fixed growth rate of the National Economic Plan in its projections of tax revenues and expenditure. With the adoption of the policy of fiscal reconstruction, however, it became concerned less with the credibility of its projection, than with emphasizing the need to constrain expenditure and reduce the amount of government borrowing. From 1981 The Medium Term Fiscal Projection also incorporated the current policies and target dates for reducing borrowing, and for eliminating the issue of special deficit-financing bonds. For FY1996 MOF produced three alternative projections, showing the implications of reducing the issue of special deficit-financing bonds from FY1997 to zero, and, to two alternative and more gradual progressive reductions. For the first time it also published a simulation, the *Medium Term Fiscal Outlook*, projecting expenditure, revenue, and borrowing forward to FY2006, in preparation for the announcement by the new Hashimoto government of its medium-term aims and policies for fiscal reform, including the aim of eliminating special deficit-financing bonds by the end of FY2003. The exercise was repeated the following year, and again in 1999, but with more elaboration. In line with the by-then published National Economic Plan for 1995–2000, the projections showed the implications of both the presumed 3.5% GDP growth, and the 1.75% growth that would result from the failure to implement the plan's recommendations for structural reform of the economy.

The Medium Term Fiscal Projection was not used directly in the preparation of the annual Budget. As even a general guide or indicator of what would or could happen to the aggregates of expenditure, revenue, and borrowing, it had little influence in the annual budgetary processes of making the Budget. At best, it provided a general backdrop for the discussions between the Budget Bureau, Cabinet ministers, and senior LDP officials which preceded the decision on expenditure and revenue aggregates, and the level of borrowing to aim for. Its main purpose was essentially political and propagandist: to focus public attention on the overall fiscal situation, by emphasizing the persistent shortfall in revenue, the increasing size and burden of government borrowing, and the continuing need to restore flexibility to the Budget by reducing dependency on the issue of bonds to finance current expenditure. More generally, MOF ministers and officials used the projection to try to create and foster a greater awareness and understanding of the continuing need for policies of fiscal restraint, for example in explanations to the LDP's Tax Policy Council, and to the Diet's budget committees when the draft budget was examined there in the spring.

THE FISCAL SYSTEM RESEARCH COUNCIL

The Medium Term Fiscal Projection was prepared in the Budget Bureau's Research and Planning Division, among whose responsibilities was that of servicing the Fiscal System Research Council, a statutory advisory body whose members were appointed by and responsible to the minister of finance. It had a formal role in the annual budget process. First, after publication of the guidelines for budget requests set by the Cabinet in June or July, the chairman of the Council commented publicly on the compilation of the next budget, for example on the need for continuing restraint, for the maintenance of ceilings on current and capital spending, and so on. Secondly, following the submission of budget requests, the Council discussed and commented on their implications for budget strategy. Thirdly, before MOF submitted its draft budget to Cabinet in December, the Council published a report with 'recommendations' for the minister of finance, normally in line with MOF's proposals, reiterating the need for 'cuts', 'rationalization', and so on.

The Council's discussions and published recommendations were strongly influenced and shaped by the Budget Bureau, whose officials in its Research Division supplied the technical and statistical data, prepared analyses and interpretations, and drafted papers, as explained in Chapter 8. The Council's formal function was mainly to support and legitimize the Budget Bureau's overall strategy. The director-general of the Budget Bureau discussed the objectives of fiscal policy, and the proposed medium-term strategy, with members of the Council, and might appear before it more formally to explain MOF's position. The Council's published recommendations provided an 'early warning' of what would follow in the Budget, an essential part of the process of building consensus.

At other times of the year, the Council, prompted by the Budget Bureau, produced reports on particular issues of fiscal policy. In February 1994 for example, it provided an outline of medium-term objectives for fiscal management, designed to restore flexibility in the Budget in order to cope with changes in economic and social conditions, such as the ageing population, the need for improved social infrastructure, and Japan's enhanced role in the international community. Those objectives—to reduce bond dependency, and to restrain the growth of expenditures by reviewing programmes and their relative priorities—were firmly in line with MOF's own policy aims and medium-term fiscal strategy. The Council proposed a medium-term target for the bond dependency ratio of less than 5%, but warned that this could be achieved only with regard to the prevailing economic conditions; progress year by year might be uneven, a signal that MOF might have to increase the number of new bonds issued in a particular year—as in fact happened soon after.

In July 1996 the Council prompted by MOF produced a report on the restructuring of the fiscal system, intended to provide the focus for the public discussion that preceded the adoption of the policy by the Hashimoto government. Here again, the intention was to alert the public to MOF's thinking, and to achieve a consensus on its preferred policies. As explained in the previous chapter, its proposals formed the basis of the recommendations of the Prime Minister's Council on Fiscal Reform in July 1997. They reflected MOF's own thinking, and that of the LDP leadership.

The Government's Tax System Research Council played a similar role to that of the Fiscal System Research Council, formally reporting to the prime minister on general matters of tax structure, and annually on issues of tax policy and changes to existing legislation. It was used by MOF as a means of propagating its own policy preferences (Ishi 1989; Katō Junko 1994). However, in the formulation of tax policy, it was much less influential than the LDP's Tax Policy Council.

THE ANNUAL ECONOMIC FORECAST

The *Economic Outlook and Basic Policy Stance on Economic Management*, published annually in December, provided the government's formal and public assessment of the outlook for the economy in the coming fiscal year, and its performance in the current fiscal year. It was normally approved formally by the Cabinet in January, by which time the Cabinet had normally approved the Budget for the fiscal year beginning in April. Shortly after, in April/May, the Budget Bureau began the process leading to the Cabinet's discussion in early summer of the size of the budget for the next fiscal year, and Spending Ministries and Agencies began to compile their budget requests for submission to it by August. Those processes got underway against the background of the economic assessment for the current fiscal year in the *Economic Outlook*, updated to incorporate revised estimates of GDP, employment, industrial production, prices, and balance of payments, in the light of both domestic and global conditions. Preparation of the new *Economic Outlook*, which influenced the budget strategy, thus began a year before the fiscal year began, and almost two years before it ended. In such circumstances there was inevitably a great deal of uncertainty, and hence opportunity for contested judgements about what was likely to happen to GDP (and other economic variables).

EPA was formally responsible for the preparation of the *Economic Outlook*, but other ministries and agencies had a direct interest in the forecasts of the main economic variables. Both MOF and MITI were key players in the process of determining the official forecast of GDP. There was as much or more politics as economics in the process of deciding, and in any year there was a greater or lesser degree of realism about the published forecast. There were two conflicting pressures. First, from the early 1980s onwards there was almost continuous external pressure on the Japanese government to expand its domestic economic activity, for example to contribute to global reflation in 1987 by increasing public spending on capital investment and lowering taxes, or to reduce the surplus on its current account. MOF needed to be seen to be sensitive to such pressures. Secondly, and concurrently, for most of that time MOF's main aims for domestic fiscal policy were to cut spending and reconstruct the tax system to generate more revenue in order to reduce government borrowing, and restore greater flexibility in budget-making. An over-ambitious or unduly optimistic GDP estimate excited expectations about the opportunity for more public spending, encouraging LDP officials and Dietmen, and ministers and their officials in the Spending Ministries and Agencies, to press and support their budget requests. MOF had to balance that consideration against the advantage that overestimating the growth of the economy, and hence the estimate of the tax revenues derived from it, meant that it could plan for a lower level of borrowing in the initial budget.

Striking a balance between demonstrable responsiveness to pressure from the USA and other G7 countries and from the international economic community for policies to stimulate higher rates of growth, and concern for its own domestic objectives of controlling public spending and reducing the level of government borrowing, provided a delicate issue of public presentation. The GDP forecast 'emerged' from the *realpolitik* in the network that linked ministers and officials from, mainly, EPA, MOF, and MITI, and senior LDP officials. EPA was not an autonomous agency. Formally within the jurisdiction and supervision of the Prime Minister's Office, in practice both MOF and MITI influenced the appointment of some senior officials, and were able to place their nominees on secondment in key bureaux. The most senior official, the deputy director-general in charge of the Secretariat, together with the director of fiscal and monetary affairs in the Coordination Bureau and the director of planning in the Planning Bureau, were all normally MOF officials serving on secondment. They contributed to the compilation of the *Economic Outlook* and its economic assessment from their own expertise, and from access to MOF's strategic thinking on expenditure, taxes, industrial production, productivity, and so on, besides EPA's own resources of data. The forecast of GDP, then, was less an estimate derived from sober analysis of the data, more a political judgement, acceptable to and formally approved by ministers, bureaucrats, and senior LDP politicians.

When economic growth was buoyant, in the years of the 'bubble' of the late 1980s, MOF's aim was to try to ensure that EPA's estimate of growth was as cautious or pessimistic as possible. That is to say, domestic policy considerations of restraining expenditure in the initial Budget were dominant. The intention was to dampen the expectations of Spending Ministries and the LDP that more expenditure could be afforded because of buoyant revenues, while at the same time allowing a margin for some growth; and, above all, to avoid a recurrence of the experience of the 1970s when expectations of the continuance of high growth encouraged still higher spending. MITI, and some other Spending Ministries and Agencies, normally had a contrary vested interest in the adoption of a higher estimate of the growth rate, to send appropriate signals not only to the international community, but to domestic business and industry, for example to encourage more spending on public and private R&D, and to support their own bids for more spending on their industrial programmes.

The tensions inherent in the roles, responsibilities and different aims of EPA, MOF, and MITI became apparent in the discussions leading up to the published GDP forecasts produced annually in the 1990s. Within MOF, there were tensions between the different policy interests of the Budget Bureau, the Tax Bureau, and the International Finance Bureau. The latter was concerned to respond, or to be seen to be responding, to its international constituency of foreign governments, while G7, IMF, and OECD were calling for an expansion of domestic demand. In the inter-bureau discussions, the Coordination Division of the Budget Bureau played the crucial role, dealing with the coordination divisions of the other bureaux, and with those of EPA and MITI as well.

Estimates of revenue from direct and indirect taxes were the responsibility of the Tax Bureau, and undue caution or pessimism could lead to conflict with the Budget Bureau's objectives for borrowing: lower estimates meant more borrowing for a given level of expenditure. To achieve its policy objectives of reducing borrowing and eliminating special deficit bonds, the Budget Bureau was normally concerned to keep estimates of borrowing as low as possible in the initial planned budget, even if in the event the out-turn was expected to be much higher, and was provided for in-year in Supplementary Budgets. Thus, throughout the 1990s the Tax Bureau was under pressure to produce more optimistic estimates of tax revenues than was warranted by best estimates of the growth of GDP.

The underlying politics of the annual economic assessment surfaced in the public discussion of the estimated growth rate for GDP in FY1993 among the three major parties, EPA, MOF, and MITI. EPA had forecast growth of 4.75% for the previous fiscal year, in line with that of the medium-term National Economic Plan; the out-turn was 0.4%. In the midst of the most severe recession since 1945, EPA's economic assessment for FY1993 pointed to growth of only 1.6%. This was unacceptable to MOF, and to a lesser extent to MITI as well. Both wanted a much higher estimate, although there was little objective evidence to warrant greater optimism. MOF's main motives were concern for its role as a responsible member of the international economic community, and the need to be seen to be responding to pressure from the USA and G7 to expand domestic demand—and, domestically, its concern to restrain public spending. EPA's proposed growth rate would provoke more calls for fiscal expansion.

At the same time, MOF was worried about the implications of a low estimated growth rate for the achievement of its policy objective of reducing borrowing and avoiding the re-issue of special deficit-financing bonds, eliminated in 1990. The level of planned borrowing in the initial budget would have to be increased to compensate for the lower estimated tax yields implicit in the lower growth rate proposed by EPA. Under protest, EPA agreed to compromise, and a GDP growth rate of 3.3% was approved. In the initial planned budget, MOF was able to show planned tax revenues at 61.3 trillion and borrowing at 8.13 trillion, the former a much lower annual increase than that planned in FY1992, the latter lower than the out-turn of that year. The Ministry could still plausibly argue that it was on course to achieve its medium-term borrowing objectives. In the event, real GDP growth was only 0.5%; tax revenues yielded only 54.1 trillion and borrowing doubled to 16.1 trillion, partly to compensate for the revenue shortfall, but mainly to finance three separate counter cyclical Supplementary Budgets.

The increasing unrealism of the annual GDP estimate, and of tax revenues and borrowing derived from it, is shown in the comparison of estimates and out-turns in Table 14.1. In seven of the eight years from 1992 to 1999, the out-turn of tax revenues

Table 14.1 *The credibility gap: estimates and out-turns of GDP, tax revenues, and borrowing, FY1992–FY2000*

FY	GDP (real terms) (annual % change)		Tax revenues (tr. yen)		Government borrowing (tr. yen)	
	Estimate	Out-turn	Initial budget estimate	Budget out-turn	Initial budget estimate	Budget out-turn
1992	4.75	0.4	62.5	54.4	7.28	9.53
1993	3.3	0.5	61.3	54.1	8.13	16.17
1994	2.4	0.7	53.5	51.0	13.64	16.49
1995	2.8	2.8	53.7	51.9	12.59	21.24
1996	2.5	3.2	51.3	52.0	21.03	21.74
1997	1.9	−0.7	57.8	53.9	16.70	18.46
1998	1.9/−1.8[a]	−2.2	58.5	49.4	15.56	34.0
1999	0.5	0.6	47.1	45.6	31.1	38.6
2000	1.0	n/a	48.7	49.9[b]	32.6	34.6

[a]The initial estimate in December 1997 was 1.9%, revised to −1.8% in October 1998.
[b]Revised Budget.

Source: *Main Economic Indicators* (monthly), Research and Planning Division, Minister's Secretariat, MOF; *Monthly Finance Review* (MOF), February 1999.

was below that estimated in the Budget, sometimes substantially so. In every year, government borrowing exceeded that estimated in the Budget.

The credibility of the annual GDP estimates was increasingly criticized outside Japan;[1] inside, Terasawa Yoshio, EPA's minister in the Hata Coalition government, was moved to protest publicly in 1994 at the constant pressure from his officials to accede to higher estimates than were warranted by economic analysis. He refused to declare that the recession had bottomed out in order 'to brighten up the general business community psychology' (JER 1994: 7).

> Growth of 2.4% in real terms was a phantom figure. I complained that I would be embarrassed to mention such a figure in front of the [House] Budget Committee, but an EPA executive shut me up by saying 'that's the figure on the basis of which tax revenues are calculated, so if you don't give that figure the budget will have trouble passing the Diet.' (*Tokyo Business Today*, January 1995)

Under threats that the entire fiscal framework would have to be revised if he officially doubted or derided the forecast, Terasawa had publicly to insist on the credibility of the 2.4% growth rate. The out-turn, as the table shows, was 0.7%. A more serious discrepancy occurred in FY1998, when an heroic forecast of economic growth of 1.8% was falsified by an out-turn of −2.2%, with a contingent reduction in the yield of tax revenues of more than 11 trillion, and a doubling of the estimate for government borrowing.

---

[1] GDP and other macroeconomic data collected by national governments on an historic time-series basis are revised and updated annually. Japan's were no exception, but those relating to the calculation of GDP were increasingly criticized in the 1990s (see e.g. IMF 1999) for technical inadequacies and possible sampling biases. There have been some obvious distortions arising from Japan's system of seasonal adjustment, and some unusually large revisions. While EPA was formally responsible for the preparation of GDP data, other ministries and agencies, such as MITI and MCA, produced related data often using different techniques. In October 2000, EPA announced a major change in its methodology to include for the first time comprehensive data on the IT sector. The effect is likely to lead to upward revisions of GDP for FY1997 and FY1998.

15

Budget Strategy, Guidelines, and Ceilings

The processes of budget-making were divided temporally by the submission of the formal budget requests by the Spending Ministries and Agencies on 31 August. Before that date MOF had to decide, and Cabinet approve: first, the upper limit on the size of the overall General Account Budget, and the amount and type of government borrowing to finance capital investment programmes, and to cover any deficit on current expenditure; secondly, the budget guidelines to be used in the preparation of budget requests; and, thirdly, within those guidelines, the upper limit or ceiling for the budget of each ministry and agency. The processes were iterative but for the purposes of analysis and explanation are treated sequentially in this and the next chapter. The budget processes of the Fiscal Investment Loan Programme proceeded in parallel, and interacted with those of the General Account Budget at several important stages. They are examined in Chapter 19.

THE BUDGET STRATEGY

Top-Down Factors

The starting point for the formulation of the budget strategy was the prevailing set of objectives for public-sector spending. As explained in Chapter 13, from at least 1981 onwards, those were concerned with fiscal reconstruction. What could be afforded consistently with those objectives was constrained partly by a number of top-down politico-economic factors, and partly by bottom-up pressures from the Spending Ministries and Agencies for more spending, both mediated by consideration and, where necessary, incorporation of party political factors.

The first top-down factor was the state of the economy currently, and its forecasted growth (or decline) for the coming fiscal year. Here the crucial factor was the forecast for GDP. As explained in the previous chapter, its determination was heavily influenced by political factors, and the competing interests of MOF's bureaus and of other Spending Ministries and Agencies, principally EPA and MITI.

The estimates of revenue from direct and indirect taxes derived from that forecast provided the second top-down factor. In Japan, as in other G7 countries, revenue did not directly determine expenditure, in the sense that what was planned to be spent was limited by the revenue to be raised through taxation and other sources. In practice, both the spending aggregate and its broad allocation among ministries and their programmes were necessarily decided in the autumn before firm estimates of the yield of tax revenues in the coming fiscal year were available. Thus, estimated revenue would influence, but not finally determine, the size and composition of planned expenditure in the General Account Budget. The extent to which it had an influence on expenditure policy was the result of a combination of both long-term factors and short-term conjunctural policies. The latter were compounded of annual tax policies which might be adjusted in response to perceptions of the business cycle, for example the rate at which the economy was perceived to be growing or declining, and whether it was thought prudent to use taxation policy in an attempt to stimulate or depress demand accordingly.

Governments might also wish to attempt to influence electoral behaviour through changes in taxation policy intended to promote or protect general or special interests, whose support, financial or otherwise, was held to give them party political advantage, for example by reducing rates of taxation, or adjusting thresholds and tax brackets. Longer-term factors included the stability of revenue, and the extent to which the tax system was sensitive to changes in economic activity, and generated surpluses or shortfall. Finally, as explained in previous chapters, estimates of tax revenues were deliberately underestimated by MOF before 1975 to provide 'natural increases' to finance tax reductions, and in the 1980s to dampen expectations about resources available to finance spending programmes.

The implications for revenue of the emerging budget strategy were discussed by the Coordination Divisions of the Budget Bureau and Tax Bureau. Argument about the revenue estimates (and hence contingently the size of the deficit to be financed) did not take place much before the EPA's GDP forecast was available to MOF and MITI in October/November prior to its formal publication in the *Economic Outlook* in December. In the 1990s the Budget Bureau tended to urge optimism in estimates of the buoyancy of revenue, counterpointed by the inherent caution and pessimism of the Tax Bureau. Here their different values and interests had to be traded off. However, both bureaux had a common interest in the reconstruction of the national finances, and the aim of reducing the burden of debt. Internally, in the early summer the Tax Bureau provided successive approximations of estimated revenue, and argued with the Budget Bureau about their reliability, their political and economic 'realism', and the need for any adjustment for the purposes of public presentation. At the same time, the Budget Bureau's Coordination Division was mindful of the need to convey purposeful signals to its budget examiners and their deputies, and through them to their Spending Ministries and Agencies about the tautness of the revenue constraints. For example, if revenue estimates were perceived within the Budget Bureau line divisions, and beyond in the Spending Ministries, as buoyant, then pressure to accede to requests, at the margin, might prove more difficult to resist. Conversely, if deputy budget examiners argued in their early informal discussions with Spending Ministries that tax revenues would be lower than earlier forecasts suggested, and hence adopted a tough posture, their credibility for future negotiations might be damaged if subsequently the revenue position proved to be a more accommodating one.

The third top-down politico-economic factor was the amount of new borrowing implied by estimates of tax and other revenues to finance the planned aggregate of expenditure. In practice, consideration of the borrowing requirement was influenced as much, and on some occasions more, by the targets set for the progressive reduction of the bond dependency ratio, and the date set for the elimination of the issue of special deficit-financing bonds. Hence estimates of revenue and borrowing were arrived at iteratively.

On the expenditure side, there were two top-down factors to be taken into account in determining the aggregate: the so-called 'fixed costs' of servicing the accumulated debt, and the statutory allocation to local government of a fixed proportion of the revenues from certain nationally collected taxes. In practice, as we shall explain in Chapter 25, MOF was able to, and frequently did, vary the size of both to relieve short-term pressures on the budget, but at the (future) cost of accumulating a greater burden of debt over the medium term.

Bottom-Up Pressures

To provide a range of options for the size of the overall budget total, the Budget Bureau's Coordination Division needed an early indication of what requirements and demands for spending were likely to come up from below, from the Spending Ministries and Agencies, and an assessment of whether they were containable within the previous year's budget shares or required additional resources of particular kinds. In the period from April to June, budget examiners and their deputies reviewed the conduct of the previous year's budget hearings, negotiations, and outcomes, and assessed the effectiveness of the tactics they had employed. At the same time, consideration was given to the progress of major policy reviews underway or contemplated in individual bureaux in particular ministries or agencies, and their implications for future spending. Budget Examiners might be engaged jointly in reviewing programmes with their opposite numbers in Spending Ministries. As the budget examiner responsible for Welfare and Labour in the 1980s, Komura Takeshi (director-general of the Budget Bureau, 1996–7) worked closely with senior officials in MHW to reform the medical care system for elderly people in 1982 and, two years later, the social security system (Komura 1993).

Concurrently, all budget examiners and deputy budget examiners were conducting informal soundings with the directors of budget and accounts divisions in their ministries and agencies, seeking information about new or revised policies, notice of obligations and commitments that entailed additional spending, and programmes that were in decline, or might be cut. These were collected and collated by the Budget Bureau's Coordination Division, and contributed to the first informal estimates of the aggregate of the spending requests of individual ministries and agencies. Formally, those processes were the First and Second Expenditure Estimates, which took place normally in March and May, from which the Coordination Division set a tentative framework (*waku*) for the whole budget. At those stages the estimates were very rough and usually exaggerated. From the imposition of negative budget ceilings in the mid-1980s, both occasions became more ritualistic than substantively important, replaced by informal and continuous consultations between the Coordination Division, the three deputy directors-general, and their budget examiners and deputy budget examiners (MOF 1993*b*). In the course of preparing the trial estimates, there might however be a formal meeting, if the director-general wanted it, to discuss major policies, projects, and programmes, and the alternative ways in which expenditures for them might be provided for and handled in negotiations. On the basis of these early rough estimates, and after discussion with the director-general, Coordination Division produced a 'lesser total' than that suggested by the earlier rough estimates of the aggregate, which provided the basis for the subsequent internal negotiations that it conducted with the budget examiners and deputy directors-general over their shares of the planned budget total (Komura 1993; MOF 1993*c*).

As more and better information and data were collected, collated, and evaluated during the course of the budget process, both top-down and bottom-up factors were progressively refined, with consequential effects on the evolving overall budgetary strategy—tighter or looser—and the tactics to be adopted by budget examiners and deputy budget examiners in their forthcoming negotiations with the bureaux and divisions of the Spending Ministries and Agencies.

THE BUDGET GUIDELINES

The budget ceiling that the Budget Bureau proposed formally to the Cabinet in June/July was derived from the application of informal guidelines prescribing the distribution of cuts and squeezes, and the allocation of additional resources. In effect, they provided the general rules-of-the-game governing the conduct of the Budget Bureau and the Spending Ministries and Agencies in the bidding processes. In practice, the decisions about the ceiling for the Budget as a whole, and those for the broad categories of spending within it, were iterated, with trade-offs and adjustments made at the margins of both.

The guidelines were reviewed annually, the lead taken by the Budget Bureau's Coordination Division. At an early stage, the director-general explored a range of options with the prime minister, the minister of finance, and senior LDP officials. How much extra spending on public works, the allocation of new monies to priority programmes, where and how cuts were to be made—all were the subject of intense political discussion. While those options were explored with LDP ministers and officials, the Coordination Division maintained a constant dialogue with the three deputy directors-general and the budget examiners in their line divisions. In turn, the latter and the deputy budget examiners kept in continuous close contact with their opposite numbers in the Spending Ministries and Agencies, discussing the implications of any possible changes in their overall budget share, and its distribution among programmes. Changes to the guidelines had consequential effects both on categories of expenditure, and on individual programmes. For example, more or fewer resources in total for investment in public buildings and facilities affected the size and composition of current expenditure on education, health, welfare, and similar programmes.

From 1961 until 1976 there was a single budget guideline, prescribing the maximum permitted increase for the aggregate of budget requests; there were no formal criteria for the allocation of resources to categories of expenditure or for individual programmes.

Strategy, Guidelines, and Ceilings

From 1977, the 'fixed costs' of debt-servicing, the assigned revenues of the local government allocation tax, and the automatic increments of pensions for former government employees were excluded from the calculation of the main control aggregate in the General Account Budget. That separation was formally marked in FY1980 by the use of the concept of 'general expenditure' to cover all programme spending, roughly two-thirds of the total.

As the fiscal crisis deepened, MOF began to develop more elaborate and discriminatory criteria. Table 15.1 summarizes the main developments to FY2000. A zero ceiling was

Table 15.1 *Summary of the main budget guidelines, FY1961–FY2000*

Fiscal year	Guidelines	Change (%)
1961–64	All expenditures	+50
1965–67	All expenditures	+30
1968–75	All expenditures	+25
1976	All expenditures	+15
1977	General administrative expenses	+10
	Other spending	+15
1978–79	General administrative expenses	
	Current office overheads	0
	Others	+15
	Other spending	+13.5
1980	General administrative expenses	0
	Other Spending	+10
1981	General administrative expenses	0
	Other spending	+7.5
1982	All Spending	0
1983	Capital spending	0
	Current spending	−5
1984–87	Capital spending	−5
	Current spending	−10
1988–93	Capital spending	0
	Current spending	−10
1994–95	Capital spending	+5
	Current spending	−10
1996	Capital spending	+5
	Current spending	
	General administrative expenses	−15
	Other spending	−10
1997	Capital spending	0
	Current spending	
	General administrative expenses	−15
	Other spending	−12.5
	Interest payment subsidies	−5
	Personnel expenses	−0.8

Table 15.1 (cont.)

Fiscal year	Guidelines	Change (%)
1998	General expenditures (statutory caps)	
	Social security	+ 300 billion
	Public investment	− 7.0
	Education	0
	Defence	0
	ODA	− 10
	Food control	0
	Science and technology	+ 5
	Energy	0
	SMEs	0
1999	Public works	0
	Science and technology	+ 5
	Social security	+ 570 billion
	Other spending	0
	Economic recovery	+ 4.0 trillion
	Public works	2.7 trillion
	Other	1.3 trillion
2000	Public works	0
	Social security	+ 500 billion
	Other spending	0
	Telecoms, science and technology	+ 250 billion

Source: *The Japanese Budget in Brief*, Budget Bureau, MOF, (annual).

imposed on the aggregate of budget requests for the first time in 1982. In principle, the amount of planned general expenditure was frozen at the level of the previous year's initial budget. The following year, a negative ceiling was imposed, with cuts applied for the first time to current expenditures up to a maximum of 5%; capital expenditures were frozen. From FY1984 to FY1987, cuts were prescribed for both kinds of expenditure, within guidelines of a maximum of −10% for current, and −5% for capital. In FY1988 the guidelines for capital expenditure were relaxed, and the standstill restored. For the following six years no changes were made to those guidelines, although the ceiling for capital expenditures was raised in FY1994 to +5% as part of countercyclical fiscal policies in response to the conditions of economic recession. Two years later, the worsening fiscal situation led to a further tightening of the limit for current expenditures, which since FY1984 had been fixed at a maximum annual reduction of −10%. General administrative expenses (mainly salaries and overheads) were separately distinguished, and a ceiling of −15% prescribed.

Until FY1998, the guidelines had no formal legal status. For that fiscal year, as part of Prime Minister Hashimoto's fiscal reforms, planned expenditure on each of the main programmes was statutorily 'capped', as explained in Chapter 13. The indefinite suspension of the legislation in December 1998 saw a return to the informally prescribed budget guidelines and programme ceilings in the planned FY1999 budget. Spending on both current and capital investment programmes was frozen, but there were some significant exceptions: 4 trillion extra was earmarked for economic recovery, with public works programmes the main beneficiaries, of 2.7 trillion; science and technology programmes were allocated a 5% increase; and social security secured an additional 570 billion. The zero guidelines for current and capital programmes were maintained in the planned budget of FY2000, with social security again attracting an extra 500 billion, and telecommunications and science and technology projects 250 billion more.

In practice, budget guidelines were always applied selectively within the total of general expenditure. From the early 1980s onwards, provision was made each year for some categories of expenditure to be wholly exempt from their application, while others were treated as exceptions, and as priority programmes, allocated additional resources. Programmes exempted were those where the level of expenditure was mainly 'demand-led', the result of the size of the clientele, the take-up of benefits, grants and subsidies, and so on. They included social security, health care, and various kinds of income maintenance, interest payments, subsidies and grants, and the reserve. Secondly, there was a group of programmes which from the early 1980s were chosen by the LDP for preferential treatment, and hence were treated 'exceptionally'.

Before deciding upon the budget ceiling, the Budget Bureau, together with the LDP leadership, reviewed the number and choice of programmes for priority in the allocation of resources. The preferences were first articulated, and evolved as priority programmes, in the period 1980–3, partly as a consequence of the work and recommendations of the Provisional Council on Administrative Reform (Rinchō), discussed in Chapter 4. From 1983 there were five programmes: personnel expenses; pensions for former government employees; overseas development aid (ODA); energy-related programmes; and defence and international treaty programmes. Both the number and choice remained unchanged until FY1998, although of course the relative priority accorded to each varied with the implementation of government/party objectives, for example as set out in five-year plans for defence and ODA.

Priority status was conferred formally for the first time in FY1982, when, together with social security and the promotion of science and technology, the five programmes were singled out as exceptions to the general freeze on all expenditure in the General Account Budget, the first year of the so-called 'zero-ceiling'. To a large extent they were self-selecting, reflecting the LDP's aims and objectives set out in successive national plans since the early 1970s. The special status for Defence and ODA accorded with the emphasis on Japan's changing international role and obligations, emphasized in the initial reports of the Provisional Commission on Administrative Reform. Energy-related programmes were given the highest priority (in percentage terms) in the FY1982 Budget. Experience of the effects of the oil crises of 1973 and 1979 had exposed the vulnerability of the Japanese economy, and underlined the need for measures to conserve energy and to exploit alternative sources. The promotion of science and technology was recognition of MITI's new industrial 'vision' of knowledge-based industries. Subsequently, social security and science and technology were relegated from the category of priority programmes to those 'exempt' from cutback, but the change made little practical difference to their budget allocations, which continued to rise annually; expenditure on social security grew faster than any other programme in the 1975–2000 period. The trends are analysed in Chapter 21.

In the 1980 summer review of budget expenditures, prior to the compilation of the FY1981 budget, MOF published a paper showing the effects of a freeze on all major expenditure programmes. The intention was partly to underline the gravity of the fiscal situation, but also to urge the need for an order of priority in cutting expenditures. The Defence Agency, supported by the defence *zoku*, urged the prescription of a special budget framework for defence spending to ensure that it was given priority. The hostility of the JSP to the security treaty and to increased defence spending, combined with the opposition of MOF in the context of the government's imminent adoption of a policy of fiscal reconstruction, were sufficient to block the proposal. Here the LDP's top leadership opposed its followers, thwarting the combined pressures of the PARC National Defence Division, its Security Affairs Research Council, and its Base Countermeasures Special Committee, not to mention the PARC chairman himself; and resisted pressure from the Defence Agency's director-general who had tried to win support from the LDP secretary general and the chairman of the LDP Executive Council (Keddell 1993).

A year later, however, with continuing US pressure for increased defence spending, there was agreement to adopt a special framework, after the defence *zoku* had been 'especially active in promoting consultations with party members' (Keddell 1993: 102). Although MOF continued to be strongly opposed, a consensus was reached, and a decision to exempt defence spending from the zero ceiling for FY1982 made after a meeting between the Prime Minister, the Chief Cabinet Secretary, and the Minister of Finance. In a wider context, the priority status was intended as a public demonstration of the responsiveness of the Japanese government to the continuing pressure of the USA for Japan to bear more of the burden of defence spending under the security treaty.

After review and agreement on the priority programmes in the budget guidelines, the Budget Bureau discussed and agreed with the LDP leadership the upper limit for the extra resources to be allocated to each of them.

Besides the priority programmes, and those exempted from the application of the budget guidelines, there was a third, looser, category, which comprised a number of capital investment programmes treated exceptionally from the general guidelines prescribing limits for capital investment as a whole. The aim was to increase spending ad hoc on specific capital programmes, and was mainly a phenomenon of the late 1980s and early 1990s, partly in response to the objective set out in the national plans and in the Structural Impediments Initiative of increasing the amount of 'social overhead capital', and partly to provide an additional pump-priming stimulus during the recession. For example, from FY1991 to FY1993, besides the general guideline which provided for a 5% increase in capital investment, additional resources were earmarked in the guidelines for schemes to improve 'social overhead capital' and 'promote public investment'. Subsequently, to stimulate the restructuring of the economy, the guidelines for FY1996 provided ad hoc sums of new money for 'basic economic development' and 'academic study and research'; those for FY1997, for the promotion of economic structural reform; and for

FY1998, for 'special adjustment measures' to provide additional funding for strategic sectors such as environmental protection, scientific research and telecommunications, and additional public works spending to improve transport, communications, and sewage systems and urban redevelopment. From 1988 to 1997, a further source of substantial extra funding was provided by the annual allocation of 1.3 trillion to some other special schemes of capital investment, initially financed with resources from the sale of government shares in NTT. The money was transferred as a loan to the General Account Budget from the National Consolidation Loans Fund. While it did not show up as spending within the head of general expenditure (and as a loan had ultimately to be repaid from the Budget), it nevertheless represented a considerable sum of new money each year for additional public works, for which eligible ministries and agencies competed. The origins, operation, and effects of the so-called NTT scheme are dealt with more fully in Chapter 23.

Top-down limits on current and capital expenditures in the budget guidelines were applied selectively, and were much less restrictive in practice than appeared throughout the period 1982–2000. If we look at the application of the guidelines to the four broad categories of expenditure, the reality was that only about 10% of the total of general expenditure was counted as current expenditure subject to the limits in the guidelines. Almost half of that total comprised spending on those priority programmes treated as exceptions to the rules; 'demand-led' programmes exempted from the guidelines accounted for about a fifth, and capital investment programmes, slightly more. If we take FY1995 as an example, out of the initial budget total for General Expenditure of 42.141 trillion, only 4.4 trillion was subject to the 10% cutback on current expenditure, and 9.6 trillion (23%) was subject to the guideline of +5% for capital investment. More than two-thirds of the total, 28.1 trillion, was excluded altogether from the application of those guidelines, either as priority or as exempt programmes of expenditure.

The base-line for the calculation of the aggregate was the previous year's initial budget expenditure, i.e. that planned; the totals for both revised and out-turn expenditure were normally higher than that planned as a result of in-year spending financed through one or more Supplementary Budgets (see below). By using planned expenditure as the base-line for budget requests, MOF obliged Spending Ministries and Agencies to bid afresh for any in-year increases above that line, agreed in the previous fiscal year. Any gains or losses incurred as a result of Supplementary Budgets were 'unwound', and not added to or subtracted from the base-line. Ceilings were negotiated and prescribed on the basis of the previous year's initial base-line. As revisions to the budget in-year were discounted, so too were the final outputs of the budget processes, the settled accounts. As many ministries and agencies regularly undershot their planned and revised budget allocations, it was important for them to establish that the base-line for the negotiations of the next year's budget was the planned (initial) spending, and not the outcome (settled) spending.

Table 15.2 shows the application of the guidelines in the formulation of the initial budget for FY1996. The base-line for the calculation of each category of expenditure (and for the aggregate) was provided by that in the initial budget for FY1995. The application of the guidelines for FY1996 set an overall ceiling for budget requests of

Table 15.2 *Guidelines for the budget requests for FY1996 (trillion yen)*

General expenditure	FY1995 base-line (initial budget)	FY1996 guidelines: maximum increase/ decrease	FY1996 budget ceilings	FY1996 Initial budget allocation
Current expenditure subject to cut-back	4.4	− 0.450	+ 3.950	4.6
Expenditure excluded from cut-back	8.8	0	8.8	9.0
Priority expenditure exempt from guidelines	19.3	+ 1.660 of which: Personnel 0.380 Pensions 0.840 ODA 0.080 Energy policy 0.040 Defence 0.320	+ 20.960	19.4
Capital investment expenditures	9.6	+ 0.480	+ 10.080	10.1
Special investment schemes[a]		+ 0.140	+ 0.140	0.040
Special factors[b]		− 0.040	− 0.040	
TOTAL	42.141	+ 1.790	43.930	43.140

[a]Economic development, and academic study and research.
[b]Reduction of expenses for general election; population census.
Source: *The Japanese Budget in Brief*, Budget Bureau, MOF (annually).

1.790 trillion above the base-line for the previous year, giving a ceiling for the Budget as a whole of 43.930 trillion. After examination and negotiation of the submitted budget requests, 1.040 trillion of that 1.790 ceiling was approved, giving an initial budget total for FY1996 of 43.140 trillion. That in turn became the base-line for the compilation of the budget for FY1997. As there was some new money every year, base-lines increased year by year.

THE INFLUENCE OF THE LDP

As successive estimates of revenue, expenditure, and borrowing were discussed and iterated, the overall budget strategy began to take shape within the Budget Bureau. But before making formal recommendations to Cabinet in June/July, the director-general of the Budget Bureau and his staff in the Coordination Division had to ensure that what they proposed was consistent with government/party objectives, incorporated any special personal initiative of the prime minister or the minister of finance, and was broadly acceptable to the LDP leadership. The difference in views between the MOF and the LDP on the appropriate strategy for the Budget was often substantial, reflecting their different perspectives and constituencies. MOF was more concerned with the broader context of the macroeconomy, of which the budget strategy was an integral part, and with the longer-term implications of the growth of public spending for the revenue base, government borrowing, and servicing the debt, urging restraint and fiscal discipline to achieve its aim of restoring a balanced budget. The LDP's preferred strategy normally reflected a shorter-term perspective dominated by party political interests, strongly influenced by the pressures of both leaders and followers to increase spending to promote agreed party policies, and to reward its supporters. Reconciling the different and often conflicting time-horizons and economic and political perspectives, and at the same time attempting to persuade the LDP of the necessity and expediency of MOF's own preferred budget strategy, was, according to one former director-general, his most important task (Tanaka Takashi 1994).

There was in the 1980s a 'colossal difference' in views between MOF and LDP. In the task of reconciliation, the director-general had the help of the director of the Budget Bureau's Coordination Division and its staff and resources, and of the director of the Research and Planning Division. Part of their task was 'to walk around', explaining and justifying the budget plan to the LDP's leaders, to try to persuade them of its suitability and relevance not only to economic and fiscal circumstances, but to the achievement of the party's own national policy objectives and its narrower political interests. More formally, both accompanied the director-general when PARC called for an explanation of the overall budgetary strategy and major policy issues.

Throughout the processes leading to the proposals, both the prime minister and the minister of finance were kept informed of the progress of the discussion of estimates, and the options for the expenditure and borrowing aggregates. Indirectly through them, and directly through MOF's administrative vice-minister and director-general of the Budget Bureau, Cabinet ministers and the three senior LDP officials—the secretary-general, chairman of the Executive Council and the chairman of PARC—were kept abreast of the evolving framework, and at various stages their reactions to policy options were sought. The director-general of the Budget Bureau was in constant touch with the minister of finance and the prime minister. The latter's role, combining that of leader of the government and the party, was to relay outwards through the LDP leadership the government's (bureaucratic-led) arguments for its preferred strategy, and to use his influence when it was necessary to gain acceptance of a tougher stance than that urged on his colleagues by the LDP rank-and-file. At the same time, as party leader he was the focus for party pressures from his senior party colleagues, both inside and outside the Cabinet. Political signals, messages, pleas, and pressures funnelled up from the party influenced his judgement about what was politically necessary and expedient to confront the macroeconomic judgements of MOF. As well, the director-general consulted informally with other prominent LDP leaders, and influential elder statesmen such as some former prime ministers—Takeshita and Nakasone in the 1990s (Kogayū 1993). Preliminary soundings, and the early incorporation of party political interests and preferences, were essential if the budget strategy was to be acceptable in June to Cabinet and to the party leadership outside, which had to mobilize support for it among rank-and-file Dietmen.

Formally, the LDP was involved in its formulation, and in the framework for the whole budget, when the Budget Bureau's Coordination Division (CD) began to firm up the aggregate and make proposals for the guidelines and allocations to each broad category of expenditure. Briefed by it, the director-general of the Budget Bureau explained formally and informally to PARC and other party and policy organs the economic context that formed the background to the budget strategy—the prospects for economic growth, the government's fiscal policy stance, projections of revenue, expenditure, and borrowing, and the proposed budget guidelines and the ceiling for each of the four categories. The interest of the LDP at that stage was less with the aggregate of the budget and the overall ceilings for each ministry, more with particular policies and programmes—the amount of priority accorded Defence, ODA, social security, and public investment and works programmes—and with particular projects and items of expenditure. CD was aware, informally, of the origin and force of party political pressures, some or most of which might already have been discounted in the evolving budget framework. Pressures for more spending that could not be accommodated within its limits often needed dampening down. In such circumstances, CD officials would urge the prime minister, minister of finance and LDP senior officials to explain, with its help, to LDP rank-and-file why not all their favoured programmes could have more resources.

According to a former director-general of the Budget Bureau, the budget guidelines, and the spending ceilings attached to those categories of expenditure excluded from their application, were decided only after intense discussion and argument with senior LDP officials (Komura 1993). The most important discussion in the formulation of the guidelines after 1982 was over the amount of the increase in public investment to be allowed as an exception to the principle of budget cuts, and the amount of new money available to finance additional ad hoc public works schemes. Here a mixture of political and economic factors had to be weighed by CD. There were continuing formal and informal pressures from the LDP to provide generally for more public investment.

Because of its political salience in the context of LDP electoral politics, and because in years of recession such as 1991–5 and 1997–9 it had been employed as a major instrument of countercyclical policy, expenditure on public works programmes was handled differently from other programmes. The budget examiner with responsibility for all MOC's public works programmes, and for parts of those programmes in other ministries and agencies, discussed his first estimates directly with his deputy director-general, and with the director-general of the Budget Bureau. Together they considered the estimates based on unchanged assumptions of the budget guidelines, and the needs and justifications of probable spending under each head, and in aggregate.

Political expediency was tempered by economic considerations. The Coordination Division discussed with the Finance Bureau's First Fund Division the proposed level of FILP investment, and estimates of local governments' own investment plans with the relevant budget examiners. It then outlined a range of possible options for total public investment, and how it was to be financed through the General Account Budget, FILP, and local government's own borrowing. Discussions with the Finance Bureau over FILP were critical. Here again, broad economic considerations had to be weighed: the desirability of more public investment, the capacity of corporations and companies in both the public and private sectors to provide it, and the likely effects on output, employment, private investment, and consumer spending. More narrowly, existing policy commitments to programmes of public investment, such as the five-year programmes for sectoral investment in roads, houses, and water, and international obligations to improve infrastructure, such as the ten-year Basic Investment Programme begun in 1991, had their own momentum and imperative.

MINISTERIAL BUDGET CEILINGS

Within the proposed overall budget total, the Coordination Division had to decide on the ceiling for each ministry and agency, within which each would be required to make its budget request on 31 August. There were three interlinked processes: first, the broad allocation by CD of a share of the total budget to groups of MOF's spending divisions managed by each of the three deputy directors-general; secondly, the allocation by them to each of their budget examiners; and, thirdly, the allocation by the latter to their deputy budget examiners, responsible for individual ministries, agencies, and programmes. From their discussions with the Coordination Division, budget examiners got a feel for the developing overall strategy, and how much in total would be available for additional expenditure. In turn, CD had a better informal appreciation of the bottom-up pressures transmitted by the budget examiners and deputy budget examiners from their ministries and agencies, and whether they were containable within the parameters of its developing strategy. In the Spending Ministries, the directors of budget and accounts divisions (BADs) through informal discussions with deputy budget examiners obtained an insight into MOF's perception of the overall fiscal situation, and began to get a feel for the possible budget ceiling within which they would be required to make their submissions to the Budget Bureau. They alerted their bureaux and divisions of what that likely outcome might be, and guided them in the preparation of their budget requests. At each level of transmission, both within the Budget Bureau and between it and the directors of budgets and accounts divisions in the ministries and agencies, the messages conveyed were overlaid with tactical considerations. For example, CD might wish to convey a more pessimistic assessment of the probable ceiling for the overall budget in order to influence the behaviour of deputy directors-general (DDGs) and budget examiners within the Budget Bureau in the 'share-out' of the budget among them; and directors of BADs in the Spending Ministries might want to make their bureaux and divisions more cautious and parsimonious in the formulation of their requests by painting a gloomier picture of their likely ministerial ceiling than perhaps warranted by informal discussions with the Budget Bureau.

In the preparation of the planned budget ceiling, DDGs negotiated with CD on behalf of their budget examiners, explaining and justifying the particular needs of the Spending Ministries and Agencies within their sphere of responsibility. At the same time, each budget examiner tried to persuade the CD of his case for a share of the additional new money for priority programmes, and for those exempted from cutback, which it was anticipated would be made available when the plans for the overall budget ceiling and the budget guidelines were complete. At the margins, through those discussions with CD, budget examiners and their DDGs contributed to the emerging judgements about the amounts to be allocated to the four categories of spending through the application of the budget guidelines.

The allocation of shares of the budget total to the three deputy directors-general was made by the director of the Coordination Division and the budget examiner in charge of budget planning after discussion with the director-general. In effect, each DDG was given a gross sum to allocate at his discretion to his budget examiners. CD influenced but did not dictate the consequential allocation by budget examiners to their deputies within the spending divisions to finance budget requests. However, CD might draw attention to the importance of particular items of expenditure, or the need to allocate additional money to accommodate particular LDP interests. A budget examiner was not obliged to accept such advice or suggestions, and might decide to allocate a larger or smaller sum to one of his deputies than the target set by CD.

Most of the allocation to ministries, agencies, and programmes was predictable from the application of the budget guidelines to the base-line expenditure in the previous year's initial budget. However, there was normally additional money to finance the priority programmes and public investment and works, and deputy budget examiners competed to obtain as large a share as possible for their ministries and agencies, and for any extra resources available in ad hoc schemes of public investment, providing evidence from their informal discussions with directors of BAD to support their claims.

The allocation to each deputy budget examiner (DBE) was indicative, a guideline within which subsequently a ministry's budget submission was examined and negotiated. Through the months of hearings and examinations that followed the submission, deputy budget examiners pressed their budget examiners to increase their allocation to meet those requests they thought irresistible and justified. Complaints to CD and to his own deputy director-general about the adequacy of his allocation were customary, ritualistic, and expected behaviour of a good DBE fighting his corner in the allocation 'game' according to time-honoured rules. Responding, DDGs could influence shares at the margin by moving small amounts between deputy budget examiners from the sum they retained from their overall allocation.

As CD began to firm up the framework for the whole budget—the criteria of the budget guidelines, the overall ceiling for the General Account Budget and, within it, for general expenditure, and the proposed ceilings for each ministry and agency—it explained the proposed principles and strategy to the minister of finance and sought his formal approval to proceed with the allocation of budget shares to DDGs and budget examiners. Shortly before the Cabinet meeting took place in June/July, the director-general of the Budget Bureau explained formally to the prime minister the principles of the proposed budget ceiling and its allocation. At this late stage the prime minister could still make changes, for instance to give a higher priority to a policy included within the exceptional category, but such was a rare occurrence. However, as explained above, the prime minister's influence was exercised less formally at an earlier stage in the process of formulating the strategy. His probable reaction to the outcome of the CD's proposals and negotiations, together with any special issue he wanted to raise, was taken into account through the network of communication between CD, his private secretaries, and MOF's Secretariat. As the strategy evolved, CD used that network to keep the prime minister and Cabinet ministers informed of what was happening, and sought their informal reactions to options and proposals which it was exploring in discussions and negotiations with other participants in the bureaucracy. By the time the Cabinet was asked formally to approve the budgetary strategy, the agreement of all the principal ministerial, party, and bureaucratic participants had been secured through the processes of continuous discussion and negotiations which had taken place in the previous three months. Because of that, changes other than minor and marginal adjustments were rarely made at that late stage.

A few days before the Cabinet met to approve the budget strategy, ministries and agencies were informed of the ceilings within which they would be required to submit their budget requests. The Cabinet did not formally approve them, in order to avoid the possibility that ministers might claim subsequently in the negotiations of their submitted requests that they were entitlements authorized by Cabinet. The ceiling was an informal understanding between each ministry and the Budget Bureau of the maximum share of the Budget that it could receive. It provided the budget examiners with the necessary flexibility to negotiate downwards (Fushimi 1994).

Where the proposed ministerial ceiling was disputed, bilateral meetings between a minister and the minister of finance were sometimes necessary to settle differences before the Cabinet meeting. By convention, three ministries whose budget ceilings normally included provision for additional expenditures on priority programmes, alone concluded formal face-to-face agreements with the minister of finance, a further illustration of the importance of ceremonial in the budget process. Defence spending through the Mutual Support Agreements and the security treaty with the USA, the ODA budget, and public works programmes (together with energy-related programmes and pensions and personnel expenses), were treated from the early 1980s as priority programmes in MOF's budget guidelines. The minister of foreign affairs, the director-general (i.e. minister of state) of the Defence Agency, and the minister of construction met ceremonially with the minister of finance, together with senior officials of the LDP and MOF. The public presentation of their budget ceilings served to focus media attention on those priority areas of the Budget, and enabled the government and the LDP to demonstrate publicly its acceptance of international obligations to the wider politico-economic community outside Japan, and to its local political constituencies. However, the ceiling announcements for defence spending in FY1994–5, delayed by the general election and formation of the coalition government led by Mr Hosokawa, were not marked by such ceremonial, because of the sensitivity of the defence issue among the JSP, at that time a member of the coalition.

The budget ceiling and guidelines were now published; ministries and agencies began the preparation of their formal budget requests for submission on 31 August, and the Budget Bureau considered its tactics for dealing with them in the months ahead in order to deliver a draft budget in December within the overall limit.

Once the budget strategy was approved by Cabinet, the director-general's role was to preside over, manage, and guide the coordination of the budget processes in the months ahead. Internally, he was concerned to achieve consistency and consensus among his staff in the Budget Bureau, to ensure that there was a common understanding of the aims of the budget, and the general strategy for the economy as a whole to which it was directed, and to guide and encourage them in achieving the aim of harmony in the processes of hearing, examination, negotiation, and 'revival' with Spending Ministries and Agencies. Externally, he was concerned to explain and justify to the officials in those ministries the purpose of the budget strategy and its appropriateness to the prevailing economic conditions, and, more widely still, to the public at large, through the media, public meetings, and lectures.

The public endorsement of the Fiscal System Research Council was a necessary ingredient in constructing a broader public consensus for the principles and policies of the initial draft budget announced at the end of December. With the advice and services of the Budget Bureau's Research Division, which provided the Council's Secretariat, the director-general in the preceding months consulted informally with the chairman and other leading members, canvassing options, testing reactions to the evolving budget strategy, and alerting them to any unusual features.

Supplementary Budgets

The process of compiling a Supplementary Budget was similar to that of the main budget, with the initiative taken by the Budget Bureau's Coordination Division prompted and guided by the director-general. The size and composition of tax and spending changes, together with the implications for government borrowing, and the timing of the Supplementary Budget were intensely politicized, the result of a continuous dialogue involving the director-general and his CD staff, the prime minister, the minister of finance, and senior LDP officials, besides the normal consultations with officials in the Spending Ministries and Agencies.

The LDP had considerable influence on the size, structure, and content of Supplementary Budgets. This was partly a function of their smaller size and simplicity compared with the General Account Budget: the relationship between revenue and expenditure was more comprehensible than the very much larger General Account Budget, and the size of the budget, its components parts and its purpose, more readily grasped. But mainly it was because, as explained in Chapter 10, Supplementary Budgets were not subject to the budget guidelines. There were no limits on the amount of additional expenditure, or its distribution between categories of spending, programmes, or ministries and agencies. They provided an opportunity therefore to finance some items of discretionary expenditure ineligible under the guidelines in the main budget, or which were cut or deferred in the budget negotiations. MOF was better able to resist some of the pressures from ministers and the LDP leadership for larger increases to the General Account Budget by its willingness to accommodate some of their demands in the institutionalized Supplementary Budget. It provided the means 'to save MOF's face' in the implementation of its policies to curtail the growth of the main budget (Kosai 1994).

16

The Budget Processes in the Spending Ministries

Ministries and agencies submitted budget requests for shares of the General Account Budget to MOF on 31 August each year. Their processes of internal compilation were concerned with two main issues: the budget limit or ceiling agreed informally with the Budget Bureau prior to submission, and, within that ceiling, the allocation of shares to each bureau, and to the programmes, projects, and items of spending of their policy divisions. Those issues were articulated through four linked and overlapping processes: first, the evolution, preparation, discussion, and negotiation of budget proposals within and between the policy divisions of each bureau; secondly, the examination of those proposals by the ministry's Budget and Accounts Division, and its negotiations with divisions and bureaux, competing for a share of the ministry's probable overall budget allocation; thirdly, and concurrently, the ministry's Budget and Accounts Division's informal negotiations with MOF's Budget Bureau of that probable budget ceiling, i.e. its putative share of the total of the planned General Account Budget; and, finally, the preparation and legitimation of formal budget requests. The four processes were iterative, but are treated here for purposes of analysis and explanation sequentially. The Budget Bureau's hearings, examination, and negotiations with ministries and agencies after the submission of the budget requests are dealt within the next two chapters.

The account provided here draws upon, and conflates material from, and the evidence of, interviews in all the Spending Ministries and Agencies, in the period 1992–9. Significant differences of organization, process, and procedure among them are explained at appropriate places in the text; the rather different budget processes in the Defence Agency and the Ministry of Home Affairs are dealt with separately at the end. Ministries and agencies use different nomenclature to describe that division in the Minister's Secretariat responsible for the preparation of the Budget as a whole, and for negotiations with the Budget Bureau. In this and succeeding chapters, the title 'Budget and Accounts Division' (BAD) is used generically.

THE KEY PLAYERS

Within the Minister's Secretariat, the key players at the centre were the director and deputy directors of its Budget and Accounts Division, and the director of its General

Affairs (or Coordination) Division. Within each bureau, the lead was taken by the directors and deputy directors of policy divisions, while the directors and staff of each bureau's General Affairs Division had a general coordinating function. The director-general of each bureau exercised general supervision, provided a conciliation and arbitration service of last resort, and undertook high-level political networking within the ministry and outside.

The director of the Budget and Accounts Division and his staff were the hub of the whole process. Throughout, the director exercised considerable discretionary authority, enhanced by his seniority—he ranked ahead of other division directors, the equivalent of a deputy director-general—and by his positional status at the heart of the Minister's Secretariat, with access to its director-general, and to the administrative vice-minister. His influence inhered in his formal and informal access to colleagues at all levels in the ministry, and to opposite numbers in the Budget Bureau of MOF. Crucially, he and his division were at the nodal point of the expenditure network, receiving and transmitting a variety of verbal and written information, guidance and instructions, both within the ministry and between it and MOF. The director acted with the implied authority of the minister, and with the implicit concurrence of the ministry's most senior officials when he played his hand in the negotiations internally with bureaux and divisions, and externally with the Budget Bureau. In theory, he could formally invoke their support, but in practice it happened rarely. There was a shared disposition to settle before such a step was taken. The process was consultative, and the aim to achieve a consensus of views, or at least to agree upon a compromise among contending parties. The director of the Budget Accounts Division alone had the total picture of what bureaux and their divisions were requesting, and the needs and justifications for their proposed expenditures. These had to be set within the context of the ministry's overall budget plan, and the strategy for maximizing its share of the General Account Budget.

BUDGET STRATEGY

The broad context for the formulation of a ministry's annual budget strategy was provided by its overall aims and objectives, and the past, present, and proposed policies designed to give effect to them. These commonly took the form of a medium-term plan or 'vision' incorporating the related activities of constituent bureaux and their policy divisions, as for example in the Defence Agency's five-year defence plans, or MOFA's medium-term plans for ODA. In MOC individual bureaux had five-year plans for capital investment in programmes for roads, housing, sewage facilities, urban parks, and erosion and flood control; MAFF had a ten-year plan for agricultural land improvement, and six-year plans for inshore fisheries and fishing ports. (Details of those and other plans are given in Table 23.2.) In the Ministry of Labour, each bureau had a five-year plan, the result of a painfully constructed consensus involving, *inter alia*, a tripartite advisory council. For example, its Employment Policy Bureau, responsible for the government's overall plan for employment policy, coordinated the interests of other affected ministries, and supervised both the initial participation of an ad hoc study group and, later, the formal involvement of two advisory councils, the Central Employment Security Council, and the Employment Council attached to the Prime Minister's Office.

Ministerial objectives were also prescribed in policy statements related to specific issues, or to several linked issues. For example, the main strategic aim of the Ministry of Education was declared formally to be the reform of education. The impetus derived from the work of the Council on Education, an ad hoc advisory committee which produced a series of reports to the Prime Minister in the period 1983–7. Strategic policy-making subsequently was guided by the Cabinet's agreement in October 1987 to a policy paper prepared by the MOE entitled *Immediate Policies for the Implementation of Educational Reform: Policy Guidelines for the Implementation of Educational Reform*.

Such plans and strategic policy documents provided the basis for the initiation of most annual budget proposals. However, their translation into an integrated and coherent budget strategy was less a process of the top-down prescription of priority between competing claims than a 'bottom-up' process, an aggregation of the separate and loosely related budget plans and proposals of individual bureaux and their policy divisions, intermediated by the Budget and Accounts Division of the Minister's Secretariat. Planning and allocating resources did not take place within a 'top management' information system designed to enable the minister to formulate a budget strategy to reflect his preferences and expenditure priorities, as happened for example in the UK, and other G7 countries from the early 1980s. While advice and guidance on the general orientation of a ministry's policy stance was provided by its Secretariat— perhaps a reminder of a Cabinet agreement committing all bureaux—the influence of the minister in shaping the budget strategy was normally marginal. In the Ministry of Construction, 'It was rare for policy or priorities to come down from the Minister or Vice-Minister' (MOC 1993a). Only rarely did the Minister of Education give a clear direction on a budget issue, or indicate a preference for more spending on an item of expenditure, most likely to occur because of pressure from constituents, individual Dietmen, or LDP influentials (MOE 1994).

Some but not all ministries had a Policy Planning and Coordination Committee, or a taskforce performing that function, usually within the Minister's Secretariat. It helped provide some broad guidance for the bureaux and their divisions on overall strategic policy, with which their budget proposals were expected to be aligned. It might also play a significant role subsequently, together with the Budget and Accounts Division, in coordinating the budget requests formulated by the policy divisions. In the mid-1990s, MITI's Policy and Planning Committee, attached to the General Affairs Division of the Minister's Secretariat, met twice a week, with a membership drawn from each General Affairs (i.e. coordination) Division of its 13 bureaux. They comprised a cohort of enthusiastic and energetic young officials, an elite licensed to 'brainstorm' on basic policies across the whole range of the Ministry's responsibilities. Above this self-proclaimed 'shadow cabinet', meetings of bureau directors-general provided more formal occasions for policy planning (MITI 1993). In the more decentralized Ministry of Construction, bureaux traditionally exercised a great deal of autonomy in policy-making and implementation. From 1990, however, senior officials provided more leadership and guidance in setting policy objectives, and deciding the priority of expenditures. A Policy Division was established in the Minister's Secretariat with responsibility for pulling together the discrete policy initiatives of the various bureaux. This was more an attempt to impose some overall coherence and direction on a list of expenditure plans compiled from the divisions, than the assumption of top-down managerial responsibility for the planning and allocation of resources (MOC 1993*a*). There was no formal Policy and Planning Committee in the Ministry of Education. Budget policies were discussed formally when the directors of 'lead' divisions in the various bureaux met with the director of BAD and coordinated on a day-to-day basis through informal contacts at various levels up to that of the administrative vice-minister.

Within the broad framework of plans and policies for the medium and long term, the director-general of a Minister's Secretariat and the director of a Budget and Accounts Division took the lead in shaping the budget strategy. They discussed constantly with each bureau director-general his aims and priorities, and involved the administrative vice-minister on major issues where necessary as the budget slowly took shape. A coordinating role might be played by bureaux other than the Minister's Secretariat. For example, in the Ministry of Transport, the Transport Policy Bureau had a Department of Comprehensive Transport Policy with general responsibility for 'basic policy'; it collected information on the main policies coming forward for the current year from each bureau, and helped the Budget and Accounts Division devise options to reflect the main expenditure priorities to put to senior officials and the minister (MOT 1994).

The capacity of a policy coordinating department such as that, or a Policy Planning and Coordination Committee, or indeed the Minister's Secretariat, to play an overarching strategic role in the formulation of the Budget was limited, constrained in practice by the traditionally powerful vertical structures that characterized the organization of all ministries and agencies. Policy, and especially budgetary policy, was made very largely bottom-up, the initiative lying with individual policy divisions within each bureaux. Proposals for additional spending on existing programmes and items, and those to finance new policies, were almost wholly their responsibility. In a real sense, a ministry's budget and its budget strategy was the sum of a number of individually compiled bureau budgets. The task of the Budget and Accounts Division was to ensure that they were consistent with the general orientation of ministerial aims and objectives as previously agreed, to contain the aggregate within the probable ceiling which it was negotiating with the Budget Bureau, and to make recommendations on the relative priority of competing bureaux' claims within that total. Priority between items of expenditure within a bureau was largely a matter for each bureau to determine. For example, the powerful River Bureau in the Ministry of Construction had four major groups of divisions, each competing for shares of existing capital investment resources, and for a share of the annual increase normally provided for in MOF's budget guidelines (MOC 1993*b*).

In the absence of formal five-year plans for each bureau, such as those in MOC, MOT, and MAFF, there were often unofficial plans. While they lacked the formal recognition of MOF, and the legitimacy conferred by Cabinet approval, they could nevertheless be significant in the determination of priority among the competing claims of bureaux, and MOF's Budget Bureau could be obliged to take cognizance of them. For example, a former director of BAD in MOFA described the 'tacit, underwater-nodding' between the directors-general of the ministry's bureaux about their claims on resources inherent in such unofficial plans (MOFA 1993). Where such understandings and informal agreements existed, they influenced the determination of the ministry's budget priorities.

THE PREPARATION OF BUDGET PROPOSALS

At the conclusion of each annual budget cycle, after the Diet's approval of MOF's draft budget, normally in March/April, bureaux and their policy divisions conducted a review of their present and future spending commitments, and considered the immediate expenditure implications of new or revised policies. They were encouraged to do this by MOF's budget examiners and deputy budget examiners, following up issues that arose in the previous round of budget negotiations, or as part of a longer-term review of a particular policy area in which Budget Bureau officials might themselves participate, or as a result of Cabinet agreement to a new policy initiative recommended by a ministry, after discussion and report by an LDP study group or an advisory council. Simultaneously, the General Affairs Division, and the Budget and Accounts Division, of the Minister's Secretariat prepared guidelines for the next budget round, incorporating new policy commitments, together with priority areas identified previously. Not all new or revised policies had expenditure implications; changes in the tax or regulatory regimes, for example, might reflect important new policy developments but had little or no expenditure implications, although of course they affected the macroeconomic context within which decisions were made about the aggregate of expenditure by MOF.

Ministry guidelines circulated to policy divisions in May/June included both general background briefing and specific instructions on the procedures to be followed in drafting and submitting the requests. The director of BAD might provide a general appreciation of the politico-economic context in which MOF's General Account Budget as a whole was being prepared, for example whether he expected it to be more or less 'tight' than the previous year, and why, and the implications for the ministry's own budget, interpreting and extrapolating the hints, nods-and-winks, and informal discussions with his deputy budget examiner in MOF. But his own tactics for the implementation of the ministry's overall budget strategy also influenced what and how much he told his colleagues at that stage, and how he expressed it. Guidelines might also include a rehearsal of the ministry's current policy initiatives, together with a restatement of any formal Cabinet agreement on major issues central to its activities. Policy divisions might be reminded of the minister's attitude towards particular issues, or those he had taken a special interest in. In MOL, the director of the Budget and Accounts Division gave each division its ceiling for the previous fiscal year, together with general information about broad contextual factors that might affect it, as a kind of base-line for the preparation of their draft requests (MOL 1994).

Instructions to divisions to begin the preparation of budget requests prescribed the schedule of dates to be followed, and outlined the procedure for meetings with the director and officials of the Budget and Accounts Division. They prescribed the format to be used in presenting the expenditure estimates for the coming financial year, and divisions were normally required to specify and distinguish between continuing commitments and those likely to arise as statutory and inescapable obligations during the coming year. They were invited to propose new or additional expenditures, i.e. what they would like to do, other than those programme expenditures to which they were committed, if resources allowed. The period of discussion and negotiation between policy divisions and BAD before the conclusion of the latter's informal discussions with MOF's Budget Bureau on the ministry's ceiling was known as the 'blue ceiling'; i.e. there was as yet no ceiling on budget requests, merely the 'blue sky' (MOC 1993b). Nevertheless, explanation of the need and justification for all types of new and past expenditures was required in writing, although the amount of detail and supporting statistical and technical evidence varied with the size of the expenditure item. The amount of discretionary authority delegated to policy divisions to allocate and commit money varied from one ministry to another. The guidelines indicated how much, and the conditions of its use.

Guidelines might also incorporate general rules prescribed by MOF about the costing of estimates in the formal budget requests, for example the rate of exchange to be used in calculating the costs of goods and services purchased overseas, but MOF's updating and revision of those rules normally occurred later in the process, towards the end of negotiations in early December. Locally, the BAD might add to them, for example by suggesting rules for calculating future movements of pay and prices.

Within each bureau the process began formally in April/May, in response to a request from the director of the Budget and Accounts Division for details of proposed new policy expenditures. Informally it started even earlier, in January and February, as policy divisions discussed their needs for the coming financial year in the light of existing commitments, additional obligations, and new expenditures they would like in order to extend or improve existing services, and to start up new programmes. The initiative here was normally taken by deputy directors and their staff within each policy division, who prepared papers, and discussed ideas and options with their colleagues. As these were firmed up, the division director became more involved, and the preferred budget strategy for the division as a whole began to evolve. While this bottom-up characterization was generally true, practice varied with the personality and management style of individual directors and bureau directors-general. Some preferred to involve themselves from the start, providing their divisions with guidance and direction on strategy and policy. Whatever the extent of the authority delegated to them, deputy directors were expected to report regularly on the progress of discussions over draft proposals.

Concurrently, discussions were held with other divisions within the bureau whose interests or responsibilities overlapped or were affected, but achieving integration and consistency often had to await the later intermediation of the bureau's General Affairs Division, and ultimately, where there were conflicts or unresolved issues of priority, the conciliation of the head of the bureau, the director-general. Some divisional issues had implications for the budgets of other ministries, and discussions preceding budget proposals often took place over a long period of time, with agreement on the share of expenditure to be borne by each whenever a policy responsibility transcended ministerial boundaries, for example the ODA budget. Where a policy area was under review, MOF's Budget Bureau might be involved on a continuing basis. Such initiatives in policy-making led by Budget Bureau officials became more common after fiscal reconstruction began in the 1980s, and were normally driven by the need to reduce the costs of programmes in the medium or long term (EPA 1993).

The initiative for new spending proposals came mainly from individual bureaux, more particularly from their divisions and sections. In the River Bureau of the Ministry of Construction, for example, throughout the year technical data and a variety of information accumulated as a result of the activities of outside groups, mainly local authorities, who urged on officials in local offices, and on bureau officials in headquarters, new or revised policies and projects requiring additional expenditure. Each year 'about a 100 proposals were floated within the Bureau' in the preliminary 'blue ceiling' period of compiling the budget request. As a result of discussion and agreement within and between its seven main divisions, the number was pruned to about a dozen, which represented the Bureau's initial request for additional expenditures within the ministry. Their need and justification were explained and argued by the director-general in a formal hearing with 'the big three': the administrative vice-minister of construction, the administrative vice-minister of construction for engineering affairs, and the director-general of the Minister's Secretariat (MOC 1993*b*).

As a result of those meetings, conducted simultaneously with all of the ministry's other bureaux, the River Bureau's proposals were whittled down to two or three, and argued again in front of the 'big three', with the deputy vice-minister for general policy coordination in attendance. Not all new policy proposals required their approval: those that were less important were later submitted to the Budget Bureau as part of the bureau's budget request.

Besides the annual reduction in current expenditures (mainly staff, salaries, and overheads)—and sometimes capital expenditures as well—that all ministries and agencies were obliged to make to comply with MOF's budget guidelines from 1982 onwards, BAD also tried to obtain additional savings selectively from programmes that it thought vulnerable to MOF's examination, taking into account the extent of continuing political interest and support, for reallocation to other programmes with a higher priority. Where a new programme of expenditure was proposed, or an existing one revised or extended, there was a strong presumption or policy 'rule-of-the-game' that the division or bureau would offer up compensating savings, by scaling down or abandoning the whole or parts of an existing programme. However, where programmes and the size of spend were demand-led, as in the Ministry of Health and Welfare, observance of this rule was more difficult.

Internal harmony within the bureau, and consistency with the ministry's general budget strategy, where that had been explicitly articulated, was the responsibility of each bureau's General Affairs Division, which encouraged the deputy directors of those divisions with related or linked policy interests and responsibilities to discuss and agree the priorities of their proposed expenditures. Coordination at this level, was primarily their responsibility. At a broader level, across the whole range of a bureau's responsibilities, the General Affairs Division collected, compiled and sought to integrate the contributions of all divisions. Where officials from General Affairs divisions participated in a broadly based Policy Planning Committee as in MITI, they tried to ensure that what emerged from their own bureau's discussions of policy and expenditures was consistent with the overall budget strategy taking shape there and in the Minister's Secretariat. In ministries where no such mechanism existed, the General Affairs Division of each bureau nevertheless performed much the same coordinating function, interpreting the ideas and strategy that were being formulated at the centre (within the Minister's Secretariat) for colleagues in its policy divisions, and transmitting to the centre the emergent policy proposals and probable expenditure implications.

In some ministries, the coordinating role within each bureau was played by a 'lead' or 'head' division. In Ministry of Education bureaux, it acted like the BAD, scrutinizing and critically examining the plans and budget proposals of the other divisions. In MITI in the mid-1990s the Machine and Information Industries Bureau had four electronics divisions with overlapping responsibilities. Their budget requests had to be mutually consistent, and in this preliminary task the Electronics Policy Division was the prime mover, the 'lead division'. In the Ministry of Labour, some of whose bureaux had departments at an intermediate level, the Working Hours Division as the 'lead division' of the Wages and Working Hours Department coordinated the budget proposals of the other divisions of the Department. The proposals then went to the Administrative Affairs Division of the Labour Standards Bureau, where they were discussed and integrated with the proposals from the other 13 divisions. When adjusted, and the priorities decided, they emerged as the Bureau's budget plan, and went to the director of the BAD in the Minister's Secretariat.

Before the draft of a bureau's budget was completed, a director-general's meeting or hearing was normally held to discuss the policy proposals and preferred strategies of each division, and to determine the budget request and underlying strategy for the bureau as a whole. The meeting also served the purpose of achieving a formal consensus, to which all were committed.

Coordinating Budget Strategy in MITI

In MITI formal coordination of the bureaux' budgets began in May/June when the two key divisions of the Ministry's Secretariat, the General Affairs Division and the Budget and Accounts Division, jointly convened the first 'hearing', chaired by the director of the former, with the director of BAD in attendance. The planning officer of the Minister's Secretariat, the director of the Industrial Structure Division, the director of industrial financing, and the counsellor on technology, all of whom had responsibilities for issues that transcended the interests of individual bureaux, also attended. Over a period of about two weeks, each bureau made a formal presentation of its current and future policies, outlined proposals for continuing and new expenditures, suggested

Budgeting in Spending Ministries

which programmes might be cut or abolished, and provided an outline of its draft budget. The director of each division attended as the business dictated. To achieve a greater degree of integration in the objectives and priorities across the whole ministry, the procedure was changed in 1992–3 to focus more attention on broad policy issues, such as trade policy, and technology policy, and policy for small and medium-sized enterprises. After the completion of the first 'hearing', the Secretariat's General Affairs Division produced a formal document summarizing the proposals in the light of the ministry's overall policy objectives. This provided the agenda for the second 'hearing', which took place in late June/early July.

The progress of the hearings in MITI (and the budget processes in all other ministries and agencies) was interrupted by the ritual of the rotation of officials which took place annually in June/July. Before the second hearing, MITI's deputy directors and directors discussed informally with those who were about to replace them their ideas and proposals for expenditure in the forthcoming budget, and briefed them on the progress made and current state of play in any informal negotiations with other divisions and with the BAD. The 'grand design' or main themes of the ministry's budget, if any, had emerged from the first hearing before the transfers took place, and were taken up in the second hearing with the transferees now in post. The latter might have new or different ideas about the policies previously pursued by their new division, or be less enthusiastic about particular policies or expenditures to which the divisions and bureau had been tentatively committed by their predecessors. As a result, abrupt discontinuities occasionally occurred in the development of particular policies, a characteristic of bureaucratic policy-making to which other writers have drawn attention (Horne 1985; Rosenbluth 1989). As transfers took place concurrently in the Budget Bureau of the Ministry of Finance, discontinuity could occur on both sides simultaneously. However, the importance of informal networking in the Japanese bureaucracy helped to minimize the effects of any serious dislocation of budget policy-making, and transferees quickly sought to establish relationships with their opposite numbers in the Budget Bureau through informal meetings and customary after-work socialization. MOF curtailed these in 1997–8, following allegations of improper and illegal behaviour of senior officials in the Banking and Securities Bureaux (and earlier also in the Budget Bureau) in various so-called 'wining and dining' scandals.

MITI's practice was to transfer the deputy director of the General Affairs Division of the Minister's Secretariat in April/May rather than June/July, ahead of both his director and the other divisional directors and deputy directors in the policy divisions. This provided for continuity in policy discussions, enabling the deputy director to familiarize himself with the current state of progress of the compilation of draft bureau budgets, to involve himself in continuing discussions with the bureau, and to continue the coordination across bureaux. It indicated the central role played by the deputy director of the General Affairs Division in the budget process. Many of MITI's elite officials served on secondment to Japanese embassies and international organizations. Postings and returns generally took place in April, but it could and did happen that some divisions had no directors for a couple of months until the general transfers took place. The Ministry of Construction also sent officials on secondment to local government in

April. On return, they had a period of 'rehabilitation' while awaiting a vacancy created in the general rotation two or three months later.

After the second hearing convened and coordinated by the Secretariat's General Affairs Division and BAD, MITI's policy divisions firmed up their plans for budget expenditures, incorporating new policies and increased spending to which the bureau had agreed. As explained earlier, within each bureau the General Affairs Division played a similar coordinating and intermediating role across divisions to that of the Budget Accounts Division across all bureaux and divisions. Hearings within each bureau conducted by the General Affairs Division took place concurrently with those convened for the ministry as a whole.

More detailed and critical hearings were conducted by the director of the BAD at the conclusion of the second general hearing. These lasted about two weeks. The director-general of each bureau, together with the directors and deputy directors of his policy divisions, was invited to attend over a one- to two-day period to explain the detail of his draft budget proposals, and argue the need and justification for any new expenditure. Those formal explanations were then followed up more informally by a member of BAD's staff who discussed and argued the detail. The role of the director of BAD in his relationship with divisions and bureaux was similar to that of the deputy budget examiner of the Budget Bureau of MOF in relation to a Spending Ministry. The director was critical, sceptical, and detached, exposing weak points, refuting arguments, and weeding out poor proposals. The process helped to refine and strengthen the arguments and evidence to be presented to the Budget Bureau subsequently, and to eliminate proposals for expenditure that would be rejected there out-of-hand.

Similar arrangements for Budget and Accounts divisions both to conduct formal ministry hearings and to examine and challenge budget proposals were found in other ministries and agencies. In MOFA, for example, there were two hearings with the 50 policy divisions, the first of which took only two to three days, but the second, more detailed of which lasted about a week. The director of BAD discussed with each director the division's major projects, and through critical inquiry obtained a broad picture of the ideas, issues, and strategies that were evolving. A similar practice was followed in MHW. At the early stages of examination, the director of BAD tried not to be too hostile, or to suppress too much. As one director explained, 'there was a need to make an attractive budget, one which will appeal to the LDP and the media'. He was on the lookout for 'good attractive items of expenditure' while discouraging proposals that were 'too fanciful' (MOFA 1993). More generally, the BAD's scrutiny was concerned to establish the feasibility and effectiveness of proposed expenditures, especially new items. Its other major concern was with achieving an acceptable balance among bureaux. This latter consideration tended to reinforce historic shares, and the innate conservatism of the process. I have more to say about that in Chapter 21.

However, this model of direct and personal interrogation by the director of BAD was not followed in all ministries and agencies. While some directors of BAD preferred to deal at first-hand with those familiar with the detail of budget proposals, others preferred to deal with those responsible for the overall budget plan of the bureau, and to rely on them indirectly to provide the detail where necessary. In the Ministry of

Education, for example, the director of BAD dealt on a day-to-day basis with the director of each bureau's General Affairs Division or its 'lead' policy division. He did not deal with individual policy divisions unless there was a very big or politically sensitive issue, as happened in 1994 with the discussion of the provision of free textbooks for pupils. But even so, the General Affairs or lead division would be informed and represented at all such meetings. In the Ministry of Labour, the director of BAD dealt with each bureau's Administrative Affairs Division, but also where appropriate or necessary directly with the directors and deputy directors of policy divisions.

As the draft budget progressed through successive stages of discussions, hearings, and examinations, the director of the Budget Accounts Division informed, and consulted constantly with, the director-general of the Minister's Secretariat and the administrative vice-minister, reporting the results of his hearings, his assessment of the proposals for additional spending in the context of the ministry's evolving budget strategy, and presenting them with successive iterations of the total budget request and its allocation. Ultimately they had to agree on the allocation of the shares to each bureau, and make recommendations to the minister. Towards the end of the process, the director of BAD presented the draft budget at a formal meeting attended by the minister, the administrative vice-minister, and the directors-general of all the bureaux.

NEGOTIATING THE MINISTERIAL CEILING

At the same time as the formal hearings and inquiries were being held within ministerial bureaux, and between their policy divisions and the Budget and Accounts Division, the director of the latter was discussing informally with his opposite number in MOF's Budget Bureau, normally the deputy budget examiner but sometimes the budget examiner, the prospects for the ministry's ceiling, the upper limit on its budget allocation within which subsequently it submitted its formal requests to MOF on 31 August. Most BAD directors believed that the decision on the ceiling in June/July was as or more significant than the negotiations over the budget requests with the Budget Bureau that followed in September–December.

In the early stages of the budget process within ministries, assumptions were made about the probable outcome of the ceiling negotiations with the Budget Bureau, and its distribution among bureaux and divisions. As a result of informal discussions with their opposite numbers in the Budget Bureau, directors of BAD obtained an early indication of their likely share, on the assumption of unchanged MOF guidelines for budget requests. At the same time, they provided budget examiners with an early warning of new or increased expenditures and major policy proposals in the pipeline, and provided them with relevant background information and explanation to enable them to argue the case within MOF for more resources for the ministry, as the Budget Bureau discussed and argued the ceiling for the General Account Budget as a whole, and its distribution among the Spending Ministries and Agencies. Those informal discussions between a director of BAD and his deputy budget examiner proceeded against the background of the formal hearings and the discussions and negotiations between the

BAD and the bureau divisions described above. Thus, a director of BAD brought to the informal discussion with the DBE his accumulating knowledge of what was being proposed by his bureaux, and his judgement of the relative priority of their competing claims. At the same time his appreciation of what the DBE might be able to deliver as the ministry's ceiling was a key ingredient of the continuing discussions about the evolving budget strategy with the administrative vice-minister, and director-general of the Minister's Secretariat, and influenced his negotiations with the directors and deputy directors of General Affairs divisions over bureau shares.

The informal discussions between the director of the Budget Accounts Division and his opposite number in the Budget Bureau were not, strictly speaking, a negotiation, although directors often preferred to represent them as such. Neither were they a detailed examination item by item of what the ministry would propose in its budget request: that came later, when the deputy budget examiner conducted his hearings in September and October. The focus was on those new or revised policies that would lead to requests for additional expenditures, and the scope for offsetting savings elsewhere in the Budget. Ministerial allocations for those categories of spending in MOF's guidelines subject to 'cut-back' or 'exempt' from it could be precisely calculated, and provided for in the director's provisional allocations to his bureau. The uncertainty occurred mainly over the ministry's likely share of the 'new money' in the category of expenditures that were to be treated as 'exceptional' in the guidelines. In discussions with the DBE, the director of BAD argued for a share of those extra resources to finance existing programmes already included within that category, and for the inclusion of other kinds of existing and new expenditures. The more he could 'move' programmes, sub-programmes, and items into the 'exceptional' category, or have them exempt from cut-back, the more likely he was to maintain or increase his overall share of the Budget. However, while it was more difficult to move existing programmes, projects, or items into those categories, new programmes or projects provided opportunities for the director of BAD to 'angle the spending' and present it in such a way as to establish a prima facie case. A DBE sympathetic to the ministry's objectives might suggest how that could be done. (MCA 1994).

The exemption of social security from 'cut-back' meant that that programme budget was discussed and negotiated afresh each year. The Ministry of Health and Welfare prepared and presented to the Budget Bureau estimates of the number of pensions to be paid in the coming year, derived from calculations of demographic trends, and the amounts to be paid per pensioner, indexed for inflation. The main burden of the argument with the deputy budget examiner turned on the appropriate rate of inflation to be used, but the analysis of demographic data might also be disputed. The costs of medical care for the elderly also fell within the category of expenditure exempt from cut-back, and here again MHW tried to persuade the Budget Bureau that its estimates of increased expenditures were both necessary and justified.

Other ministries and agencies had an interest in obtaining a similar exempt or priority status for their programmes. MAFF for example sought to have the costs of pension schemes for farmers included within the general pensions programme accorded priority status, rather than funded through current expenditures subject to cut-back

(MAFF 1993). Most ministries tried to obtain a share of the increased allocation for the three other priority programmes—defence, energy, overseas development aid. The expansion of the latter's budget in the 1980s prompted a number of ministries to take an interest in overseas economic cooperation. The MHW created an Office of International Cooperation in 1989 'designed to deal with the growth of the ODA budget in the 1980s related to the health aspects of aid directed at basic human needs' (Orr 1990: 20).

There was also some flexibility in the allocation of monies between categories prescribed in MOF's budget guidelines. A director of the Budget and Accounts Division helped his bureaux and divisions to exploit the classification and definition of expenditure, and to switch items between them to reflect the priorities of the ministry and/or individual bureaux. For example, expenditure could be cut and 'saved' for reallocation elsewhere by delaying payments from one financial year to the next, or by attempting to transfer expenditures to a more favourable category. In MAFF some areas of expenditure, such as 'food credits', the Special Accounts for food management, and paddyfield farming, were exploited to enable it to switch expenditures (MAFF 1993).

To attract extra resources, or even to maintain resources at current levels, the Budget and Accounts Division was acutely attuned to the 'atmospherics' of 'ideas-in-good-currency'. Apparent changes in ministerial policy were often presentational rather than substantive, reflecting what was currently fashionable. Thus, if there was a greater emphasis in national budgeting on 'environmental protection' or the 'quality of life', as happened in the late 1980s and early 1990s, when both attracted additional resources, mainly for public works programmes, Budget and Accounts divisions encouraged bureaux and divisions to present their arguments for new (and some old) expenditures in those terms. The substance of the projects, and perhaps their number and cost, might remain relatively unchanged. If there was more money for capital investment in 'improving living standards', then bureaux wanted their share of it, and could produce arguments to demonstrate that projects of erosion control or dam construction would have that effect, equally with new projects from other bureaux and ministries, where the contribution to the improvement of quality of life derived less from the 'changing colours' (*oironaoshi*) of old policies and projects than from bright new colours. The Mori government's priority for IT projects in the planned budgets for FY2000 and FY2001 encouraged keen competition among ministries for a share of new money, worth 1 trillion in the latter year. In many ministries conventional budget requests were dressed up in the new IT colours. MAFF for example requested 28 billion for the promotion of IT projects in forestry and fishing villages. MOC redefined a scheme to improve sewage systems as an 'IT project' because sewage pipes could carry fibre-optic cables. Playing the allocation game within and among ministries according to such rules partly helps to explain the rigidity of the allocation of public works and capital investment, characteristic of the Japanese budgetary system. That issue is discussed in more detail in Chapter 23.

The allocation of resources within a bureau could change also to reflect a new purpose or the political salience of an issue. For example, the establishment of the new Quality of Life and Culture Division in MITI's Industrial Bureau in the early 1990s meant the allocation of bureau monies for wholly new purposes. While the total budget for the bureau was little affected, 'how it was used changed considerably' (MITI 1994). Because of the relevance of the work of the new division to other MITI bureaux—textiles for example, and the Agency for Science and Technology—the composition of their budgets reflected the appearance of a wholly new set of policy issues.

In June/July, Cabinet formally approved MOF's budget criteria and guidelines prescribing the ceilings for the four broad categories of expenditure: current, capital, exempted (from cut-back), and exceptional (priority). Before that occurred, ministries and agencies were informed of their ceilings. The director of BAD did not disclose to his bureaux and divisions whether the ministry's prescribed ceiling was more or less than that assumed in earlier discussions and negotiations with them. Within it, he normally had some room for manoeuvre, to make marginal adjustments to provisional bureaux allocations, to reflect agreed priorities. As well, he tried to retain a proportion of the negotiated ceiling to provide for the later reallocation of some monies where bureau negotiations with the Budget Bureau in November proved less successful on those programmes with high priority that the ministry wished to protect. One element of his budget strategy was also to provide a 'reserve', an undisclosed sum from the total ceiling, which he could draw on subsequently to make marginal increases to the budgets of some divisions treated harshly or disappointed in his original provisional allocation. The tactics of some directors were to be strict initially, and subsequently, if resources allowed, more generous. This helped to enhance their authority, and to build up credit and goodwill to be drawn on in future negotiations with bureaux and divisions. A director might also use a portion of his 'reserve' to finance some of those appeals from bureau directors-general against the provisional allocation.

Each bureau was informed of its share of the ceiling, and its distribution by broad categories of spending. In the Ministry of Construction the administrative vice-minister personally informed each director-general, but the practice varied. One former director of MOFA's Finance Division used to call in each bureau's director of General Affairs Division, and inform him of the bureau's share and its proposed allocation among the divisions. Those were not inflexible. He could be persuaded after discussion to agree to marginal adjustments, but only within the overall total. Occasionally, a director of BAD might attach conditions or 'strings' to monies allocated to a particular project or programme within a bureau's budget, but normally the bureau's director-general in consultation with his director of General Affairs Division had discretion to adjust at the margin the proposed allocations to reflect priorities agreed internally by the bureau, especially where the BAD had allocated less than requested to a particular division, programme, or project. He might with the agreement of BAD move monies between divisions, or top up allocations from a small 'pot of gold'. For example, in MAFF the director-general of each bureau had a 'special disaster prevention reserve' which could be drawn upon. With the introduction of the zero and minus ceilings in the 1980s, and the stricter observance of the policy rule of 'scrap and build', new policies did not necessarily entail additional spending. As bureaux 'consumed their own smoke', the director of the Budget and Accounts Division intervened less in the reallocation between projects and programmes within them.

Once the allocation of the ministry's ceiling had been made to each bureau, and divided among the divisions within them, each bureau completed its draft budget requests. The director of the BAD collected and collated them and produced a draft budget for the whole ministry, submitted to the administrative vice-minister and/or the director-general of the Minister's Secretariat for approval, and shown to the minister. Where the latter had earlier expressed particular policy preferences, or identified projects where he had a personal interest, those would already be reflected in the allocation or, if made known subsequently, provided for partly out of BAD's retained monies. Most ministries and agencies had a formal minister's meeting attended by all bureau directors-general, at which the director of BAD presented the draft budget for the whole ministry. It was a largely ceremonial and symbolic occasion, with little discussion of substantive issues. The main purpose was formally to confirm and legitimize the allocation of shares of the ceiling made by BAD, and the budget requests to be made to MOF at the end of August. Only minor changes would be made at such a late stage; although the minister might ask for additional spending in some areas, or suggest changes in particular programmes, it was a rare occurrence, because his views, together with particular sectional interests, would have been incorporated reflexively, or accommodated by 'anticipated reaction', much earlier. It could happen though. One director of BAD in MOL confessed that he had been 'surprised' by a ministerial intervention at a formal hearing. The painfully constructed 'balance' between bureaux had to be readjusted, and some agreements, concluded much earlier, renegotiated (MOL 1994).

THE INFLUENCE OF THE LDP

Before a ministry's budget request was submitted to MOF on 31 August, the LDP was formally consulted. At the end of the process of formulating the Budget after long, complex and sometimes painful *nemawashi*, that formal consultation was more ritual than substance, and a week or less was scheduled, leaving little time to reopen and reorder allocations around which a consensus had been carefully constructed over the previous three months. Before 1993 that formal consultation involved only the LDP. In the period of coalition governments the procedures became more complicated, as were described in Chapter 10.

At those earlier stages in the preparation of draft budget requests, PARC divisions and their numerous sub-committees, together with associated special committees, councils, and research societies, met formally on several occasions to hear divisions and bureaux make formal presentations of their policies and expenditure proposals. Those meetings were invariably and necessarily preceded by informal networking between officials from the Spending Ministry and senior members of the relevant PARC division and committees, and characterized by intensive *nemawashi*. The main focus of the LDP's attention was the Spending Ministry, not MOF's Budget Bureau. Officials from the Spending Ministry attended the formal meetings: budget examiners and deputy directors-general never attended, and evinced a lofty disdain for their activities (MOF 1994c). However, at later stages in the budget process there was a great deal of informal contact between Budget Bureau officials, senior LDP officials, and PARC influentials.

As explained above, budgetary policy was made very largely bottom-up as policy divisions and their bureaux brought forward proposals for spending on existing programmes, and those to finance new, agreed ministerial policies. The direct influence of the LDP, and other interests such as local governments and producer groups, at that stage was represented by the accumulation within policy divisions of their pleas and proposals for additional spending on particular projects and programmes, besides those generated internally. At that time, when policy divisions were competing for the inclusion of items of additional spending within their bureau's budget request, *zoku* and rank-and-file Dietmen might press claims on behalf of sectional interest groups, or in support of the party's or their own preferred options for more spending, or for the inclusion of new projects or items.

As the budget requests began to take shape in July and August, and were firmed up within the Spending Ministry, there was constant interaction to ensure that any objections and reservations the PARC division might make had been discussed informally. At meetings of the division and its Research and Special Committees, directors-general of bureaux outlined and explained their proposed budget submissions, to seek support and to allay complaints. As one MOFA director of BAD explained:

it was necessary that Diet Members' support be secured, their wishes catered for but their zeal for individual projects or items often restrained. The political limits within which ministry officials had to work were often narrow and the intricate relationships built up between ministries and Diet members, while often beneficial to both, involved delicate bonds of obligation. (Rix 1980: 168)

The aim was to avoid the element of surprise, through prior notification of the intentions of the Spending Ministry: to alert the PARC division to the principles and major policy items of the budget request to be laid before them formally in late August. Depending upon the politico-electoral salience of the ministry and its individual bureaux, modifications to the requests of some bureaux might be made as a result of *nemawashi*. A former chairman of the PARC Division for Post and Telecommunications explained: 'We intervened on some items and policy ideas at this stage', but normally the views and probable reactions of the leading members were well known to the officials from the Minister's Secretariat, and to individual bureaux, and, where appropriate or necessary, had been taken into account much earlier in the process (Kondo 1994). The broad thrust of policy, and the priorities of spending, were normally well established and familiar to the PARC division from its activities, and those of research commissions, special committees, and ad hoc study groups, in reviewing general policy proposals and legislation throughout the year.

At the formal meeting of a PARC division to discuss the draft budget, the director-general of the Minister's Secretariat, accompanied by the director of the BAD and supporting staff, explained the principles, strategy, and major features of the ministry's budget request. Explanation and subsequent discussion were both general and formal; there was no detailed examination or interrogation. All policies had to be approved by the party, and at that stage the PARC division was giving formal approval for the proposed budget to proceed as a recommendation to the Deliberation Commission, and then to the Policy Affairs Research Council. The formal and ceremonial occasion also served to involve formally all the PARC division members in the decision, and to provide the opportunity for any of them to express formal disagreement. Such action was unlikely, first because of the informal substantive discussions that preceded the meeting, and secondly, because of the cultural inhibition on public dissent, reinforced here by the consequence of the rule that party Dietmen could attend any division, whether a member or not. Most LDP rank-and-file were deterred from registering objections or disagreements formally and openly before their peers.

There was no evidence that PARC divisions formally or informally attempted to influence the initiation and formulation of budget proposals within bureaux and their divisions when discussion began there in April/May; nor that they tried to influence the negotiations between the director of the Budget Accounts Division and the Budget Bureau over the ceiling in June/July. However, at both stages, as explained, *zoku* or an individual Dietman might attempt to do so.

Zoku played two main roles, first supporting their Spending Ministry's attempts to maximize its budget, and secondly as supplicant. Both *zoku* and the Spending Ministry shared a common interest (with the PARC division) in maximizing budget share. General support for its budget aims and policies through the media, and in the Diet, helped in the formation of a favourable climate. But *zoku* played almost no part in the shaping of the ministry's budgetary policy and strategy, although along with other Dietmen they might press the claims of groups they represented, and their own constituencies, in April and May when divisions and bureaux discussed their budget proposals.

A Spending Ministry threatened by MOF cuts to its budget in the informal negotiation of its ceiling in May/June, or at a later stage as a result of the examination of its budget request by budget examiners, sometimes took the initiative in mobilizing political support. It tried to enlist the help of senior *zoku*, especially those who had held Cabinet posts in the ministry and were known to be sympathetic to its objectives. The extent to which it could do so effectively varied with the status of the ministry, and the politico-electoral salience of its spending programmes. It was easier for those like the Defence Agency or MAFF or MOC, with influential networks of public and private constituents to tap into, and with prominent LDP supporters to call upon. For others whose budgets or programmes evinced little outside interest it was either more difficult or, like MOT's Marine Safety Agency, impossible to mobilize external opposition to budget cuts proposed by MOF (MOT 1994). MOC kept a list of potentially useful *zoku*, ranked by status, seniority, and experience. Grade A influentials included former ministers of construction, Diet committee chairmen, and PARC chairmen. The most junior *zoku* were graded C. Anxious to create a favourable impression with the ministry by their support, energy and reliability, they would undertake mundane, 'floor-mopping' (*zōkin-gake*) activities on its behalf; prompted and encouraged, they might even petition Budget Bureau officials in support of specific budget requests from a policy division, though such lobbying was normally ineffective (Koga 1994; Arai 1994). But even friendly and supportive *zoku* were not always willing to be drafted to intercede on the ministry's behalf.

The more important role for most *zoku* was that of supplicant, representing the interest of special groups and their own electoral constituencies. This was most obviously the case where there was a direct link between the budget policies of a ministry and benefits or votes, as explained in Chapter 10 and illustrated in Table 10.2. Here *zoku* sought to influence the allocation of a bureau's budget, where the director-general had discretion to make marginal adjustments. More generally (with the PARC division), they pressed for the maintenance of grants and subsidies, the construction of more houses and roads, and other kinds of public works. When budget proposals were discussed in April and May, *zoku* and other LDP Dietmen might visit bureau directors-general, their deputies and directors of divisions, and put the case for a particular policy, project, or item of expenditure relevant to their interests. Senior *zoku* could offer in exchange information about the circumstances, needs, and anxieties of the groups and constituencies they represented, the sentiment within the party, the attitude of special Diet Committees, and, from long experience of the policy area, advice, information, and political guidance. In MAFF one director of BAD encouraged bureaux and divisions to establish close relations, and to liase continually with *zoku-giin* in formulating their budget requests in order to anticipate and incorporate their views and reactions, and thus avoid the need for major changes later in the process, when the draft budget was presented formally to the PARC Agriculture Division (MAFF 1993).

THE DEFENCE AGENCY

The budget process in the Defence Agency, while broadly similar to that in other ministries and agencies, had some important differences. First, the rationale underpinning most of its activities—the implementation of the security treaty with the USA—was the subject of continuing political dispute, with the JSP/SDP (until 1994) declaring the Self-Defence Forces unconstitutional. Secondly, the size of the defence budget as a proportion of GDP had historically been an issue of similar continuing political debate. From November 1976 until 1986, the policy objective enshrined in the *National Defence Policy Outline*, followed by successive prime ministers and their LDP governments, was to hold the defence budget below 1% of GDP. Thirdly, there were important organizational differences which affected the budget process and the outcomes. The Defence Agency did not have full ministerial status; its director-general held rank as a minister of state, below the prime minister, within whose policy jurisdiction the Agency was formally established. Further, as explained in previous chapters, some of the most senior posts in its civilian bureaux were normally held by officials seconded from MOF, MITI, and MOFA.

The Defence Agency was also unusual in its organizational structure, reflecting the incorporation of parallel and unintegrated civilian and military hierarchies. The latter comprised three Self-Defence Forces (SDFs) and a Defence Facilities Administration Agency, equivalent to the policy bureaux and divisions found in other ministries. Some 90% of the Defence Budget was divided among the three SDFs, after each negotiated with the Budget and Accounts Division of the Defence Agency's Finance Bureau.

Like most other ministries, policy-making in the Agency was based upon a series of five-year plans. However, because of the political salience of defence policy and the security treaty with the USA, the five-year plan was a more detailed statement of objectives, plans, costs, and forward commitments than found in those elsewhere. One consequence of that was that the three SDF organizations sought funds annually to implement agreed plans, in which the annual priorities were largely predetermined. Bureaux were not competing for additional funds to finance new and revised policies, as happened for example in MITI and MOE, where formal and informal hearings and negotiations were part of the process of determining priorities.

The overall size of the Defence Agency's budget request was discussed between the director-general of the Finance Bureau, the director-general of the Defence Bureau, the administrative vice-minister, and the minister; while the content of the front-line procurement budget was always discussed and agreed with senior officers of the three SDFs. The threshold was set by MOF's estimate for GDP, revised after the formulation of its draft General Account Budget in early December. Before each of the three SDF organizations and the Defence Facilities Agency submitted budget requests, the director-general of the Finance Bureau formally allocated shares of the ceiling negotiated by the director of the Budget and Accounts Division with his opposite number in the Budget Bureau. His discretion to vary the historic shares, other than marginally, was limited. In the internal negotiations conducted by the director of the BAD and his seven deputy directors, the director of each General Coordinating Division in each of the SDF organizations and the Defence Facilities Agency sought to protect those shares, mobilizing political support outside the Defence Agency where they perceived them to be threatened. The director-general of the Finance Bureau did not normally take part in the negotiations within the Defence Agency, but where there were difficulties or conflicts with the SDFs he might be brought in by the director of BAD to 'persuade them' (DA 1994). More commonly, the use of his discretionary authority was invoked as a threat, a deterrent to ensure their compliance. But in any case, most of the defence expenditures allowed little room for variation in the short term, for example the fixed military personnel costs, and 'current-year obligations' incurred from contractual commitments undertaken in previous years. The trends of defence budget allocations are analysed in Chapter 21.

MINISTRY OF HOME AFFAIRS

The budget process in the MHA was different from all other spending ministries and agencies, reflecting its role as a central ministry, coordinating the plans and expenditures of all those ministries that provided finance for local government. It occupied a central position in the budget-making process for both the General Account Budget and the Local Government Finance Plan. The latter, drawn up by MOF, prescribed the aggregates for revenue and expenditure for local government as a whole, as explained in Chapter 11. MHA advised, and had a major input through, three funding sources. First was the local allocation tax, calculated by a fixed formula. In some years in the mid-1990s, because of financial stringency, the full entitlement was not made available to local governments: instead, a proportion was 'borrowed' by MOF to help reduce the size of the deficit on the General Account Budget. Such loans had to be repaid in later years. Secondly, the MHA negotiated trilaterally with the responsible Spending Ministries and MOF the respective burden of central and local government expenditures in the delivery locally of national services, such as education, and health and welfare services. Thirdly, MHA negotiated with those ministries the size of local loan programmes to finance capital investment and public works schemes. Together, those three central sources of funding provided about 40% of the total annual revenue of all local governments.

As a coordinating ministry, MHA had very few executive functions; it had no policy divisions or bureaux. Almost the whole of its budget was to enable other Spending Ministries and Agencies to 'transfer', through grants, subsidies, and taxes, funds for local governments to deliver local and regional services, and to pay grants and benefits of various kinds under national programmes. It did not have a ceiling share for the latter, although it negotiated with MOF over the local allocation tax, the loans programme, and the overall Local Government Finance Plan. Its claim to support other ministries and agencies in their negotiations with MOF over their ceilings, and subsequently in the Budget Bureau's examination and hearings on their budget requests, was disputed by some of them, who complained that 'it never supports us'. Unlike other ministries, it dealt with several rather than one Spending Division of the Budget Bureau.

CONCLUSIONS

The processes of compiling an annual ministerial budget were almost wholly a bureaucratic activity, dominated by the bureaux and their constituent policy divisions. While their individual contributions were intermediated and coordinated by the Budget and Accounts Division of the Minister's Secretariat, in general, strategic horizontal coordination was weak. While ministers might intervene ad hoc to influence the outcome of a particular issue in which they had a personal interest, their role and that of administrative vice-ministers was mainly to confirm and legitimate the budget strategy, and the priorities and allocations that evolved from the coordination of the independent and often disparate initiatives begun in the policy divisions and bureaux.

The budget processes within ministries and agencies were characterized by a mixture of formal and ceremonial procedures on the one hand, and informal discussions, consultations, and negotiations on the other; the former served mainly to confirm and legitimate the consensual agreements reached in the latter. Formal 'hearings' took place at four different levels: at bureau level; between the Budget Accounts Division and individual bureaux; across all bureaux; and at ministerial level. Their main purpose was to provide for the formal participation and 'hearing' of those with a direct interest, in order to ensure their formal agreement, commitment, and compliance with policy positions constructed from earlier informal discussions and negotiations. The degree of formality and ritual varied with the organizational level, and the number and seniority of the participants. Bureau hearings might be less formal, and provide the occasion for some substantive discussion on issues where there were differences of opinion, or where there were competing or conflicting interests within or between policy divisions that had not yet been reconciled. It was rare at higher levels. The formal demonstration of consensus was significant: it confirmed face-to-face what the core participants had agreed previously, and committed both them and peripheral participants subsequently. Substantive discussions, negotiations, hard-bargaining, and the achievement of agreement between contending interests underpinned the formal processes, and took place in a continual succession of informal meetings where a variety of verbal and written directions and information were exchanged within divisions and bureaus, and between both and the director and staff of the Budget and Accounts Division.

Formal structures and arrangements, and informal processes, characterized the contribution of the LDP as well, and served similar purposes. It was important for the party to be seen to be consulted, and its views formally 'heard', if it was to commit its rank-and-file members to formally concluded agreements. The main vehicle of communication was PARC and its divisions, committees, and study groups. At the same time, to exert influence, the LDP needed to have its collective views, and those of individual influential and senior politicians, brought to bear early enough in the budget process within each ministry and agency while options remained open and before positions were taken up. The LDP's influence on the composition and allocation of individual bureau budgets, and its incidence and effectiveness, varied with the politico-electoral salience of the particular ministry and its programmes, and the extent to which political intervention might also be required to resolve jurisdictional conflicts between ministries on issues that proved irreconcilable by bureaucratic coordination. The LDP's direct influence resulted mainly from the representation of party interests to directors and deputy directors of policy divisions, and to the bureau's director-general, and indirectly by the incorporation of their discussions, and through the 'anticipated reaction' of the collective interests of the party and the particular local, electoral interests of influential Dietmen. I have more to say about the direct and indirect modes of exercising influence in Chapter 20.

17

The Budget Bureau's Hearings, Examination, and Negotiations

After Cabinet approved the budget strategy, and ministries and agencies were informed of their ceilings in June or July, the initiative within the Budget Bureau passed to the budget examiners and deputy budget examiners. The broad aim was to deliver by December a draft MOF budget within the budget ceiling, and consistent with the guidelines approved by Cabinet for the different categories of expenditure. There were four main stages of compilation following the formal submission of budget requests at the end of August: the hearings, examination, negotiations, and 'revival negotiations'.

THE SUBMISSION OF BUDGET REQUESTS

MOF prescribed the date and the form in which the budget requests were submitted. For the whole of the period 1975–2000, and earlier still, this was 31 August. The date had a ceremonial significance. Requests were dispatched by the director of the Budget and Accounts Division of the Minister's Secretariat of each Spending Ministry and Agency, and were addressed to the relevant budget examiner in the Budget Bureau, who passed them to his DBEs. Where policy jurisdiction was shared among ministries or agencies, for example ODA programmes, and some public works, requests were divided as appropriate between different Budget Bureau divisions. Officials of such ministries had subsequently to negotiate with several BEs/DBEs. The requests were voluminous and detailed, covering every item and sub-item of expenditure for the coming fiscal year, together with the initial, revised, and settled budget figures for past years.[1] At that stage no supporting explanations and data were submitted in evidence, nor arguments advanced to justify their requests.

There were normally no surprises or unanticipated bids. Deputy budget examiners knew informally, from prior discussions with directors of Budget and Accounts divisions, about policy changes in train, the priority attached by bureaux, ministers, and the LDP to certain items of expenditure, and the likely size and composition of the bids for the 'new money' allocated in the budget guidelines to priority programmes. Rough estimates of the costs of the bids for programmes subject to cut-back or exempt from

---

[1] The volumes of the initial budget for FY1999 measured 15.5 cm × 12.7 cm × 18.5 cm and weighed several kilograms. Budget details were not computerized until 1996.

Hearings, Examination, and Negotiations

it could be calculated from the base-line of the previous year's initial budget, and from the out-turn expenditures of each programme, item and sub-item, available in the settlement of accounts three months after the end of the fiscal year.

HEARINGS

In September, Budget Bureau officials conducted a series of 'hearings', at which their opposite numbers from the Spending Ministries and Agencies formally outlined and explained their budget requests. Their significance was partly symbolic, signalling to all the participants and the world outside Kasumigaseki that the process of examination had begun. More importantly, they reflected a general cultural norm, providing the opportunity for the supplicant to explain face-to-face the purpose, need, and justification for the expenditures requested before a decision was reached by the Budget Bureau. As a senior official in the Minister's Secretariat explained, 'A visit is polite and shows respect. The form and the procedure of the visit is symbolically important, even if the substance is known and nothing was changed by the visit' (Maruyama 1993). But more than that: 'for the Deputy Budget Examiner it was vital to listen long and hard and often to what the Spending Ministry said; they like to be heard' (Horié 1993). Budget officials had to try to understand their point of view, what they were trying to do in the particular context of the ministry's aims and objectives. The hearings provided the formal opportunity to do so.

The hearings were held at four hierarchical levels, with Budget Bureau officials dealing with counterparts in the Spending Ministries at one level above, as is customary in many budgetary systems. Figure 17.1 shows the relationships. Hearings at the first

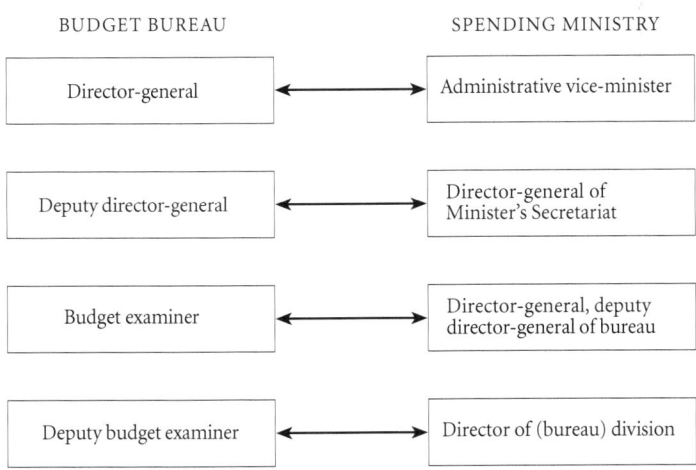

Figure 17.1 *The Budget Bureau's formal hearings, 1975–2000*

three levels were largely ceremonial, took up little time, and might involve at the most senior level little more than 'courtesy calls'. For example, the director-general of a Spending Ministry's Secretariat would call upon the relevant deputy director-general in the Budget Bureau, and briefly outline the budget for his ministry as a whole, drawing attention to those programmes or particular items of expenditure that were thought to be especially important. Such points of emphasis might be repeated by the appropriate bureau directors-general before individual budget examiners. The hearings conducted by the deputy budget examiners were substantively more important. The agenda for those, and for hearings at the other levels, was set by the director of the Budget and Accounts Division of each Spending Ministry and Agency by arrangement with the DBE.

At that working level, each divisional director would attend the hearing with his supporting staff, perhaps five to ten in number. Facing him across a desk in a crowded and cramped MOF office would be the DBE, alone or with a single member of his staff. A hearing might last several hours, frequently all day, the corridors of MOF's first and second floors crowded with waiting officials. Each DBE might have a dozen or more policy divisions to hear, and his time and that of his support staff would be fully occupied throughout September. The staff of the Spending Ministry's Budget and Accounts Division (BAD), but not the director, would accompany the divisional directors at all hearings before the DBE. The ministry's BAD was thus able to observe, record, and monitor their progress, and its director could be kept abreast of progress and developments across the whole range of the ministry's divisions and bureaux, providing essential background information to enable him to adjust and refine his overall strategy for maximizing the ministry's budget in response to the progress of the hearings (and, later, the negotiations). Interposed between the DBE and each divisional director, he had a broader perspective than either, and at the conclusion of the hearings he and his staff advised each policy division on the tactics to be adopted in the negotiations that would follow—when and how to yield, remain firm, compromise, and so on.

Additional information and evidence in support of the request would be sent by divisional directors to DBEs after the formal submission on 31 August; additional information and written explanation justifying particular proposed expenditures would be brought to the hearing by the director and his accompanying staff. DBEs were reliant on the Spending Divisions and Agencies for most of the specialist and technical information and data. Although they also had access to other kinds of information independently, for example from the specialist press or personal research, MOF itself provided little in the way of institutional help with analysis and evaluation, or through specialist staff services such as management accounting or Operations Research (OR), as happens for example in the UK and elsewhere. However, the Budget Bureau had access to reports of its budget inspectors, together with those of administrative inspections carried out by the Management and Coordination Agency; and MOF's Institute of Fiscal and Monetary Policy occasionally helped with the analysis of capital investment projects.

Directors were accompanied by the appropriate technical staff, whose evidence was heard and cross-examined by the DBE. This mode of face-to-face inquiry was held by

DBEs to be especially helpful in establishing the degree of support, commitment, and enthusiasm of the ministry's specialists for the proposed expenditures. One former DBE explained that an important part of the justification for an item of expenditure was the ability of directors to explain the need and justify the costs and benefits in plain language that could be understood by a layman with 'common sense'. 'If they were not able to explain and convince the DBE in language he could comprehend, then perhaps they shouldn't have public money' (Horié 1993).

From the perspective of the DBE, the purpose of the hearing was to acquire sufficient information from the Spending Ministry to enable him to assess the need and justification for the request, and crucially to arm himself sufficiently to argue for or against particular expenditure proposals when cross-examined in turn by his own deputy director-general at the Budget Bureau meeting that followed the hearings. One former DBE maintained that the amount and quality of the evidence brought forward in support of the justification for an item of expenditure was more important in the assessment than the amount of money itself. As each ministry had a ceiling on its total budget, the issue was not one of by how much it could or should be increased, but how within that ceiling it should be distributed at the margins on programmes, projects, and items; there was, however, competition among eligible ministries for the 'free money' available in priority policy areas.

At the hearings, the DBE questioned and probed the explanations and arguments presented by the director and his staff; requested additional information, and provided some indication of his preliminary reaction. At that stage, while nothing was conceded or given away, a DBE could convey in appropriately coded language signals about probabilities and possibilities. If those signals were correctly interpreted, the director (and the BAD staff) might get some feel for the DBE's attitude towards particular proposals: 'promising'; 'promising, if more convincing data are forthcoming'; or 'unpromising', as a deputy budget examiner explained (Ueno 1993). How was it possible to communicate a firm rejection of a budget request in a socio-cultural context where conflict was avoided? One budget examiner explained: 'If I said "yes" it was "yes", if I didn't say "yes" in some form or other, it was probably "no".' What happened subsequently would depend on the reaction of the Spending Ministry's officials. If they interpreted his response as a rejection, and did not return to argue further, then he would conclude that they were not seriously committed to the project or item. The purpose of that ritual of claim and counter-claim was to 'test out their purpose, intent and commitment. It can be done effectively only face-to-face' (Shiga 1993). That particular budget examiner had had experience of working in the London Embassy, and at OECD in Paris, and preferred the Anglo-Saxon tradition of adversarial discourse, with short, sharp questions and unambiguous responses; but such a preference was a singular one among most of his colleagues.

The DBE avoided specifying in detail the kind of data that would satisfy him, in order to avoid a commitment that he might be unable to sustain and deliver later on. Nevertheless, a director might get a strong hint and react accordingly. The explanation and response at the hearings (and the examination and negotiation that followed) were part of the formal game, a necessary ritual, with its own sequence, rhythm, and language. It was similar to the conduct of the bidding processes and negotiations between the expenditure controllers of the UK Treasury and the Spending Departments with whom they dealt. The rules of the very formal and elaborate game played between them were well known to both sets of contestants and were scrupulously observed, but rarely openly discussed (Thain and Wright 1995).

The main focus of the DBE's attention at the hearing, and subsequently in detailed examination of the request, was those new programmes or projects and new items of expenditure within existing programmes. While the formulation and initiation of a new programme, or the revision to an existing one, had normally been discussed between officials in the Budget Bureau and the Spending Ministry at an earlier stage, sometimes over a long period of time, the DBE nevertheless scrutinized the request for new or additional money in the broad context of the particular pressures and 'tautness' of each spending round, set by the top-down macroeconomic factors discussed in Chapter 14. He also paid particular attention to any rapid buildup of expenditure on an existing programme, and to any items of expenditure that appeared unusual or contentious. He was on the lookout for the 'thin end' of a wedge of future expenditure. Weak or poorly argued proposals attracted special attention. The DBE's main task was 'to pick away at the Spending Ministry's data and argument to find "inconsistencies", to expose errors of fact, to reveal flaws' (Mimura 1993). Scrutiny and examination was mainly an exercise of finding loopholes and gaps in the arguments made in support of the bids, and then 'digging in' (Hayashi 1993). The DBE also raised questions about the continuing need for expenditure at the levels proposed on those programmes specifically targeted in the Budget Bureau's preliminary internal discussions on strategy and tactics. Subsequently, informal meetings with his deputy director-general to review the submitted requests, and discuss the proffered explanations, gave the deputy budget examiner a feel for the 'soft bits', where cuts might be made, and those bits that were 'hard'. (Tanami 1993).

A DBE could be helpful and constructive where the objectives of a programme or project were thought worthwhile and he was broadly sympathetic to the request. He might suggest or propose ways in which a programme could be financed at the level requested, even though it exceeded the limit informally discussed at the time of negotiating the ceiling. One former DBE distinguished two types of response to a request: linear and cubic (Horié 1994). Normally his reactions were located on a line running from acceptance to rejection, but sometimes there were several 'faces' to a request which could be examined and adjusted without increasing or decreasing the total (cubic) volume of expenditure. For example, if a programme could not be financed wholly through the resources of the General Account Budget, the DBE might suggest or propose a joint venture with private-sector firms, or the introduction of private money to offset the costs, as happened in the financing of some space exploration programmes, and the construction costs of deep-sea exploration vessels. Alternatively, a sympathetic DBE might be prepared to help finance a programme through savings made in other programmes elsewhere in his sphere of responsibility.

On such issues, and concerning those proposals that involved very large expenditures, the DBE might refer to his budget examiner for advice on how to proceed, or to the deputy director-general for guidance after prior consultation with the former. The deputy director-general stood between the Budget Bureau's Coordination Division (CD) and his DBEs. His role was partly that of coordinator, concerned as was the CD with ministerial ceilings and overall budget limits, and partly that of senior examiner, concerned with the supervision of the exercise of control of the expenditures of those ministries and agencies that fell within his sphere of responsibility. He was pulled in two directions, allocating shares of resources and imposing limits on his DBEs on the one hand, and scrutinizing their examination of budget requests and providing advice and guidance on strategy and tactics on the other. In both he had a key political role, meeting with LDP officials, Dietmen, and representatives of interest groups to explain, clear the ground, and, where appropriate, persuade them of MOF's preferred position.

The role and *modus operandi* of budget examiners varied, partly determined by the policy area and programmes for which they had overall responsibility. For example, the BE in charge of the welfare budget, public works, or agriculture necessarily spent more time in politicking with LDP officials and consulting with party organs, and more time 'putting himself about' in the Diet, than the BE with responsibility for the Ministry of Justice. He had also to keep in close touch with his opposite numbers in the Spending Ministry who might be similarly engaged, to avoid 'crossed wires'. A BE whose responsibility included a programme where a policy review or reform was in progress necessarily spent more time on detailed policywork before, during, and after the process of hearing and examination. How much a BE involved himself with the detail of those processes was also partly a function of temperament, personality, and style. Some BEs delegated a substantial amount of authority to their DBEs, allowing them discretion to exercise their own judgement, and to settle on their own account all but the most important or politically sensitive issues. Practice on referral upwards varied with a DBE's time in the job, his experience, confidence, and personality, and with the extent to which BEs were prepared to involve themselves in the detail of particular requests. Very large projects or programmes tended to involve the deputy director-general, who provided a broader perspective, especially where political as well as budgetary considerations were in play. He was concerned with the overall budget of the ministry or agency, and with its objectives. Part of his task was to ensure that DBEs (and BEs) had an appreciation of what a ministry was trying to do as a whole, and not merely a grasp of those of its programmes and items for which they had responsibility.

Ad hoc informal hearings or meetings between the DBE and the divisional director of the Spending Ministry took place as needed after the formal hearings were concluded. The agenda was more limited and specific, dealing with particular issues or items of expenditures where the DBE wanted further explanation or information. The attendance was much smaller, and the proceedings more 'colloquial', with more 'cut and thrust' (Mimura 1993). But the DBE would give nothing away at that stage.

EXAMINATION

After the conclusion of the formal hearings and informal meetings with the directors, the DBEs and their staffs examined and assessed each item of expenditure in the light of the evidence and information provided by the ministry, and the verbal explanations and arguments advanced at the hearings. In so doing, the DBE began to form firmer judgements about the need and justification of particular items of expenditure, and the priority attached to them by the Spending Ministry. At that time he might meet informally with the Spending Ministry's director of the Budget and Accounts Division and discuss the progress of the hearings overall, and the performance of the divisional directors. From such discussions, the director of BAD would obtain an impression of the DBE's initial reaction to the budget as a whole, or that part of it for which he had responsibility, and perhaps would give some hints about the likely outcome overall, together with particular strengths and perceived weaknesses. Such off-the-record discussion would provide useful pointers for the director of BAD in his subsequent briefing of the divisional directors on how to play their hands in the negotiations that followed. Before that, however, the Budget Bureau would hold its own internal review.

Budget Bureau Meetings (Kyokugi)

Budget Bureau meetings were held in October, after the conclusion of the formal and informal hearings. Each of the three deputy directors-general would draw up and announce a schedule of interviews with his DBEs, allotting so many days to each. The order was important, because those coming first had less time for preparation after the end of the hearings in September. New DBEs tended to be taken later in the schedule; those with lighter work-loads, or with less important policy areas, earlier. Each DBE would present the budget requests within his sphere of responsibility, together with an assessment of the need and justification for each, and his judgement of what should be allowed or disallowed on each item of expenditure; he would also outline and present his proposed budget draft. Prior to the meeting, the DBE would have consulted informally with his budget examiner about any large or contentious items of expenditure, and sought guidance on how to present particular issues. The BE attended the meeting, but his role was mainly that of an observer, paternalistically listening to the presentation and argument of his DBEs, and occasionally offering comments to elucidate or clarify points being made.

The Budget Bureau meeting was primarily a dialogue between the deputy director-general and each DBE. While the DDG knew the outline of the budget request of each ministry or agency, and their ceilings, he knew little or nothing of the details of the proposed expenditure item by item, or the background, apart from any knowledge acquired from his own previous experience as DBE or BE, and from any direct involvement with a particular project or programme. In a process lasting several days, each DBE was subjected to detailed and expert cross-examination on each item of expenditure by the DDG, who listened to the evidence and argument submitted in support of each bid, and questioned the DBE on his assessment of it, and his proposed course of action. Cross-examination might last several hours; in 1993, the two DBEs with responsibility for the ODA budget were grilled for twelve and seven hours, respectively (Sumi 1994). One former DBE likened the DDG to a drill sergeant putting the raw recruits through their paces (Yonezawa 1994*a*). Through cross-examination, the DDG would find out what was going on, how the bids were being handled, and would be alerted to those issues where it might be necessary or desirable to take political soundings or involve party leaders directly. For the DBE it was also an 'educational process', and an opportunity to demonstrate his mastery of the subject-matter, and provide evidence of his analytical skills and judgement.

The DBE received approval or criticism for his basic ideas and thinking, and for his proposed tactics for handling the bids, especially relating to large projects or those with a high profile. But there was not time, nor was it necessary, to explain and justify his proposed course of action on every detailed item of expenditure (Sumi 1994). The DBE's normal strategy was to submit a budget draft at a level slightly above the total sum allocated to him by the DDG earlier in the process. If he planned to deliver a budget below that assigned level, there would be scepticism about his ability to make the necessary cuts and savings to achieve it. He tried to persuade the DDG of the credibility of his draft, and to convince him of the need and justification for allowing additional expenditures above the target level. Other DBEs argued similarly, and competed for additional funds. The DDG had to be selective if he was to bring in the overall budget for his spending divisions at or around the level agreed earlier with the Coordination Division. His own strategy in the initial allocation of shares and targets to his DBEs provided a margin for slippage, and for later reallocations.

After the imposition of zero and minus ceilings in the budget guidelines in 1982, Bureau meetings were 'less exciting' than was once the case (Takeshima 1993). When there was opportunity to argue the case for increasing shares of a rapidly rising annual budget, DBEs competed with each other to obtain the support of the DDG for additional resources for particular programmes and projects. From 1982 onwards, both the DDG and DBE were mainly looking for ways to secure cuts to ensure that each ministry and agency kept within its ceiling. During a long, intense, and exhausting interrogation, the DDG gave advice and guidance where necessary on how particular issues might be handled by the DBE in his forthcoming negotiation with the Spending Ministry. His context and perspective was broader than that of any individual DBE, and his judgement of what might be cut, or cut further, was informed by an appreciation of the overall aims and objectives of each ministry and agency, and the degree of priority that each attached to particular programmes and projects. While DBEs were not obliged to accept such advice and suggestions, in practice, the DDG's comments and opinion were not lightly ignored. After the formal presentation, the DBE might take up an issue informally with him, or respond to a suggestion made at the meeting. The DDG's 'lieutenants', chosen from among the staff of the Coordination Division, took formal notes of the Bureau meeting and chased the progress of agreed action subsequently.

As a result of their explanations to the DDG in the Bureau meeting, DBEs hoped to increase their original allocation. Additional monies for those who were successful came from the DDG's unallocated reserve, his 'pocket money' (*futokoro*: literally, inside money-pocket), and/or from the director of the Coordination Division who had his *pokketo* too (Sumi 1994).

Sometimes there was a second Bureau meeting, where the DBEs reported on their progress in the negotiations, the likely outcome, outstanding issues to be resolved, and the strategy and tactics to be adopted to deliver the draft budget on target. Following the conclusion of the Bureau meetings, each DDG reported to CD on the likely outcome of the DBE's examination of the bids. The Coordination Division pulled together their three reports to create a picture across the nine spending divisions.

The Important Items Meeting, convened and chaired by the director-general of the Budget Bureau, was held concurrently with the Bureau meetings, and before the negotiations with the Spending Ministries took place. Each BE together with his DDG made a formal presentation of the budget requests for those 'important items' (*shuyō keihi*)—the major programmes of social security, education, defence and so on—with the focus on politically sensitive issues of policy, and those where substantial changes had taken place or were proposed. The director of the Coordination Division and his staff attended, together with the director of the Legal Affairs Division, the director of the Research Division, and the director of Research and Planning. Each meeting was conducted mainly as a dialogue between the director-general and the budget examiner, supported by the relevant DBE, although in theory anybody could contribute. What occurred depended very much on the personality and experience of the director-general. Most, but not all, had had recent experience as DDGs in the Budget Bureau, and earlier in their careers as BEs or DBEs. But where the director-general lacked recent knowledge or experience of budgeting, he delegated more of the task of examination and oversight to his DDGs, and the meeting was more formal. An experienced and knowledgeable director-general provided explicit guidance or direction where he thought it necessary and appropriate, but normally his reactions were conveyed more as 'signals' to be picked up and processed than as formal instructions. In some cases he was more explicit, where for example he thought that reforms in a particular programme contemplated for the years ahead should be brought forward in time. The Coordination Division pulled together the conclusions of the discussions and indicated programme totals to each BE, where these had been revised in the light of those discussions.

After the introduction of tighter budget guidelines in the early 1980s the significance of this occasion declined, and became more ritualistic than substantive, according to those who attended it. However, it had a greater symbolic significance outside MOF, to the Spending Ministries, where it was seen as a process of legitimation. In negotiations with their opposite numbers, it was very useful for budget examiners and DBEs to be able to say that the decision about what could be allowed or disallowed on a major item of one of the big programmes had been made formally by the director-general in the Important Items Meeting, and that they were therefore obliged to carry it out.

In recent years, there were more frequent, informal meetings to discuss progress and any difficulties arising, between the director-general and DDGs, BEs, and DBEs, as the negotiations proceeded in late November and early December. The hierarchical level of such meetings was determined by the issue, the size of spend, political sensitivity, or the extent to which an item was unusual in some way (Takeshima 1993). A BE could go directly to the director-general as of right if he was anxious about some aspect of a programme, but would normally first discuss the matter with his DDG who would then accompany him. The director-general was kept informed of the handling of all important or politically sensitive issues, such as the rice subsidy, the size and composition of the public works budget, and the defence programme, where the consequences of proposed action by the Budget Bureau involved ministers and senior LDP officials. At all such meetings the director-general's 'staff' from the Coordination Division attended.

The Minister of Finance's Meeting

There was normally one formal meeting—the budget ministerial conference (*yosan shōgi*)—usually in early November, attended by the minister of finance and the two parliamentary vice-ministers, together with the administrative vice-minister, the director-general of the Minister's Secretariat, the director of the Coordination Division of the Secretariat, and the minister's private secretaries. The Budget Bureau was represented by the director-general, the three DDGs, the director of its Coordination Division, and the BEs and DBEs from the line divisions. Discussion centred on the budget framework of each ministry and agency, the big programmes such as social security, and those in which issues of political sensitivity had arisen, or where the proposed expenditure might prove controversial. In turn, each BE took the lead and explained the tentative allocations to his Spending Ministries and Agencies (agreed before the negotiations), his DBEs providing detailed information and further explanation where necessary. The role played by the minister would depend very much on his personality, methods of working, and experience. 'Takeshita never said very much, but he remembered details of expenditure items and allocations from previous years ... rarely communicated his preferences and intentions, but was highly effective as a persuader and negotiator with other Ministers and LDP officials' (Horié 1993). He influenced the allocations on some items not by issuing directions or giving guidance to the BE or DBE, but by doing deals with ministers personally, and then communicating the outcome as a *fait accompli* to the DBE. Hayashi Yoshirō (1992–3), appointed in December 1992 after the Budget was complete, spent his first week immersed in the revival negotiations (see below). Fujii Hirohisa, minister of finance in the Hosokawa Coalition government, as a former MOF official was content to allow the Budget Bureau to make the running without much guidance or direction. His successor, Takemura Masayoshi (1994–6), was much more active and involved, both because of his party (Sakigake) and his position as its leader, and because of his personality. He provided much more political input. There were more ministerial meetings where he indicated what he wanted done on particular programmes. He introduced an element of unpredictability into the budget process which, according to one DBE, made it more exciting (Nakagawa 1995).

As the hearings and examination of budget requests got underway in the Budget Bureau in September and October, PARC divisions and sub-committees examined the details. PARC senior officials, but especially the acting chairman, looked at the balance of the Budget among ministries and between important programmes such as social security, defence, housing, and public works. Some attempt was made to identify those items of expenditure that might cause difficulty in the upcoming negotiations between the Budget Bureau and the Spending Ministries later on in November. But for the most part, discussion in each division was general rather than a line-by-line scrutiny of budget allocations. Members tended to focus upon, and know about, those few items that they were interested in, either because of their affiliation to interest groups or because of a direct constituency interest. Most were too busy with other business to have the time, energy, or inclination to get a detailed grasp of the overall General Account Budget, with its dense and complex structure of items and sub-items (Kondō 1994). The chairman of each division reported to PARC's Deliberation Council, where he was interrogated on important policy issues, other issues discussed by his division, and those issues that aroused controversy or proved difficult in some way. Agreed recommendations were submitted to PARC itself, whose formal approval was necessary before submission to the party's Executive Council.

NEGOTIATIONS

The negotiations between a DBE and the relevant directors of divisions in the Spending Ministries took place in November and lasted for about a month. In the light of the conclusions of the Budget Bureau meeting, the DBE aimed to negotiate a settlement along the lines of the draft budget agreed there with his DDG. If he had meanwhile obtained some additional resources from him or the Coordination Division, he had more flexibility to deal with some requests, and to try to work out acceptable packages; he could afford to be more generous on some programmes, and negotiate changes and adjustments at the margin. But he could not change those allocations agreed to at the Bureau meeting without reference to the DDG.

There was pressure on both sides to secure agreement to ensure that the 'pace' of the budget process was maintained. DBEs were frequently cross-pressured, by individual divisions arguing for additional increments (within the ministry's overall budget ceiling), by the Budget Bureau's Coordination Division, and by his own DDG looking for further cuts, perhaps to finance increases elsewhere. Where there was disagreement with the Spending Ministry, the DBE might refer an issue upwards to his budget examiner; but the latter had only about a week to deal with such cases from all of his deputies, and there was less time still where an issue rose to ministerial level. Moreover, in referring upwards, the DBE risked losing credibility with his opposite number, an important ingredient in the continuing relationship, and drew the attention of his superiors in the Budget Bureau to his competence and ability to settle matters at his own discretion. The DBE trod a fine line between strictness and generosity in conducting the negotiations. If he took a too tough line with a division too early, and subsequently obtained a far larger than expected share of any additional monies available to his DDG/BE, he and his opposite number risked damage to their credibility. For example, where the divisional director or the director of BAD had created the expectation of tight funding among his colleagues in a Spending Ministry, he would be embarrassed, at the conclusion of the negotiations, if more money was available from the DBE for some programmes, and hence his earlier judgement was shown to be mistaken; next time round, his advice and judgement might carry less weight with his colleagues.

The DBE negotiated separately with each director of a policy division, focusing mainly on those items of additional spending that were novel or contentious, weak or poorly argued. The purpose of the negotiation was less to agree on allocations for each item than to discuss and negotiate the relative priorities: those expenditures that were absolutely necessary, necessary, and simply desirable. When the ministry's final framework was settled, he would then draw the line appropriately in the light of the total available. Part of the DBE's context was the thrust or theme of the overall budget strategy. During the course of each negotiation, the DBE explained the 'atmosphere of the discussion' in the Budget Bureau, and advised: 'such and such items are promising', or 'forget items two and three' (Ueno 1993). However, the ministry might want to press the case for the latter, and return with more supporting data. The proposed expenditure on some of the new items was approved earlier, but about a quarter to a third normally remained for negotiation. Where the DBE had good relations with the Budget and Accounts Division of the Spending Ministry, he could obtain an informal indication of the priority attached to spending proposals across several divisions, and was better able to gauge the importance of a particular proposal brought forward by the division(s) within his own sphere of responsibility. Such information provided an element of the context within which he conducted the negotiations, and helped him to form a judgement about the size of negotiating margins and 'bottom lines'.

For example, MOFA wanted an increase of 8% on its ODA budget in FY1994, and had submitted a request of 7.9%. The Budget Bureau's Coordination Division had prescribed a ceiling of 4.6% in its allocation of new monies to priority programmes. In September and October in the hearings, the DBE dampened expectations about the probable outcome, while simultaneously arguing with the CD for a larger share in the final budget framework. Sympathetic to the objectives of the programme, and supportive of the case made out by his opposite number in MOFA, he argued in the Budget Bureau meeting for an increase of 6%. By the beginning of December, the CD was convinced of the need for some further increase above its earlier ceiling, and agreed to raise it to 5%. The DBE did not disclose to MOFA how much extra he had won from CD, and continued to argue in the final negotiations that his 'bottom-line' figure was 4.6%. Reluctantly (or so it appeared to MOFA), he conceded an additional 0.2%, and the negotiation was concluded, the MOFA official satisfied at having won a little more. The DBE was then able to use the remaining 0.2% to finance some additional expenditures on other MOFA programmes (Nakagawa 1994).

In the course of the negotiations, the DBE might indicate very broadly to the director of the Budget and Accounts Division in the Spending Ministry what the likely outcome of the negotiations would be—not item by item, but in general terms. This enabled the director to advise those divisions whose budget margins were at risk on the best course of action to limit the damage, or to negotiate a deal. For example, where the DBE was defeated on an issue internally in discussion within the Budget Bureau, and failed to obtain additional funding from his DDG, it would be difficult or impossible to persuade him to change his mind subsequently. Knowledge of that was important to the director of BAD in fine-tuning his overall strategy, for example by advising one division to accept a deferral, another to re-submit with more evidence to support its argument along lines hinted at informally by the DBE.

The director of BAD also had to decide whether, when, and how to involve his more senior colleagues, either with the concurrence of the DBE, who might himself have suggested it, or on his own initiative, because of the significance of the issue, or to demonstrate to political constituents the importance attached to it by the ministry. Involving senior bureaucrats or ministers required a response at the corresponding level from the Budget Bureau, and each side needed to define and agree the procedures for doing so, the agenda, and, if possible, the rules of the engagement, to try to ensure that the outcome was predictable, preferably predetermined by arrangement between the two sides.

Throughout the negotiations, each DBE reported progress to the Budget Bureau's Coordination Division, which maintained a watching brief, and advised on tactics where appropriate. Where difficulties occurred in the negotiations with a particular ministry, the CD acted as an intermediary between the DBEs/BEs and MOF's director-general and administrative vice-minister. Where necessary, the latter two would be briefed and advised to 'move among' the LDP leadership to explain why particular requests had to be cut, deferred, or rejected. Adjustments to the internal allocations made to DDGs earlier in the process might become necessary as negotiations proceeded, and as DBEs pressed for additional funds to finance bids made by their ministries which were squeezed initially, and for which a convincing and persuasive case had been made by a ministerial bureau or division.

Towards the end of November, as more accurate information about the prospects for economic growth and, contingently, the estimated yield of revenue from direct and indirect taxes become available, derived from EPA's *Economic Outlook*, the Budget Bureau's Coordination Division issued detailed, precise, and comprehensive guidelines which prescribed the principles, procedures, and the 'rules-of-the-game' to be followed in the final stages of the examination and scrutiny of the budget requests by the DBEs and BEs. They included guidance on the treatment of particular kinds of costings (for example the yen–dollar rate of exchange), the appropriate rates to be used in calculating salary and related costs, and (in liaison with the Budget Bureau's Allowance Control Division) the rates for social welfare payments. The rate of interest to be applied in capital investment projects was also 'guided', and a common assumption made about oil prices. Spending Ministries were advised accordingly, and re-based their budget requests, submitting revised calculations to the DBEs. No general GDP deflator was used. Ministries made their own estimates of future price movements in specific programmes, and incorporated them in their unit cost calculations. DBEs challenged, and argued for lower cost estimates during the course of the examination.

By the beginning of December, the framework for the whole budget was being firmed up, and each DBE had a more accurate estimate of the size of his overall allocation, and hence his negotiating margins and 'bottom-lines'. The earlier skirmishes gave way to hard-bargaining over those margins. If the overall politico-economic context was more favourable, for example if there was to be a higher than estimated revenue yield, he might be able to be more generous towards some of the budget requests, especially if, as a result, he had obtained additional resources from his DDG. On the other hand, if the economic outlook was gloomier than earlier anticipated, the CD might oblige DDGs to squeeze their ministries and programmes and look for more cuts, and ask their DBEs to adopt a tougher stance. As the negotiations proceeded towards settlement, the CD drew upon its small 'reserve', 'held back' at the time of the allocation of budget shares to the DDGs, to fund some additional or unanticipated expenditures.

At the conclusion of the negotiations, the DBE informed his DDG of the aggregate outcome, i.e. whether he had delivered below or above the budget allocated to him, and sought to obtain the approval of his BE and DDG for that outcome. Except on a few important items, or those in which the DDG had taken a particular interest, the DBE would not provide him with the details of each settlement, and how it was achieved. Each DDG then prepared an estimate of the outcome of the negotiations in his divisions, ministry by ministry, together with an estimate of his ability to deliver the budget aggregate assigned to him earlier in the process. The Coordination Division was alerted to any potential difficulties, and the director-general was kept abreast of progress through informal meetings with his DDGs, or indirectly through the CD. The latter kept a 'score-card' of the results of the negotiations across all of the Budget Bureau's divisions, and compared the probable or anticipated outcome with the ceiling for the General Account Budget as a whole. It aimed to deliver a total less than that ceiling, partly to provide an adequate margin for the 'revival negotiations' that took place later towards the end of December, discussed later in the chapter.

THE LDP'S INFLUENCE ON THE ALLOCATION PROCESSES

After the submission of budget requests, the LDP, through its policy organs, formally maintained a watching brief on the progress of the negotiations. Informally, senior party leaders, PARC officials, and senior *zoku* tried to influence particular outcomes, or to get involved as a Spending Ministry solicited and mobilized political support for its bid, or a particular programme or project. How that could occur, and the different roles and influence of LDP leaders and Dietmen, a PARC division, and *zoku* in the negotiations of budget shares, is illustrated in the following brief account of defence spending in the 1980s.

Most of the PARC and *zoku* pressure for increased defence spending in the 1980s occurred after the submission of the Defence Agency's annual budget request to MOF, constrained until 1986 by the policy rule-of-the-game of a budget–GDP ratio of 1%. This was a useful budget norm for MOF, enabling it to constrain pressures for more spending in the 1980s, against the backdrop of the government's commitment to its policies of fiscal reconstruction, and its sensitivity to the opposition within the Diet, and more widely outside, to the continuance of the security treaty. The Defence Agency's budget request invariably exceeded the ceiling agreed with MOF. PARC's National Defence Division, the Security Affairs Research Council, and the Base

Countermeasures Special Committee, normally supported the Defence Agency's claim in its negotiations with the Budget Bureau. Defence *zoku* were active too, attempting to build a consensus within the LDP where the issue of more defence spending divided party factions, and rank-and-file Dietmen. Influence was a function of access to the top leadership. In most years, a trade-off between the Defence Agency's request and the Budget Bureau's lower counter-claim was bargained after extensive consultations and brokerage by defence *zoku*. The prime minister was normally involved at the end of the process, but his intervention served more to politicize and ratify the compromise worked out informally between MOF and the Defence Agency, supported by PARC and the defence *zoku*.

It was more difficult for MOF to resist the Defence Agency's request for budget increases above its predetermined ceiling when the politico-economic context of the budget process was informed by particular pressures from the US government, and the argument for more spending supported by a consensus of PARC influentials, the top leadership of the LDP, and MOFA. Nevertheless, even then, the compromise tended to be 'split-the-difference', or tilted more towards MOF's counter-claim rather than the Defence Agency's bid. The final outcome reflected earlier calculations made within the Budget Bureau of what that compromise would be when negotiating the Defence Agency's budget ceiling earlier in the process, and reacting to its initial budget request. If MOF appeared to concede some budgetary ground when confronted by a consensus urging more defence spending, the 1% limit helped it to contain those pressures to incremental rather than quantum increases. The political imperative of that limit meant that in practice MOF had to manage the presentation of the GDP ratio, massaging the figures for example by manipulating the calculations of the base for measuring GDP, excluding pensions and other items included in standard NATO calculations, and deferring payments on procurement contracts to future years. In reality, Japan spent about 2% of GDP on defence in this period (Samuels, 1994: 323). From 1987, the National Defence Programme Objectives, and the 1% limit, were replaced by Mid-Term Defence Plans.

Throughout the stages of the compilation of the budget, the director-general of the Budget Bureau was in constant touch with the LDP leadership—the chairman of PARC, the secretary-general, and the chairman of the Executive Council—to discuss progress and any difficulties arising, and to ensure that the probable outcome was consistent with the aims of the party. One director-general in the 1980s was 'constantly opposing the views expressed by [the three], rebutting their arguments, and explaining the need and justification of MOF's position' (Tanaka Takashi 1994).

In November, before the conclusion of the negotiations between the Spending Ministry and the Budget Bureau, PARC issued a formal statement on the budget prospects, the balance between programmes, and the priorities of spending. This, the General Plan for Budget Formulation (Yosan Hensei Taikō), was the conclusion of its own examination and coordination of the reviews carried out by the 17 divisions. It was cast in general terms, bland, even anodyne in tone. It was more a public demonstration of the apparent political virility of the party, exemplified by its participation in the budget-making process, than a detailed statement of the party's aims and preferences for the Budget.

As the negotiations between the Budget Bureau and Spending Ministries and Agencies drew to a close in early December, a draft of the whole Budget went to the administrative vice-minister and the minister of finance. Over the following two weeks there was a continuous and frenetic round of informal discussions involving officials of the Budget Bureau and the Spending Ministries, ministers, and senior LDP officials. First, the nine budget examiners and the three DDGs of the Budget Bureau made repeated, daily visits to the LDP top leadership, the acting chairman of PARC, and their respective PARC division chairmen and vice-chairmen to explain, item by item, what the Budget Bureau proposed, and the underlying needs and justification of the allocations to each Spending Ministry and Agency, and to their main programmes. One former DBE attested that his 'BE was never in the office', but spent a great deal of time in informal discussions with the PARC acting chairman and other senior LDP officials, making as many as twenty different daily visits to the offices of LDP senior officials in the members' Diet buildings, the Diet, and even their private residences (Horié 1994). Secondly, the chairmen and vice-chairmen of PARC divisions and committees petitioned and pleaded special cases in visits to BEs and DDGs, often very late at night, when the latter had concluded their own hectic daily rounds. 'The Chairman of the [PARC] Research Society for Small and Medium-sized Business came to the office of the DDG once a week to plead for more resources and special treatment', and a way had to be found to try to accommodate him (Shiga 1994).

Nemawashi at this stage in the budget process entailed careful preparation of the ground for the subsequent publication of the MOF's draft budget, and the detailed results of the negotiations between the Budget Bureau and the individual Spending Ministries when the latter were formally 'shown' their allocations, in mid-December. The aim was to provide advanced notice and warning, to inform, and where necessary to persuade, coax, and cajole. It was neither a consultation nor a negotiation. Where necessary, the Budget Bureau officials tried to persuade LDP leaders and officials to abandon their support for a principle or policy or a favoured item of expenditure that had been cut or squeezed. If there were unwelcome cuts and squeezes, senior LDP officials had to be alerted to the 'shocking outcome' soon to be publicly revealed, and given the opportunity to discuss their reservations and register objections, and the time to bring their rank-and-file into line. Figures were not disclosed—'it would be too risky at this stage', before the whole budget had been agreed and each ministry's negotiated allocation settled—but principles, main policies and items were discussed (Yonezawa 1994*b*). At the same time, BEs and DDGs were taking soundings, gathering 'political' information, testing, and evaluating the reaction of the senior and influential LDP and PARC officials to the principles of items allowed, cut, and rejected, getting a feel for political sensitivities and pressures that might be building up, in order to assess the climate for the reception of the draft budget; identifying what issues would prove difficult; and assessing how serious politicians were about their commitment to a policy or a principle, and the extent to which they would press objections after publication, and hence what concessions or compromises it might be prudent to make beforehand. All of this informal politicking was necessary to ensure that the Budget was broadly acceptable to the party, and to ensure that the formal ceremonial of the revival negotiations that followed its publication proceeded smoothly and predictably, along predetermined lines. Some minor adjustments and modifications might be made to some items of expenditure at that late stage, before the draft budget was formally approved by the LDP through PARC and the Executive Council, prior to its presentation to Cabinet. On a few items where the negotiations with a Spending Ministry proved difficult or inconclusive, a BE might seek the help of PARC's acting chairman, and try to persuade him of the need and justification for MOF's tough and uncompromising line. If he could be persuaded, then the hope was that he would use the authority of his office, and his political skills, to influence his colleagues—senior LDP officials and ministers—to exert pressure on the Spending Ministry to back down. In such circumstances, the BE might have to offer an inducement or incentive which the Acting Chairman could 'trade'. For example, in return for the deferral or postponement of the contentious item of expenditure, the BE might suggest that the LDP should set up a special committee to discuss it, and to bring forward a proposal for sympathetic consideration in the next budget cycle.

The acting chairman of PARC (or other LDP notable) was not always responsive to such arguments, or might be unwilling to use his authority to try to influence the Spending Ministry. Where the issue was sufficiently important—a point of principle or a precedent for example—and the BE unwilling to back down, the latter might feel obliged to raise the issue to a higher level in the Budget Bureau, asking his DDG to intervene, and visit the acting chairman. Further escalation could involve the director-general of the Budget Bureau, or even the minister of finance.

Senior LDP officials, PARC members, and/or individual *zoku* were sometimes lobbied by the Spending Ministries to use their influence with Budget Bureau officials in an attempt to restore some expenditures, and increase others beyond levels approved in the negotiations. Knowing when to play that card and whom to approach were critical decisions for the director of a ministry's Budget and Accounts Division. The timing and the manner of the intercession was crucial. The strategy of one director-general of the Defence Agency's Financial Bureau, a former budget examiner in MOF, was to delay the deployment of such political support as he could muster until December, when MOF was compiling the draft budget (Akiyama 1994). But MOF was sensitive to *ex parte* representations and pressure, and such tactics could prove counter-productive if Budget Bureau officials reacted by stiffening their opposition. On the other hand, they could benefit from early warning of the likelihood of senior political intervention, of an awareness of their stance on particular policy issues, and of the pressure they might bring to bear. If there were to be such pressures, and from influential sources, better for the Budget Bureau officials to know sooner than later, and to react accordingly—by anticipating and allowing for pressure where it was likely to prove irresistible, or by preparing arguments to counter or oppose it, or by mobilizing countervailing political force, for example by involving the minister of finance or the prime minister.

On a very few items of particular importance, where a DBE/BE was unable to agree on a compromise with the director of the BAD of a Spending Ministry, and the intervention of more senior officials from both sides had also failed to achieve an acceptable settlement, ministers could become involved, and a substantive bilateral negotiation would take place. The minister of finance would use both ministerial and party channels to try to influence and persuade his colleague in the Spending Ministry. As minister of finance, Takeshita was particularly adroit, and was admired within the Budget Bureau for his back-stairs wheeling and dealing on its behalf. In most cases ministers were able to settle their differences, but it did happen that occasionally one or both, with different pressures, found it difficult to back down, concede, or agree a compromise. The gap between their respective 'bottom-lines' might be unbridgeable. Such conflicts tended to be over matters of principle or high policy. In such circumstances, the issue might then be raised to the party political level for resolution, at a meeting presided over by senior LDP officials. A former budget examiner described the procedure followed on such occasions:

The meeting was convened at the PM's official residence. The secretary-general presided, flanked by the chairman of PARC and the chairman of the party's Executive Council. Sometimes the vice-president of the party would attend as well. The minister of finance sat alongside them. Behind him sat the director-general of the Budget Bureau, together with the responsible deputy director-general, and the budget examiner from the Budget Bureau's Coordination Division. Less senior LDP officials—the deputy secretary-general, the acting chairman of PARC, and so on—sat behind their seniors.

The spending minister sat across the table and was interrogated by the secretary-general and his senior colleagues. The minister of finance explained the ministry's case, and commented upon the points made by the spending minster. Officials would not speak. The procedure was ad hoc and improvised. One single hesitation or slip or surprise statement by either minister could be damning. Each had to be fully armed and briefed, and make no mistakes, if he hoped to win. (Yonezawa 1994*b*)

That procedure and the behaviour of the participants was highly unusual in the context of the budget-making processes: neither the proceedings nor the verdict was rehearsed or predetermined: the outcome was unpredictable, contrary to the entrenched behavioural rules-of-the-game, scrupulously observed in both formal and informal budget processes. The method of settling the dispute was redolent of traditional martial culture. As the BE described it, '364 days' preparation; an instant clash of swords; one wins, the other loses.' Both the Spending Ministry and the Budget Bureau preferred the certainty and smoothness of customary procedures in which the outcome was controllable by them and normally predictable.

The new politics of party dissolution, de-alignment and realignment, and the unstable and short-lived coalition governments that followed the LDP's defeat in the Lower House election of 1993, profoundly affected the processes of budget policy-making over the following three years. The next section examines the changes in the interactions between the principal participants in those processes in the broader context of the changing relationships between bureaucrats and politicians in the policy processes.

THE COALITION GOVERNMENTS AND THE BUDGETARY PROCESSES, 1993–1996

Strategic decisions about the size of the General Account Budget, and the broad allocation of ministerial ceilings for FY1994, had been agreed by the Budget Bureau in the last weeks of the Miyazawa government, and were presented as a *fait accompli* to the incoming Hosokawa Coalition. Thereafter the main task of the Spending Ministries and the Budget Bureau was to secure the compliance of the new government's coalition parties. The progress of the compilation of the Budget was maintained during the autumn of 1993, and the stages of request, hearing, examination, and negotiation were completed on time. But by December it was apparent that the coalition partners were divided over the issue of its general orientation and strategy, and disagreed on allocations to some expenditure programmes, notably defence. Unable to agree, they gave priority and time instead to discussion of political reform, according to the Deputy Prime Minister and Foreign Minister (Watanabe 1994). Cabinet consideration and approval of MOF's draft budget was deferred until February 1994, six weeks later than was customary. Further delay occurred after its presentation to the Diet, when the LDP blocked its passage to extract concessions on the proposed legislation to reform the electoral system and party fund-raising. That achieved, further delay ensued as the LDP sought successfully to bring down the Prime Minister over alleged corrupt activities while governor of Kumamoto Prefecture. The Diet's discussion of the draft budget did not begin until mid-May; it was finally passed in July. Temporary supply was voted to provide for government expenditure in the new fiscal year beginning 1 April. The Hata government was defeated on a no-confidence motion by the combined votes of the LDP and the JSP shortly after the Budget was passed, its main task; and the third coalition government within a year took office on 30 June 1994 headed by the JSP leader, Murayama Tomiichi.

The uncertainty and delay in obtaining Cabinet's approval of the draft budget, and its protracted and difficult passage through the Diet, were the most significant short-term effects of the influence of the coalition parties on those processes in the preparation of the Budget for FY1994. Three other issues affected the budgetary processes. First, the use of public works programmes to fuel the LDP's electoral machine in the rural constituencies was strongly criticized by the incoming Hosokawa government, which instructed MOF's Fiscal System Council to review the principles and practice of the budget allocation of grants and subsidies to agricultural projects, roads, ports, and bridges and to recommend a reordering of priorities to give greater emphasis to housing projects and leisure facilities. This was accomplished in time to influence decisions on the amount and distribution of the public works budget in November 1993, and is discussed in Chapter 23. Secondly, the participation of the JSP in the Hosokawa Coalition government created uncertainty about the objectives, size, and allocation of the defence budget, a contributory cause of the delay over the Cabinet's consideration of MOF's draft budget.

The third issue—the abortive attempt to introduce a national welfare tax in February 1994—displayed many of the characteristics of the new political instability.

The coalition of seven parties with differing views on policy provided a more open, public discussion of policy options. As we have seen in Chapter 16, before 1993 the symbiotic relationship between bureaucrats and senior LDP politicians had ensured that options were canvassed, discussed, and selected through informal party channels between bureaucrats, senior LDP and PARC officials, *zoku*, and, where appropriate, special interest group leaders. Policies were announced formally as *fait accompli*.

For both the Prime Minister and MOF, the immediate withdrawal of the proposal to introduce the new tax represented a humiliating climb-down. The rebuff to MOF on such an important issue was evidence of more general uncertainty in the bureaucracy of what was practicable and politically acceptable in the changed conditions of multi-party government. The management of parties with opposed views on tax, spending, and financial regulation required skills of a different order from those honed by familiar routines over the previous 38 years. The background to the JSP's repudiation of the proposal is disputed. But whether the party knew of the Prime Minister's intention, and if so when and how it was consulted, is less important than what the episode revealed of the changed conditions of policy formation. With several parties, it was more difficult for bureaucrats to 'clear the ground'; construction of a consensus among leaders who could commit and deliver their supporters to an agreement took longer, and was more complex, and less predictable.

The manner in which the proposed tax reform was initiated was a vivid demonstration of the collapse and removal from influence in the budgetary processes of the LDP's PARC divisions, committees, and commissions. One of the most powerful of those bodies before 1993 (and after 1996) was its Tax System Research Council, more influential even than the government's own Advisory Tax Commission. Not only was it denied a pre-eminent role in the discussion preceding the proposed tax reform, a role now assumed by the latter: in opposition, its chairman lost authority to control rank-and-file LDP Dietmen, some of whom publicly opposed any increase in consumption tax. Commenting on the fiasco, the Chairman of the government's Tax Commission said: 'The members of their tax panel have lost their clout... Yamanaka [the Chairman] probably was powerless to prevent such behaviour. After all, his authority came from his position as the person to go to when you want a concession, and he doesn't have that position now.' The change was dramatic: 'People who used to take their petitions to LDP politicians don't know where to go and they've been calling on me and asking whether I'll give them a hearing' (Kato Hiroshi 1994).

Power sharing in the Murayama and Hashimoto Coalitions meant that budgetary policy-making had to be shared also. The participation of the three coalition parties in the formulation of the budgets for FY1995 and FY1996 occurred at two levels: separately, within each party's policy-making bodies, and collectively, in the tripartite bodies, mainly the Policy Coordinating Council (PCC) and its divisions, shadowing the ministries and agencies. The composition of those bodies, and their roles and functions in the policy-making processes generally, was explained in Chapter 10. Before formal submission to the Budget Bureau at the end of August, the Spending Ministries explained their requests formally to PARC divisions, and to the equivalent organizations in the other two coalition parties, having earlier consulted and discussed important items and issues with the senior officials of each party as the budgets were being prepared within bureaux. The procedure was similar to that followed before 1993, described above.

After the formal submission to the Budget Bureau on 31 August, PARC divisions and their equivalents in the other two parties discussed, and reported to their Deliberation Commissions, their views on the important items. Each 'PARC' then made a formal and general statement about those items. Until each of the three parties had discussed and agreed its position on the Spending Ministries' budget requests, and the general composition of the Budget overall, the PCC and its 19 divisions could not begin the attempt to produce a coordinated response, first within each division and then in the Council as a whole. In that process, there was a great deal of informal consultation and discussion between each party's 'PARC' divisions and the corresponding PCC divisions. The LDP's policy positions were often couched in general, even vague, terms, to avoid difficulties for their representatives on the PCC (Hori 1995). Both the PCC and its divisions worked towards a consensus. Decisions were taken after agreement had been reached, but without formal votes. One consequence was that policy pronouncements on the Budget (and other issues) tended to be even blander than those produced formally by PARC when commenting on MOF's draft budget in the period before 1993.

During the examination and negotiation stages, there was some informal consultation between officials in the Spending Ministries and party representatives on the tripartite bodies, to alert them to the progress of budget-making and to sound out their probable reactions to outcomes of particular negotiations. At the conclusion of the negotiations, MOF's draft budget was submitted to the Cabinet, and ministries and agencies were 'shown' their budget allocations. Each party then discussed those few items outstanding, or for which political resolution was required. The PCC's 19 divisions discussed and coordinated the views of the three parties, and agreed with the relevant Spending Ministry and Budget Bureau officials the agenda and procedure for the revival negotiations. The procedure followed was similar to that of the pre-1993 period, discussed below. However, at the highest level of formal revival negotiation, between the minister of finance and the relevant spending minister, each party was represented by its 'PARC' chairman and two other senior officials.

The formal tripartite bodies had no part in determining the size of the overall General Account Budget and the FILP Budget, or the ceilings for each ministry. Those decisions were reached after agreement between senior ministers and party officials from all three parties. The venue for formal consultation among the leaders of each party was the Consultation Council, but informal discussion between those and other party officials, and the director-general of the Budget Bureau, preceded formal ratification. Budget-making for FY1995 and FY1996 was shaped by a number of general politico-economic and administrative factors, of which the most immediately relevant were the fiscal consequences of the deep and prolonged economic recession: the revenues from direct and indirect taxation declined simultaneously with increased domestic and international pressures for more public spending to stimulate the economy. Further pressure resulted from the loss of industrial production and GDP consequent upon the devastation caused by the Great Hanshin–Awaji earthquake in January 1995: a Supplementary Budget totalling 2.7 trillion to finance immediate disaster relief, and to underwrite longer-term capital investment programmes, was introduced in April 1995. A second Supplementary Budget totalling 5.3 trillion provided additional expenditure for public works, agricultural subsidies, and small businesses, besides further support for disaster relief.

The reform of taxation was an urgent priority for the Murayama government, as it had been for its two predecessors. The JSP soon abandoned its opposition to the principle of increasing indirect taxation, along with almost all its other long-held beliefs, as the yield of tax revenues declined for the fourth successive year. The Coalition government agreed to a prospective increase in the national consumption tax from 3% to 5% in April 1997, softened by temporary cuts in income tax in FY1995.

Overall, the three years of coalition governments had a profound, if temporary, effect on the budget processes. Processes that were known, predictable, and programmed, and in which the roles of Cabinet, LDP organization, and *zoku* were institutionalized in formal and informal arrangements, became uncertain, inchoate, and protracted. The behaviour of fissiporous coalition parties, inexperienced in government and lacking a cohesive consensus on budget principles and strategy, were unpredictable. Above all, the long established formal and informal relationships in the budget processes, between bureaucrats in MOF and the Spending Ministries, and senior LDP officials, PARC divisions, and *zoku*, were abruptly halted in 1993. The channels of informal contact were closed, at least until the LDP's participation in the Murayama Coalition. Bureaucrats in MOF and the Spending Ministries were cut off from prime sources of information about political attitudes and sentiments, and denied access to the advice, counsel and specialist advice (and of course demands) they had routinely relied upon.

THE LDP AND THE BUDGET PROCESSES, 1996–2000

Normal relationships were not resumed with the return to one-party LDP government in November 1996 (with the support of the SDP and Sakigake). While most of the changes in the structures to accommodate multi-party government proved temporary, changes in the relationships between the LDP and MOF proved more enduring. They were partly the cause of MOF's loss of authority, as the LDP began to play a more independent and assertive role in policy-making, and attempted to replace bureaucratic domination of the budget processes with political control. Generally, MOF's prestige and authority were weakened by public and political criticism of its handling of the economic recession, and its perceived inability to resolve the crises in the financial system; moreover, the reputation and integrity of its officials was damaged by mounting evidence of improper and corrupt behaviour, culminating in a succession of arrests of MOF officials by the Tokyo Prosecutor's Office in the 'wining and dining' scandals of 1997–8.

The dominant and dominating role traditionally played by MOF in the budgetary processes was now disputed by LDP politicians intent on wresting the initiative from bureaucrats, and establishing political control of the formulation of the budgetary strategy, and the aggregates and composition of the General Account and FILP budgets. Prime Minister Hashimoto was personally committed to fiscal reform, and campaigned on that platform in the Lower House elections of July 1996. The initiative that led to the Fiscal Structural Reform Act of 1997 was politically inspired, and the legislation implemented in the FY1998 budget was determined by the politically dominated Administrative Reform Council. The origins of the legislation and its effects on the budgetary processes were dealt with in Chapter 13. In the paralysis of policy-making that infected the Hashimoto government in the second half of 1997 and the spring of 1998, as the economy moved deeper into a recession, exacerbated by the ill-timed increase in the consumption tax in April 1997, MOF was slow or reluctant to respond to growing international and domestic pressure for cuts in taxation and increases in spending. Fiscal expansion conflicted with the priority it attached to the implementation of the process of fiscal reform begun in the budget of FY1998. The initiative in the formulation of successive packages of countercyclical fiscal measures, especially those with implications for tax, was seized by LDP committees and commissions. The party was seen publicly to have taken charge (if not actual control) of fiscal policy, a reversal of budgetary practice before 1993. However, the issue of fiscal expansion versus fiscal restraint continued to be disputed among the leadership of the party until Prime Minister Obuchi's commitment to fiscal policies aimed at economic revival.

THE 'REVIVAL' NEGOTIATIONS

The ritual element that pervaded the whole of the budgetary process was nowhere more evident than in the so-called 'revival' negotiations (*fukkatsu sesshō*) which took place between Budget Bureau officials and their opposite numbers in the Spending Ministries and Agencies, and between the minister of finance and his Cabinet colleagues following the submission of MOF's draft budget to the Cabinet in mid-December. After the conclusion of the negotiations, Spending Ministries and Agencies were formally 'shown' their allocations. They then had an opportunity to re-request those bids or parts of bids that were unsuccessful. The original intention was to allow them a further opportunity for appeal, and an attempt to persuade budget examiners to agree to additional expenditure. As the LDP became more involved in policy-making in the 1960s, the period of 'recovery' provided an opportunity for senior party officials, and rank-and-file Dietmen, to obtain additional funding for favoured projects and local schemes. Campbell (1977) provides a detailed account of the origins of the revival negotiations, and an analysis of their implications for the budget and MOF's control up to 1974. Mabuchi (1997) provides a somewhat different explanation, arguing that they arose from MOF's aim to curb the use of Supplementary Budgets, which were vulnerable to political influence, and were in exchange for an overtly political allocation in the final draft of the initial budget.

Whatever their origins and effects in the earlier period, from 1980 onwards, the revival negotiations became less important in the process of allocating expenditures, but no less significant symbolically as a public demonstration of the (apparent) power and influence of LDP politicians. Once the principle of imposing a stricter ceiling on the aggregate of the General Account Budget was accepted by ministers and the LDP leadership, there was no longer an opportunity to increase the size of the overall budget total as a direct result of political intervention after the submission of MOF's draft budget proposals to Cabinet in mid-December. As explained in this and earlier chapters, from that time political influence in the budget process was exercised much earlier in the process; the LDP could and did influence the size of the total budget and its composition in the discussions leading up to the June/July ceiling decisions. The revival negotiations were less important substantively, and less necessary, because any adjustments to reflect, explicitly and demonstrably, the LDP's priorities of public spending were now made when the ceiling was calculated, and the amount of resources allocated to the different categories of spending programme—priority, cut-back, exempt, and so on—was provided in the guidelines. That process incorporated the views of ministers and the LDP leadership, and, more generally, reflected the pressures of the relevant *zoku* and interest groups. Party priorities were reflected not only in the ceiling and the allocations to each category of expenditure, but also as an important constituent element of the broader politico-economic context within which requests were heard, examined, and negotiated by budget examiners and their opposite numbers.

Nevertheless, the formal rituals and the accompanying ceremonial of the revival negotiations were preserved. All but one of the six 'typical stages' or levels identified by Campbell (1977) in the early 1970s remained, although their *raison d'être* was transformed for the reasons explained above. Aside from the cultural significance of being seen to allow a disappointed or frustrated supplicant a further opportunity to persuade the DBE or BE in a face-to-face meeting, there was the political symbolism of the LDP being seen publicly to decide certain budget allocations. The reality was of course otherwise. Officials, ministers, and party leaders confirmed in interviews that they were well aware that the LDP's power to change the budget allocations in MOF's draft budget was a fiction. The LDP leadership 'plays to the gallery', and played up the apparent conflict between the party and MOF. In a stage set for 'theatricals, MOF writes the scenario for the enactment of the drama at the end of December' (Arai 1994). 'All LDP from old to young, influentials to back-benchers, are able to say and claim publicly that they had personally influenced the outcome of the budget' (Hatoyama 1994).

MOF's draft budget was shown and explained formally to the LDP's PARC divisions, which met to hear from the director-general of the Minister's Secretariat of each ministry what had been allowed, cut, rejected, and so on in the negotiations with the Budget Bureau. Each PARC division then discussed and agreed on four or five items of the Spending Ministry's budget that had been cut or disallowed by the Budget Bureau, and which the division wished to see 'revived', renegotiated, and hopefully recovered in the last week of December. The chairman and vice-chairman of each had previously discussed and agreed those informally with the Spending Ministry, which in turn had normally agreed them beforehand with the DBE in the Budget Bureau (see below). The large number of potential revival items generated across the 17 divisions and numerous committees was not formally coordinated by PARC. No division wished to be seen publicly to surrender some of its proposals, or to risk the embarrassment of its proposals being accorded a lower priority than any other. Informally, the top three LDP leaders advised by PARC's acting chairman decided on a rank order, and agreed on it and the procedure and the items for the recovery processes, with the Spending Ministry, the Budget Bureau, and ministers. Both before and after that agreement, senior LDP officials, *zoku*, and members of PARC divisions were active in attempts to recover particular projects and items of expenditure 'lost' in the earlier negotiations.

Immediately following the presentation of MOF's draft budget to Cabinet, Spending Ministries and Agencies formally re-requested those expenditures agreed formally with PARC. Once again, this was more ritual than substance: even where a Spending Ministry or Agency had no prospect of obtaining additional funds for a programme or project, it was nevertheless anxious to demonstrate to its constituents that it had attempted to do so. In most cases the initial bid was resubmitted at this stage without additional explanation or supporting information. Each DBE in consultation with his opposite numbers—the directors of divisions in the Spending Ministries and Agencies—drew up the schedule of arrangements for the negotiations on re-requested items at each hierarchical level. The agenda for each was discussed and agreed between the DBE and the director of the Budget and Accounts Division of his Spending Ministry. Before formal negotiations began, there was 'furious *nemawashi* by each budget examiner, deputy budget examiner, and director of budget and accounts, separately and sometimes collaboratively to smooth the passage' (Yonezawa 1994*a*). DBEs did not however agree on the content of the financing of revival expenditures without consultation with and the approval of the BE and the DDG, and in some cases the Coordination Division and the director-general himself. Likewise, the director of budget and accounts in the Spending Ministry consulted with his bureau directors-general and the administrative vice-minister. The Budget Bureau had its own preferences for the size and allocation of the margin, and tried to build a consensus with LDP senior officials and *zoku* before and during the period of the revival negotiations. It tried to persuade LDP rank-and-file members indirectly through the intermediation of senior LDP officials, and directly by lobbying during the course of the negotiations. While it was not always successful, provided it had good relations with LDP influentials, it could always hope to steer and manage the course of the revivals. The stages of the revival negotiations, and the major players are shown in Table 17.1.

The formal proceedings would begin with a meeting at MOF between the BE and the director-general of each bureau, who read out formally the main priorities of the spending bids. The BE responded, accepting some further (agreed) additional spending on items in the programme, and indicating which expenditures he was unable to accept of those re-requested (also agreed). He gave a formal undertaking that the two sides would continue to discuss and negotiate. The administrative vice-minister of the Spending Ministry now waited upon the deputy director-general and explained the priorities of the spending bids, and those further items on which agreement had been secured. Finally, in the Daijin Sesshō (Ministers' Negotiations) the Spending Minister would discuss and 'negotiate' face-to-face with the finance minister the two or three items or programmes to which he attached the highest priority. The finance minister would be accompanied by his administrative vice-ministers, deputy vice-minister

Hearings, Examination, and Negotiations

Table 17.1 *The stages and main players in the Revival Theatricals, 1975–2000*

Stage	MOF	Spending Ministry
1. Naiji	BE/DBE	Director, Budget and Accounts Division
2. Kachō	DBE	Director of division (of Bureau)
3. Kyokuchō Sesshō	BE	Director-general of Bureau
4. Jikan Sesshō	DDG	Administrative vice-minister; deputy vice-minister; director of Budget and Accounts Division
5. Daijin Sesshō	Minister of finance; administrative vice-minister; director-general and deputy directors-general of the Budget Bureau	Minister

from the Secretariat, the director-general of the Budget Bureau, relevant DDGs, and numerous other more junior officials. The chairman of the LDP's Policy Affairs Research Council, and sometimes the acting chairman as well, would be present, as witnesses to the agreement and as 'go-betweens'. DBEs would queue up outside the minister's office awaiting their summons. The 'show' would be illuminated by the presence of TV and the press, to whom ministers announced their successful 'recoveries'.

These meetings at all levels were mostly formal, the outcomes predetermined by informal prior arrangement between the two sides. The rehearsal of requests, the restatement of priorities, and the repetition of explanations to justify spending were (mostly) empty rituals whose observance and meaning had only a ceremonial and symbolic significance. It was important for every level, administrative as well as ministerial, to have, and to be seen to have secured, some concession. It was especially necessary at ministerial level, to enable ministers to emerge from the negotiations with a public and demonstrable 'recovery', and to claim that it was obtained only by their personal intervention. The public ceremonial was politically necessary, a symbol of the LDP's manifest influence and power in the compilation of the Budget.

While it was evident to all the participants that the budget total was fixed, and the allocations between ministries virtually settled, nevertheless, a small margin was available within that total to provide the stakes for the rituals of the revival games. It had already been provided and discounted within the budget ceiling decided in June. The size of the margin varied very little, year to year. From FY1988 to FY1996, it totalled between 177.7 billion and 223.2 billion each year. (Wright 1999*e*: table 20). This was equivalent to about 0.5% of the total budget for the mandatory and discretionary general expenditures, a still smaller percentage of the gross budget. Nevertheless, the sums were large enough to enable individual ministers and senior LDP officials (and some backbench Dietmen) to claim publicly personal and party success in obtaining additional resources for favoured programmes and projects. Three programmes—social security, education and science, and pensions for former officials—between them annually attracted about 75%–80% of the total recovery.

How did MOF manage the financing of the margin within the budget ceiling? The costs of the revival negotiations were funded partly by sums set aside in the budget allocations to each ministry and agency. By agreement between the DBE and the director of each Budget and Accounts Division, a small unallocated sum was assigned under the heading of 'administrative expenses' in the Budget for the Minister's Secretariat. This was then drawn upon to adjust some expenditures at the margin in the revival negotiations. At an earlier stage in the budget process, the two sides discussed and agreed which projects and items were to be reserved for 'revival', and the amounts needed to finance them. The Budget Bureau also had its own 'hidden reserves', a small sum set aside by the Coordination Division in its initial allocations to the DDGs. Shortly before the revivals began, BEs formally transferred the earmarked margins to MOF's own budget allocation, where they were temporarily 'lodged' for the five or six days of the revival negotiations. The publication of MOF's draft budget showed the total revenues and borrowing available to finance the negotiated totals for each ministry and agency within the ceiling for the Budget as a whole. There was apparently no more money available to finance additional expenditure without raising revenue or increasing borrowing. Reluctantly, MOF reduced its own (temporarily inflated) budget allocation to finance those political projects and items of expenditure insisted upon by the LDP. MOF had apparently 'lost' by having its Budget cut; politicians had apparently 'won' significant concessions.

To what extent did politicians influence the distribution of the 'revival' margin between projects and programmes? The LDP's known political priorities and interests had already been taken into account by both sides in the setting of the ceiling for each ministry and agency, and the relative degrees of priority between programmes expressed in the guidelines. In the revival negotiations, emphasis was given to particular projects and items which had electoral appeal, such as social welfare and educational programmes. For example, in the revival negotiations of FY1995, an 'additional' 31.5 billion was allocated to social welfare, and the so-called Gold Plan for the welfare of the elderly, and further subsidies were made available for private educational institutions. While MOF was normally able to agree and predetermine with the Spending Ministries the distribution of the margin before the revival negotiations began, it occasionally happened that political pressure for a project proved irresistible, despite its opposition. That occurred on several occasions with the financing of extensions to the Shinkansen railway lines, which were a powerful totem of political pressure: tangible, highly visible, geographic, hi-tech, and prestigious. The combination of pressures from local politicians, national LDP influentials, and MOT and its interest groups sometimes overwhelmed MOF's traditional scepticism about the cost-effectiveness of many such proposals. More rarely, a real 'recovery' of an expenditure occurred which was not predetermined. One budget examiner with responsibility for health and welfare cited an example of pensions for the families of injured and handicapped war veterans, where a 'real open negotiation' took place with the LDP, whose special committee had representatives of four interest groups (Watanabe 1994).

At the conclusion of the revival negotiations, normally towards the end of December, the Cabinet formally approved the revised draft of MOF's budget, and MOF and the Spending Ministries prepared the formal budget documents for presentation to the Diet, normally towards the end of January. The minister of finance formally introduced the Budget in speeches to each House, after which the Budget Committee of the House of Representatives began its examination. The director-general from the Budget Bureau attended most sessions, flanked by the two budget examiners from the Coordination Division, one with responsibility for the frame of the whole budget, the other for the contents of programmes, and the distribution between the Spending Ministries and Agencies. The details and specific information on parts of the Budget were provided by DBEs who attended as appropriate; BEs from the line divisions did not normally do so. The Budget Committee reported to the House, and after approval in plenary session, the Budget passed to the House of Councillors, where a similar process was followed. Either House could formally amend the Budget, but in practice that had not occurred since 1956. But from time to time the government was obliged to offer or negotiate amendments to overcome opposition parties' obstruction of the passage of the bill procedurally, examples of which were given in Chapter 3. The House of Councillors was required to approve the draft budget within 30 days after transmission, failing which it was automatically given legal effect. Within that period, differences between the two Houses were discussed by a joint committee. The decision of the Lower House prevailed in the event of disagreement.

18

Rules-of-the-Game: Managing Relations with the Spending Ministries

What rules-of-the-game governed MOF's relationships with the Spending Ministries and Agencies? What norms of behaviour guided Budget Bureau officials in their interactions with opposite numbers? First, there were the general bureaucratic norms or universal principles that guided bureaucratic conduct, embedded historically in the institution of bureaucracy. Inoguchi (1997) and Ooms (1985) argue that those norms that characterize the modern Japanese state were grounded in Tokugawa ideology, for example the emphasis on discipline, diligence, and devotion to the ideal of public service; the 'propensity for inclusionary aggregation of societal institutions and interests'; and, a concern with the individual needs and conditions of 'locality'.

Secondly, within the general contours described by such norms were those that distinguished the behaviour of MOF officials from those in other ministries and agencies, the distinctive habits and customs of work, and standard operating procedures. They were partly institutionalized in the formal and informal structures of the ministry established to enable it to perform its distinctive functions and to fulfil its 'mission'. They were also partly socio-cultural—the embedded collective identity of the ministry inculcated and nurtured by socialization in the 'MOF-family': tradition, work experience, training, secondment and postings, and peer pressure. For example, while the rotation of officials was a general bureaucratic characteristic, intended to expose the generalist administrator to a variety of different experiences, to broaden his knowledge and understanding (and to avoid the risk of 'capture' and corruption), in MOF it was also linked to a set of unwritten rules which precisely determined promotion and career development, discussed in Chapter 9.

Thirdly, within the contours of those ministry norms, and the more universal bureaucratic ones, were the specific norms of behaviour, which guided and regulated the conduct of officials in the Budget Bureau compared with their colleagues in, say, the Tax Bureau or (until 1998) the Banking Bureau and Securities Bureau. Again, they derived from both formal and informal institutional structures (for example the leading role of the Coordination Division, and its links to the Minister's Secretariat through the roles played by the deputy vice-minister for overall policy coordination and the two special officers for planning); from the spending control function, and how it was defined and revised over time; and, from the socio-culture of life in the Budget Bureau divisions.

Budget examiners and deputy budget examiners were essentially reactive. It was for Spending Ministries and Agencies to propose expenditure; the Budget Bureau's task was to save money. 'If DBEs are not unpopular, then we are not doing our job' (Sumi 1994). Other key norms of behaviour were scepticism, detachment, and informed criticism. Detachment was institutionalized in the structures of the Budget Bureau, and in MOF as a whole. Frequent movement between posts was partly intended to minimize the risk of a DBE or BE becoming too sympathetic to the aims of a Spending Department and being 'captured' by it, as for example happened in the 1990s in the professional relationships between some senior officials in the Banking and Securities Bureaux and private banks and securities firms. The dilemma for the deputy budget examiner was that:

In order to cut, he must get close to the ministry; he must know the detail. But the closer he gets, the more he knows, the greater the risk that he is unable to act because he empathises with the aims and needs of the Ministry's programme, and has a better understanding and appreciation of what it was trying to do and why. (Sumi 1997)

Budget officials were not equipped by qualification or training to match the specialist knowledge and expertise of the Spending Ministries they shadowed, or to challenge their professional and technical competence. The norm of critical inquiry required skills, expertise, and professional judgement that were different from those of the Spending Ministry's officials, but they were neither technically superior nor a substitute. The DBE had to be sufficiently informed to probe and pick away at the case put up to him; he had to know enough to ask the right questions, and to ask for relevant kinds of information. He was however dependent upon the Spending Ministry for most of the specialist and technical information, and had no comparable, independent source of his own to match it. Part of his skill was the acquisition of other kinds of information by exploiting the resources of networks within MOF, and between different parts of it and outside groups such as the LDP, the Diet, and the media. These provided him with essential background, helped to 'contextualize' specific expenditure issues that arose in the hearings and examination, improved his understanding of the relevant issues, and perhaps helped him to develop an alternative point of view.

Those and other norms that guided the behaviour of Budget Bureau officials were for the most part unwritten but well understood, if not always scrupulously observed in practice. They can be inferred from observable behaviour, and from what officials in the Budget Bureau and Spending Ministries said and did. There were also some other kinds of evidence. A list of 'ten commandments' for DBEs, drafted many years ago, was still in circulation in the Budget Bureau in the 1990s. It comprised a series of written exhortations, cast in the imperative mode, addressed to some aspects of behaviour that were often the cause of common complaint among Spending Ministries, and in the Budget Bureau itself. Some of those, of course, had a wider application, characteristic of bureaucratic behaviour generally. Each commandment was addressed to a dysfunctional behavioural trait, the obverse of a prescribed idealized behavioural norm. For example, the commandment 'don't be soft' was to avoid the risk of 'capture' by a Spending Ministry; the prescribed idealized behavioural norm was scepticism: 'what are they really after?' Table 18.1 lists the commandments and idealized behavioural norms. The derived dysfunctional behaviour to which they were addressed is shown in the third column.

Table 18.1 *The behavioural norms of Budget Bureau officials (Yosan Tantosha Shitsumu Jukkai)*

'Commandment'	Behavioural norm	Dysfunctional behaviour
1. Don't be arrogant (*Ibaccha ikenai*)	Respect for the other's status and responsibility (*Aite wa posuto ni keirei da kokoro shiyō*)	Arrogance
2. Don't get angry (*Okoccha ikenai*)	Understanding of the other's position and argument (*Aite no tachiba o rikai shiyō*)	Intolerance
3. Don't be soft (*Amaku naccha ikenai*)	Scepticism: what are they really after? (*Aite no yokyu o mikiwameyō*)	Giving in too easily; 'capture'
4. Listen to them even if you are opposed to their ideas (*Ue o muicha ikenai*)	Open-mindedness (*Aite o settoku shiyō*)	Overbearing; closed mind
5. Don't be too demanding (*Tsuraku naccha ikenai*)	Logical assessment (*Satei wa suji o tōsō*)	Over-zealousness
6. Don't round the numbers (*Maruku irecha ikenai*)	Factual and statistical accuracy (*Satei wa tumiageyō*)	Carelessness
7. Don't decide on your own (*Dokudan senkō shicha ikenai*)	Consult with colleagues and superiors (*Yoko no rennraku, jōshi no kessai chūi shiyō*)	Independence
8. Be organized and orderly (*Rūzu ni shicha ikenai*)	Methodical (*Nenniwa nen o ire seiri shiyō*)	Disorder
9. Don't antagonize them (*Kiraware cha ikenai*)	Calm; discreet; modest (*Mi o tsutsushimō*)	Hostility; antagonism
10. Don't be behind schedule (*Osoku naccha ikenai*)	Strict compliance with the budget timetable (*Shigoto wa kijitunai, jikannai, kufū shiyō*)	Dilatoriness

Above all: be sensible; don't kill yourself.
There's nothing more important than your health
(*Kenkō daiichi, heijō no chūi kanyō*)

Source: 'The Ten Commandments', Budget Bureau, MOF, 1994.

The norms were very similar to those that characterize the behaviour of Treasury expenditure controllers in the budgetary system of the UK central government (see Thain and Wright 1995). More generally, an effective and successful deputy budget examiner had a 'sound and healthy judgement', was a persuasive and effective negotiator, and was not too negative or hostile towards spending. In some policy areas—health and welfare or pensions, for example—he needed also to be innovative with a long-term perspective, able to stimulate and contribute to the review and reform of large programmes (Horié 1993; Kormura 1993; Kubono 1993). An individual DBE could also 'add value', where he had an option, and decide to allow more spending or less (Sumi 1994).

The key to a satisfactory outcome of the budget process for both the Budget Bureau and the Spending Ministry was the relationships between the DBE and the divisional directors, and above all between the DBE (and BE) and the director of the Spending Ministry's Budget and Accounts Division. Those relationships cannot be characterized as either inquisitorial or cooperative or collaborative or adversarial: they might be any or all of those simultaneously, depending upon the nature of the issue, the priority accorded it by either side, the experience and mutual understanding of the parties, and their preferred strategies. Occasionally, as we have seen, those relationships were also confrontational or conflictual. They also varied over time, influenced by those broader political, economic, and administrative contextual factors, to which attention was drawn in previous chapters, and with the different stages of the budget processes. For example, while the preliminary probings of DBEs at the formal hearings were inquisitorial, negotiations towards the end of the process were more adversarial, as the two sides explored and bargained over their margins and bottom lines, and mobilized support among the LDP, interest group leaders, and the electorate at large.

In whatever mode the relationship was conducted—inquisitorial, negotiative, cooperative, collaborative, adversarial—there was a general disposition on both sides to seek agreement through accommodation. Each had the incentive of mutual self-interest in ensuring that relationships were, and remained, workable and effective. The two sides needed each other; they were interdependent. There were two main elements to that interdependence, the first of which was the constitutional and cultural context in which budgeting took place. Even more so than the UK, Japanese central government was a loose federation of autonomous 'states', as we have explained in previous chapters. While MOF was invested with the constitutional responsibility for coordinating the Budget, it was rarely able to impose its preferences on ministries and agencies that possessed and deployed independent and countervailing sources of authority—constitutional, statutory, and political. In practice, decisions about the allocation of resources were as much or more informed by a political as an economic or fiscal rationality. Secondly, neither MOF nor the Spending Ministries and Agencies could discharge functions or provide services statutorily imposed upon them, achieve their policy aims, and try to optimize their values without exchanging the resources of finance, information, and expertise. Their behaviour was mutually constrained; they were obliged to negotiate their discretionary room for manoeuvre.

All divisional directors and DBEs emphasized (in interviews) the need for good working relationships founded upon mutual trust, confidence in each other, openness, and honesty. Both expected each other to be *shōjiki*—honest, upright, frank, and straightforward. The establishment and maintenance of good relations were deliberately cultivated professionally, and socially 'after hours' (although the latter became more difficult in the late 1990s as MOF's 'wining and dining' scandals made officials more cautious in 'getting close' to their opposite numbers). In the small world of

Kasumigaseki, it was likely that these bureaucrats knew each other before taking up appointment, through common educational and social experience, and perhaps also through secondment and cross-ministry postings. In the mid-1990s, one director of BAD in MOFA had served previously on secondment in the Budget Bureau as a BE; another had been attached to the Securities Bureau of MOF; the director-general of the Defence Agency's Finance Bureau was on secondment from MOF where he had served as a budget examiner. Such experience was not uncommon. Where previous acquaintance was slight, arrangements were quickly made on both sides to establish close and friendly relationships in early summer, well before the hearings and negotiations began. This was especially important where the annual rotation of officials in June/July resulted in new appointments on one or both sides. An official in the Spending Ministry closely identified with the initiation of a new policy or an expenditure proposal might be replaced by someone unable or unwilling to pursue the same initiatives. DBEs and their opposite numbers worked hard to build relationships of confidence and trust, especially in the first two months of their new appointments. But there was no implied commitment on either side that that relationship would be collaborative or collusive. 'If there were good relations between the director of a Budget and Accounts Division and a deputy budget examiner, and the director convinced of the reasonableness of his argument and stance, he might be able to say "we will persuade the politicians why they can't have [the expenditure]. Leave the matter to me"' (Horié 1993).

The observance of informal policy rules-of-the-game, such as 'fair shares', 'balance' or 'equal misery', and of those prescribed more formally in the budget guidelines, and of conduct regulated by behavioural rules-of-the-game, impelled the parties to consult, discuss, argue, negotiate, and agree on outcomes, formally and informally, face-to-face. Nevertheless, frustrations and tensions would arise where, for example, the normal channels of communication were not used, or where one or other side bypassed or cut out the other. Informal ground-clearing and *nemawashi* were intended to keep both sides fully informed of each other's actions and probable reactions. The avoidance of misunderstanding, uncertainty, and unpredictable behaviour was a deeply embedded behavioural norm. Nevertheless, sometimes directors-general in Spending Ministries 'jumped the gun', taking up positions publicly, or committing the ministry without prior notification and discussion with the Budget Bureau. Tension in the relationship could also arise where the deputy budget examiner failed to discuss and persuade a disappointed director whose budget request, or a part of it, had not been given priority. Part of the DBE's task was to convince unsuccessful applicants that it was right that they had been turned down. If they were not convinced, or felt that another, worse, project or policy had been given a higher priority, then that could create tension in the relationship (Sumi 1994).

The rules-of-the-game were so drawn and observed to preclude the element of surprise, especially important in the Japanese budgetary context, where it had a different cultural connotation than in the UK budget process. In both, it represented a breakdown in the 'workable' relationships between participants, and perhaps was indicative of a lack of trust. For the UK participant 'surprised' by budgetary behaviour or outcome, it was mainly the consequences that were significant—the repercussions of such action, having to explain to a superior or a minister why he was not alerted, and picking up the pieces, limiting the damage (see Thain and Wright 1995). Such consequences might follow equally in the Japanese context, but here there was an additional crucial dimension: the social consequences of lack of trust were more serious, and were evidence of culturally aberrant behaviour. The 'surprised' participant might not be certain how to respond because the expected and appropriate social signals and cues had not been made beforehand, leaving inadequate time for him to adjust socially, to prepare the appropriate response, to behave in the appropriate social context. The aggrieved Japanese participant might be obliged to construct a different context to deal with the 'surprise' and its consequences. Ground-clearing and *nemawashi* were intended partly to avoid such situations, and face-to-face meetings, to confirm formally what had been decided, perhaps verbally and informally, to avoid future misunderstanding, and to enable those participants who were not at the core to share in the formal responsibility for the decision-making. Binding them in through a carefully constructed consensus made it more difficult for them subsequently to act in a contrary fashion.

From the perspective of the Budget Bureau, the main frustration in the relationships, according to one DBE, occurred when the Spending Ministry's Budget and Accounts Division 'mishandled the process'—for example where the DBE adopted a customary and ritualistic negative, even hostile, stance towards spending proposals, and urged still greater economy. Despite clearly signalling his willingness to continue talking and negotiating, the BAD overreacted, 'flying to the Diet' in an attempt to mobilize support for its case against that argued by the Budget Bureau (Nakagawa 1994). Such behaviour was a breach of the rules-of-the-game, whereby differences were settled whenever possible by agreement and consensus was reached through the shared values of the Kasumigaseki expenditure community. Involving politicians unilaterally, without prior agreement to do so, risked an unpredictable outcome, and damaged the relationship. As in all budgetary systems, there were a variety of stratagems, and occasional 'dirty tricks', to which all Spending Ministries resorted from time to time. 'Trying it on' was normal and expected behaviour, although the Budget Bureau kept an unofficial 'black list' of those policy divisions and directors who did so, for example by soliciting political support and bringing it to bear up the hierarchy without prior consultation (Hayashi 1993). 'Bouncing' the Budget Bureau into a decision contrary to an informal understanding, or without due warning and exhausting procedures through the normal channels, was a serious breach of the rules-of-the-game. 'We were raped', says the frustrated DBE. Relationships often became more tense towards the end of the process, when the press of events and the shortage of time led to a short-circuiting of the usual channels of communication. 'I have not been informed' would be a common complaint among participants at that time.

19

Making the FILP Budget

THE FILP POLICY COMMUNITY

The community of organizations whose members contributed to the processes of making and carrying out the FILP Budget was extensive. Its membership, drawn from a wide variety of statutory and non-statutory organizations and groups, was broadly of two kinds, distinguished by the concentration of resources of authority, information, and organizational expertize, and the regularity of interaction. Those (parts of) organizations, and groups within them, that interacted on a regular and routine basis in the processes of making and/or carrying out of FILP policy had 'insider' status. 'Outsiders' had some contact irregularly with other members of the policy community, over some policy issues or problems, but their interactions tended to be formal or ad hoc and non-routinized (Thain and Wright 1995).

Figure 19.1 shows the membership of the FILP policy community before the reforms of 2000–1. Insider organizations and groups were of two broad types: statutory and non-statutory. Statutory groups with a direct responsibility for making FILP policy included pre-eminently MOF's Financial and Budget Bureaus, MPT's Postal Savings Bureau, and MHW's Pensions Bureau, together with the FILP agencies, and their sponsoring ministries and agencies. Statutory organizations and groups primarily responsible for carrying out FILP policy included those FILP agencies—the 11 public banks and finance corporations, and the 50 or so eligible public corporations and special companies—and local governments and local public enterprises.

Non-statutory groups with insider status included pre-eminently the LDP's top leadership; PARC and its relevant divisions, research committees, and study groups; the LDP's postal *zoku*; city and regional banks and their representative associations; local postmasters and the Association of Commissioned Postmasters; and some private sector contractors and clients and their representative associations. Outsider groups included those whose role or function in the policy processes was mainly formal, for example the legitimation of policy-making through formal meetings of the Cabinet and the Fund Operation Council that advised it, or plenary sessions of the Diet; the formal function of scrutinizing draft budget legislation performed by the Budget and Standing Committees of each House; the supervision and inspection of the Board of Audit; and the formal advice and recommendations of advisory councils and ad hoc committees. Outsider groups also included some international organizations and groups, for example the US federal government and its agencies, G7, IMF, and the World Bank.

FILP Budget-making

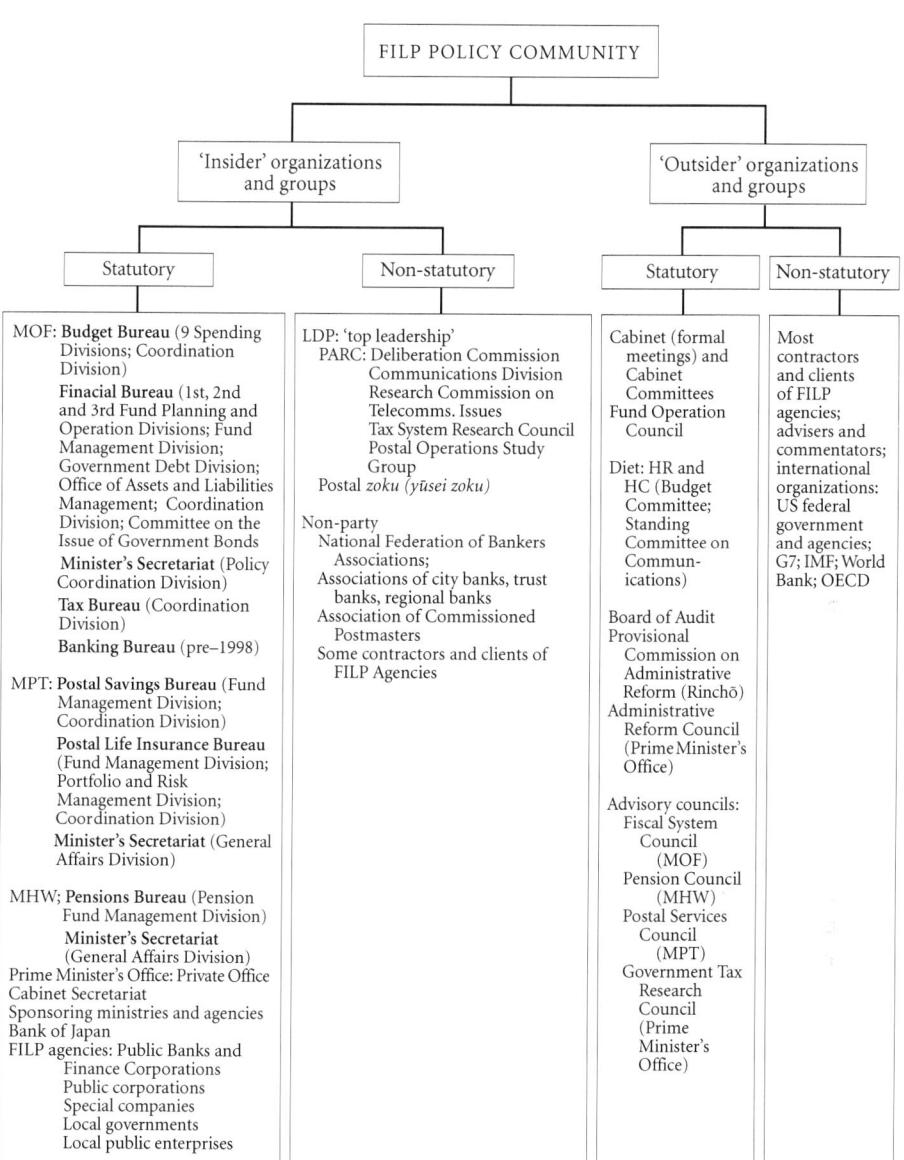

Figure 19.1 *FILP policy community, 1975–2000*

There were three main issues to be determined by interaction among the members of mainly insider organizations and groups of the policy community in the making and carrying out of the FILP Budget in the period 1975–2000. The first of those was the size of the FILP Budget. That decision was taken within the broader context of the government's macroeconomic strategy, and its short- and medium-term fiscal objectives, and was inextricably linked with the decision on the size of the General Account Budget, the size and financing of the deficit, and servicing the debt. The processes of formulation were initially begun in different bureaux of MOF. The Financial Bureau took the lead on FILP, the Budget Bureau on the General Account.

The second set of issues had to do with the raising, sourcing, and costs of funds to finance the planned FILP Budget. Logically prior to the decision about the size of the planned budget, in practice, the availability of postal, pension, and other funds, and the prescription of interest rates for their use, was only one of several determining factors. The third set of issues concerned the functional composition of the investment and loan programme, and its allocation to FILP agencies, Special Accounts, local authorities, and the General Account Budget. In practice, the three sets of issues were interconnected, elements of a continuous, iterative process; here each is dealt with separately. But first we begin with a brief analysis of the politics of the accumulation and deployment of postal savings and pension deposits. This both illustrates the interactions among the members of the organizations of the policy community, and provides the background to the events leading up to the changes in the FILP system initiated in 1997 and implemented in April 2001, among which was the severing of the historic statutory link between postal savings, pension deposits, and FILP.

THE POLITICS OF POSTAL SAVINGS

The postal savings system was from its inception in 1875 characterized by a high degree of political sensitivity. The amount and significance of household savings in the Japanese political economy, the diffusion of the collection, and the investment potential of the accumulated deposits ensured that the issues of regulation and control were fiercely contested within the bureaucracy. The historical privileged status enjoyed by postal savings deposits, insulated from competitive banking services, jealously protected by savers and small investors, by local postmasters, and by constituency Dietmen, and (for most of the second-half of the twentieth century) opposed by the banking community, added to that salience. The political history of the postal savings system throughout the twentieth century was characterized by periodic jurisdictional struggles, between MPT (and its forebears) on the one hand and MOF on the other, over the control of the use of the accumulated deposits available for investment; the interest rates paid depositors, and the terms and conditions of various kinds of deposits; and the tax status of the income earned on those deposits. Jurisdictional conflict was exacerbated by the expansion of the FILP Budget from the 1970s onwards, partly to relieve pressure on the General Account Budget, at a time when interest rate differentials between the public and private sector were narrowing with the liberalization of financial markets, and the deregulation of long-term deposit rates.

The politics of the management and control of postal savings during the last quarter of the twentieth century was both complex and sensitive. The welfare objectives of encouraging domestic savings with high and guaranteed returns for small savers in a secure national system of postal (and pension) savings protected by MPT (and MHW), and supported by LDP Dietmen, became increasingly difficult to reconcile with MOF's developmental objectives of providing government credit at preferential rates for capital investment and for public works projects, financed through FILP, heavily dependent upon those savings. Failure to resolve the tension led to the increasing politicization of the issue, with adjudication and temporary settlements achieved through the intervention of the LDP.

The identity of interest which historically brought some of the members of the FILP policy community together in a network focused on the issue of the raising of FILP funds was the preservation through the postal savings system of a means to accumulate the savings of small investors, and to use them to promote national development goals. While members differed on the methods to be used to attract and reward depositors (and, increasingly, on the uses of their deposits to maximize returns on investments), they agreed broadly on the desirability of continuing to do so. That core value held the network together until the mid-1990s. The principal agenda of issues with which it dealt was concerned with policies to encourage the continued growth of deposits. The underlying issue was the extent to which depositors should be privileged compared with investors in other financial products and institutions. Here the values and objectives of the members of the network differed. Their mutual interdependence within the network, exchanging resources of authority, information, finance and expertize, ensured that their discretionary room for manoeuvre on each issue was mutually constrained, and had to be negotiated.

Historically, the policy issue of FILP fund-raising centred on control of the rate of interest paid on postal saving deposits, and the privileged tax status enjoyed by depositors. The main protagonists were MOF and MPT, although from the mid-1970s the LDP became a major player in the regulation of the relationships between them and other members of the policy network. MHW was also involved as the ministry responsible for pensions and welfare insurance, and for control of the Pension Welfare Services Public Corporation, a conduit for the investment of funds in the Special Accounts for Welfare and National Insurance, and the Social Welfare and Medical Service Corporation, both substantial beneficiaries of Trust Fund Bureau Fund. MOF's responsibility for economic, financial, and fiscal policies pulled it in different but sometimes overlapping directions. Organizationally, the objectives of its different bureaux, and their different constituencies, dictated different attitudes and policy responses to the issue. Responsibility for macroeconomic policy meant, for example, that it gave high priority to the problems presented by the continuing large current account surplus, a contributory factor of which was the high level of domestic savings. Encouragement of continued savings through the postal system was partly at the expense of domestic consumption of home-produced and imported goods. Simultaneously, responsibility for financial policy also pushed it towards a preference for a unitary structure of interest rates and for the abolition of preferential rates for postal savings, which acquired additional salience after the deregulation of financial markets and services. As the supervisor and regulator of the banking system until 1998, MOF's Banking Bureau was pressed by its constituents to remove the competitive disadvantages of commercial banks. The International Financial Bureau shared the interest in deregulated interest rates, from the perspective of its constituents of foreign governments and international organizations pressing for the liberalization of Japanese financial markets. The Financial Bureau's responsibility for the raising of FILP funds pulled it in the opposite direction: it was concerned to see that its main source, the Trust Fund Bureau Fund dependent upon postal savings, accumulated adequate funds and revenues year by year. MOF's Tax Bureau also had an interest—in the raising of revenue through existing taxes, in the elimination (before 1987) of tax evasion through illegal but widespread multiple deposit accounts in the postal savings system, and in the discussion of proposals for new taxes to alleviate the pressures of increasing public spending and debt in the General Account Budget.

MPT was less cross-pressured organizationally than MOF. It managed and controlled the postal savings system, and aimed to maintain its attractiveness to small investors by maintaining favourable differential interest rates, and by offering terms and conditions on deposits not available elsewhere. The main source of funds from 1941 was ten-year savings certificates, which attracted fixed interest calculated every six months, redeemable six months after the initial deposit. Investors could also exercise a cancellation option, allowing them to move into and out of postal savings as interest rates fluctuated, an option too expensive for most private-sector financial institutions to offer. In addition, the size and significance of the accumulated deposits was a source of political influence and power for the MPT. With the expansion of local post offices under a former minister, Tanaka Kakuei, the appointment of local postmasters provided a means of influence and potential control of an electoral machine in 24,000 localities, which gave the ministry bargaining power within the LDP. With the growing importance of telecommunications, and the size of its capital investment programmes, the expansion of the postal business contributed to the ministry's claim to be a front-rank policy ministry. In its control and protection of the postal savings system, it enjoyed the support of the Association of Commissioned Postmasters, and from time to time, depending upon the issue, that of formal and informal groups in the LDP, PARC, and the Postal Affairs *zoku* (which with a potential membership of over 300 made it the second largest up to 1993), and of small investors who could be mobilized to bring pressure on LDP Dietmen.

MPT and its predecessors repeatedly and successfully resisted attempts by MOF to take over responsibility for the control of postal savings and the determination of interest rates. The two ministries were obliged to negotiate and achieve an accommodation of their different values and objectives. With the growing strength of MPT in the 1970s following the Tanaka initiative, and the increasing importance of telecommunications, MOF found it more difficult to influence the flow of postal savings into the Trust Fund Bureau Fund, and to resist MPT's demands for greater autonomy in the investment of those savings more profitably elsewhere. The tax-free status of interest income earned on postal savings deposits, and the use of multiple tax-free savings accounts to evade the tax to which it gave rise, became major policy issues within the policy network, issues that MPT had fought successfully to keep off the agenda through the 1970s.

Conflict between MPT and MOF intensified as the latter sought to remove those privileges. There were two kinds of pressure: first, MOF (the Budget Bureau and the Tax Bureau) was looking to raise additional revenue through the control of both tax evasion and tax exemption, as part of its broader fiscal strategy to reconstruct national finances to reduce the deficit on the General Account Budget and the issue of government bonds to cover it, and to lower both the bond dependency ratio and the GDP–debt ratio. Its failure to raise additional revenue through the introduction of a consumption tax in the early 1980s made it keener still to remove the tax privileges of postal savings depositors. Secondly, MOF's Banking Bureau was under pressure from city, trust, and regional banks, whose activities it then supervised and regulated, to remove 'unfair' competition in the market for the business of small and medium-sized businesses, and small investors. Preferential rates of interest on some kinds of deposits, and the special terms and conditions offered, favoured those small investors in the postal savings system. Preferential rates of interest charged on loans to small businesses by the FILP agencies disadvantaged private-sector financial institutions. As financial services were deregulated, demands for their removal became more insistent. A further source of pressure was the desirability of a unitary structure of interest rates in managing the Japanese economy, an aim of both the Budget Bureau and the International Financial Bureau.

The conflict broadened as MOF sought to wrest control of postal savings from MPT. The latter's growing political power and influence, and its skilful orchestration of the campaigning of local LDP politicians, postmasters, and small savers, enabled it to successfully defend its jurisdictional control of the accumulation and management of postal savings. While the 1988 Tax Act removed much but not all of the privileged status of postal savings deposits, MPT's *quid pro quo* was MOF's concession of an element of independence in the investment of postal savings. However, the size of the discretionary investment was not large enough to constrain the revenues available to the Trust Fund Bureau Fund, and hence the financing of MOF's investment programmes through the FILP Budget. Moreover, MOF insisted that half of MPT's annual discretionary investment had to be used for the purchase of government bonds, to help finance the deficit on the General Account Budget.

The politicization of the dispute between the two ministries became an issue in its own right, as LDP Dietmen exploited the potential of posts and telecommunications business to promote and protect their own electoral interests through local personal networks. In turn, conflict over the collection and management of postal savings became part of the wider jurisdictional dispute over telecommunications policy preceding and following the sale of NTT shares, and the regulation of telecommunications business which precipitated the 'telecom wars' of the 1980s over the privatization of NTT, VANs, and several other policy issues, fought principally between MPT and MITI, but with MOF closely allied to the latter (Johnson 1989). The conflict took a different turn with the appointment of Koizumi Junichirō as minister of post and telecommunications in the Murayama Coalition government in 1994. Echoing the criticisms of many radical analysts, he called for the privatization of postal savings. At the same time, with the envisaged reduction in pension funds as the number of elderly beneficiaries in the population increased, MHW was anxious to increase capital values through more profitable investment in the market. The reform of FILP became inevitable, a part of the broader administrative changes initiated by the Hashimoto government in 1997. The historic statutory link between FILP and postal savings and pension funds was broken. The origins and implications of that and other changes to the FILP sytem are discussed in Chapter 28. The interaction among members of the policy community in the making and carrying out of the FILP Budget is examined next.

DETERMINING THE SIZE OF THE FILP BUDGET

The Trust Fund Bureau Fund

In determining the size of the FILP Budget, both top-down macroeconomic considerations and bottom-up pressures were in theory constrained by the amount of funds available for investment. A prudential judgement was made by the First Fund Division of the Financial Bureau, dependent partly upon the amount of new deposits in the postal savings system and other funds, partly upon the annual cash flow generated by the income from interest payments and the redemption of past loans to the FILP agencies, but principally by the need for 'sound management' of the Trust Fund Bureau Fund.

Recommendations about the amount to be made available for the Fund, and the contributions to it of postal savings, pensions, and other minor sources, were made to the Fund Operation Council, a statutory advisory council attached to the Prime Minister's Office. The Council was formally responsible for the unified management of those funds, and for advising the Cabinet on major decisions of policy governing their use, within the legal requirements of the Trust Fund Bureau Fund Law. Its membership was regulated by tacit agreement on rules-of-the-game which provided for 'representatives' of MOF, MPT, MHW, and local government (Yonezawa 1995). In the 1990s there were in addition an ex-official of the Bank of Japan, the chairman of the Federation of Banks' Associations, three senior academics, and an analyst from the *Japan Economic Journal*. The Secretariat was provided by the Financial Bureau's First Fund Division. The Council made recommendations to Cabinet on the amount of TFB funds to be made available to finance the FILP Budget, advised on the appropriate deposit rate for fund investments (the same rate of interest it paid to the various savings funds for its loans), and (after 1987) managed the TFB Fund investment portfolio. It received annual reports from MOF, MPT, and MHW on the operations of the funds that each managed.

The initiative on most decisions lay with the First Fund Division of the Financial Bureau, which undertook necessary research and analysis. The potentially contentious issue of the prescription of the TFBF deposit rate was normally negotiated and agreed informally between its senior officials and those from fund management divisions in MPT and MHW before the formal meeting of the Council; a joint recommendation was brought to it by the secretariat. A former director of the First Fund Division recalled only one occasion when the ministries failed to resolve their differences prior to the Council meeting, and agreed to allow it to decide; thereafter, they took care to avoid a repetition of what proved to be a thoroughly disagreeable occasion (Yonezawa

FILP Budget-making

1995). In a like manner, the three ministries consulted and agreed on the use of the funds for which each had responsibility, which collectively comprised the agreed TFB Fund total. The Council's recommendation to Cabinet on the size of this total to finance the FILP Budget was made towards the end of December, after the conclusion of the negotiations between the Financial Bureau and the FILP agencies on their allocations, and the projects and programmes to be funded by them. At about the same time, decisions were made on the amount of central government borrowing needed to finance the deficit on the General Account Budget, and the proportions to be financed by the Trust Fund Bureau Fund and the market, decisions that again involved the First Fund Division, which provided advice to the Committee on the Issue of Government Bonds, which formally decided.

With the deregulation of interest rates in 1987 and 1993, which linked postal savings deposit rates and the Trust Fund Bureau Fund rate more closely to market rates, it became increasingly difficult for MOF to ensure an adequate supply of funds for the TFB Fund at a cost that could be recovered by charges for investments and loans made by the FILP agencies. The management of assets and liabilities, and the financing of risk, became major issues. Their implications for the continued viability of the FILP system are discussed in Chapter 28.

The principal participants in the processes of deciding the size of the FILP Budget were formally the prime minister and Cabinet, which had to approve recommendations about the size and composition of FILP funds from the Fund Operation Council; the Budget Bureau, whose recommendations to Cabinet for the size and allocation of the General Account Budget were made in the context of the general strategy for the economy in both the short and medium term, which necessarily included consideration of the need and desirability for a particular FILP aggregate, and the implications for the economy of the capital investment programmes financed there and in the General Account Budget; the Finance Bureau, which managed the TFB Fund and negotiated the allocation of the FILP funds with the FILP agencies; their sponsor ministries and agencies; and MPT and MHW, which controlled the postal savings and pension funds.

The FILP Budget was the direct responsibility of the Financial Bureau, 'the third floor', in the Ministry of Finance. It took the lead, although the Budget Bureau was closely involved in all stages of its formulation. Three divisions, supervised by a deputy director-general, handled all the FILP business: the First and Second Fund Planning and Operations divisions, and the Local Fund Operations Division. A Fund Management Division was responsible for the management of the flow of funds into and out of the Special Account for the Trust Fund Bureau Fund. The First Fund Planning and Operations Division, with a staff (in 1998) of 49, supervised and coordinated the work of compiling FILP undertaken in the other two divisions, and was responsible for consulting and negotiating with the Budget Bureau to ensure that the two budgets were integrated and consistent with overall policy objectives. The division set the framework within which the FILP business was conducted by the other two divisions, and provided general direction for them within the government's prescribed macroeconomic policy. An Office of Asset and Liability Management was set up within the First Fund Division in the mid-1990s, reflecting the growing importance attached to that function in the TFB Fund Special Account, and in the financial management practised by each of the FILP agencies.

The size of the FILP Budget depended upon a number of related factors. First, FILP was an integral part of the government's macroeconomic strategy to achieve national economic and social goals. In conjunction with the General Account Budget, it was also an instrument to implement policies to achieve short- and medium-term fiscal objectives, and of countercyclical fiscal and monetary policy. The aggregate for each budget was set concurrently and interdependently within that broad politico-economic context, influenced by similar factors: the current and projected levels of economic activity; and the government's strategy and policies to implement the economic and social policies set out in the Five-Year National Economic Plan, for example that for 1992–7, designed to enhance living standards by creating and improving social overhead capital, and that for 1996–2000, which emphasized the structural reform of the economy.

The size and composition of the FILP Budget, and the emergency fiscal packages partly funded through in-year revisions to it, conveyed signals to the outside world. Its determination and timing had therefore to take into account the response that the government thought politically expedient and fiscally appropriate to the prevailing international economic and financial climate, and to specific pressures from foreign governments and international financial organizations. As well, the size of FILP was influenced by specific international commitments, such as that of the Structural Impediments Initiative, and the Basic Plan for Public Investment, which subsequently committed the government to public investment of 430 trillion over the ten-year period 1991–2000, increased in 1994 to 630 trillion for 1995–2004.

Secondly, the size of the FILP Budget was strongly influenced by MOF's judgement of the size of the total capital spending programme envisaged for the public sector as a whole, in which consideration had to be given to the economic impact of the combined total of proposed public-sector and probable private-sector capital investment, some of which, it was hoped, would be induced by the former. Here the demand for capital and the capacity of the labour market and of the construction and plant capacity industries were material factors. The effect on both prices and wages was also taken into account.

A third factor was the need to provide for the priorities and preferences of the LDP, and to respond to backbench pressures for more public spending in general, and for public works projects and programmes in particular. Here again, consideration alongside the General Account Budget was inseparable, but, given the political salience and visibility of some kinds of public investment—especially public works—the amount, timing, and geo-electoral location of the projects financed by FILP funds were crucial decisions.

Fourthly, although Finance Bureau officials formally emphasized that the size and composition of the FILP Budget were determined by the number of viable projects brought forward each year by the FILP agencies, this was only one of several factors. 'Bottom-up' pressures and demands for FILP funds were iterated in a continuous process with the evolving 'top-down' macroeconomic and political strategic limits for both FILP and the General Account Budget. While the criterion of profitability that ostensibly governed the allocation of funds to those agencies was in principle a constraint on the number of projects nominated by them, and was supported by their sponsoring ministries and agencies as likely to generate sufficient future revenue to repay the interest on loans and the principal, the criteria for determining profitability—how much and over what period of time—were not disclosed. Most loans, and hence repayment periods, were long-term, many for 35 years or more, and the assessment of potential profitability over such a long lead time was in practice a matter more of subjective judgement than of objective analysis (discussed in Chapter 28). Where the government's objective was to stimulate the level of economic activity in times of recession, the criteria employed to justify the allocation of some FILP funds were more relaxed still, for example extending the maturity of the loan, sometimes several times over as happened with some projects.

'There are no bad debts', the director of the First Fund Division explained (First Fund Division 1993). Technically, that was the case, for if losses occurred the sponsoring ministry was formally responsible for covering them via repayments through the General Account Budget. The reality was that several FILP agencies, and a larger number of projects financed by them, had large, recurring, and accumulating debts. Japan National Railways, for many years financed through FILP, had its loan periods extended several times, and its losses on revenue subsidized by payments from the General Account Budget to FILP. After privatization, the huge accumulated debt was subsidized by annual payments from FILP into a Special Account for Debt Settlement until 1998. As will be shown in Chapter 28, the criterion of profitability was increasingly relaxed to allow more investment in several other unprofitable social capital projects. In theory, the amount of money available through the Trust Fund Bureau Fund and related resources could constrain the size of the FILP Budget, but together, the accumulating reserves, interest payments on outstanding loans, redemptions, and fresh deposits in the postal and pension funds were more than adequate to continue the funding of FILP at levels comparable to historic rates of growth throughout the period 1975–98. Indeed, until 1999 the revenues available to the TFB Fund, and other sources of FILP finance, normally exceeded the total of planned FILP Budget expenditures. Foreshadowing the implementation of the decision taken in 1997 to end the statutory link between postal savings and pension funds in 2000, the revenues from both sources were scaled down in the planned budget for FY1999.

It is evident from the analysis of the historical trend of FILP Budgets in Chapter 24 that there was a general presumption that FILP would grow each year incrementally, and would absorb a predictable and stable share of estimated GDP growth. In deciding the total of the FILP Budget, therefore, the current estimate of GDP, and FILP's historic share, were major considerations. While subsequently the initial FILP Budget total was normally revised several times during the course of the fiscal year, generally upwards, this occurred less because of the demand for additional funds from the FILP agencies—although this did happen towards the end of the year, when some had exhausted their initial allocation—and more often because of MOF's response to changed or changing economic circumstances, for example providing a further fiscal stimulus by increasing capital spending, as happened on numerous occasions in the 1990s.

THE PROCESS OF ALLOCATION

The allocation of the funds to the FILP agencies was the responsibility of the Second Fund Planning and Operations Division of MOF's Financial Bureau. Five deputy directors worked under its director; two other deputy directors engaged on allocation were, for historical reasons, attached to the First Fund Division. The work was divided between the seven deputies on lines corresponding to those in the Budget Bureau divisions, by ministry and agency, and they worked closely on a day-by-day basis with their opposite numbers, the deputy budget examiners. In approving projects, the deputy directors of the Second Fund Division worked generally within the framework of the FILP Budget drawn up by the First Fund Division, reflecting the priorities determined by the government, some of which were made explicit in the five-year National Economic Plan, others of which were indicated more generally both there and in the annual *Economic Outlook*, and by the preferences of the LDP leadership and Dietmen, articulated formally through PARC and its divisions. MOF's close control of the 11 public banks and finance corporations ensured that their lending strategies, and hence their requests for funds, were consistent with government, and party, objectives and priorities. Apart from the JDB and the Export–Import (EXIM) Bank, all of them had prescribed and limited policy goals set by government—in practice, MOF and its co-sponsoring ministries—and every quarter had to obtain ministerial approval for their projects and funding programmes.

Senior officials in the First and Second Fund divisions claimed (in interviews) that the guidance on the allocation of the FILP Budget given to them by their deputy directorgeneral, and through him by the director of the First Fund Division, was qualitative rather than quantitative, and that explicit limits were not laid down. While it is true that the demand for funds from the FILP agencies was a factor in determining the size of the Budget and its allocation, the prior identification of priorities in both national and sectoral plans, 'visions', and policy statements was an explicit encouragement to bring forward certain kinds of capital projects. More directly, sponsoring ministries and agencies were encouraged to look for such projects to support among their FILP agencies, consistent with national objectives and agreed ministry priorities. That the Second Fund Division did more than simply react to demands is apparent from the size and composition of the allocations made. In the 1980s and 1990s the number of capital projects to improve the 'quality of life'—housing, water and sewage-disposal facilities, parks and recreational facilities—increased, while those for industrial development and road transport either increased less rapidly or declined (see Chapter 24). By whatever means—direct or indirect encouragement through the network; by tightening or relaxing the criteria for approving loans—the Financial Bureau broadly reflected the priorities of MOF and the LDP for the size, composition, and allocation of the FILP Budget.

The Third Fund Division of MOF's Financial Bureau, the Local Fund Operations Division, was responsible for the compilation of the annual Local Bond Plan, which prescribed the amount of local government loans, the main sources of finance for them, and allocations to broad policy categories, roads, water supply, sewage facilities, and so on (Local Fund Operations Division 1998). Its staff of 20 worked in close concert

FILP Budget-making

with the First and Second Fund divisions, and with their counterparts in the Budget Bureau preparing the General Account Budget and the Local Finance Plan (which prescribed the aggregate of revenue and expenditure for the whole of local government). There were formal five-year investment plans for most policy sectors (see Chapter 23 for details). Each responsible ministry or agency decided each year, in consultation with MOF and MHA, the volume of public works and public facilities to be allowed in the light of past allocations and present priorities, and the respective contributions of central government through the General Account Budget and FILP, and from local governments' own sources of revenue income and local borrowing. The allocations sector by sector were closely connected with the amount of grants and subsidies from the General Account Budget for specific schemes and projects, water, sewerage, roads, and so on.

The process of budget-making was similar to that of the General Account Budget, described in previous chapters. Budget requests were submitted to the Financial Bureau's Second Fund Division by eligible FILP agencies in August. At an earlier stage, each request would have been submitted to the appropriate sponsoring ministry or agency and discussed with it. Some were revised in the light of those discussions, others withdrawn (where the ministry withheld its support). Prior approval was not a legal requirement, but in practice all requests for FILP funds made to the Financial Bureau were approved by the sponsoring ministry or agency. As the latter had by law to approve the budget for each sponsored organization within its jurisdiction, requests for FILP funds were scrutinized along with other revenues and expenditures in bids for the General Account Budget and the Special Accounts. This process served to filter out some proposals, and led to the modification of others. Sometimes a ministry expanded or added to the FILP agency's request because of political pressure, or because it wanted to enlarge its capacity or responsibility to serve the broader objectives of the ministry. The agency might be reluctant to do so, and have to be 'persuaded' (Yonezawa 1995).

Hearings were conducted by the seven deputy directors of the Second Fund Division. Practice varied. In some there was a separate hearing for the sponsoring ministry alone, followed by that for its agency. In others, officials from both were present. Who took the lead depended on the status and strength of the agency. The most powerful, like the JDB or EXIM, took the lead, with the sponsoring ministry playing a supporting role. Conversely, the weaker agencies tended to be subordinate to their ministries. Most of those within the Ministry of Construction's jurisdiction were weak 'colonies of the colonial power', according to one former director of the First Fund Division (Yonezawa 1995). The procedure was very similar to that of the Budget Bureau hearings described in Chapter 17, and took place also in September. Examination and negotiation by the deputy directors followed in October and November. At that time there was close contact at all levels with 'opposite numbers' in the Budget Bureau. Information, analysis, and background were exchanged as both budgets began to take shape. Deputy directors of the Fund divisions stayed particularly close to the DBEs in the Budget Bureau. In negotiations between them to cut, amend, or approve requests, each was guided by the mandate from his respective formal bureau meeting and, as issues arose, by guidance and advice from ad hoc meetings with senior colleagues. Large projects, or those that caused some technical or political difficulty, were handled by the director of the First Fund Division, or the deputy director-general of the Financial Bureau. Where there was a serious conflict of interest between it and the Budget Bureau, an issue might rise up the hierarchy and be dealt with at the director-general level. This was most likely to occur where there was a change in the structure or substance of a policy, or where such a change was consequential on agreement to a bid. For example, the Financial Bureau and the Budget Bureau differed in their attitude towards the subsidization of FILP projects and programmes in the 1990s. The former took a much stricter, more principled view, reluctant to allow subsidies for road construction projects, for example. Generally, it disliked subsidies or loans to Special Accounts because once agreed they were difficult to end and recoup, as happened with those for forests, national hospitals, and national universities and schools. The Budget Bureau, with its broader responsibility for managing the whole economy, and for devising an overall fiscal strategy to achieve national objectives, was more pragmatic and flexible in its approach. Where a serious difference of opinion led to an impasse, the views of the director-general of the Budget Bureau ultimately prevailed because of his seniority and status: the Financial Bureau was obliged to give way.

Although the costs of the aggregate of bids submitted by the FILP agencies normally exceeded the provisional parameters of the FILP Budget, the financing of those approved was largely a contingent issue. Projects and programmes of which the Financial and Budget Bureaux approved because of their relevance to declared national (and party) policies, for example housing, welfare, or the environment, could be financed in a variety of ways. FILP funds could and were used increasingly with subsidies from the General Account to finance jointly projects that could not earn profits to cover the full costs of FILP loans. The most significant example in the 1990s was that of the Government Housing Loan Corporation, which lent money to prospective house purchasers at rates of interest below the rate at which it borrowed from the Trust Fund Bureau Fund. The deficit was covered by subsidies from the General Account Budget. That and other examples are discussed in Chapter 28.

Some FILP projects were financed as joint ventures, so-called 'third sector projects' involving contributions from on the one hand the FILP Budget and the General Account Budget, and on the other from private-sector financial institutions. As well, most FILP agencies could raise money on their own account in domestic or international financial markets to finance a part of their investment and loan programmes. The JDB and EXIM could do so only in international markets, while the Government Housing Loan Corporation was not allowed to do so in either. Those, and other sources, were regarded by the Financial Bureau as 'buffers', allowing it to authorize financing arrangements for viable projects of which it and the Budget Bureau approved, but for which sufficient FILP funds were unavailable or, rather, could be more effectively (and tactically) allocated to other projects. A further 'buffer' was available to the Financial Bureau through accumulated carry-forward and unspent allocations from the FILP Budget for the previous fiscal year, which enabled it to finance additional approved bids.

The FILP agencies were all charged the same interest rate for their loans and investments: that approved by the Fund Operation Council. The terms and conditions in each case were discussed and negotiated between the Second Fund Division and each agency. The contents of the policy and the location of the capital investment were critical issues. It is in that context that the issue of independent FILP funding or FILP plus General Account subsidy arose, especially on those projects and programmes that involved the creation or improvement of social overhead capital where the expectation of profit was low, long-term, or uncertain. For example, the budget examiner in the Budget Bureau might try to persuade his opposite number in the Financial Bureau to use FILP funds to co-finance a part of an existing expenditure programme charged on the General Account Budget. One budget examiner successfully persuaded his opposite number in the Financial Bureau to charge to FILP as low-interest repayable loans a proportion of the cost of financing educational scholarships, formerly a charge borne wholly upon the General Account, thus partly relieving pressure on the latter. As an example of the budget-making process, we look briefly at that in the Housing and Urban Development Corporation (HUDC) in the mid-1990s.[1] In 1999 it relinquished responsibility for the provision of public housing and housing land to the private sector, and was renamed the Urban Development Corporation.

The Budget Process in the Housing and Urban Development Corporation (HUDC)

HUDC was one of the some fifty or sixty eligible FILP agencies. It was created in 1981 from the merger of the Japan Housing Corporation (1955) and the Land Development Corporation (1975). It was responsible, with the Government Housing Loan Corporation at central level and Local Housing Supply Corporations at prefectural and municipal levels, for the implementation of the government's housing policies. It provided low-cost housing and housing sites for rent and purchase and urban infrastructure such as roads, parks, and sewage facilities, and it undertook schemes of urban renewal and development. At the end of FY1996 it had capital of 219 billion and a staff of 5,000. Its activities were financed mainly through FILP, but also through private-sector loans from life insurance companies, rentals and loan interest and repayments, and subsidies from the General Account Budget.

At the end of each year, HUDC prepared and submitted to the Ministry of Construction an annual plan of its present and proposed activities, organization, staff, and financial balances. The Ministry's approval of it provided the broad framework of revenues and expenditures flowing from past decisions, accumulated land-holdings, housing stock, and other fixed and current assets and liabilities within which the budget requests for the coming financial year were prepared. As in ministries and agencies, that process got underway in late spring with the discussion and compilation of requests in HUDC's headquarters departments and branch offices. Key roles in the discussion and negotiation of competing claims were played by its Finance Department and Planning and Coordination Department. In the preparation of their requests, heads of those departments liased with the supervisor of the Housing Department at the Ministry of Construction, to ensure that HUDC programmes and projects were

---

[1] This account is based mainly on interviews with the director-general of the Planning and Coordination Department of HUDC in March and November 1997 and March 1998.

consistent with government policy, and integrated with the Ministry's housing, urban development, and road programmes. Unlike ministerial requests for resources from the General Account Budget, there were no budget ceilings for FILP agencies, and hence no informal discussions between HUDC finance officials and those in MOF's Financial Bureau before the formal submission of the budget request at the end of August.

The first hearing was held in front of the Budget Bureau's examiners, with other MOF officials present. The director-general of HUDC's Planning and Coordination Department, accompanied by the director of the Finance Department, provided a general overview and explanation of its plans and projects, and the costs of policies to give effect to them. The budget request was examined in the broader context of MOC's programmes, and HUDC's continuing programmes of land acquisition, house-building, and rental management. The aim of the first hearing was to explain and justify what HUDC was doing, and the scale and cost of its proposed future activities.

The second-stage hearing was with Financial Bureau officials, whose Second Fund Division was responsible for the allocation of FILP funds to FILP agencies. HUDC's dependence on FILP funding, and its response to the exercise of discretionary authority by the Financial Bureau, varied with the state of the market for alternative sources of finance from private financial institutions; in the 1990s, as those became more competitive, HUDC was much less dependent on FILP funding.

The third stage was the formal agreement by MOF's Budget and Financial Bureaux to the size of HUDC's planned budget, and to the contributions from both public and private sources. In FY1997 the total planned budget was 1,398 billion, of which FILP contributed 985 billion. Subsidies from the General Account Budget totalled 248 billion, largely to enable HUDC to continue to provide low-cost rented accommodation, consistently with declared government policy.

In the allocation of its agreed budget, HUDC enjoyed a greater degree of flexibility than many other FILP agencies. For example, MOC kept the Japan Highway Public Corporation on a very short and tight rein, instructing it on what and how much to build and where. By contrast, HUDC had discretion to adjust its activities to respond flexibly to changing market conditions. For example, although there was agreement, and FILP finance, to build 5,000 housing units in FY1995, depressed market conditions led it to build only 2,200. The letting of contracts, and the allocation of funds to approved schemes and projects, was left largely to the regional branch offices.

Local Governments

The process of allocating FILP funds to local governments began with each indicating its capital needs on its own account, together with those of the local public enterprises (electricity, water, and other utilities) that it managed. Requests for capital were made to MOF's local offices. The latter then aggregated them, sector by sector, and bid to MOF's central Local Fund Operations Division. Along with other factors, the bids comprised elements in the determination of the size and composition of the Local Bond Plan and the (Budget Bureau's) Local Finance Plan. When both had been decided centrally, MOF gave each of its local offices a quota for each policy sector, such as water and housing, usually but not invariably less than the amount they had requested, after the latter had received bids from local governments. Local offices then examined those bids in detail and made allocations to each local government within the broad guidelines of the relative priority prescribed for each policy sector by the Financial Bureau. Local offices had some discretion to approve changes at the margin between policy sectors and projects within a local government's total allocation. From the mid-1990s there were fewer complaints or appeals to MOF's headquarters by local governments disappointed at the local allocation, because of the relative ease of obtaining loans elsewhere, and at much the same or even lower cost. The difference between the rates charged in the private-sector money markets and those for government funds, once 1½%–2% in the 1960s and 1970s, had all but disappeared. From 1994 the long-term prime rate was lower than the rate charged on government funds, the rate on loans through the issue of local bonds, comparable to that of the government's rate, while that charged by the Japan Finance Corporation for Municipal Enterprises (JFCME) was only 0.1% higher than the government rate (JFCME 1997*b*).

One of the 11 public banks and finance corporations within MOF's jurisdiction, the JFCME was established in 1957 to provide low-interest, long-term finance for local public enterprises. Both the scope of eligible recipients and the scale of its lending activities expanded over the following forty years. In the 1990s it also lent to regional road corporations and local development corporations established by local governments, and directly to the latter for certain general projects, such as public housing and local road construction. As a FILP agency, the JFCME bid annually to the Second Fund Division for funds from the Trust Fund Bureau Fund. It absorbed the major share of the sum allocated in the FILP Budget for central government borrowing, i.e. government-guaranteed bonds and loans. In FY1997, of the 3 trillion earmarked for that purpose, 2 trillion was allocated to guarantee the issue of bonds by JFCME to finance loans to local public enterprises, and to some projects undertaken by local governments themselves. Apart from the central government itself, it was the largest issuer of bonds. The Financial Bureau's rule-of-thumb was that JFCME's allocation was roughly equal to a quarter of the total FILP funding for the whole of local government borrowing (Local Fund Operations Division 1998). As Table 12.4 shows, it was allocated 2.2 trillion from the total of 8.6 trillion in FY1997.

CABINET AND DIET APPROVAL

The draft FILP Budget was submitted to Cabinet at the same time as the draft General Account Budget, normally in December. 'Revival negotiations' similar to those for the General Account Budget followed. Fewer issues were dealt with at that stage because the interests and preferences of LDP politicians were discussed and settled in consultation with the relevant sponsoring ministry or agency much earlier on (First Fund Division 1993, 1994). More generally, the priorities of the party were reflected or anticipated in the Budget Bureau's early estimates of the General Account Budget in May and June, and in parallel discussions at the same time on the forthcoming FILP budget-making. Because most of FILP funds were used for capital projects, the content, allocation, timing, and location were issues of great interest to constituency Dietmen, and more generally to the LDP leadership. The primary focus of their attention was not however the size of the FILP Budget or its composition. There was no special PARC division for FILP. Rather, through individual PARC divisions and research commissions their concern was with discrete policy sectors, housing, welfare, public works, and so on, and with the contents of those policies and the geo-electoral location of projects and programmes to implement them. How they were to be financed—through FILP, the General Account or Special Accounts—was of much less interest.

After approval by Cabinet, the draft FILP Budget was submitted to the Diet together with the draft General Account Budget, normally in January. The 1973 Long-Term Funds Operation Law required Diet approval for all investments and loans of more than five years financed by the Trust Fund Bureau Fund, the Postal Life Insurance Fund, and government-guaranteed bonds and borrowings. The fourth main source of FILP funds, the Industrial Investment Special Account, was provided by allocation in the General Account Budget. The Diet was not required to approve the Fiscal Investments and Loans Programme as such, but was furnished with material for reference. It comprised three tables (Zaitō-sanpyō) and supporting references: the FILP financing plan, which showed the budgetary allocations; the estimate of FILP funds required from the main sources, postal savings, pension reserves, and so on, to finance those allocations; and the functional allocation, classified by policy areas, housing, environment and so on (see Table 24.1). In practice, there was no discussion or debate of the FILP Budget, and the requisite resolutions were a formality.

Each of the 11 public banks and finance corporations submitted for the approval of the Diet its budget of revenue and expenditures, but not its funding programmes, material on which was appended for reference only. Details such as the scale of loans and the breakdown of targeted loan fields were not discussed.

IN-YEAR BUDGET REVISIONS

While the annual budget process was formally completed with the Diet's resolutions, in practice, budget-making, as for the General Account Budget, was virtually continuous. In-year revisions to the initial (planned) FILP Budget were common, especially in times of recession, when the government might have one or more Supplementary Budgets to finance additions to the General Account and provide funds for 'Emergency Economic Packages', as happened on ten occasions between 1992 and 2000. In FY1995 the initial budget for FILP was revised five times, on three occasions partly to fund additional expenditure in Supplementary Budgets and twice to provide additional 'follow-up' funding (FILP 1996); in FY1998 on four occasions, twice in June and again in November and December, adding more than 10 trillion (2% of GDP) to the planned budget. Whereas supplementary General Account Budgets had to be submitted and approved by the Diet, FILP's greater flexibility allowed increases of up to 50% of initial budgets using funds from the Trust Fund Bureau Fund, Postal Life Insurance Fund, and the government-guaranteed borrowing for public corporations and public finance corporations, without reference to the Diet.

The procedures for revision were similar to those used in dealing with the initial bids from the FILP agencies. Hearings, examinations, and negotiations between the Second Fund Division and each of the FILP agencies followed a similar pattern, but both the duration and the substance were abbreviated. The initiative was normally taken by the Financial Bureau rather than the FILP agencies in those circumstances where MOF had decided that a further increase in public investment was needed as part of a countercyclical package of measures; although, independently of that, those FILP agencies that had exhausted their allocations before the end of the year often submitted requests for additional funding.

IMPLEMENTATION

Most of the FILP Budget was allocated to the 11 public banks and finance corporations, which in turn provided finance for programmes and projects implemented by private-sector contractors and public-sector organizations. None of the 11 undertook capital development projects itself. Other FILP agencies—public corporations, local enterprises, and special companies—could do so, or could subcontract with private-sector firms. The basic terms and conditions of investments and loans made to FILP agencies, and by them to their prospective clients, were determined during the negotiations with the Second Fund Division. Normally the interest rate, and the maximum lending ratio, were prescribed for each public finance corporation, and applied subsequently to each successful applicant granted a loan from it under the same investment programme. Each FILP agency was responsible for carrying out the programme(s) agreed and funded by FILP as negotiated with the Second Fund Division. Apart from the JDB, all public finance corporations had to obtain the approval of their sponsor minister each quarter for the proposed programme of funding. JDB was not restricted, and within the limits of its budget had discretion on the selection of projects and the size of loan. However, the general outline of its planned operations was subject to annual Cabinet approval. In practice, this meant that MOF (its sponsor ministry) was able to influence its policy objectives, its overall lending strategy, and the allocation of funds to particular policy areas. Informal consultation between the JDB and MOF's Financial and Budget Bureaux ensured consistency in the implementation of the broad policy aims of both.

The process by which FILP agencies allocated FILP funds to projects was similar to that followed by private financial institutions, qualified by the need to ensure that decisions were consistent with the aims of government policy. The procedure followed by the JDB provides a brief example. After submission of an application, JDB conducted a hearing with the client to discuss the outline of the proposed project, details of the desired loan conditions, the financial status and reliability of the firm, and the size of the loan. If the request was eligible within the terms of one of the JDB programmes, the Bank had to decide whether it could and should provide financing. That decision was partly a judgement of the compatibility of the project with government policy, and partly a financial judgement about viability, risk, ability to repay, and so on. In deciding 'policy compatibility' JDB consulted with relevant ministries and agencies, who made recommendations about its suitability.

CONCLUSION

The factors that determined the size of the FILP Budget were similar to those that governed the decision-making on the General Account Budget. Indeed, both sets of decisions were taken concurrently, and the processes interlinked and iterative. Apart from the context provided by medium- and short-term macroeconomic objectives, and the fiscal strategy to achieve national economic and social goals, other determinants were the size of the 'capital budget', i.e. the amount of public capital investment and public works spending, and its division between the two budgets; prudential judgement of the availability of investment funds from the Trust Fund Bureau Fund; the number, size, and policy relevance of projects brought forward by the FILP agencies, supported by their sponsor ministries and agencies; and the priorities and preferences of the LDP. In practice, neither the availability of funds nor the number of projects constrained the growth of the FILP Budget; throughout the period 1975–2000 there was a strong presumption that the FILP Budget would continue to grow at rates consistent with those of its past absorption of GDP. The composition and distribution of the FILP Budget were similarly characterized by historic, secular trends of 'balance' among policy sectors and FILP agencies, although a longer time-horizon revealed changes in priorities, reflecting the switch in national economic and social objectives after the end of the high-growth era. Both of those issues are taken up in Chapter 24.

There was no shortage of funds to finance FILP Budgets at historic levels. The accumulated assets of the Trust Fund Bureau Fund totalled 436.0 trillion in March 1999 (FILP 1999). The annual operating balance available for investment normally exceeded the total of the planned expenditures—so much so that in 1997 MOF publicly acknowledged that the size of the FILP Budget had been driven more by the supply of funds and the need to invest the accumulated deposits than by appropriate economic and financial judgements of the need for loans and investments, and their viability (Fund Operation Council 1997). Secondly, there appeared to be no shortage of viable projects—or, more accurately, there was no lack of demand for FILP funds from FILP agencies on the preferential terms and loan conditions that were generally available up to 1993. The rate of interest charged on long-term FILP loans had been historically lower than the long-term prime rate offered by private-sector financial institutions. For example, the JDB's 'most preferred lending rate' was 2%–3% less in the 1960s, and about 1%–2% less in the 1970s. Revision of the Trust Fund Bureau Law in 1987 linked TFB Fund deposit rates and postal savings rates more closely to market rates, thereby reducing the historic preferential advantage enjoyed by FILP agencies. Towards the end of the 1980s, in fact, there was a temporary inverse relationship, with private-sector interest rates lower than those offered by the public banks and finance corporations, a trend that re-emerged in the 1990s. The threat to the privileged status of postal savings, and the continued viability of the FILP system, are issues discussed at the conclusion of Chapter 28.

20

The Role and Influence of the LDP in the Budgetary Processes

Budgets distribute benefits, and (through taxation) impose burdens differentially. Targeted on particular socio-economic classes, interest groups, and industries, the management and manipulation of budget outputs helped the LDP to maintain itself in power for 38 years until 1993 and, less certainly, after its return to the leadership and domination of the coalition governments from 1996.

OPPORTUNITIES FOR INFLUENCE

Through governmental and party organizations, the LDP had begun to play a more active and interventionist role in policy-making generally from the early 1970s. Previous chapters have explained and explored the opportunities it had to exercise influence in the budget processes during the following quarter of a century, and have assessed the contribution made by the party leadership, PARC officials, *zoku*, and rank-and-file Dietmen.

Opportunities for the LDP to influence those processes and their outputs occurred at four main stages. The first was at the time of the formulation of the overall budget strategy, and the prescription of the ceilings for the General Account and FILP Budgets. Here the party had to decide, or approve, MOF's proposed budget guidelines which determined the priority of types of expenditure—current and capital—and the allocation of new money to those programmes selected for preferential treatment. The second opportunity for influence occurred at the stage of compiling budget requests within each Spending Ministry and Agency. Here its influence was constrained by the contours of the informally agreed ministerial ceilings, and the proposed allocation to functional bureaux and their constituent divisions, derived from the application of the budget guidelines. The third opportunity for the LDP to exercise influence occurred after the submission of formal budget requests, at the successive stages of hearing, examination, negotiation, and 'revival' conducted by MOF's Budget Bureau. Finally, the LDP could seek to influence the implementation of approved budget expenditures at the point of delivery of benefits, services, investments, grants, subsidies, and so on.

This chapter draws upon the accounts in previous chapters of the LDP's role in each of those four stages to contrast its influence through the formal structures and informal processes. It argues that the influence exercised formally and directly through party and governmental structures, and particularly at the time of the 'revival' negotiations, was more apparent than real. The purpose was mainly to demonstrate publicly the party's involvement in budget-making, and its apparent influence. The reality was that formal arrangements served mainly to legitimize agreements concluded elsewhere informally through networks of politicians and bureaucrats, and indirectly and implicitly through 'knowing the LDP's mind', and through 'anticipated reactions' to the known priorities and preferences of LDP leaders, and PARC influentials.

Influencing the Size and Allocation of the General Account and FILP Budgets

Before the emergence of the fiscal crisis in the mid-1970s, the LDP was able to influence the size and allocation of the two budgets by exerting pressure on individual ministries, and their bureaux and divisions, to increase spending on particular projects and programmes as the budget process proceeded through its several stages. The size of both budgets was determined largely bottom-up, through the politics of negotiation that took place between September and mid-December, constrained top-down by what MOF thought could be afforded in the context of its macroeconomic policies. Despite that, it was largely a win–win game, as budget guidelines were drawn generously to provide for annual increases of up to 50%, financed by the 'natural increase' of revenues that accrued from double-digit economic growth.

With the end of the high economic growth era, and of the high and rising public spending that buoyant revenues had made possible, the LDP became committed in principle, although much less so in practice and in detail, to a policy of fiscal restraint. The imposition of negative ceilings on current and capital expenditures in 1982 changed the rules-of-the-game by which budgets were made and allocated. In the new zero-sum game, there were in principle both winners and losers, as top-down limits were imposed on the total of the General Account Budget, on types of expenditure, on the main programmes, and on each ministry and agency. As the *policy* rules governing the budget process were changed by MOF in response to the perceived need to tighten fiscal policy, the *behavioural* rules followed by bureaucrats and politicians were adjusted contingently. The LDP was obliged to change its collective and individual behaviour, and to play a more strategic role.

First, it was obliged to take a more strategic view about the desirable total for the General Account and its distribution among ministries and agencies, and, about FILP and its use to finance additional public works and other capital spending. To some extent, this obliged ministers and senior party officials collectively to pay more attention to the priorities of public spending. Some programmes—ODA, energy, defence, and (at first) science and technology—were accorded higher political priority, as a result partly (but not wholly) of LDP intervention in the early 1980s, and were allocated new money year by year. Secondly, to influence the size and distribution of the General Account Budget, the LDP was obliged to switch its attention to the period *before* Cabinet approved the budget guidelines and the allocation to broad categories of spending in June/July. As those criteria were progressively tightened by MOF in the middle of the 1980s, with the concurrence or acquiescence of the LDP leadership and the formal approval of the Cabinet, the focus of most ministerial and party interest became those programmes and policies prescribed as exceptional, i.e. accorded priority status—those exempted from the cut-back (imposed on ordinary expenditures), such as health or social security, or, like public works programmes and agricultural subsidies, accorded an ad hoc preferential status. Thirdly, the LDP had to focus more attention on the earlier stages of the budget process in the Spending Ministries and Agencies, before requests were formally submitted to the Budget Bureau at the end of August.

The extent to which the LDP collectively as a party, and individually through senior party officials, elder statesmen, and *zoku*, influenced the allocation of the Budget in the budgetary processes was constrained by a number of factors. Competition among them to ensure that their ministries, and favoured policy areas and projects, maintained existing budget shares, and wherever possible secured a slice of the additional money allocated to those priority and exempted policy programmes, was in practice often moderated by the influence of the LDP's senior leadership. While political pressure through PARC divisions, and the activities of *zoku* and backbench Dietmen, occasionally succeeded in changing an allocation substantially, more commonly the effect was marginal and was limited to its distribution among bureaux and their constituent divisions. Confronted by competing ministries, supported by networks of PARC divisions, research committees, *zoku*, interest-groups, and bureau officials, it was often easier for the Budget Bureau and the LDP's top leadership to agree to maintain the existing relativities among ministries and among programmes. This was most strikingly the case in the allocation of new monies to the most politicized policy area, public works, where additional expenditures were allocated to reflect and reinforce the existing relativities between the principal beneficiaries, MOC, MAFF, MOT, and MHW. However, as Chapter 22 will show, even here there were, over time, changes in the distribution between sectors. Elsewhere, among other policy areas in both the General Account and FILP Budgets, there were both winners and losers, as the next four chapters demonstrate.

The Budget Process in the Spending Ministries

The LDP's influence on budget-making in the Spending Ministries varied with ministry and policy area. It was potentially least significant in those ministries and agencies with international programmes to support—foreign (diplomatic) policy, national security, and trade. The size of ministerial budgets for those policy areas tended to be small, and the benefits collective or national. For example, MITI's budget was historically small, although it did fund science and technology projects through the Science and Technology Agency (STA). While the LDP was active in the promotion and protection of business interest groups, many of whom were among the largest contributors to party funds, particularly in the sphere of government regulation and the licensing of business activities, the level of government subsidy was small and hence was not a major focus for attention in MITI's budget. Small and medium-sized businesses whose production and markets were mainly regional or local, rather than national and international, and were located mainly outside Tokyo, were however of much greater interest. LDP Dietmen pressed claims on their behalf collectively for grants, subsidies, and tax breaks.

The LDP was much more active and influential in those Spending Ministries and Agencies with programmes of expenditure for domestic public works and public investment, to be found mainly in the budgets of the MOC, MAFF, and MOT, but also in the public 'facilities' programmes of MOE (school building) and MHW (hospital building). Those ministries were the main beneficiaries of annual earmarked new monies in the General Account Budget. Together with FILP-financed projects, their programmes provided for locally and regionally distributed benefits: road construction and maintenance, public housing construction and loans, ports and harbours, land improvement, water conservation, and the provision of leisure and amenity facilities. ODA, with its potential for private-sector contracts through grants and tied aid, attracted the attention of politicians as well. 'Project-oriented ODA was similar to domestic public works and construction where inter-locked bureaucratic–political–private sector interests manage the allocation of contracts' (Arase 1994: 192).

Thirdly, there were those ministries and agencies with programmes that provided other kinds of tangible benefits, such as income maintenance, support programmes for small farmers, rice subsidies, social security, and pensions (particularly those for widows and the war-disabled). Fourthly, there were those ministries and agencies supporting programmes of expenditure that financed the provision of services collectively to special clientele, e.g. health, welfare, and social services, and which also affected the interests of producer groups, such as doctors, social workers, and teachers.

The LDP's influence was potentially greatest in the latter two categories, but with some qualification. Within ministries, the pressure from LDP and interest groups varied with the salience of discrete policy issues; some bureaux were the target of more and sustained pressures than others. For example, in MOFA the bureaux dealing with ODA were the focus of more attention than those responsible for diplomatic and trade relations with other countries; in the Defence Agency, the Equipment Bureau responsible for procurement was targeted by companies manufacturing weapons and equipment in the private sector seeking to influence the size and composition of budget requests (Chinworth 1992; Samuels 1994).

Influence on the Budget Bureau's Negotiations

After the submission of budget requests, the LDP, formally through PARC and its divisions, maintained a watching brief on the progress of the negotiations. PARC's formal statement on the budget prospects, the balance between programmes, and the priorities of spending was a general summary of the party's previously stated aims and preferences, intended more for public consumption than to influence the Budget Bureau's handling of the requests. Informal arrangements for discussion, pre-notification, and warning between PARC influentials and senior officials of the Budget Bureau were more significant, especially in early December, when MOF was preparing the ground to ensure that the draft budgets were broadly acceptable to the party, and to ensure that the formal ceremonial of the revival negotiations that followed their publication proceeded smoothly and predictably along agreed predetermined lines.

The formal ritual of those revival negotiations at the conclusion of the Budget Bureau's negotiations was a vivid demonstration of the appearance and reality of LDP influence and the reality of its exercise. The formal exchanges at the level of both officials and ministers were stage-managed theatricals where the outcomes were predetermined by informal prior arrangement between the two sides. Nevertheless, the public ceremonial was politically necessary, a symbol of the LDP's (apparent) manifest influence and power in making the budgets.

Influence on the Implementation of the Budgets

The LDP's influence both formally and informally was more effective when focused on the implementation of outputs of the two budgets. How, where, and by whom monies were to be spent were questions of greater political interest to PARC division members, *zoku*, and backbench Dietmen than the quantum obtained by a bureau and its divisions in the budget negotiations between the Budget Bureau and ministerial bureaux and divisions. The role of all those LDP members was mainly to endorse budget requests, and to attempt to counter any demands from the Budget Bureau for cuts and squeezes in particular favoured programmes. Faction-leaders, *zoku*, and backbench Dietmen were more concerned with geo-electoral considerations—where the money was to go, and who would benefit. This was especially true of public works expenditure, where they sought to influence the allocation to prefectures and electoral districts, the choice of projects and schemes, and the contractual arrangements for their implementation (issues discussed at greater length in Chapter 23). But to provide for a continual flow of public works projects to sustain the party's politico-electoral machine, the LDP leadership had to ensure that its influence was exercised first at the strategic level of budget-making, and, secondly at the level of the allocation of shares among bureaux in ministries and agencies. This was true too of FILP, which provided a rich, additional source of local and regional expenditure on public works projects and programmes, and hence a source of tangible benefits for local LDP Dietmen. Self-financing, the expansion of FILP enabled the LDP to increase the flow and volume of benefits without incurring the political costs of increasing taxation, and the economic and financial costs of an increasing burden of debt necessary to (partly) finance any additional spending through the General Account. PARC divisions and *zoku* did not target the FILP Budget directly (there was no dedicated PARC division or commission; there was no FILP *zoku*); they were less interested in the method of financing the expansion of the public works budget than in where and on what the money was to be spent.

FORMAL AND INFORMAL MODES OF INFLUENCE

The formal structures, arrangements, and procedures for involving the LDP in the four stages of the budget processes, mainly through its Executive Council, PARC's Deliberation Council, and divisions and research committees, were mainly ceremonial, a public demonstration of the party's apparent influence and control. But they also provided for the necessary functions of legitimization and commitment. For example, a bureau director-general accompanied by his policy division directors was called before the relevant PARC division to explain, defend, and justify his budget request, and the policies and new items of expenditure contained within it. Formally, that provided the opportunity for the party to be seen publicly to influence the request before it was submitted to MOF. In practice, there was too little time for revision and amendment at that stage. Nor was it intended that there should be. The role of the PARC division hearing was more ceremonial and ritual than substance, intended to demonstrate to the electorate, and to its own supporters, the influence and control of the party, and its acceptance of political responsibility. It served also to commit and bind members of the division formally to an agreed consensus.

While mechanisms for formal consultation and decision-making such as those were institutionalized into the budget processes, so equally were the opportunities and occasions for informal consultation and discussion that preceded them and were necessary prerequisites. For example, senior members of PARC, especially PARC's acting chairman, played an informal coordinating role to achieve coherence and consistency in the formal endorsements by divisions of ministerial budgets; at an earlier stage they could constrain demands of the rank-and-file for more spending; and they played a key role in establishing the priorities of the 'revival negotiations'. As channels of potential political influence and control, informal processes of consultation, discussion, and consensus-building were substantively more important in the budget-making processes: (*a*) before the size of the budget had been decided and approved formally by Cabinet, and the ministerial ceilings informally agreed between the Budget Bureau and the Spending Ministries and Agencies; (*b*) before the budget requests had been drafted and sent to PARC for its formal approval; (*c*) before the Budget Bureau's examination of the budget requests was concluded and the framework for each ministry decided; and (*d*) before the revival negotiations began. The cultural obligation to inform and consult, and to pre-notify and signal intentions, was essential to avoid the unacceptable elements of surprise and unpredictability, and to ensure certainty and consensus. The frequency of formal meetings, and the processes of informal consultation and *nemawashi* that preceded them, served rather to build a coalition, or construct a broad consensus in which all interests that 'need to know' were consulted, than to provide opportunities for negotiation or hard bargaining. What in other national cultural contexts might be conducted mainly on paper, by telephone, fax, and e-mail to ensure that all interested or affected parties were kept informed had normally also to be done in the Japanese politico-administrative culture face-to-face.

The incorporation of the LDP leadership, senior officials of the PARC divisions, and *zoku* into the budget processes through the institutionalization of informal consultation did not mean that they controlled or even necessarily influenced the outputs. Direct participation, which sought to influence an outcome mainly through face-to-face discussion, less often by telephone or written communications, was not necessarily successful. An obligation to consult because of the 'need to know', to explore policy preferences and attitudes, to listen to petitions and representations, did not mean that an official would necessarily respond by changing a policy agreed earlier by his bureau, or giving preference to an alternative option canvassed by an LDP politician. The seniority of both officials and politicians, and the weight and timing of the arguments deployed, would partly determine what happened subsequently. Direct petitions and representations from chairmen or senior members of PARC divisions and special committees, or from one of the three LDP leaders, an elder statesman, or a *zoku* 'don' or 'boss', had to be taken more seriously than those from most ordinary LDP members. Some *zoku* known personally to budget examiners and their deputies tried to obtain special consideration for a project or an item of spending. Here, familial, secondary education, and prefectural connections were more significant than those of university or bureaucratic cohort. 'If X [a very senior LDP politician] comes to me, I will try to help', explained one budget examiner, because the two had attended the same high school and were classmates. 'If the request can be accommodated within the existing budgetary framework, then all right.' But he also emphasized that such pleas were directed primarily at the stage of implementing an agreed budget allocation, and hence were normally addressed to the relevant officials in a Spending Ministry's bureau.

Much depended on the issue and the timing, and on the strength of any countervailing bureaucratic arguments. For example, an informal meeting between the director-general of the Budget Bureau, the prime minister, and the top leadership of the LDP—the chairman of PARC, the chairman of the Executive Council and the secretary-general—at which the overall level of the Budget, and the allocation to some ministries, was discussed could influence the outcome in ways that were held most advantageous to the party. But influence and pressure was not one way. Such meetings provided the opportunity for the director-general and Budget Bureau officials to argue their case, and to urge restraint. LDP leaders might choose to reject that advice, or to give it less weight than other politico-electoral factors, but MOF had to be listened to. Mutual benefits and expectations also influenced the exchange and the outcome. Without accepting the contention that the LDP controlled all bureaucratic behaviour through the expectation of future benefits, such as promotion and post-retirement positions (Ramseyer and Rosenbluth 1993), such factors could enter into some informal relationships of consultation—indeed, could influence bureaucratic behaviour more generally, indirectly and implicitly.

INDIRECT AND IMPLICIT INFLUENCE ('THE GHOST IN THE MACHINE')

Thus far we have discussed the potential for the exercise of influence through the direct, explicit interaction between politicians and bureaucrats in both formal structures and arrangements, and in informal processes. The LDP also exercised an indirect influence generally on budget policies: through its known and publicly stated policy aims, preferences, and priorities, it influenced the formulation of the budget strategy, the composition of the Budget, and its allocation to ministries. More specifically, in particular policy areas, or on particular issues, its political preferences and objectives were well known and influenced outcomes without direct interaction. Relationships between LDP leaders and senior officials on the one hand, and directors-general of bureaux and directors of policy divisions in policy areas of high LDP interest or sensitivity on the other, were deliberately cultivated by both sides; the views, policy positions, and responses of politicians were well known to bureaucrats. Moreover, senior officials were aware and sensitive to the general orientation of LDP policies. Budget policy evolved within the general context of the party's broad aims and objectives.

Knowing the LDP's 'mind', and working within the grain of party policies, ensured consistency between what bureaucrats proposed to do and what the LDP wanted them to do. Some options were precluded or foreclosed or ruled out because of the context of a policy framework, or general guidelines articulated by the party in a particular policy area. For example, the LDP's generally hostile attitude towards increases in direct taxation constrained MOF's policy options in financing the fiscal deficit throughout the 1980s. Specifically, within particular policy areas, bureaucrats in Spending Ministries and Agencies anticipated or took into account the probable reactions of a PARC division or its leading officials, or a senior *zoku*, where their policy preferences or attitudes towards proposed items of expenditure, a policy change, or the priorities embedded in a budget request had been clearly articulated. In such ways, without overt, direct, and explicit intervention, either formally or informally, the LDP influenced budget policy. Like Adam Smith's 'invisible hand' or 'the ghost in the machine', the LDP established the parameters within which policy options were discussed and initiated. The anticipated reaction was a factor weighed and assessed alongside other non-political factors by bureaucrats in the Spending Ministries and Agencies, and by Budget Bureau officials. It might or might not be incorporated. To the extent that it was, without direct formal or informal intervention, the LDP influenced the outcome.

But care is needed in making such judgements. From the outside, it is impossible to tell, or to assess, what weight was given to the political factor relative to other considerations, and the extent to which the outcome reflected the interests of other participants both within the bureaucracy and outside—interest groups, clients and consumers, opposition parties in the Diet, other national governments and groups. More difficult still, where the anticipated reaction of the LDP was incorporated indirectly and implicitly, it might correspond to an independently determined bureaucratic preference: there was an identity of interest between bureaucratic and political values. Again, it would be impossible to distinguish, without knowing and weighing, the values and preferences of both. It follows from this that routine policy issues with 'low visibility', which excited little or no interest from LDP leaders or followers, might or might not be influenced indirectly or reflexively by political preferences; there is normally no means of knowing. Ramseyer and Rosenbluth (1993) argue that bureaucrats will *always* make decisions in the interest of the LDP, because of the latter's monitoring and control mechanisms, and the availability of sanctions for non-compliance. It is evident, however, that the LDP traditionally took little or no interest in some policy sectors, had no preferred policy position, provided no policy framework or guidelines, and was uninterested in attempting to influence directly what was proposed; while within almost all policy sectors there were issues that it was content to leave to bureaucratic regulation. The extent to which, even here, bureaucrats were influenced indirectly, by consideration of a general but unarticulated interest of the LDP, is impossible to judge. Their motivation equally might be that they were serving an elected, responsible government accountable to the Diet, rather than the promotion of their own self-interested values; the two might of course coincide.

'CREDIT-CLAIMING'

Whatever the reality of their influence, directly through formal structures and informal processes or indirectly through 'anticipated reactions', ministers and politicians of all parties claimed credit, seeking to be identified publicly and personally with a particular budget policy or output, whether or not the claim was justified. Credit-claiming was an important and necessary function of the budget relationship between politicians and bureaucrats. The LDP needed not only to provide a flow of benefits, favours, services, and facilities to targeted groups and clienteles, but to be seen, publicly and manifestly organizationally, to be responsible for doing so, whether or not it actually had exercised any direct influence in the budgetary processes. Through formal institutions and processes, ministers, party leaders, *zoku*, and rank-and-file appeared publicly to influence, or to have been readily identified with, particular budgetary outcomes, and were able to claim credit for them in their representations to special interest groups and local electorates; more widely, they were seen to be influential in the delivery of demonstrable benefits by the constituencies of small businessmen, construction companies, farmers, and rice-growers to whom they appealed in their grand electoral strategy. To realize the potential political benefits to the party of their electoral and financial support, it was necessary only that the party's claim to wield influence in the budgetary process *appeared* credible, as judged by outcomes favourable to those clients.

NEGOTIATED DISCRETION

The involvement of politicians to promote, support, or protect budget requests might appear from the outside as confirmation of the LDP's control of budget-making. On the other hand, if bureaucrats were exploiting their relationships with politicians to achieve their ministerial, bureau, and division objectives, it could be interpreted as evidence of bureaucratic dominance. The argument throughout this book rejects the crude polarities of bureaucrats versus politicians: the reality of the budget (and other policy) processes was altogether more complex and subtle. Rather, it emphasizes their shared interest, and the mutual interdependence of their relationships.

The paradigm of the politics of public spending in the last quarter of the twentieth century was negotiated discretion. There was an expectation that politicians, not just ministers, would or could be involved formally and informally at all stages of the budgetary processes, and not just at the time of their most public involvement during the revival negotiations. Both Spending Ministries and MOF accepted that that was a legitimate rule-of-the-game. Conversely, the rules-of-the-game allowed and legitimized bureaucrats' contact with politicians. They inhabited the political world as players operating in an overtly political fashion, as we saw for example at the conclusion of the budget negotiations, when Budget Bureau officials built a *political* consensus for the Bureau's proposed budget allocations. While they might operate discreetly and informally, that was not because such conduct was illegitimate, but because behavioural norms decreed it,[1] and because it was more efficient and effective to do so. From a broad cultural and societal perspective, there was nothing unusual in politicians and bureaucrats keeping in touch with each other, exchanging information, alerting each other of their interests and intentions. It was a necessary condition of consensual budget-making, and it was essential for bureaucrats in both MOF and the Spending Ministries to build support for a policy position, and to try to achieve the highly prized 'smooth procedure' for the process of budget-making in order to deliver an agreed outcome 'on time'. Secondly, it showed that potential political influence could be exploited constructively and adroitly by officials in Spending Ministries to serve bureaucratic interests, as well as by LDP leaders, PARC divisions, and *zoku*, to further the short and longer-term interests of the party collectively, and of the factions, groups and Dietmen that comprised it.

The predictable and programmed processes of making the Budget, in which the roles of the Cabinet, the LDP's organization, and *zoku* were institutionalized in formal and informal structures and arrangements, became uncertain, inchoate, unpredictable, and protracted in the period of multi-party government during 1993–6. The profound changes to the budget processes during those years proved temporary, but the restoration of the LDP did not mark the resumption of 'business as usual' with MOF and other bureaucrats. MOF's status, prestige, and authority, already progressively eroded by the economic, financial, and fiscal events following the collapse of the bubble economy, were now further degraded as the LDP relieved it of formal responsibility for monetary policy, management of the banking crises, and the regulation and supervision of financial services. The maintenance of its pre-eminent and dominating role in the budget processes was challenged in the reorganization of the central government initiated by Prime Minister Hashimoto in 1997, intended to relieve MOF of the responsibility for formulating budget policy, and to invest it instead in the Cabinet's new Council for Economic and Fiscal Policy. The implications of that and other changes are discussed in Chapter 30. But first, in the next part of the book, we examine who and what won and lost in the budgetary processes, returning to the themes explored here in the conclusion to Chapter 22.

---

[1] An example of the cultural difference in the relations between politicians and bureaucrats in Japan and the UK is illustrated by the social/educational networks that connect them. In Japan I obtained access to senior politicians through bureaucrats with whom they had social, educational, or ministry links; in the UK, access was through a political network from which bureaucrats were rigidly excluded. Indeed, UK bureaucrats normally have no entrée to that network, even though they might share the same or similar social/ educational/ ministerial backgrounds.

PART IV

THE OUTPUTS OF THE BUDGETARY PROCESSES

21

Who Wins, Who Loses?

Government in Japan, as elsewhere, used fiscal (and other) policies to influence the supply and demand for goods and services in the economy, through changes in corporate and personal taxation, public investment, subsidies, and welfare payments, most obviously when it attempted to stimulate or depress the level of economic activity countercyclically. Both then and more generally, through the annual General Account and FILP Budgets, it distributed benefits and imposed burdens differentially on economic and social groups, clienteles and individuals. Who and what won and lost in the central budgetary processes were determined mainly by the size, composition, and distribution of the mandatory and discretionary expenditures in the General Account and Supplementary Budgets, that is the budget total excluding the 'fixed costs' of debt-servicing, the issue of new bonds, and the statutory transfer of a proportion of some nationally collected taxes to local government.

The chapter begins with an assessment of MOF's performance in delivering a budget total of general expenditures in December within the ceiling prescribed six months earlier—in short, the extent to which it won or lost in the autumnal bilateral negotiations with Spending Ministries and Agencies. Next, I look at the changes in the distribution of current and capital spending as the policies of fiscal reconstruction, consolidation, and expansion were implemented. Here there are two main issues. First, there is the extent to which capital spending was cut and current spending protected; this commonly happens in conditions of fiscal stress, it proving easier to cut future spending than current spending. The second issue is the extent to which after 1982 formal policy rules-of-the-game prescribing the differential treatment of current and capital spending were observed in practice, measured by the outputs of both. Next, budget outputs are analysed organizationally, broadly by examining the distribution of expenditures between central and local governments. The main issue here is the extent to which MOF and the Spending Ministries protected their own budgets at the expense of the transfers to local governments of grants and subsidies. Again, experience of fiscal stress in other comparable countries suggests that central governments try to protect their own budgets, and deflect pressures to cut and squeeze expenditures elsewhere, to local and regional governments and to quasi-governmental organizations (see Thain and Wright 1995). The analysis that follows of outputs attributable to Spending Ministries and Agencies shows which of them won and lost, and by how much, in the annual budgetary processes.

Finally, a functional analysis of outputs proceeds through a progressive disaggregation of the total of general expenditures by broad policy groups, major programmes, and some constituent sub-programmes, to determine the extent to which changes occurred over time, and how benefits and losses were distributed among them. The concluding section summarizes the analysis, and discusses the general conclusions to be drawn from it in the context of McCubbins and Noble's (1995a) quantitative analysis of budgeting from 1952 to 1989. Because of their special place in Japan's political economy, the outputs of the budget programmes for public works are dealt with separately in Chapter 23, and those for FILP in Chapter 24.

THE AGGREGATE OF GENERAL EXPENDITURES

The aggregate of planned general expenditures in MOF's draft budget, approved by Cabinet in December, is a measure of MOF's performance in delivering, through the autumnal bilateral negotiations with Spending Ministries and Agencies, a total within or close to the ceiling prescribed in June/July. Analysis of changes in the aggregate over time provides the means to assess whether MOF won or lost relatively to all the Spending Ministries in the implementation of policies of fiscal reconstruction and consolidation.

There was a very sharp reduction in the rate of growth of planned expenditure from FY1980, the first year of fiscal reconstruction, halting the double-digit growth that characterized the 1970s.[1] With the introduction of a general freeze on all spending in FY1982, and the still tighter controls introduced the following year, there followed five years in which the size of the planned budget remained virtually unchanged. As controls were relaxed after FY1987, there was a resumption of growth, but within a range of 3%–4%, historically a modest rate. On that evidence, MOF's claim that its policies were effective appeared to be justified, although it should be emphasized that in no year, apart from FY1984, was the amount of planned general expenditures cut, other than by a token amount. Nevertheless, MOF had 'won' in one important respect: it had changed the expectations among Spending Ministries that the amount of those expenditures would continue to grow substantially year by year; MOF had reined back and contained the rate of planned growth.

That picture of apparent success is, however, subject to substantial qualification. The planned expenditure recorded in the initial budget did not accurately predict the total amount of spending that would be approved by MOF in each fiscal year and would be allocated to the Spending Ministries. In every year from 1975 to 2000, the net effect of the annual Supplementary Budget(s) was to increase the total of planned general expenditures. From FY1984 onwards, between 2% and 15% per annum was added to the planned budget in-year. Even in the years of the most stringent budgetary controls, MOF approved changes after the initial budget worth several hundred billion each year, equivalent to between 1% and 2½% of the planned total (Wright 1999e: table 1).

---

[1] The analysis here and throughout the chapter is drawn from statistical data presented in tables in Wright (1999e).

Figure 21.1 compares the planned rate of change year-on-year with the real rate, measured by comparing the revised budget totals with those of the planned budget for the *previous* fiscal year. Instead of planned marginal cuts and standstill, as the policies of fiscal reconstruction were implemented after 1980, spending continued to grow year-by-year, albeit at more modest rates than those that characterized the earlier period. Nevertheless, between 1983 and 2000, the real rate of change was always greater than the planned rate of change in every year except 1991. While the measurement of planned budget growth shows a period of standstill followed by a small increase after FY1987, the rate of annual growth measured by the revised budget rose rapidly. In FY1988 the resumption of growth, measured by the initial budget, registered a modest 1.2%; the real rate of growth was 8.9%. The following year the latter had almost doubled, with an increase of 4.9 trillion equal to a growth rate of 15%; planned expenditure had provided for an increase of only 1.1 trillion, 3.3% more than the previous year. As the size and frequency of additional spending packages financed by Supplementary Budgets increased with the onset of the recession, the contrast between the planned and revised totals for general expenditures became more marked. In 1995 there was an increase of more than 9 trillion, a 22% increase on the planned budget for the previous year; in 1998 a 28% increase, worth more than 12 trillion.

The outcome of those revised budget totals, i.e. the amount actually spent, is recorded in the annual settlement of accounts. The pattern is very similar to that for the revised budget; unlike the initial budget, the latter is an accurate predictor of the final outcome. We would expect to find, and do find, an element of under-spending on the aggregate of expenditure, characteristic of most centralized national budgetary systems. This occurred regularly and predictably, but was generally less than 1% of the revised budget total. Exceptionally, in FY1997 the whole budget was overspent, the out-turn producing a deficit of 1.6 trillion, the result of a much greater shortfall in revenue than estimated in the revised budget. This was repaid in the initial budget for FY1999.

The slower rate of the annual growth of general expenditures in the period 1980–8 was reflected in the ratio of settled, out-turn totals to GDP. Here again, MOF's claim that a reduction from 12.6% to 9.3%, and by 1991, to 8.2%, was the result of its policies for fiscal reconstruction requires some qualification (MOF 1992*b*). During that period MOF benefited from continuous economic growth, and at rates higher even than those for out-turn expenditures. To that extent, the declining ratio was due as much or more to the increase in GDP as to lower rates of growth of general expenditures resulting from the implementation of MOF's policies. Conversely, the slowing down of economic growth from 1990 and the simultaneous expansion of the Budget combined to move the ratio upwards once again.

Thus, who won or lost in the determination of the aggregate of general expenditures is affected to a large extent by what is measured. MOF's claimed success in halting the growth of spending depicted by the pattern of *planned* initial budgets is qualified by the reality of what in total MOF actually agreed to, and what finally was spent by the Spending Ministries. On that evidence, MOF was unsuccessful in practice in cutting public spending, and failed to arrest its growth. The effect of annual Supplementary

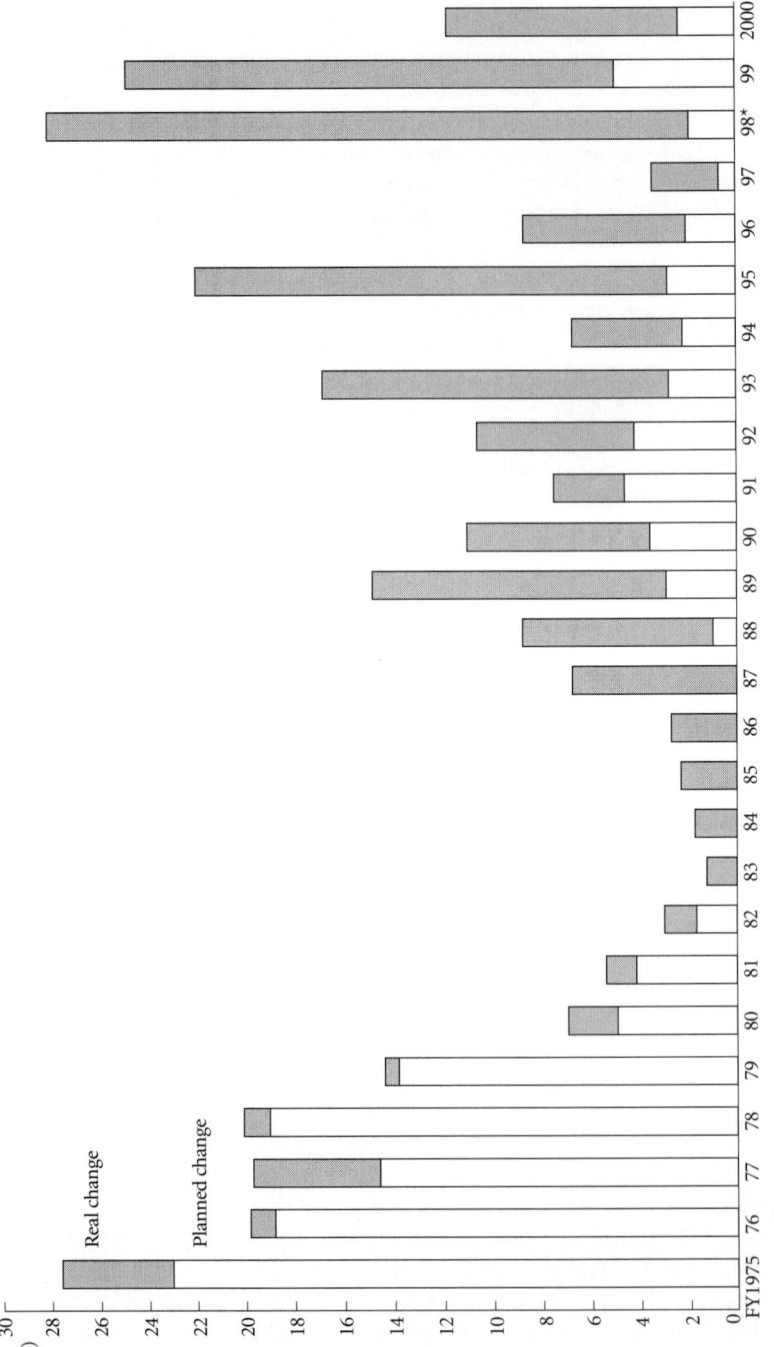

Figure 21.1 *Planned and real changes in the General Account Budget, FY1975–FY2000*
General expenditure in the General Account Initial and Revised Budgets: percentage annual change

For consistency in the calculation and composition of the totals for Initial and Revised Budgets, all expenditures associated with the NTT scheme—loans, repayments, and subsidies, and other transfer payments—have been stripped out.
*MOF's calculation of the figure for planned change for FY1998 (−1.3%) has been adjusted for reasons explained in the text

Source: Zaisei Tōkei (annually), Research Division, Budget Bureau, MOF.

Budgets, which crucially were not subject to the restriction of the formal policy rules-of-the-game prescribed in the annual budget guidelines, was to add substantially each year to the planned budget, whether or not an additional fiscal stimulus was required on the grounds of economic management. What MOF planned was substantially different from what it allowed in practice.

THE OUTPUTS OF THE BUDGET NEGOTIATIONS

The total of general expenditures in the initial draft budget approved by Cabinet, normally at the end of December, and submitted thereafter to the Diet, can also be read as the 'score-card' of the game between MOF on the one hand, and the Spending Ministries and Agencies collectively on the other: first, in setting the ceiling in June/July, and secondly, in delivering it, as the outcome of the autumnal bilaterals.

How successful was MOF in setting a control total that effectively constrained the growth of general expenditures? Throughout the whole of the period 1975–2000, the years of the most acute fiscal reconstruction notwithstanding, the ceiling prescribed for the aggregate always exceeded that of the total in the initial budget of the previous year (Wright 1999e: table 2). The latter became the base-line for the budgetary processes of the next round. In other words, there was an expectation of continuous incremental growth. MOF was unable or unwilling to prevent an annual increase in the planned aggregate by cutting the base-line total when the overall budget strategy was discussed and determined in the period leading up to the June/July Cabinet decision. There was always some 'new money' to be competed for, never a total freeze. Before the introduction of the policy of fiscal reconstruction those annual increments were substantial, between 8% and 20% of the base-line total between 1975 and 1981. Thereafter the application of the tighter budget controls reduced them to less than 2%. With the collapse of that policy in 1987–8, more new money was made available each year, up to 5% of the base-line between 1989 and 1997. Those annual increments of 'new money', resulting from the application of the budget guidelines for current and capital spending, were not inevitable, inescapable increases arising from existing policy commitments. While that was true of some kinds of spending exempt from cut-back, for example demand-led social security programmes, other categories of expenditure were treated exceptionally, and allocated additional resources—personnel expenses, the pensions of former government employees, and the priority areas of defence, economic cooperation, and energy for example, and from time to time capital expenditure programmes as well. In broad terms, MOF was unable and/or unwilling to prevent the annual growth of general expenditures through the application of formal restrictive budget guidelines: Spending Ministries and Agencies collectively were net beneficiaries of the informal budget processes leading up to the prescription of the ceilings in June and July. Thereafter they competed for additional amounts of both current and capital spending, although the latter was financed partly through other means as well.

MOF did however succeed, through the ceiling, in slowing the annual rate of increase of the aggregate, most obviously in the period of acute fiscal reconstruction in the period 1983–7. From 1980, there was no recurrence of the huge amounts of 'new money' made available in the 1970s when budget guidelines provided for increases up to 20% above the base-line. While the expectation of growth was not removed, MOF had succeeded in changing the policy rules-of-the-game. But even that success needs qualification: it was achieved partly at the cost of an expansion of FILP, and also through substantial amounts of new money for additional public works programmes in annual Supplementary Budgets, through the exploitation of the Special Accounts, and by various stratagems of 'creative budgeting'. These are discussed in detail in Chapter 25.

MOF's performance in the autumnal bilateral negotiations was however more impressive. Despite the continual pressures for more spending from ministries and agencies, supported by political lobbying through the LDP's PARC divisions and ad hoc interventions of ministers and senior party officials, and backed by formal and informal lobbying of special interest groups and clientele—despite all that pressure, in most years from FY1980 to 1998, as Figure 21.2 shows, MOF was able to deliver a planned total within the ceiling, or only very marginally above. To achieve that outcome, it juggled competing bids, trading off increases and cuts. MOF was a beneficiary; the

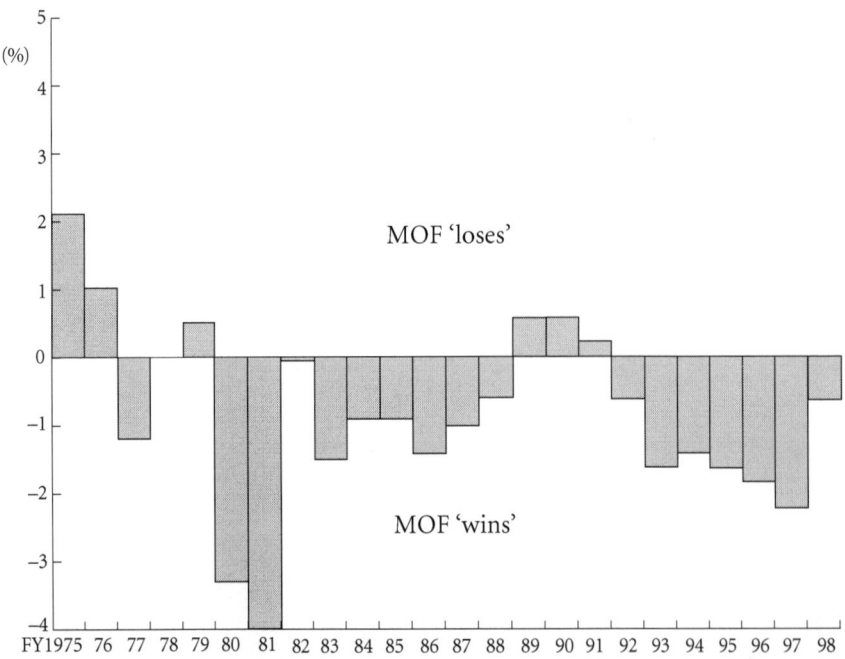

Figure 21.2 *Outcome of MOF's negotiations with Spending Ministries and Agencies: delivery of the budget ceiling, FY1975–FY1998*
General Account Initial Budget: percentage of budget ceiling

Source: Wright (1999e: table 2).

Spending Ministries and Agencies were collectively marginal net losers. This is evidence of MOF's control of the budgetary processes after ministries and agencies had submitted their requests: it could deliver within a narrow tolerance a 'control total' for general expenditures in the overall Budget, but subject to the proviso that it always approved additional spending in Supplementary Budgets, some of which were prepared concurrently in the course of the current fiscal year. There is also evidence that some pressures in the bilaterals were contained or 'bought off' by the promise of further favourable consideration after the compilation of the Budget.

CURRENT AND CAPITAL SPENDING OUTPUTS

Throughout the period 1983–2000, the formal policy rules-of-the-game were drawn to protect capital spending relative to current (see Table 15.1). Their application produced outputs from the budget processes that were almost the reverse of those formally prescribed. Current spending was to be cut: it grew annually. Capital spending was to be protected through smaller cuts or standstill: it was cut each year from 1980 until 1989. The capital budget of 8.6 trillion in 1980 was not achieved again until 1993. As a result, the ratio of current to capital spending in the aggregate of general expenditures increased from 2.6:1 in 1980 to reach a peak of 3.9:1 in 1990, declining marginally thereafter as the consequence of the expansion of investment programmes in the countercyclical policies that began in 1991 (Figure 21.3).

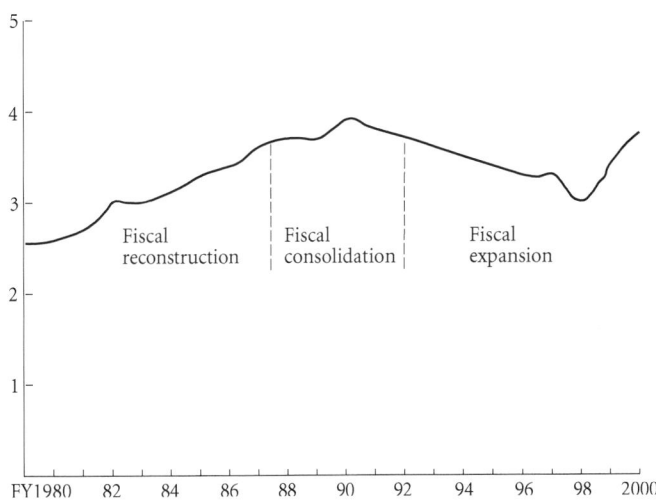

Figure 21.3 *Ratio of current to capital expenditure in the General Account Budget, FY1980–FY2000*
General Account Initial Budget

Source: Medium-Term Fiscal Projection (annually), Research Division, 2001, Budget Bureau, MOF; Cabinet Office.

The explanation for this contradiction between policy aims and outputs is that the policy rules-of-the-game provided categories of exemption and exception, loopholes for ministries and agencies to exploit in their bids for current spending on many programmes. In practice, the guidelines for cut-back applied to only about 12%–16% of the total current expenditures, mainly overheads. Both priority programmes treated exceptionally, and demand-led programmes exempted from the guidelines were allocated additional resources in almost every year from 1980 onwards. Moreover, the guidelines were implemented flexibly. Provided ministries and agencies kept within their agreed ceilings, they could, with the agreement of the Budget Bureau, switch between capital and current, and within the latter between priority, demand-led, and other programmes.

The outputs of the planned budget show that capital investment 'lost' both in real terms, and relative to current spending. The reality was that capital investment programmes continued to benefit substantially from the resources allocated elsewhere in the overall fiscal system. First, the transfer of a proportion of the funds from the sale of NTT stock provided 1.3 trillion additional finance for capital projects in each of the three years 1986–9. Secondly, some investment programmes, such as housing and school and hospital building, were financed increasingly through FILP loans to agencies such as the Government Housing Loan Corporation, and to Special Accounts such as those for national universities, schools, and hospitals. Thirdly, additional resources for public investment, mainly public works, were commonly provided in the regular annual Supplementary Budgets, which were not subject to the budget guidelines.

The resumption of the growth of capital spending in the General Account Budget from 1989 onwards was financed partly by the use of various ad hoc special initiatives, as explained in Chapter 15. Even in the planned budget of FY1998, which capped most spending programmes, the 7% reduction in capital investment was offset by ad hoc measures for economic structural reform and public works totalling 550 billion. In FY1999, a 5% nominal increase in the public works budget was translated into a real increase more than double that rate by the inclusion of various special schemes and programmes.

In the wider context of the whole budgetary system—the General Account, FILP, Supplementary Budgets, and the 38 Special Accounts—capital spending was a net beneficiary, simultaneously with the continued growth of current spending through the General Account. Miraculously, MOF succeeded in squaring the fiscal circle, achieving simultaneously a reduction in the annual growth of the planned aggregate of general expenditures in the General Account Budget and an increase in both of its constituent elements, current and capital spending. While the margins of additional resources for current spending in the General Account Budget were much smaller than in the period of high economic growth, nevertheless, ministries and agencies continued to compete throughout the 1980s for annual increments, rather than trying to limit and avoid the effects of annual cuts. Of course, as I shall show, there were differential rates of growth (and some of decline) in the allocations to individual ministries and particular programmes. But the conclusion is inescapable: the implementation of the prescribed and apparently strict budget guidelines for the General Account Budget had the opposite effect to that apparently intended and proclaimed in MOF's rhetoric: current spending continued to grow, and capital spending was cut—albeit amply compensated by expansion elsewhere in the fiscal system.

CENTRAL/LOCAL SPENDING OUTPUTS

It is more difficult to determine the extent to which central and local government won and lost. An apparent loss could be compensated elsewhere, for example by MOF/MHA approval of additional local government borrowing, or by financing outputs through local sources of revenue. But the purpose here is not to determine the relative position of local to central government spending in SNA calculations of overall general government in the period of fiscal reconstruction, which I reserve for discussion in Chapter 26. Rather, it is to examine the trends of the distribution of central and local government spending in the general expenditures of the General Account Budget: to determine whether the effects of MOF's policies of fiscal reconstruction disadvantaged local government relative to the central ministries and agencies. It excludes, as definitions of general expenditures exclude, those revenues from certain national taxes assigned to local governments. Those revenues fluctuated with the buoyancy of the economy and tax yields; both central and local government were disadvantaged by lower yields. However, local government 'lost' relative to central government, when from time to time MOF suspended statutory payments of those assigned revenues to local government as a temporary expedient to relieve pressure on the General Account Budget (discussed in Chapter 25).

The outputs of the general expenditures can be divided between central government's 'own spending programmes' and transfer payments to local government. The latter were of three kinds: central government's obligatory share in some local authority services, such as compulsory education, public works, and disaster-relief projects; payments to local governments acting as agents of the central government in the provision of some national services, for example the conduct of national elections and the collection of statistics; and grants-in-aid for the support, encouragement, and promotion of the implementation of local services. Those outputs attributable to central government's own spending programmes increased annually throughout the period 1975–96, although the rate of that growth slowed in the period of fiscal reconstruction. Those of the transfer payments to local governments were cut during the latter period. Modest growth was resumed in 1989, and was sharply increased in the years of recession that followed. Overall, in the share of general expenditures, central government 'won' and local government 'lost'. In 1975 the ratio of central to local in the initial budget was 1.86 : to 1; by 1993 it was 2.3 : 1. The margin was greater still if measured by the out-turn of expenditure after revisions through Supplementary Budgets, increasing from 1.82 : 1 in 1975 to 2.55 : 1 in 1990 (Wright 1999*e*). The burden of fiscal reconstruction and consolidation fell more on local government spending financed through the General Account Budget than on central government's own spending, an issue explored in more detail in Chapter 25.

ALLOCATIONS TO MINISTRIES AND AGENCIES

The 'bottom line' for each Spending Ministry and Agency, comparable to the profit maximization criterion of private–sector companies, was the maximization of their budget resources. In the post mortem of its performance in the budget process, each Spending Ministry (and its clientele and supporters) asked itself how well it had done: better or worse than last year? How did its performance compare with competing Spending Ministries and Agencies? Had it gained or lost budget share?

There was no change in the number of Spending Ministries and Agencies between 1975 and 1998, and only marginal changes in their formal policy jurisdictions through the acquisition of new functions and the transfer of existing ones. Nevertheless, care is needed in the analysis and interpretation of the budgetary outputs attributed to each of them. The total resources available to finance their programmes included not only those derived from the General Account Budget, but also allocations from FILP, while the jurisdiction of some ministries and agencies also included responsibility for one or more of the 38 Special Accounts, whose revenues were sometimes topped up by transfers from either the General Account or FILP or both. Thus, whether a Spending Ministry or a programme won or lost in the budgetary processes was not wholly represented by changes in its share of general expenditures in the General Account Budget. As the squeeze on the latter became tighter with the growth of the fiscal deficit in the 1980s, increasingly, MOF negotiated with the ministries and agencies to finance some parts of ministerial programmes by substituting FILP finance, and the exploitation of the hypothecated revenues in some Special Accounts, for example that for road construction.

Allocations to ministries and agencies have been quite commonly calculated by analysts as a proportion of the gross total of the Initial General Account Budget, conflating the totals for both 'fixed costs' and general expenditures. To do so presents a misleading picture of the distribution of the Budget, and the success/failure of ministries and agencies in the budget process. The inclusion of 'fixed costs', for which there was no competition (although MHA negotiated with MOF over the total of assigned tax revenues to local government), distorts the allocations. This applied principally, but not exclusively, to the budget shares of MOF and MHA, which for the former included the costs of government borrowing and servicing debt, and for the latter the allocation of assigned revenues (from certain nationally collected taxes) to local governments. The difference between their gross and net allocations is substantial. For example, for FY1994 MOF's gross allocation was 17.7 trillion, larger than any other ministry. The element of 'fixed costs' comprised the greater part: 16.0 trillion, or 90%, most of which was the allocation of the total debt-servicing costs. MOF's net allocation (of general expenditures) was 1.65 trillion. The gross allocation to MHA was 12.8 trillion, of which all but 0.69 trillion was the aggregate of the fixed proportion of national taxes assigned to local governments. The analysis that follows removes those and other distortions by using the net totals of general expenditures allocated to ministries and agencies.

The assessment of which ministries and agencies won and lost in the budget process is based on an analysis of changes in the volume of their annual allocations, and in their annual percentage share of the total over the period 1975–97. These reveal trends of growth or decline, and the relative performance of ministries and agencies. While the same indicators could be used to identify winners and losers in each annual budget round, the occurrence of temporary or special factors biases annual budget outcomes; short-term fluctuations and distortions are smoothed over the longer term.

Winning and losing measured in this way is not necessarily an indication of perceived success or failure in the budget process. The perception of either by a ministry or agency (which might be different from that of MOF) depends upon its judgement of the effectiveness of its budgetary strategy to achieve its budgetary aims. For example, a ministry that had won more resources might nevertheless consider its performance in the budget process as a qualified success, or even a failure, if it had received not only less resources than it had requested—a common and expected occurrence—but less than its undisclosed 'bottom-line'. Conversely, a ministry losing resources and suffering a cut in the size of its budget might judge its performance as successful because it had avoided a greater loss still. Public perception of success or failure could differ from judgements made internally. For example, a ministry allocated a larger budget might be perceived as successful, or proclaimed so publicly by its minister, although that budget represented a smaller share of the total. Factors that influenced who won and who lost in a particular round included the degree of priority accorded to particular programmes, the size of the ministerial budget ceiling informally negotiated with MOF prior to the submission of the formal bid, and the conduct of the negotiations with MOF over the latter.

Analysis of the allocation of general expenditures at the conclusion of each ministry's and agency's negotiation with the Budget Bureau on its formal submitted request reveals three general profiles for the period as a whole: first, that of budget growth, roughly 1975–82; secondly, restraint, 1982–8, and, finally, a resumption of growth from 1989 onwards.

The years 1975–82 were years of growth for the budgets of all Spending Ministries and Agencies, despite the recognition of an acute fiscal crisis at the beginning of that period. The allocation of resources in the budget process was a positive-sum game. No Spending Ministry or Agency had its budget allocation cut before FY1983. However, budget growth was experienced differentially. While all were winners, some won more than others. MOC made huge gains, increasing its budget from 1.816 trillion in 1975 to 4.063 trillion in 1982; similarly, MOE almost doubled its budget from 2.403 to 4.584 trillion. MAFF's budget increased by a third, from 2.032 to 3.333 trillion, while MHW enjoyed the largest gains of all, from 3.906 to 9.016 trillion.

The implementation of the tighter controls associated with the policy of fiscal reconstruction from 1982 changed the game from one in which all were winners to zero-sum, as total budget resources were progressively squeezed, albeit within an annually increasing budget. In each of the following nine years, between three and seven of the 20 Spending Ministries and Agencies suffered cuts to their budgets. The most consistent losers, with the largest budgets cuts, were MAFF, MITI, MOL, MOT, and MOC; MPT's small budget was also cut, but for a shorter period of time. MHA and MOF lost resources in some years, but these were exceptional cases, as their budgets were used to juggle resources between Special Accounts and local governments. All other Spending Ministries and Agencies increased the size of their budgets. The 'misery' of fiscal reconstruction was not therefore equally shared; cuts were not imposed 'across the board'—there were both winners and losers. Among the latter the cuts were not evenly distributed. Some Spending Ministries like MAFF and MOT lost substantially: MAFF's budget declined from 3.330 to 2.915 trillion between 1982 and 1986; MOT suffered even greater losses, from 1.437 to 0.890 trillion.

Others lost continuously but less, like MOC and MOL; and MITI lost almost a quarter of its much smaller budget between 1983 and 1988. While those ministries had their budgets cut, others enjoyed continued annual growth, as resources were channelled to priority programmes exempted from the cut-back guidelines or were treated exceptionally. Continuous and substantial growth were enjoyed by MHW, MOFA, and the Defence Agency. More modest gains were made by the other agencies comprising the Prime Minister's Office; while the budgets of MOE and the smallest agencies, such as the Imperial Household, Diet and so on, were largely static, or grew only marginally.

The third profile is associated with the resumption of the pattern of general budget growth from 1989 onwards, as fiscal reconstruction was succeeded first by policies of 'consolidation' and then, more explicitly, by expansion. Those Spending Ministries and Agencies whose budgets had been cut gradually joined the ranks of those that had enjoyed uninterrupted growth. By FY1989 only three Spending Ministries still experienced budget cuts—MAFF, MOT, and MOC—and those cuts were small. By FY1991 there were none, apart from the special case of MHA. The allocation of budget resources had become once again a positive-sum game. As before, the gains were not evenly distributed. MOFA continued to attract substantial additional resources; while budget growth was resumed in MOE, MAFF, and MOC. The latter's budget increased from 3.681 trillion in FY1988 to 5.172 in FY1996, reflecting the massive increase in public works spending in the period of economic recession that began in FY1991. For partly the same reason—an increase in spending on agricultural infrastructure—MAFF's budget picked up again after FY1990. While the Defence Agency's budget had continued to grow annually, with the end of the cold war the rate of that growth began to slow down after FY1991.

Budget Shares

Success in the budget process is only partly measured by budget growth and failure by budget cuts. While a ministerial budget might continue to grow in size, the rate of that growth might be more or less than that needed to maintain its existing share of the overall total of general expenditures in the General Account Budget. On that criterion, the winners are those Spending Ministries and Agencies that increased or maintained their share relative to others; losers are those whose budget share declined. The relative performance of ministries and agencies is measured by dividing them into three groups differentiated by the size of their share of the total general expenditures (Wright 1999*e*: table 4). The first group comprises those whose share was less than 1% of the Budget. Here the shares remained unchanging, allocations throughout the period of fiscal reconstruction determined largely by past decisions. For example, MPT's share year-by-year remained constant between 0.07% and 0.08% until FY1992; that of the Cabinet Office, between 0.03% and 0.05% throughout. The second group comprises those ministries and agencies with shares of the Budget in a range between 1% and 4%: MOJ, MOFA, MOF, MOL, MITI, MOT, and MHA. By contrast with the smaller ministries and agencies, fiscal reconstruction (and, later, consolidation) was experienced differentially. MOFA gained additional resources each year, and increased its share of the total budget from 1.03% to 1.7%, rising from thirteenth to tenth in the rank order between 1982 and 1990. The MOJ also improved its share of the Budget, but marginally. MOT, MITI and MOL all lost budget share; MOT and MITI recovered some of the lost ground in the years of fiscal expansion that followed, but MOL's relative decline continued.

Six ministries and agencies each attracted more than 10% of general expenditures in 1982, or achieved that share subsequently; between them, they accounted for more than 80% of the total. MHW and the Defence Agency had the largest shares, and increased their position relative to the others consistently throughout the periods of fiscal reconstruction and of the expansion that followed. MHW's share of the budget rose from 27.64% in 1982 to 33.2% in 1996. The Defence Agency gained budget share each year until the end of the cold war, rising from 7.92% in 1982 to 11.8% in 1991. All the other large ministries lost ground, strikingly so in the case of MAFF whose share declined annually from 1982 to 1994, with a loss of 4% of the total. The relative decline of other ministries and agencies was smaller, but that decline was consistent throughout the period of fiscal reconstruction. Thereafter, the trend of decline of MAFF, MOT, and MOC was halted, and they experienced modest budget growth for the first time in a decade. MOE continued to lose resources relative to other ministries, but MOC's share of the Budget grew at a faster rate than any other ministry, almost regaining the ground lost in the years of fiscal squeeze.

The evidence of this analysis demonstrates, first, that among the Spending Ministries and Agencies there were both winners and losers in the budget process; moreover, there was substantial variation within each of the three groups, and over time. Secondly, there is little evidence to support the contention that the principle of balance was a major factor in determining the allocation of resources *organizationally*. Only among the very smallest ministries and agencies is there evidence that historic patterns of allocation determined current decisions. Apart from MPT, the Cabinet Office, and the Imperial Household Agency, this group comprised organizations such as the Diet, Courts, and the Board of Audit, whose status was constitutionally distinguished from the Spending Ministries and Agencies. That partly explains their treatment in the budget process; but more important was the fact that their very small budgets comprised mainly current rather than capital programmes, with salaries and administrative expenses providing the major component of the former. Personnel and pension costs were exempt from the policies of cut-back, although of course the number of staff was subject to those personnel reduction plans discussed in the next chapter. While token cuts could be made in other parts of their budgets, deeper cuts were not feasible. Conversely, as budget restraint eased, the opportunity for more than very marginal growth was limited.

Thirdly, cut-back in the period of fiscal reconstruction was experienced differentially among both the medium-sized and the large ministries and agencies: the 'misery' was not equally shared. Not all ministries and agencies experienced cuts; those that did, experienced it differentially. Fourthly, with the relaxation of the policies of fiscal restraint after 1988, most but not all ministries and agencies enjoyed a period of continuous budget growth, albeit at different rates, reflecting the continuance of the priorities prescribed in the budget guidelines.

As there is not an exact fit between ministries and programmes—some, like ODA and public works, were shared among several—it is not possible to explain the whole of ministerial and agency growth and decline in terms of the degree of priority, or lack of it, accorded to particular programmes in MOF's annual budget guidelines. Nevertheless, in some cases it explains quite a lot. MHW's success was due in large measure to the exemption of the social security and health and welfare programmes from cut-back; that of the Defence Agency, to the priority accorded security programmes, which attracted additional resources year-by-year. Exemptions and exceptions to the cut-back guidelines also provided potential loopholes for all ministries and agencies to exploit, and are part of the explanation why most ministries and agencies continued to enjoy incremental budget growth.

Those ministries that 'lost' in the budget process were those with programmes mainly or wholly subject to the policies of cut-back, implemented through the budget guidelines—at their most rigorous, 10% cuts on current and 5% on capital expenditure. Agriculture, transport, and labour services, and most of the industrial support services provided by MITI, were not prioritized. While MAFF, MOT, MOL, and MITI could compete to win a share of new money available to finance other priority programmes, their claims for example for a share of the ODA budget or defence procurement were not always easy to establish and justify to the Budget Bureau. While they were eligible to compete for additional resources provided for capital investment, in the early years of fiscal reconstruction their capital programmes were subject formally to the guidelines on cut-back, and obtaining a share of any new money served mainly to prevent further decline in their overall budgets. However, the deep cuts and sharp losses of budget share suffered by those ministries, especially MAFF, MOT, and MOC, need to be set in a broader fiscal context. All three were the principal ministerial beneficiaries of the public works programmes financed through annual Supplementary Budgets and FILP, and also some Special Accounts. While their capital programmes and budgets were being eroded in the General Account Budget, the cuts were more than compensated from those two sources, providing them with substantial additional resources to finance, for example, road construction, agricultural infrastructure, ports, harbours, bridges, and airports. In Chapter 23 I shall show that the allocation to ministries and agencies of public works programmes and projects was determined almost wholly by their historic shares, and here the principle of balance was rigidly adhered to. Other ministries also benefited from the expansion and allocation of FILP funds. Some capital investment projects for the creation of 'public facilities' such as university and school buildings and hospitals, previously—and properly—a charge on the revenues from taxation in the General Account Budget, were now partly financed through the use of Special Accounts, while the element of FILP loans in several capital programmes increased during the 1980s. Care is needed, therefore, in the interpretation of the evidence of 'losing' ministries and agencies in the budget processes of the General Account Budget.

OUTPUTS OF MAJOR POLICY GROUPS

Programmes in the General Account Budget were aggregated and classified into nine policy groups, together with administration and overheads, and a contingency reserve. Those groups conflated the expenditures on programmes, sub-programmes, and 'items' into which the Budget was divided. There was no exact correspondence between policy groups and individual ministries and agencies, and therefore allocations to the former were not necessarily an indication of success or failure of the latter in obtaining resources for their policy functions. For example, most expenditures within the social security policy group fell within MHW's budget, but constituent programmes of employment insurance and unemployment benefits were the responsibility of the MOL. The resources allocated to Overseas Economic Cooperation, to Energy, and to Education and Science were distributed among several ministries and agencies; the budget for the Public Works policy group was shared among programmes devised and implemented mainly by four ministries—MOC, MOT, MOL, and MHW.

Analysis of the trends in the outputs of general expenditures at the broad level of policy groups reveals the extent to which the functional composition of the Budget changed over time. Moreover, it was at that broad level that LDP politicians and bureaucrats in MOF and the Spending Ministries signalled preference and accorded priority to particular policies.

A clear pattern of differential growth and decline among the nine policy groups is observable over the whole period 1975–2000. That pattern is closely related to the three time-profiles of budget growth, restraint, and expansion mentioned earlier, and in particular to MOF's policies for fiscal reconstruction, consolidation, and expansion associated with them. All nine policy groups benefited from the annual guidelines of budget growth up to 1980, although the rates of growth among them differed. Thereafter, the implementation of the policy of cut-back (together with exemptions and exceptions) to specific programmes and types of expenditure produced a mixed pattern of budget outputs conflated in the policy groups. Social Security, excluded from cut-back, enjoyed continuous annual growth at above average rates, increasing its share of the total in every year but one between 1975 and 1998; by 1998 it was absorbing more than a third of the total of general expenditures, compared with a quarter 20 years earlier. Overseas Economic Cooperation enjoyed similar continuous annual growth until FY1998, more than doubling its share of the overall budget. While sharing a similar priority, the allocations to Energy-related programmes were more erratic. While the Energy budget grew annually throughout the period, its steadily increasing share of the Budget was halted in 1987 when two years of heavy cuts marked a period of standstill.

The Defence budget was *sui generis*, nominally regulated by constitutional prescription, and for most of the period 1975–98 by ostensible observance of policy rules-of-the-game—for example that expenditure should not exceed 1% of GNP, introduced in 1976 and abandoned in 1987. In practice, as discussed in Chapter 16, there were various 'creative' budgetary stratagems to ensure compliance with that ratio. Figure 21.4 shows the size of the annual defence budget, its annual percentage change, and its share of the total general expenditures for the period 1975–2000.

After small reductions in the period 1975–9, thereafter defence claimed an annually increasing share of the total, rising from 7.2% in 1980 to 11.8% in 1990–1. Its growth was unaffected by the period of cut-back between 1981 and 1987, defence having been chosen as a priority programme, and one exempt from the increasing tightening of expenditure controls. The continuous annual growth varied between 5% and 6% for most of the period, but this was cut to less than 1% in the period of coalition governments in 1993–6 involving the JSP. Supplementary Budgets made very little difference. Defence normally received only a very small increment, less than 1%, and occasionally lost a still smaller proportion of its initial allocation.

Those policy groups whose constituent programmes were wholly or mainly subject to cut-back after 1982 either display patterns of lower, slower growth, like Education and Science, or show a trend of decreasing budget share. In both cases the result was a loss of budget share over the period as a whole. The budget output for Public Works conflates the allocations of a number of programmes of capital investment. Nevertheless, the trend over the whole period is also closely related to changes made in the criteria prescribed for budget requests for capital investment. The effect of the tightening of controls in the period of fiscal reconstruction is evident, as is the gradual relaxation thereafter, and the fiscal stimulus provided later, in the years of recession in

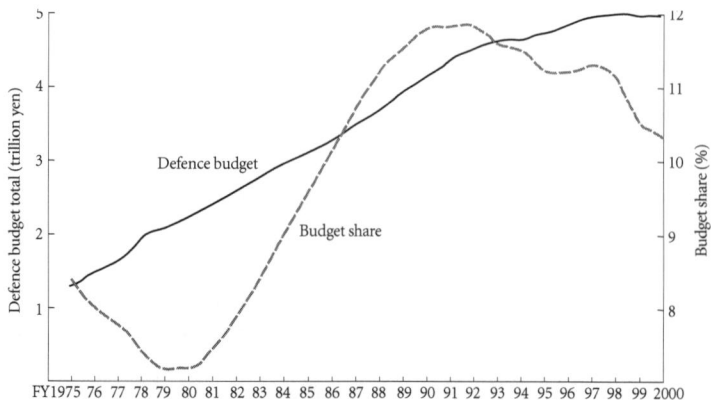

Figure 21.4 *The Defence budget: size and share of general expenditures, FY1975–FY2000*
General Account Initial Budget

Source: *Zaisei Tōkei* (annually), Research Division, Budget Bureau, MOF.

the mid-1990s. Between 1979 and 1997 the Public Works share of the total of general expenditures declined from 22.4% to 19.7%.

A similar pattern is observable in the programmes conflated in the policy group Measures for Small Businesses, although here the loss was sharper. There was a gradual but continuous loss of budget share in planned expenditures from 1980 to 1996, the greatest losses occurring during the period of fiscal reconstruction; in most years, there was a loss of volume as well. Those losses were sustained even in the years of recession in the 1990s when MOF took repeated action to pump-prime the economy. By 1996, Measures for Small Businesses had lost a half of its share of the planned budget.

Figure 21.5 compares the budget shares of each of the nine policy groups, and that for Administration and Overheads, at three-year intervals from 1975 to 2000. Taking the period as a whole, there were four clear winners: Social Security gained 10% more of the total budget for general expenditures; Defence, 2.5%–3%; Economic Cooperation, about 1.5%; and Energy (from 1978) about 0.5%. While the Public Works budget share was greater in the years 1996–2000 than in 1975, its share had contracted throughout the

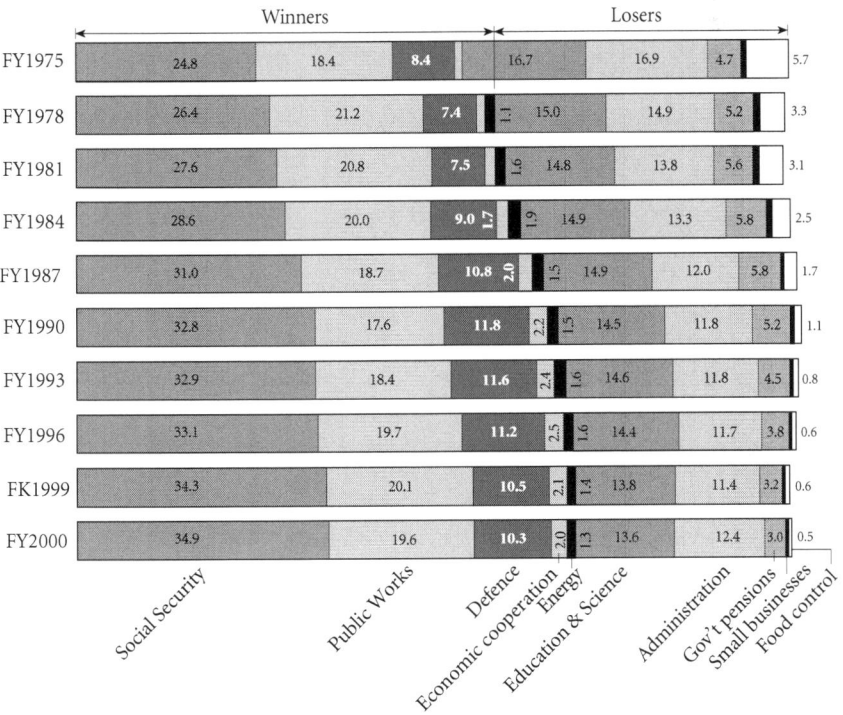

Figure 21.5 *'Winners and losers': policy groups, FY1975–FY2000*
General Account Initial Budget: percentage of general expenditures
Source: Zaisei Tōkei (annually), Research Division, Budget Bureau, MOF.

1980s. There were five clear losers: Food Control lost 5% of the total; Administration and Overheads, about the same; Education and Science, 3%; and Measures for Small Businesses, 0.4%. Government Employee Pensions increased its share until 1987, thereafter losing more than 1% of its 1975 total.

The profiles of winners and losers presented here provide an incomplete account of the total resources allocated to some policy groups. Public Works was a consistent loser in the planned budget from 1981 to 1990, but a major beneficiary of annual Supplementary Budgets, which were not subject to the controls imposed on budget requests. A comparison of the planned and revised allocations for Public Works (Table 23.2) shows that the initial allocation was revised upwards through Supplementary Budgets in every year throughout the period 1975–2000. The effect was to offset—indeed, outweigh—the apparent standstill and loss of resources measured by budget share in the planned allocations of the initial budget during the 1980s. If Supplementary Budgets, and other sources such as FILP and the NTT scheme, are taken into account, Public Works emerges as a clear, consistent winner throughout the years 1975–2000.

The profile of progressive cuts in the planned expenditure on Measures for Small Businesses, the result of deliberate fiscal discrimination in the budget guidelines, is on the face of it surprising. The LDP apparently acquiesced in the continuous erosion of a group of programmes hitherto regarded as a crucial element in the broad politico-electoral strategy to maintain itself in power. As so often, appearance is belied by the reality of expenditure-politics. First, as Figure 21.6 shows, from 1986 substantial additional resources were made available through Supplementary Budgets not subject to the budget guidelines. The trend of decline scored in the initial General Account Budget was reversed, although this occurred only towards the end of the period of fiscal reconstruction, from FY1986 onwards, during which time the squeeze was tightened as further cuts to the programmes were made through the Supplementary Budget. Throughout the whole of the 1990s, substantial additional resources for the Small Businesses programme were made available in Supplementary Budgets; in FY1995 and again in FYs1998, 1999, and 2000, those increases were huge—in 1998 there was a five-fold increase, from 185 billion planned expenditure to 1,015 billion.

Secondly, the annual losses sustained in the period of fiscal reconstruction, were compensated by the use of FILP funds; loans for small businesses increased from 15.6% of the net FILP Budget in 1975 to 18% in 1985. Thirdly, the budgets of public finance corporations providing such loans for small businesses (the People's Finance Corporation, the Finance Corporation for Small Businesses, the Environmental Sanitation Business Finance Corporation) were financed not only through FILP, but also through indirect transfers from the General Account Budget via MOF's own planned budget, and through their own internally generated revenues. Fourthly, local governments provided funds in support of local small businesses directly on their own account, and through the Japan Finance Corporation for Municipal Enterprises, financed mainly by loans from FILP. The availability of those off-budget resources, and the expectation that they would be used, were factors that influenced the allocation of planned expenditures for small businesses in the initial General Account Budget. MOF was able to 'cut' the planned budget allocations while simultaneously ensuring a

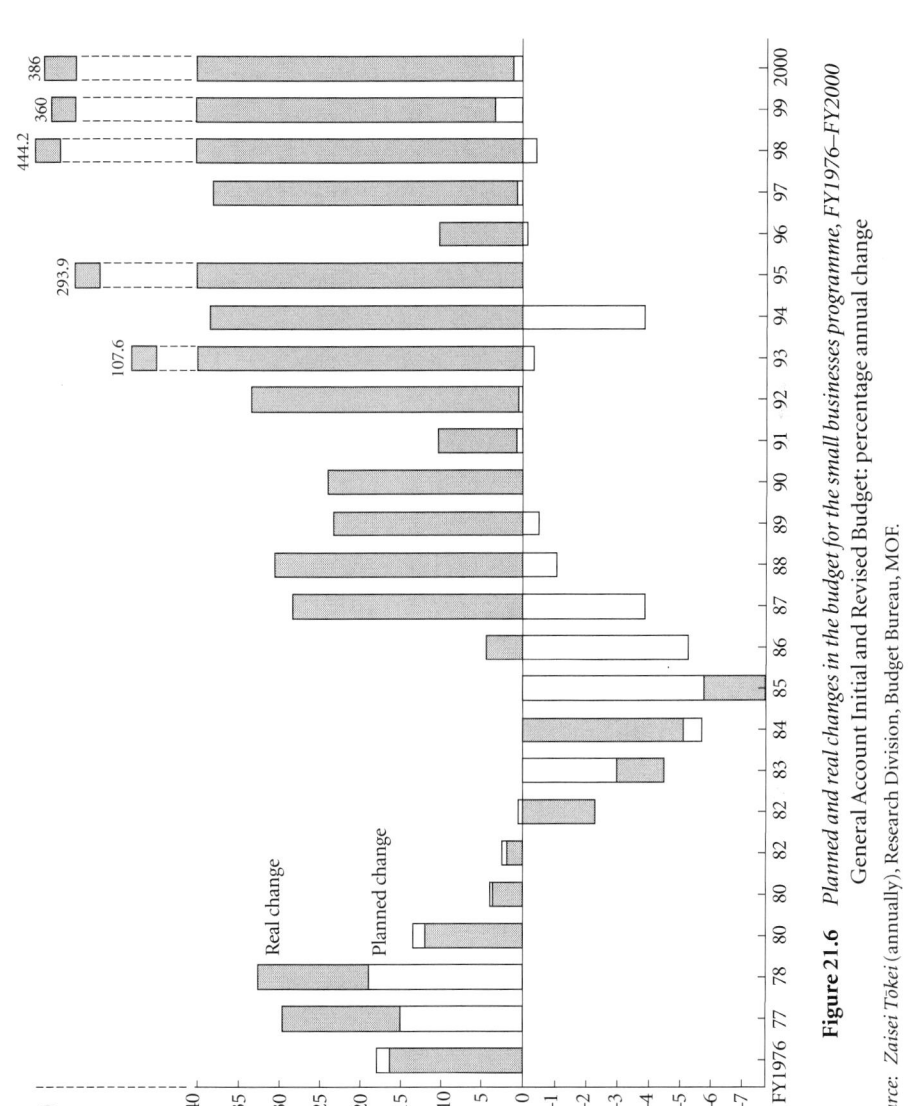

Figure 21.6 *Planned and real changes in the budget for the small businesses programme, FY1976–FY2000 General Account Initial and Revised Budget: percentage annual change*

Source: Zaisei Tōkei (annually), Research Division, Budget Bureau, MOF.

continuous flow of funds from other sources. In the 1990s, despite repeated substantial additional increments through Supplementary Budgets, the planned allocation in the initial budget hardly varied from one year to the next, while its share of the planned budget actually declined.

Food Control, the biggest loser, also benefited from additional allocations made to its initial budget. While those were not large enough to arrest its progressive loss of overall budget share, nevertheless, in nine of the 20 years losses were offset by the extra resources made available in Supplementary Budgets, while in four other years it had very small increments. Education and Science, another loser, acquired additional resources in all but three years, but these were only marginal gains, and not sufficient to compensate for its loss of budget share. Administration and Overheads benefited as well from Supplementary Budgets, and rather more substantially in the period 1986–96. Those 'compensations' for losers were not offset by deductions from winners, although some of the latter sustained minor losses in Supplementary Budgets from time to time.

Broad allocations to the nine policy groups were the gross aggregates of a number of constituent programmes with contrasting profiles of growth and decline. We turn now to an examination of the pattern of budget allocations within those groups.

PROGRAMME OUTPUTS

Net changes at the macro level of policy groups conceal a variety of gross movements among the constituent programmes and sub-programmes into which each is divided. Sub-programmes are further divided, in all incorporating some 400–500 'items' comprising the planning, management, controlling, and accounting units of the General Account Budget. Here I do not attempt a comprehensive analysis of all programmes and their constituent parts. My intention is, first, to compare changes in programme outputs over time, and to test assumptions about the criteria of allocation; and, secondly, to show that the level at which the analysis is conducted reveals contrasting rates of growth and decline *within* a broadly defined programme. I take the four largest policy groups—Social Security, Defence, Public Works, and Science and Education—and one of the smallest, Measures for Small Businesses. I begin with a comparative analysis of the trends in the budget allocations to the constituent programmes of each policy group, and then analyse the changes within a selected sub-programme.

Unpacking the Social Security budget reveals that the annual gains, and the overall increase in its share of the General Account Budget, were not shared equally by all five constituent programmes (Wright 1999*e*: table 6). While all enjoyed substantial annual growth up to 1980, albeit at substantially different rates, thereafter the implementation of policies of fiscal reconstruction, consolidation, and expansion were experienced differentially. The Unemployment Assistance Programme attracted a declining share of resources year by year, a fate shared by the Public Assistance Programme generally after

1985. The other three programmes—Social Welfare, Social Insurance, Public Health—all benefited substantially, enjoying almost uninterrupted annual growth, but at different and annually fluctuating rates. Figure 21.7 shows that the 'misery' of the period of fiscal reconstruction between 1980 and 1987 was not shared equally or proportionately. There were differential rates of both decline and growth around the average rate of change of 3.6%. The Programme for Unemployment Assistance was a consistent loser, and heavy losses were sustained by the Programmes of Social Insurance and Public Assistance.

A breakdown of the budget allocations for the fast-growing Social Welfare Programme shows that neither growth nor decline was evenly distributed among its six constituent sub-programmes (Wright 1999*e*: table 7). The slow-down in the rate of annual growth of the budget for the programme as a whole after 1980 was unevenly

Figure 21.7 *'Unequal misery': changes in the budget allocation for Social Security Programmes in the Period of Fiscal Reconstruction, FY1980–FY1987*
General Account Initial Budget: percentage annual change

Source: *Zaisei Tōkei* (annually), Research Division, Budget Bureau, MOF.

distributed. Some sub-programmes received large annual increments, while others were simultaneously cut back substantially, clear evidence of deliberate choice and discrimination. Sub-programmes for the care of the elderly received the highest priority, increasing their share of the programme budget from 36% in 1975 to more than 60% by 1995. This result was a combination of 'inertial growth', the rising number of elderly people in the population as a whole making demands upon existing services, and the result of the implementation of new policies to improve the amount and quality of those services most obviously through the Ten-Year Gold Plan, which aimed to increase the number of home helps, beds in nursing homes, and so on between 1989 and 1999. Sub-programmes for the protection of the physically handicapped also grew at above-average rates for the budget as a whole, but there were occasionally fluctuations, for example two successive years of substantial loss of resources. The child protection sub-programme lost ground steadily after 1980, suffered two successive years of substantial losses in 1985 and 1986, recovered thereafter, but overall by 1995 had lost half of its 1975 budget share. The most marked variation was in the trend of allocations for the construction and maintenance of various social welfare institutions—old people's homes for example. The large annual increases before 1980 were not sustained through the period of fiscal reconstruction, as the slow-down and cut-back in capital expenditure was applied to the sub-programme. The resumption of growth thereafter was modest and erratic. The allocation of resources for child benefit fluctuated wildly; huge increases up to 1980 were followed by more modest growth, as the sub-programme was protected from the full rigour of fiscal constraint, and then by continuous decline. Between 1985 and 1995 it lost half of its share of the budget for the Social Welfare Programme as a whole.

While this analysis of the resources allocated to programmes and sub-programmes within the Social Security policy group reveals the consequences of decisions made in the budget process, caution is needed in drawing conclusions about the relative political priority of those programmes. As I have explained, the budget outputs of the central government's General Account Budget are not necessarily an index of the total resources allocated to provide for a particular service or benefit. Local governments shared the costs of some programmes, or provided related services. For example, central government provided half the capital costs of building and improving facilities for the elderly in municipalities, while prefectures contributed a quarter. To repeat, my purpose here is not to determine the amount and allocation of resources as a proportion of general government expenditure, but to identify and compare those outputs attributable to the central government's budgetary processes.

As we saw above, the Education and Science policy group lost ground to other policy groups between 1987 and 1993. The distribution of its budget among six constituent programmes from 1975 to 1996 shows that all of them grew very substantially between 1975 and 1980 (Wright 1999*e*: table 8). Thereafter there was considerable variation in the annual allocations among them, and in the trends over time. Figure 21.8 shows the annual fluctuations among and within the programmes in the period of fiscal expansion from 1988 to the end of the century. The average annual rate of growth was 2.5%. There was wide variation around that figure. Subsidies for schools built by

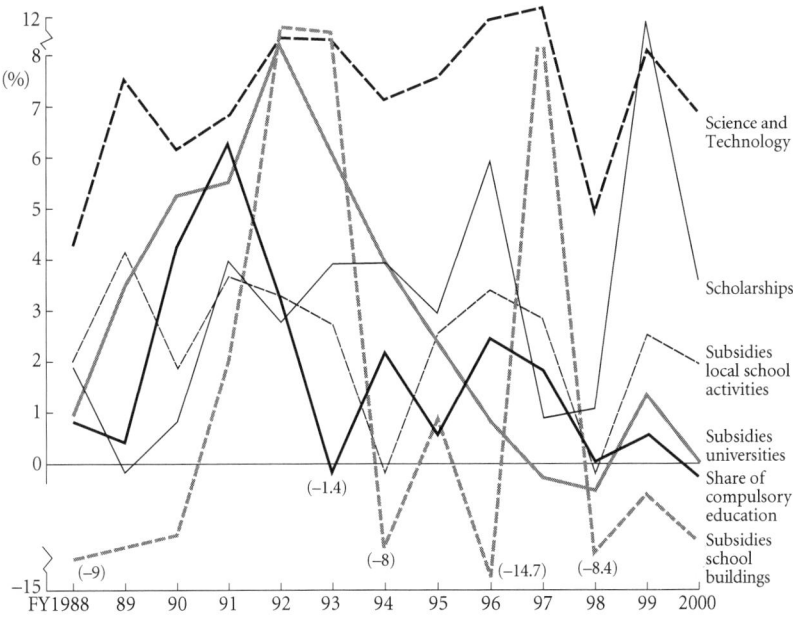

Figure 21.8 'Swings and roundabouts': changes in the budget allocations for Education and Science Sub-programmes in a Period of Fiscal Expansion, FY1988–FY2000
General Account Initial Budget: percentage annual change

Source: *Zaisei Tōkei* (annually), Research Division, Budget Bureau, MOF.

local governments fluctuated wildly. There were two peaks of growth shared by most but not all programmes, in 1991–3, and 1996–7, both coincident with the runup to the general elections for the Lower House.

The programme for the promotion of Science and Technology enjoyed continuous growth well above that rate. Together with the central government's share of the cost of providing compulsory education, it was protected from the cut-backs sustained during the period of fiscal reconstruction. Transfers to both the Special Account for Education and the Scholarship Programme grew continuously but less quickly; the latter was cut back sharply in the period of fiscal reconstruction. The School Building Programme was cut more deeply still in the same period, a direct consequence of the general budget policy of slow-down and then cut-back in capital expenditure. However, the size of the cuts for both programmes was also the result of the availability and use of an alternative means of finance, through FILP subsidy.

Unpacking the most successful of those programmes—that for Science and Technology Promotion—reveals a substantial shift of resources among the six sub-programmes, reflecting changes in priority (Wright 1999b: table 9). Figure 21.9 shows very different budget profiles over the 20-year period. The fastest growing sub-programmes were those for Oceanic R&D and Space R&D. The latter enjoyed continuous

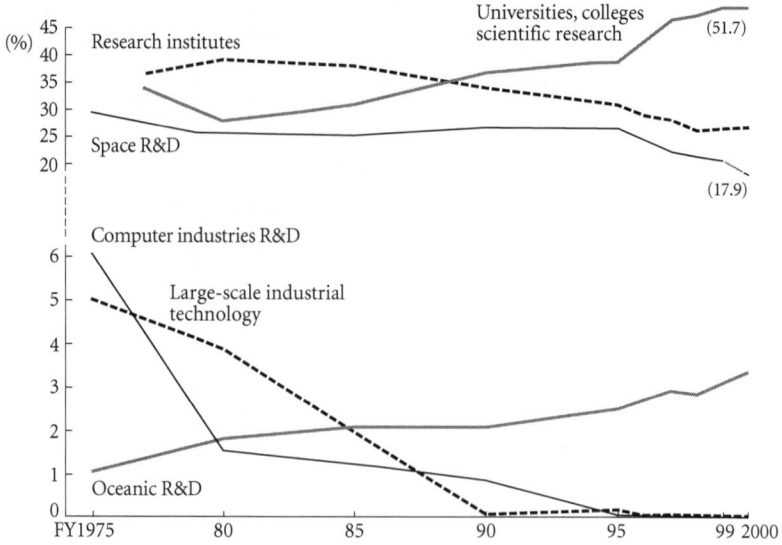

Figure 21.9 *Changes in the Budget Shares of the Science and Technology Sub-programmes, FY1975–FY2000*
General Account Initial Budget: percentage annual change
Source: *Zaisei Tōkei* (annually), Research Division, Budget Bureau, MOF.

annual growth, at modest rates until 1989, when there was an annual increase of 10% per annum. Despite this, overall, the sub-programme lost almost 3% of its share of the Science and Technology Programme budget between 1975 and 1995. The profile of the Oceanic R&D sub-programme was very different, fluctuating between periods of modest growth, cuts in the years of fiscal reconstruction, and very large increases at rates of between 10% and 20% from 1988. Overall it more than doubled its share. The budgets for Research Institutes, and for a group of other small sub-programmes grew continuously, but at less rapid rates. However, whereas the former lost 6% of its budget share, the latter gained 15%. The two other sub-programmes, for Large Scale Industrial Technology and for Computers, both experienced continuous annual decline. But again, their profiles were different. The implementation of the general budget policy of cut-back hit the former much harder. Between 1981 and 1988 its annual budget was reduced from 13.322 to 2.172 billion, a loss of 84%. Decline in support for research and development in the computer industry had set in much earlier, before the cut-back of the fiscal reconstruction period, from the full rigours of which it was more protected. However, the long-term trend of decline continued, as MITI abandoned the policy of underwriting the full R&D costs of firms collaborating in hi-tech consortia (Callon 1995). By 1995 the programme had been virtually wiped out, claiming less than 0.2% of the total budget for the Science and Technology Programme, compared with over 6% twenty years earlier. To some extent, those losses were offset by the establishment of agencies for specific R&D programmes and projects, whose capital requirements were financed partly through FILP, for example the New Energy and Industrial Technology Development Organization.

Within the Defence budget, the allocation of shares organizationally between the Defence Agency and the Defence Facilities Administration Agency, and within the former among the three Self-Defence Forces, remained fairly stable for much of the period. With the slow-down in budget growth after 1991, the Ground Self-Defence Force tended to gain budget share at the expense of the Maritime Self-Defence Force and the Air Self-Defence Force; the 'misery' of the squeeze was not equally shared. On a programme basis, there was a shift of resources from personnel expenditure to contracts and matériel, although after 1987 the proportions remained fairly stable (Wright 1999*e*: tables 12 and 13).

The fourth major budget is that for the Public Works policy group. The changes in the outputs of that budget, its distribution between ministries, and the allocation to constituent programmes are dealt with in detail in the next chapter. The budget for Measures for Small Businesses was the smallest of the nine policy groups, but, like that of public works, politically important to the LDP. It was distributed among three ministries, and a number of programmes. MITI provided subsidies and assistance to the Small Business Finance Corporation, and to small businesses and their representative associations. Most of that spending was for the instruction and training of employees and managers, the promotion of the activities of chambers of commerce, the creation of shopping centres, and the improvement of the working environment of small and medium-sized businesses. MOF provided subsidies for the People's Finance Corporation and the Small Business Credit Insurance Corporation. The remainder of the budget was allocated to MOL. Figure 21.10 shows the annual incremental gains and losses through the period 1975–2000. As a result, MITI's share of the initial budget, and hence the programmes it financed, declined from four-fifths to two-thirds by the mid-1990s; MOF gained, increasing its share from 18% to 30%. Towards the end of the century, MITI regained some of the lost ground. As explained earlier, with annual cuts in the overall programme for Small Businesses from 1982 onwards, both lost resources, but the misery was not equally shared between them. Although MOL's share was tiny in comparison with MOF and MITI, the effects of annual incremental changes are clearly shown. From a position of steadily diminishing budget share in the 1970s, it improved its relative position in every year from 1984 to 1995.

PARTY POLITICAL OUTPUTS

The final category of outputs from the budgetary processes of the General Account Budget examined here are those attributable specifically to the political 'revival negotiations', the annual ritual that took place at the conclusion of the budget process, after the submission of MOF's draft budget to the Cabinet in December. Its purpose, procedure, and political significance were explained in Chapter 16. Relative to the aggregate budget of each of the nine policy groups, the annual increments resulting from the

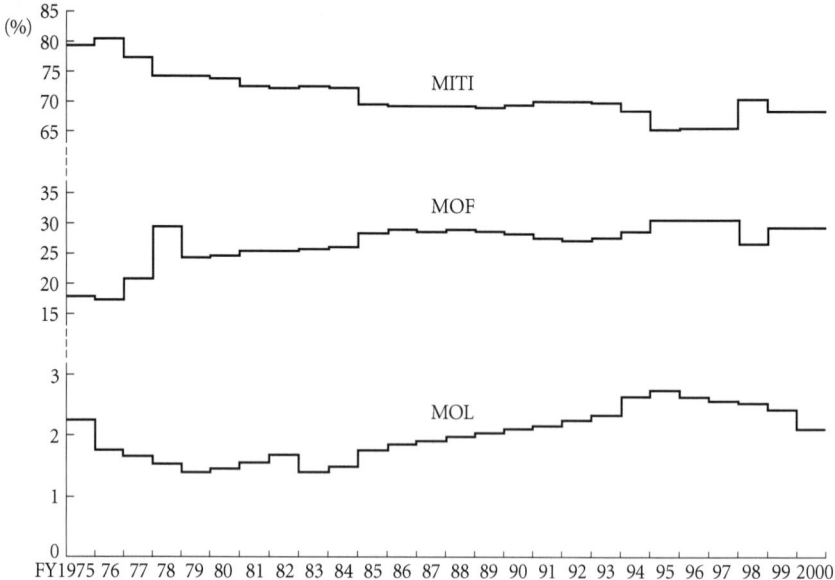

Figure 21.10 *Ministerial shares of the Budget for the Small Businesses Programme, FY1975–FY2000*
General Account Initial Budget: percentage
Source: *Zaisei Tōkei* (annually), Research Division, Budget Bureau, MOF.

revival negotiations were very small. But, as explained in Chapter 20, their symbolic value far outweighed their substantive importance. Nevertheless, the sums involved were large enough to enable individual ministers and senior party officials to claim publicly personal and party credit for success in obtaining extra resources for favoured programmes. For example, the minister for health and welfare could claim in FY1993 that his personal intervention had secured an additional sum of some 35 billion for the Social Security budget, and the minister for Education and Science, 105 billion for his programmes—sums sufficiently large to impress political supporters, clients, and backbench Dietmen on the LDP's PARC division, tangible evidence of the party's influence on the size and composition of the budget.

The reality is otherwise. The aggregate of the increments for ministerial programmes in the nine policy groups combined fell within a range of about 180–225 billion each year, but that total was always offset by compensating, across-the-board reductions in administrative and operating expenses, and in the miscellaneous category of small programmes of an equivalent amount (Wright 1999*e*: table 16). The net cost of overt political intervention was therefore nil; the size of MOF's draft initial budget was unchanged by the revival negotiations. Further, the small increases to the budget shares of policy groups and their constituent programmes were more apparent than real. As explained in Chapter 17, both the size and distribution of those political outputs were almost wholly predetermined in the later stages of the bilateral negotiations between MOF officials and their counterparts in the Spending Ministries, and already discounted in the aggregate of the initial budget draft submitted to the Cabinet. In brief, they were institutionalized within the budgetary processes.

The distribution of the 'negotiated' political outputs among policy groups was equally predictable. The 'winners' were those with large programmes of the greatest political salience and visibility: Education and Science, Social Security, Social Welfare, and Pensions for Government Employees (including programmes for widows and the families of former servicemen, for example). Between them they accounted for three-quarters of the total additions each year. In percentage terms, they were marginal: less than 0.5% of the Social Security budget, within 2% for Education and Science, and 3% for Pensions. Other programmes, such as Defence, Economic Cooperation, and Measures for Small Businesses, benefited but by smaller margins. Within policy groups, particular programmes and projects were 'chosen' by ministers and LDP officials to obtain maximum political advantage, or to demonstrate their concern with issues of political sensitivity or policy priority, or because of their high visibility—'last minute' negotiations to secure additional resources for an extension of the Shinkansen rail network, or a further expansion of pension programmes for veterans or war widows. Extra provision for Public Works at this stage in the budget processes was rare: normally it would have already benefited either from the General Account Budget, or from the annual expansion of FILP, or both, and especially from the expectation of further gains in the ensuing Supplementary Budget.

CONCLUSIONS

By attributing budget outputs to types of expenditure, organizations, and functions of central government, and by measuring their size, distribution, and change over the period 1975–2000, I have shown who and what won and lost in the budget processes. Both MOF and the Spending Ministries collectively benefited from the planned aggregate of general expenditures within the General Account Budget. While MOF did not succeed in cutting its size, it nevertheless succeeded in restraining the rate of planned (but not actual) growth, and in the period of fiscal reconstruction achieved a virtual standstill. The Spending Ministries benefited collectively from the continuous growth of the aggregate, even if the benefits in total for which they competed were smaller in size, and the process of their distribution more competitive and discriminatory, than in the years before 1982.

Spending Ministries also benefited from a control regime that ostensibly discriminated more against current than capital spending. In practice, despite the apparently tough controls, less than one-sixth of the total current spending was subject to cut-back guidelines; for the period 1982–7, the whole of capital spending was subject first to standstill and then cuts. The reality was that both current and capital spending continued to grow; apparent cuts in capital spending programmes through the initial budget were offset by the additional resources provided off-budget through Supplementary Budgets, FILP, and some Special Accounts.

Ministries and agencies benefited from the uneven distribution of cuts and squeezes which fell disproportionately on the transfer payments to local governments to implement the central government's national programmes. Their 'own' spending programmes were more protected.

Among ministries and agencies, there were both clear winners and losers in the competition for annual resources in the initial budget. Neither growth nor decline was shared equally, or in relation to historic shares. Only among those ministries and agencies with the smallest budget share is there some evidence that past allocations were a major influence on budget decisions. Among most ministries and agencies, planned cuts and squeezes in the period of fiscal reconstruction were not shared equally, nor were they proportionate to historic budget shares; some enjoyed continuous and substantial growth. Nor did all ministries and agencies share in the fiscal expansion that occurred after 1987; some continued to lose resources.

Who won and who lost was determined mainly by the composition of each ministry's budget—the types of expenditure, and the degree of political priority accorded particular policy groups and programmes in the annual budget guidelines. However, where two or more ministries shared policy jurisdiction, and competed for resources to fund joint programmes, the allocation was influenced, sometimes determined, by the observance of the principles of 'balance' and 'fair shares'. As I shall show in the next chapter, in the Public Works policy group the historic 'balance' among MOC, MAFF, MOT, and MHW was maintained inflexibly throughout the whole period. However, the allocation of the budget for Measures for Small Businesses was less obviously determined by historic patterns: MITI lost resources to MOF almost continuously throughout the period 1975–2000; cuts and squeezes in the period of fiscal reconstruction were experienced differentially.

It is more difficult to establish whether principles of balance and fair shares were observed in the distribution of budgets *within* ministries and agencies. The Defence Agency is perhaps a special case, but it does provide some evidence that, both organizationally and functionally, historic trends of budget share were a factor in allocation. Empirical evidence of the allocation of the Public Works budget within the four recipient ministries is ambiguous (and is discussed in detail in the next chapter). The evidence of interviews with officials in other Spending Ministries suggests that, while 'balance' was a factor influencing the allocation of programme budgets among bureaux and divisions, in practice there was often more flexibility than is apparent from inspection of the aggregated data of the initial budget.

Functionally, budget outputs display characteristics of both growth and decline, with clear winners and losers closely related to changes in budget guidelines and the relative political priority accorded spending programmes between 1975–2000. Measured by the outputs of the nine policy groups, allocation in the annual budget processes was determined not mainly by past decisions, nor by historic shares of the budget. Fiscal reconstruction, consolidation, and expansion were experienced differentially among them. Cut-back was managed simultaneously to reduce some allocations, and to protect and promote other functions of government. The effects of the budget process were highly discriminatory, and variable between functions of central government. Annual rates of growth varied even when all policy groups were allocated budget increases, as happened before FY1981. With the introduction of the policy of fiscal reconstruction, there was greater variety still among the budget outputs. On the one hand, some policy functions experienced a sharp and sustained decline in the resources allocated to them; on the other, some enjoyed substantial and continuous growth. Throughout the 1980s, LDP governments gave the highest priority to defence, economic cooperation, and social security, health, and welfare, preferences reflected in their continuous exclusion from the policies of cuts and squeezes, and in the implementation of the prescribed objectives of successive medium-term sectoral plans. That conclusion is qualified for some policy groups, where the impact of annual Supplementary Budgets was substantial, reversing an apparent decline in the trend of budget allocations.

Within policy groups, the variation among programmes and sub-programmes was more marked still. The annual allocation of resources was both 'unbalanced' and often disjunctural: neither growth nor decline was evenly distributed. There is substantial evidence that programme outputs were more the result of policy choice, and political and bureaucratic priority, than they were determined by the observance of principles of the maintenance of budget shares, previous decisions, 'balance', or 'equal misery'.

Those broad conclusions support, qualify, and in some cases contradict the results of the quantitative analysis of outputs undertaken by McCubbins and Noble (1995). In a sample of 88 of the 400–500 budget 'items' for the period 1952–89, they tested hypotheses about the conventional norms of Japanese budgetary behaviour, such as 'fair shares', 'incrementalism', and 'non-retrenchment'. They concluded that there was 'no evidence at all that Japanese budgets conform to a fair-shares notion of budgetary stability' (p. 91); rejected the incrementalist budgetary model as inconsistent with their historical analysis; and found ample evidence to disprove the contention that Japanese budgets do not retrench. 'Existing explanations for Japanese budgeting, therefore, cannot account for the dynamism ... found in the budgetary data.' The analysis of this and other chapters broadly supports their conclusions, but also qualifies them in some important ways. In particular, the evidence of retrenchment in the period of fiscal reconstruction is more apparent than real when the planned, initial budget data on which they rely are compared with the revised data of Supplementary Budgets, the outcome data of the settlement of accounts, and the budgetary context widened to include off-budget sources.

McCubbins and Noble conducted their analysis at the basic level of 'item' of expenditure, where evidence of change, variation, and fluctuation is most likely to be found, because by definition 'items' fall within the policy jurisdiction of a single ministry or agency, with greater discretion from 1982 to allocate expenditures within an overall budget ceiling negotiated with MOF. Their analysis does not distinguish or compare organizational outputs, or aggregate allocations to 'items' into sub-programmes,

programmes, and policy groups. From 1982 and the prescription of more restrictive and discriminatory budget guidelines, top-down limits on ministerial and programme budgets became more significant, with ceilings for both negotiated before the submission of formal budgetary requests. Bottom-up pressures on allocations at the level of 'items' were now moderated more within ministries, among and within bureaux, than between them and MOF's Budget Bureau examiners. The latter were now as much or more concerned with the prior informal negotiation of individual ceilings for the ministries they shadowed, as with the formal examination and negotiation of the requests submitted by them.

Ministries and agencies competed for a share of a prescribed quantum of new money assigned to priority programmes, and argued the case for the maintenance of entrenched entitlements elsewhere. They negotiated ministerial ceilings, and submitted requests within them. The allocation of resources in the initial budget approved by the Cabinet in December was therefore a record or 'score-card' of the 'success' or 'failure' of each ministry's negotiation to maximize its share within a prescribed ceiling, and an indication of whether it had won or lost relative to other ministries. An analysis of budget allocations by 'item' does not capture that organizational dimension, or reveal the extent of discrimination between policy groups and their constituent programmes. As I have shown, where programmes are shared organizationally, the principles of 'balance' and 'fair shares' are more significant in determining budget outputs.

A second qualification to the general conclusions of the analysis of this chapter, and to those drawn by McCubbins and Noble, is methodological. Size, distribution, and change of output vary with the base-line used. Some planned expenditures in the initial General Account Budget are very different from revised spending plans in the Supplementary Budget; both, especially the former, are usually different from the out-turn expenditures. As I have shown, the planned expenditures of some programmes were often and substantially revised upwards in annual Supplementary Budgets—not only in periods of fiscal expansion, when additional resources were allocated to the spending plans of some ministries to stimulate economic activity, or to relieve economic and social hardship resulting from natural disasters such as the Great Hanshin–Awaji Earthquake, but also in the period of so-called retrenchment in the mid-1980s. McCubbins and Noble's reliance (1995: 111) exclusively on the data provided by *initial* budgets, and their exclusion of the 'relatively unimportant' Supplementary Budgets,[2] excludes the substantial amount of additional resources made available to the total of general expenditures. The apparent retrenchment of the General Account Budget measured in terms of planned expenditure which they detected was in reality no more than a slow-down in the rate of that growth; apparent decline in the trend of budget outputs of some policy groups was in reality transformed by regular annual supplementation into continuous growth. The evidence of the revised budget data referred to earlier in this chapter, and

---

[2] The basis for that judgement is their calculation that the 'net addition to main budget expenditures was about 4.2%, in the 1980s only 3.1%'. This refers to the total of the General Account Budget. If, as I have argued, debt service and other fixed costs are excluded, the annual supplementation of general expenditures is very much larger.

discussed in more detail in the next, contradicts their conclusion that 'spending on public works was cut drastically in the 1980s' (McCubbins and Noble 1995: 105). It actually increased annually throughout that period, and by very substantial amounts. While it is true that some ministries lost budget share, as they demonstrate, those like MOC, MOT, and MAFF benefited substantially from Supplementary Budgets and FILP allocations. It is worth repeating that neither the Supplementary Budget nor FILP was subject to the annual budget guidelines, and hence both were exempt from all formal spending controls.

Finally, McCubbins and Noble's analysis is restricted to one part of the budgetary system: the outputs of the General Account Budget, together with a sample of the Special Accounts. As I have emphasized, increasingly throughout the period 1975–2000 MOF relieved pressure on that budget caused by the accumulating deficit by substituting other sources of finance (and by expedient manipulation of cash flows, discussed in Chapter 25). Outputs of the initial General Account Budget attributed to ministries and agencies therefore understate their relative success (and failure) in obtaining resources to fund their activities. Not only Supplementary Budgets, but also some Special Accounts were sources of additional funds, while FILP provided an alternative to the General Account for some kinds of capital spending. For example, the programme of capital expenditure on school buildings was apparently in decline, measured by the allocation of resources within the Education and Science policy group in the General Account Budget. However, that decline was offset by the financing of construction and improvement through the Special Account for Schools, partly subsidized through FILP.

That qualification applies also to the functional classification of the outputs of the budgetary process: policy groups, programmes, and sub-programmes. Thus, the total output for a programme negotiated in the General Account Budget process might not score all the agreed resources allocated to it, for the reasons explained above. It follows that interpretation of change in such outputs over time is subject to the same caution: an apparent trend of growth or decline in the General Account Budget might not represent the reality of even the planned total resources (let alone the additional resources through Supplementary Budgets) allocated to a programme over time. One problem with the analysis and interpretation of budget outputs is that the three elements of General Account Budget, FILP, and the Special Accounts are not brought together, at least not in the public, official data.[3]

Despite those qualifications, it is true that the primary focus of political, bureaucratic, parliamentary, and public attention was, and continues to be, the allocations of the general expenditures in the initial General Account Budget to ministries and agencies and their major programmes. Ministers, or rather their officials, competed for shares of that element of the initial budget, and the publication in December of the outcome of that competition in the budgetary processes, both before and after the 'revival negotiations', was the focus of a great deal of public attention and critical

---

[3] The construction of conflated data is bedevilled by problems of definition and methodological problems of netting off expenditures in 'trades' between the General Account and Special Accounts, and between central and local governments.

comment. Analysis and judgements were made about which ministries and programmes had won/lost, and by how much. Accordingly, there were pressures on the Spending Ministries and Agencies to try to finance as much as possible of their programmes through the General Account Budget, in order to be able to claim credit for 'head-line' budget totals, but also to secure a higher base-level in the negotiations in the next budget cycle.

The tightening of the annual budget guidelines after 1981 had two major effects on planned budget outputs. First, their effect was less to reduce the total of general expenditures, although the rate of their growth was cut, than to make the process of allocating scarcer resources more discriminatory. The division of the aggregate of current expenditures into three categories of priority meant that most but not all programmes could establish a prima facie case for continued growth, albeit at different rates. As a result, a substantial redistribution of budget resources occurred over the period 1975–2000. The effect of the continuous priority given to programmes of defence and ODA resulted in a substantial shift of resources, as did the exemption from cut-back of the demand-driven programmes of social security, health, and welfare.

Secondly, after 1982 the win–win game that had hitherto characterized the processes of the compilation of the initial budget became to a large extent a zero-sum game, in which a finite amount of resources—the overall budget ceiling—was competed for. There were both winners and losers measured by the initial budget outputs. Competition for annual shares of scarcer additional resources was intensified; and those ministries and agencies whose budgets were vulnerable to cut-back, comprised mainly or substantially of policy groups and programmes with a lower priority— agriculture, public works, labour services, industrial support—competed to retain previous allocations, and shares of the total budget, or to slow down trend rates of decline. Ministries and agencies competed to establish prima facie cases of eligibility for priority funds, and for shares of ad hoc special programmes of capital investment. The effects of both fewer additional resources to compete for and the threat of cuts to existing allocations forced ministries and agencies to think harder about the allocation of their budgets within negotiated ceilings, and to decide on a rank order of priority both between programmes and within them. One result of greater prioritization was a redistribution of resources within programmes and sub-programmes, the budget dynamism detected by McCubbins and Noble among 'items'. Another effect of the tightening of formal expenditure controls was that both MOF and the Spending Ministries and Agencies paid more attention to the informal budgetary processes that preceded the prescription of ministerial budget ceilings. Those ceilings set the upper limits to their formal budget requests.

The Role and Influence of the LDP

What role did the LDP play more generally in the new zero-sum game in which, after 1982, there were now potential losers among Spending Ministries, policy groups, and programmes? Committed to the principles of MOF's 'sound management' of the national finances that underlay the policies of fiscal reconstruction, it approved and supported MOF's attempts to cut and restrain the growth of the General Account Budget. Each year it formally approved or reaffirmed the budget guidelines proposed by MOF, which incorporated the political priority it wished to accord to particular policy groups and programmes, pre-eminently defence and ODA, and the protection it wished to afford others, such as social security, welfare, and health programmes. In so doing, it appeared to approve implicitly also the adverse implications of those discriminatory budget guidelines: that those ministries and agencies, policy groups, and programmes without priority, or lower in the rank order, were to be subject to cut-back or budget restraint. At risk were some of those programmes that the LDP had maintained at high and rising levels of expenditure as crucial elements in the politico-electoral strategy that had helped to maintain it in power. Why did it approve or acquiesce in a regime of spending control which apparently threatened that strategy, risked alienating the electoral support of groups such as farmers, small businessmen, and local builders, and apparently denied itself the demonstrable electoral benefits of more spending on local roads, harbours, bridges, and the improvement of social and environmental infrastructure?

The explanation is only partly that the LDP had less need of the support of such groups after the reorientation of its electoral strategy in the early 1970s, focused more on urban and metropolitan electorates. While support for (the declining number of) small farmers through the subsidization of rice production through the Food Control Programme was progressively reduced after 1980, the LDP continued to provide subsidies and grants for agricultural improvement schemes, most conspicuously in the 6.2 trillion compensation for the projected opening of domestic markets following the GATT agreement of 1994. It was able to do that, and to continue to deliver other traditional budget benefits and favours, by exploiting the potential of supplementary and alternative sources and methods of public finance. Some evidence of the use of Supplementary Budgets to allocate additional resources to programmes cut and squeezed by the application of formal budget guidelines to the initial budget has been presented in this chapter. Chapter 23 examines the budget outputs of public works, and explains how off-budget sources of finance were used to maintain a profile of continuous growth throughout the period 1975–2000.

22

Cuts and Squeezes in the Bureaucracy

Japan's public sector is small compared with other G7 countries. With a ratio of less than 40 public employees per 1,000 population, in 1998 it was a half the size of that in the UK and the USA, and a third of that in France. By March of that year there were nearly 5 million employees distributed between the national government, local government, public corporations, and organizations affiliated to government, as shown in Table 22.1.

There are four broad organizational categories of central government officials, shown in Table 22.2. The first category (non-industrial) comprises the staffs of ministries, agencies, and commissions, with which we are mainly concerned in this chapter. It also includes teachers, doctors, nurses, and related educational and medical staff employed in national schools, colleges and universities, and hospitals and medical establishments. As national government employees, their salaries and running costs were borne on the Special Accounts controlled by the ministries that supervised them. Nearly two-thirds of all non-industrial officials were employed outside Tokyo, in regional, prefectural, and local offices of various ministries and agencies. In March 1998 there were 233 regional 'block' offices, 599 prefectual offices, and about 5,500 local offices (excluding post offices). Their expenditure was counted on the budgets of the parent ministries and agencies.

The second category (industrial) comprises the staff of four (previously five) government enterprises, each supervised within the jurisdiction of a ministry. Both the Self-Defence Armed Forces, and the independently appointed staff of the Diet, the courts, and the Board of Audit are normally excluded from the definition of 'central government', as we do hereafter.

Table 22.1 *Public-sector employment, March 1998*

Organizational category	No. employed
Central government[a]	1,156,290
Local government[b]	67,118
Public corporations[c]	528,553
	4,951,961

[a]31 March 1998.
[b]1 April 1997.
[c]1 January 1996.

Source: *Annual Report*, MCA, 1998.

Table 22.2 *Central government employees, March 1998*

Sub-sector		No. employed
Non-industrial		533,770
Ministries, agencies, and commissions	345,068	
National schools, universities, hospitals, etc.	188,702	
Industrial (Government enterprises)		319,107
Self-defence forces		292,358
Diet, Court, Audit, etc.		31,055[a]
		1,156,290

[a] Includes 148 ministers, parliamentary vice-ministers, chairmen, and full-time members of commissions, the director-general of the Cabinet Legislation Bureau, the two deputy chief secretaries of the Cabinet, and some of the Imperial Household staff. They are all included in the category 'Special Services' under the National Public Service Law, differentiated from the remainder of national government employees who are categorized as 'regular services'.

Source: *Annual Report*, MCA, 1998; IAM (1999).

A concerted attempt to reduce the number of central government employees began in 1967, a decade or so earlier than the cuts and squeezes that occurred in most other G7 countries. In 1965 the General Account Budget became unbalanced for the first time since the implementation of the Dodge Line, and government bonds were issued to cover the deficit. To restrain the growth of the size of central executive, the Government enacted the Total Staff Number Law in FY1967, which limited the numbers of full-time staff employed in ministries and agencies, and in national hospitals and schools. The following year the first of a continuous series of personnel reduction plans was initiated, prescribing a planned reduction of the total number of staff; the Eighth, for 1992–6, provided for a planned reduction of 39,048, although the actual reduction was greater, 42,362, mainly in the National Forestry Service, MAFF, and the Hokkaido Development Agency. The Ninth Plan for 1997–2001 provided for a planned reduction of 35,122 posts, 4.11% of the total at the end of FY1996.

Each ministry and agency negotiated with the Management and Coordination Agency (MCA) a target reduction for each plan period, based on assessments of the trends in staffing, volume of work, potential productivity improvements, turnover rates, the possibility of rationalization (abolition, contracting out, etc.), and taking into account changes in working practices. Targets were prepared by MCA and the whole reduction plan was submitted to Cabinet. After the Cabinet's formal decision, the internal distribution of the agreed cuts to achieve the target was left largely to the discretion of each ministry and agency. Each year they submitted their plans for reduction to the MCA, indicating the target to be achieved in the following fiscal year. At the same time, to provide flexibly for the expansion of services in some areas, and to staff new functions and programmes, each organization could bid each year for new posts. In practice, the implementation of planned reductions created a 'pool' of surplus employees in a 'staff size account' which MCA drew on to staff agreed new posts, normally within the same ministry or agency or their satellites, but also among them. What remained in that account became the total number of personnel cut in each fiscal year. Both proposals for the implementation of the reduction plan and bids for new posts were submitted by each ministry and agency to the MCA at the end of August. Bids were examined by its Administrative Management Bureau with a view to need, efficiency, practicability, and enforceability.

As a result of the implementation of eight successive plans from FY1967, the size of the central executive was reduced by a net total of 46,456 posts, just over 5%, from 899,333 to 852,877, by the end of March 1998. That apparently modest achievement after nearly 30 years of concentrated and sustained effort to reduce the number of national government employees presents a misleading picture, because it is the *net* result of a large number of *gross* movements of both increases and reductions among central government organizations. The implementation of the plans resulted in a gross reduction of 284,494 posts between FY1967 and FY1996, offset by the creation of new posts to provide for expansion in different policy areas to make a total of 240,257. The gross reduction helped the government to respond flexibly to the demands of new and expanding policy areas. Crucially for the budget, salary and related costs were contained in the early 1980s when fiscal pressures became acute, and, in the period of fiscal reconstruction that followed, were even reduced. In 1981 pay and other costs absorbed 4.8% of the gross General Account Budget, reduced progressively to 4.3% in 1991.

This chapter examines the extent to which policies of fiscal reconstruction in the 1980s resulted in cuts and squeezes to the number and distribution of officials in the Spending Ministries and Agencies, compared with those employed in other parts of the central government—the staffs of national hospitals, schools, and government enterprises. Secondly, it looks at the distribution of those cuts among the Spending Ministries and Agencies to determine which of them gained or lost, and to test the familiar proposition that policies were implemented 'evenhandedly', to maintain 'balance', and to avoid competition and conflict. Thirdly, it looks at the distribution of those gains and losses within Spending Ministries and Agencies to assess the extent to which the central core of the executive—senior, managerial, and professional staff employed on central policy-making functions at headquarters (HQ) offices—was protected or protected itself from the full rigour of cuts and squeezes. Experience of cut-back management in comparable G7 countries has shown that the effects of sustained cuts tend to be felt more severely at the periphery, than at the centre—by local and branch offices, by subordinate agencies of the central executive, and by junior, ancillary, technical, and industrial staff, rather than by senior management and professional staff (Thain and Wright 1995).

From 1968 to 1982, the burden of the planned cuts was shared between the 'non-industrial' officials in the Spending Ministries, Agencies and national schools and hospitals on the one hand, and the 'industrials' in the government enterprises on the other. However, the latter's 64,138 lost posts represented a 17.2% reduction of their total staff, compared with 13.2% (69,653) in ministries and agencies. National hospitals and schools lost a total of 17,876 (12.2%) posts from a staff of 146,070 in 1968 (AMA 1982). Between 1982 and 1995 a further 137,883 posts were lost overall as a result of the implementation of planned cuts. It is not possible to calculate the

Cuts in the Bureaucracy

distribution between the three categories, but the evidence suggests that ministries and agencies shared the burden of cuts with other central government organizations, although more cuts were imposed on 'industrials' in the government enterprises.

How were those planned cuts distributed within ministries and agencies? From 1968 to 1983, most of the cuts were made outside the central core staff, in regional, prefectural, and local branch offices, and in subordinate agencies. The prime examples were MAFF's Food Agency and Local Statistical Offices, which together contributed the greater part of the planned reductions in its total staff; its central HQ staff suffered fewer cuts. A similar phenomenon is observable in the Ministry of Construction, where the deepest cuts occurred in the staffs of local construction offices. A similar trend is observable in the decade after 1983. As we saw in Chapter 4, in its First Report the Provisional Commission for Administrative Reform had recommended in 1981 an across-the-board reduction of 5% in staff numbers, subsequently incorporated and implemented through a revised personnel reduction plan for 1982–6. Slightly more reductions were achieved than planned, and the 49,934 posts were shared proportionately between ministries and agencies collectively on the one hand, and government enterprises on the other. Some of the former lost more than 5% of their staff, with MAFF and the Hokkaido Development Agency being the biggest losers, although MOL, MOC, and the AMA/MCA also suffered above-average cuts. Again, those losses were borne more by local and regional offices and satellite agencies than by HQ staff in the ministry. As a result, between 1984 and 1988, 54 regional 'block' offices were abolished, together with 178 offices at the prefectural level and 809 offices at other levels. This experience of the incidence of planned cuts was repeated more widely, though less sharply, across the whole of the central executive.

Planned cuts were implemented concurrently with bids for new posts. Responding flexibly to the needs and demands of new government functions (for example telecommunications and biotechnology), the changing priority between some services and activities (for example housing and industrial support), the decline of established policy areas such as agriculture, and the emergence of new issues on the national policy agenda (the environment), MCA and MOF were prepared to accede to bids from Spending Ministries and Agencies for additional staff where a case could be made out that they were necessary and justified. In the period 1968–82, 141,068 new posts were authorized. The largest increase (40%) took place in the staff of national hospitals, schools, colleges, and so on, reflecting the increased priority given to higher education and affiliated institutions, and to nationally provided highly advanced medical services, such as national cancer centres. The remainder was shared evenly between ministries, agencies, and government enterprises. After the adoption of the policy of fiscal reconstruction, and the imposition by MOF of negative ceilings on the General Account Budget in 1982, the ceiling for new posts was halved. Comparable data for the gross numbers of new posts from 1982 to 1997 is unavailable, but the continued increase in the net totals of staff in hospitals and schools suggests that the earlier trends of distribution were maintained.

The net effects of planned cuts and annual increases on the size and distribution of staff within the central executive is shown in Table 22.3 at five stages in the period from FY1967 to the end of FY1997. The first shows the position at the introduction of the

Table 22.3 Squeezing the central government, FY1967–FY1997 (fiscal year end)

	FY1967	FY1982	FY1991	FY1995	FY1997	Change, FY1967–FY1997 (%)
Non-industrials	525,849	536,190	533,246	534,369	533,770	+7,921 (+1.5)
Ministries and agencies	379,769	354,758	344,993	345,766	345,068	−34,701 (−9.1)
National hospitals, etc.	44,517	52,243	53,547	53,598	53,596	+9,079 (+20.4)
National universities, schools	101,563	129,189	134,706	135,005	135,106	+33,543 (+33.0)
Industrials (government enterprises)	373,484	352,541	330,008	322,836	319,107	−54,377 (−14.6)
Mint and Printing (MOF)	9,738	8,420	7,800	7,563	7,451	−2,287 (−23.5)
National Forestry (MAFF)	41,148	31,623	17,671	11,331	8,991	−32,157 (−78.1)
Postal Service (MPT)	321,347	312,498	304,537	303,942	302,665	−18,682 (−5.8)
Alcohol Monopoly[a] (MITI)	1,251	0	0	0	0	−1,251 (−100)
Total central government	899,333	888,731	863,254	857,205	852,877	−46,456 (−5.2)

[a] Abolished 1982.

Source: IIAS (1982); Masujima and O'uchi (1993); Horié (1996); *Annual Report*, MCA, 1998.

Total Staff Number Law. The second stage shows the net effects of the implementation of that law, and of the plans for personnel reduction and annual staff reviews immediately following the adoption of the policy of fiscal reconstruction, and the imposition of zero budget ceilings. The third and fourth stages show the net effects on staff numbers after more than a decade of tighter budgetary and manpower control. Finally, staff numbers are given for FY1997.

The net reduction of 46,456 posts between FY1967 and FY1997 represented a little over 5% of the total for the central government as a whole. More than three-quarters of that reduction occurred in the period after the adoption of the policy of fiscal reconstruction, and the imposition of zero and negative budget ceilings in 1982. From the middle of the 1990s, there was a much sharper net loss of jobs than at any time since 1968, the consequence of the deterioration in the condition of the national finances in the circumstances of the deep and prolonged economic recession. Secondly, the total non-industrial staff showed a net gain over the whole period of 7,921 posts, but unevenly distributed. National hospitals (20%) and schools (33%) were net beneficiaries, while ministries and agencies were net losers (-9.1%). Thirdly, the largest contribution to the reduction in the size of the central government as a whole was made by the industrial staff of the government enterprises, which between them lost a net total of 54,337 posts (14.6%) between FY1967 and FY1997.

The net loss of 34,701 posts by ministries and agencies represented a 9% fall on the staff numbers for FY1967, compared with a loss of 14.6% for government enterprises. However, if allowance is made on the one hand for the creation after 1968 of the new ministerial agencies for Okinawa, National Land, and Environment, and hence new posts, and the abolition of one of the five government enterprises (and loss of posts on another), the net effects of staff changes are very little different between the non-industrial and industrial categories. Ministries and agencies were not markedly more favourably treated than government enterprises. Nor were they able to deflect manpower cuts from their HQ and local office staff to their enterprises. The latter were set planned targets for personnel reduction independently of the former, and it was not possible to protect central core staff by weighting overall ministry targets more heavily against individual enterprises. In practice, their planned target reductions tended to be very similar in percentage terms to those set for their supervising ministries and other ministries and agencies.

Within the industrial category of government enterprises, the net changes produced the greatest losses in the National Forestry Service. Total staff numbers declined by 78% between FY1967 and FY1997, reflecting the diminishing political salience of domestic agricultural policy generally, but, more specifically, the result of policies agreed by Cabinet in 1990 and 1991 to improve the management and financial control in the Forestry Service itself. By March 1998 its accumulated debts and liabilities totalled 3.5 trillion. A further reorganization and reduction of staff was enacted in October 1998. Net losses of staff sustained by MOF's Mint and Government Printing Enterprises, and from a very much larger base by MPT's Postal Service, were much more modest by comparison. The latter's 6% reduction was much less than that of Spending Ministries and Agencies generally. Whether this was the result of the LDP's concern to protect a traditional source of local electoral influence through local postmasters, or was due to the influence of the strong postal *zoku* and the local postmasters' association is impossible to determine. MCA (unsurprisingly) denies that such considerations influenced its judgements.

The size and distribution of the net losses suffered by the Spending Ministries and Agencies between FY1967 and FY1997 are shown in Table 22.4. The totals for MOE and

Table 22.4 *Spending ministries and agencies: staff numbers, FY1967–FY1997* (fiscal year end)

	FY1967	FY1982	FY1997	Change, 1967–97 (%)
Prime Minister's Office and agencies				
Cabinet Office	172	190	253	+81 (47.0)
PM's Office proper	4,007	3,306	589	−3,418 (85.3)
MCA/AMA	1,667	1,459	3,576	+1,909 (114.5)
Defence Agency	30,469	27,359	24,926	−5,543 (18.2)
EPA	594	515	514	−80 (13.5)
STA	2,003	2,171	2,123	+120 (6.0)
Environmental Agency (1971)	—	907	1,008	—
Hokkaido Development Agency	11,848	9,861	7,554	−4,294 (36.2)
National Land Agency (1974)	51	447	467	+416 (815)
Okinawa Development Agency (1972)	—	1,110	1,148	—
Others[a]	9,702	9,776	9,948	−246 (2.5)
Sub-total	60,513	57,101	52,106	−8,407 (13.9)
Ministries				
MOJ	47,819	49,938	51,208	+3,389 (7.1)
MOFA	2,746	3,632	5,094	+2,348 (85.5)
MOF[b]	67,506	68,084	72,358	+4852 (7.2)
MOE[f]	2,934	3,297	3,104	+170 (5.8)
MHW[g]	21,092	21,907	22,494	+1402 (6.6)
MAFF[c]	62,139	48,541	36,508	−25,631 (41.2)
MITI[d]	12,933	12,974	12,404	−529 (4.1)
MOT	34,898	38,207	37,689	+2,791 (8.0)
MPT[e]	3,325	2,971	2,789	−536 (16.1)
MOL	27,621	25,340	24,983	−2,638 (9.5)
MOC	35,719	28,128	23,742	−11,977 (33.5)
MHA	524	549	589	+65 (12.4)
Sub-total	319,256	303,568	292,962	−26,294 (8.2)
TOTAL	379,769	354,758	345,068	−34,701 (9.1)

[a] Includes non-ministerial agencies and commissions within the Prime Minister's Office.
[b] Excludes staff in Mint and Government Printing Offices.
[c] Excludes staff in National Forestry Service.
[d] Excludes staff in Alcohol Monopoly.
[e] Excludes staff in postal services.
[f] Excludes staff in national schools and universities.
[g] Excludes staff in national hospitals.

Source: IIAS (1982); Horié (1996); *Annual Report*, MCA, 1998.

MHW exclude the staffs of national schools and hospitals; and numbers for government enterprises are excluded from the totals for supervising ministries. Staff numbers for the subsidiary agencies within the jurisdiction of Spending Ministries (e.g. MOF's NTAA, MAFF's Food Agency and Fisheries Agency, MOT's Marine Safety Agency) are conflated with those for HQ, local, and branch offices.

Cuts and squeezes were experienced differentially among the Spending Ministries and Agencies. Gains and loses were unevenly distributed. Seven Spending Ministries and two ministerial agencies emerged as clear winners, increasing the size of their staffs over the period 1967–97. Substantial volume gains were made by MOJ, MOFA, MOF, MOT, and MHW, and marginal gains by MOE and MHA. The latter was however a small office, and on that account its central core received some protection from cuts—besides which, the increase was explained partly by the additional work created by the new local electoral system. If the staff of national hospitals and schools are included in the totals for their parent ministries, MHW and MOE emerge as very clear winners. There were three clear losers: MAFF, MOL, and MOC. Overall, ministries lost almost 8.5% of their work-forces, compared with losses of 13.9% in the Prime Minister's Office and its agencies as a whole. Within the latter, the Defence Agency and the Hokkaido Development Agency were substantial losers. No agency, apart from the MCA, which was reconstructed and reorganized with the abolition of the AMA in 1984, added other than very marginally to its staff. Part of the explanation is that most agencies within the Prime Minister's Office have mainly coordinating and staff functions rather than line management responsibilities. The acquisition of new functions, and the growth (and decline) of others, occurred largely but not entirely within ministries, rather than ministerial agencies. The decline in staff of the Defence Agency (especially the Defence Facilities Agency) and the Hokkaido Development Agency was mainly the result of significant policy changes. In the former, as the number and size of US military and air bases declined, the number of support staff was reduced.

CONCLUSION

The analysis of the size and distribution of the implementation of planned cuts and annual increases from 1967 to 1998 provides some qualified support for the hypothesis that in a climate of cut-back the core staff of senior, managerial, and professional staff employed on policy-making functions and activities in the central government tends to be protected or to protect itself from the full rigour of cuts and squeezes. First, while the headquarters staffs of ministries and agencies were not wholly insulated from the regime of planned cuts, the net effects on their numbers were less severe than on the 'industrials' in the government enterprises. Secondly, net losses among Spending Ministries tended to be concentrated in regional, prefectural, and local offices or satellite agencies rather than at HQ. The sharp losses in MAFF's Food Agency and in MOC's local construction offices have already been mentioned. Many local and regional offices carried out national policies for public (construction) works, regulated economic and social activities, and provided assistance and information services to business and citizens. There was more scope for potential cuts outside headquarters offices

Table 22.5 *Administrative core of the central executive, FY1967–FY1995 (fiscal year end)*

	No. of officials		Change	
	FY1967	FY1995	No.	%
Administrative service I[a]	251,467	240,973	−10,494	−4.2
Administrative service II	62,479	21,045	−41,434	−66.3
Total administrative service	313,946	262,018	−51,928	−16.5

[a] Includes staff employed as professional/specialized, a category distinguished separately from ASI in 1986. It includes patent examiners, air traffic controllers, etc., whose numbers increased from 6,708 in 1986 to 7,931 in 1995.

Source: Horié (1996).

because of the larger numbers employed, and because of the nature of the work performed there; the implementation of policy lent itself more readily to rationalization through, for example, contracting out and computerization. It was more difficult to make cuts in the numbers of those employed in policy-making functions without a radical shift of policy jurisdiction—privatization for example. But by the same token, the implementation of new policies or new functions took place mainly outside headquarters or in executive agencies, and hence more new posts were created in local than in headquarters offices, and in the staff of national hospitals and schools. Thirdly, cuts and squeezes were distributed unevenly. The 'misery' was not shared: there were both winners and losers.

Fourthly, the core policy-making staff at HQ offices maintained their position. The analysis of the composition of the non-industrial staff of Spending Ministries and Agencies in Table 22.5 shows that the effects of changes in staff numbers were experienced differentially between senior and junior administrators. Manual workers, machine operators, janitors, messengers, and so on (Administrative Service Level II) contributed four-fifths of the total net reductions between FY1967 and FY1995. By comparison, officials, diplomats, and other office workers employed in the making and carrying out of policy suffered far fewer net losses (4.2%). And as we have seen, those losses tended to occur mainly at local and branch offices or in satellite agencies rather than at HQ.

In the reorganization of central government implemented in 2001, the government was committed to further reductions in the number of officials. Prime Minister Obuchi had announced the intention to reduce the number of officials by a quarter within ten years. The implementation of this goal would require larger annual reductions throughout the first decade of the new millennium than had been achieved in the previous 40 years. However, proposals to privatize national universities if implemented could provide the greater part of that reduction, some 120,000 posts.

23

A 'Public Works State'

Historically, Japan invested, and continues to invest, a greater proportion of its GDP in gross fixed capital formation than comparable industrialized countries. Public and private investment combined averaged about 30% of GDP from 1982, twice the level achieved in the USA and UK, while the remaining G7 countries managed only two-thirds of the Japanese ratio. General government gross fixed capital formation accounted for about a fifth of the total, but on a rising trend in the 1990s, reaching 6.7% of GDP in FY1995, as government made repeated attempts to kick-start the economy with public works spending. As private investment declined after the collapse of the bubble economy, general government claimed an increasing proportion. Table 23.1 shows the details for FY1990–FY1997.

Public investment by central government was planned and financed partly through the General Account Budget, partly through FILP, and partly through some of the 38 Special Accounts. The investment provided through the General Account Budget was financed largely by government borrowing through the issue of government 'construction' bonds, while FILP funds were provided mainly by the Trust Fund Bureau Fund, the largest element of which was postal savings. Local governments' public

Table 23.1 *Gross domestic investment in the public and private sectors, FY1990–FY1997 (current prices, trillion yen)*

FY	Public and private sectors' gross fixed captial formation[a]		General government gross fixed capital formation[b]		General government % of total public and private investment
	Total	% GDP	Total	% GDP	
1990	140.085	31.9	21.914	5.0	15.6
1991	143.924	31.1	23.909	5.2	16.6
1992	143.141	30.3	28.033	5.9	19.5
1993	139.231	29.2	31.158	6.5	22.3
1994	136.428	28.5	30.501	6.4	22.4
1995	140.883	28.8	32.517	6.7	23.2
1996	147.736	29.3	31.327	6.2	21.2
1997	141.007	27.9	28.987	5.7	20.6

[a] Excludes increase in stocks.
[b] Excludes residential buildings and plant and equipment, and increase in stocks.
Source: *Annual Report on National Accounts*, 1999, EPA; Economic Research Institute, 2000, EPA.

investment was financed through transfer payments and subsidies from the General Account Budget, and through their own independent sources of revenue and borrowing, including loans from FILP agencies. Finally, some of the public investment schemes financed by public banks and finance corporations, and public corporations and special companies, apart from substantial FILP funding, were self-financed and/or financed by approved borrowing in domestic and overseas capital markets.

PUBLIC WORKS EXPENDITURES

There were two main categories of public investment programmes: public works (*kōkyō jigyō*) and what the Japanese call 'public facilities' (*shisetsu-hi*). The latter included the creation of fixed capital—for example in school-building and related facilities, hospitals and social welfare facilities, and government buildings. In FY1994 investment in such facilities financed through the General Account was approximately 1 trillion, compared with nearly 9 trillion for public works. The remainder of this chapter is concerned with public works, which includes *inter alia* investment in roads, bridges, railways, ports, airports, and harbours; agricultural infrastructure and land improvement schemes; parks, open spaces, and recreational and cultural facilities; urban regeneration; housing; water and sewage facilities.

There are four main categories of public works: first, public works under the jurisdiction of the central government, which provided two-thirds of the finance to local government's one-third; secondly, public works under the jurisdiction of local governments, half the finance for which was provided by them and half by central government; thirdly, public works under the jurisdiction of local governments alone, with no central government subsidy; and fourthly, public works provided by public corporations and companies, for example the Japan Highway Public Corporation, partly funded by FILP. We are concerned here with those public works financed wholly or partly by the central government through the General Account Budget, Supplementary Budgets, FILP, and some of the Special Accounts. Apart from those Special Accounts that helped finance investment in public facilities such as school buildings and hospitals, there were five others—for roads, harbours, improvement schemes, and national forests and fields projects. Some of those (e.g. roads and airports) had hypothecated revenues derived from specific indirect taxes (e.g. petrol and aviation fuel), but all derived most of their funds for public works from transfers from the General Account and FILP Budgets. With depreciating assests, all six became increasingly dependent on subsidies from the General Account Budget in the 1990s. More than half of the annual finance of the Special Accounts for harbours, flood control, and land improvement schemes was provided in this way.

Two-thirds of all public works programmes and projects were carried out by local governments, mainly prefectural and municipal authorities; the central government was responsible directly for only 11%, while public corporations and companies provided most of the remainder. Local governments accounted for about 80% of Japan's annual public capital formation in the calculation of general government expenditure in the National Accounts. Public works projects, and the construction of public facilities such as hospitals and schools, together absorbed about a third of all local government expenditure annually, the total of 31 trillion (in the FY1995 settled account) amounting to more than the combined amount of social security and education, the other two big local spending programmes. The size and composition of the programmes for public works and public facilities at the local level were closely related to the objectives and priorities set by central government.

Seen in the context of other G7 or OECD countries, Japan's national (and local) politics traditionally had a strong distributive orientation. The emphasis on public works (and agricultural subsidies) was one of the most enduring and significant characteristics of its post-war political economy. Japan spent five times as much on public works as other OECD countries (OECD 1997). With approximately a fifth of the total of general expenditures in the General Account Budget, public works was regularly the second largest programme, after social security. The rationale of a continuous pre-emption of such a large share of the Budget was a mixture of socio-economic and political factors. Throughout the period 1975–2000, MOF repeatedly justified the scale of resources devoted to public works by reference to the lack and poor quality of Japan's social infrastructure compared with other G7 countries. For example, despite continuing high levels of investment, only half of domestic households outside Tokyo and other main cities were connected to main sewage systems, compared with 70% in the USA and 90% in the UK, Germany, and elsewhere; only 74% of roads other than national highways were paved, compared with 90%–100% in other G7 countries; while the number and distribution of parks, open spaces, and local environmental, cultural, and educational amenities also compared unfavourably (MOF 1998c). In Tokyo there were only 2.9 square metres of city parks per resident compared with 25.6 in London, 27.4 in Berlin, 29.3 in New York, and 11.8 in Paris (MOC 1997a). Such comparisons are not however unambiguous justification for more public works spending. Such 'shortages' might have been compensated by other related investment, or reflected previous inefficient allocations.

Whatever the merits of the social argument, the *political* rationale for the continuing high levels of public works spending derived partly from the LDP's response to those and other perceived deficiencies of 'social overhead capital', and the priority given to their improvement in its re-oriented policy aims and objectives from the 1970s onwards. At the same time, public works spending was an instrument of the party's grand electoral strategy, a means to distribute benefits generally to rural and urban electorates through highly visible projects of local investment and specifically targeted special interest groups and clientele, in exchange directly and indirectly for electoral and financial support. Finally, the expansion of the public works budget was justified by MOF and LDP governments economically as a means of stimulating the economy at times of slow-down and recession, and at other times in response to international pressure to increase the level of domestic demand to contribute to faster growth in G7 and other industrial countries.

This chapter seeks to answer three questions. First, how were decisions made to determine the aggregate of the public works budget, and to allocate it among the competing needs and demands of the Spending Ministries and Agencies? Secondly, what criteria determined the distribution of shares among policy sectors, ministries, and bureaux? To what extent were they relatively fixed over time, the result of the observance of informal rules-of-the-game? Thirdly, to what extent did the LDP influence the size, composition, and distribution of the public works budget? The first part of the chapter outlines the main policy sectors, the jurisdiction of the Spending Ministries and Agencies, and their five-year investment plans. It then goes on to analyse the trends of budget outputs in the initial and revised General Account Budgets, and to draw attention to the significance of Supplementary Budgets and other 'off-budget' sources as a means of financing additional public works spending. The third part of the chapter examines the allocation of the public works budget among and within competing ministries, policy sectors, and functions. The conclusions of the analysis are summarized in the next section which contrasts the appearance and reality of public works spending. This leads into a discussion, first, of the efficiency and effectiveness with which resources were used; and, finally, of the role and influence of the LDP in the construction and maintenance of a 'public works state'.

PUBLIC WORKS SECTORS

Public works programmes and projects were distinguished sectorally. Each was the sole or shared responsibility mainly of three ministries—MOC, MAFF, and MOT—which between them accounted for about 96% of the public works budget in the General Account. The remainder was shared mainly by MHW, MITI, and the Environment Agency. Each of the three main ministries, with jurisdictional authority for one or more sectors, had a number of medium-term investment plans, the overall planned costs of which it negotiated and agreed with MOF's Budget Bureau. Until 1989, the orientation and scale of the resources allocated to those plans were prescribed in the national goals and objectives in successive five-year National Medium Term Economic Plans. That for 1979–85 was the last to do so. As MOF embarked upon fiscal reconstruction in the early 1980s, the details of sector-by-sector planned investment were omitted. With a continuing crisis in the financing of a growing deficit on the General Account Budget, MOF was unwilling to commit resources to particular sectoral plans for future years. In an uncertain and difficult financial climate, it wanted to be able to respond flexibly and contingently to changes in the economic and fiscal environment as they occurred. As public finances improved in the years of the 'bubble economy', MOF felt more confident to underwrite the government's objective expressed in the 1988–92 National Plan to improve 'social overhead capital', particularly to enhance living standards and the quality of life. Resources were allocated sectorally in the 1990 Basic Plan for Public Investment, which provided also a major part of the formal response of the Japanese government to US demands for increased domestic investment in the concluding agreement of the Structural Impediments Initiative in 1990 (EPA 1994*b*). It provided for the commitment of 430 trillion over a ten-year period from FY1991 to FY2000. In October 1994, the Coalition government of Prime Minister Murayama committed additional funds for public investment, and those for the Basic Plan were increased to 650 trillion from FY1995 to FY2004. Table 23.2 shows the ministerial responsibility for public works sectors, together with the investment plans and planned total investment for the period up to the year 2000. Each year, the Spending Ministries and Agencies bid for shares of the General Account Budget to

Table 23.2 Ministries' long-term sectoral plans and investments, 1996–2006 (trillion yen)

Ministry	Sectors	Plan	Duration	Total planned investment	Planned investment per annum
MOC	Flood control	9th Flood Control Plan	1997–2003	24.0	3.43
	Roads	12th Roads Plan	1998–2002	78.0	15.6
	Sewage	8th Sewage Plan	1996–2002	23.7	3.39
	Urban parks	6th Urban Parks Plan	1996–2002	7.2	1.03
	Housing	7th Housing Plan	1996–2000	[7.3 million units; 3.6 with public funds]	[1.46 units]
	Traffic safety[a]	6th Traffic Safety Plan	1996–2002	2.69	0.38
	Slope failure prevention	4th Slope Failure Protection Plan	1998–2002	1.19	0.24
MAFF	Fishing ports	9th Fishing Ports Plan	1994–2001	3.0	0.38
	Land improvement	4th Land Improvement Plan	1993–2006	41.0	2.93
	Forestry improvement	2nd Forest Improvement Plan	1997–2003	5.38	0.77
	Inshore fishery	4th Inshore Fishery Plan	1994–2001	0.6	0.08
	Erosion control	9th Programme of Forest Conservation Projects	1997–2003	3.77	0.54
MOT	Airports	7th Airports Development Plan	1996–2002	3.6	0.51
	Ports	9th Plan for Improvement of Ports and Harbours	1996–2002	7.49	1.07
MOC/MAFF/MOT	Shore protection	6th Shore Protection Plan	1996–2002	1.77	0.25
MHW	Waste disposal	8th Plan for Waste Disposal Facilities	1996–2002	5.05	0.72
TOTAL				208.44	31.31

[a] Shared with the National Police Agency.

Source: constructed from data supplied by MOC.

PUBLIC WORKS OUTPUTS OF THE GENERAL ACCOUNT BUDGET

Public works spending in the General Account Budget was in principle controlled by the limits prescribed annually in the formal budget guidelines. In practice, for most of the period 1975–2000 those limits were exceeded, often by substantial amounts. Figure 23.1 compares the changes in the guidelines with those of the planned allocations in the initial budget. In the period of fiscal reconstruction, after two years of success in achieving standstill, MOF failed to cut the allocation by 5% annually as prescribed for the four years 1984–7. Thereafter, apart from the special circumstances of FY1995, the planned allocation was almost always greater than the prescribed limits.

Spending on public works programmes planned in the initial General Account Budget increased from 2.9 trillion in 1975 to more than 9 trillion in 2000, accounting annually for between 18% and 20% of the total of general expenditures. The rapid expansion of the public works budget initiated by Prime Minister Tanaka in the early 1970s continued

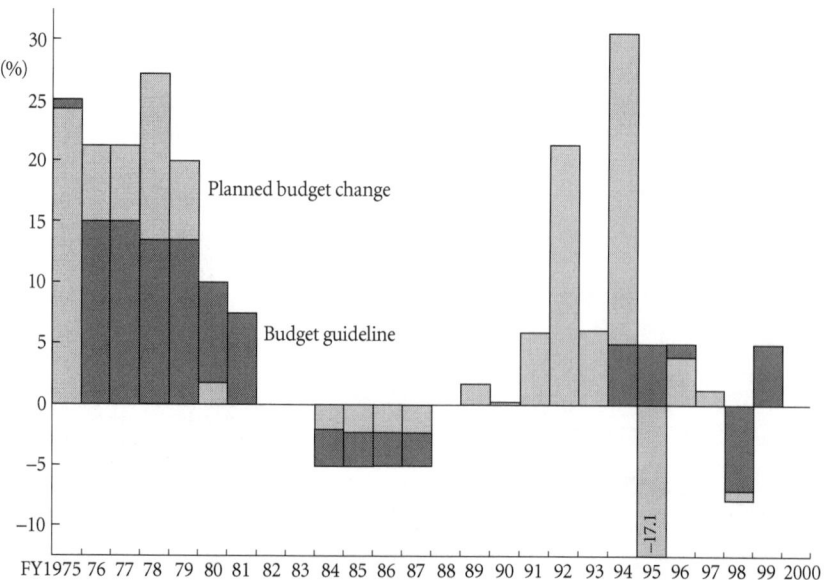

Figure 23.1 *Budget guidelines and planned allocation of public works expenditure, FY1975–FY2000*
General Account Initial Budget: percentage change
Source: *The Japanese Budget in Brief* (annually), Budget Bureau, MOF.

until FY1980, with annual increases of more than 20%, well in excess of the prescribed budget guidelines. In cash terms, the planned budget for public works spending was frozen in the early 1980s, and then marginally cut during the four years 1984–7, although those cuts were less than half of the maximum reduction of 5% prescribed in the annual budget guidelines. This was the period of the public recognition and politicization of the fiscal crisis through the activities of Rinchō, set up in 1981 (discussed in Chapter 4). In 1988 budget controls were relaxed, and a standstill budget was restored for public investment. Despite that intention, the planned initial allocations began to rise once again.

With the onset of economic recession in 1991, the government introduced several ad hoc schemes of public works expenditure aimed at the promotion of public investment, the improvement of living standards, and the expansion of educational and scientific research. By FY1993 those were worth 500 billion of additional public works. After the report of the MOF's Fiscal System Council in November 1993 recommending greater prioritization in the allocation of the public works budget (discussed below), the schemes were conflated within a new budget guideline for FY1994 permitting a general increase of public works expenditure up to a maximum of 5%. With other sources of off-budget finance available (see below), MOF was able to contain planned allocations within that figure for the next three years. (The extraordinary increase of 30% in FY1994 was due mainly to the repayment of debt on previous loans to finance public works spending, again discussed below.) In FY1998 the public works budget was cut by 7.7%, one of the 'caps' prescribed in the Fiscal Structural Reform Act of 1997. Further cuts were planned for each year of the 'intensive reform period' up to 2001. However, the controls in that legislation were suspended in the following year, and the planned cuts abandoned. The expansionary trends of the earlier years of the decade were resumed. The restoration of budget guidelines provided for a planned increase of 5% in the initial budget for FY1999 and 0% in FY2000. In both years, there was an additional planned allocation of 500 billion for public works contingencies.

The overall effect of the implementation of cuts and squeezes to public works programmes in the period of fiscal reconstruction from 1980 onwards meant that their rising share of general expenditures in the planned General Account Budget was halted and then reversed (Wright 1999*a*: table 3). In turn, the trend of gradual decline gave way to gradual increases as government responded to the conditions of economic down-turn from 1990 onwards. The annual expansion was modest compared with the 1970s: the years of high and rising public spending on public works had apparently ended. That appearance of fiscal prudence was belied by the reality. Planned public works expenditure was supplemented by three additional 'off-budget' sources: annual Supplementary Budgets, the so-called 'NTT Scheme', and FILP. I deal with each in turn.

'OFF-BUDGET' SOURCES

Supplementary Budgets

Supplementary Budgets were not subject to the restrictions of the budget guidelines. In one or more annual Supplementary Budgets, public works programmes were allocated additional resources in every year throughout the period 1975–2000; the main beneficiaries—MOC, MOT, MAFF, and MHW—could always rely on their initial planned allocations in the initial budget being increased subsequently.

Supplementation occurred in years of economic growth as well as at times of economic slow-down or recession, when additional public works projects were often deemed necessary, and for which there was a plausible economic rationale. A comparison of the planned initial allocations in the General Account Budget with the revised totals after the passage of annual Supplementary Budgets shows that the planned standstill, and then reduction, of the public works budget between 1980 and 1988 was in reality a period of continuous growth. Figure 23.2 compares the planned changes with those of the revised budget. Cuts and squeezes were more apparent than real; the additional resources allocated in the Supplementary Budgets more than compensated for the amounts 'lost' in the cuts imposed in the planned initial budget in accordance with the budget guidelines. In each of the four years 1984–7 the initial planned allocation was cut by more than 2%; Supplementary Budgets increased it by, respectively, 5.5%, 8.6%, 11.5%, and 20.3%. The resumption of modest increases in annual planned allocations in the period of fiscal consolidation and expansion from 1988 onwards was outweighed by the huge extra resources provided through the Supplementary Budgets. From 1992 the effects of countercyclical fiscal policies financed through Supplementary Budgets was especially marked. In FY1993, for example, a planned increase of 6.2% in public works spending was converted into a real increase of more than 87% through Supplementary Budgets.

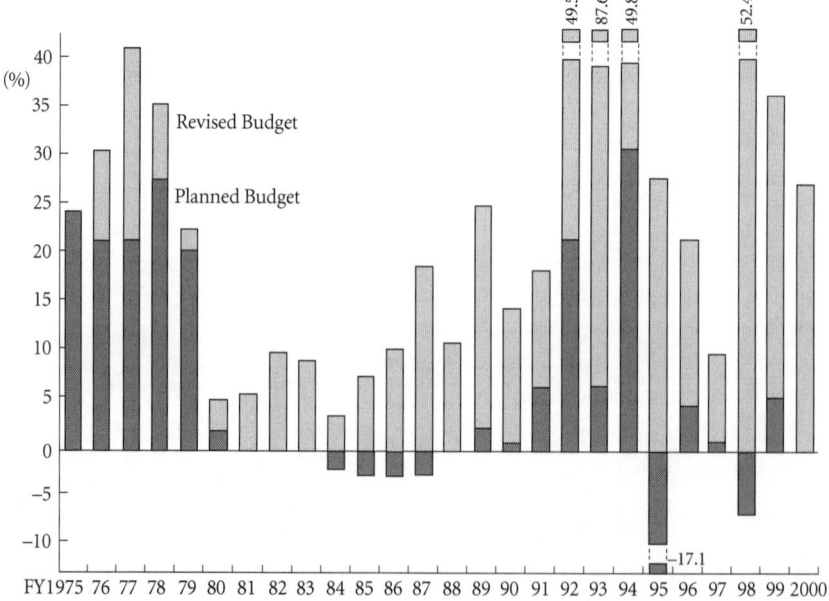

Figure 23.2 *Planned and real changes in the public works' budget, FY1975–FY2000*
General Account Initial and Revised Budgets: percentage annual change

Source: *Zaisei Tōkei* (annually), Research Division, Budget Bureau, MOF.

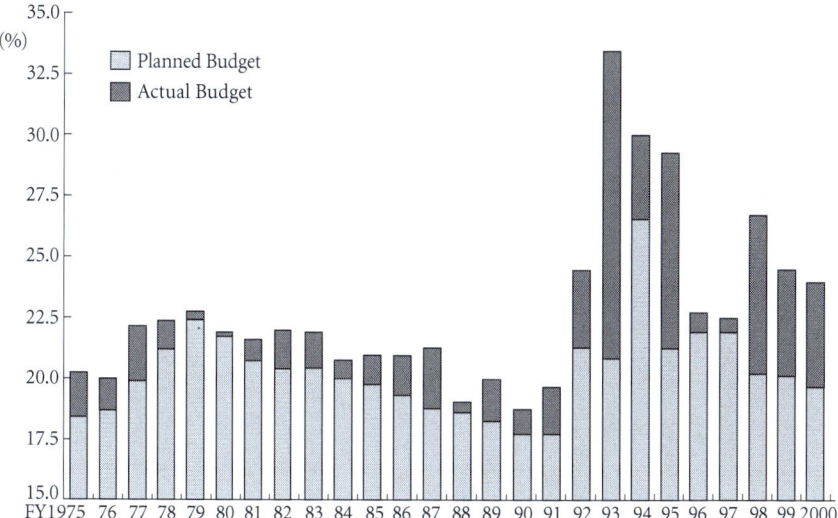

Figure 23.3 *Planned and real changes in public works' share of the budget, FY1975–FY2000*
General Account Initial and Revised Budgets: percentage annual change

Source: *Zaisei Tōkei* (annually), Research Division, Budget Bureau, MOF.

MOF claimed that the share of general expenditures allocated to public works declined from 21.7% in 1980 to 17.7% in 1990. In reality, through supplementation, the actual allocations to public works increased as a proportion of general expenditures by between 0.1% and 2.3% annually throughout the period of fiscal reconstruction, and very substantially thereafter. Figure 23.3 compares the changes in those shares measured by the initial and revised budgets. Despite the *apparent* reduction of public works in the planned budget, Spending Ministries could not only look forward to an annual increase in the amount allocated in every Supplementary Budget: they could also expect that the public works budget would increase its share of general expenditures.

With the collapse of the economic bubble in 1991, the Japanese economy entered the deepest recession since the war. Successive attempts to stimulate the economy through countercyclical fiscal policies incorporated substantial amounts of additional public works expenditures. Besides the increases in the General Account Budget allocations, there were 14 major packages of supplementary fiscal measures between August 1992 and October 2000. Ten of those provided tax and spending changes, financed through Supplementary Budgets.[1] The main elements are shown in Table 23.3. Additional planned infrastructure investment in those packages totalled 55.737 trillion, of which

---

[1] Of the other packages of countercyclical policies, those of October 1997 and February 1998 contained no direct tax or spending measures, providing a series of proposals to improve competition through deregulation; those of December 1997 and October 1998 provided mainly for the recapitalization of private commercial banks.

Table 23.3 Public works planned spending in countercyclical fiscal packages, 1992–2000 (Project cost basis, trillion yen)

	28 Aug. 1992	13 Apr. 1993	16 Sept. 1993	8 Feb. 1994	14 Apr. 1995[a]	20 Sept. 1995	24 Apr. 1998	16 Nov. 1998	11 Nov. 1999	19 Oct. 2000	Total
(1) *Infrastructure investment*											
General public works	3.4	3.64	1.0	3.59	0.205	3.93	4.5	5.7	4.486	n/a	30.451
Disaster relief	0.5	0.53	0.45	0	0.718	0.70	0.20	0.60	0.700	0.500	4.898
Local government (own public works)	1.8	2.3	0.50	0.30	0	1.0	1.50	0	0	0	7.400
Total public works	5.7	6.47	1.95	3.89	0.923	5.63	6.20	6.30	5.186	n/a	42.749
Building and equipment	0.55	1.150	0	0.61	0.154	0.910	1.50	1.8	1.614	n/a	8.288
(2) *Total infrastructure investment*	6.25	7.62	1.95	4.50	1.077	6.540	7.706	8.10	6.800	5.200	55.737
(3) *Other economic and fiscal measures*[b]	4.45	5.43	4.20	4.90	3.543	6.270	4.350	9.80	11.200	5.800	59.943
(4) *Tax measures (net revenue lost)*	0	0.15	0	5.85	0	0	4.60	6.0	0	0	16.600
(5) *Total fiscal package (1)–(4)*	10.700	13.200	6.200	15.300	4.600	12.800	16.700	23.900	18.000	11.000	132.400

[a] OECD estimates.
[b] e.g. lending by public financial institutions to promote industrial investment, housing, and SMEs; land acquisition; employment promotion; regional promotion coupons.

Source: EPA and MOF; OECD (1993, 1996, 1998, 1999b, 2000).

42.749 trillion was allocated directly to public works projects, and a further 8.288 for building and equipment related to them. The April 1998 package of 16.7 trillion, then the largest ever introduced by the Japanese government, included temporary tax cuts of 2.0 trillion for FY1998 and FY1999, and additional public works spending of 7.7 trillion. But even that huge sum was dwarfed by the 24 trillion of nominal tax and spending measures announced by Prime Minister Obuchi in November 1998. A further 8.1 trillion was allocated for the creation of social infrastructure, of which planned general public works projects totalled 5.7 trillion. In November 1999 yet another package of fiscal measures provided for additional spending of nearly 18 trillion, of which nearly a third was allocated to public works. But care is needed in the interpretation of those and other apparently substantial increases in the volume of public works expenditures, and their impact on the economy. We return to that issue later in the chapter.

The NTT Scheme

For a period of four years beginning with the Supplementary Budget of FY1987, the implementation of the so-called 'NTT Scheme' provided a substantial annual addition to the total of public works expenditure, financed *outside* the General Account Budget. When the Telephone and Telegraph Public Corporation was privatized in April 1985, two-thirds of the shares of the new NTT were deposited in the Special Account for the Consolidation of the National Debt. Revenue from the sales in the bull market of the 'yen bubble' between 1986 and 1988 of some of those shares, totalling 10.2 trillion, led to an accumulation of surplus funds in that account. MOF and the LDP government agreed to use some of them to provide an additional stimulus for public works investment to implement the priority of improving 'social overhead capital' announced in the National Plan for 1988–92.

Each year 1.3 trillion was made available as loans from the Special Account for the Consolidation of the National Debt, passed through the General Account Budget as self-cancelling revenue and expenditure items, and deposited in a new Special Account for Social Infrastructure, within the long-established Industrial Investment Special Account. Repayment of loans on maturity was made through the same channels to the Special Account for the Consolidation of the National Debt, where they were legally required to be used for debt redemption.

There were three types of loan. 'A-loans' were interest-free; they were extended to public corporations for the construction of public projects yielding profits for repayment within 20 years, for example national roads built by the Japan Highway PC. 'C-loans' were available to the 'third sector': to private-sector companies capitalized partly by local governments and public finance corporations such as the Japan Development Bank. NTT 'B-loans', the largest component, were extended to local governments for carrying out public works projects. These latter loans yielded no profits, and the cost of their repayment was ultimately a charge on the General Account Budget—in effect, a direct subsidy from the central government.

All ministries and agencies were eligible to compete for the additional funds, but they did so mainly as sponsors of public banks and finance corporations, public corporations, and local government services, rather than to obtain additional funds for their own capital investment programmes. The major beneficiaries of the scheme were local governments, which between them received more than 85% of the annual total; public corporations claimed between 8% and 9%, with the 'third sector' loaned the remainder (Wright 1999a: table 6).

The expansion of the public works programme through the mechanism of the NTT Scheme in the late 1980s was motivated by a combination of domestic and international factors. The LDP wanted to give a higher priority to the improvement of living standards and the environment, and made it a principal concern of the National Plan for 1988–92, published in 1987, the year that marked the transition from fiscal restraint to more relaxed policies signalled by the Supplementary Budget of that year, following the Louvre Accord. In conditions of the depressed world economy, Japan had come under renewed and sustained pressure from the USA and other leading members of the international economic community to increase the level of domestic public investment in order to expand demand in the economy, and (later) help to reduce the huge surplus on its current account by increasing the demand for imported goods. The availability of an off-budget source to finance a large increase in public works provided the means for an immediate rapid expansion of some 20%. At the conclusion of the Structural Impediments Initiative in 1990, the Japanese government was able to announce the Basic Plan for Investment for the ten-year period 1991–2000, and commit resources to it totalling 430 trillion. The decision to expand public works expenditure had of course already been taken, and thus to a large extent the government was able to make an international virtue out of the domestic politico-economic imperative. Both the Basic Plan and its revision in 1994 further emphasized the priority to be given to the improvement of 'social overhead capital', mainly environmental, welfare, and cultural facilities—housing, water, sewage plants, parks, local roads, agricultural infrastructure, green spaces, welfare facilities, schools, research and academic facilities, and sports and cultural facilities. Together, it was planned to increase their share of the public works budget from 50%–55% in the 1980s to some 60%–65% between 1995 and 2004, with corresponding reductions in other sectors (EPA 1994b).

A key factor in the international–domestic equation was MOF's policy aim to reduce government borrowing and eliminate the issue of special deficit-financing bonds, targeted for 1990. The years from 1986 to late 1990 were years of economic growth; the 'bubble economy' of speculative stocks and land prices, and consequential buoyant tax revenues, helped to defray the costs of rising public spending. Pressure on the General Account was also relieved by the use of the NTT Scheme to finance almost the whole of the annual increase of public works. In FY1988 an increase of almost 20% was financed wholly through NTT; the allocation to public works in the General Account Budget—the 'head-line' total—was frozen (Wright 1999a). In 1989 the General Account contributed 117 billion additional funds (a 1.9% increase), the NTT Scheme 1,300 billion, worth an additional 21.2%. In 1990 the General Account contributed a mere 0.3% increase and the NTT Scheme, more than 20%. In its first four years, the effect of the NTT Scheme was to transform the modest annual increases allocated in the initial planned General Account Budget into totals averaging more than 20%. To put it the other way round, the 1.3 trillion of additional public works financed off-budget allowed MOF to constrain the growth of public works in the Budget as the guidelines were relaxed. From FY1992, the costs of continuing the NTT Scheme were borne directly by the General Account Budget, and were conflated in the programme total for public works. Repayments of the loans from the National Debt Consolidation Fund began in 1993. The effect of those repayments was to inflate the 'head-line' total of public works in the General Account Budget for the next three years. The planned allocation of 11.146 trillion in FY1994 was in reality only 8.881 after allowances for repayments; the apparent annual increase of nearly 30% was in reality only 3.2%. In FY1995, a reduction of 17.1% in the initial allocation became -27% after deduction for repayments. Repayments of outstanding loans were suspended in FY1996.

The NTT Scheme provided a means of ratcheting up the total public works budget without, in the short-term, adding to the deficit on the General Account and the level of outstanding debt. The importance of the 'cost-deferred' increase of public works programmes was two-fold. First, FY1990 had been set as the target year for the elimination of the issue of special deficit-financing bonds. Using revenues from NTT did not add to the size of the deficit on the General Account Budget, *in the short term*. Repayment of the loans could be deferred until after 1990, when MOF hoped that conditions of continuing economic growth would generate additional tax revenues.

Secondly, the increase in 'cost-deferred' public works expenditures provided welcome relief to the LDP's party managers, and rank-and-file Dietmen. After four years of a declining 'head-line' total for the public works budget, the additional public works expenditures financed through the NTT Scheme from 1988 provided further means to oil the wheels of local electoral machines, gearing up for the election to the Lower House in February 1990. Those were difficult years for the LDP. The Recruit–Cosmos scandal broke in 1988–9, and forced the resignation of Prime Minister Takeshita and four LDP ministers; his successor, Uno, resigned after a brief period, with the exposure of sexual indiscretions in his private life. Contributions to party funds declined: those to six of the seven leading factions declined between 1988 and 1989; those collected by Takeshita's faction fell from 1,969 million in 1987 to 831 million in 1988. However, this decline partly reflected a switch in reporting contributions collected from factions to individual senior party members, in order to deflect attention from Takeshita's factional role (see Hrebenar 1992). The 1989 election for the Upper House brought defeat for the LDP, and the expectation that it would suffer a similar reverse in the Lower House in 1990.

There is then a convincing *political* rationale for the expansion of the public works budget before the economy began to enter recession in 1991, and one to which the MOF could accede because the cost of doing so did not add to the deficit, or inhibit its fiscal objective of achieving the elimination of special deficit-financing bonds by 1990. More broadly, the political imperative matched the perceived governmental need expressed in the National Plan to improve living standards by investing in social and environmental infrastructure. As MOC, MAFF, and MOT were keen to do so, there occurred in those years an identity of party political, national governmental, and bureaucratic interests.

After FY1991, the continuation of the NTT Scheme presented MOF with two problems. First, the accumulated surplus of revenues from the sale of NTT stock was almost exhausted. Either more stock had to be sold to generate additional revenues, or an alternative source of funds had to be provided. With the collapse of the yen bubble, further sales of stock in the depressed market conditions were not an option. The costs of most of the scheme had now to be borne directly on the General Account, adding further to a rising trend of public spending at a time of declining revenues and renewed government borrowing to cover the resulting deficit. From 1992 onwards, more than four-fifths of the annual 1.3 trillion costs of the additional NTT public works—loans to local governments for B-type projects—were underwritten by the General Account Budget as a straight subsidy; the remainder, as before, was provided by loans from the small surplus remaining in the Special Account for National Debt Consolidation, and by the repayment of previous loans to the 'third [private] sector'. Each year a sum of approximately 1.13 trillion was incorporated *within* the planned budget allocation for public works to finance the continuance of the NTT Scheme.

MOF's second problem was the redemption of the earlier loans from the National Debt Consolidation Fund to finance the scheme, which by the end of FY1991 totalled more than 5 trillion. Now that it had achieved (albeit temporarily) its objective of eliminating the issue of special deficit-financing bonds, it could contemplate repayment. A start was made with a token repayment of 78.3 billion in the budget of FY1993; in the following year 2.26 trillion was allocated for that purpose. Together with the continuing subsidization of the NTT Scheme, the effect of the latter repayment was to swell the size of (gross) public works planned spending in the initial budget to 11.146 trillion, and to contribute to the inescapable resumption of the issue of special deficit-financing bonds in the same year, as the size of the deficit on the General Account Budget increased rapidly. In FY1995 a further tranche of 1.108 trillion was repaid.

As explained above, the planned totals in the initial General Account Budget for these years thus distort the picture of public works growth and decline. The NTT Scheme was drastically curtailed in FY1998 with the ending of its major component, the financing of B-type projects, mainly local government. Both A- and C-type projects continued to receive funds within the overall public works budget, but combined they totalled no more than 0.1595 trillion. Underspending on the public works budget was becoming serious, especially at the local level, where in FY1998, of 19.3 trillion planned public works spending in the Local Finance Plan, only 15.2 trillion was used.

FILP

The third additional 'off-budget' source of public works expenditure was FILP, which annually provided funds for public works organizations controlled by the central government. As explained in greater detail in Chapter 12, those included five organizations for road and bridge construction, the Housing and Urban Development Corporation, and the 11 banks and public finance corporations whose loan and investment activities included the financing of public works projects. The allocation of funds in the initial FILP Budget for those purposes increased in every year but one from 1976 to 1994, absorbing between 13% and 18% of the total FILP Budget. In cash terms, that represented an increase from 1.86 trillion in FY1976 to a peak of 6.08 trillion in FY1993. This is almost certainly an underestimate of the amount available to finance public works, as

A 'Public Works State' 433

the initial FILP Budget was always revised upwards in-year, but no data were published about the amount of additional resources made available to finance public works.

The 'Off-Budget' Effects

Collectively, the three additional 'off-budget' sources—Supplementary Budgets, the NTT Scheme, and FILP—had a considerable impact on the amount of finance available for public works projects provided by central government. Figure 23.4 shows the total, and the contribution of each source. For example, the initial allocation in the General Account Budget for FY1995 of 9.239 trillion represented a reduction of 17% year-on-year. However, resources allocated through the other three off-budget sources produce a grand total of 19.583 trillion, representing an annual increase of more than 75% over the planned allocation in the General Account Budget of the previous year.

The first general conclusion to be drawn from this analysis is that the planned allocation in the initial General Account Budget was an inaccurate prediction of the total resources available to finance public works spending. The three off-budget sources together accounted for between 30% and 60% of the total of public works planned expenditures each year in the period 1975–96. (The totals in Figure 23.4 for

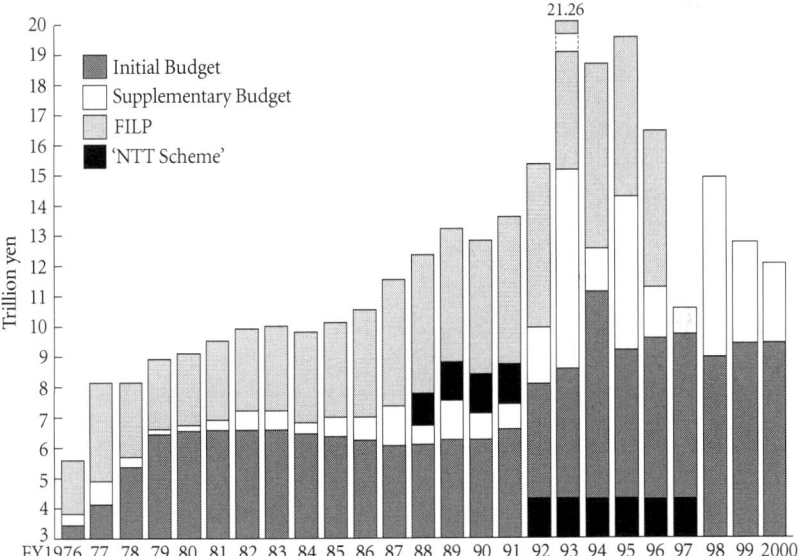

Figure 23.4 *Budget and 'Off-Budget' public works' spending, FY1976–FY2000*
General Account Initial and Revised Budgets, FILP Initial Budget: trillion yen

General Account Initial Budget totals for FY1992–FY1997 include repayments of money borrowed from the Special Account for the Consolidation of the National Debt to finance the NTT Scheme between FY1988 and FY19991.

FILP data are unavailable for FY1997–FY2000

Source: *Zaisei Tōkei* (annually), Research Division, Budget Bureau, MOF.

FY1997–FY2000 are understated because those for FILP-financed public works are not available.) Secondly, contrary to the appearance of a regime of cuts and squeezes and a trend of decline, the reality was that the resources to finance public works increased every year from 1976 to 1993 with the exception of small reductions in 1984 and 1990. Thirdly, in the period of fiscal reconstruction, 1980–7, while the allocation in the initial General Account Budget was frozen and then cut, continuous growth was ensured by the substantial additional resources provided by the combined off-budget sources. Controlled by MOF, they were not subject to the guidelines that regulated the amount and composition of the allocation of the main budget. Fourthly, those three sources combined became progressively more significant relative to the planned allocation in the General Account Budget. In FY1979 almost three-quarters of public works financed by the central government was made available through the General Account Budget; ten years later it financed less than a half. In most years in the 1990s more public works were financed off-than on-budget. Finally, what was prescribed in the formal budget guidelines, and planned in the General Account Budget, bore little relation to the total of public works spending. Throughout the whole of the period 1975–2000, MOF agreed to actual changes of between 40% and 160% each year.

THE ALLOCATION OF PUBLIC WORKS BUDGETS

The conventional interpretation of the outcome of the budget processes is that the allocation among competing ministries and agencies was determined mainly by adherence to the principles of balance and 'fair shares'. The argument runs thus: public works programmes were the responsibility of autonomous, verticalized bureaucratic organizations. Compartmentalization was fostered by vested interests comprising producer groups, local constituents, ministers, LDP officials, Dietmen, and the bureaucrats themselves. Reliant on the benefits and favours conferred by public works projects as an important source of local influence in the maintenance of personal electoral networks, LDP politicians competed through PARC divisions, research committees, special commissions, and through their influence with senior LDP officials, to maintain existing shares for construction, agriculture, and transport. Confronted with competing demands from rank-and-file Dietmen, PARC officials and the LDP leadership opted for the safer course of maintaining the existing balance. As explained in Chapter 15, within MOF, budget examiners competed for shares of the planned total of the General Account Budget (to finance approved programmes and projects of their ministries and agencies), and for a share of any additional resources for public works. Coordination by the Budget Bureau's deputy directors-general, director-general, and the Coordination Division, intermediating the political pressures from PARC and the LDP leadership, reinforced the status quo distribution. In brief, political and bureaucratic discretion to change, other than very marginally, the allocation of the public works budgets between ministries, or to establish and implement new priorities between sectors, was tightly circumscribed in practice.

The evidence of the historical trends in the allocation to public works programmes in the General Account Budget confirms that conventional interpretation. It was inflexible. Over the past 30 years, the proportion of the Budget allocated to each of the big three (MOC, MAFF, and MOT) and to MHW and MITI scarcely changed, as Table 23.4 illustrates.

The implementation of policies of fiscal reconstruction in the 1980s served to entrench further their existing shares. For almost the whole of the decade, the five ministries negotiated with the Budget Bureau for shares of an apparently fixed or declining allocation within the General Account Budget. In a zero-sum game, an increase in one ministry's share would have meant a compensating reduction in another. Unsurprisingly, MOF opted for the principle of 'equal misery', the negotiations resulting in the maintenance of existing shares. Thus, between 1981 and 1990 MOC's share fluctuated within a margin of 0.07%; MAFF, of 0.11%; MOT, of 0.01%. No change at all was made in MHW's share during the same period.

That extreme rigidity began to change, albeit marginally, in the 1990s. As explained above, the aggregate of planned public investment increased substantially, with the adoption and gradual implementation of the ten-year Basic Plan for Public

Table 23.4 *Allocation of public works spending among ministries and agencies, FY1965–FY1999 (%)*[a]

FY	MOC	MAFF	MOT	MHW	MITI	Environment agency
1999	69.29	18.98	7.08	3.92	0.13	0.18
1998	69.19	19.34	6.93	3.88	0.13	0.15
1997	68.51	20.05	6.94	3.85	0.14	0.13
1996	68.63	20.28	6.86	3.78	0.16	0.12
1995	68.50	20.54	6.87	3.65	0.17	0.11
1994	68.35	20.83	6.86	3.47	0.23	0.16
1993	68.61	21.49	6.24	3.26	0.24	0.16
1992	68.47	21.68	6.24	3.20	0.25	0.16
1991	68.31	21.85	6.24	3.13	0.25	0.16
1990	68.19	22.04	6.24	3.10	0.26	0.16
1989	68.19	22.04	6.24	3.10	0.26	0.16
1988	68.19	22.04	6.24	3.10	0.26	0.17
1987	68.20	22.02	6.25	3.10	0.26	0.17
1986	68.20	22.02	6.25	3.10	0.26	0.17
1985	68.20	22.01	6.25	3.10	0.26	0.17
1984	68.26	21.95	6.24	3.10	0.27	0.17
1983	68.25	21.95	6.24	3.10	0.29	0.18
1982	68.23	21.94	6.24	3.10	0.31	0.18
1981	68.22	21.93	6.24	3.10	0.33	0.18
1980	68.14	21.88	6.35	3.06	0.36	0.21
1975	68.47	20.38	7.23	—	—	—
1970	69.77	20.41	7.70	—	—	—
1965	69.36	20.14	7.46	—	—	—

[a]General Account Initial Budget.

Source: data supplied by Budget Bureau, MOF; Planning Division, EPA; MOC.

Investment, aimed at increasing the proportion of total public investment allocated to improving living standards and environmental and cultural facilities. Secondly, from FY1988 investment funds of 1.3 trillion from the sale of NTT stock were made available annually, in addition to the main public works programmes of the General Account. Thirdly, for the three years 1991–3, additional investment funds were made available under an initiative to fund 'special measures' to improve living standards. The sectors most affected by those three initiatives were housing, sewage facilities, city parks, and urban redevelopment, all of which fell mainly within MOC's jurisdiction. From 1991, the priority accorded to them began to be reflected in marginal changes in the budget allocation between MOC and MAFF. For example, MOC obtained some 75% of the total available for 'special measures', i.e. a share about 8% greater than its historic allocation.

A further contributory factor to changing priorities was the decline in domestic agriculture, and the continued fall in the number of farmers, from 6.1 million in 1960 to 3.7 million in 1985, with a further fall to 3.1 million in 1990. This was reflected in the progressive reduction of subsidies for domestic rice growers, while public works spending on agricultural infrastructure began to decline in 1991. Those trends are partly to be explained by the reorientation of LDP's electoral strategy in the 1970s to give greater weight to the demands of voters in cities, towns, and metropolitan areas. Nevertheless, the political salience of domestic agriculture in the composition of the Budget remained significant. After the breakup of the LDP in 1992–3, the defection of many of the more liberal, progressive, and urban-based Dietmen led by Ozawa Ichirō and Takemura Masayoshi left a rump in the Lower House that was both more rural and more conservative in its orientation than the old, unreconstructed LDP. The rump was more sensitive and sympathetic to agricultural interests, and more responsive to the pressures brought to bear by the still powerful agricultural cooperatives. Evidence of this was provided by the generous compensation for farmers, necessary to secure the ratification of the agreement in the Uruguay Round of GATT to open domestic markets to foreign rice. Subsidies, loans, and additional money for public works to help them adjust to foreign competition totalling 6.01 trillion over the period 1995–2000 was approved by the Coalition government in October 1994, after MOF had tried to limit the package to 2.7 trillion. Nearly 60% of that total was earmarked for public works.

Secondly, the strength of the agricultural interests represented in both the LDP and the JSP/SDP obliged the Coalition governments of, first, Murayama and, then, Hashimoto to seek a solution to the collapse of the housing associations (*jusen*) in 1995, which minimized the costs to the agricultural cooperatives, major shareholders, and (with some of the city banks) guarantors of a large proportion of their non-performing loans and bad debts. Their opposition to sharing the burden of the costs of the proposed bail-out by writing off a proportion of the 5.5 trillion owed them was a major factor in the Murayama–Hashimoto proposal to use 635 billion of public money in a joint public–private rescue plan. The subsequent public furore provoked the opposition parties to stall the passage of the FY1996 budget.

The historic rigidity of public works spending allocations attracted increasing criticism at home and abroad in the 1990s. There was growing public scepticism voiced in the media about the economic efficiency, rather than the political benefits, of increasing amounts of local infrastructural investment. There was also continuing criticism from foreign governments and international organizations about the closed access to construction markets. That criticism was fuelled by the revelations of bribery and corruption in the Sagawa Kyūbin scandal which erupted in the summer of 1993. The Tokyo District Prosecutor's Office began to unravel and expose a complex set of corrupt relationships between construction companies and local politicians in the bidding system, and the award of contracts for local public works projects (for details see Woodall 1996). In January 1994 the Hosokawa Coalition government announced measures to improve access for foreign companies to public works markets, and to increase the transparency of the bidding system, to allow for open and competitive bidding for public works projects above a prescribed threshold. New guidelines for public tendering were drawn up by the Fair Trade Commission, which also began an investigation into alleged bid-rigging in contracts for ODA infrastructural projects overseas. The government's commitment to reform public works budgeting had led to a reformulation of the criteria for allocation in November 1993, discussed below.

Long-Term Sectoral Flexibility

The rigidity of the budgetary outputs represented by the trends of ministry shares in the period 1975–2000 obscures evidence of long-term flexibility in the *sectoral* distribution of public works investment. Figure 23.5 shows the changes measured as a proportion of the General Account Budget over the period 1946–99. The roads and disaster relief investment programmes declined sharply from peaks in the 1950s and early 1970s, respectively; rivers, flood control, and erosion showed a long-term decline from the 1960s. The two growth sectors—housing, and the sewage facilities and environmental programmes—reflected the reorientation of national goals and objectives in the 'welfare era' inaugurated by Tanaka Kakuei in the early 1970s, and reaffirmed in the National Economic Plans of 1983–7 and 1988–92. Those long-term sectoral changes are illustrated in more detail in Figure 23.6, which shows the changing composition of the annual planned public works budget. In the 20 years from 1975, the most striking changes are the decline in the share of the roads programme (B), and the increase in that of water and sewage facilities and environmental programmes (E). The surprisingly small increase in the housing programme (D) is explained by the greater use of FILP funds to finance the expansion that occurred in the 1980s and 1990s. It should be emphasized that those trends and changes relate only to those public works financed through the General Account Budget, and exclude the contributions from the three off-budget sources discussed earlier in the chapter. Hence the apparent decline in the roads programme, shown in historic trends of the General Account Budget, was offset by the spending on national roads and expressways through FILP agencies, and on local roads through local governments, partly financed by FILP loans through such agencies as the Finance Corporation for Municipal Enterprises.

The Allocation of Public Works Budgets within Ministries

To what extent were the long-term trends in the distribution of public works spending among sectors reflected in the allocation of shares within ministries? Here there is a

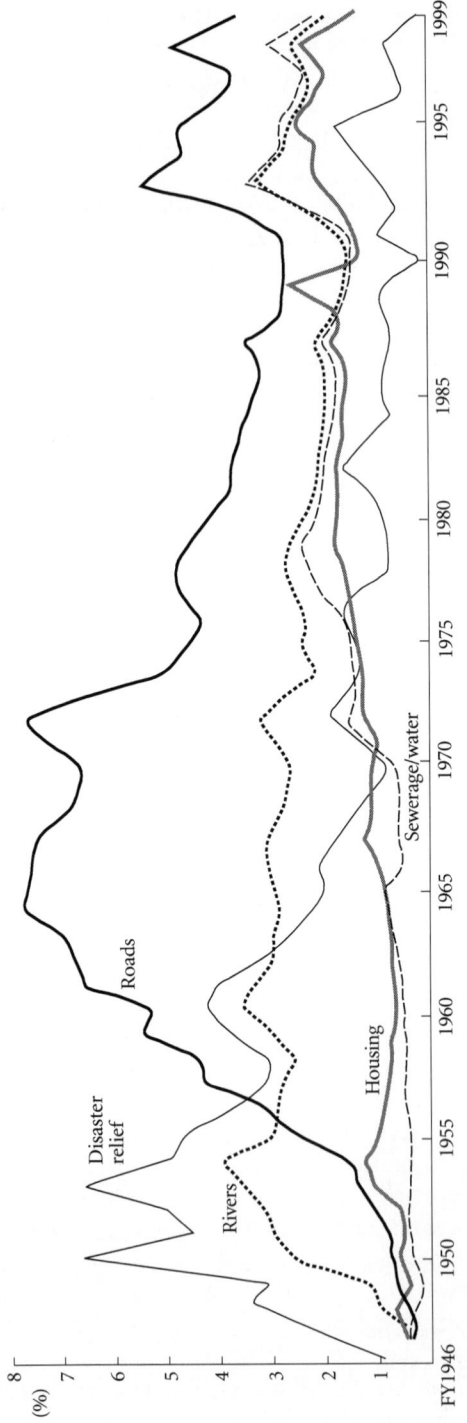

Figure 23.5 Changing allocations to public works' programmes in the General Account Budget, FY1946–FY1999 General Account Revised Budget: percentage share

Source: based on data provided by Coordination Division, Minister's Secretariat, MOC.

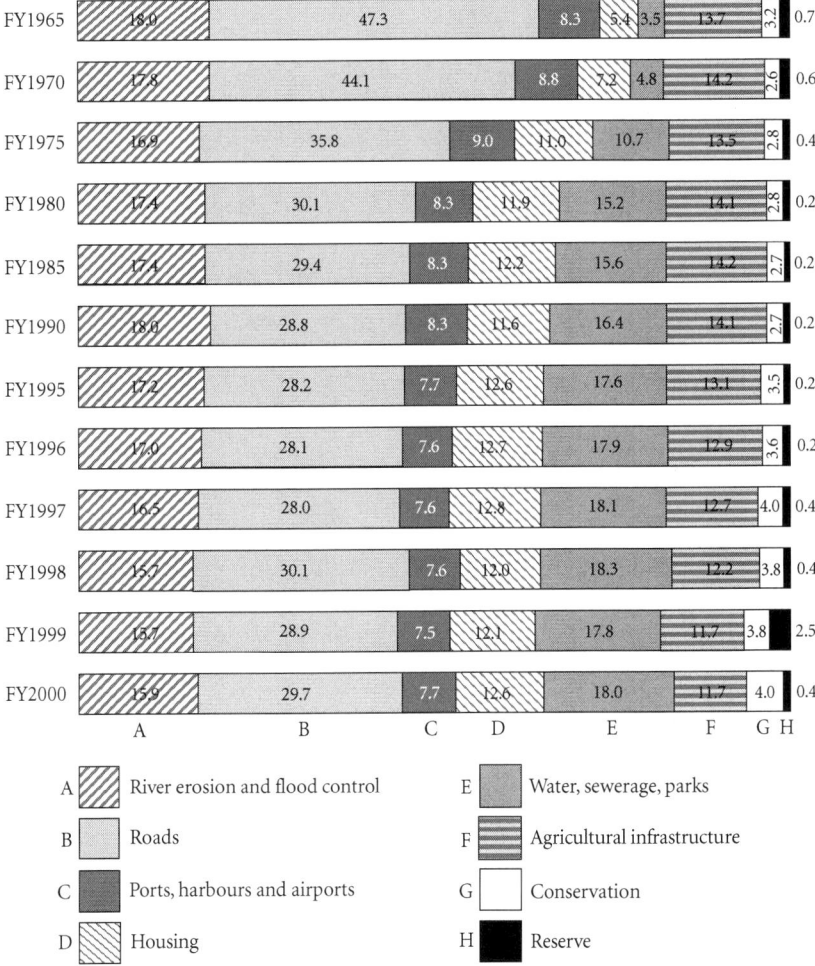

Figure 23.6 *Changing composition of the public works' budget, FY1965–FY1999*
General Account Initial Budget: percentage shares of the total allocated to public works
Source: *Zaisei Tōkei* (annually), Research Division, Budget Bureau, MOF.

similar conventional argument to explain the apparently fixed shares among bureaux to that invoked in the explanation of the rigid allocation among the five ministries. Briefly, verticalized, autonomous bureaux competed for shares of a fixed public works budget within the ministry's ceiling negotiated with MOF, and solicited the support of LDP PARC divisions, and the lobbying of LDP *zoku*. With weakly coordinated policies at ministerial level, the director of the Budget and Accounts Division and senior Secretariat officials preferred to allocate according to principles of balance and 'fair shares' to maintain the historic patterns of distribution, rather than face the organizational and political implications of applying more difficult and contentious principles of choice and discrimination with win–lose outcomes. Moreover, ministry bureaucrats had professional career interests vested in the maintenance of existing budgets. For example, all three ministries had large numbers of engineers and related technical staff in their bureaux, and in local and regional offices, whose employment was dependent upon the continuation of a flow of public works projects (MOC 1996). MAFF had an estimated 18,000 *gikan* technical staff specializing in public works; MOC, 14,000; and MOT, 12,000.

The empirical evidence of the historic trends is less supportive of that explanation, but it needs to be borne in mind that a change in allocation did not necessarily mean that a change had occurred in the priority accorded a particular sector or function. A decline or an increase in share might represent a 'book transfer' of a proportion of the financing of that sector/function from the General Account Budget to FILP or a Special Account. The financing of housing subsidies is an obvious and important example of this, referred to below, where both the General Account (through MOC's budget) and FILP provided funds for the Housing and Urban Development Corporation, and the Government Housing Loan Corporation, both of which fell within that ministry's jurisdictional authority. We now examine the distribution of public works within each of the three main ministries in the period 1975–99.

The allocation of the public works budget in the Ministry of Construction was divided among four functional bureaux: (i) the City Bureau, responsible for urban policy, city planning, urban renewal, parks and open spaces, and sewage facilities; (ii) the River Bureau, responsible for water use, flood control, water systems, seacoasts and erosion; (iii) the Roads Bureau, responsible for road planning and administration, and national and local road construction; and (iv) the Housing Bureau, responsible for the supervision of the Government Housing Loan Corporation, the Housing and Urban Development Corporation, and public and private housing construction. While there is not an exact correspondence between the organizational responsibilities of those four bureaux and the functional categories shown in Table 23.5, the overall pattern is clear.

First, reflecting changing national priorities, the Roads Bureau experienced a long-term, incremental decline in its allocation (column 1); secondly, the Housing Bureau attracted an increasing share of resources for housing subsidies in the period 1980–7, followed by a short period of reductions and a return to incremental growth from 1992. The reduced allocations were less the result of a lower priority for the construction of public and private houses, more a change in the method of financing those subsidies. The amount of subsidy to finance the loans made by the Government Housing Loan Corporation, which borrowed at a higher rate (6% in 1994) and lent at a lower rate (4.5%), increased throughout the whole of the period 1980–98. To reduce the burden on the General Account of MOC's contribution, a greater proportion was transferred to FILP. The allocation to the City Bureau to finance public works expenditure on sewage facilities, parks, and urban renewal increased slowly throughout the period (columns 4, 5, and 7), with a greater rate of increase observable in sewage programmes after 1988, as greater priority was accorded them in national plans. Urban renewal was

Table 23.5 *Functional composition of the ministry of construction's public works budget, FY1980–FY1999* (% of total public works in the General Account Initial Budget)

FY	Road construction (1)	Flood control (2)	Housing subsidies (3)	Sewage schemes (4)	Parks (5)	Seashore (6)	Urban renewal (7)	Total (8)
1999	28.19	13.39	12.31	12.32	1.77	0.39	0.91	69.29
1998	28.53	13.23	12.18	12.47	1.77	0.40	0.62	69.19
1997	27.97	13.24	12.19	12.35	1.76	0.41	0.60	68.51
1996	28.12	13.34	12.16	12.27	1.74	0.41	0.58	68.63
1995	28.20	13.44	12.06	12.11	1.71	0.42	0.56	68.50
1994	28.30	13.54	11.95	11.92	1.68	0.42	0.54	68.35
1993	28.72	13.81	11.77	11.70	1.66	0.43	0.51	68.61
1992	28.78	14.00	11.65	11.49	1.63	0.43	0.50	68.47
1991	28.80	13.99	11.61	11.45	1.61	0.43	0.47	68.31
1990	28.77	14.02	11.61	11.35	1.58	0.44	0.42	68.19
1989	28.85	14.02	11.61	11.35	1.56	0.44	0.37	68.19
1988	28.95	14.03	11.61	11.29	1.54	0.44	0.34	68.19
1987	28.92	13.72	12.44	10.91	1.45	0.44	0.33	68.20
1986	29.13	13.64	12.33	10.94	1.45	0.44	0.27	68.20
1985	29.42	13.57	12.21	10.92	1.44	0.44	0.20	68.20
1984	29.66	13.56	12.14	10.91	1.40	0.44	0.15	68.26
1983	29.72	13.56	12.08	10.93	1.40	0.44	0.12	68.25
1982	29.72	13.56	12.07	10.92	1.40	0.44	0.12	68.23
1981	29.85	13.56	11.95	10.91	1.40	0.44	0.12	68.22
1980	30.07	13.56	11.87	10.71	1.37	—	0.12	68.14

Source: data supplied by Budget Bureau, MOF; Planning Division, EPA; MOC.

increasingly financed through FILP, for example in lending by the JDB. The allocation to the Rivers Bureau for flood control, water resource development, sediment control and seashore schemes (columns 2 and 5), roughly stable until 1987, experienced gradual decline throughout the 1990s.

The distribution of the public works budget in MOT changed very little over this period until 1994. Then, in the reordering of priorities under the Hosokawa and Murayama Coalition governments, ports lost budget share, while the programme for railroad protection acquired additional resources (Table 23.6). The slow, marginal decline in the allocation to airports is accounted for partly by the transfer of some of the costs of financing public works schemes to other agencies, both public (FILP) and private, for example in the construction of the Kansai International Airport, and the New Tokyo International Airport.

Unlike MOC and MOT, the distribution of the public works budget among MAFF bureaux remained virtually unchanged throughout the period 1980–90. Thereafter there was a progressive decline in the priority accorded to the provision of agricultural infrastructure, reflecting the changing politico-economic salience of domestic agriculture referred to earlier. Table 23.7 shows the details.

Table 23.6 *Functional composition of the ministry of transport's public works budget, FY1980–FY1998* (% of total public works in the General Account Initial Budget)

FY	Ports	Airports	Seashore	Railroad protection	Shinkansen	Total
1998	3.72	1.53	0.42	0.70	0.33	7.08
1997	3.75	1.59	0.43	0.74	0.35	6.93
1996	3.81	1.48	0.43	0.74	0.32	6.94
1995	3.84	1.44	0.44	0.73	0.29	6.86
1994	4.01	1.39	0.44	0.72	0.30	6.87
1993	4.18	1.39	0.45	0.01	0.21	6.86
1992	4.18	1.39	0.46	0.01	0.21	6.24
1991	4.20	1.40	0.46	0.01	0.17	6.24
1990	4.24	1.41	0.46	0.02	0.10	6.24
1989	4.25	1.41	0.46	0.05	0.07	6.24
1988	4.25	1.41	0.46	0.12	—	6.24
1987	4.18	1.47	0.46	0.14	—	6.25
1986	4.16	1.48	0.46	0.14	—	6.25
1985	4.15	1.49	0.46	0.15	—	6.25
1984	4.13	1.50	0.46	0.15	—	6.24
1983	4.10	1.52	0.46	0.15	—	6.24
1982	4.10	1.52	0.46	0.15	—	6.24
1981	4.10	1.53	0.46	0.15	—	6.24
1980	4.20	1.53	0.46	0.16	—	6.35

Source: derived from data supplied by MOC.

The Allocation of Public Works Budgets within Bureaux

A further dimension of potential flexibility was provided by the opportunity for departments, divisions, and sections to bid for shares of the allocation made to each bureau, within the overall ceiling fixed for each ministry. To what extent were such allocations concerned with 'balance' and the maintenance of fixed shares? Here, the evidence is less easy to come by. At the stage of the compilation of budget requests in the summer, in principle the director-general had discretion over the whole budget of his bureau. Before the ministry's Budget and Accounts Division had agreed the bureau's allocation he could, if he so wished, attempt to change the distribution of the putative allocations between the constituent departments and divisions. But in the negotiations of the bureau's allocation and its distribution, divisional directors competed to maintain (and where possible to increase) existing shares. It was at the divisional and section levels that new schemes, projects, and ideas were discussed and argued about, as explained in Chapter 16. Here the role of each bureau's General Affairs Division in the coordination of proposals, and in the determination of the bureau's priorities, was crucial. In practice, the scope for the exercise of such discretion was limited, circumscribed by the representations and pressures of vested interests within the

Table 23.7 Functional composition of MAFF's public works budget, FY1980–FY1998
(% of total public works in the General Account Initial budget)

FY	Agricultural infrastructure	Mountains afforestation	Fishing ports	Forest restoration[a]	Coastal fisheries construction	Seashore	Forest environment[b]	Total
1998	12.15	2.06	2.22	1.93	0.34	0.33	0.30	19.34
1997	12.69	2.09	2.25	2.08	0.34	0.34	0.30	20.05
1996	12.86	2.50	2.30	2.06	0.34	0.34	0.28	20.28
1995	13.05	2.52	2.36	1.27	0.34	0.35	0.66	20.54
1994	13.25	2.54	2.44	1.27	0.34	0.35	0.64	20.83
1993	13.76	2.58	2.55	1.28	0.34	0.36	0.63	21.49
1992	13.88	2.62	2.57	1.26	0.35	0.36	0.63	21.68
1991	14.00	2.65	2.59	1.26	0.35	0.36	0.64	21.85
1990	14.13	2.69	2.61	1.26	0.35	0.37	0.64	22.04
1989	14.13	2.68	2.61	1.27	0.35	0.37	0.64	22.04
1988	14.13	2.67	2.61	1.27	0.35	0.37	0.64	22.04
1987	14.13	2.64	2.61	1.27	0.34	0.37	0.64	22.02
1986	14.15	2.62	2.61	1.28	0.34	0.37	0.65	22.02
1985	14.16	2.60	2.61	1.29	0.34	0.37	0.65	22.01
1984	14.13	2.57	2.60	1.31	0.34	0.37	0.65	21.95
1983	14.13	2.56	2.60	1.32	0.33	0.37	0.64	21.95
1982	14.12	2.55	2.59	1.32	0.33	0.37	0.64	21.94
1981	14.12	2.55	2.59	1.32	0.33	0.37	0.65	21.93
1980	14.12	2.55	2.58	1.30	0.32	0.37	0.64	21.88

[a]Title changed from Forest Roads in FY1996.
[b]Title changed from Reafforestation in FY1996.

Source: Budget Bureau, MOF; Planning Division, EPA.

bureau and outside—the LDP, local politicians, and interest groups. After the budget was allocated, there was no such flexibility. Directors-general could not move expenditures, even marginally, between items because the allocation item by item had been approved by MOF and the Diet. However, in the implementation of planned public works schemes, MOF allowed the director-general and his bureau officials some discretion at the margin to vary the details of site, location, design, and so on.

Nevertheless, priorities within bureaux could and did change to reflect preferences and choices within policy sectors, for example about the types and locations of road schemes, flood prevention projects, and infrastructural projects for the development of ports and harbours. Where these occurred, they tended to be subsumed within broader functional categories, and not reflected in gross data. For example, within the broad allocation for public works on fisheries and harbours projects, some marginal adjustments were made in the 1990s by spending more on parks and green spaces associated with such projects (MOF 1994*d*).

The reorientation of public works programmes within the broad sectoral allocation for agricultural infrastructure is another example. As the programmes for the enlargement and rationalization of paddy fields were almost completed, in order to justify the continuance of the budget for agricultural improvement, MAFF argued the need of resources to improve the associated agricultural sewage facilities to prevent pollution, and the need for agricultural roads and local airports to improve communications. The result was a shift within the overall public works budget towards agriculture. Contingent on that change was an exacerbation of competition with MOC for the construction of roads, and accompanying budget resources. However, there were both organizational constraints and political pressures inhibiting such changes within sectors, as local and regional governments, and individual LDP Dietmen from rural constituencies, sought to enhance and reward their local networks by claiming credit for a new road, bridge, or land improvement scheme. Criticism of MAFF's competition with MOC for the construction of rural roads led to a change of classification (and increased resources) from 'forest roads' to 'forest restoration' in FY1996.

While it should not be exaggerated, there was more flexibility in the allocation of public works within ministries and among functional categories than was apparent. However, criticism of undue rigidity in the shares between MOC, MAFF, and MOT, and in the distribution between the main sectors, was nevertheless justified; this attracted growing public attention in the 1990s, and resulted in some attempts to prioritize projects.

The Prioritization of Public Works Programmes

The perceived inflexibility of the composition of the public works budget was thrown into sharp focus by the events triggered by the exposure of corruption and bribery in the Sagawa Kyūbin scandal, and the accumulating evidence presented by the Tokyo Prosecutions Office of corrupt practices in the letting of public works contracts at the local and regional levels. Shinseitō, formed in 1993 after the break-away of dissident LDP members following the arrest and prosecution of Kanemaru Shin, campaigned mainly on electoral reform to destroy the alleged money–votes–favours nexus that had characterized the relationship between faction leaders and LDP rank-and-file constituency members on the one hand, and special interest groups and bureaucrats on the other. As leader of the Japan Renewal Party, Hosokawa promised in his general election campaign to change the distribution of the public works budget. On taking office, as prime minister in the Coalition government in July 1993, he quickly announced the intention to examine and reform the criteria used in determining the allocation of public works expenditure.

A sub-committee of MOF's Fiscal System Council, under the chairmanship of Professor Ishi Hiromitsu of Hitotsubashi University, was set up to examine the allocation of public works expenditures. The four ministries prepared and presented evidence at a series of hearings conducted by it in the autumn of 1993. In its 'Report on Reforming Public Works Appropriations' of 26 November 1993, the sub-committee proposed the adoption of three broad criteria to distinguish the relative priority of public works programmes and projects, and classified them, A, B or C. The highest priority was to be given to projects to improve living standards and the environment, such as subsidies for house-building, sewage facilities, agricultural irrigation, water supply, waste disposal facilities, and parks. Group B projects were those concerned with the conservation of land, such as afforestation to prevent soil erosion, and to protect lives and property from national disasters, such as flood control and the maintenance of coasts. Group C, the lowest priority, encompassed projects to improve the industrial infrastructure, for example fishing ports and other coastal fishing facilities, agricultural roads, and water supply for industrial use.

The Fiscal System Council approved the proposals, and its report was accepted by the minister of finance; indeed, the Budget Bureau had participated in the review, and those budget examiners with responsibility for public works programmes, in anticipation of the report, had already employed the criteria in their examination and negotiation of the bids from ministries for the budget for FY1994. Those with projects categorized as a low priority within Group C, particularly MAFF, campaigned to repeal the criteria and to frustrate their application in the budget round, mobilizing the support of the powerful interests of producer groups and members of the LDP *zoku*. Initially, the Cabinet had set aside a small sum of 100 billion to allocate more specifically according to the new criteria, but in the event it was subsumed within the general appropriations. While some effort was made to change the allocations to accord with the rankings suggested by the Council, the effect in the FY1994 budget was marginal. The Ministry of Construction's share fell by only 0.26%, and that of MAFF by 0.66%, but these nevertheless represented their largest annual losses since 1980. However, the Ministry of Transport increased its share by 0.62%, and sustained that gain through the budgets for FY1995–FY1998. Subsequently, MOC regained its share. In FY1996, at 68.63%, it achieved its highest ever proportion, increasing it still further two years later. The gradual erosion of MAFF's share from FY1991 continued, MHW being the main beneficiary. In terms of function, Group A projects such as housing, urban development, water supply, and parks received increases well above the average of public works as a whole; Group B projects received below-average increases, and Group C, only marginal increases, which in the case of ports meant a sharp reduction in overall budget share. This prioritization was repeated in FY1995, although there was a 24% cut in the budget for the improvement of water supply facilities for industry (Group C) (MOF 1995).

The effects on the trends of historic sectoral-shares were modest. In FY1994, Group A projects such as housing increased their share marginally, from 11.8% to 12.0%, and water supply and sewage facilities were up from 17.1% to 17.6%. Group B and C projects lost resources marginally. While those were modest adjustments, their political importance was very much greater, given the fierce interministerial competition referred to earlier. 'During the annual budget process, interested groups [of politicians and bureaucrats] made a great fuss over a variation as small as 0.1%' (Ishi 1995: 407). Opposed by the major ministerial beneficiaries, the scheme was quietly abandoned after FY1995, allegedly because of the objection of backbench members of the Coalition government led by Murayama (MOC 1997*b*). Nevertheless, MOF felt obliged in subsequent annual budgets to demonstrate that, in the allocation among and within broad functional categories, it had given due weight to the priority of particular projects and schemes.

The commitment of the Hashimoto government to fiscal structural reform in the 1997 Act focused still more attention on the issue. In June 1997 the duration of the ten-year Basic Plan for Public Investment was extended by three years to 2007, resources were reduced from 600 to 470 trillion in the initial ten-year period, and the content and duration of ministerial sectoral plans were reviewed. In the FY1998 General Account Budget, public works spending was capped, being set a target of a minimum of 7% reduction. In the event it was cut by 7.7%. Special funds were earmarked for two priority programmes: 150 billion for the improvement of the efficiency of distribution networks, and 250 billion for infrastructural programmes contributing to improved living standards. However, the criteria were so widely drawn that almost all existing schemes and projects were eligible. With the statutory suspension of the Fiscal Structural Reform Act in December 1998, budget controls were dismantled, and MOF announced a countercyclical fiscal stimulus of more than 16 trillion, of which 7.7 trillion was allocated to social infrastructure investment. Priority was given to three policy areas which between them accounted for about 60% of the total: environment and new energy sources were allocated 1.6 trillion; telecommunications networks, and science and technology, 1.0 trillion; social welfare, medical care, and education, 1.0 trillion. Nevertheless, roads and transportation attracted a further 0.8 trillion, and public works projects to prevent natural disasters a similar sum (MOF 1998*c*).

The General Account Budget for FY1999 was planned for a 15-month period, from 1 January 1999, in order to incorporate the third Supplementary Budget passed by the Diet late in 1998, providing for 23 trillion additional spending and tax changes to stimulate further the depressed economy. The public works budget was planned to increase by 5% (10.6% if the 500 billion allocated to the public works reserve fund is included). Because of the carry-over of unspent allocations from the General Account Budget for FY1998, and from the first and third Supplementary Budgets for FY1998, the outlays for the 15-month period of the FY1999 Budget were estimated at 13.4 trillion, representing an increase of 18% on the estimated outlays of FY1998 (MOF 1999). On the initiative of Prime Minister Obuchi, a public works reserve of 500 billion was created to help break down the entrenched allocations to MOC, MAFF, MOT, and MHW, to give greater priority to specific programmes, and to make the processes of allocation more transparent, rational, and accountable. The funds were open to bids from all ministries and agencies, adjudicated by the Prime Minister's Office. As a result, allocations among ministries changed by 2.3%. The experiment was repeated for FY2000 with a further 500 billion set aside, but the process of allocation was both politicized and opaque. For example, initially 100 billion was earmarked for the construction of *shinkansen* railway lines, and 50 billion for agricultural infrastructure. After public criticism, both were subsequently substantially reduced, and the allocation for IT projects increased. The two priority programmes identified in the main budget for FY1998 attracted further resources of 150 and 250 billion each, and a third, environmental and welfare projects, was added, and allocated 100 billion. The total of 500 billion represented a tiny proportion of the overall public works budget, most of which continued to be shared among the four main ministries in historic proportions. The General Account Budget for FY2000 was similarly spread over a 15-month period, again to provide for the carry-over of unused public works funds in the second Supplementary Budget of FY1999. Despite the continuance of under-spending, the budget guidelines for FY2001 provided for the same level of public works spending as the previous year, and a doubling of the reserve fund to 1 trillion. Greater priority was given to the extension of the *shinkansen* rail network on the initiative of senior ministers and politicians of the three coalition parties. The 75 billion allocated represented an increase in its share of the public works budget from 0.37% to 0.8%.

APPEARANCE AND REALITY

The political economy of public works expenditure provides a graphic illustration of the importance of distinguishing appearance from reality in Japanese budgetary politics. This chapter has shown that the real amount of resources provided by central government to finance public works projects was always much larger than the 'head-line' planning total in the annual (initial) General Account Budget. As a consequence, the trends of the latter were an incomplete guide to what actually happened to the aggregate of public works spending throughout the period 1975–2000. While MOF halted, and then reversed, the trend of rising public works spending *planned* in the General Account Budget in the 1980s, that apparent evidence of restrained growth and cuts was contradicted by the occurrence of continuous annual real growth in the overall volume. Public works projects were financed increasingly 'off-budget'. In consequence, there was a progressive decline in the role of the General Account Budget as the main source of finance for public works programmes; in most years after 1988 it provided less than half of the annual real aggregate. Further, I show in the next section that the appearance of the aggregate of on- and off-budget public works spending was itself deceptive. 'Head-line' planned totals grossly inflated the reality of new net spending, while the resources actually committed and consumed were constrained by regular under-spending and carry-forward, as projects were deferred, uncompleted, or cancelled.

Why did the LDP and MOF pursue two apparently contradictory policies after 1980, on the one hand restraining and cutting the growth of planned public works spending in the General Account Budget and on the other financing its continuous growth through other means? First, MOF's main budgetary aim from 1976 was to cut the budget deficit and reduce the level of government borrowing. As public works claimed nearly 20% of the total General Account Budget, and spending had risen sharply in the 1970s, restraining its further growth was an essential element of the implementation of the policy of fiscal reconstruction. Secondly, in practice, that policy was difficult to reconcile with sustained domestic and international pressures for more public works spending throughout the period 1975–2000. Domestically, public works had become an essential ingredient of the LDP's successful politico-electoral strategy in the era of 'machine-politics' inaugurated by Tanaka in the early 1970s. The LDP's policy priorities were changed to give greater emphasis to social, health, and welfare programmes, part of which was a concern to improve living standards by devoting more resources to the creation of social overhead capital—houses, urban development, and the environment—and fewer to the support of industrial infrastructure. Those domestic pressures were compounded by others from the international economic community at various times in the 1980s and 1990s, urging an expansion of public investment to generate domestic demand in the economy. Responding to those pressures, budgetary controls were gradually relaxed from 1987; in 1990 the government committed itself to a ten-year programme of public investment, and it increased the size of this four years later, responding to the recession that followed the collapse of the bubble economy. As international pressures became more insistent following the collapse of the economies of several East Asian countries in 1997, and as the Japanese economy once again moved into recession, the government responded once again with more public works spending.

Through Supplementary Budgets, FILP, and the NTT Scheme, MOF sought to provide the additional resources to accommodate those pressures for more public works spending. By so doing it relieved pressure on the General Account Budget. FILP was in principle self-financing, although in practice the central government provided, through the General Account Budget, for the continual subsidization of some FILP agencies, for example the Government Housing Loan Corporation. The costs of the NTT Scheme were ultimately a charge on the General Account Budget, but repayment of the interest-free loans from the Consolidated Fund was deferred until FY1992, after MOF had achieved its aim (albeit temporarily) of eliminating the issue of special deficit-financing bonds. Together, the 'off-budget' sources provided a means of ratcheting up the aggregate of public works spending without, in the short term, adding to the budget deficit.

While it is true that in principle the provision of additional resources for public works in annual Supplementary Budgets added to the out-turn expenditures of the General Account Budget, in practice the net costs of so doing were often quite small, and were partly offset by higher than (deliberately) underestimated revenues, and by institutionalized annual supplementary cuts to current expenditures. Until the years of recession in the 1990s, MOF was generally able to meet most of the costs of additional public works financed through Supplementary Budgets with only a marginal increase in government borrowing. That strategy was first squeezed, and soon overturned, as declining revenues and huge increases in public works combined to raise the deficit and government borrowing to levels higher even than even those of the late 1970s which prompted the policy of fiscal reconstruction. While some of the increasing pressure on the General Account Budget continued to be relieved through the financing of additional public works through FILP and the NTT Scheme, there were limits to the expansion of both. Public works projects financed through FILP were in principle expected to yield profits, although as we have seen the element of subsidization for some kinds of projects had grown through the 1980s. The further expansion of FILP thus depended on the number of viable projects, and the long-term costs and risks of funding or subsidizing others where the expectation of future profits and repayment was low. Expansion of the NTT Scheme depended upon the sale of a further tranche of shares, which was impracticable in the conditions of a depressed market. Moreover, public works financed by such additional loan capital contributed to a greater future burden on the General Account as loans matured.

The processes of allocating public works expenditures through the General Account Budget (which from 1992 included the cost of subsidizing the NTT Scheme) and FILP were influenced, sometimes determined, by the observance of the principles of balance and 'fair shares'. While those served to entrench the existing entitlements of the four main ministerial beneficiaries, there was greater flexibility in the allocations among policy sectors. Long-term trends show significant changes in the relative priority of some major programmes—roads and housing for example. There was no such flexibility in the long-term trends of the allocation to the four ministries. Within them, there was some evidence of marginal changes in the distribution among bureaux, reflecting changes in national objectives and priorities. To some extent, the relatively fixed shares of ministerial bureaux obscured changes in priority, and annual allocations between constituent divisions. But even at that level, discretion to vary historic allocations was constrained by the vested interests of bureaucrats, politicians, and special interest groups in maintaining the status quo. The application of the criteria prescribed in 1993 for the determination of priority in the functional allocation of public works expenditures in the General Account Budget had only a marginal effect, but it served to emphasize further the emerging trends of the greater weight given to housing, urban development, and environmental infrastructure, with corresponding less weight to roads, harbours, ports, and facilities for industrial infrastructure.

Finally, it is necessary to repeat that many public works programmes and projects, pre-eminently housing but also roads, ports, harbours, rivers, and land and agricultural infrastructure, were financed not only through the General Account Budget, annual Supplementary Budgets, FILP, and the NTT Scheme: but through Special Accounts as well, with substantial subsidies from the General Account Budget, and revenues from hypothecated taxes. As well, local governments financed public works on their own account, in addition to those supported by General Account transfers and FILP loans. The fungibility of those sources complicates the analysis of allocation. An apparent decline in a public works sector or programme in the General Account might be compensated by an allocation through FILP or a Special Account, or through local governments' own borrowing.

EFFICIENCY AND EFFECTIVENESS

Evaluation of the efficiency and effectiveness of public works spending is similarly complicated. Different, often conflicting, criteria can be used. First, it is possible to measure the achievement of general objectives prescribed in medium-term national and sectoral plans, where targets were laid down for their implementation—for example the number of houses built, connections to main sewers. But such measurement does not indicate whether the use of resources for those purposes was efficient: it does not measure and assess the opportunity cost of their use for those purposes compared with alternative uses of the same funds or the cost of providing for those purposes in other ways, for example through the private sector, public–private joint ventures, or loans.

There was little attempt at cross-sector or inter-project assessment in determining the size and allocation of the public works budgets in the General Account and FILP. Analytical techniques of project appraisal, such as cost–benefit and cost effectiveness analysis and discounted cash flow, were rarely used in the selection and comparison of projects on a regular and systematic basis before the end of the 1990s; where they were used, as in economic assessments of land improvement projects from the 1980s, they were often ignored (Shōgenji 1999). A legal attempt by environmental protectionists in 1997 to force the government to abandon a reclamation project on the grounds that the costs far outweighed the potential benefits elicited the response from the official in charge of the project that no cost–benefit analysis had been undertaken (Nikkei 1999a). The Japan Highway Corporation used a 'pool system' to determine the tolls of newly built roads, but never published the actual and anticipated surplus or deficit on each road. One reason for its recurring deficits, subsidized by the central government, was that it had to buy from its 66 protected, affiliated joint-stock companies, mostly owned by the Road Facilities Association, and to lease land and facilities to them at below-market prices (Inose 1997).

MOC introduced new methods of economic assessment on a trial basis in FY1997 in an attempt to prioritize new road and river basin sewage projects, and to evaluate their need and effectiveness by using 'comprehensive and objective evaluation criteria, including cost-benefit analysis'. It was to be applied not only in initial decision-making, but also intersectorally, to compare the costs and benefits of alternative schemes for road and rail, for example (MICHI 1998: 208). Five other ministries followed suit the following year, after an initiative from Prime Minister Hashimoto. In April 1999 this was put on a formal basis with the announcement that MOC, MOT, MAFF, NLA, and the Okinawa and Hokkaido Development Agencies would initiate cost–benefit analyses on all new public works projects in FY2000, and publish the results. But by 2000 there was still no formal, regular, independent, and comprehensive *ex post* review of the efficiency and effectiveness of the public works spending as a whole, without which it was impossible to determine whether it represented value for money.

Secondly, in any such overall assessment of efficiency and effectiveness, it is necessary to distinguish between the appearance of planned and approved public works projects, and the reality of their implementation. Underspending on the public works budget was normal, and the carry-forward of unimplemented projects customary practice. In the early 1990s only some 90%–95% of the planned total in the General Account Budget was actually carried out in the fiscal year, with underspending running at some 1 trillion a year. By FY1998 the completion rate had fallen to 74.7%. In other words, through delay, deferment, and cancellation, a quarter of the annual planned public works projects remained unimplemented at the end of the fiscal year. As mentioned earlier, the position became so acute that the time-horizons of the budgets for both FY1999 and FY2000 were extended to a 15-month period in order to incorporate the unspent allocations in the numerous Supplementary Budgets of the previous fiscal years.

Local governments' public works projects were funded partly with subsidies from the central government and partly from their own sources, including borrowing from FILP and its agencies. Until FY1988 the subsidized element was greater, but thereafter (partly to implement policies of fiscal reconstruction and consolidation) local governments were required to bear a greater share of the burden. By FY1998 the ratio of unsubsidized to subsidized public works was roughly 2 : 1. But with the huge and recurring increases in countercyclical spending, local governments were experiencing greater difficulty in implementing their unsubsidized projects. In FY1997, for example, some 4 trillion of a total of 20.1 trillion remained unspent or was carried forward.

Falling completion rates were especially noticeable in rural land schemes, where farmers were required to contribute a large proportion of the costs of reclamation and improvement. With falling rice prices, they were reluctant to undertake such schemes, 'and a large portion of the budgeted funds end up not being used' (Kase 1999). In urban areas, public works schemes were often delayed because of the difficulty of acquiring land. Those trends were exacerbated at the end of the 1990s. After a review of the efficiency and effectiveness of some 90 current public works projects in the compilation of the FY1999 budget, 26 approved projects were cancelled, 15 were scaled down and a further 51 were put on hold (MOF 2000*a*). The exercise was repeated in FY2000, and a further eight projects were cancelled and 14 suspended, worth some 24.5 billion. In the same year, MOC had 185 projects not begun within five years of budget approval, and 5,461 not completed within ten years of starting (*Nikkei Weekly*, 7 August 2000).

Thirdly, it is possible to assess the efficiency and effectiveness of public works spending as contributing to the improvement of productivity and the expansion of demand, and hence to the growth of GDP. Public investment, especially public works spending, results in greater economic efficiency if it contributes to or creates the conditions for more industrial activity through the provision of new or improved basic infrastructural facilities, and thereby increases productivity in the private sector. Generally, the 'productivity effect' was declining from the second half of the 1970s (EPA 1996*b*). The very high levels of public spending both on public works and on public facilities—mainly national schools and hospitals—in the 1990s were not a major factor in increasing productivity (Ostrom 1996). Central and local spending on public investment provided only modest stimulatory (and contractionary) impulses to GDP in the 1990s (Muhleisen 1999). Locally, there was no significant positive relationship between public investment and economic growth (Nakazato 1999).

It is a little more difficult to assess the effectiveness of public works spending used explicitly as a countercyclical stimulus to domestic demand in the economy. Political as well as economic considerations often dictated the timing of the announcement, the presentation of the package of measures, and the political rhetoric with which they were supported. The appearance of the large-volume increases listed in Table 23.3 was deceptive. Estimates of the macroeconomic effects of an increase in public works spending vary with definitions of net new spending, so-called 'clear water', or *mamizu* to use the Japanese vernacular. For example, estimates of 'clear water' in the September 1995 package of 14.22 trillion ranged from 3.5 to 9.4 trillion, representing a 0.7%–2% boost to GDP over the following 12 months. MOF preferred to define new spending as fresh public-sector investment, excluding loans by public finance corporations on the grounds that they might simply be replacing private-sector lending. On that definition, the 14.22 trillion package was reduced to 10.87 trillion, of which 7.9 trillion was to be financed by the issue of central and local government bonds, the remainder provided by the Trust Fund Bureau Fund through FILP allocations. In the financing of the package through a Supplementary Budget, provision was made for a total of only 5.325 trillion of new money. Overall, between August 1992 and October 2000 there were 14 packages of fiscal measures, with a nominal 'head-line' value of 132.4 trillion; but the 19 Supplementary Budgets to finance those (and other) measures provided for only 40.721 trillion of planned expenditure.

In the analysis of the effect of those countercyclical measures, the narrower definitions preferred by many private-sector economists and analysts distinguish new projects and programmes from those already planned but advanced in 'front-loading' schemes; they also exclude loan programmes offered by FILP agencies recycling postal savings, whose main effect was on the allocation of funding among investment projects rather than on the total of investment in the economy; exclude transfers of assets, within the public sector, such as government purchases of land and other assets, which merely redistribute ownership without creating any income or wealth; and allow for the time lag between the announcement of additional spending, the approval of projects, the commitment of resources to them, the letting of contracts, 'starts', progress, and completion. There is a lag in the official statistics showing public works starts, and the formation of new fixed capital assets based on the progress of projects.[2]

The stimulatory effect of countercyclical packages was hugely overstated by MOF, by a factor of two or more. Only about a third—some 23 trillion of the 65–75 trillion head-line figures for those introduced between 1992 and 1997 (see Table 23.3)—provided a real stimulus to the economy (Posen 1998). The package of public works and other measures introduced in September 1995, mentioned above, provided a real stimulus to economic activity of less than 60% of the amount claimed by MOF; three others had no stimulatory effect whatever.

Part of the explanation of this dichotomy is that, while MOF could request, it could not oblige or force, local governments to implement planned public works expenditure.

---

[2] For a discussion of these and related issues, see sect. 1–6 of *Economic Survey of Japan, 1992–93* (EPA 1994*a*).

A 'Public Works State'

From the middle of the 1990s, the local governments were increasingly reluctant to provide some or all of the finance from their own resources, or via the issue of local government bonds. Their fiscal crisis of deficit and debt was, if anything, more acute than that of central government. Declining tax revenues, cuts in central government grants and subsidies, and massive borrowing to finance public works in earlier packages had contributed to liabilities estimated at 184 trillion by the end of FY2000. In the April 1998 package of 16.7 trillion (Table 23.3), MOF asked them to provide additional public works of 1.5 trillion from their own resources, and to contribute a further 2.4 trillion to projects funded jointly. There was no realistic expectation that they would do so. Nor did they. In fact, local governments *cut* their public works from the last quarter of 1998 to the end of 2000 (OECD 2000). Apart from front-loading previously committed expenditures, MOF inflated the head-line total of the 1998 package by including the purchase of land and other assets, 'asset reshuffles' totalling 4.35 trillion. Excluding those, and the planned but unrealistic contributions of local governments, the real value of public works spending was reduced to 3.8 trillion. Even if local governments had paid their full share of joint projects, that total rises to no more than 6.2 trillion. With temporary tax reductions worth only 2.0 of the 4.60 trillion claimed by MOF, the head-line total of 16.7 trillion was worth no more than some 8 trillion of 'clear water' (Posen 1998: 51–3).

If the positive effects of countercyclical stimulation on demand in the economy were in reality marginal, to what extent did the increase of public works spending have an adverse effect, for example by 'crowding out' investment in plant and equipment in the private sector, as the sale of government debt forced up interest rates? While EPA found no such evidence in its econometric analysis of such short-term adverse effects, nevertheless, it warned that the medium-term consequences of a rising fiscal deficit, largely the result of continued heavy government borrowing to finance public works, could affect confidence in the future of the economy, and hence lead to a reduction in the economic growth rate—the so-called 'non-Keynesian effect'. The positive effect on consumption of stimulatory fiscal policies was not apparent when the deficit continued to rise above 5% of GDP. In its Economic Survey for 1996, EPA warned that 'the emergence of a continuing, large fiscal deficit in future could cancel out the effect of enlarged fiscal policy on stimulating competition' (EPA 1996*b*: 142).

As the deficit rose above that level in 1996 and 1997, to reach 7.4%, the Hashimoto government, returned to power in October 1996, committed itself to a reduction of 10% per year in the level of public works spending as part of its fiscal reform policies to reduce the deficit to 3% of GDP by FY2003. The Ministers for Construction and Agriculture both fiercely opposed the proposal, and argued to retain the revenues that accrued from hypothecated taxes. At the same time, it was argued that public works projects were more costly than those in the USA, partly because of the lack of competition, and the collusion between designated bidders in the *dangō* (agreement by consultation) system, an institutionalized system of bid-rigging. An MCA Survey for FY1994 listed 276 reports of collusive bidding, of which only 52 were reported to the Fair Trade Commission. In April 1997 the Cabinet ordered a review of pricing standards to include labour costs, design services, costs of materials, and the introduction of numerical targets for each ministry. Action guidelines were issued, aimed to reduce the costs of public works projects by at least 10%. In a comparison with the USA, contract prices were found to be a third higher in Japan, something that is only partly explained by price and cost-of-living differentials. OECD's own estimate was higher still: 40%, after allowing for Japan's higher prices (OECD 1997). With hindsight, the criticism of the short-lived Hosakawa government that there was 'too much public works spending', and that too many projects for which the need on grounds of strict economic efficiency was difficult to justify, appeared to be confirmed by the analysis of the positive and negative effects discussed above, and the decision to cut the budget by 10%. Takemura Masayoshi, minister of finance from June 1994 to January 1996, declared in a rare act of contrition: 'I regret the fact that I allowed an increase of the government's debt by approving public works projects worth 40 trillion' (*Nikkei Weekly*, 2 June 1997).

Finally, the effectiveness of public works spending can be assessed in terms of the actual or perceived political benefits to the LDP. To what extent did the party influence the size, composition, and distribution of public works spending?

'A PUBLIC WORKS STATE'

By the 1990s, Japan had become a 'public works state' (*doboku kokka*) in the words of Sakakibara Eisuke, MOF's vice-minister for international finance, its post-war economic system characterized by a level of fixed capital formation in the public sector greater than any other industrial country (Sakakibara 1998: 32). As we have seen, the core and greater part of that investment was provided by public works, nominal spending on which by both central and local governments totalled about 50 trillion a year at the end of the 1990s, roughly 10% of GDP.

The origins of the public works state can be traced to the beginning of industrialization in the Meiji era, sustained and enlarged subsequently by heavy road and rail investment in the succeeding Taishō era, and the implementation of neo-Keynsian fiscal policies to counter the Depression of the inter-war years. To that tradition, the LDP added an explicitly political dimension in the second half of the twentieth century. It became the ruling majoritarian party, and achieved and sustained its dominant position, through a combination of distributive politics and economic development. Public works was central to both. It provided the 'third leg' of a grand electoral strategy which included agricultural subsidies, and tax breaks and spending measures for small businessmen. From the early 1970s, national policy objectives designed to improve living standards, welfare, educational and cultural facilities, and the quality of the environment widely throughout Japan were combined with the narrower party political interest in providing a flow of benefits and favours targeted at farmers and rice-growing domestic householders, small businessmen, local construction and property developing firms, and the electorates of rural constituencies. The construction industry, with more than 560,000 companies employing 6 million people directly, and providing jobs indirectly for 10 million more, was heavily dependent on public works contracts and looked to the LDP at the central level to provide them (Igarashi 1999). Public works schemes and projects—roads, bridges, houses, ports and harbours, local and national airports, parks, recreational and cultural facilities, waste disposal facilities, water conservation, and agricultural land improvement and infrastructure—were more 'visible' and had greater political salience than many other budget outputs of central government's expenditure programmes.

It has become next to impossible to find either a coastline that hasn't been covered by *tetorapotto* (concrete blocks used to protect coastlines and make artificial harbours), or a river without a dam or a mountain without a planned cedar forest. In urban areas, roads are excavated with the regularity of annual festivals, and ever taller buildings and deeper subways are being constructed. (Igarashi 1999: 4)

Last-minute extensions to *shinkansen* rail lines, approved politically in the 'revival negotiations' at the end of the compilation of Budget, despite MOF's opposition, were a classic and recurring case of highly visible, prestigious local and regional projects.

Political benefits are impossible to quantify or weigh precisely in terms of a calculus of votes/seats and the distribution of public works, although the votes cast for a former deputy director-general of MAFF's Bureau of Land Structural Reform, who ran in a nationwide electoral district in the 1980 election for the House of Councillors, were almost directly proportional to the distribution nationally of agricultural subsidies for land improvement (Hirose 1981). At the very least, the size, composition, and distribution of public works contributed to the continued electoral success of the LDP up until 1993, or—what is more crucial to the Budget—were perceived to have done so by both the leadership of the LDP, and rank- and-file Dietmen. There is a relationship between changes in the public works budget from off-budget sources, and the runup to Diet elections (Kohno and Nishizawa 1990).

Why, then, did the LDP approve the exclusion of public works from programmes accorded formal priority status in the budget guidelines from FY1982 onwards? How did that exclusion affect the implementation of its grand electoral strategy through budget policies? Investment expenditure (mainly public works) was separately identified and categorized in the budget guidelines for the first time in FY1983, and the implementation of those guidelines in the next decade squeezed and cut the volume of public works spending, and its share of the initial General Account Budget. The LDP approved, or at least acquiesced in, those (apparently) restrictive guidelines, because MOF was willing or persuaded to make available additional resources to finance public works through the institutionalized Supplementary Budgets, and through FILP and the NTT Scheme. As we have seen in this chapter, the combined annual total of those additional resources more than compensated for the cuts imposed through the application of the budget guidelines in the compilation of the annual General Account Budget. They provided the means for the LDP to square the circle: to support the implementation of MOF's budget policies for fiscal reconstruction while ensuring a continued flow of resources to achieve its broad objectives of improving living standards and distributing benefits and favours targeted on groups, clients, and locations.

Deciding how much extra resources to provide annually for public works involved both economic and political judgements: the need to respond, and to be seen to respond, to domestic and international pressures for more public investment to expand the level of domestic demand in the economy in the short term was constrained by a consideration of how much could be afforded in the context of a recurring fiscal deficit on the General Account Budget, the size of government borrowing and the accumulation of debt, the availability of resources to finance the expansion of FILP, and the probable profitability of projects financed through it. Political factors included the accommodation of pressures from faction leaders (especially the Tanaka–Takeshita–Obuchi faction, which traditionally had specialized in public works), and more formally from the PARC divisions and Special Committees for Construction, Agriculture, and Transport. In practice, the weight given to economic rather than political factors is difficult to determine, as the economic justification for additional public works spending often obscured those allocations that were mainly or wholly politically inspired. Occasionally, the political influence was more overt, or at least the justification was more transparently political.

How did the LDP influence the allocation of the aggregates of public works resources? The empirical evidence presented above shows that the organizational distribution among ministries and agencies remained largely unchanged. Whatever the strength of political support for MOC, MAFF, MOT, or MHW in the budget process, demonstrated formally for example through PARC divisions, and informally through interaction between the senior bureaucrats of those ministries, PARC influentials, *zoku*, and the LDP leadership on the one hand, and MOF's Budget and Finance Bureaux on the other, it did not materially affect the outcome. Their relative shares remained unchanged. It is possible, of course, that without the maintenance of such support networks, one or other of the ministries might have lost resources. Thus, political support served to reinforce their competing claims to maintain their existing shares. As aggregate resources on- and off-budget were increasing annually, and by substantial amounts, all could 'win', and be seen to be doing so. MOF was not obliged to trade off among the competing ministries: it could satisfy those claims by distributing the additional resources *pro rata* according to historic patterns.

Within ministries and agencies, individual bureaux built and nourished links with those politicians favourably disposed towards them, and sought to mobilize and exploit their potential for influence within the party and government, formally and informally, at certain stages of the budget process, for example prior to the formal meetings of the PARC divisions to 'hear' the explanation of the ministry's budget request. The extent and effectiveness of any such influence should not be exaggerated. It served more to help maintain existing entitlements than to secure for a bureau or division an increased share of the ministerial allocation. Long-standing bureaucratic rivalry, such as that between the Rivers and Roads Bureaux in MOC, was about jurisdiction and resources; both had their supporters in the LDP. But judged by the historic trends of budget allocations to the functions for which they were mainly responsible, only over the medium or long term is there an apparent change. The extent to which that is attributable directly to LDP influence is impossible to judge.

The sectoral distribution of public works spending was influenced more by the LDP's politico-electoral strategies. In the general reorientation of priority between 'social' and 'industrial' capital investment in the 1970s and early 1980s, housing and local infrastructural projects for leisure, amenity, educational, and other purposes attracted an increasing share of the total budget, industrial and technological capital projects much less. (In the next chapter I show how and to what extent the FILP Budget was reoriented.) The shift undoubtedly reflected the LDP's changed electoral strategy to widen the basis of its support, expressed in changed national objectives in successive five-year plans. Nevertheless, the LDP continued to rely heavily on the electoral support of rural areas, and rural interests remained over-represented in the LDP and in the Diet. While the total amount of land under cultivation shrank from 6.09 million hectares in 1961 to 4.8 million in 1999, agricultural-related public works continued to attract a substantial share of the overall budget. Agriculture, forestry, and fisheries accounted for nearly 10% of GDP in 1965 when MAFF obtained nearly 20% of the total allocation of public works; by 1993, although agriculture contributed little more than 2% of GDP, MAFF's share had increased to 21.5%. Rural public works spending, mainly schemes of land improvement, pre-empted half of the agricultural budget (Shōgenji 1999). As the scope for more large-scale projects of irrigation and drainage diminished, resources were shifted into the creation of a social infrastructure, such as rural sewage schemes and village roads.

The LDP was not obliged to choose between urban and rural interests, other than very marginally; the huge expansion of public works expenditure through off-budget sources enabled it to reward both of them. At the same time, it was able through those sources to continue to distribute political benefits to small businesses as loans, subsidies, tax reliefs, and public works contracts. However, its support in urban areas appeared to be declining in the 1990s. In the Lower House elections of 2000, only one-tenth of urban voters supported the party.

It is more difficult to establish the extent of the LDP's influence on the geographic distribution of public works projects, to prefectures and, within them, to particular electoral districts. There is a relationship between public works spending and the political salience of prefectures. Several econometric studies concluded that the rate of return on public investment was positively related to the level of income in the 47 prefectures, and twice as large in those with high as with low incomes (see OECD 1997 for a summary). Yet the distribution of public investment was four times greater in low-income prefectures. They tended to be those in rural areas, where non-agricultural employment was more reliant on the construction industries than in those metropolitan prefectures such as Tokyo, Osaka, and Tokai, with the highest incomes. While such a distribution tended to reduce the economic efficiency of public investment, it could be regarded as a redistribution of income and public goods contributing to employment, improved living conditions, and a better environment. But if that was the main effect, what was the opportunity cost of redistributing income through public works spending? Could it have been done more effectively by health, welfare, and income maintenance policies?

The distribution among rural and urban prefectures remained relatively fixed. Thus, Hokkaido, Niigata, and Shimane Prefectures consistently attracted more public works spending throughout the period 1975–89; Tokyo, Osaka, and Saitama, the least. (Woodall 1996: 177). This suggests that either the Dietmen from the rural prefectures were more influential than those from more urban prefectures, or that the priority among the 47 prefectures reflected, through 'anticipated reactions', the indirect influence of the LDP's electoral strategy. The over-representation of rural interests in the LDP, the location of the constituencies of prime ministers (Tanaka and Taskeshita, for example), and the activities of LDP paymasters such as Kanemaru help to explain the maintenance of that priority. In FY1992 Shimane Prefecture had more public works per capita than any other prefecture; Takeshita Noboru, leader of the most powerful LDP faction in the 1980s and prime minister in 1987–9, had his home there. When Tanaka Kakuei was head of the same faction, and prime minister, Niigata Prefecture (where he lived) topped the list of prefectures; by 1992 it had fallen to eleventh place. There is also some evidence that the prefectures and constituencies of former ministers of construction attracted a greater share of public works projects (Woodall 1996).

Evidence of the influence of individual LDP politicians on the distribution of public works projects within prefectures, to particular electoral districts, is more difficult to come by. The conventional wisdom is that many rank-and-file Dietmen were successful in attracting particular public works projects to their electoral districts, and that such demonstrable benefits were crucial to the maintenance of their local personal networks, and local support organizations (*kōenkai*), for organizing and mobilizing electoral support. Public works, it is claimed, were an essential link in the politics of compensation: crudely, votes-for-favours.

It seems more likely, however, that the LDP's influence was aimed less at the attraction of public works projects to particular electoral districts and much more at securing projects for individual construction companies. In awarding a contract, there were three interrelated decision points where political or bureaucratic discretion was exercised: first, the choice of designated bidders from among those qualified and eligible; secondly, the ceiling price within which the contract was to be let; and thirdly, the award of the contract at a price bid by one of the designated firms. Under the (then) 'designated competitive tendering system', a small number of qualified firms were invited to submit bids for a public works project. The *zenekon* (general contractors) scandal in 1993 revealed the active intervention of politicians to influence the choice of the firms selected to bid. Large construction firms categorized politicians according to their perceived influence. Some of those firms then provided large personal and party donations to senior politicians in return for the exercise of that influence in their favour. The interest of construction firms in securing a nomination to bid is obvious enough, as was their equal interest in limiting competition through the *dangō* system the number of eligible bidders. In May 2000 the Fair Trade Commission served 'cease and desist' orders to 203 construction companies and 94 surveying companies concerning collusive bidding for agricultural projects of a local office of the Hokkaido local government (OECD 2000).

Construction firms had an interest too in obtaining information about a ministry's ceiling price for a contract. While there is the evidence from the Sagawa Kyūbin scandal of a money-for-favours relationship between firms and some national, regional, and local politicians, the evidence of political or bureaucratic influence on the disclosure of the ceiling price to designated bidders, i.e. that the contract price was commonly very close to the ceiling-price, is circumstantial (Miwa 1998).

The revelations of political intervention in a series of bribery and corruption scandals in the 1990s indicated that the scope and opportunity to influence decisions in exchange for cash contributions to party and factional funds had proved irresistible to some prominent LDP politicians. Apart from Kanemaru, in 2000 Nakao Eiichi, a former minister of construction, was convicted of receiving 50 million from the Wakachiku construction group in exchange for awarding them contracts for public works. Here it is unnecessary to enter into the debate about the extent and significance of corruption in the procurement system, and the involvement of individual national, regional, and local politicians. (For a provocative analysis, see Woodall 1996.) The incentive to attempt to influence the process at one or all three decision-points was a powerful one. Leaving aside illegal payments, construction firms were historically among the largest corporate donors to the LDP, and contributed to the campaign funds of local Dietmen.

Local public works helped to attract and mobilize voters benefiting from projects such as housing, local roads and bypasses, bridges, sewage and water schemes, agricultural improvement schemes, and the creation of local jobs in the construction industry (Cox and Thies 1998; Meyer and Naka 1998). Whether or not they had any direct or indirect influence on their location, LDP politicians, especially those in rural constituencies, stood to benefit if they could be personally identified with them. Through formal membership of PARC divisions for Construction, Agriculture, and Transport (all heavily over-subscribed), an active *zoku* member of the construction or agricultural tribe with access and informal connections to the bureaucracy could claim, and be seen publicly (apparently), to be influencing the size and allocation of the public works budget. A former MOF official, Yamamoto Kōzō, who resigned at the age of 47 to enter the Diet, explained:

My basic priority now is to build roads and sewage systems in my district' ... local mayors ask me for help. I call the ministries [of Finance and Construction] and ask them about it. Then I call my colleagues in the Finance Ministry—specifically the budget examiner in charge of the relevant budget allocation. And I usually get the information I want; not always, but they usually co-operate. And if they have room to negotiate, then they pay attention to my request ... I pass the information to my local district. (quoted in Hartcher 1998: 48)

Dietmen, especially those in rural constituencies, could 'claim credit' when road or housing projects were allocated to their electoral districts, whether or not their attempt to influence decisions had affected directly or indirectly those allocative decisions. As we saw in Chapter 20, 'credit-claiming' was an integral part of the mutual relationships between Dietmen and their personal support organizations (*kōenkai*), their success in attracting public works projects given prominence in 'newsletters' and the local media.

Whether continuing budget deficits and mounting debt will force a radical reappraisal of the role of public works in Japan's political economy in the twenty-first century is uncertain. There were some signs of political responsiveness to growing public criticism of wasteful and inefficient projects, and to local protests such as that in Tokushima in January 2000 which led to the abandonment of a planned MOC project to dam the Yoshino River. A former administrative vice-minister of MOC, Sumitya Shōji (1998), attested that much of the ministry's investment in large-scale facilities in commercial seaports was wasteful. Besides the internal ministry reviews mentioned earlier, the coalition partners of Prime Minister Mori's government agreed in August 2000 a plan to cancel 233 projects, nearly half of which were MOC's. However projected cost savings were small, less than 2% of the annual public works budget. Moreover, there was evidence that MOC and other ministries switched lost-spending into other projects, while local governments both sought reimbursement for the costs incurred on cancelled projects, and pressed for new projects as compensation.

24

Winning and Losing in the FILP Budget

Analysis of FILP Budget outputs is beset with definitional traps and methodological hazards. Different values for FILP can be derived, depending upon the definition and the budget base used in time-series data. First, the FILP Budget can be, and is, defined gross or net. The gross budget included all expenditures for whatever purpose attributed to FILP and financed through deposits, mainly with the Trust Fund Bureau Fund and the Postal Life Insurance Fund. By contrast, the net budget included only those funds used to finance the investments and loans of the FILP agencies—the investment and loan programme proper. It also excluded those funds allocated in the FILP Budget for other general finance purposes, mainly to underwrite a part of central government's borrowing requirement to cover annual fiscal deficits on the General Account Budget, and (from 1987) to finance capital management operations designed to generate additional income for the Postal Savings, Postal Insurance, and Pensions Special Accounts. Secondly, as with the General Account Budget, the measurement of the size and changes of gross and net FILP budgets varied with the budget base—the initial planned budget, the revised budget, the out-turn of those planned and revised budgets, and the amount actually spent, allowing for both underspending and expenditure carried forward.

This chapter distinguishes those definitions and budget bases in an examination of the trends of the aggregate budget outputs, and shows their allocation and distribution, organizationally, among FILP agencies and, functionally, among broad policy areas. The issue of the extent to which the FILP Budget supported industrial and technological development, despite the reorientation of national objectives to give greater weight to social and environmental objectives, is dealt with in detail.[1]

AGGREGATE BUDGET OUTPUTS

The Gross FILP Budget

The planned gross FILP Budget grew annually and rapidly from 9.730 trillion in FY1975 to 57.759 trillion in FY1998, a six-fold increase, twice the rate of the growth of the planned General Account Budget (Wright 1998*a*: table 5). Figure 24.1 compares the trends of the two budgets. In the mid-1970s FILP was less than half the size of

---

[1] The analysis in this chapter is based on statistical and other data in Wright (1998a,*b*).

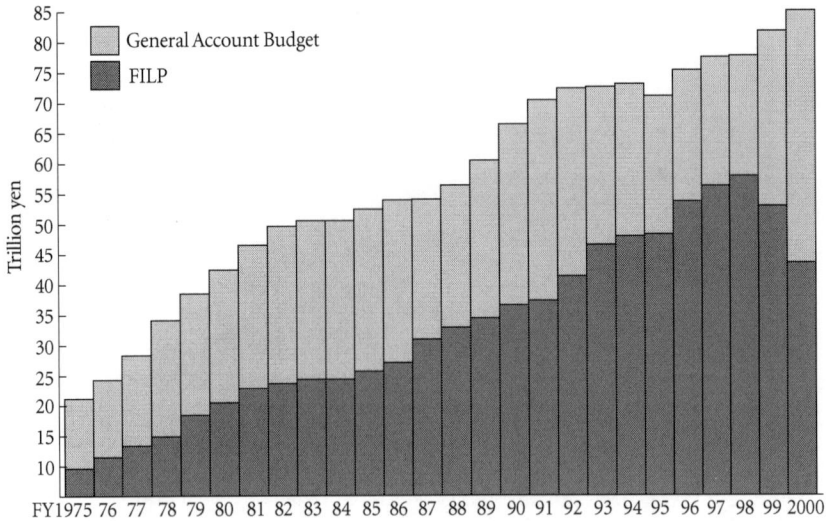

Figure 24.1 *The growth of FILP and the General Account Budget, FY1975–FY2000*
FILP and General Account initial Budgets: trillion yen

Source: *Zaisei Tōkei* (annually), Research Division, Budget Bureau, MOF.

the General Account Budget; a decade later it was nearly 60%; by 1998, after the exceptionally severe economic recession of the previous seven years, it had reached over 70% of the size of the General Account. If central government borrowing and capital management operations are excluded, the net FILP Budget in 1975 was 9.3 trillion and the General Account Budget net of debt costs, 15.8 trillion. By 1996, before the initiation of FILP reform, the difference had narrowed substantially. At 40.5 trillion, the amount allocated to capital investment and loans projects in FILP was fast approaching the total allocation in the main budget for all programmes of general expenditures, 43 trillion. A continuation of those historical trends of growth experienced in the 1980s and 1990s would have seen more spent on capital development through FILP than on all programmes combined in the main budget. In terms of size, the 'second budget' would have become the 'first budget'.

There were three phases of growth (Wright 1998b: table 5). From 1975 to 1981, annual increases to the gross FILP budget averaging between 11% and 23% were associated with a continuation of sustained high economic growth, and with the high government spending inaugurated in the 'welfare era' begun under the premiership of Tanaka Kakuei in the early 1970s. The profile of the second phase, from 1982 to 1991, is one of much lower growth, consistent with MOF's policies for fiscal reconstruction and consolidation. However, annual growth rates of between 1.2% and 6.5% were still much larger than those of the initial General Account Budget. The increase of 14.5% in FY1987 was the one-off effect of the introduction of those capital market operations discussed in Chapter 12. In the third phase, covering the years of the 'bubble economy' and the subsequent severe economic recession, the annual growth of the FILP Budget reached double figures again, reflecting policies of fiscal expansion, and the use of FILP as an instrument of countercyclical policy. Growth was reined back after FY1996, as the aims, purpose, and role of FILP were questioned in the reform of the institutions of central government. In FY1999 the initial budget was cut for the first time for more than 25 years, prior to the implementation of statutory FILP reforms.

FILP consistently absorbed more than 8% of nominal GDP from 1979 to 1992, rising thereafter to more than 10% per year until the implementation of reform in FY1999. Figure 24.2 shows the ratio of FILP to GDP, and compares it with the General Account Budget–GDP ratio. The remarkable stability of FILP's share throughout the 1980s shows that it was little affected by the policies of fiscal reconstruction in that period. While the rate of annual increase slowed, it nevertheless grew at a faster rate than the General Account Budget and, after the onset of recession in FY1991, at a faster rate than GDP.

This analysis of the FILP Budget using an initial budget base understates its size and significance in national budgeting, and its absorption of GDP. Changes could be made to the planned budget in-year more easily and flexibly than to the General Account Budget: up to 50% of the initial budget could be added without obtaining statutory

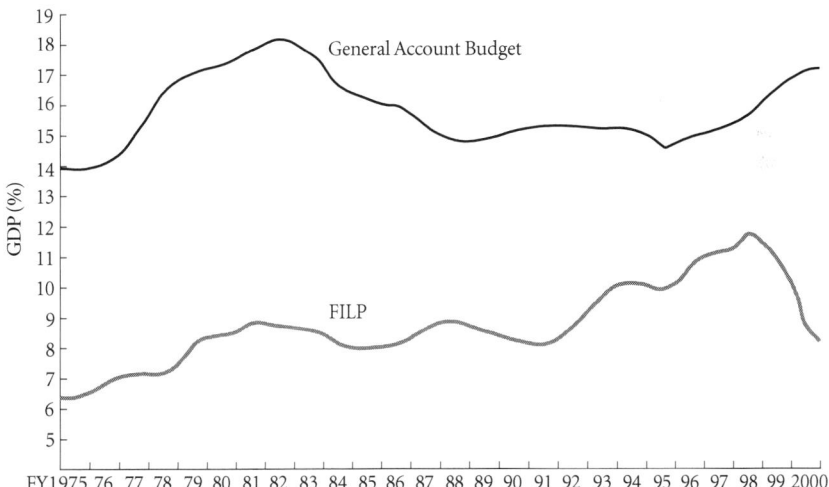

Figure 24.2 *FILP and the General Account Budget: proportions of GDP, FY1975–FY2000*
FILP and General Account Initial Budgets: percentage nominal GDP

Source: *Zaisei Tōkei* (annually), Research Division, Budget Bureau, MOF.

464 Budget Outputs

authority. The planned budget was revised upwards, sometimes on several occasions, every year from FY1975 to FY1999, apart from 1984 and 1996, when small reductions were made. In-year changes were substantial in the mid-1970s and from FY1987 onwards, as FILP was exploited to help finance countercyclical fiscal policies, adding between 0.5% and 1% per year to FILP's absorption of GDP. For example, in FY1992 the initial planned budget claimed 8.7% of GDP; after all in-year revisions totalling 4.8 trillion were included, that proportion rose to nearly 10%. Figure 24.3 shows the planned and real changes in the FILP Budget for 1975–2000.

The Investment and Loan Programme

The 'head-line' total of the gross FILP Budget was very much larger than the amount actually allocated to finance the Investment and Loan Programme. First, up to 20% of the initial planned budget was used annually to purchase central government bonds to help underwrite the recurring deficits in the General Account Budget (Wright 1998*b*: table 7). Secondly, from FY1987, a proportion of the initial budget was also set aside to

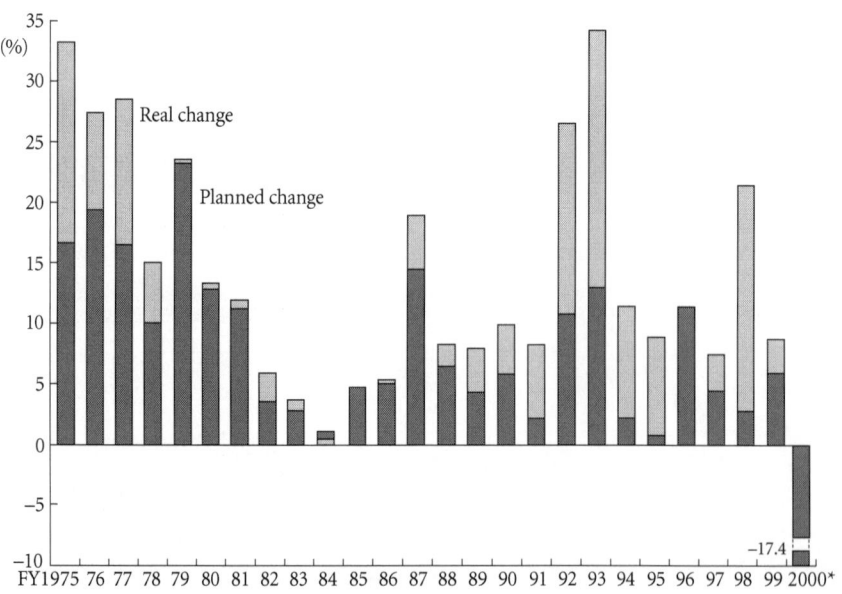

Figure 24.3 *Planned and real changes in the FILP Budget, FY 1975–FY2000*
FILP Initial and Revised Budgets: percentage annual change

Gross Budget inludes, besides the investment and loan programme proper, allocation for purchase of central government bonds, and (from 1987) portfolio investment of postal savings and pension funds.
*Planned budget change only

Source: FILP Report (annually), First Fund Division, Financial Bureau, MOF.

finance capital market operations for some of the postal savings and pension reserves deposited with the Trust Fund Bureau Fund. The funds for those operations were substantial, increasing three-fold, from 3.35 trillion, to 13.5 trillion, by FY1999. Figure 24.4 compares the gross FILP Budget with the budget for the investment and loan programme for the period 1975–2000. It shows that the combined effect of the two 'offsets' was to erode progressively the amount of the initial planned FILP Budget available to finance the Investment and Loan Programme. Whereas nearly 90% was available in the 1970s and early 1980s, the proportion was less than 80% after FY1987, falling as low as 63% in FY1998. FILP had thus become an integral part of the overall fiscal system, with FILP funds providing a vital 'lubricant'. We look at that changing role and purpose in more detail in Chapter 28.

There was a four-fold increase in the resources allocated to the Investment and Loan Programme in the initial FILP Budget, from 9.3 trillion in 1975 to 39.349 trillion in 1999. The annual rates of growth mirrored the three profiles associated with the policies of growth, reconstruction, and expansion mentioned earlier for the gross budget. However, the real rate of change, measured by the inclusion of all in-year changes to planned allocations, was much greater for all three. The real growth rate was roughly double that planned for the five years of the bubble economy, while still larger real increases occurred subsequently as FILP was used to help finance the ten

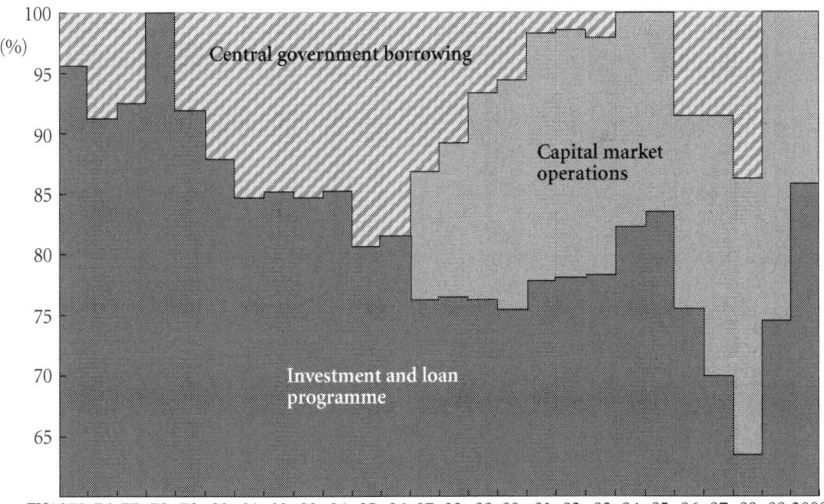

Figure 24.4 *The squeeze on the Investment and Loan Programme in the FILP Budget, FY1975–FY2000*
FILP Initial Budget: percentage shares

Source: *FILP Report* (annually), First Fund Division, Financial Bureau, MOF.

countercyclical fiscal packages of 1992–2000. In FY1993, for example, a planned increase of 13.4% was converted into a real increase of more than 40% as a result of successive in-year revisions. Figure 24.5 compares the planned and real changes in the expenditures allocated to the Investment and Loan Programme within the FILP Budget for the period FY1987–FY1999.

What was actually spent in each fiscal year on the Investment and Loan Programme differed both from what was planned initially, and from the revised allocation made in-year. Here the distinction between gross and net FILP is crucial. Netting out central

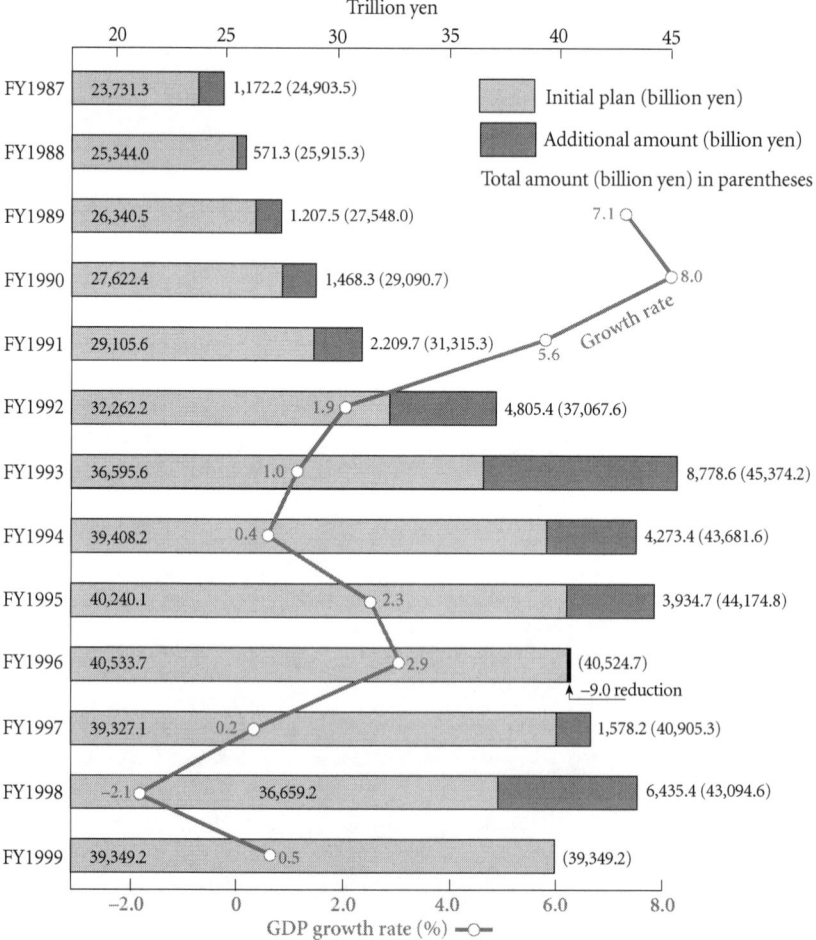

Figure 24.5 *Planned and real changes in the Investment and Loan Programme in the FILP Budget, FY1987–FY1999*
FILP Initial and Revised Budgets: trillion yen

Source: *FILP Report 2000*, First Fund Division, Financial Bureau, MOF.

government borrowing and portfolio management, the out-turn (settled budget) showed that between 15% and 30% of the revised budget for the Investment and Loan Programme remained unused or was carried forward at the end of each fiscal year (Table 28.2). Projects deferred, abandoned, or cancelled accounted for about 3% of the allocation of the revised budget total (Wright 1998b: table 9). In the mid-1990s, as FILP was used increasingly to help finance the costs of successive countercyclical measures, more substantial amounts remained unused. At the end of FY1995, for example, only just over a half of the revised plan for investment and loans was carried out; more than a fifth (9.8 trillion) was unused.

Besides unused allocations, some 15%–22% of the allocations in the revised budget were carried forward each year, and added to planned expenditures in the initial budget for the next fiscal year. Except where the amount carried forward was unusually large, as in FY1995 (9.8 trillion) and FY1996 (8.9 trillion), the net effect on the out-turn of the Investment and Loan Programme cancelled out, taking one year with another (Financial Bureau 1998b).

ORGANIZATIONAL OUTPUTS

FILP was used mainly to finance investments and loans to central rather than local government organizations. On average, more than four-fifths of the planned expenditure was allocated each year to the 50–60 FILP agencies: the public banks, finance corporations, public corporations, and special companies, controlled or supervised by central government ministries. Nevertheless, FILP provided almost half of local governments' annual capital requirements by buying or guaranteeing bonds issued by them or their local public enterprises—transport, gas, and water. Indirectly, through the financing of one of the FILP agencies, the Japan Finance Corporation for Municipal Enterprises (JFCME), it also provided a further tranche of funds. For example, in FY1997 FILP funds provided 8.6 trillion of the total of the Local Bond Plan drawn up by MOF. The JFCME provided a further 2.2 trillion in government guaranteed bonds and its own bonds (JFCME 1997a). The allocation of the FILP Budget between central and local government organizations did not however determine whether FILP funds would be spent on national or local projects. While some of the investments and loans financed by the centrally controlled public banks and finance corporations, and public works organizations (public corporations and special companies for road and bridge construction, for example), was for the creation of national infrastructure, such as highways and national airports, most was allocated for local or regional projects.

How were those outputs distributed organizationally among FILP agencies? The 11 public banks and finance corporations attracted between 65% and 70% of the total of the Investment and Loan Programme, the budget for which increased year by year until FY1996. However, the distribution of that budget varied. The allocated resources were concentrated in a handful of FILP agencies. In order of budget size, in 1975 they were: the Government Housing Loan Corporation, the People's Finance Corporation, the EXIM

Bank, the Small Business Finance Corporation, the Japan Development Bank, the Finance Corporation for Municipal Enterprises, the Pensions and Welfare Services PC, and the OECF. Together they accounted for 60% of the Investment and Loan Programme, rising to 70% by FY1985 (Wright 1998*a*: table 17). Their rates of growth and budget shares varied. The principal beneficiary was the GHLC, which between 1975 and 1996 more than doubled its share of the programme, from 11.5% to about 30%. That striking growth was largely at the expense of the allocations to other PFCs and FILP agencies. Figure 24.6 shows who had won and lost among the main PFCs in 1996 compared with 1976. Besides the GHLC, the Pensions and Welfare Services PC, the OECF, and the People's Finance Corporation enjoyed growth above the rate of the Investment and Loan Programme as a whole, and also captured a larger share of the Budget. By contrast, the JDB, Small Businesses Finance Corporation, the EXIM Bank, and the JFCME all grew at below the rate for the programme as a whole, and also lost budget share.

Who won and lost intertemporally within the 20-year period, in each annual spending round, is shown in Figure 24.7 which plots on the x-axis the number of years (in the 20-year period) in which the PFCs maintained or increased their allocations, and on the y-axis, the number of years in which they maintained or increased their budget share. Four PFCs both acquired additional resources and increased their budget shares in most years: the GHLC, the Pensions and Welfare Services Public Corporation, the People's Finance Corporation and the JNR Debt Settlement Corporation. Five PFCs—the JDB, EXIM Bank, Small Businesses FC, the OECF, and the JFCME—both won and lost. The additional resources secured in most years were insufficient to prevent reduced budget shares.

The analysis shows that, organizationally, there were both winners and losers as resources were allocated differentially in the budget processes. Budget share was a guide to allocation, but did not determine it. However, no PFC lost both resources and budget share consistently through the period.

Allocations to other FILP agencies were also concentrated. About 80%–85% of the budget share of those agencies responsible for public works was accounted for by five undertaking road and bridge construction (the Japan Highway PC, the Metropolitan Expressway PC, the Hanshin Expressway PC, the Honshu–Shikoku Bridge Authority, the Trans-Tokyo Bay Highway Corporation); by the Housing and Urban Development Corporation, which provided public housing for sale or rent; by two corporations responsible for major airport construction, and by the Special Account for airport development (Wright 1998*a*: table 16). The three-fold increase in their combined allocation between 1975 and 1993 was about the same as the growth rate for the Investment and Loan Programme, but the distribution among individual agencies changed significantly. More FILP funds were allocated to those agencies responsible for road and bridge construction than for housing or airports, rising from 805 billion in 1976 to 3.5 trillion in 1993, with HUDC's share of the Budget for public works organizations falling from nearly one-half in 1975 to less than one-quarter by 1993. The allocation for airport construction averaged 1% or less until the mid-1980s, when the financing of the Kansai International Airport and the redevelopment of Narita claimed some 4%–5% of the budget share of FILP public works organizations.

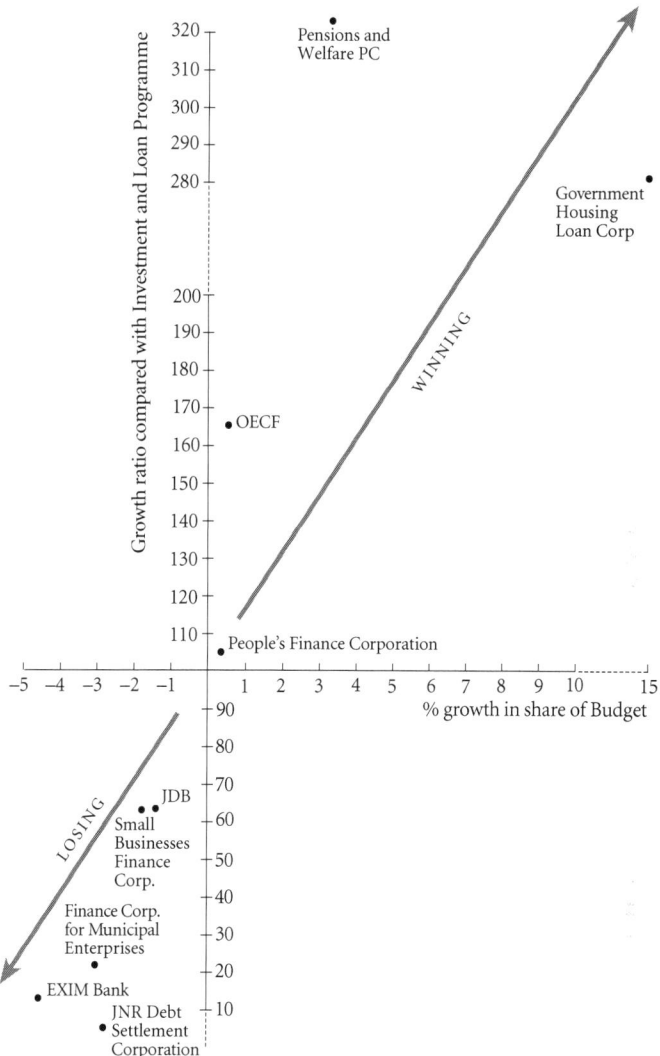

Figure 24.6 *FILP agencies: winners and losers in FY 1976 compared with FY 1996 FILP Initial Budget*

Excludes central government borrowing and portfolio management.

Source: derived from data provided by the First Fund Division, Financial Bureau, MOF.

POLICY AREAS

FILP investments and loans to eligible agencies were classified into 13 policy areas which MOF reported annually to the Diet (Table 24.1). The continuous and substantial

470   *Budget Outputs*

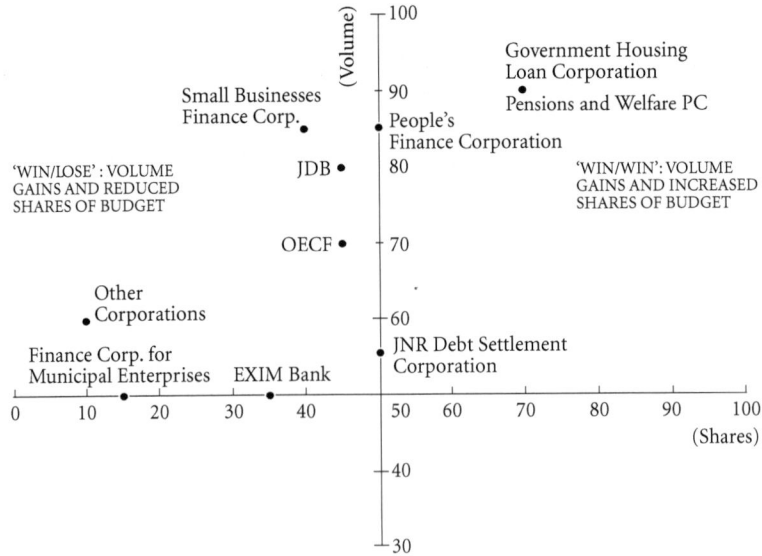

Figure 24.7 *Annual allocations to FILP agencies: 'Winners and Losers', FY1976–FY1996*
FILP Initial Budget

Excludes central government borrowing and portfolio management.

Source: derived from data provided by First Fund Division, Financial Bureau, MOF.

growth of the Investment and Loan Programme throughout the period 1975–99 provided the means to finance the annual growth of resources allocated to all policy areas. However, not all of them were winners, and both winners and losers gained and lost resources differentially. We look first at the rates of growth and decline of the budget allocations to each, and at changes in their shares of the Budget for the Investment and Loan Programme as a whole, in 1975 and 1996, before the reform of FILP.

The *x*-axis in Figure 24.8 measures the growth rates of each policy area compared with the budget as a whole. The *y*-axis measures the change in the share of the budget for each policy area. In the 'Win/Win' box, five policy areas—housing, welfare, land, environment, and roads—enjoyed above-average growth in their budgets, and claimed an increased share of the Budget. By contrast, in the 'Lose/Lose' box, six policy areas—regional development, SMEs, agriculture, education, trade, and transport—had both lower than average growth and a reduced budget share. Industry both 'won' and 'lost': it increased its share of the budget marginally, but enjoyed lower than average growth.

This analysis demonstrates not only that there were both winners and losers, but that policy areas won and lost differentially. Rates of growth and shares of the Budget were very different. Among the winners, the budget for housing policy grew at a rate almost twice that of the Investment and Loan Programme as a whole, and increased its share of the budget by 14.2%. By contrast, roads and environment benefited much less.

Table 24.1 *Functional classification of the allocation of FILP funds by policy area, FY1975–FY2000*

I PA 'directly enhancing the quality of national life'	II PA 'building the foundation for national life'	III Industry and technology PA	IV Trade and economic cooperation PA	V Fund management
Housing Living environment improvement Public Welfare Culture and education Small businesses Agriculture, forestry, and fisheries	National land conservation and disaster relief Roads Transportation and communication Regional development	Industry and technology	Trade and economic cooperation	Portfolio investment[a]

[a]From 1987.
PA: Policy area.
Source: *Zaito-Sanpyō* (annual), Financial Bureau, MOF.

Transport's growth was only 24% of the average for the Investment and Loan Programme as a whole, and by 1996 its share of the budget was 7.5% less than that of 1975. Among the losers, losses were distributed unequally, with trade and transport losing most.

Success and failure in the budget allocations are now analysed intertemporally. In Figure 24.9 the x-axis measures annual volume increases in the allocation for each year of the period 1975–96. The maintenance or increase in volume is measured on a scale from 0 to 100%, the latter representing success in each of the 21 years. The y-axis measures the maintenance or increase in the share of the Budget for each year.

On a year-by-year basis, there were no clear losers in the annual allocative process: most of the time all policy areas gained something, and some benefited considerably. No policy area lost both volume and share in more than 10 of the 21 years. To put it another way, in most years all policy areas maintained or increased their budget allocations. However, they did so differentially, with the result that allocations to some policy areas—SMEs, agriculture, transport, and trade—were insufficient to prevent a loss of budget share in most years. For example, the annual allocation to SMEs was maintained or increased in 19 of the 21 years, but those allocations were not large enough, relative to those made to other policy areas, to prevent a loss of budget share in 12 of those years. The result, as we have seen in Figure 24.8, was that by 1996 SMEs had become an overall loser relative to other policy areas, compared with its position 20 years earlier. Among those other policy areas in the 'Lose/Lose' category in that figure,

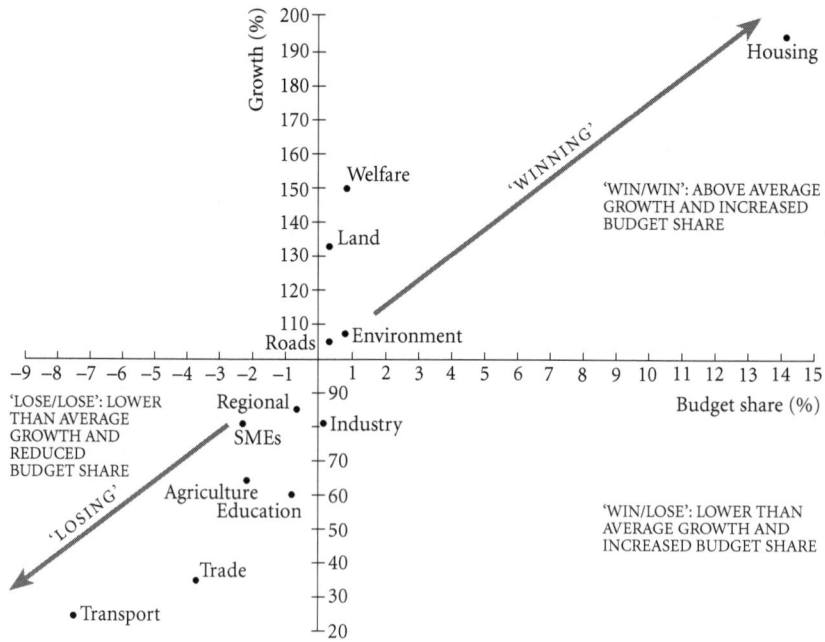

Figure 24.8 *FILP policy areas: 'Winners and Losers in FY1975 compared with FY1996 FILP Initial Budget*

Excludes central government borrowing and portfolio management.

Source: derived from data provided by First Fund Division, Financial Bureau, MOF.

there are some striking differences when success or failure in each annual budget allocation is assessed. Regional development acquired more resources, and increased its share of the Budget annually for the greater part of the period. Agriculture, transport, and trade also enjoyed increased allocations in most years, but not sufficiently to prevent a loss of budget share.

In short, year by year through the period 1976–96, no policy area lost both resources and budget share consistently. No policy area fell into the Lose/Lose category in Figure 24.9. In most years, all policy areas gained additional resources, but they did so differentially, and hence some increased their budget share annually as well. Resources were not allocated on a 'fair shares' or historic pro rata basis, nor were they distributed consistently in incremental (or decremental) steps.

To what extent did those changes in the composition of the Investment and Loan Programme justify MOF's claim of a broader, longer, sustained, and substantial shift of resources, away from rebuilding the economic and industrial base and providing the accompanying infrastructural services, and towards the improvement of living standards and the quality of life? Table 24.2 shows that that change was well underway in the 1960s, and was maintained throughout the period 1975–99. FILP funds to

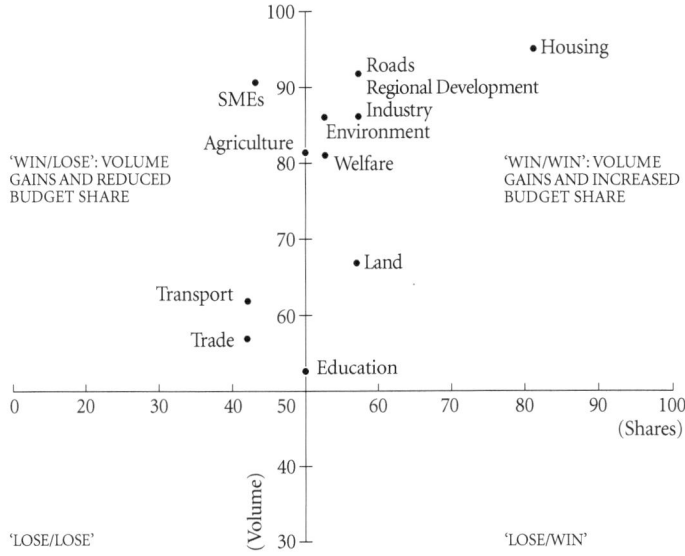

Figure 24.9 *Annual allocations to FILP policy areas: 'Winners and Losers', FY1975–FY1996*
FILP Initial Budget

Excludes central government borrowing and portfolio management.

Source: derived from data provided by First Fund Division, Financial Bureau, MOF.

Table 24.2 *Changing priorities of the FILP Budget: budget outputs by policy areas, FY1955–FY2000 (%)*[a]

Policy area	1955	1965	1975	1985	1995	1996	1997	1998	1999	2000
Quality of life	45.1	52.8	64.1	69.8	76.0	75.6	75.7	78.3	74	77.4
Building the foundation of life	32.1	31.9	25.2	21.9	16.2	17.9	18.0	15.2	15.7	15.9
Industry/ technology	15.8	7.8	3.0	2.9	3.1	2.5	2.4	2.4	3.6	1.8
Trade/economic cooperation	7.0	7.5	7.7	5.4	4.7	4.0	3.9	4.1	6.7	4.9

[a] *FILP Initial Budget; fiscal years.*

Source: First Fund Division 1998, 2000, Financial Bureau, MOF.

promote policies broadly designed to enhance the quality of life—for example housing and welfare programmes—were less than one-half of the total budget in 1955; by 1995 they absorbed three-quarters. Conversely, support for industrial and technological development fell sharply, from 15.8% to 1.8% in 2000, while policies of infrastructural investment—land, roads, transport and communications, and regional development—attracted less than one-sixth of the budget in 2000 compared with one-third 40 years earlier.

That analysis and representation of the allocation of the annual FILP Budget were largely the Financial Bureau's *ex post facto* stylization of the outcome of the allocation processes, and enabled it to claim that FILP plans had 'shifted priority from industry to daily life' by reducing financing for industry and technology from 16% of the FILP Budget in FY1955 to less than 3% in FY1996–7 (FILP 1997: 28). We now examine the validity of that claim.

SOCIAL AND INDUSTRIAL INVESTMENT

The rapid growth of 'social investment', and the decline of financial support for industry and technological development, in the FILP Budget was partly the result of the reorientation of national objectives that occurred at the beginning of the 1970s. It was also partly a reaction to the continuing criticism through the 1980s of the Japanese government's role in the economy. The growth and size of the FILP Budget, and its use to provide loans and subsidies for industrial and technological development, was a particular target of the US government and international economic organizations such as the OECD. MOF was sensitive and defensive about the purposes served by FILP, and in official and semi-official publications repeatedly emphasized that, whatever might have been the case in the 1950s and 1960s, there had been a marked and continuous decline in the amount of industrial support as national economic and social objectives had changed.

MOF's stylized presentation of the outcome of the budget processes, dividing allocations among five broad policy groups, exaggerated the extent to which resources were shifted away from the support of industry and technology. MOF's repeated claims (FILP 1996, 1997, 1998) that the FILP system 'effectively allocates funds with an ever greater priority on improving the quality of the people's lives', supported by reference to the resources allocated to the six programmes grouped in the first policy area, 'quality of life', is disingenuous. It included those resources allocated to small and medium-sized enterprises and to agriculture forestry, and fisheries. MOF admitted that resources for the former were used 'to expand lending to aid business-creation and technology and product development'; while the latter included loans related to business, and to the food processing and distribution industry (FILP 1996: 32). Both are categorically distinct from the social, environmental, welfare, and education programmes in Table 24.1 (programmes 1–4). They should more properly be bracketed with those programmes in the policy areas for 'building the foundation of national life', and for industry and technology. Moreover, while the construction of public housing for rent and sale, and the provision of loans for home purchase, were legitimately 'social investment', such capital investment also supported the construction industry and its suppliers.

A more accurate representation of the allocation of FILP investments and loans between social and industrial investment is shown in Table 24.3, which groups the budget outputs for the programmes for small and medium-sized enterprises and agriculture with other industrial, trade, and technology programmes. This analysis shows that, despite the doubling of resources allocated to social investment between 1955 and 2000,

Table 24.3 *Social and industrial investment in the FILP Budget, FY1955–FY2000 (%)*[a]

Policy area	1955	1965	1975	1980	1985	1990	1995	1996	1997	1998	1999	2000
Social												
investment	28.1	33.0	44.4	48.2	47.5	50.7	57.7	59.4	60.1	59.2	55.7	58.4
Housing	13.8	13.9	21.4	26.2	25.4	30.3	35.3	35.6	35.3	35.6	32.7	34.1
Environment	7.7	12.4	16.7	14.1	15.7	15.3	16.4	17.5	18.5	17.5	17.1	17.8
Welfare	2.1	3.6	3.4	3.5	2.8	3.1	4.0	4.3	4.2	4.0	3.8	4.2
Education	4.5	3.1	2.9	4.4	3.6	2.0	2.0	2.0	2.1	2.1	2.1	2.3
Industrial												
development	71.9	67.0	55.6	51.8	52.5	49.3	42.3	40.6	39.9	40.8	44.3	41.6
Small												
businesses	8.1	12.6	15.6	18.7	18.0	15.7	15.3	13.3	13.0	16.7	16.1	16.7
Agriculture	8.9	7.2	4.1	4.9	4.3	3.1	2.9	2.9	2.6	2.4	2.2	2.3
Land	7.7	3.1	1.2	1.7	2.3	1.2	1.3	1.5	1.4	1.5	1.7	1.9
Roads	3.7	7.9	8.0	5.7	8.8	9.8	7.8	8.3	9.7	9.1	8.6	9.3
Transport	12.2	13.9	12.7	9.6	8.4	8.3	4.6	5.2	4.2	1.7	1.9	1.8
Regional												
development	8.5	7.0	3.3	2.6	2.4	2.5	2.6	2.9	2.7	2.9	3.5	2.9
Industry	15.8	7.8	3.0	3.0	2.9	2.9	3.1	2.5	2.4	2.4	3.6	1.8
Trade/												
economic												
cooperation	7.0	7.5	7.7	5.6	5.4	5.8	4.7	4.0	3.9	4.1	6.7	4.9

[a]FILP Initial Budget; fiscal years.
Source: First Fund Division 1998, 2000, Financial Bureau, MOF.

some 40% of the FILP Budget continued to be allocated to support industry, trade, and technology development. Loans and investments in SMEs doubled their budget share in the same period. To illustrate those trends, we look more closely at the changed roles of the Japan Development Bank and the EXIM Bank, and their lending practices.

The roles of the JDB and the EXIM Bank

The Japan Development Bank (JDB) and the Export–Import (EXIM) Bank were the main instruments in the high-growth era for implementing the strategy of using FILP funds to promote and develop Japan's four basic industries: coal, electricity, shipbuilding, and iron and steel. In 1955 almost half of the annual FILP loans and investments made by the public banks and finance corporations were made by them. By 1965 however their share had fallen to a third, and by 1995, to less than 20%. That decline was largely accounted for by the rapid expansion of the Government Housing Loan Corporation, whose share of the budget rose from 6.8% in 1955 to around 40% in 1995. Those changes were less pronounced if measured by the total of loans outstanding, with the two banks claiming a quarter in 1980.

The decline in the lending of these two banks relative to the other finance corporations was partly a reflection of the change in national economic and social objectives, which in turn was partly due to the decreasing significance of the role of the four basic industries in the economy, as Japan gave greater priority to the manufacturing sector and the emergent hi-tech industries. It was also partly the result of the increasing availability of other sources of private finance for capital investment, with the progressive liberalization of domestic financial markets from the mid-1970s onwards. The manufacturing sector became less dependent on FILP for investment capital, as city, commercial, and regional banks became more active in financing loans to industry in the more competitive financial environment of the 1980s.

To reflect those changes, the JDB's legal terms of reference were changed in 1973 to allow it to finance social welfare projects and to contribute to the improvement of living standards. In 1994 its overall budget was 2.292 trillion, of which about half was provided by FILP funds and half from the payment of interest and the repayment of principal on loans outstanding; it also raised a small amount of money by issuing bonds in foreign markets. It was not therefore wholly reliant on FILP for its income, but its budget strategy was nevertheless determined within the framework of the government's national economic and social objectives, and the annual economic and fiscal strategy determined by MOF. While the role of the JDB undoubtedly changed, and with it its lending practices, most of its funding supported, directly and indirectly, private-sector industries and technology. Table 24.4 shows the distribution of its planned allocations for FY1994. In its annual report, the JDB claimed that a quarter of its budget was allocated to the 'improvement of living standards and urban infrastructure'. But only a very small amount of that sum was used explicitly for the creation and improvement of 'social capital'—environmental conservation, and social welfare facilities (JDB 1995); the greater part was used for urban development, the construction and improvement of private rail systems, and to provide facilities for the retail and wholesale distribution industry. Budget allocations to the other five policy areas were more narrowly focused still on industrial and technological development, between them accounting for more than two-thirds of the total budget. Loans for regional development supported the construction of urban facilities and transportation, and the relocation of industries, especially in the service sector.

To enable the private sector to undertake R&D in advanced technologies, the JDB provided loans for projects in electronics, biotechnology, and new materials, and for developing telecommunications and broadcasting infrastructure. Loans for national resources and energy absorbed more than a third of the annual budget, and the JDB actively promoted nuclear power generation, supporting projects to 'consolidate and strengthen the petroleum industry', and the construction of power plant facilities using alternative energy sources. Some of the projects were subsidized by government grants, and by loans provided at special preferential rates. Loans to support the expansion of imports became increasingly important, but the level of support for foreign firms directly investing in Japan was small. The programme for the adjustment of industrial structure was larger, mainly for those industries adversely effected by the strong yen. Transportation industries, railways, shipping, and aircraft and airports collectively attracted over 13% of the budget. Loans were provided for construction with the privatized rail companies, and at 'special preferential rates' for the expansion of Shinkansen rail-lines. Privatized airlines were also provided with funds to purchase aircraft.

Table 24.4 *Japan Development Bank: planned allocations, FY1994*

Allocation	%	bn yen	%
Improvement of living standards and urban infrastructure		582.685	26.5
Urban development	49.1		
Private railroads	35.8		
Retail and wholesale distribution	1.9		
Conservation of environment and social welfare	12.2		
Regional development		151.698	6.9
Development and promotion of technology		274.496	12.5
Advanced telecommunications and IT networks	69.5		
Industrial technology	30.4		
Resources and energy		805.923	36.6
Nuclear power	31.5		
Energy	14.0		
Diversification of energy resources	34.1		
energy conservation	20.4		
Internationalization of Japan and adjustment of industrial structure		69.601	3.2
Loans for foreign companies	20.5		
Adjustment of industrial structure	79.5		
Transportation		298.292	13.6
Railways	41.5		
Shipping	10.4		
aircraft and airports	48.1		
TOTAL		2,199.005	100

Source: *Annual Report, 1995*, Japan Development Bank.

The balance of JDB's loans and investments outstanding in 1994 totalled 15 trillion, distributed among the six project areas in almost identical proportions to its new loans.

As the Japanese government responded to the continuing economic recession in the late 1990s, and to the increasing domestic and international pressures for radical economic restructuring, the retitled Development Bank of Japan (DBJ) gave still more explicit support to 'economic revitalization' through support for new businesses, product development, innovation, regional development, and the promotion of foreign direct investment, allocating almost half of its new loans to them in FY1998 and FY1999 (DBJ 2000).

The role and functions of the EXIM Bank changed radically after the end of the high-growth era, when its main business was to provide loans to facilitate and promote exports. After 1975, the promotion of imports to help reduce the growing surplus of the trade balance became an important additional function, but both were overtaken and ultimately dwarfed by the emphasis after 1985 on the promotion of overseas direct investment, and the implementation of government programmes for overseas economic cooperation and aid. By 1994 untied loans under the latter absorbed 46% of the bank's annual budget; financial support for exports and imports had fallen to about a third. The extent to which those and other of its activities can be said to support Japanese industrial development is difficult to estimate precisely. If untied loans and import loans are excluded, about 45% of the budget comprised export loans and overseas investment loans. The latter became more significant subsequently with the appreciation of the yen, and the movement 'offshore' of production and R&D facilities by Japanese companies. EXIM Bank provided foreign currency loans for small and medium-sized companies, and 'two step investment loans, whereby loans are provided to local financial institutions in the countries concerned, which in turn provide finance to the operations of Japanese companies in those countries' (EXIM 1995: 35).

Besides the JDB and EXIM Bank, the Japanese government provided financial support for private-sector industrial development through other FILP agencies. New post-Ford modes of industrial production saw a decline in the significance of large-scale, basic industries, and the rise of SMEs with flexible methods of production exploiting new technologies. Six of the nine public finance corporations supported with FILP funds provided investments and loans directly to private-sector industry and small and medium-sized businesses. *The Small Businesses Finance Corporation* established in 1953 provided loans to SMEs for equipment and long-term working capital, loans of long-term funds to small business investment companies, and loans to organizations that lent equipment. Eligible businesses had to have capital of less than 100 million and employ fewer than 300 people. *The People's Finance Corporation* provided loans to small businesses, and to pensioners. *The Agriculture, Forestry, Fisheries Finance Corporation* made loans to related businesses, and to the food processing and distributing industry. Both the *Hokkaido–Tōhoku* and *Okinawa Development Finance Corporations* provided loans and finance for private-sector development businesses, and the latter, also for industrial development, SMEs, and business operations. The *Environmental Sanitation Business Finance Corporation* set up in 1967 provided loans to restaurants, barbershops, hotels, cleaners. The total FILP allocation to those six organizations in FY1994 was 6.777 trillion, about 17% of the total net FILP Budget.

An estimate of the level of industrial and technological support provided by those and other public finance corporations, and other FILP agencies, is obtained by dividing them into three groups: those whose functions and lending practices supported private-sector industrial development; those whose functions supported the creation or improvement of social capital; and those whose functions involved the support of aid and economic cooperation to other countries (Wright 1998*b*: appendix I). We look at the distribution of new investments and loans for FY1994, and then at the composition of their outstanding balances.

FILP's Winners and Losers

Table 24.5 shows that, while the distribution of the FILP Budget for FY1994–5 among the agencies was mainly to support the provision of social capital (60%), more than a third of the loans and investments contributed to industrial and technological development. Those proportions almost certainly understate the amount of indirect industrial support. The net figures for JDB and EXIM loans to support industry are cautious; the total for social capital is boosted by the inclusion of 2.778 trillion loaned to the Special Account for Pensions and Welfare (net of portfolio management), only some of which was used directly to finance housing. It is arguable whether the remaining loans should be counted as capital. The inclusion of loans to local authorities, mainly through the underwriting of bonds for capital schemes and projects, assumes that the whole was used for the creation and improvement of local 'social capital', i.e. public works projects for houses, roads, environment. The exclusion from industrial and technological support of the whole of overseas economic aid and cooperation provided by the JDB, EXIM Bank, and OECF understates the amount of direct and indirect industrial support from loans and investments. For example, while 98% of all ODA loans were 'untied', and the recipient countries free to procure goods and services from any country, more than a quarter did so from Japanese firms. Most ODA grants were bilateral rather than multilateral, and Japanese firms provided medical services

Table 24.5 *Composition of the FILP Budget by allocation to agencies, FY1994[a]*

	tr. yen	tr. yen	%
Industrial and technological support		13.902	35.2
6 public finance corporations	6.777		
JDB (40%)	0.829		
EXIM (20%)	0.345		
24 other agencies	5.951		
'Social capital'		23.796	60.37
GHLC	8.963		
HUDC	1.423		
JDB (60%)	1.243		
Pensions and Welfare Services Corporation	2.778[b]		
17 other agencies and special accounts	1.440		
Local authorities, public works etc.	6.500		
Finance Corporation for Municipal Enterprises	1.449		
Economic aid and cooperation		1.710	4.2
EXIM (80%)	1.035		
OECF	0.641		
Other	0.034		
TOTAL		39.408	100

[a]FILP Initial Budget.
[b]Net of portfolio management.

Source: derived from data in *FILP Report, 1996*, and from classification of agencies in Wright (1998*b*: app. I).

and public health, water supply, rural and agricultural development, and infrastructural projects such as roads, bridges, and telecommunications.

A similar distribution between social and industrial investment emerges from an analysis of the balance of outstanding loans and investments (net of portfolio management) at the end of March 1998 for all recipient FILP agencies. Table 24.6 ranks them by size. Twenty-nine agencies accounted for 97% of the total; more than half of which was contributed by four agencies, none classified as industrial. Excluding those providing finance wholly or partly for the portfolio management of capital market operations, and loans to the General Account, the total of the balance of outstanding loans and investments is divided between social and industrial capital roughly in the ratio of 60:30, with overseas economic cooperation and aid loans making up the remainder. This ratio is slightly higher than that for new loans and investments in the annual FILP Budget analysed above, partly because those for social capital schemes and projects are newer: less time had elapsed to redeem them than for industrial loans and investments. But it might also indicate the greater difficulty of redeeming loans on social capital, where the returns on investment were insufficient to meet the costs of borrowing, and repaying the principal, because of the lower expectation of profits. However, some loans for industrial schemes and projects were mainly to meet the costs of continuing debt, for example the JNR Debt Settlement Corporation. The implications of the distribution of outstanding balances between industrial and social capital are discussed in Chapter 28.

We may conclude, therefore, that the Japanese government continued to support industrial and technological development with loans and investment through FILP, notwithstanding the change of national economic and social objectives in the 1960s. The level of that support was much greater than MOF's claim of less than 3% by 1996–7. Between about one-third and two-fifths of FILP funds were allocated annually to finance directly and indirectly new industrial capital schemes and projects.

EFFICIENCY AND EFFECTIVENESS

On the aggregate annual profit and loss account, the Trust Fund Bureau Fund Special Account normally showed a small profit. At the end of FY1998, the returns on the management of the Fund—mainly interest paid on loans and securities—totalled 18.3 trillion; operating expenses were marginally less, almost wholly the payment of interest on deposits. There was a surplus of 1.6 trillion, substantially larger than in previous years because of the lower rates of interest paid on deposits, in line with falling market rates. The Postal Life Insurance Fund Special Account also normally showed a small surplus on its operating account (FILP 1999). What was not disclosed in the published accounts of either funds, or those of the FILP agencies, was the efficiency and effectiveness of loans and investments in a (net) FILP Budget totalling some 40 trillion a year—8% of GDP. There was no published evidence of the returns on the capital invested in particular programmes and projects, although each FILP agency was said to carry out its

Table 24.6 *Functional balance of outstanding loans and investments among FILP agencies, 31 March 1998*

	tr. yen	%
Local authority organizations	73.8	18.7 (Social)
Government Housing Loan Corporation	71.8	18.2 (Social)
Special Account for Postal Savings	45.6	11.6 (Portfolio)
Pension and Welfare Services PC	34.8	8.8 (Social/Portfolio)
Japan Highways PC	20.9	5.3 (Industrial)
Finance Corporation for Municipal Enterprises	14.5	3.7 (Social)
Japan Development Bank	14.3	3.6 (Social/industrial)
Housing and Urban Development Corporation	14.0	3.5 (Social)
Postal Life Insurance Welfare Corporation	14.0	3.5 (Portfolio)
Japan National Railway Settlement Corporation	11.7	3.0 (Industrial)
People's Finance Corporation	8.6	2.2 (Industrial)
EXIM Bank	8.2	2.1 (Economic cooperation/industrial)
General Account Budget	8.2	2.1
Small Businesses Finance Corporation	6.9	1.7 (Industrial)
Corporation for Advanced Transport	4.7	1.2 (Industrial)
OECF	4.4	1.1 (Economic cooperation/industrial)
Agriculture, Forestry, and Fisheries Finance Corporation	4.2	1.1 (Industrial)
Metropolitan Expressway Public Corporation	3.7	0.9 (Industrial)
Special Account for National Forests	3.6	0.9 (Industrial)
Hanshin Expressway Public Corporation	3.1	0.8 (Industrial)
Honshū–Shikoku Bridge Authority	2.1	0.5 (Industrial)
Social Welfare and Medical Service Corporation	2.0	0.5 (Social)
JR Construction Public Corporation	1.7	0.4 (Industrial)
Okinawa Development Finance Corporation	1.6	0.4 (Industrial)
Hokkaido-Tōhoku Development Finance Corporation	1.4	0.4 (Industrial)
Water Resources Development Finance Corporation	1.4	0.4 (Social)
Special Account for Government Land	1.2	0.3 (Social)
Environmental Sanitation Business Finance Corporation	1.1	0.3 (Industrial)
Airport Development	1.0	0.3 (Industrial)
	384.5	97.4
Others	10.3	2.6
Total balance of outstanding FILP loans	394.8	100

Source: *FILP Report 1998*; categories from Wright (1998*b*: app. I).

own internal evaluation. There was cross-subsidization between more and less profitable projects, and the period of repayment of principal on projects was often extended. In theory, each agency had to repay its debts on loans and investments made to it through FILP, although some, like the JNR Debt Settlement Corporation and the National Forestry Service, were unable to do so for most of the 1980s and 1990s. In its examination of bids for further funds, the Financial Bureau's Second Fund Division took into account the general track record of each agency; but which projects proved viable, returned profits, and repaid loans on the terms initially agreed were not disclosed publicly. As most such loans were long-term, the justification and effectiveness of funding decisions were not apparent for some considerable time. But FILP had been in operation for more than 40 years, and by the 1990s the results of long-term loans and investment in the 1950s and 1960s should have been available, at least within each agency, and in the Financial Bureau. What would be more interesting is an assessment of the effects and effectiveness of funding decisions since the reorientation of national objectives, and the emphasis on the creation and improvement of social overhead capital, where the criterion of profitability had been judged inappropriate or interpreted flexibly. We return to that and other issues of efficiency in Chapter 28 which examines the origins, content, and implications of the reform process begun in 1997.

The efficiency with which FILP funds was used directly and indirectly to promote and support industrial and technological development, and their effectiveness in achieving declared policy objectives, are important issues in the continuing debate about the contribution of government credit policies to Japan's economic performance after 1945. Briefly, Calder (1993) has challenged the conventional explanation of the dynamism in the political economy in the post-war period in which FILP-funded agencies such as the JDB and the EXIM Bank are accorded key roles in state developmental leadership. He argues that the sectoral pattern of government credit support changed little between 1953 and 1986, and concludes that industrial growth in both the high-growth era and since owes much more to 'corporate-led strategic capitalism' in which the private-sector institutions of companies and businesses are accorded the pre-eminent role. 'State allocation of credit in post-war Japan ... had much less importance in stimulating Japanese economic development—especially the promotion of emergent industries—than developmental state theorists such as Chalmers Johnson suggest' (Calder 1993: 261).

If valid, that alternative explanation raises important questions about the rationale for the continued growth of FILP after the end of the high-growth era, when Japan had caught up with the West, and also about the efficiency and effectiveness of the use of ever larger FILP budgets to promote new industries, slow the rundown of those in decline, and provide funds for R&D, new products, technologies, and processes, and support for small and medium-sized businesses. FILP funds for industry, and especially for the latter, provided a traditional source of electoral and financial support for the LDP. Calder (1993), drawing upon Hirose Michisada (1981), has commented that 'The bulk of People's Finance Corporation loans, for example, have since 1974 been tendered on an unusual non-collateralized basis to more than two million small, often unstable firms, on the mere recommendation of LDP Diet members and the formalistic recommendation of local chambers of commerce officials serving as a front for conservative political interests' (pp. 122–3). Throughout the period 1975–99, the Corporation absorbed 11%–12% of the net FILP Budget; by FY1996, with an allocation of 3.25 trillion, it was the second largest recipient of FILP funds.

CONCLUSIONS

The analysis of the trends in the size, composition, and distribution of budget outputs in the period 1975–2000 suggests six broad conclusions.

First, the 'head-line' total of the planned Budget, normally that used by MOF and outside analysts and commentators, presents a misleading picture of the size, significance, and role of FILP in central government budgeting and the national economy. The use of *gross* planned and revised totals produced high values for FILP, those of *net* out-turn expenditure totals for the investment and loan programme, lower values. For example, in FY1991 the gross revised planning total was 39.614 trillion; the net out-turn expenditure total, adjusted for central government borrowing, portfolio fund management, carry-forward and underspending, was 29.105 trillion, a difference of some 36%. Its share of GDP fell correspondingly by more than 2%. The potential for misunderstanding, misrepresentation, and manipulation is obvious enough. For example, the OECD, using data supplied by MOF, understated the proportion of FILP funds allocated to public works, and to the 11 public banks and finance corporations, by including both central government borrowing and portfolio management in calculations of the FILP total (OECD 1993: table 25).

Secondly, whatever measure is used, the continuous growth of FILP from 1975 is indisputable. Part of the explanation of that growth is that FILP was used increasingly for purposes other than those for which it was originally intended: to finance central government borrowing, and to undertake capital market operations designed to provide better returns on some of the Trust Fund Bureau Fund investments. More significantly, however, the reorientation of the government's economic and social objectives outlined in successive National Economic Plans in the 1980s, and itemized in terms of specific policy objectives in the annual economic and fiscal strategy, refocused the targets of FILP funds. While the need for publicly provided industrial investment through such FILP agencies as JDB and the EXIM Bank declined sharply in the 1960s, other social investment needs—housing, welfare, and environmental and leisure facilities—were given higher priority. The purposes served by FILP and the agencies through which its investment funds were allocated changed radically. The criterion of future profitability, which ostensibly distinguished projects financed through FILP from those financed through taxation and borrowing in the General Account and some Special Accounts, where no such return was expected as a condition of investment, was less strictly observed in practice than was once the case. Increasingly, FILP was used to finance social capital projects and high-risk technological projects, which formerly would have been financed, if at all, through the General or Special Accounts. The expansion of the FILP Budget helped to relieve pressure on the General Account

Budget, providing an alternative source of funding for some of its programmes—especially public works, but also the construction of 'public facilities' such as schools and hospitals—and a means of subsidizing loss-making organizations such as JNR and, after its privatization, the JNR Debt Settlement Corporation. As programmes of capital investment and public works were squeezed in the planned General Account Budget, the expansion of FILP provided the means for the LDP to continue to distribute benefits and favours to local small businesses, the real estate and construction industries, and farmers and agricultural workers. Funds allocated to FILP agencies for road and bridge construction, a common source of politico-electoral favours, increased five times by volume in the period 1976–92, and their share of all FILP-financed public works increased from two-fifths to two-thirds.

The third broad conclusion is that most FILP funds were allocated to organizations controlled by central rather than local government, although of course particular local and regional areas benefited from the distribution of investments and loans made by central FILP agencies. Fourthly, the allocation of FILP funds to organizations and policy areas was characterized by choice and discrimination; priorities reflected declared changes in national (i.e. LDP) economic and social objectives. While the major reorientation from industrial development and infrastructure to social, welfare, and environmental policies had taken place before 1975, there was a continued and continuing shift of FILP resources over the following twenty years in support of those policies. Greater priority still was accorded to housing programmes, while education, transport, and communications attracted fewer resources.

Fifthly, despite that shift from the support of industrial to social investment, the extent of the change was less than MOF claimed or was apparent. Between one-third and two-fifths of FILP funds continued to be used to support industrial and technological development throughout the whole of the last quarter of the twentieth century. Finally, there is little evidence of 'balance' and 'fair shares' in the distribution of the FILP Budget among the FILP agencies. The major beneficiaries of the expansion of the Budget were a handful of the public finance corporations, mostly controlled by MOF or supervised jointly with other central ministries. Among public works agencies controlled by the central government, those for roads and bridges attracted a greater share of resources than those for housing. This trend of concentrating resources among a small number of agencies became more pronounced in the period 1975–99. The continued expansion of the FILP Budget at annual rates of growth above those of the General Account Budget provided a painless means to give effect to those changing priorities. The annual budget process was a positive-sum game in which most but not all policy areas and programmes and agencies, enjoyed continuous budget growth, albeit at differential rates.

PART V

EFFECTS AND EFFECTIVENESS

25

Fiscal Reconstruction: 'Smoke and Mirrors'

MOF's main aim from the emergence of the fiscal crisis in 1975 onwards was to reduce the fiscal deficit on the General Account Budget and, in the longer term, to eliminate it, and restore the balanced-budget characteristics that prevailed in the high-growth era. This chapter assesses its claim to have made substantial progress towards the achievement of that aim by the end of the 1980s, until the onset of economic recession in the early 1990s first slowed then halted that progress, and ultimately reversed it as the economic imperatives provoked more public spending, higher levels of government borrowing, and tax cuts and concessions. It analyses and assesses the effects and effectiveness of the policies that MOF initiated, and attempted to implement, under the broad banners of 'fiscal reconstruction' and 'fiscal consolidation' in the 1980s and early 1990s, and the countercyclical expansionary policies that succeeded them in the recessionary conditions that prevailed for most of the remainder of the decade. The contribution to fiscal reconstruction of successive Provisional Councils for Administrative Reform, and the Management and Coordination Agency, notably through policies to reduce the scope of the public sector through privatization of some public corporations and government enterprises, and to reduce its size and costs—those and other policies to improve efficiency and economy in the central executive were discussed and evaluated in Chapters 4 and 22.

The chapter begins with an examination of the effectiveness of MOF's policies to raise more revenue, and its attempts to change the tax structure by achieving a better balance between direct and indirect taxation; then (in the second part of the chapter) MOF's attempts to close the fiscal gap, specifically to eliminate the issue of special deficit-financing bonds, which became a symbol of its control of public finances. The third section examines MOF's control of the growth of the expenditures in the General Account Budget, contrasting the surface appearance of control with the underlying reality. I then show how MOF's adroit and successful manipulation of the flows of public expenditure between the General Account Budget, FILP and some of the 38 Special Accounts, and its creative accounting and the use of 'temporary special measures', combined to relieve pressure on the General Account Budget. The conclusion summarizes the evidence and provides an overall assessment of MOF's performance, reserving for discussion in Chapter 29 the explanation of why it was not more successful.

RAISING REVENUE

I am not concerned here with the efficacy of taxation policy as a tool of macroeconomic policy, nor with the distribution, burden, and equity of particular taxes, nor with the components of the tax structure as such, all of which were issues with which MOF grappled throughout the period (see Ishi 1993), nor with the fiercely contested debate about the extent to which Japan's tax system is either 'pro-growth' and regressive, or hostile to capital and re-distributive (for summary and analysis see DeWit and Steinmo 2001).

The interest in revenue-raising is limited to those aims set out in the policy of fiscal reconstruction relevant to MOF's planning and control of public spending described in Chapter 13: first, to raise more revenue to finance rising public spending, and to close the fiscal gap; and secondly, to change the structure of the tax system to provide for greater long-term stability in tax revenue. The bureaucratic politics and 'rationality' that underlaid both the strategy and tactics to achieve those aims, and their effects and effectiveness, most notably in the three major attempts to introduce a consumption tax, have been dealt with adequately elsewhere (Katō Junko 1994; Ishi 1992; Muramatsu and Mabuchi 1991), and were summarized in Chapter 13.

MOF's policies for raising additional revenue in the period of fiscal reconstruction from 1980 to 1987 enabled it to cover the costs both of the constrained growth of general expenditures, and of servicing an increasing proportion of outstanding debt. Apart from FY1982, tax and other revenues (excluding government borrowing) grew annually at faster rates, both in volume and as a percentage, than the General Account Budget as a whole, and general expenditure within it. As a result, MOF was able, first, to contain the size of the fiscal deficit in FY1981 and FY1982, and then gradually to begin to close the gap. Nevertheless, a gap of more than 11 trillion remained at the end of the period of fiscal reconstruction. MOF was more successful in reversing the trend, which had characterized the 1970s, of the costs of general expenditures exceeding total revenue (Figure 25.1).

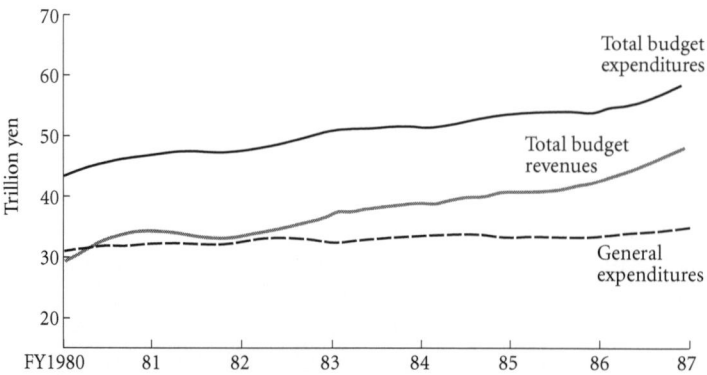

Figure 25.1 *Revenue and expenditure in the period of fiscal reconstruction, FY1980–FY1987*
General Account Revised Budget: trillion yen

Source: Zaisei Tōkei (annually), Research Division, Budget Bureau, MOF.

Success in narrowing the fiscal gap was due only partly to the buoyancy of revenues in conditions of sustained, albeit modest, economic growth. Changes in tax rates and thresholds were important contributory factors. Table 25.1 shows that the burden of taxation (national and local) as a proportion of national income increased by 4%, from 22.2% in FY1980 to 26.4% in FY1987, and absorbed an increasing share of GDP. Social security contributions as a proportion of national income increased too, but much less quickly. Taxation and social security together accounted for 31.3% of national income in FY1980 and for 37.3% in FY1987.

The increasing burden of taxation was subject to prudential parameters set by the Second Provisional Council for Administrative Reform in July 1982, which laid down that the ratio 'must be kept at a level considerably lower than that of European countries (around 50%)', and to the political constraints of the LDP's electoral strategy (MOF 1996b: 21).

Despite that anxiety about the rising tax burden in the context of an increasingly elderly population, Japan in the mid-1980s was (and remained thereafter) lightly taxed compared with other G7 countries. Only the USA had a lower ratio than Japan; the other G7 countries all had ratios near to or above 50%. More worrying for MOF was its anomalous tax structure, with its much greater dependence on the revenues from direct taxes than in those countries.

Direct and Indirect Taxes

Throughout the period 1975–2000, MOF repeatedly drew attention to the instability that resulted from its dependence on direct rather than indirect taxes, arguing that in other industrialized countries the adoption of VAT and similar taxes had produced more stable sources of revenue, which were less reliant on progressive income tax

Table 25.1 *Increasing burden of taxation in the period of fiscal reconstruction, FY1980–FY1987[a]*

FY	National and local taxes as % of national income	Social security contributions as % of national income	Tax burden (%)
1980	22.2	9.1	31.3
1981	22.8	9.8	32.6
1982	23.1	10.0	33.1
1983	23.4	10.0	33.4
1984	23.9	10.1	34.0
1985	24.0	10.4	34.4
1986	24.9	10.6	35.5
1987	26.4	10.6	37.0

[a]General Account Settled Budget.

Source: The Japanese Budget in Brief, 1996, Budget Bureau, MOF.

(where the yield varied more with changes in the levels of economic activity than was the case with indirect taxes). In its campaign to 'educate' politicians and the electorate in the benefits of a national consumption tax that it was actively promoting during the period of fiscal reconstruction, it contrasted the current yields of direct and indirect taxation with those of the inter-war period, when twice as much was collected in indirect as in direct taxes.

In the years immediately preceding the adoption of the policy of fiscal reconstruction, the ratio of direct to indirect taxes was more than 2:1. In 1981 direct taxes contributed 70.1% and indirect taxes 29.9%. The ratio of the revenues from corporation tax and income tax in the former was 31.5% : 38.1%. Between 1981 and the tax reforms of 1988, the proportion from direct taxes increased by 3% to 73.2% with a corresponding reduction in indirect taxes. Thus, MOF had been unable to halt the trend observable before 1980 of increasing weight of direct to indirect taxes. Revenues from the latter, and especially from commodity taxes, grew much more slowly: the imbalance deteriorated from a high point of 32.5% in FY1976 to a low point of 25.8% in FY1989, fully justifying MOF's concern in the 1980s of the need to increase the revenue from indirect taxation.

In reality the situation was even worse, as that analysis was based on an interpretation of the gross data for all taxes collected nationally by the government. A more accurate assessment of the effectiveness of MOF's fiscal policies to achieve its aim of reducing the deficit on the central government's General Account Budget is obtained by adjusting that data to show the total amount of tax revenues available to MOF to finance the General Account Budget. Each year between 2% and 5% of the total of indirect taxes collected nationally (equivalent to about 3 trillion in FY1993) was hypothecated revenue assigned statutorily to local governments directly or indirectly through Special Accounts, and hence unavailable to finance General Account expenditures. (Only a very small, statistically insignificant, proportion of direct taxation revenues was hypothecated.) For example, in FY1993 the ratio of gross revenues from direct taxes collected nationally to gross revenues from indirect taxes was 69.4 : 30.6. Adjusted for hypothecations, the ratio rises to 73.3 : 26.7. Hypothecation of indirect taxes had two effects relevant to the present discussion. First, it reduced the total tax revenues available to MOF for the General Account Budget, and hence added to the problem of revenue shortfall. Secondly, the inclusion of hypothecated revenues distorted the picture of the composition of the tax structure.

Table 25.2 adjusts the official statistical series published by MOF to allow for hypothecation. On this basis, in the year preceding the adoption of the policy of reconstruction, the ratio was 3 : 1. Thereafter it changed very little until the buoyant revenues (mainly from corporation tax) of the economic 'bubble' pushed it still higher, to reach a ratio of nearly 4 : 1 in 1989. Thus, despite MOF's repeated attempts to change the tax structure in the 1980s culminating in the reforms of 1988, almost no progress was made in changing the balance between direct and indirect taxation revenues available to finance expenditures in the General Account Budget.

The more concerted and, ostensibly, fundamental reforms of income tax in 1988 were intended to address some of the underlying weaknesses of the tax structure, and

Table 25.2 *Ratio of direct and indirect tax revenues in the General Account Budget, FY1980–FY1989*[a]

FY	Direct tax revenues (%)	Indirect tax revenues (%)	Ratio
1980	75.0	25.0	3 : 1
1981	73.7	27.0	2.7 : 1
1982	74.2	25.8	2.9 : 1
1983	73.6	26.4	2.8 : 1
1984	75.2	24.8	3 : 1
1985	74.6	25.4	2.9 : 1
1986	73.0	27.0	2.7 : 1
1987	74.8	25.2	3 : 1
1988	75.2	24.8	3 : 1
1989	79.0	21.0	3.8 : 1

[a]General Account Settled Budget.

Source: calculations derived from table 14-7, *Japan Statistical Yearbook*, annually, MCA.

to provide a broader base to offset the effects of a progressively ageing population. Tax structures had departed substantially from principles of economic neutrality and horizontal equity, as the income tax base became more narrowly focused on the taxation of labour income. The reforms aimed to extend the scope of the tax base by bringing more personal and corporate tax income into the tax net, and increasing the weight of individual tax through a national consumption tax. Table 25.3 compares the effects of the tax structures before and after the legislation. Income tax rates were restructured, the rate of corporation tax reduced, personal income tax bands simplified, and rates of tax revised. Despite those changes, the tax burden remained concentrated on income taxes rather than on goods and services.

The national consumption tax implemented in 1989 was intended to help redress that imbalance, and to mitigate the problems of horizontal equity and compliance. It was also intended to raise more revenue, and to provide a more stable future source of revenue. The gross total revenue from excise taxes between 1980 and 1988 had grown only slowly, contributing less than 4% of total taxation revenues per annum. With the introduction of the national consumption tax there was a sharp increase both in the total, and in its share of total tax revenues. However, not all the revenues collected were available to MOF to finance expenditure programmes in the General Account Budget. Almost a quarter were statutorily allocated annually through the Local Allocation Tax to local governments. In FY1997 the tax was raised to 5%, and divided into a national consumption tax (4%) and a local consumption tax (1%), the latter assessed and collected by prefectural governments. Central government's share of the national consumption tax was, however, now only 70.5%, with the remainder allocated to local governments through the Local Allocation Tax in the General Account Budget. Table 25.4 shows the

Table 25.3 Composition of central government tax revenues, FY1988 and FY1990 (%)[a]

	FY1988 Pre-tax reform	FY1990 Post-tax reform	OECD average
Taxes on personal income as			
% of GDP	7.0	8.4	11.9
% of total taxation	32.2	37.8	30.5
Corporate income taxes as			
% of GDP	7.5	6.8	2.8
% of total taxation	34.3	30.4	8.0
Total taxes on income			
% of GDP	14.5	15.2	13.7
% of total taxation	66.5	68.3	38.5
Tax on goods and services			
% of GDP	3.9	4.1	12.6
% of total taxation	17.7	18.6	30.1

[a] General Account Settled Budget.

Source: Economic Surveys: Japan 1993, OECD, 1993.

Table 25.4 National consumption tax, FY1989–FY1999[a]

FY	Total collected (trillion) (1)	Annual change (%) (2)	% of total tax revenues (3)	Central government's share of total collected (trillion) (4)
1989	4.09	100.0	7.2	3.27
1990	5.78	41.6	9.2	4.62
1991	6.22	7.6	9.8	4.98
1992	6.55	5.3	11.4	5.24
1993	6.98	6.5	12.2	5.59
1994	7.04	0.9	13.0	5.63
1995	7.24	2.8	13.2	5.79
1996	7.57	4.6	13.7	6.06
1997	10.11	33.6	18.2	9.30
1998	12.62	24.9	24.7	10.07
1999	14.15	12.1	28.8	10.45

[a] General Account Settled Budget.

Source: data supplied by Tax Bureau, 1997, MOF; EPA, 2000; Cabinet Office, 2000.

amount of consumption tax revenues collected, and central government's share of that total before payment of the assigned proportion through the Local Allocation Tax.

From 1990 to 1996 there was a steady growth in the amount collected (cols. 1 and 2), accounting for a progressively increasing proportion of total tax revenues (col. 3). The changes in 1997 resulted in a sharp increase in both. By 1998 the consumption tax contributed a quarter of tax revenues, although that rise is explained only partly by the increases in rates. As MOF predicted, the yield of indirect taxes proved more buoyant than income and corporate taxes in times of recession. As total tax revenues fell sharply in 1998 and 1999, so the proportion contributed by the consumption tax rose.

The effects of the introduction and changes to the national consumption tax were threefold. First, they helped to redress the imbalance between direct and indirect axation. Secondly, although central (and local) government finances became more dependent on indirect taxation, more than 60% of revenues continued to come from income and corporate taxes, still significantly more than the G7 average. While the rate of corporation taxation was reduced sharply from 1998, at 41% it remained higher than most G7 countries. Thirdly, central government's share of the revenues collected from the national consumption tax (col. 4) increased only modestly until the introduction of the higher rate in 1997.

In FY1999 the budget rules for the use of the revenues from the national consumption tax were changed to provide for hypothecation. The whole of central government's share was allocated specifically to finance spending on social welfare programmes, partly to help allay public hostility to the tax. The yield however was inadequate to finance the full costs of social security, medical care for the elderly, and nursing care. In FY2000 the estimated revenues of 6.9 trillion fell short of the 9.1 trillion planned expenditure on those programmes. Together with a sharp fall in other revenues resulting from the 10 trillion cut in income and corporate tax rates, the continuing inadequacy of tax revenues refocused attention on a reform of the tax structure. In February 1999, the Prime Minister's Economic Strategy Council criticized its inadequacy, and this was echoed in the report of the Government Tax Commission's triennial survey of the whole tax system the following year. The OECD (1999*b*) called for comprehensive reform, urging an increase of 3.5% in the tax–GDP ratio over the next ten years by increasing the rate, broadening the base of the consumption tax, and broadening the base of personal income tax.

Fiscal 'Consolidation', 1987–1991

With the transition from fiscal reconstruction to fiscal consolidation in 1987, and then the relaxation of fiscal policy in the bubble economy that ensued, there was a substantial growth of both revenue and expenditure (Wright 1999*b*: table 6). The annual growth of revenues continued to run ahead of the annual growth of both the budget total and general expenditures until FY1992, and the surpluses generated allowed repayment of some of the earlier outstanding debt, 'borrowings', and transfers between the General Account Budget and Special Accounts (see below). As economic growth slowed thereafter, and then declined into recession, revenues fell and were inadequate to cover the annual increase in general expenditures until FY1997.

Revenues from taxation for the General Account Budget fell in 1991 for the first time for over 25 years, and continued to fall for four successive years. As a proportion of GDP, they declined in eight of the nine years, from 13.7% in 1990 to 9.5% in 1999 (MOF 2000*a*). The estimate of 45.678 trillion in the revised budget for FY1999 was the lowest for more than a decade, and represented a 20% fall on that for the FY1997 Budget (Wright 1999*b*: table 7). The sharpest fall occurred in the revenues from corporation tax, down from 18.9 trillion in 1989 to 12.1 trillion in 1993, reflecting the reduction in company profits. The yield from income taxes fell by more than 25% between 1991 and 1994. Revenues from indirect taxes continued to rise throughout the recession, albeit more slowly, the greater part contributed by the new consumption tax, as mentioned earlier. The contrasting trends of direct and indirect taxes provided ample vindication of MOF's claim that revenues from the latter were more stable, and less subject to cyclical variation. Without the revenues of the new consumption tax, the disastrous shortfall of revenue would have been still worse. It was in the context of a revised revenue estimate of a shortfall of nearly 5 trillion in the spring of 1994 that MOF launched (through Prime Minister Hosokawa) its pre-emptive, and ultimately abortive, strike to introduce a national welfare tax to raise more revenue.

To summarize, the problem of the shortfall of revenue, which the policy of fiscal reconstruction was intended to remedy over the longer term, persisted throughout the 1980s, exacerbated by the slow-down in economic activity in the recessionary years that followed in the 1990s. For a time, sufficient revenue was raised to finance the constrained growth of general expenditures in the General Account Budget, and for a brief period during the years of bubble economy some modest progress was made towards liquidation of the outstanding debt. MOF's longer-term aim to change the balance of direct to indirect taxation was almost wholly unsuccessful. Even the substantial increase in indirect taxes resulting from the national consumption tax did little more in the early 1990s than reverse the trend of increasing dependence on direct tax revenues, and to restore the 5 : 2 ratio that obtained in the late 1970s. In reality, that ratio was closer to 4 : 1 for the net tax revenues available (after hypothecation to local governments) to finance the General Account Budget.

Finally, while the burden of national taxes as a proportion of national income (and GDP) increased marginally year by year, rising from about a quarter in 1975 to over a third by the end of the century, the Japanese electorate remained more lightly taxed than any other G7 country, and well within the self-imposed parameters of an acceptable burden for an ageing population. Figure 25.2 shows the comparison with some other G7 countries. The inclusion of social security contributions raised the burden to 36.9% of national income, comparable to the USA, but lower than the UK (48.9%), Germany (55.9%), and France (64.6%).

THE FISCAL DEFICIT AND GOVERNMENT BORROWING

The Effects of Estimated Revenue Shortfall and Surplus

The difference between total revenues and expenditures is conventionally treated as the budget deficit covered by government borrowing. MOF treated and measured that

'Smoke and Mirrors'

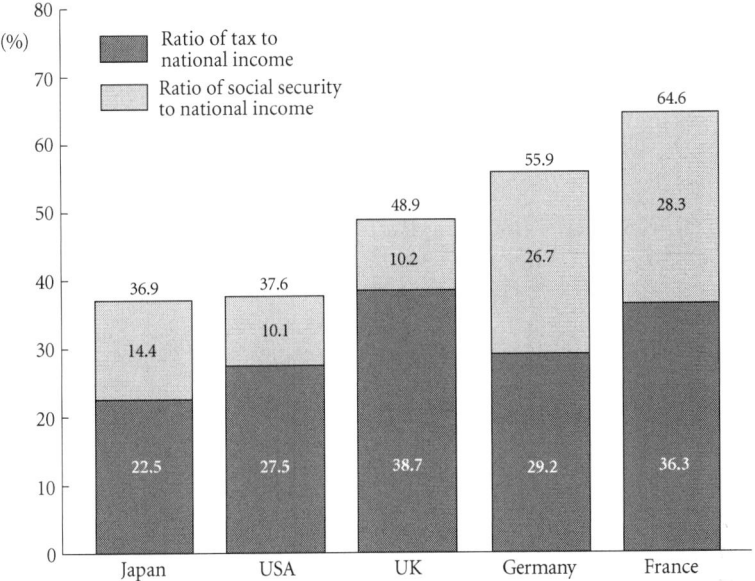

Figure 25.2 *Tax burden in Japan and G7 countries, 1996–2000*
Tax and social security contributions: percentage of National Income

Japan: planned budget FY2000; USA, Germany, France: actual budget, CY1997; UK: actual budget, CY1996.

Source: *Annual National Accounts, 2000*, OECD; *The Japanese Budget in Brief 2000*, Budget Bureau, MOF.

difference as a bond dependency ratio, the proportion of the total expenditure in the General Account Budget covered by the issue of government bonds. By defining the deficit thus, it was able to distinguish and demonstrate to politicians, bureaucrats, and the clienteles of both the difference between borrowing to cover capital investment, through the issue of ordinary construction bonds, and borrowing to cover the costs of current expenditures not covered by the revenues from taxation and other sources, through the issue of special deficit-financing bonds.

The distinction was an important one legally and economically. 'Construction bonds' (*kensetsu kokusai*) were issued under Article 4 of the 1947 Public Finance Law for the first time in FY1966, when the Budget became unbalanced for the first time since the imposition of the Dodge Line, and in every year subsequently. In FY1975, with the emergence of the fiscal crisis, a special law was enacted to allow the issue of special deficit-financing bonds (*akaji kokusai*) to cover shortfall in revenues. As an 'exceptional' and temporary measure, the law had to be re-enacted each year it was planned to issue such bonds. Economically, the distinction drawn by MOF between the different purposes of the two kinds of borrowing was similar to the concept of the so-called 'golden rule', whereby governments seek to avoid borrowing to cover current revenue expenditures, either annually or over the period of a medium-term economic cycle.

MOF's main policy objective in the period of fiscal reconstruction was the reduction of the overall bond dependency ratio, and the elimination of the issue special deficit-financing bonds within that total. The Medium Term Fiscal Projection of the National Budget published annually in February set out the projections of expenditure and revenue for a five-year period to achieve prescribed target levels for the issue of new government bonds. Various assumptions were made about future GDP and the elasticity of revenue growth. To accommodate irresistible pressures for more public spending, especially the rising fixed costs of debt servicing, the projections for tax revenues were calculated as the difference between estimated expenditure and the borrowing target. The difference between total expenditure and total revenue (including borrowing) was the adjustment necessary to balance the account, which was treated as a nominal target for the reduction of expenditure in negotiations between Spending Ministries and the Budget Bureau. The revenue projection was incorporated into the initial Budget, and subsequently adjusted in the revised Supplementary Budget after the updated *Economic Outlook* was published in December. From 1981 to 1986, that adjustment resulted in a lower estimate of tax revenues than in the initial Budget, and a correspondingly higher one for borrowing. In the period of the bubble economy, revised estimates of tax revenue in Supplementary Budgets were higher than the totals of those planned in the initial Budget (and the Medium Term Fiscal Projection from which they derived), but those for government borrowing were lower only in FY1988. That was because MOF used the additional revenues generated to redeem more of the national debt, and pay back some of the temporary loans and cash transfers from various Special Accounts.

From 1991, MOF's estimates of tax revenues in the initial Budget were once more unduly optimistic. In the prevailing conditions of economic recession, they required substantial adjustment downwards in revised Supplementary Budgets. Huge gaps opened up between the revenues actually collected by the time of 'settlement' after the end of the fiscal year, and the earlier estimates projected in the Medium Term Fiscal Projection on which the initial General Account Budget was planned. Figure 25.3 measures those differences.

In the high-growth era, MOF deliberately underestimated tax yields in order to maintain the informal rule-of-the-game (discussed in Chapter 2) that the tax burden should not exceed 20% of national income, and contingently to provide, through 'natural increases' of revenues generated by higher than forecasted economic growth, the means to finance the LDP's annual tax reductions. Why then did MOF deliberately and consistently overestimate the yield of tax revenues in most years from 1975 onwards, apart from the period of the bubble economy in the late 1980s? First, by so doing it could present, in the Medium Term Fiscal Projection and the initial Budget based on it, a correspondingly lower estimate for government borrowing, consistent with the principal policy objective of reducing the bond dependency ratio. Published in February for the fiscal year beginning 14 months ahead, the projection of revenue in it demonstrated both MOF's intention and its intended progress towards the borrowing target. With the achievement of that target as the principal policy objective, and given a constrained but rising level of expenditure, the revenue projection became almost

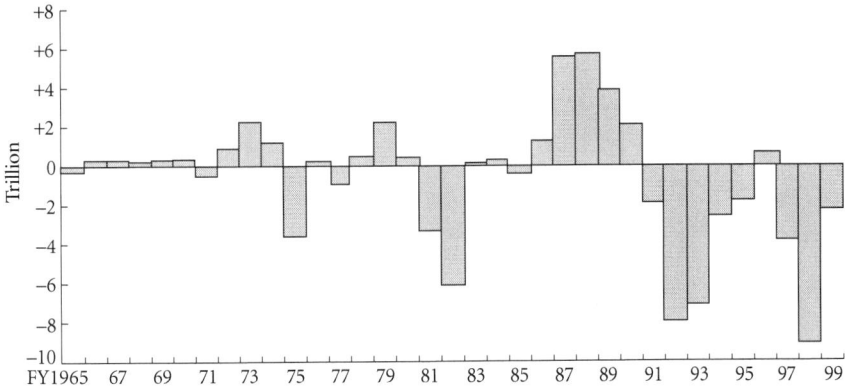

Figure 25.3 *Tax revenues: shortages and surpluses, FY1965–FY1999*
Source: Ishi (2000); Tax Bureau, MOF.

(but not quite) a residuum. If government borrowing had to be cut, and expenditure could be restrained but not cut, then the estimate of revenue had to rise. Secondly, by inflating the estimates of revenue, MOF could avoid drastic cuts to the total and to the distribution of general expenditures. The resultant shortfall in revenue was normally compensated by increased borrowing in Supplementary Budgets, by short-term financial expedients, and by the manipulation of budgets and accounts. We examine those later in the chapter.

Government Borrowing

During the period of the economic expansion in the bubble years of 1987–91, MOF deliberately and consistently underestimated the yield of tax revenues in the Medium Term Fiscal Projection, and in the initial Budget. By so doing, it sent a signal to Spending Ministries, at the time of the preparation and negotiation of their budget ceilings in the spring and early summer, that revenue resources would constrain expenditures. But it did so in the knowledge that there would be an actual surplus of revenues at the time of settlement to carry forward to the next fiscal year to redeem the national debt, and to pay back temporary loans and transfers. We look at the use and manipulation of those surpluses later in the chapter.

MOF's failure to raise revenue sufficiently to cover even the more modest rates of growth of the General Account Budget, which characterized the period from the late 1970s onwards, made the achievement of its borrowing and expenditure objectives crucial to the success of fiscal reconstruction. As explained in Chapter 13, the targets for the reduction of government borrowing were explicit, more so than those for either revenue or expenditure. But the prescription of precise targets and dates for their achievement made it difficult for MOF to conceal failure, although it could and did— through the manipulation of cash flows between the General Account Budget, the

Trust Fund Bureau Fund of FILP, and various Special Accounts—reduce the *apparent* level of government borrowing, and hence represent more favourable progress towards the achievement of a particular target. I have more to say about that later.

The use of special deficit-financing bonds to finance *current* expenditure was contrary to those principles of the 'sound management' of the national finances articulated and reiterated by MOF during the 1980s, described in Chapter 13. The elimination of such bonds was MOF's main aim from the start of fiscal reconstruction, and the success and failure of its policies was assessed by it according to the progress made towards the achievement of that objective. As we have seen, it failed twice to achieve it by prescribed target dates, in 1980 and 1984, succeeding finally in 1990, when for the first time in 15 years no special deficit-financing bonds were issued to cover a part of the fiscal deficit.

However, the combination of countercyclical spending and declining revenues that characterized the recessionary years that followed led to a rapid deterioration in the financing of the General Account Budget, and MOF was obliged to resume their issue in FY1994, and to continue to do so in large and ever increasing amounts for FY1995 and the next five years. In FY1996 nearly 12 trillion of special deficit-financing bonds were issued, at that time the largest amount ever recorded, and more than the total of construction bonds. But that total was exceeded in FY1998, when 17 trillion were issued, while the total of 25.5 for the following year represented more than 5% of GDP. As the temporary conditions of the bubble economy had provided the means—through additional revenues—to eliminate the issue of special deficit-financing bonds, so the conditions of a much longer period of recession enforced their resumption. It represented a humiliating failure of MOF's reconstruction policies. Their elimination once again became both the prime objective and the symbol of the effectiveness of its policies.

That aim was part of the broader objective of reducing the proportion of total expenditures financed by government borrowing, measured by the bond dependency ratio. MOF attached almost as much weight to reducing the ratio as to the elimination of special deficit bonds. The two were closely connected: reducing the bond dependency ratio invariably meant a reduction in the number of new bonds issued. The converse was not always true: when the bond dependency ratio rose, MOF was able sometimes to provide for the necessary additional borrowing wholly through the issue of ordinary construction bonds.

MOF was successful in reducing the bond dependency ratio during the greater part of the period of reconstruction, mainly because of its improving control of total expenditure in the General Account Budget, but also because of some modest success in revenue raising. The revised bond issue was always larger than that planned in the initial budget, apart from 1979 and 1988. The three distinct phases in the trends of the ratio of the total of those issues to the total expenditure of the General Account Budget is shown in Figure 25.4. First, there was a period of rapid increase, as the fiscal crisis emerged in 1975 and the economic events associated with the effects of the two oil crises precipitated a sharp increase in public spending. The high point was reached in 1979, when the ratio of government borrowing to total expenditure reached nearly 40% of the planned (initial) General Account Budget. The second phase, from 1980 to

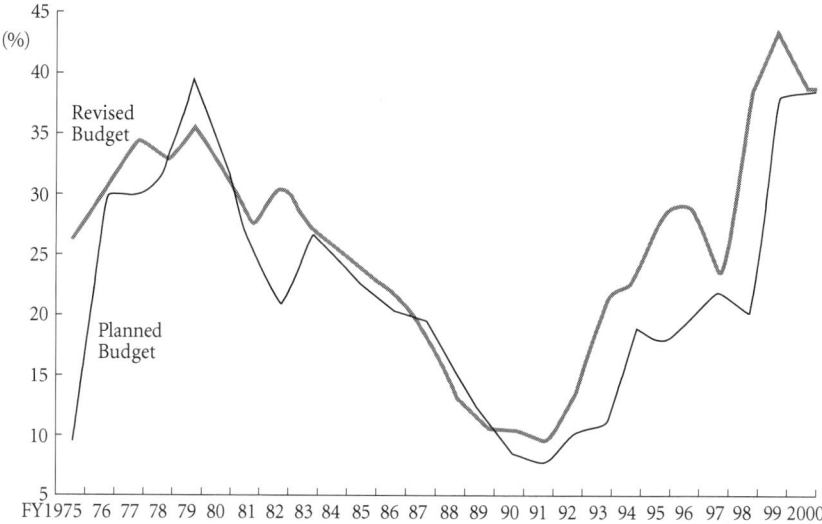

Figure 25.4 *Ratio of central government bonds issued to planned and actual budget totals, FY1975–FY2000*
General Account Initial and Revised Budgets: percentage
Source: Zaisei Tōkei (annually), Research Division, Budget Bureau, MOF.

1991, marked a progressive annual decline in the ratio to a low point of 7.6%. Encouraged by that success, MOF set a precise numerical target for a further reduction in the ratio of less than 5% by 1995.

The third phase is coincident with the beginning of the economic recession, and is marked by a sharp upward annual progression in the ratio, to reach 28% of the planned Budget in 1996. With the introduction in-year of six mini-budgets between 1992 and 1995, the ratios for the revised issue of bonds became much larger than those for the planned issue in the initial budgets, reflecting the large increase in the amount of additional government borrowing to finance capital investment and public works projects. For example, in FY1993 there was a doubling of the number of bonds issued after the initial Budget, the bond dependency ratio rising from a planned (initial) 11.2% to (revised) 20.9%, its highest level for a decade. Even that level was exceeded in each of the next four years, as the revised issue totalled nearly 30% of the Budget. Reducing the bond ratio to less than 5% was now little more than a pious hope. The target date was deferred, and the planned annual reductions to achieve it by 1999 revised sharply upwards. It was now targeted as a 'medium-term benchmark' (MOF 1994*b*: 17). However, a more ambitious target of 3% to be achieved by 2003 was incorporated into the Fiscal Structural Reform Act of 1997. Once again, the achievement of that target was deferred, as Prime Minister Hashimoto executed a reluctant policy U-turn in the spring of 1998 to respond with countercyclical measures to deal with the deep recession. In the revised Supplementary Budgets of FY1998, the number of bonds issued doubled from a planned 15.57 to 34.00 trillion, equivalent to almost 40% of the total expenditure in the General Account Budget. The planned issue in FY1999 of 31.050 trillion was the highest ever recorded in an initial Budget, equivalent to more than 6% of forecasted GDP. More than two-thirds were special deficit-financing bonds. Supplementary Budgets added a further 7.5 trillion to take the total to 38.616 by the end of March 2000, more than 43% of the total Budget. The new century was marked with yet a further increase as the planned issue pre-empted almost 40% of the Budget.

MOF had two other related but broader objectives for government borrowing: to reduce the size of the accumulated debt outstanding, and to cut the costs of its annual servicing. Those annual costs were (ostensibly) 'fixed'. Absorbing an increasing proportion of the total General Account Budget, they caused 'fiscal rigidification', which MOF had earlier declared contrary to its principles of 'sound financial management'. Throughout the periods of reconstruction and consolidation, it had continually emphasized that the restoration of fiscal flexibility could be achieved only by the gradual redemption of bonds as they matured. The longer it took to do so, for example by refunding bonds on maturity, the greater the burden bequeathed to future generations, a further source of anxiety with the progressive ageing of the population. No targets were set for optimal or acceptable levels of debt or annual service costs until the Fiscal Structural Reform Act of 1997. Figure 25.5 shows the trends of debt outstanding during the period 1975–2000, rising from a total of 14.9 trillion to 327 trillion (planned), an increase in the proportion of GDP from below 10% to 75%. The value of

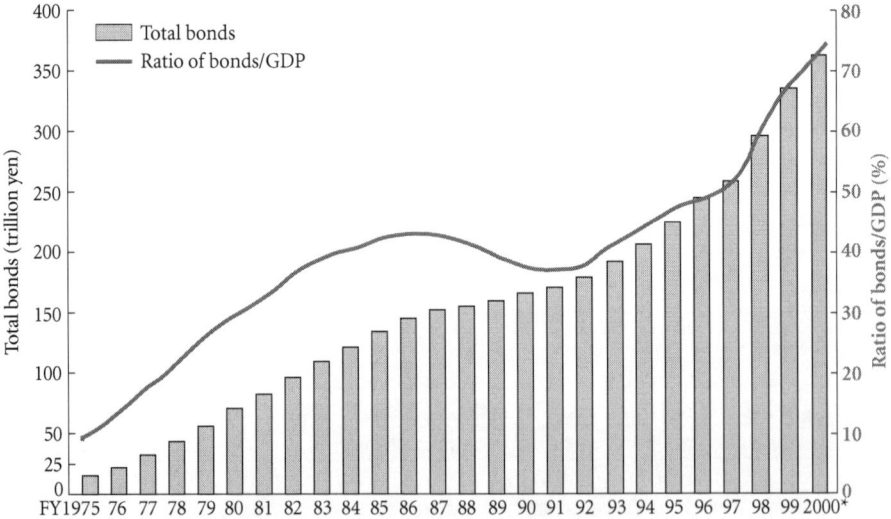

Figure 25.5   *Central government bonds outstanding, FY1975–FY2000*
General Account Settled Budget: trillion yen

*Initial Budget

Source: *Zaisei Tōkei* (annually), Research Division, Budget Bureau, MOF.

the total government bonds outstanding increased year by year by substantial amounts through almost the whole of the period of fiscal reconstruction. From the middle of the 1980s annual growth slowed, as the generation of surplus revenues in the period of the bubble permitted higher rates of redemption. But that improvement was not sustained in the conditions of the recession.

Figure 25.6 shows for the period 1975–2000 the annual costs of servicing the central government's debt, i.e. debt redemption and interest payments on bonds outstanding, and those costs as a proportion of the total General Account Budget. From 1 trillion and almost 5% of the Budget in FY1975, the costs rose annually to reach almost 22 trillion, pre-empting more than a quarter of the budget in FY2000. Those figures understate the real costs of servicing the debt. As we shall see later in the chapter, from time to time MOF suspended statutory annual payments to redeem the national debt in order to relieve pressure on the General Account Budget.

For more than 25 years, a fifth or more of the total General Account Budget was pre-empted by the fixed costs of debt servicing, exerting a considerable and continuing squeeze on general expenditures. 'Fiscal rigidification' increased throughout the whole of the period 1975–2000, as Figure 25.7 shows: in FY1975 general expenditures accounted for more than three-quarters of the total budget; by FY2000 they had fallen to just over one-half.

To summarize, MOF failed to achieve its main aim of eliminating the issue of special deficit-financing bonds for all but four years of the period 1975–2000. It achieved steady progress in reducing the bond dependency ratio, but did not succeed in reducing it to less than 5% by the prescribed target date of 1995. Although it had come close

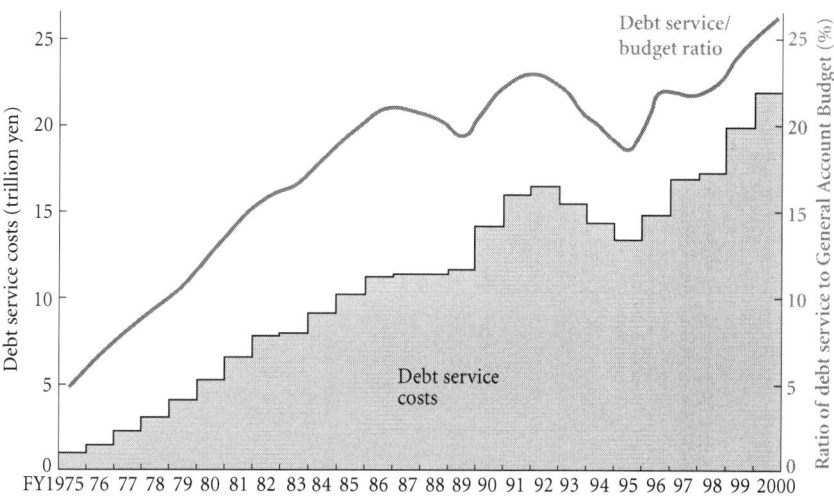

Figure 25.6 *Servicing central government debt, FY1975–FY2000*
General Account Initial Budget: trillion yen

Source: Zaisei Tōkei, (annually), Research Division, Budget Bureau, MOF.

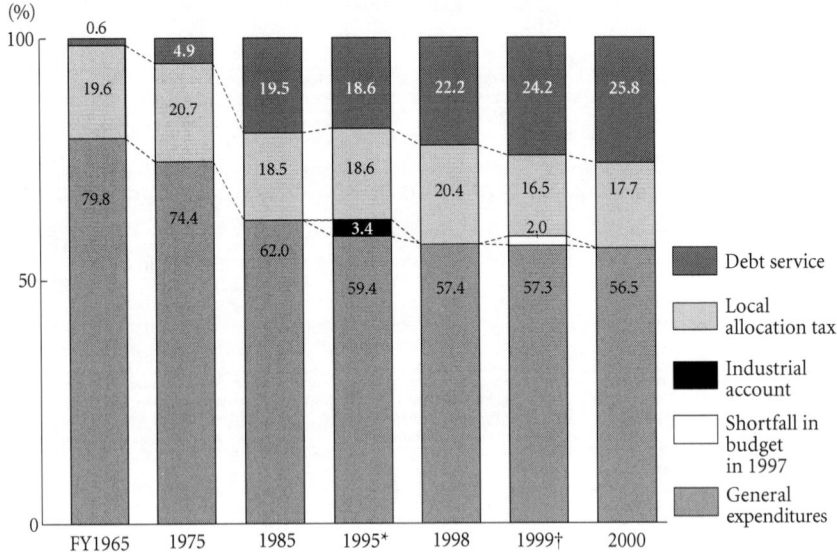

Figure 25.7 *Fiscal rigidity: the squeeze on general expenditures in the General Account Budget, FY1965–FY2000*
General Account Initial Budget

*3.4% for transfer to Special Account for Industrial Investment under the NTT scheme.
†2% for repayment of shortfall of revenue at budget settlement in FY1997.

Source: The Japanese Budget in Brief (annually), Budget Bureau, MOF.

to doing so in 1991, thereafter the ratio moved sharply upwards. Both the size of the accumulated debt and the annual costs of servicing it grew inexorably through almost the whole of the period. MOF failed in its aim to reduce the 'fiscal rigidification' identified at the time of the emergence of the crisis in 1975.

In reality, even the modest achievements of some of those aims of reconstruction and consolidation were more apparent than real. As I shall show below, by exploiting FILP as an alternative source of funding, through creative accounting, and the manipulation of cash flows between the General Account Budget and 'off budget' Special Accounts, MOF's presentation of the state of central government finances concealed a more serious and fundamental deterioration. But first we look at the effects and effectiveness of its policies for controlling the growth of expenditure in the General Account Budget.

RESTRAINING THE GROWTH OF PUBLIC EXPENDITURE

MOF's objective for public spending was set, and constantly reaffirmed, only in the broadest terms: to restrain the growth of public expenditures as much as possible. No numerical targets were prescribed, and no dates for the achievement of some desirable state of restraint set, until the short-lived Fiscal Structural Reform Act of 1997. Assessment of performance is therefore more difficult to make, and is to a large extent implicit in the various time-series data that accompanied the presentation of the Budget. It depends, first, on what is measured and, secondly, on the budget base used. On the revenue side, total revenues are divided broadly into the receipts of taxes and stamps, and government borrowing. Expenditure can be measured gross, with the total budget including the fixed costs of the servicing of debt and the issue of bonds, together with the transfer of statutory revenues to local government, and net, with the primary budget total excluding those fixed costs.

The budget base used in the measurement of those aggregates affects the results in three ways. First, planned expenditure in the initial Budget provides an incomplete picture of the total of expenditure because of in-year changes made to those plans financed by Supplementary Budgets. Secondly, the total of planned expenditure in the initial and revised budgets is different from what is actually spent or committed in the fiscal year. Thirdly there is normally a difference between the out-turn of spending and the out-turn of revenue, i.e. the revenues actually collected in the fiscal year. While the former is normally under-spent, the latter is normally greater than revenue estimates in the initial and revised budgets, and greater than the out-turn of expenditure. The resulting surplus is normally carried forward (after statutory deductions for the repayment of national debt) to the next fiscal year. For example, the initial budget for FY1998 provided for planned expenditures of 77.669 trillion. That total was revised upwards during the course of the fiscal year in three Supplementary Budgets to 87.991 trillion, but the final out-turn was only 84.391 trillion. Revenues to finance the planned expenditures comprised 58.522 trillion of tax revenues, and borrowing of 15.57 trillion; the remainder comprised fees, charges, and so on. The additional spending in the three Supplementary Budgets was financed by additional borrowing totalling 34.0 trillion, part of which was to compensate for a revised estimate of tax revenues, down by more than 8 trillion to 50.165 trillion. Of the 34 trillion, half was special deficit-financing bonds. The out-turn of revenues including borrowing was 89.782 trillion.

MOF's preferred performance indicators were, firstly, a comparison of the changes in the totals for the expenditure *planned* in the initial General Account Budgets, in the hope thereby to be able to show lower growth rates year-by-year as reconstruction policies were implemented; secondly, more narrowly, a comparison of changes in *planned* general expenditures within the Budget, net of borrowing and the statutory assignment of a fixed proportion of national and local taxes to local governments; and, thirdly, a comparison of the trends of the growth of the gross aggregates of central and local expenditure.

Judged on those criteria, MOF was undoubtedly successful in restraining the growth of expenditures for much of the periods of fiscal reconstruction and consolidation during the 1980s. First, while planned expenditure in the initial General Account Budget increased in every year from 1975 to 1987, the rates of increase were progressively reduced from 24.5% to 4.8%. Thereafter, the economic growth enjoyed in the years of the bubble economy allowed, and the conditions of recession that followed obliged, MOF to increase public spending substantially, and the annual percentage changes moved upwards once again. Secondly, MOF's performance was more impressive still when measured by its narrower preferred definition of 'general expenditures'. As fixed costs claimed an increasing share of the total budget, focusing upon them enabled it to present a more favourable picture of control. From a high point of annual growth of 23% in FY1975, the change in the annual total of those general expenditures was almost halved by FY1979. The next eight years saw MOF's most determined efforts at reconstruction, in which it enlisted and exploited the support of the Administrative Reform movement led by the Provisional Councils. By 1982 the annual rate of increase was less than 2%, and in each of the next five years MOF claimed, for the first time, to have achieved real cuts in the total of general expenditures, albeit within a margin of 1%. Growth resumed in 1988 and began to rise steadily thereafter. But MOF had apparently succeeded in changing expectations, and was able to contain the annual increases within 5%, compared with rates of more than 20% in the early 1970s. Thirdly, MOF's comparisons of the growth rates of gross expenditure in the General Account Budget and local government's aggregate expenditure showed the latter rising faster annually from 1984.

MOF was also successful in reducing the proportion of GDP absorbed by the planned General Account Budget as a whole during the 1980s, from 18% to 15.5%. On the more narrowly defined general expenditure, it could claim a more impressive reduction still, as the ratio fell from 12.6% in 1980 to 8.4% in 1994. The latter, it emphasized, represented 'less than 67% of the FY1980 peak', approximately the same proportion as that of FY1970 (MOF 1994b: 19). The inference that MOF wished to draw was clear: its performance had returned the public finances to the *status quo ante* that prevailed before the era of welfare spending began.

'SMOKE AND MIRRORS'

MOF's public demonstration of its achievement in restraining the growth of public spending as measured by its preferred performance indicators is subject to substantial qualifications. First, it was able to make only small cuts in planned general expenditures for a brief period; no such cuts were made in the overall planned totals for the General Account Budget for 20 years from 1975. Secondly, even that restraint of the growth of general expenditures is less impressive when a revised rather than a planned budget base is used as an indicator. MOF was much less successful in controlling expenditure demands and pressures *in-year* than in the budget-making processes preceding the initial Budget. This is partly because it was more willing to acquiesce in some of the demands for additional spending financed in Supplementary Budgets which were not subject to the strict controls of the budget guidelines and ceilings, and partly because the pressures to stimulate the economy in-year often proved irresistible. Thus, the cuts in the total of general expenditures claimed for five successive years in the mid-1980s were cuts in *planned* expenditure which MOF was unable (or unwilling) to deliver.

Table 25.5 compares the annual percentage change in planned and revised totals for general expenditures in the Initial and Supplementary Budgets for the period of fiscal

'Smoke and Mirrors'

Table 25.5 *Planned and actual changes in general expenditures in the General Account Budget, FY1981–FY1988*[a]

FY	Planned Total (tr. yen)	(%)	Actual Total (tr. yen)	(%)
1981	1.317	4.3	1.698	5.5
1982	0.570	1.8	1.070	3.3
1983	−0.001	−0.0	0.485	1.5
1984	−0.034	−0.1	0.625	1.9
1985	0.000	−0.0	0.767	2.3
1986	−0.001	−0.0	0.840	2.6
1987	−0.001	−0.0	2.234	6.8
1988	0.399	1.2	2.906	8.9

[a]General Account Initial and Revised Budgets.

Source: *Zaisei Tōkei*, 1997, Research Division, Budget Bureau, MOF.

reconstruction. The effect of in-year changes was to add between 485 billion and 2.9 trillion to planned expenditures each year, representing year-on-year increases of the initial Budget of between 1.5% and 8.9%. After 1988, the difference between planned and revised totals for general expenditure was even more marked. While MOF proclaimed modest annual increases in planned expenditures for 1989 and 1990 of just over 3%, it subsequently agreed revised spending worth 4.9 and 3.8 trillion, representing real annual increases of 15% and 11.4%. As Supplementary Budgets became more frequent to fund successive ad hoc packages of countercyclical measures in the recession of 1992–5, and again from 1997 to 2000, the unreality of expenditure plans became plainer still. While the economic argument for additional ad hoc spending in response to the experience of the deepening recession justified extra in-year spending, those were not exceptional years. Over the whole period 1975–2000, MOF always revised its initial planned spending upwards: it was never cut.

As explained earlier, revised Budgets were also used to finance an increase in 'fixed costs' when revenues were overestimated in initial Budgets and MOF was obliged to cover the wider-than-planned deficit with more borrowing. A comparison of planned and revised expenditures in the General Account Budget as a whole shows a similar pattern to that of general expenditures for the whole of the period 1975–2000. Only in 1995 was there a planned cut in the budget total; the reality was a large increase in-year of some 5 trillion.

A third qualification to MOF's apparent achievement in controlling expenditure is that the reductions in the general expenditure–GDP ratio were achieved more as a result of the growth in GDP than as a reduction of the former. In times of sustained economic growth, a reduction in the ratio is easier to achieve. Indeed, public spending can continue to rise (as it did), and simultaneously absorb a smaller proportion of GDP. That combination was significant in the politics of the budgetary process in the period of fiscal reconstruction, allowing MOF to accommodate politico-bureaucratic pressures for more spending without sacrificing its fiscal objectives, measured by the general expenditure–GDP ratio. The converse—the combination of economic decline and a rise in spending (boosted by demands to stimulate the economy)—has an opposite and disastrous effect on the ratio. When that happens, governments understandably prefer to emphasize other more favourable performance indicators, or to re-define public spending to exclude certain of those items less susceptible to control (as in the UK in 1992). MOF began to experience those adverse effects in 1992, when the ratio rose for the first time since 1980; thereafter the trend was upwards.

Control of the growth of the planned total of the initial General Account Budget claimed by MOF was attributed to its successful implementation of policies of fiscal reconstruction. While it is true that budget norms and guidelines were contributory factors, in reality fiscal pressures were relieved as much or more so by MOF's adroit manipulation of revenues and expenditures within the General Account Budget and between it, FILP, and the 38 Special Accounts, and by its skilful management of the presentation of that performance. There were three main budgetary stratagems designed to relieve pressure on the General Account Budget: first, the deflection of part of the burden of cuts and squeezes to local governments; secondly, the manipulation of the statutory provision for 'carry-forward' of surplus revenues on the General Account Budget at the end of the financial year to redeem the national debt; and, thirdly, the manipulation of cash flows between the General Account Budget, some of the 38 Special Accounts, and FILP. As explained in earlier chapters, fiscal pressure on planned budgets was also relieved by the postponement of the repayment of loans under the NTT scheme, as well as by the exploitation of that and other off-budget sources of finance.

Shifting the Burden of Cuts and Squeezes

Many of the functions undertaken by local governments were 'agency-delegated' functions, and as such they were carried out as directed by the relevant Spending Ministries and Agencies. In addition, for almost all activities of local government, those ministries and agencies set standards, regulations, and guidelines, compliance with which was ensured through various financial controls and inducements. At a general level, MOF (with MHA) exercised a comprehensive and detailed control of the aggregates of revenues and expenditures of local government as a whole. It had a number of instruments with which to influence and control them. One was a Local Government Finance Plan, an annual official estimate of standard targets for the aggregates of revenues and expenditures based on formal criteria. This guaranteed sufficient financial resources to local government, coordinated national and local public finances in the context of the national economy, and provided guidelines for local government's own financial management. In estimating total revenues, MOF prescribed the amounts to be contributed locally through taxes, charges, and fees, and nationally through transfer payments and the assignment of proportions of nationally collected taxes. Secondly, individual local governments had to obtain 'loan permits' from the MHA. Thirdly, funds for those approved loans were provided mainly from the Trust Fund Bureau Fund managed by MOF's Financial Bureau, and from the Finance Corporation for Municipal Enterprises which it co-sponsored with MHA. Larger, mainly city, local authorities were allowed to issue local bonds on the open market, and to borrow long term from the private sector. The number and size of loans from all those sources were controlled in aggregate through the Local Loans Programme, MOF's fourth instrument of influence and control.

The policies of fiscal reconstruction adopted and implemented by MOF in the 1980s were a response to a perceived fiscal crisis of central government. Local government finances were experiencing similar difficulty: their expenditures were rising at an even faster rate than those of the central government, and were suffering a chronic shortage of tax revenues. But MOF's prime concern was to restore the balance on the General Account by increasing central government revenues and reducing expenditures. At that time, there was no official acknowledgement of a broader fiscal crisis of the state to which both central and local government finances were contributing, and in which FILP played a key role. Public recognition of that was to come much later, after the collapse of the bubble economy. Official published targets for the reduction of general government outlays and of the gross debt of the whole public sector were not set until the initiation of fiscal structural reform in 1997.

What evidence is there that MOF exploited the use of its instruments of influence and control of local government finance to shift the burden of cuts and squeezes from central to local government? Central government took about two-thirds of the total national gross revenues collected as taxes, local government collectively, the remaining third (Wright 1999*b*: table 12). That ratio changed very little between 1975 and 1998, not enough to suggest that, as a result of the implementation of MOF's policies for fiscal reconstruction, central government acquired a larger share of tax revenues at the expense of local governments. Over the period as a whole, there was a small upward drift in the trend of tax revenues claimed by local government, but there is no one, simple factor that accounts for that. From time to time, however, as the opportunity arose, MOF did attempt to secure a greater share of those tax revenues that were shared between the two levels of governments. It happened for example over the discussion of the distribution of the proposed increase to the national consumption tax in 1994, and again in 1997.

MOF argued that central government's spending grew more slowly than that of local government over almost the whole of the period, 1975–2000, although not significantly in the mid-1970s, when the rapid buildup of expenditure in the General Account precipitated the fiscal crisis and MOF's response with policies of fiscal reconstruction in the years 1980–7 (Wright 1999*b*: table 13). The *apparently* superior performance of central government is however deceptive. What is measured here is gross expenditure of the General Account Budget, and of the Ordinary Accounts of local government.[1] If debt servicing and other fixed costs are excluded and allowance is made for intergovernmental transfers, almost wholly from central to local government, the trends of net expenditures tell a different story (Wright 1999*b*: table 14). Taking the period 1975–2000 as a whole, roughly two-thirds of the total net expenditure of central and local governments was attributable to the latter. However, in the period of the emergence of the fiscal crisis and the implementation of policies of fiscal reconstruction with which MOF responded, that share was reduced, while central government's rose from 33% in 1977 to over 38% in 1983. In other words, central government's net spending grew faster than that of local government.

This analysis suggests that central government's 'own spending', that is the amount of policy expenditures on the programmes of ministries and agencies net of transfer payments, not only continued to grow during the period of fiscal reconstruction, but did so partly at the expense of local governments. The analysis of budget outputs in Chapter 21 concluded that the ratio of central to local government spending rose from 1.82 in 1975 to reach 2.55 by 1990. That hypothesis is tested by looking first at the composition of the Local Government Finance Plan, to examine the changes in the distribution of the revenues from central and local sources, and secondly at changes in the aggregates of two components of that Plan, i.e. the assigned proportions of nationally collected taxes, and grants and subsidies, to assess their effect on the net General Account Budget.

The three main sources of locally generated revenues were: (1) locally imposed and collected taxes on individuals, businesses, land and property, and some specific goods and services; (2) local bonds; and (3) charges, fees and miscellaneous payments, transfers, and adjustments. Central government contributed to local revenues in three main ways. First, it allocated a proportion of certain nationally collected taxes: 32% of the total yield of personal income tax, 35.8% of the corporate income tax, 32% of the liquor (alcohol) tax, 29.5% of the consumption tax, and 25% of the yield of the tobacco tax. The resulting aggregate, the Local Allocation Tax, was distributed as general grants to local authorities according to a formula that reflected needs and resources, and was intended to maintain a minimum uniform standard of local services. Secondly, the Local Transfer Tax transferred to local governments a proportion of various nationally collected taxes, on local roads, motor vehicles, petrol, and aviation fuel. The third source of revenue was the aggregate of central government's local transfer payments from the General Account and Supplementary Budgets, comprising statutory contributions to the costs of providing certain national services, such as education, welfare, and public works projects; discretionary grants-in-aid for certain current expenditures; and subsidies for agency-delegated functions.

There was a substantial shift in the contributions of local and central governments to the total revenues of local government (Wright 1999*b*: table 15). In 1975 central

---

[1] The aggregate of local governments' expenditures, the Ordinary Accounts, includes the consolidated account for general administrative services such as education and police, and several special accounts for services such as housing, whose expenditures are financed partly by fees and charges. It excludes the accounts of 'local public enterprises'.

government contributed 47% of the total; 20 years later, that had fallen to 37%. The shift is marked precisely by the introduction of MOF's policies for the fiscal reconstruction of central government finances in 1980. By the beginning of the years of the bubble economy seven years later, central government's share of local government revenues had already fallen by 10%. That sharp reduction was due partly to the loss of revenue from national taxes, as the economy slowed down in the 1980s, reflected in the declining proportions of the assigned revenues from the Local Allocation and Transfer taxes. But, more significantly, it was due mainly to a sharp fall in the proportion of total revenues provided by transfer payments from the central government. Grants-in-aid and subsidies fell from 25.8% of total local revenues in 1979 to 17.0% in 1988. Despite the economic boom that followed, that trend of continuous annual decline was sustained, although it was now partly offset by a rise in the share of the assigned taxes, as revenues grew strongly. The contribution of the new national consumption tax almost doubled revenues from local transfer taxes after 1988.

The converse of central government's falling contribution to total local revenues was the greater fiscal burden borne by local government, in particular by local taxes. Before 1980 revenues from local taxes contributed on average between 33% to 36% of total revenues. That proportion moved sharply upwards to reach almost 46% by the end of the period of fiscal reconstruction; there was only a marginal reduction in local borrowing, while the contribution from other local sources remained unchanged. From 1994 the contribution of local bonds rose sharply, as local governments borrowed heavily to finance public works in successive countercyclical economic and fiscal packages determined nationally by MOF.

There is, then, evidence of local government bearing more of the burden for the financing of its expenditures, both during and after the period of fiscal reconstruction. What was the effect of that shift on the General Account Budget? The Local Allocation (but not the Local Transfer) Taxes were counted as expenditure in the General Account Budget, offset by the total revenues collected for those assigned taxes. In principle, the proportion of nationally collected taxes assigned to local government was a fixed cost, which varied only with the yield of those taxes. Thus, an increase in the yield of those (and other) taxes increased the total revenues available to finance the General Account Budget; but at the same time, they increased the total of those budget expenditures, because more had to be paid as assigned revenues to local authorities. Revenues from the assigned taxes were paid into a Special Account, and then transferred to local government. In preparing the initial General Account Budget, MOF estimated the yield of national taxes, and included the proportion to be assigned to local authorities in the initial Budget (and in the Local Government Plan). Where that estimate proved to be too low, i.e. when the yield from taxes was higher than estimated, then provision had to be made for additional expenditure to be paid to local government (as assigned revenues) in the Supplementary Budget. Where the yield was overestimated, and the settled out-turn proved lower, then MOF had less revenue to cover the costs of planned expenditures in the initial Budget (including those already assigned revenues to local government). As a result, there were insufficient funds in the Special Account to cover the revenues allocated in the Local Government Plan, and MOF had to finance the deficit by borrowing from the FILP Trust Fund Bureau Fund (which it controlled) at current rates of interest.

In practice, when MOF's estimates of local revenues and expenditures in the Local Government Finance Plan showed a shortfall in revenue, it commonly made additional revenues available by increasing the amount assigned as local allocation taxes, as well as obliging local authorities to increase their local borrowing. Between 1975 and 1984 MOF borrowed a total of 5.8 trillion from the Trust Fund Bureau Fund to top up the revenues assigned to local government from the Special Account. Conversely, when local authorities showed substantial surpluses on their current accounts, as in 1991–3, MOF cut their proportion of assigned revenues from the Special Account. This represented negative spending in the General Account Budget for three successive years, worth a total of 1.7 trillion. However, in FY1994 there was a sharp decline in the estimated revenue from local (as well as national) taxes, and MOF was obliged once again to use its discretionary authority to top up revenues assigned from the Special Account by borrowing from the Trust Fund Bureau Fund.

The economic recession of 1991–5 affected local revenues adversely in two ways. First, because of the general slow-down in economic activity, revenues from local taxes, and those assigned from the Local Allocation and Transfer taxes, were depressed. MOF estimated the loss of revenue for local government for the three years 1994–6 at 2.988, 4.260, and 5.750 trillion. Secondly, MOF's countercyclical fiscal measures included cuts in national income tax and local residence tax, which had the effect in the same period of an additional loss of income for local government, totalling 2.889, 2.690, and 2.870 trillion for the three years. Those huge shortfalls in income for local government were covered mainly by transfers from the Special Account for the Allotment of Local Allocation and Transfer tax, and by obliging local authorities to issue additional local (construction) bonds and, exceptionally, local deficit-financing bonds as well. Money transferred from the Special Account was borrowed from the Trust Fund Bureau Fund, and appropriate rates of interest charged on it.

Only a small proportion of this huge loss of income for local government was borne directly as a cost on the General Account Budget: in 1995 a mere 181 billion was appropriated additionally from the Budget, and in 1996, 839 billion. In short, while MOF was obliged to make additional revenues available to local government to avoid a collapse of local finances, it did so without adding substantially to the rising costs of the central government's budget. By borrowing from the Trust Fund Bureau Fund, by postponing the repayment of some of the loans incurred then and previously, and by obliging local authorities to issue deficit-financing as well as ordinary construction bonds, MOF was able to finance local government's estimated lost revenues through the worst of the recessionary period without great cost to the General Account Budget. Indeed, if MOF's estimate of the loss of income from the assigned taxes was accurate, the effect of the tax cuts in the period 1994–6 was to reduce expenditure in the Budget. To that extent, the rate of growth of the overall General Account Budget was lower than it might have been. Of course, the deficit was increased as a result of the loss of revenues from the central government's share of income tax and other indirect taxes. The longer-term consequences of debt incurred though those short-term expedients were substantial. By the end of 1996, MOF estimated that 10.5 trillion was outstanding (part of the estimated 'hidden debt' of central government, then approximately 43 trillion), 'requiring budgetary treatment in the following years' (MOF 1996b: 32). As MOF candidly admitted, many of those and other 'special measures to reduce expenditures and increase revenues of the General Account ... are stop-gap transactions between the General Account and various Special Accounts'. Thus, MOF had relieved pressure on the General Account Budget in the short term, but had stoked up the fires of a longer-term debt conflagration.

What was the effect on the General Account Budget of the central government's declining contribution to local government's revenues? Transfer payments to local government increased rapidly in the 1970s, helping to finance the implementation of new social, welfare, and environmental policies; the total doubled between 1975 and 1979. From 1980 that growth was virtually halted, and then for six consecutive years the total was cut. Incremental growth was resumed in the years of the bubble economy, and accelerated as MOF reacted to the conditions of economic recession with repeated countercyclical fiscal policies. As a proportion of the total of general expenditures in the General Account Budget, transfer payments to local government fell from around 34% in 1980 to just under 29% in 1991 (Wright 1999b: table 16). Measured on an out-turn basis, the reduction was greater still.

The exclusion of transfer payments to local government thus transforms the picture presented by MOF from one of marginal cuts to the annual total of general expenditures in the General Account Budget to one of continuous growth throughout almost the whole of the period 1975–2000. From 1987, which marked the transition from reconstruction to consolidation (expansion), those annual increments on an out-turn basis were substantial. Revision in Supplementary Budgets added an extra 1 trillion in FY1987, and more than 2 trillion in FY1988. Local government did not share in that expansion, other than very marginally, until 1992.

The conclusion is inescapable: pressure on the General Account Budget was partly relieved during the 1980s by imposing a greater burden of cuts and squeezes on both the revenues and expenditures of local government. By reducing central government's contributions to local revenues, by 'stop-gap' transactions designed to reduce the short-term costs of transferring statutorily assigned revenues from national taxes, and by cutting transfer payments, MOF constrained the growth of the overall General Account Budget, and was able to present a picture of marginal cuts in the total of general expenditures in the period of fiscal reconstruction. Central government's planned and actual 'own spending' increased not only through those years, but in every year throughout 1975–99, and at a faster rate than the annual transfer payments to local government until the explosion of public works spending in the recessionary years of the 1990s.

Settlement and 'Carry-Forward' of Surplus

MOF's second budgetary stratagem to relieve pressure on the General Account Budget involved the manipulation of the statutory provisions for the carry-forward of surpluses on the General Account Budget at the end of the fiscal year, and their use for the redemption of the national debt. At the end of each financial year, the Spending Ministries and Agencies accounted for their spending to MOF by 31 July. MOF then produced an account of the final out-turn or settlement of the revenues and expenditures of the General Account Budget. After formal approval by the Cabinet, it was sent to the Board of Audit for scrutiny and certification. In December the Cabinet submitted the audited accounts, together with the Board's report, for the Diet's consideration.

Until the onset of the fiscal crisis in the mid-1970s, the normal expectation was that the settlement of the General Account Budget would generate a surplus of revenues as a result of 'natural revenue growth', the difference between revenues collected and those estimated yields in the initial and revised budgets. In the era of high economic growth, 'natural revenue growth' had generated large surpluses. Under the 1947 Public Finance Law, at least 50% of any surplus had to be transferred to the Special Account for National Debt Consolidation to redeem the national debt. The persistence of revenue shortfall from the mid-1970s led to the occurrence of a deficit rather than a surplus on the settled accounts. To cope with the 'unforeseeable decline in tax revenue', a Settlement Adjustment Fund was set up in 1977 with an initial capital of 200 billion. The intention was that future deficits on the settled accounts would be covered by payments from the Fund, which would be replenished by payments in years when there were surpluses, after the statutory transfers to redeem the national debt, at the discretion of MOF. In fact, very little was paid into the Fund, and the deficits on the settled budget accounts that occurred in the 1980s were almost wholly covered by transfers from the Special Account for National Debt Consolidation Fund.

The shortfall in revenue after the collapse of the bubble economy in 1991 put a particular strain on the process of settlement. FY1992 and FY1993 were the first two consecutive years since 1945 in which a deficit had occurred on the settlement of the General Budget Account. In the former fiscal year the shortfall at settlement was substantial, 1.544 trillion. As the Settlement Adjustment Fund was exhausted, MOF borrowed an equivalent sum from the Special Account for National Debt Consolidation. The relief on the General Account Budget afforded by such a loan was temporary, for repayments had to be made statutorily within two years; MOF made such provision in the initial budget for FY1994. In FY1993 a similar shortfall at the time of settlement was covered partly by lower-than-estimated expenditures, but mainly by the savings that accrued from the lower costs of debt-servicing resulting from the fall in interest rates. Nevertheless, there still remained a shortfall of 568 billion. As in the previous year, MOF was obliged to cover it by borrowing once again from the Special Account for National Debt Consolidation; but extraordinarily, 'in the light of the currently severe fiscal situation', MOF postponed repayment until FY1996, i.e. three years later instead of two. In the event, MOF was able to repay the loan earlier, in the second Supplementary Budget of FY1995. The use of the Special Account for National Debt Consolidation to make up revenue shortfalls by transferring funds to the Settlement Adjustment Fund was not intended originally, and was allowed only as a temporary expedient. It was also exploited by MOF in other ways, to relieve pressure on the General Account Budget (MOF 1995: 112).

The Redemption of the National Debt

Government bonds issued to cover the deficit on the General Account Budget were redeemed in two ways: by purchase on maturity, and by issuing refunding bonds. MOF operated a 60-year redemption rule whereby one-sixth of bonds issued were redeemed in each ten-year period, the remaining five-sixths being refunded five times before the real redemption. Sixty years was taken as the average economic depreciation period of the assets purchased by those bonds. Redemption payments were made through the Special Account for National Debt Consolidation in three ways: first, statutorily, by a fixed-rate appropriation from the General Account Budget of one-sixth of the value of bonds outstanding at the beginning of the previous fiscal year; secondly, and again statutorily, by the transfer of not less than half of the surplus on the settlement of the General Account Budget; and, thirdly, by discretionary transfers from the General Account Budget. The Special Account was also endowed from the proceeds of fund investment, and from sales of stock.

Pressure on the costs of debt redemption in the General Account Budget emerged in the mid-1980s, as the (mainly ten-year) special deficit-financing bonds issued for the first time in the crisis conditions of FY1975 approached maturity. Faced with the prospect of massive and recurring annual redemption costs borne on the General Account, MOF applied the principle of 'refinancing' to special deficit-financing bonds in FY1984. In the following year, bonds worth 1.865 trillion were refinanced. To cope with the scale of the underwriting operations, the capacity of the main source of loans, the Trust Fund Bureau Fund, was expanded. At the same time, MOF introduced two other related initiatives to ease the pressures on the General Account Budget, and on the market for long-term government bonds: the issue of short-term refunding bonds, and the flotation of refunding bonds in advance of their maturity.

Those measures helped to spread the burden of repayment over a longer period, and to relieve immediate cost pressures on the General Account Budget. But more urgent action had been needed earlier to constrain the rising costs of servicing the national debt, which by FY1982 was pre-empting nearly 16% of the General Account Budget, three times more than in the crisis year of FY1975. In 1982, and for eight consecutive years, MOF suspended the statutory requirement of the fixed-rate appropriation from the General Account Budget to the National Debt Consolidation Fund. Payments were resumed in FY1990, but were suspended again from 1993 to 1995. From time to time MOF, under special legislation, also suspended the statutory transfer to the Fund of the surplus on the settlement of the General Account Budget, the legislation permitting the priority of the allocation of the surplus to general purpose funds over that of debt redemption. Thus, throughout almost the whole of the periods of fiscal reconstruction and consolidation, MOF was able to relieve some of the pressures on the General Account Budget by suspending the statutory arrangements for the liquidation of a part of the national debt. The resulting savings from the suspension of the fixed-rate transfer alone were considerable, averaging annually some 1.5 to 2.5 trillion yen throughout the period of fiscal reconstruction, as Table 25.6 shows. Added to other fixed costs in the Budget, they would have had the effect of further squeezing the amount available

Table 25.6 *Deferred liquidation of the national debt, FY1982–FY1998*[a]

FY	Deferred payments (tr. yen)
1982	1.37
1983	1.60
1984	1.82
1985	2.02
1986	2.24
1987	2.41
1988	2.53
1989	2.61
1990	Payments resumed (2.62)
1991	Payments resumed (2.56)
1992	Payments resumed (2.63)
1993	3.04
1994	3.08
1995	3.20
1996	Payments resumed (4.54)
1997	Payments resumed (5.20)
1998	Payments resumed (5.53)

[a]General Account Settled Budget.

Source: data provided by Budget Bureau, MOF.

for general expenditures, and hence exacerbating 'fiscal rigidification'—or, if not offset, would have resulted in larger budget expenditure.

The budgetary significance of the suspension of payments to redeem the national debt is illustrated by the effects of the costs of their resumption in 1990, when the fixed-rate appropriations for that year totalled 2.623 trillion, equivalent to half of the total increase in the FY1990 Budget over the previous year. Together with those of the Local Allocation and Transfer taxes, the annual fixed costs of debt redemption accounted for 80% of the annual increase of the General Account Budget. Reducing the scale of the fixed costs, either of local assigned taxes or of debt redemption, or both, was thus a very effective means of 'cutting' public expenditure. It was also a useful means of partly financing additional expenditures in Supplementary Budgets. For example, the suspension of the fixed-rate appropriation totalling 3.04 trillion in the second Supplementary Budget for FY1993 helped to finance a package of special economic measures. Suspending the arrangements for redeeming the national debt had the further short-term advantage for MOF that (unlike local assigned taxes and some other 'temporary special measures' for postponing payments), it was not required to make up repayments in subsequent years. But such suspension contributed to longer-term difficulties. MOF's dilemma was that short-term budget reductions to achieve fiscal reconstruction were purchased at the expense of longer-term costs: unredeemed debt imposed a burden on future generations, a further example of the triumph of expediency over the proclaimed principles of 'sound management' of the national finances.

A further unintended consequence of the use of the National Debt Consolidated Fund as a makeshift was that the suspension both of fixed-rate transfers into it and of surpluses on the settlement of the General Account Budget seriously depleted its funds and weakened its capacity to perform its original function of redeeming the national debt. By the early 1990s, the Settlement Adjustment Fund was exhausted, and unable to provide funds to cover the shortfall of revenues on the annual settlement of the General Account; and the balance of the National Debt Consolidation Fund was inadequate to provide temporary compensation for those shortfalls, or even to fulfil its original purpose of redeeming the national debt. Unable to exploit and manipulate those two resources, MOF was obliged to resume the issue of deficit bonds in 1994 to cover the revenue shortfall. A similar crisis had been averted in the mid-1980s, when the balance of the National Debt Consolidation Fund had shrunk from 3.6 trillion in 1980 to 1.3 trillion in 1985. On that occasion, however, the privatization of NTT was accompanied by legislation to allow the transfer to the Fund of the proceeds of the sale of some NTT stock. Besides the welcome relief provided by that new source, some of the proceeds were used to finance public works expenditure without short-term cost to the General Account Budget, as explained in Chapter 23.

The Manipulation of Special Accounts and FILP

MOF's third budgetary stratagem to relieve pressure on the General Account Budget involved the manipulation of cash flows between it, some of the 38 Special Accounts, and FILP. From time to time during the period of fiscal reconstruction, MOF (with the formal approval of the Diet) suspended the payment from the General Account of some statutory annual subsidies into various Special Accounts, most notably those for welfare insurance and national pensions, as well as for redeeming the national debt. Acknowledging this publicly in 1990, it undertook to 'deal with postponed public expenditure and long-term debts belonging to the JNR [Debt] Settlement Corporation' (MOF 1990: 113), and to repay money 'borrowed' from other Special Accounts or 'owed' to them. The significance of those 'bridging loans' to the General Account Budget can be gauged by the assignment in the Supplementary Budget of FY1988 of approximately 1.5 trillion for the resumption, in part, of the central government's contribution to the Employee's Pension Insurance Scheme, previously suspended. By the end of FY1997, those so-called 'hidden debts' amounted to some 45 trillion, about 9% of GDP, of which the long-term debt of JNR alone totalled 28 trillion.

Most of MOF's stratagems to relieve pressure on the General Account Budget were 'special temporary measures'. Of greater significance for the longer-term viability of the public finance system as a whole was the exploitation of FILP as an alternative source of funding for some public expenditure programmes, and as a 'lubricant' for the public finance system as a whole.

In Chapter 24 I explained how the allocation and distribution of FILP's capital investment changed after the end of the high-growth era, and the FILP Budget was used for other purposes. As the original concept of FILP changed, its initial insulation from general expenditure financed through the General Account Budget and numerous Special Accounts became blurred. From the 1970s it was used increasingly as an instrument of general expenditure purposes in the overall public finance system, as the demands for more public goods and services outstripped the supply of tax revenues. It became an essential 'lubricant' for government finances, providing both short- and long-term cash-flow to support both central and local government finance. At the end of FY1992, nearly 40% of all government bonds outstanding (180 trillion) were guaranteed by FILP funds. FILP underwrote a substantial proportion of the special deficit-financing bonds issued from 1975 to cover the deficit on the General Account Budget, amounting to 20% of the FILP Budget by 1985; it also guaranteed increasing amounts of local government bonds. Another 'lubricating' cash-flow function was the provision of temporary loans and financial accommodations for the General Account Budget and some Special Accounts. The balance of outstanding loans to the former totalled 8.245 trillion at the end of FY1997, mainly outstanding loans transferred from the former JNR and the JNR Debt Settlement Corporation (FILP 1998). Cash so borrowed had of course to be repaid, but, as happened in 1992, scheduled repayment could be deferred to relieve pressure on the General Account Budget.

As a substitute for general finance, FILP funds were used both 'actively' and 'passively'. Passive use included the supply of funds to repay debts, and to defer repayments of both principal and interest on accounts in deficit elsewhere in the financial system. Various Special Accounts, whose activities were formerly and properly a charge on the General Account Budget and hence on taxation when their operating budgets were in deficit, or when they needed an injection of fresh capital, were subsidized through FILP. The principal beneficiary was the JNR Debt Settlement Corporation, set up in 1987 to liquidate the long-term debts of the former national railway system. By FY1997 these totalled 28 trillion. For a decade FILP had provided more than 1 trillion annually to subsidize the costs of servicing that debt, making the Corporation the eighth largest recipient of funds among the fifty or so FILP Agencies. By the end of 1995–6 its accumulated loans totalled 15.4 trillion, the sixth largest outstanding balance of the FILP agencies. The Special Account for National Forests managed funds for the development and preservation of national forests. Changed market conditions in the 1970s led to a loss of income, and from 1976 the account was subsidized annually from both FILP and the General Account Budget. By 1997 it had accumulated loans from FILP of more than 3 trillion, and continued to receive further annual loans of approximately 300 billion. The Honshū–Shikoku Bridge Authority had outstanding FILP loans of nearly 2 trillion in 1995, and was borrowing at a rate of 250 billion a year to subsidize its loan repayments. There was little prospect of any of those three Special Accounts being able to repay their FILP loans.

The 'active' use of FILP loans as a substitute for general finance occurred when investments that should properly be charged to taxation, and hence to the General Account, were financed through FILP. The intention, as with 'passive' funds, was to relieve pressure on the General Account Budget. As MOF publicly and candidly admitted, 'FILP reduces policy costs in terms of the tax burden on the public' (FILP 1997: 5).

As the targets of FILP lending changed after the end of the high-growth era to reflect the reorientation of national economic and social objectives towards the improvement of living standards, infrastructure, and the environment, the expectation of profits on such capital developments and public works projects was a much greater risk. Some of those, like housing, had previously been financed mainly through the General Account Budget. In the 1980s and 1990s more than a third of the FILP Budget was used to finance housing construction and to provide loans for house purchase. In FY1994 the government's housing programme was financed partly through the General Account Budget, at a cost of 1.053 trillion (a 6.6% increase over FY1993), but mainly through FILP, at a cost of 13.205 trillion (a 22.3% increase). Had the General Account Budget been obliged to fund more of those public works projects and capital development schemes undertaken by FILP to improve 'social overhead capital', several trillion would have been added annually to it through the period of fiscal reconstruction, and beyond. There were also, of course, the effects on FILP of providing loans at rates of interest lower than those at which it borrowed money from the Trust Fund Bureau Fund, partly compensated by subsidies from the General Account Budget. That issue is discussed in Chapter 28.

MOF also sanctioned the allocation of FILP funds to some Special Accounts for investment programmes, such as national universities and schools and hospital building, which were normally (and more properly) financed out of tax revenues in the General Account Budget. By the end of 1995–6 they had accumulated loans from FILP of 831 billion and 769 billion respectively, and continued to receive annual loans of almost 100 billion. Repayment was unlikely, as the creation and maintenance of such 'social capital' was unlikely to generate sufficient profits to cover the annual costs of the investments and repay the principal. FILP funds were also used to top up the Industrial Investment Special Account, although, as explained in Chapter 12, its main source of income from 1985 was provided by the dividend income from the stock of the privatized NTT held by the central government.

The use of FILP funds as an alternative source of capital investment, and to subsidize operating losses and accumulated debts of those and other Special Accounts, increased in the 1980s and 1990s. In most cases there was little prospect of the loans being repaid from profits earned, or from operating revenue. As a senior official of MOF's Financial Bureau candidly admitted, 'It is a way of keeping the General Account down and reducing pressure caused by less tax revenue' (MOF 1993*d*). It is impossible to estimate from the published data the size of those subsidies and transfers, but combined they provided significant annual relief of a burden that otherwise would have been borne on the General Account; hence they reduced the level of government borrowing or taxation needed to finance general expenditure. The financial propriety of this growing practice was questionable and questioned, and raised issued of parliamentary control and accountability. In FY1998, as part of the reform of FILP, the financing and debts of the JNR Debt Settlement Corporation and the Special Account for National Forests were transferred to the General Account Budget.

Managing the Presentation: Fiscal Sleight-of-Hand

I have explained above how and why MOF chose those indicators of its performance in controlling public spending and the amount of borrowing that put it in the most favourable light. We have seen as well the systematic and regular use of fiscal sleight-of-hand in estimating tax revenues in the planned Budget in order to limit the issue of deficit-financing bonds, and to avoid deep cuts in spending programmes. From time to time, MOF also engaged in 'creative' accounting, to put a gloss on the public presentation of its budget performance. FY1998 provides a case in point. For the first time, statutory differential caps were imposed on all programme expenditures. The effect, MOF claimed, was to cut the total of general expenditures by 1.3% on the previous year, the largest reduction ever made in Japan's fiscal history (MOF 1997b). This was accomplished by some adroit sleight-of-hand. The total of general expenditures for FY1997 was swollen by the inclusion retrospectively of 1.3 trillion NTT expenditures, instead of the usual practice of charging it to the Budget as a separate item, outside the total of general expenditures. Conveniently, with the virtual abandonment of the NTT scheme, only 0.159 trillion of NTT subsidies was planned for FY1998 and hence charged to general expenditures. Comparison of the initial Budget for general expenditures in FY1998 with those of the now inflated FY1997 total produced the reduction claimed by MOF. The apparent reduction of 1.3% in FY1998 was in reality an increase of 2.06%, if existing accounting practices had been observed.

CONCLUSIONS

The conventional explanation of MOF's performance in response to the fiscal crisis of the mid-1970s is that, through policies of fiscal reconstruction and consolidation, it gradually regained control of public spending in the 1980s, successfully re-established the principles of fiscal discipline and sound management of the national finances relaxed in the years of Tanaka Kakuei's dominant and dominating leadership of the LDP, and in consequence presided over a decade of declining deficits and debts (e.g. Pempel and Muramatsu 1995; OECD *passim*). The culmination of that *apparently* successful period of budget retrenchment was the elimination of special deficit-financing bonds briefly in the 1990s, an event mistakenly perceived by some academic writers to be the achievement of MOF's main fiscal objective, the restoration of the balanced Budget (Brown 1999; Suzuki 1999). The analysis of this chapter, and the evidence presented elsewhere in the book, has shown that MOF's achievement in reconstructing and consolidating central government finance after 1975 was more apparent than real. The principles of 'sound management' of the national finances articulated in 1977, which underpinned the policies of fiscal reconstruction, were honoured more in the breach. The underlying reality of the critical state of the national finances was little changed as a direct result of the implementation of the policies of fiscal reconstruction and consolidation in the 1980s.

The problem of the shortfall of revenue was continually addressed but never solved; MOF's longer-term campaign to change the balance of direct to indirect taxes was almost wholly unsuccessful. It never attempted to disguise that failure; indeed, the constant reiteration of the underlying weaknesses of the tax structure was an important element in its annual strategy to persuade ministers and their LDP supporters and bureaucrats in Spending Ministries to exercise self-restraint in their demands for more public spending, and to convert them to its cause for the reform of the tax structure. The LDP was eventually persuaded of the need for tax reform, even if its conversion came too late, and at the cost of damaging compromises in order to carry its rank-and-file in the Diet, and to assuage the grievances of special interest groups. Even the accomplishment of that limited tax-reform proved more difficult and time-consuming than MOF envisaged.

More than a decade after it had begun its campaign, the 1988 legislation proved too little and too late to remedy the underlying structural weakness. Although rates of income tax were reduced, and a national consumption tax introduced, 'the relative weight of taxes on labour income, capital income and consumption have not changed much, and the income tax base remains narrowly focused on the taxation of labour income via a withholding system' (Ishiyama 1994: 12). Temporarily obscured by the 'windfall revenues' that accrued from the frenetic and speculative economic activity of the bubble, that weakness was cruelly exposed by the recession, that followed. So serious was the deterioration on the revenue side of the fiscal equation that MOF tried twice in 1994 to raise the rate of the consumption tax, arguing that an increase in the flat rate from 3% to 7% was needed merely to maintain existing yields. Simultaneously, it had to try to reconcile the need to raise more revenue with demands to cut taxes to stimulate the depressed demand in the economy. The trade-off agreed by the Murayama government in September 1994 provided a reduction of 5.5 trillion in estimated tax yields in FY1994, and an increase in the flat rate of the national consumption tax from 1 April 1997, but limited to 5%.

MOF was more successful in reducing the bond dependency ratio. That was partly the result of its tighter control of the planned expenditure total of the General Account Budget after 1982, but mainly the result of the calculated manipulation of cash flows between it, FILP, and some of the 38 Special Accounts. Nevertheless, it failed to achieve the target of a ratio less than 5% by 1995, although it came close to doing so by 1991, helped by the revenues of the bubble economy; thereafter the ratio moved rapidly and sharply upwards. MOF failed to achieve its policy aim of eliminating special deficit-financing bonds; the target date was twice deferred in the 1980s and achieved only after the end of the period of fiscal reconstruction and the relaxation of spending controls. Success proved temporary; the bonds were re-introduced in 1994 and re-issued in increasing and record amounts for the following six years. Their projected elimination by FY2003, statutorily provided in the Fiscal Structural Reform Act of 1997, was deferred for a third time in the following year, as the Hashimoto and Obuchi governments responded to the deepening economic recession with countercyclical fiscal policies financed by massive borrowing.

While MOF continued to emphasize the importance of 'fiscal responsiveness and flexibility', their restoration proved elusive. The accumulation of debt, and the annual costs of servicing it, grew inexorably throughout the period of fiscal reconstruction and beyond, and continued to squeeze the amount available to finance general expenditures. 'Fiscal rigidification' increased. Debt servicing and other so-called fixed costs absorbed 43% of the Budget in FY2000 compared with 25% in FY1975.

The tighter control of public spending was more apparent than real. MOF achieved some modest success in containing the planned growth of general expenditures, less so the General Account Budget as a whole, but neither was cut in real terms. The totals for both were revised annually in-year, and out-turn expenditures provided profiles of continuous growth throughout the whole of the period 1975–2000. The pressures for more public spending were relieved but not dissipated by a variety of budgetary stratagems and 'special temporary measures'. While those measures were expedient in providing short-term relief for the General Account Budget, they were palliatives for the symptoms of the underlying structural weaknesses.

MOF's pragmatic and expedient response to continuous fiscal stress throughout the period of fiscal reconstruction and beyond was understandable, and from its perspective politically rational. By such short-term expedients as exploiting the potential of FILP as a 'second budget', using it and several Special Accounts as alternative sources of finance to the General Account Budget, cutting and squeezing local government's assigned revenues and transfer payments, suspending statutory payments, by temporary 'borrowings' and 'special measures', and the adroit manipulation of cash flows, MOF was able to present an image and foster an illusion of public spending control consistent with apparent steady progress towards the achievement of its main policy objectives. With a consensus on the need for a radical reform of the tax structure impossible to achieve, the alternative—other than cutting general expenditures in real terms, which political and bureaucratic pressures made difficult or impossible to sustain—was to finance continuous growth with still more government borrowing. Not only would that have added immediately to the rising costs of debt servicing, but the issue of more special deficit-financing bonds would have made the task of their eventual elimination even more difficult. The achievement of that aim, and of restoring balance to the Budget, would have become a still more distant prospect.

MOF's short-term strategy was founded on the belief that it was dealing with conditions of acute fiscal stress that were temporary, the symptoms of which would be relieved by the resumption of higher rates of economic growth in the near future, generating a sufficient surplus of tax revenues to enable it to repay the various loans and borrowings, liquidate the inherited and accumulated debts of Japanese National Railways and other public corporations and Special Accounts, and contribute to the redemption of the national debt. In the 1980s that was not an unreasonable expectation. Revenues grew faster than expenditures in the years of the economic bubble (1987–91), encouraging MOF to make a start on repayment. But the buoyancy of those revenues also encouraged expectations among Spending Ministries and their clienteles of the continued growth of planned expenditures, at rates higher than those experienced for a decade. Moreover, huge increases were approved in-year through Supplementary Budgets, especially in the period preceding Diet elections. In FY1988 the General Account Budget was planned to rise by 4.8%: it increased by 14.3%; in FY1989 a planned rise of 6.6% was converted into a 17% increase through the

Supplementary Budget; and in FY1990, the year of the Lower House election, the largest annual increase in the planned Budget since the beginning of fiscal reconstruction, 9.6%, was raised still further to 15.3%. While it is true that some of the planned and revised growth resulted from MOF's provision for modest repayments and redemptions, general expenditures continued to grow rapidly, accounting for between one-quarter and one-half of the annual budget growth in those years. When tax revenues (on a revised basis) fell in the recession of 1991–5, expenditures continued to grow.

Why was an apparently 'strong' Ministry of Finance, at least until the early 1990s, unable or unwilling or frustrated in its attempts to implement agreed policies to constrain the growth of public spending, the main cause of fiscal stress? This issue is taken up in Chapter 29, but first we examine MOF's performance with the central government budget in the broader context provided by the concept of general government, and then in Chapter 27 compare it with the experience of other G7 countries.

26

Deficits and Debt

In 1978 Japan adopted the new System of National Accounts (SNA) recommended by the UN a decade earlier. It integrates, *inter alia*, five major consumption accounts of the national economy, of which the income and outlay accounts for various institutional sectors include those for 'General Government'. This concept is used by most governments, and provides a common framework and criteria by which to measure, assess, and compare national and international fiscal and financial performance. Broadly, the definition includes all producers providing but not selling government services to the community in three main categories: central government, local government, and social security funds (for details, see ERI 1990). I use General Government in this chapter to analyse the trends of spending in those three categories in Japan throughout the period 1975–2000; in the next, to compare Japan's fiscal performance with other G7 countries.

There are three main performance indicators of General Government: outlays, fiscal balance, and the balance of assets and liabilities (gross and net debt). The results from using them are compared with those obtained by applying MOF's own preferred narrower definition of fiscal balance and debt, which excluded social security funds and included the accounts of public corporations. The definition and measurement of debt is subject to some other qualifications discussed later in the chapter.[1]

GENERAL GOVERNMENT EXPENDITURE

Nominal General Government expenditure increased in every year throughout the whole of the period 1975–2000, apart from FY1997, when the implementation of the Fiscal Structural Reform Act and the caps on most central and local government spending programmes produced a small reduction. Figure 26.1 shows that growth was fastest in the period preceding the declaration of a fiscal crisis in central government's finances in 1980, when annual rates of between 10% and 18% exceeded even the double-digit growth in GDP. Growth slowed in the period of fiscal reconstruction that followed, but nevertheless continued to increase faster than GDP in most years. That trend was reversed briefly in the bubble years of 1988–91, when the growth of GDP

---

[1] In October 2000 the system of collecting and analysing data in the SNA was changed, and time-series for the national accounts revised. The data used here and throughout the book are those available and published in EPA's annual *National Accounts* before that date.

Deficits and Debts

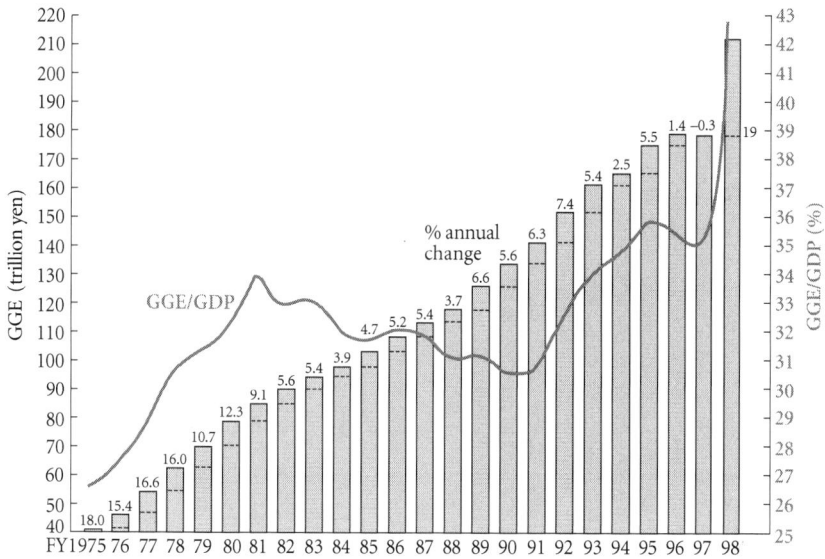

Figure 26.1 *General Government expenditure, FY1975–FY1998*

Nominal values and prices at fiscal year

GGE = current outlays plus net capital outlays. Historic valuation for GDP revised to 1999.

Source: Report on National Accounts (annually), EPA.

outpaced that of General Government (GG). In the recessionary years of the 1990s, GG growth rates were modest compared with those of the previous decade, but now absorbed a larger share of GDP. The GG–GDP ratio increased from 30.7% in 1990 to almost 36% five years later. Over the period as a whole, the ratio increased by more than 10%, half of which occurred before 1980 and was attributable directly to the rapid growth of central and local expenditure in the inauguration of the 'welfare era'. In most years GG outlays increased at a faster rate than GDP. In FY1998 the GG–GDP ratio increased to 42.6%, but that sharp rise was attributed mainly to the one-off capital transfer of 27 trillion debt of the JNR Debt Settlement Corporation, and the Special Account for the National Forestry Service.

The distribution of GG between central and local government spending from 1975 to March 1999 is shown in Figure 26.2. The slow-down in the growth of GG during the period of MOF's fiscal reconstruction was attributable wholly to the retrenchment of local government spending. By the end of 1986 its share had fallen 5% on the 1980 figure, and over 10% on that at the beginning of the fiscal crisis in 1975. Conversely, central government's share of GG actually increased year by year from 1975, and right through the period of fiscal reconstruction. By the end of FY1985–6, its share of 26.3% was 2% higher than in FY1979. Far from cutting and squeezing central government spending, MOF's policies of fiscal reconstruction actually resulted in the continuous

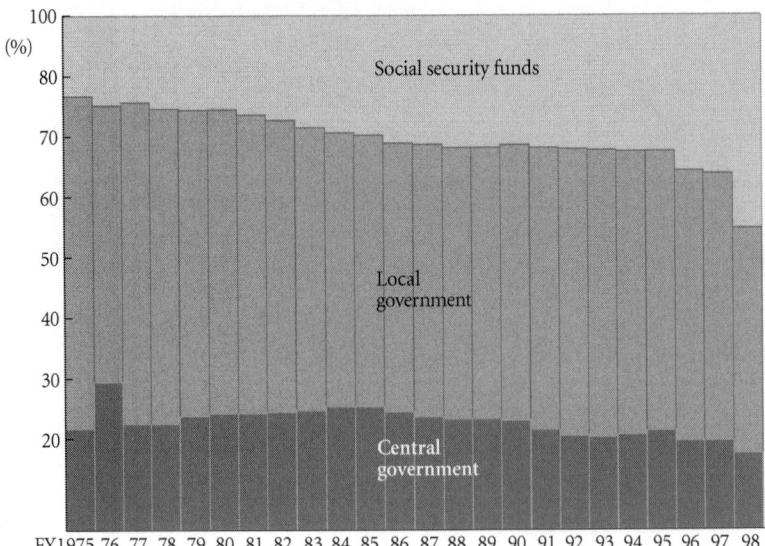

Figure 26.2 *Central and local shares of General Government expenditure, FY1975–FY1998*
Settled Budgets: percentage
Source: *Report on National Accounts* (annually), EPA

growth of both current and capital spending, while those of local government fell sharply. Not until the 1990s did central government's share of GG begin to fall. By FY1996 it was less than 20%; local government's share was about 40%.

The combined outlays of central and local government fell year by year, from almost 77% of GG in 1975 to less than 64% in FY1997. (The figure for 1998 was distorted by the capital transfers from the central government to the private sector, mentioned above.) That declining share reflected the changing functional composition of GG between 1975 and March 1999. Table 26.1 shows that, over the period as a whole, social security increased by more than 10% relative to final consumption expenditure and gross capital formation, to claim 40% of total GG by FY1997. That gain was almost wholly at the expense of the goods and services provided by central and local government, which, after taking more than a third of total GG in 1975, had fallen twenty years later to little more than a quarter. Nevertheless, both final consumption expenditure and gross capital formation continued to grow, albeit at slower rates, during the period of reconstruction in the early 1980s and thereafter. There were no real cuts. As was shown in previous chapters, the sharp fall in the share of GG claimed by gross capital formation in the years of fiscal reconstruction was 'compensated' by the continuous growth of capital investment in the FILP programme, the outlays of which are excluded from the calculation of GG (see below). The relative shares of GG are distorted in FY1998 by the doubling of the 'other' category, the principal cause of

Table 26.1 *Changing composition of General Government expenditure, FY1975–FY1998[a]*
(trillion yen)

FY	Final consumption expenditure Total	%	Gross capital formation Total	%	Social security funds Total	%	Others[b] Total	%	GGE total
1998	50.910	24.0	29.919	14.1	73.042	34.4	58.222	27.5	212.091
1997	50.028	28.5	28.987	16.5	70.144	40.0	29.130	15.0	178.269
1996	48.587	27.0	31.327	17.5	68.169	38.0	30.751	17.5	178.863
1995	47.673	26.9	32.517	18.4	65.170	36.8	29.865	18.0	175.227
1990	39.520	29.0	21.914	16.1	47.452	34.8	25.992	20.0	134.878
1985	31.038	29.6	15.357	14.7	35.762	34.1	20.999	21.6	103.156
1980	24.122	29.7	14.938	18.4	24.907	30.7	14.984	21.2	78.951
1975	15.261	37.4	8.103	20.0	11.826	29.0	5.526	13.8	40.716

[a] General Account Settled Budget.
[b] Includes subsidies, property income, net purchase of land, and some current transfers.
Source: *National Accounts*, 1999, EPA.

which was the net capital transfer to the private sector from central government of 27.4 trillion, mentioned earlier.

THE MEASUREMENT OF JAPAN'S FISCAL PERFORMANCE

MOF consistently argued against the use of the standard definition of General Government to measure its fiscal performance. Its reasons were set out in a paper provocatively entitled 'Why a Discussion of Japanese Government Finances Should not be Based on the General Government Financial Balance' (MOF 1992*a*). Written in 1992 and directed primarily at the audience of foreign governments, especially the USA, and international bodies such as OECD, its aim was to rebut demands for further fiscal expansion because of the continuing surplus on its GG financial balance. During the periods of fiscal reconstruction and consolidation in the 1980s, Japan had come under such pressure, as the economies of the leading industrial countries slowed down. As a party to the Louvre Accord in 1987, it had responded with cautious fiscal expansion.

MOF argued that 'the general government financial balance does not accurately reflect the government's actual fiscal position and should not be the basis for a discussion of government fiscal policy' (MOF 1992*a*: 1). GG was 'an artificial concept constructed and used out of accounting convenience', and 'of questionable value in understanding national financial situations' (p. 3). This was so for two reasons. First, conventionally, the concept of General Government included social security funds. The pension system in Japan was funded differently from elsewhere. It was based on the 'partially funded system' designed to accumulate funds in advance before the system reached maturity to the benefit of future claimants. MOF insisted that the surplus on the social security account arising from the historic accumulation of funds was 'a debt owed to future beneficiaries and should not be drained to cover shortfalls in the central government's budget account' (MOF 1994*b*: 13). The surplus on the balance of the social security funds arose because 'the Japanese pension system is still at a lower level of maturity than systems in the other leading countries. Given that the Japanese demographic structure is ageing with unprecedented speed, it is fully expected that this social security surplus will be rapidly eroded' (MOF 1992*a*: 5). MOF further argued that the USA, some of whose analysts were among its fiercest critics, excluded the social security surplus from the calculations of its overall financial balance; since legislation in 1990, it had been 'off-budget', and so excluded from estimates of the fiscal deficit.

Social security funds were deposited in several Special Accounts[2] and were not counted as receipts or revenues to be used *directly* to finance expenditure in the General Account Budget. In practice, the distinction between pension funds and General Account revenues is perhaps less clear-cut than MOF's rhetoric suggests. First, as we saw in the previous chapter, from time to time MOF suspended statutory payments from the General Account Budget into the various Special Accounts for pension and insurance funds, tantamount to treating those funds as negative expenditure. Secondly, about a half of the funds in the Special Accounts were subsequently deposited with the Trust Fund Bureau Fund, and used (by MOF) to finance FILP loans and investments. Some of those funds were used to underwrite some of the General Account Budget debt bought by FILP. There is in practice little difference between exploiting the surpluses in those ways and using them directly as revenue to finance purchase of government bonds to cover the deficit on the General Account. Partly, and for those reasons some analysts argued that MOF's claim to exclude social security funds from GG calculations was invalidated by their use to finance debt elsewhere in the public sector.

The second reason for MOF's objection to the use of the standard definition of General Government was that conventionally it excluded the balance on the financial accounts of public corporations. In Japan these 'undertake public works and other investment as part and parcel of government policy and at direct government initiative ... and it is not right that their figures should be excluded' (MOF 1992*a*: 7). Public corporations, especially the 11 public banks and finance corporations, implemented capital investment programmes amounting to one-fifth of the total public-sector fixed capital formation. Collectively, they were in deficit for all but one year of the period 1975–96. As I shall now explain, the exclusion of social security funds, and the inclusion of the financial balances of public corporations, have a marked effect on the calculation of Japan's fiscal deficit and debt, and hence on the assessment of its performance here and, in the next chapter, compared with other countries.

---

[2] Special Account for Welfare Insurance; Special Account for National Pensions; Special Account for Seamen's Insurance; Special Account for Workmen's Insurance; National Government Employee Mutual Aid Associations; and various Employees' Pension Funds.

GENERAL GOVERNMENT FISCAL BALANCES

From FY1956 until the first oil crisis in FY1973, the fiscal balance of General Government was in deficit only twice, in FY1958 and FY1966. After 1973 deficits rose steadily, to reach a peak of 4.45% of GDP in FY1979, prior to the initiation of MOF's policies of fiscal reconstruction. Figure 26.3 shows the trends for the whole of the period from 1975 to March 1999, and those of the balances as a proportion of GDP. After 1979, there was a progressive annual reduction of deficits until the achievement of a surplus in 1987, sustained for the following five years. Deficits re-emerged as the economy moved into recession, and the government responded with countercyclical fiscal policies. By volume, deficits were now greater than any previously experienced. By FY1996 the total of over 20 trillion was equivalent to more than 4% of GDP. That was dwarfed two years later by deficits that had swollen to nearly 55 trillion, absorbing 11% of GDP. Not only was that the largest ratio for 50 years, it was greater than that of any of the other 25 OECD members.

A disaggregation of GG in Figure 26.4 reveals the distribution of fiscal balances between central and local government, and social security. The substantial surplus on the latter throughout the period from 1975 to March 1999 accounts almost wholly for the overall surplus on GG achieved over 1987–92. The balances of central and local government combined remained in deficit throughout, although the size of that deficit was progressively reduced in the period of fiscal reconstruction. Local government was

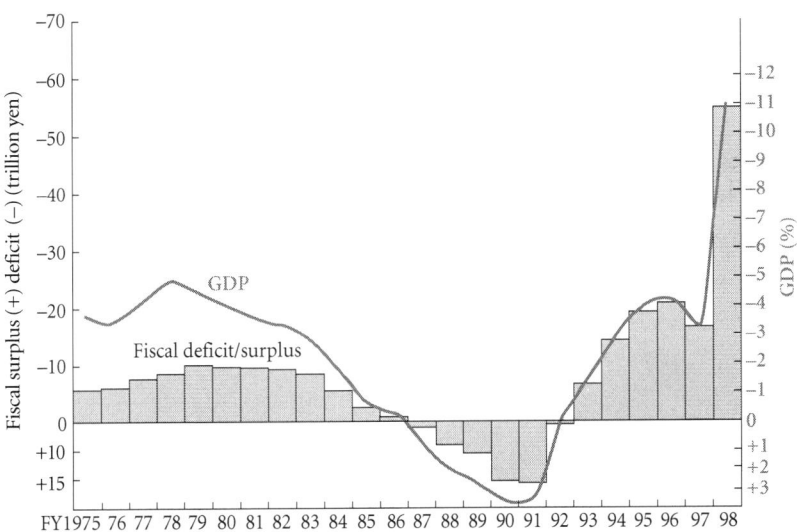

Figure 26.3 *General Government fiscal balance, FY1975–FY1998*

Nominal GDP; Settled Budgets: trillion yen

Source: Report on National Accounts (annually), EPA.

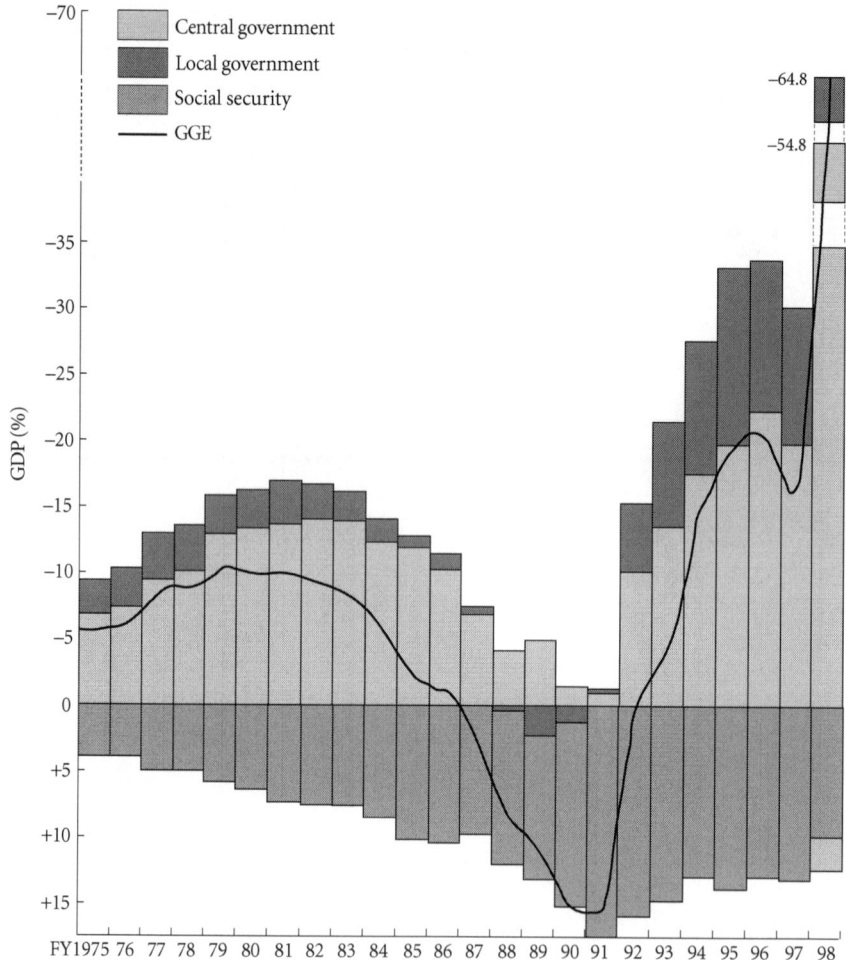

Figure 26.4 *Composition of the fiscal balance of General Government, FY1975–FY1998*
Settled Budgets: surplus (+) or deficit (−) as percentage of nominal GDP
Source: *Report on National Accounts* (annually), EPA.

more successful in reducing its deficit than central government and began to do so four years earlier, in 1976 (Wright 1999c: table 7). Moreover, it achieved three years of surplus in the late 1980s, a performance unmatched by central government. However, the latter began from a much larger base: at its peak in 1982 the deficit totalled 14.21 trillion; that of local government never exceeded 4 trillion until the 1990s. Two-thirds of the combined fiscal deficit was contributed by central government in 1975, and that proportion increased annually throughout the period of fiscal reconstruction to reach more than 90% by the end of the decade. The sharp rise in local government's share of the combined deficits from 1992 was the result mainly of additional local spending on public works and investment projects in MOF's countercyclical fiscal policies.

Nevertheless, for a decade after 1982 there was an annual progressive reduction in the size of central government's deficit, of a magnitude to justify MOF's claim that it was on course to achieve a surplus before the fiscal implications of the recession overwhelmed that progress. By 1991 the deficit was less than a trillion yen, absorbing 0.21% of GDP compared with 5.67% in 1979. By whatever means of budgetary manipulation and sleight-of-hand that had been accomplished, it was an impressive achievement and, as I shall show in the next chapter, bears comparison with other G7 countries. However, the largest and sharpest reduction in the deficit on its own budget occurred *after* the abandonment of MOF's policies of fiscal reconstruction in 1987, when the bubble economy generated substantial growth in revenues, more than matching the accelerating growth of spending. The improvement was the result less of MOF's budgetary policies than of the short-term adventitious benefits of GDP growth. 'Windfall revenues', estimated at 63.5 trillion of additional increments over a six-year period, contributed substantially to the reduction of the deficit. Half of these were assigned specifically to debt reduction and servicing the remaining debt (Ishi 2000).

As explained in earlier chapters, the aggregate of expenditures and revenues of central and local government, social security, and public corporations (together with FILP) were determined and controlled by MOF, and cash flows between them were manipulated expediently to relieve pressure on the General Account. A more balanced assessment of General Government would perhaps then allow the inclusion of the financial balances of public corporations, as MOF and some analysts have argued (see e.g. Atoda 1994). Figure 26.5 compares three profiles of GGE–GDP ratios using different definitions of expenditure: the standard SNA measurement of GGE (including social security); GGE plus balances of public corporations; and MOF's preferred indicator, GGE plus public corporations and minus social security. The profiles are very similar, but with the significant difference that MOF's definition produces no years of surplus in the period of the bubble economy, and of course higher values for deficits throughout the period.

There is a nice irony in that the narrower definition, which MOF argued was more appropriate to the singularity of Japanese public finance (at least in the 1980s), produced trends of fiscal deficits and surpluses that were less favourable to an assessment of the effectiveness of its policies of fiscal reconstruction in the 1980s than the SNA definition of GG. Why then did it object to the use of the conventional GG–GDP ratio, employed by many of the other G7 countries at that time, to measure its fiscal performance? Because to have done so would have put at risk the achievement of a broader politico-economic objective: to resist international pressure to stimulate domestic demand through policies of fiscal expansion. From the middle of the 1980s, the Japanese government was under continual pressure from industrialized countries, particularly the USA, and international economic organizations such as G7, IMF, and the OECD to contribute to policies designed to alleviate the economic effects of global recession by expanding its public sector. Japan was urged to increase public spending because its fiscal balance as measured conventionally by GG was in surplus, or was

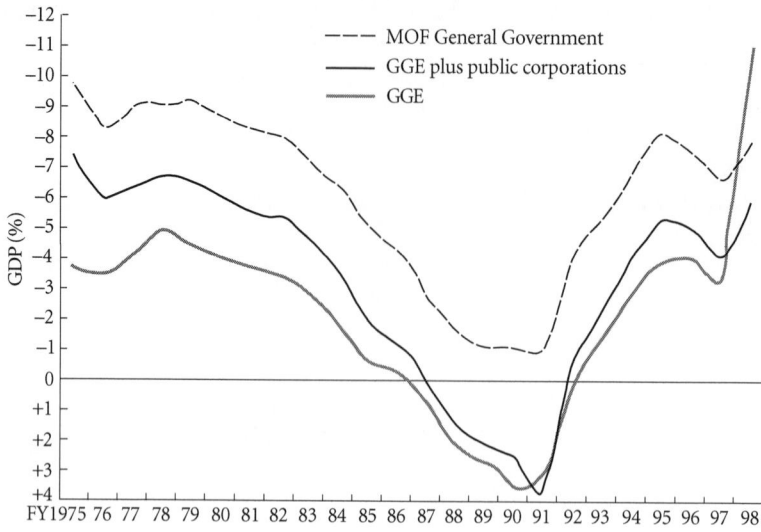

Figure 26.5 *Profiles of fiscal balances of General Government, FY1975–FY1998*
Settled Budgets: surplus (+) or deficit (−) as percentage of nominal GDP
Source: Report on National Accounts (annually), EPA.

running only a small deficit. As explained earlier, MOF counter-claimed that the concept of General Governmnet was inappropriate to Japan, and that the exclusion of the social security surplus and the inclusion of the deficit on public corporations produced an overall and substantial deficit on the financial balance. MOF also had to contend with growing domestic pressures from MITI, MOFA, and senior LDP officials to relax fiscal policy (see Funabashi 1988). As we have seen, its reluctant concession of a 6 trillion stimulus in the Supplementary Budget of May 1987 effectively brought the period of fiscal reconstruction to an end.

Resistance to such pressures both before and after the Louvre Accord in 1987 was partly because of the primacy afforded to the domestic imperatives of fiscal reconstruction—restraining the growth of the General Account Budget, and avoiding an increase in dependence on government borrowing, set in the broader context of the fiscal implications of an ageing population. But MOF was also concerned with the broader implications of expanding demand in the domestic economy through fiscal measures. Expansion was linked to the growing international pressures to open its domestic markets to foreign competition, and to deregulate economic activity. Pressure from the international economic community for fiscal expansion was part of the broader agenda of economic reforms that dominated the trade talks between Japan and the USA in the 1980s and early 1990s, and which led to the Structural Impediments Initiative concluded in 1990, and the agreement to open the domestic rice market

Deficits and Debts

concluded with the GATT in 1995. Paradoxically (but conventionally), as the recession of the 1990s in the Japanese economy persisted and deepened, and proved stubbornly resistant to countercyclical economic, financial, and fiscal measures, MOF justified a succession of ever-larger mini-budgets of public investment and public works partly by reference to such 'foreign pressure' (*gaiatsu*).

GENERAL GOVERNMENT FINANCIAL LIABILITIES: GROSS AND NET DEBT

The direct consequences of the almost continuous trend of deficits described above was that Japan's accumulated debt increased rapidly throughout the period 1975–2000. 'Debt' can be defined and measured in several different ways, producing very different results (see OECD 1998 for a discussion). The financial liabilities of General Government are calculated both gross and net, and conventionally are represented as a ratio of GDP. In Japan's case, the substantial difference between them (more than 60% of GDP in FY1998) is mainly the result of the exclusion (gross) and inclusion (net) of social security funds mentioned earlier. At the simplest level, Japan's 'unconsolidated' gross debt (including social security) as a proportion of GDP rose from 24% in 1975 to an estimated 132.9% at the end of March 2001 (Figure 26.6). 'Consolidation' of *real* financial assets and liabilities produces very much higher estimates of both gross and net debt (OECD 2000). For example, the inclusion of

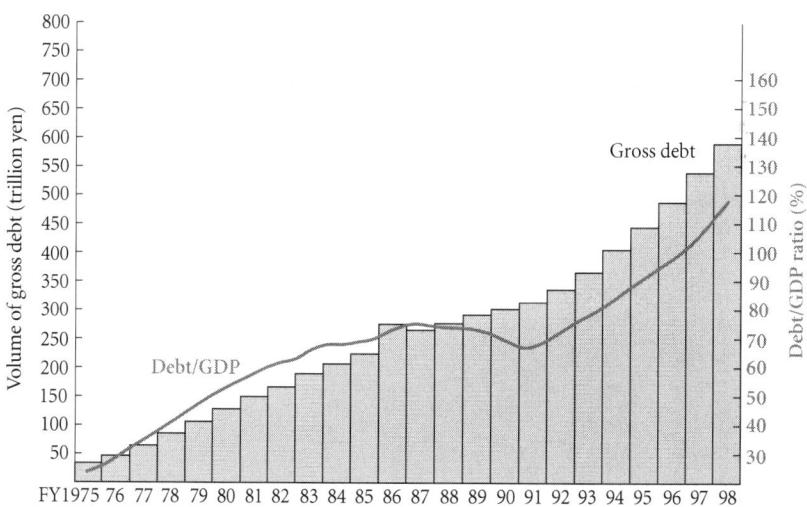

Figure 26.6 *General Government gross debt, FY1975–FY1998*

Nominal GDP: trillion yen

Source: *Report on National Accounts* (annually), EPA.

implicit gross liabilities such as those of the welfare pension system would add more than 700 trillion to official calculations of gross debt; and contingent liabilities, for example government guarantees of the external financing of government-affiliated institutions, would increase that still further.

MOF underestimated net debt, first, because the definition of 'social security funds' until October 2000 included some 50 trillion of corporate pension funds; and, secondly because it excluded the cost of the future payments of subsidies by central government to FILP agencies, a significant offset of their estimated financial assets. Published data are unavailable, but the total is unlikely to be less than the 6.4 trillion estimated in MOF's pilot study of the policy (subsidy) cost in 14 of them in 1998 (to be discussed in Chapter 28). Figure 26.7 compares MOF's definition of unadjusted gross debt (A) with that of the OECD definition (B), which includes some consolidation of the assets and liabilities of public corporations. The latter produces lower values throughout the range of the time-series. But whatever definition and method of

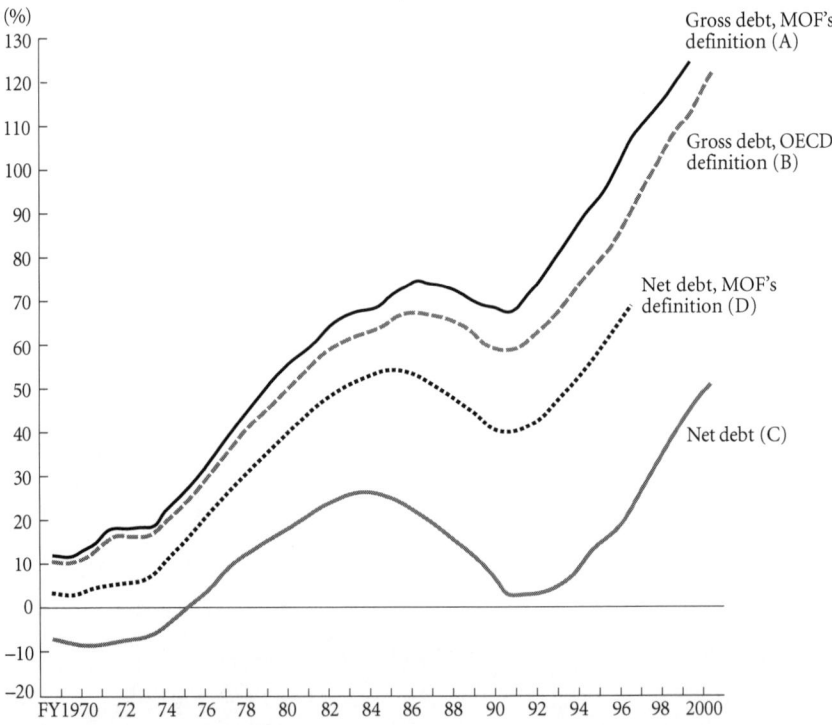

Figure 26.7 *Profiles of General Government gross and net debt, FY1969–FY2000*
Nominal GDP: percentage
FY1998–FY2000 are OECD estimates.
Source: EPA and OECD, 1999 and 2000.

calculation is used, the profile of gross debt is similar to that shown in Figure 26.6, with a steeply rising trend in the 1990s.

The net financial liabilities of General Government are more difficult to calculate. What counts as assets and liabilities is arguable, and how both are valued and incorporated into the balance sheet of GG is contested (OECD 1998; Ostrom 2000). Using MOF's definition, the net debt was 3.1 trillion in 1975, 2% of GDP. A decade later, in the period of fiscal reconstruction, that had reached 88.5 trillion, equivalent to a quarter of GDP (Wright 1999c: table 10). Thereafter there was a progressive fall in both the amount and the net debt–GDP ratio. As with the trends of deficit and gross debt, the improvement did not really begin until the late 1980s, *after* the abandonment of MOF's policies of fiscal reconstruction. By the early 1990s the net debt figure was less than 4% of GDP, but by 1998 the total of net debt had risen sharply and at 164 trillion was equivalent to a third of GDP.

The basis of those calculations almost certainly understates the size of the financial liabilities. The quality of some of the assets included by MOF is questionable. For example, as I have argued in earlier chapters, many of the loans and investments made through and by FILP agencies are unlikely to be repaid, and were sustained as assets only by continual operating subsidies. Any lower valuation of those and other assets in 'residual categories' in the national accounts results in an increase in the trend of net debt throughout the whole period.

The inclusion or exclusion of pension funds has a more marked effect still. It can plausibly be argued that they should be excluded from calculations of net debt (as MOF urged in calculations of gross debt and fiscal deficits) because they are not available in the medium term to meet GG budgetary obligations. The result is a steep increase in the trend of net debt throughout the period. As Figure 26.7 shows, on that basis net debt (D) had reached 60% of GDP by FY1996, compared with the 16.6% in the official calculation (C).

The significance of those and other measurements of financial liabilities is the extent to which debt of that magnitude is sustainable without provoking a situation of acute fiscal crisis. Continual deficits increase the amount of debt, which in turn increases the costs of servicing that debt, which in turn contributes to an increase in the size of the deficit. The risk is that deficits and hence debts might spiral out of control. There is also the issue of increasing difficulty in financing debt through the issue of government bonds, and the effect of doing so on domestic and international financial markets. In Japan's case, the rising trend of debt is compounded by the under-funding of publicly provided pensions with a progressively ageing population. There is as well the vexed question of the extent to which public debt of that size is a burden on future generations in a declining population (see Komiya 1999). The next chapter compares Japan's debt position with that of other G7 countries. Here we are concerned mainly with the contribution of central government to the accumulation of gross debt, and use the unconsolidated definition and measurement.

The gross debt–GDP calculations in Figure 26.6 combine the liabilities of central government and local government and the social security funds. In FY1975 these totalled 36 trillion, rising annually throughout the next 25 years. In the period of fiscal reconstruction, 1980–7, the amount of debt doubled, the proportion of GDP rising from 53% to 75% (Wright 1999c: table 9). It fell back during the succeeding years of the bubble economy, but rose sharply from FY1992 as the growth of the economy slowed, tax revenues declined, and public spending increased.

Central government's financial liabilities contributed most to the accumulation of that debt and its growth during the period 1975–99. Figure 26.8 shows the composition of gross debt, omitting the contribution of the gross liabilities of social security averaging between 0.3% and 1.3% per annum. In 1975 the ratio of central to local government debt was less than 2:1; the gross debt of the social security funds was insignificant (Wright 1999c: table 9). By 1989 the ratio was over 3.5:1. Not only was the size of central government's debt the major determinant of overall general government debt, but its share increased faster than local government's. In the period of fiscal reconstruction, its debt–GDP ratio increased by 50%, while that of local government grew by less than 20%. In the 1990s local government's share of gross debt increased faster than central government's, although the huge volume increases of the latter represented a sharp acceleration in its debt–GDP ratio.

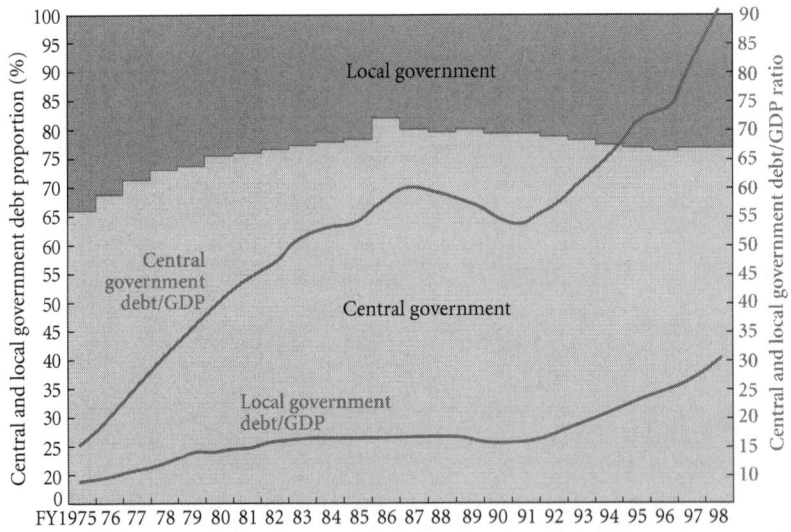

Figure 26.8 *Composition of General Government gross debt, FY1975–FY1998*

Nominal GDP: percentage

The gross liabilities of social security averaged less than 0.5% per annum throughout the period and are omitted.

The aggregates for central and local government (and social security) are slightly larger than the total for general government owing to the netting out of some liabilities in the latter.

Source: *Report on National Accounts* (annually), EPA.

CONCLUSIONS

The apparent turn-around in Japan's public finances in the 1980s is attributed by most analysts to the effective implementation of MOF's policies of fiscal reconstruction of the central government budget (see e.g. Asako *et al.* 1991; Shibata 1993; Kawai and Onitsuka 1996; Ihori 1996; Suzuki 1999; Alexander 1999*a*). Failing to distinguish the appearance from the reality, some have even credited MOF with achieving its goal of a balanced budget by 1990. It is true that by manipulating cash flows MOF had succeeded in that year in eliminating (temporarily) the issue of special deficit-financing bonds; but the General Account Budget remained in deficit as a whole, with MOF continuing to borrow to cover capital expenditure and to finance the costs of servicing the debt as a whole. In any case, even that relief proved temporary, as MOF was forced to issue deficit bonds once more in 1994.

The analysis in this chapter of the organizational and functional composition of the trends of GG outlays, fiscal balances, and debt points to a different conclusion, and shows that conventional assessment is subject to some important qualifications. First, while MOF's policies of fiscal reconstruction certainly helped to slow the secular trend of GG growth generally, they did not reverse it. For most years in the period 1975–2000, the rate of growth of outlays exceeded that of GDP, with the result that the GG–GDP ratio rose from a quarter to more than a third. While both central and local government spending contributed to that growth, social security funds grew faster than either, increasing its share of GDP from a quarter to more than a third. Secondly, the slower rate of growth of GG in the years of fiscal reconstruction was attributable almost wholly to the retrenchment of local government spending. Central government's current and capital spending continued to grow throughout the period of fiscal reconstruction and beyond.

Thirdly, the fiscal balances of central government, local government, and public corporations remained in deficit for almost the whole of the period 1975–2000. While MOF's policies of fiscal reconstruction undoubtedly helped to reduce the magnitude of those deficits in the 1980s, the surplus on GG conventionally measured was achieved (briefly) only after the abandonment of those policies in 1987, and was attributable almost wholly to the substantial and accumulating surpluses on social security funds, and to the rapid growth of the economy in the bubble years (increasing the size of the GDP denominator) and the growth of 'windfall' tax revenues (depressing the size of the debt numerator). Fourthly, central government's financial liabilities contributed most to the accumulation of debt, and its rapid growth, throughout the whole of the period 1975–2000. From 1992 onwards, both central and local government were obliged to borrow larger amounts of money to compensate for shrinking tax revenues and to finance the implementation of countercyclical policies. A sharp rise in the stock of public debt, and a slow-down in economic growth, combined to produce a surge in the debt–GDP ratio.

Finally, although this chapter has been concerned mainly with spending, as I have emphasized in earlier chapters, MOF's failure to reform the tax structure to generate additional revenues, combined with falling tax revenues in the economic recession of the 1990s, meant that central government's deficits and debts were as much or more driven by shortages of revenue, apart from the 'windfalls' of the unsustainable 'bubble economy'.

FILP spending is not counted in General Government. Its revenues were derived not from taxation and borrowing, but (until April 2001) mainly from postal savings and pension funds compulsorily deposited with MOF's Trust Fund Bureau Fund. Its inclusion would have no effect on the overall financial balance of GG, nor on the GDP–fiscal deficit, as revenue and expenditure were balanced annually. However, as shown in Chapter 23, FILP was used increasingly as an alternative to the General Account Budget as a source of finance for some kinds of public investment, and more generally for public works—for example the financing of the activities of the public banks and finance corporations and some public works organizations through its control of Special Accounts, and the underwriting of a proportion of both central and local government debt. It was used also increasingly to subsidize some central government capital expenditure programmes. Some of the contingent liabilities incurred in FILP were implicitly guaranteed by government, for example loans to subsidize operating costs. There is then an argument for the inclusion of a proportion of FILP expenditure in annual calculations of GG. Its continued exclusion therefore understates the GG aggregate, and also the amount of public debt. The Trust Fund Bureau Fund held a large proportion of pension funds which it invested through FILP agencies. Those assets are not consolidated in the accounts of GG. Their inclusion, it is estimated, would raise the gross debt by between 5% and 10% through the period 1975–96 (OECD 1998). The net debt position would be unaffected, as the Trust Fund Bureau held no net assets itself. However, as I have argued, the total of net debt is affected by the valuation of unconsolidated assets and liabilities, among which are those of FILP agencies.

27

Japan's Fiscal Performance in an International Context

All G7 (and most other) governments experienced a profound shock to their fiscal systems in the mid-1970s. The proximate cause was the first oil crisis, resulting in a general slow-down in economic activity, unstable and rising levels of inflation, and balance-of-payments difficulties. The effects were experienced differentially, but for most countries the fiscal consequences of rising deficits and debt were symptoms of a longer-term progressive deterioration in national finances. Although the severity of those symptoms differed, and the combination of historical factors contributing to rising public spending varied, the experience of fiscal stress provoked similar responses. Most G7 governments embarked upon policies of fiscal reconstruction in the late 1970s and early 1980s to cope with the symptoms of persistent deficits and rising levels of debt caused by rising public spending and revenue shortages. At the same time, there was a crisis of confidence in the ability of governments to deliver 'successful' economic policies, and in the Keynesian economic theories that had underpinned them since 1944. Policies of fiscal reconstruction were legitimated ideologically by the 'end of Keynesianism', and by the end of the political consensus among contending political parties of the strategic role of the public sector in managing the economy.

The spread and subsequent dominance of neo-liberal ideas on the management of industrialized economies affected all aspects of the public sector. Applied to the administrative context of budgets and budget-making, they brought, in all G7 countries in the 1980s (but later in Italy), a reassessment of the role of the public sector, and of the size, scope, and purpose of publicly provided universal benefits and services. There was a process of continuous change in the administrative context within which budgetary systems were operated, while those systems themselves were reformed to re-centralize control so as to achieve more effective short-term control of the budget aggregates. Policies to cut and squeeze programme expenditures, and to constrain the growth of total spending, were implemented at the federal level in the USA, Canada, and Germany, and at the central level in France, Italy, the UK, and Japan. There were profound effects as well on the provision of public services at the local, regional, and provincial state levels, as all G7 governments sought to curb subnational spending.

This chapter sets the trends of Japan's public-sector spending, examined in the previous chapter, in the broader context of those of other G7 countries, and assesses the effectiveness of MOF's policies to reconstruct the finances of central government compared with the performance of other central and federal governments. It does not deal with the broader issue of why neo-liberal economic reforms were taken up by most G7 countries in the 1980s but not by Japan (or Germany).

Before we begin, it needs to be emphasized that, despite all the economic and fiscal vicissitudes of the 1990s, Japan's economy remained the world's second largest, and cumulative growth in real terms compared very favourably with that of the other G7 countries from 1989 to 1996 (Figure 27.1); only Germany out-performed it. But the slow-down in the Japanese economy after 1991 allowed first the USA and then all but Italy to catch up, and by 1998 to overtake it.

GENERAL GOVERNMENT: EXPENDITURE, DEFICITS, AND DEBTS IN G7

Outlays

In the aftermath of the first oil shock in the 1970s, and the slow-down in economic growth, general government expenditure (GGE) in G7 countries as a whole increased from a third of GDP to more than 40% by 1982 (Figure 27.2). Retrenchment in the 1980s produced a gradual reduction, but a further increase in the first half of the next decade. By 1993 it stood at 41%. Japan's GGE profile was little different, but from a much lower base-line of roughly 20% in the early 1970s. Outlays in Japan subsequently

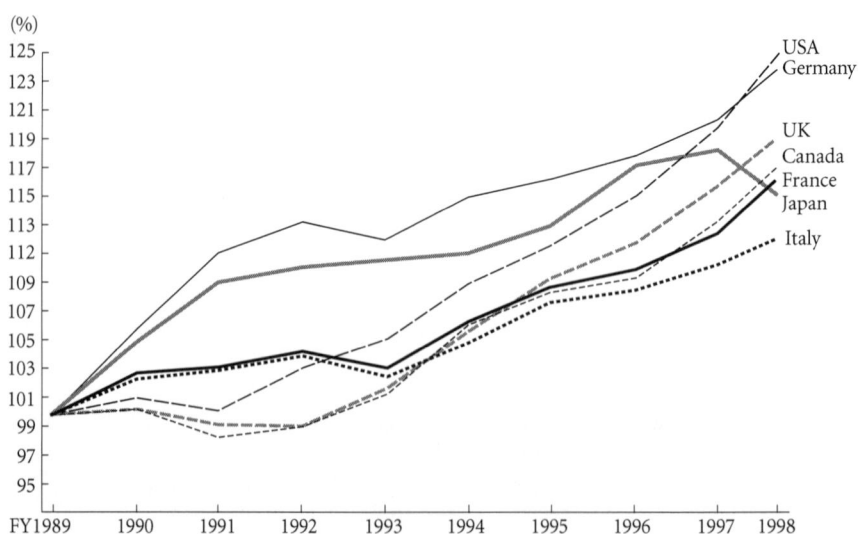

Figure 27.1 *Cumulative economic growth: Japan and G7, FY1989–FY1998*
Annual percentage; 1989 = 100

Source: *Economic Outlook, 1999*, OECD.

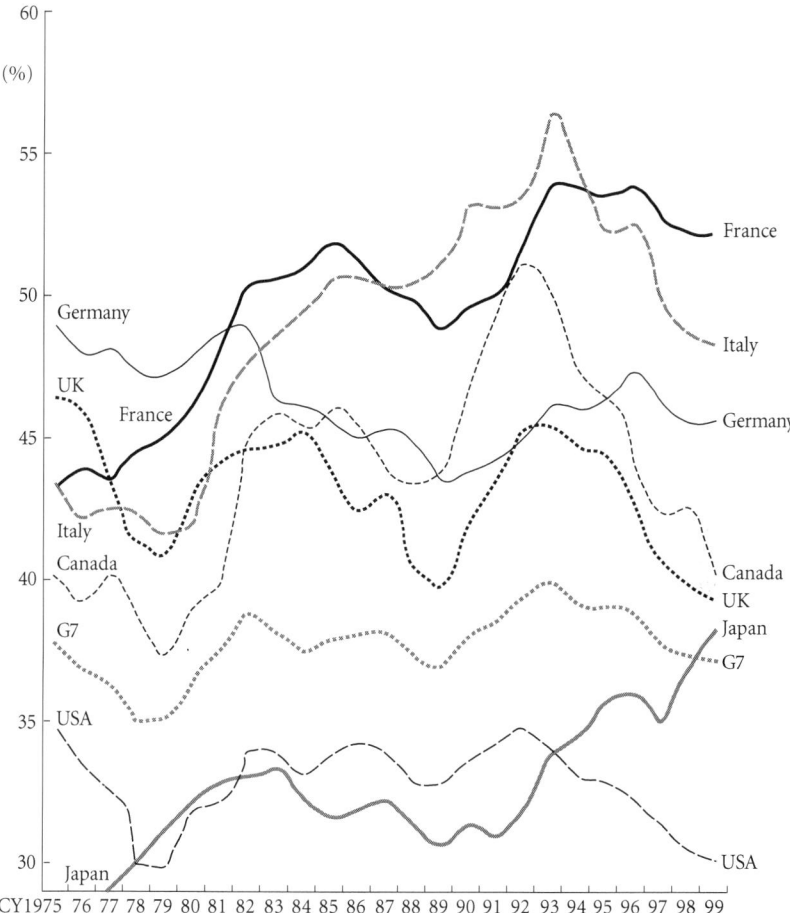

Figure 27.2   *General government expenditure in G7, CY1975–CY1999*
Annual percentage; nominal GDP

GGE = current outlays plus net capital outlays. Calendar year basis—Japan FY converted to CY. Numbers are subject to revision for countries that have changed the basis of their National Accounts.

Source: *Economic Outlook*, no. 67, June 2000, OECD.

grew at a faster rate than in other G7 countries, to stand at more than 33% by 1982. Japan allocated a smaller but increasing proportion of its GDP to GGE than other G7 countries throughout the period 1975–2000, although the differentials with the USA and the UK narrowed in the last two decades. MOF was neither more nor less successful in containing the growth of public spending in the period of fiscal reconstruction in 1975–86 than other comparable countries. In the 1990s as a whole, Japan's public spending grew faster than other G7 countries, and MOF was less successful than its counterparts. However, the cyclical component of that growth accounted for about 25%, the consequence of repeated fiscal stimuli.

Composition

Japan's final public consumption expenditure was only a half of that of European G7 countries, and lower still compared with the USA, accounted for partly by its lower level of defence spending. Japan spent less of its GDP on each of the main functions of government—education, health, and social services for example—than other G7 countries apart from the USA, though even the USA spent marginally more on public health, and considerably more on public education. However, Japan's capital spending in each category exceeded that of almost all of them (OECD *Annual National Accounts*).

Balances

General government budget balances can be measured and compared as shares of GDP in four main ways: (1) the ordinary or conventional balance, expressed as a deficit or surplus; (2) structural balance, which attempts to remove the effects of the business cycle on the ordinary balance, expressed as a share of potential GDP; (3) inflation-adjusted balance, which corrects the ordinary balance for the impact of inflation; and (4) the primary balance, which removes from government expenditure the interest payments made to holders of public debt. An analysis of the trends of balances using those four measures for G7 countries (OECD *Annual National Accounts, passim*) points to four broad conclusions. First, the fiscal situation deteriorated in all seven countries from about the mid-1970s, in the recessionary conditions induced by the effects of the first oil crisis. Influenced by Keynesian theories, governments responded with fiscal policies to increase expenditures and cut taxes. Revenues fell and fiscal deficits widened.

Secondly, the poor fiscal performance continued for about a decade until governments began to take corrective measures, helped by more favourable conditions for economic growth. The combined deficits of G7 countries fell by about 3% over 1983–9. Japan alone ran a surplus for six consecutive years between 1987 and 1992, eight years on a primary balance basis. (The UK achieved a small surplus in 1988 and 1989.) That improvement occurred after the relaxation of MOF's policies of fiscal reconstruction from 1987 onwards, and was due mainly to the generation of increased revenues in the period of the bubble economy, which helped to reduce the deficits of both central and local government. Thirdly, after 1989 the fiscal situation among G7 countries deteriorated once again, partly for cyclical reasons; 1993 was among the worst years fiscally for the period from 1975.

A fourth general trend became apparent in the second half of the decade: from 1994, all G7 countries (apart from Japan) experienced a dramatic and sustained improvement in their fiscal performance, moving towards or achieving a surplus on the general government balance. As the Japanese economy moved into recession, the falling revenues and increased spending of both central and local government combined to produce a sharp and sustained deterioration in the financial balance. Deficits increased for seven consecutive years to reach −10.7% by FY1999. A comparison of the primary balances shows Japan's fiscal situation in a worse light still. While all G7 countries show substantial and rising surpluses on their financial balances so measured, Japan is alone in deficit and substantially so. The exclusion of social security funds produces an even worse performance, with larger deficits (and no years of surplus) on the general government financial balance for the whole of the period 1975–99, reaching −8.9% of GDP (on a calendar year basis) by the latter date. Figure 27.3 compares Japan's financial performance with other G7 countries in the 1990s, excluding social security funds for both Japan and the USA, as MOF argued. More significantly, it shows all of the G7 countries but Japan showed a trend from the early 1990s of improving financial balances.

The Growth of Public Debt

Fiscal deficits that persist over time result in the growth and accumulation of public debt, with important economic and financial consequences such as the possible crowding out of private investment as increasing government expenditure and/or tax cuts pre-empt potential investment funds; the absorption of savings that might

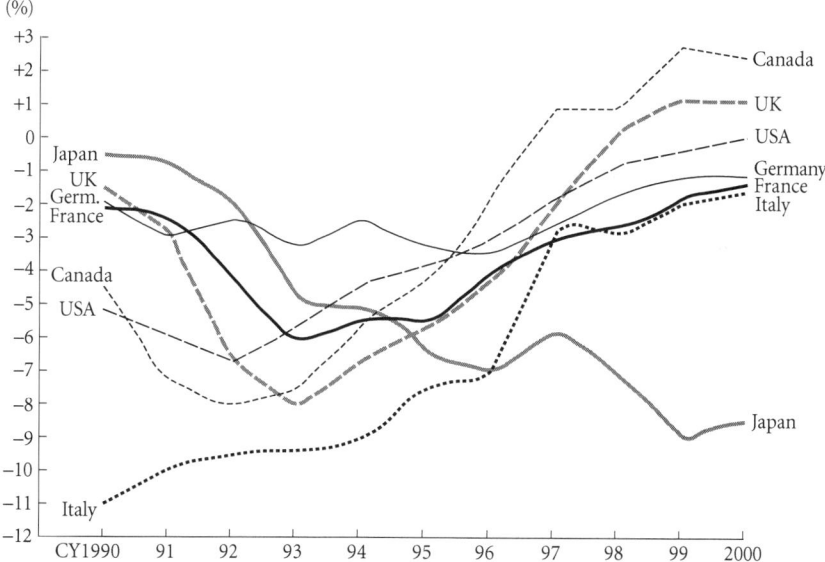

Figure 27.3 *General government fiscal balances in G7, CY1990–CY2000*
Settled Budgets: surplus (+) or deficit (−) as percentage of nominal GDP
USA and Japan exclude social security funds.
Source: Economic Outlook, no. 67, June 2000, OECD; *National Accounts* (annually), OECD.

otherwise be attracted to overseas projects; the adverse effects on interest rates and employment, and the risk of instability in financial markets. In the G7 countries as a group, there was little change in the ratio of gross public debt to GDP throughout the 1970s, but in the following decade it increased from 42.9% to 61.3%, and rose rapidly to over 76% by 1998. Thereafter the trend was a declining one (OECD 2000).

MOF repeatedly compared Japan's unfavourable gross debt with that of the USA and other G7 and OECD countries. Figure 27.4 shows that as a proportion of GDP it was throughout the 1980s consistently some 5%–10% greater than the USA, and larger still compared with all G7 countries, apart from Italy and Canada. It was also higher than both G7 and OECD averages, although the difference here was less marked. The rising trend of gross debt among G7 countries from 1975 was mirrored in Japan, apart from the years of the bubble economy when the reduction in borrowing, and the retirement of some debt, produced a gradual fall from the high point of 67.5% in 1987. The total began to rise again with the resumption of heavy borrowing during the recession of the 1990s. Overall, in the period 1975–2000 Japan's gross debt performance was considerably worse than that of other G7 countries, apart from Italy and, after the mid-1980s, Canada, until 1998. From the middle of the 1990s, the long-term trend of

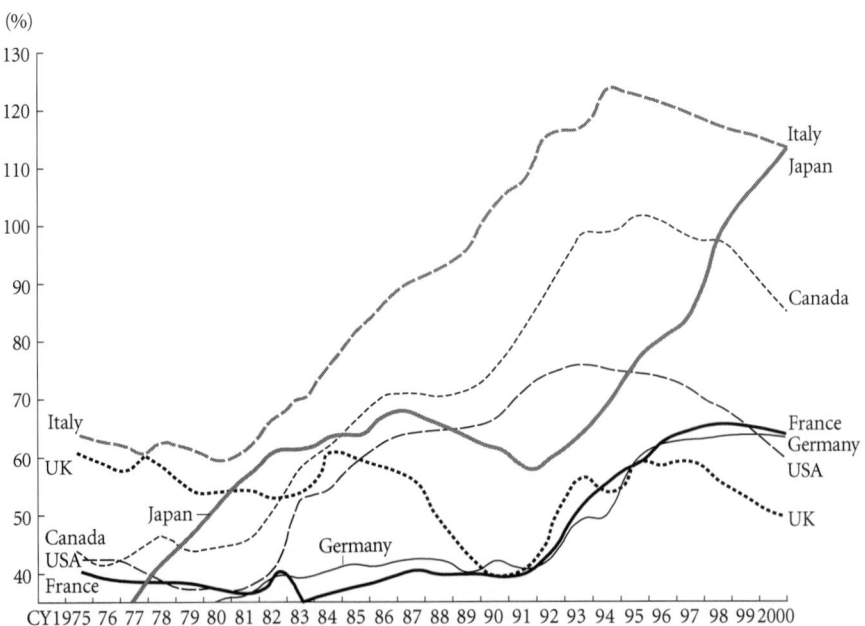

Figure 27.4 *General Government Gross Financial Liabilities in G7, CY1975–CY2000*
Settled Budgets; nominal GDP: percentages

Figures for some countries are estimates in CY1999 and CY2000.

Source: *Economic Outlook*, no. 67, June 2000, OECD; *The Japanese Budget in Brief 2000*, Budget Bureau, MOF.

rising debt in G7 countries levelled out, and then began to fall, in the UK, France, Germany, and Italy, influenced by the Maastricht criterion for membership of the European Monetary Union (EMU). Japan was a striking exception to that trend. By 1999 its gross debt totalled more than 100% of GDP and was set to rise to 130% at the end of FY2000, as MOF borrowed heavily to finance ever larger packages of countercyclical fiscal policies.

Japan's net debt position was superior to that of all other G7 countries throughout most of the period 1975–2000, where there were rising trends of between 20% and 50%; Italy's increased from 67% in 1983 to more than 100% by the end of the century. By contrast, Japan's trend of net debt was downwards, from 26% in 1983 to 4.2% in 1992 (OECD 2000). Apart from the UK in the 1980s, there was no comparable progressive reduction elsewhere. Japan's performance was due mainly to the different methods of collection and accumulation of social security funds, as explained in the previous chapter. Overall, the substantial and continuing surpluses on the financial balance of its social security funds—greater than those in other countries—together with MOF's heroic valuation of financial assets and liabilities (discussed in the previous chapter), combined to produce a performance greatly superior to that elsewhere until 1996, when Japan's net debt alone continued on a rising trend.

CENTRAL/FEDERAL GOVERNMENTS' FISCAL PERFORMANCE

How did MOF's performance with the central government's General Account Budget compare with that of other G7 countries? For the purpose of comparison here, I refer to three performance indicators used by MOF: the central government's fiscal deficit[1] as a ratio of total central government expenditure; its long-term outstanding debt as a ratio of GDP; and the ratio of interest payments to total central government expenditure. Those three were targeted explicitly in the mid-1990s because they served the strategic purpose of drawing attention to the rapid deterioration of Japan's fiscal situation that had taken place from 1991 (in comparison with other countries), and hence underlined to both domestic and foreign audiences the need for remedial action.

A fourth performance indicator, not explicitly targeted by MOF, is central government's financial balance (fiscal surplus/deficit) as a ratio of GDP. As we have seen in the previous chapter, there was a gradual reduction in Japan's deficit on the central government budget during the period of reconstruction, from 1980 to 1986 followed by a much shaper reduction *after* the relaxation of reconstruction, the result of a combination of GDP growth and surplus revenues available to finance additional spending. There were broadly similar trends for the UK and Germany, but beginning from a lower base-line. Conversely, the USA and France had rising deficits from 1980 to 1986, but shared similar experience of decline with Japan, and the UK, and Germany

---

[1] Strictly speaking, the bond dependency ratio. As explained in Chapter 12, the fiscal deficit (the difference between total revenues and total expenditures) was smaller than the bond dependency ratio because MOF financed some capital expenditures through government borrowing by the issue of long-term bonds.

thereafter. Japan's central government deficit, larger than any other country for most of the period, was transformed into the smallest by the early 1990s. But, like the trend of GGE, that improvement occurred mainly during the period of the bubble economy. Thereafter, as Figure 27.5 shows, the deficit on Japan's central government financial balance was on a steeply rising trend, whereas that of all other G7 countries, was set firmly on a downward path from the mid-1990s, with the UK, the USA, and Canada achieving surpluses.

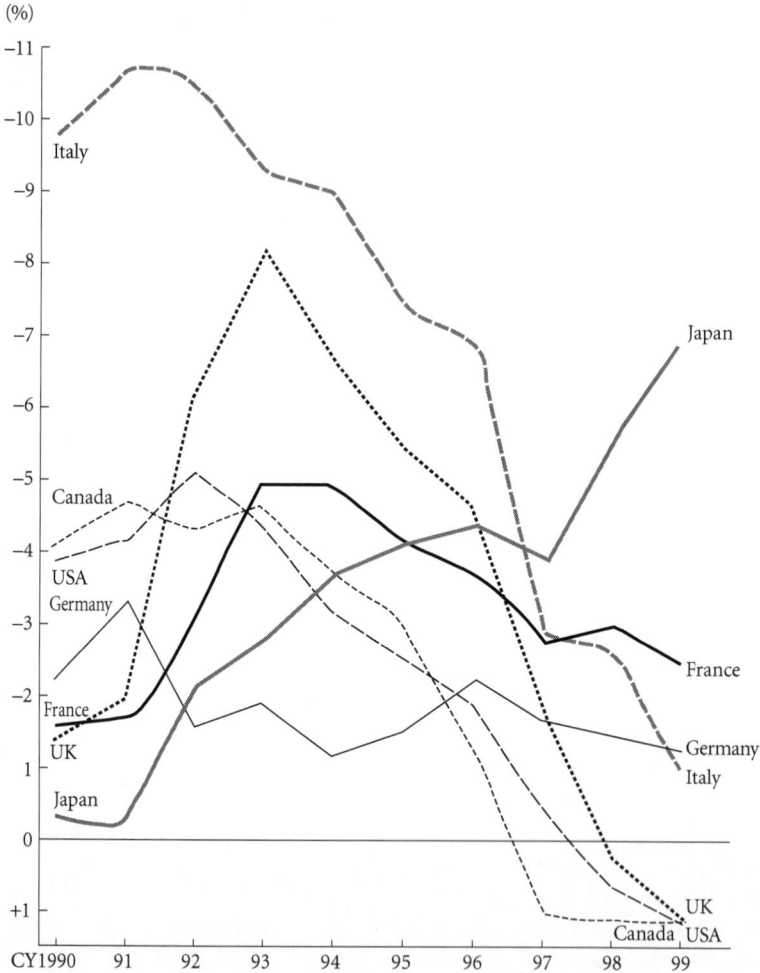

Figure 27.5 *Fiscal balances of central/federal governments in G7, CY1990–CY1999*
Settled Budgets: surplus (+) or deficit (−) as percentage of nominal GDP
Source: *Economic Outlook*, no. 67, June 2000, OECD.

The measurement of the fiscal deficit (i.e. the bond dependency ratio) as a proportion of the General Account Budget was explicitly targeted by MOF in the era of reconstruction. Figure 27.6 shows the sharp rise in fiscal deficits on central/federal budgets that occurred in the mid-1970s among five of the G7 countries, alongside the even sharper rise for Japan, reaching a high of 34.7% in 1979 compared with less than 20% for the other countries. Japan's deficit on the General Account Budget continued at a high but declining level, a trend observable in all other G7 countries apart from the USA until 1989. The decline was sharpest in the UK, where the proceeds of privatization, and the 'Lawson boom', contributed to the surplus enjoyed during 1987–9. In the 1990s the deficits of all countries rose again, with Japan's again exceeding all the rest. Measured in this way Japan's comparative position was the worst of all five countries over the period as a whole. MOF's performance during the period of reconstruction was not markedly different from that of other countries.

The trends of central/federal government's long-term debt as a ratio of GDP in the same five countries are shown in Figure 27.7. Japan's steeply rising curve from 1974 to 1986 was matched only by that of the USA. From a roughly similar base-line, Germany and France had more gradual levels of rising debt. By the 1990s when the volume of debt outstanding was rising again in all five countries, Japan's debt had increased more than fivefold in 20 years compared with a doubling in France, Germany, and the USA. The UK alone achieved a substantial reduction, and overall a relatively stable performance.

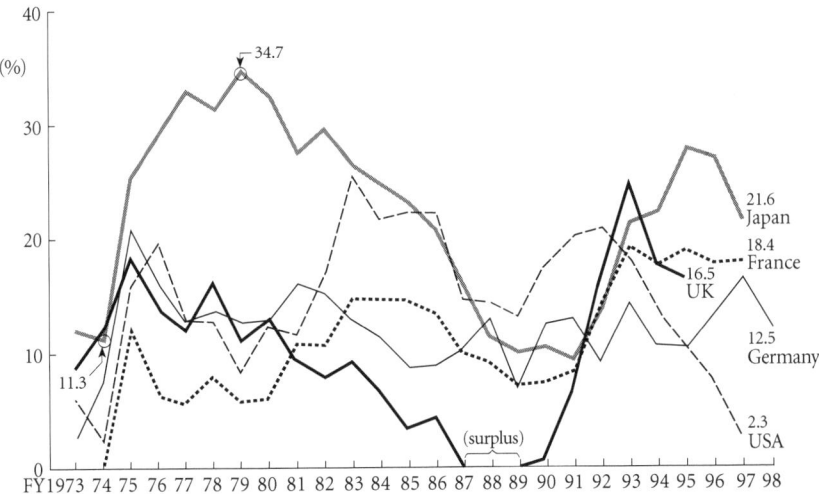

Figure 27.6 *Ratio of fiscal deficits to budget expenditures in central/federal governments in G7, FY1973–FY1997*

Settled Budgets: percentages.

Source: The Japanese Budget in Brief 1997, Budget Bureau, MOF.

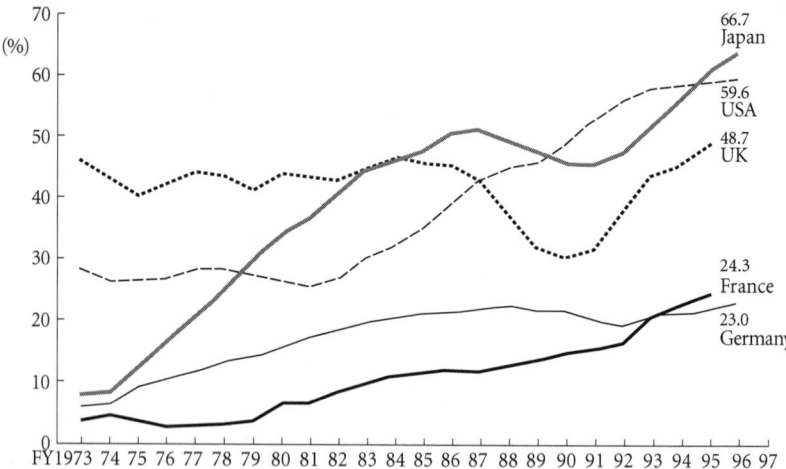

Figure 27.7 *Government bonds outstanding in G7, FY1973–FY1996*
Settled budgets nominal GDP: percentages

Includes local and state governments.

Source: *The Japanese Budget in Brief 1997*, Budget Bureau, MOF.

The profiles of the ratio of interest payments to the total expenditures of central/federal government were very similar for all five countries, but Japan's costs were higher for almost the whole period (Figure 27.8). The sharp increase registered by all of them from the mid-1970s was greater still in Japan. During the period of fiscal reconstruction, Japan's debt costs were absorbing nearly twice as much of total central government expenditure as elsewhere, although thereafter the differential narrowed.

On the evidence of the four performance indicators of deficit–GDP, deficit–Budget, debt–GDP, and interest payments–Budget, MOF's performance with the central government's Budget compared unfavourably with that of its counterparts in other central/federal governments in G7 for most of the period 1975–2000. Moreover, whereas all the rest were improving their budget performance from the mid-1990s, Japan's alone was deteriorating.

THE FAILURE OF FISCAL RECONSTRUCTION IN THE 1980s

Despite the adoption of policies of fiscal reconstruction and retrenchment in the 1980s, GGE continued to rise in all G7 countries. Central/federal budgets contributed the major part of that growth, some (like those in the UK and Canada) at rates even faster than before the crisis. Rising public spending was accompanied by a growing shortage of tax revenues, as the successful application of the principles of economic

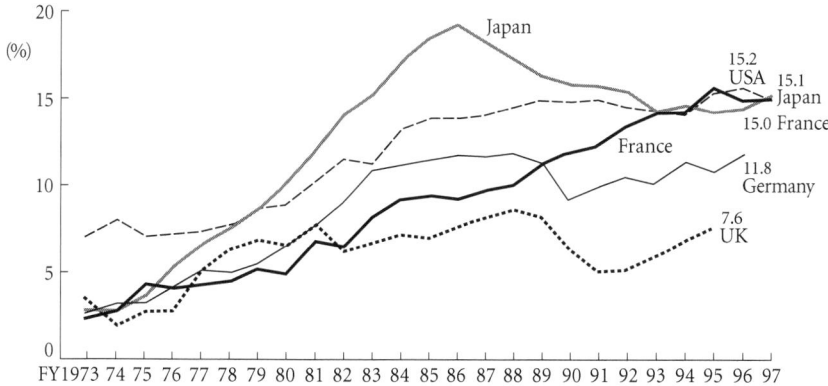

Figure 27.8 *Ratio of interest payments to Budget expenditures in central/federal governments in G7, FY 1973–FY1997*
Settled budget: percentages
Source: *The Japanese Budget in Brief 1997*, Budget Bureau, MOF.

liberalism to taxation, epitomized by 'supply-side' Reagonomics and Thatcherism, lowered rates of personal and corporate taxation and (with the exception of Japan) shifted more of the burden on to indirect taxes. There was an illusion of discipline and control. Heroic objectives to cut public spending in real terms were scaled down or (as in the UK) re-based to 'better reflect the reality' of inexorable growth (Thain and Wright 1995). In reality, G7 countries were able to do little more than to slow the growth of central/federal spending, except for very short periods of time. The underlying secular trends of continued expenditure growth and revenue shortfall were obscured but not remedied by budget stratagems and fiscal sleight-of-hand designed to manage the public presentation of an apparently effective performance.

More spending accompanied by a shrinking revenue base exacerbated conditions of continuous and, in most countries, widening fiscal deficits, increasing government borrowing and accumulating levels of gross government debt. Japan's performance in achieving a surplus on its GG financial balance was superior to other G7 countries only with the inclusion of the large surplus on social security funds, accumulated on a different basis from most of them. The gross financial liabilities of G7 countries, averaging 42% of GDP in 1980, had reached nearly 60% a decade later. Japan's gross debt position compared unfavourably, and by 1997 was the worst in G7, apart from Italy; in FY1999 its gross debt surpassed even Italy's. Paradoxically, MOF's performance was worse where it had more control, i.e. over gross borrowings; the apparently impressive performance in restraining the size and growth of net debt was the result more of the method of financing pensions than of MOF's policies for reconstruction.

More narrowly, a comparison of central/federal governments' financial balances shows that Japan was not markedly more successful in reducing the deficit on the General Account Budget in the 1980s, while over the period 1975–2000 as a whole

MOF's performance was the worst. The costs of servicing debt exerted a continuous squeeze on all central/federal budgets, as the fixed costs of interest payments and redemption reduced the discretion of budget-makers to vary programme expenditures. The squeeze was compounded as demand-led mandatory expenditures (for example social security) absorbed a growing proportion of the latter. Budgets became more inflexible. Politicians had less discretion to influence the composition and allocation of the residual resources. The costs of servicing central government's debt in Japan were a heavier burden than elsewhere, and fiscal discretion was progressively diminished throughout the period 1975–2000.

From about the mid-1980s (following the Plaza and Louvre Accords), fiscal policies in G7 were relaxed in conditions of 'boom' and 'bubble'. While deficits improved, only the UK achieved (briefly) a surplus on its overall financial balance, largely the result of the revenues from the sale of assets; Japan's was distorted by the inclusion of a massive social security surplus. But the improvement there and elsewhere was the result more of the rapid (and unsustainable) growth of the economy than of the effectiveness of earlier policies of reconstruction, or the continuation of the reform of the administrative context within which budgets were made and carried out.

Conditions of worldwide recession in the late 1980s and early 1990s exposed once again, as in the mid-1970s, the fragility of the state of the public finances of most G7 countries. Deficits rose sharply and levels of government debt exceeded those at any time in the previous 20 years. By 1995 all seven countries had gross debt above the Maastricht threshold of 60%; in Italy it was more than 100% of GDP. Responding to the renewed but deeper crisis of deficit and debt, all G7 governments committed themselves to a restoration of balanced budgets as a medium-term aim, and to the introduction of short-term policies of budget control to achieve annual targets for reduced deficit and debt linked to that aim. Unlike the crisis of the mid-1970s, for EU members there were now broader political as well as economic and fiscal factors which made it imperative to act urgently. For them, entry into EMU in 1999 was conditional on a satisfactory economic and fiscal performance. Those of the convergence criteria prescribed in the 1992 Maastricht Treaty that were aimed specifically at budget discipline included a level of deficit on the balance of general government of not more than 3% of GDP, and a gross debt ratio of not more than 60%. To comply with those and other economic criteria, EU governments were obliged to introduce and implement policies of unparalleled financial stringency, and to maintain them over a period of years prior to entry. Contingently, budgetary systems, budget norms, and rules-of-the-game had to be reformed and recast (and in some cases manipulated by fiscal sleight-of-hand) to ensure that the central/federal ministries of finance could deliver a fiscal performance consistent with the criteria in time for the formal assessment in July 1998.

Similar changes to budgetary systems, and to fiscal policies, took place in the non-EU countries in G7, as they too became politically committed to a restoration of balanced budgets. There was among them (and other OECD countries) an implicit acknowledgement of the Maastricht budget criteria as standards by which to judge the effectiveness of their short-term budget performance. While they strove to meet these criteria partly for domestic reasons of political economy, they were also responding to increasing international pressures of fiscal convergence among industrialized countries, such as competitiveness in business tax regimes, and the sale of government debt. Japan adopted one of the Maastricht criteria in the Fiscal Structural Reform Act of 1997, setting a target date of FY2003 for the achievement of a fiscal deficit of 3% or less of GDP on the combined financial balances of central and local government (excluding social security). The amount of public debt was to be held to its 1997 level, and the issue of special deficit-financing bonds reduced annually to achieve their elimination by FY2003. However, as the economic recession worsened, the Act was amended in 1998 to extend the target date for the deficit to FY2005, i.e. by March 2006. The target date for the elimination of the issue of special deficit-financing bonds was deferred once again, the fourth time since 1980.

Fiscal convergence of deficit and debt levels was also further stimulated by growing political awareness and concern at the effects of the 'fiscal time-bomb' ticking below the surface of all G7 (and other OECD) fiscal systems. It threatened to undermine with varying force the stability of the fiscal base in the early years of the new millennium. Of several elements, the most important was the fiscal consequences of progressively ageing populations. The increase in the number of elderly and retired, relative to those of working age, exerted a double fiscal squeeze: falling tax revenues on the one hand, and rising costs of providing pensions, social security, and health and welfare and social services on the other. Here again, Japan's situation compared unfavourably with most other G7 countries, and was projected to deteriorate rapidly from 2000. The ratio of population aged 60 and over to that aged 20–59 was nearly 40% in 1998; only Italy had a larger ratio. The estimated change in the ratio between 1998 and 2025 would rank Japan ahead of all other G7 countries, and third highest in the whole of the OECD area. The ageing population has profound implications for the economy: on the labour supply, household savings, the level of investment—and on the public finances, especially the costs of providing public pensions, and rising public health expenditure. One consequence, exacerbated by the cost of financing public debt in the future, was intergenerational inequity—the excess of the net tax paid by future generations over that paid by those born today—unless radical changes were made, for example by cutting rates of benefit, raising the retirement age still further, broadening the base of contributors (Takayama *et al.* 1998; EPA 1995*a*).

The provision of both private and public pensions in Japan was in a serious state throughout the 1990s. Expenditure on public pensions was estimated to rise from 6.8% of GDP in 1995 to 14.3% in 2020, 'an increase probably unequalled in any other OECD country' (OECD 1998: 146). From FY2000, pension funds were to be managed with greater concern for returns in the market. Private pension funds were in no better state. Employee pension funds were grossly underfunded.

Towards the end of the 1990s, the trends of unsustainable growth in public spending of the previous two decades had been halted in all G7 countries apart from Japan, and in some had been sufficiently reversed to make realistic and credible their aspirations for balanced central and federal budgets. The most remarkable turn-around occurred in the USA, where a deficit of $290 billion on the federal budget in 1994 had shrunk to $22 billion in FY1998, and the first surplus for 30 years was declared in the budget (excluding social security) for the fiscal year ending in September 1999. The Congressional Budget Office forecasted a cumulative surplus of $1,000 billion (excluding social security) over the first ten years of the new century. In his final Budget, for FY2000, President Clinton proposed the elimination of all federal debt by 2013. If implemented, the US federal government would then be debt-free for the first time since 1835. Canada achieved a balanced federal Budget even earlier, returning surpluses in FY1997– FY1999; the UK's central government Budget was in substantial surplus in FY1999 and FY2000; and the budget deficits of France, Germany, and Italy were set on a downwards path. Japan's balance alone was moving sharply upwards. Its fiscal situation was the worst of all G7 countries, and the prospect of a balanced central government budget was more remote than at any time since 1965.

28

FILP under Stress

The original purpose of FILP was to contribute to fixed capital formation by allocating funds to dedicated functional organizations at the national, regional, and local levels to enable them to provide finance for capital investment and loans for mainly three types of public-sector projects. The first of those was for projects where loan periods were too long for private-sector institutions to bear the interest-rate risk, such as some key industrial sectors financed by loans from the Japan Development Bank and the EXIM bank in the post-war period. Secondly, FILP finance was intended to finance those projects whose potential profitability was too uncertain for private-sector institutions to bear the risk. The third main type was projects where low-interest loans were offered for purposes of income redistribution, and the interest rates were too low to be handled by private-sector financial institutions, such as the loans made by the Government Housing Loan Corporation, by the Small Businesses Finance Corporation to small and medium-sized firms, and by the regional development agencies.

Through its funding of development organizations in the high-growth era after the end of the Allied Occupation, FILP provided resources for the rapid development of basic industries such as steel, shipbuilding, coal, and electricity, to promote industrial and technological development. With the end of high growth, national economic goals were reoriented in the 1970s and 1980s to reflect a greater concern with the social, welfare, and environmental policies set out in successive national plans. The number of FILP agencies (and the purposes served by them) increased, reflecting those changed objectives. The priorities of FILP allocations changed, both in the allocation to the agencies and in the functional distribution which their investments and loans brought about. In 1953, the first year of the FILP, the JDB absorbed more than a quarter of the total funds allocated to agencies other than local governments; by 1991 its share was less than 5%. Over the same period, the Government Housing Loan Corporation increased its share from less than 10% to nearly a quarter.

Whatever the need and justification for FILP and its agencies in the post-war reconstruction of Japanese industry, the continued need for such an institution in an advanced industrial economy was increasingly challenged in the 1980s. As we have seen in Chapter 12, FILP provided MOF and other ministries with leverage to influence the amount, direction, and flow of capital into both public and private sectors. Whether they were able to determine the efficient use of those resources better than financial institutions in the private sector is arguable. Whether they should have tried to do so, in order to implement a strategy for achieving national goals, is a fundamental question of the purpose of government, which advocates and critics of a 'positive industrial policy' debated in the USA in the 1980s, and which underlay the trade disputes between the USA and Japan at that time. Central guidance and control of the allocation of credit to key industries, technologies, and processes became less necessary and more difficult to justify as the economy was progressively liberalized, and private-sector financial institutions became better able and more willing to provide finance for medium- and long-term investments in deregulated markets for financial services and products. Equally, FILP's provision of finance for social capital projects 'to improve living standards' and the 'quality of life', and to service the debts on funds so employed, was criticized as inappropriate. Such expenditures, it was argued, should be met out of general taxation and/or government borrowing, and be subject to the scrutiny and examination of the Diet (e.g. Miyawaki 1993).

While few inside Japan advocated the outright abolition of FILP, the need to redefine its purpose, scope, and operational criteria became urgent as tensions arose in the system. From the early 1980s, it became increasingly difficult to reconcile two conflicting principles: the 'profit principle' guiding the management of funds deposited with the Trust Fund Bureau Fund, which needed to earn sufficient revenue on its investments and loans to cover its operating costs, principally the payment of interest on the deposits from the postal savings system; and the 'low-cost principle' guiding the provision of funds by the Trust Fund Bureau Fund to the FILP agencies for public policy purposes—the achievement of national economic, social, and welfare objectives. The tension between those two principles was exacerbated by the further difficulty occasioned by the expansion of FILP to provide 'lubrication' for the operation and management of the public financial system as a whole. The consequences were increasing difficulties first at the 'entry' stage, in maintaining the attractiveness of postal savings in an era of deregulated interest rates and financial products and services; secondly, at the 'intermediate stage', in the prescription of interest rates for funds deposited with the Trust Fund Bureau Fund, and hence the rates charged for loans to the FILP agencies; and finally at the 'exit' stage, in the efficiency and effectiveness of the use of FILP funds. We look at each in turn, before discussing the background to the reform process initiated in 1997, and at the principles of 'New FILP' introduced in April 2001.

THE COLLECTION AND SUPPLY OF FUNDS

As traditional bank lending to large companies in basic industries declined in the 1970s and 1980s, city and commercial banks began to compete with the public banks and finance corporations for the investment business of medium and small-sized firms in new high-tech industries, and for the household savings of small investors. In direct competition with the PFCs and the Postal Savings System, they pressured their sponsor bureau in MOF, the (then) Banking Bureau, to support their demands for the de-privileging of some kinds of postal savings deposit accounts. As discussed in

Chapter 12, they were partly successful, in that the Tax Act of 1988 removed the tax-exemption status of interest income earned on those accounts.

Interest rates on large denomination deposits were deregulated in 1979, and that on small denomination deposits was completed in 1993. Private-sector financial institutions were then in theory able to raise the rates of interest paid on deposits, making them more attractive to small investors. For a time in the mid-1980s there was a temporary decline in the attractiveness of postal savings as, first, private banks started to issue new money certificates and other kinds of deposit certificates; secondly, the stock market boom after 1985 diverted some funds away from postal savings; and thirdly, there was a continuance of the trend from 1979 of an increase in life insurance savings. Those shifts were attributed to more attractive yields of interest, and to the substitutability among small investors of postal savings and bank deposits. But the expectation that competition for the savings of small investors might result in a diminution of postal savings, and hence in the supply of potential funds for the Trust Fund Bureau Fund and FILP, proved unfounded. Despite interest rates being set slightly lower than both private-sector three-year fixed deposit rates and government bond coupon rates, postal savings fixed deposits continued to attract household savings in record amounts. At the end of FY1993, the outstanding balance of postal savings totalled 183.5 trillion, representing nearly a quarter of all domestic savings, and a third of all domestic savings by individuals. The rate of increase in the previous three years averaged between 7% and 12%.

There were three main reasons for this growth. First, most postal savings were in *teigaku chokin* (postal savings certificates), comprising some 85%–90% of the total from 1980. Although they offered interest rates lower than those of comparable instruments in the private market, they provided guaranteed interest rates for variable terms from six months to ten years, and a cancellation option. Depositors could move their funds in and out, as interest rates in the market fluctuated, to enjoy the benefit of higher rates. Private-sector financial institutions could not, or were unwilling to, bear the costs/losses by offering similar conditions on fixed deposits. Further, they argued that the costs to the government of the *teigaku chokin* accounts were greater than the simple interest rate calculations suggested, because of the option premium. The difference between them and those of similar deposit instruments available from commercial banks was estimated to be worth as much as 1.5 points. That spread helped to explain the growth of postal savings despite nominal interest rates below those offered by banks (Kamada 1993).

Secondly, bank failures in Japan (and the USA) were a powerful determinant of the attractiveness of postal savings (Kuwayama 1999). The failure and bankruptcy of several regional banks, the publicized weakness of credit associations, credit cooperatives and agricultural banks, and the *jusen* in the continuing crisis of the banking sector in the 1990s further encouraged small investors to plump for the security of the government guaranteed postal savings system.

Thirdly, the attractiveness of postal savings *vis á vis* the financial products offered by other financial institutions in the more competitive market conditions after the liberalization of financial markets in the mid-1980s and the linking of public and private rates from 1994 was sustained because post offices were able to provide a wide variety of postal as well as banking and insurance services, compared with the limited range of financial services that the banks then provided. Moreover, postal savings accounts were more convenient and were accessible through the 24,000 local offices compared with 16,600 bank branches. Post offices also benefited from economies of scale and lower overheads and salaries; they paid no corporation tax, were not required to make deposits with the Bank of Japan, and did not have to contribute to insurance for investors' deposits. Thus, they could generate higher revenue than banks, and operate on thinner profit margins.

The continuous expansion of postal savings was the major cause of the historic growth of FILP. Over-endowed with postal savings, which provided 57% of its total supply of funds, the Trust Fund Bureau Fund had to seek more and more investment outlets among FILP agencies for those deposits in order to cover the interest payments and its operating costs. In turn, FILP agencies were encouraged to look for more investment schemes and projects. The accumulation of postal savings also partly accounted for the inauguration of the Financial Liberalization Fund in 1987, although in the capital market operations undertaken through it there was also the motive of earning higher profits for the more efficient management of the Postal Savings Special Accounts in the new deregulated regime.

One effect of the liberalization of financial services and products in the 1980s, and the consequential deregulation of interest rates completed in 1994, was that the privileged position hitherto enjoyed by the public banks, financial corporations and other FILP agencies was threatened by an increase in the costs of their borrowing from the Trust Fund Bureau Fund and a narrowing of the differential between the interest rates they charged for their own loans and those of the private financial sector. It became more difficult for MOF to ensure that the cost of funds deposited with the Trust Fund Bureau Fund could be recovered by the charges for investments and loans made by the FILP agencies to public and private-sector clients and customers. The continued attractiveness of postal savings depended upon the maintenance of advantageous terms and conditions for (mainly long-term) deposits; while the continued attractiveness of FILP investments and loans depended mainly upon the maintenance of the differential between the FILP rate of interest and the long-term prime rate offered by private-sector financial institutions. As long-term interest rates fell, and domestic and international competition in financial services and products intensified, MOF (and MPT) were squeezed at both the 'entry' and 'exit' stages of FILP funds.

The erosion of interest rate differentials between public and private financial institutions after deregulation in the 1980s was but one part of the problem. Fluctuations and volatility in long and short-term interest rates produced variable yields, both positive and negative for postal savings and Trust Fund Bureau Fund deposits. Those difficulties were compounded by the mismatch of assets and liabilities in the Postal Savings Special Account and the Trust Fund Bureau Fund (and the principal FILP agencies), and the absence of asset/liability management schemes similar to those that private banks operated to deal with the effects of fluctuating interest rates. MOF's First Fund Division began to address this problem only in the early 1990s.

THE USE AND MANAGEMENT OF FUNDS: THE TRUST FUND BUREAU FUND

The Trust Fund Bureau Fund, administered by MOF's First Fund Division of the Financial Bureau, was a non-profit-making intermediary between the inflow of savings and the outflow of FILP loans and investments. There was no 'spread' between the interest rate it paid on the postal savings deposited with it and that which it charged for its investments and loans to the FILP agencies. Until March 1987 the deposit interest rate was fixed by law. Thereafter there was greater flexibility to adjust the Trust Fund Bureau Fund rate in response to changes in the private financial sector. One consequence was that changes in the Trust Fund Bureau Fund rate and the FILP rate fluctuated almost monthly, where once, especially in the 1950s and 1960s, such changes took place infrequently. As a general rule, the Trust Fund Bureau Fund deposit rate was set in line with the market interest rate on long-term government bonds. The rate was determined by the First Fund Division in the light of market conditions, and the prevailing interest rates for postal savings deposits.

The minimum contract term for deposits with the Trust Fund Bureau Fund from postal savings and other sources was one month, earning the lowest rate of interest. Most of the deposits were for longer than seven years, and earned the maximum rate, which was the rate commonly referred to, and was the same as its lending rate to the FILP agencies. The terms of its loans provided for a maximum of 35 years, but varied with the nature and purpose of the FILP programme and individual loans. The purchase of central government bonds was for the same ten-year term as government-backed purchases of bonds by local government and FILP agencies, and at the same 'coupon rate'.

Inherent Interest Rate Risk

The changing role of FILP, and the deregulation of interest rates, combined to make it more difficult for the Financial Bureau to manage the flow of funds through the Trust Fund Bureau Fund to avoid a negative spread on the rates it paid for its borrowed capital, and the charges it made for its loans to FILP agencies. First, progressive interest rate deregulation, and increased competition among private-sector financial institutions, made them more efficient, and reduced interest rate differentials; those in the public sector narrowed correspondingly. Secondly, when interest rates were regulated, long-term rates were set at a higher level than short-term rates, and a positive yield could be guaranteed. With deregulation, there was frequent fluctuation of differentials between long-term and short-term rates, increasing the degree of risk for the Trust Fund Bureau Fund with periods of asset and liability mismatch.

The final and most critical decision for FILP was the rate of interest to be charged by the FILP agencies. Required to pay interest on their loans from the Trust Fund Bureau Fund, they had in turn to seek a higher return on most of their loans and investments to the projects and programmes they financed. In practice, the decision was constrained by the supply of private-sector funds for comparable long-term projects.

The benchmark here was provided by the long-term prime rate. Historically, the margin between it and the standard FILP rate was of the order of 1% or 2%, a significant inducement to clients and customers. With interest rate liberalization in the 1980s, and the subsequent deregulation of financial services and deposits, the spread became very much smaller, with brief periods in the 1980s when the FILP rate was higher than the private-sector long-term rate. In 1993–4 and for three years, 1995–7, the FILP rate was consistently higher than the long-term prime rate and the ten-year Japan government bond rate.

The public banks and finance corporations normally had a lower, 'preferential', rate besides the standard FILP rate of interest. The JDB for example had a 'most preferred lending rate' set at a lower level. Before 1987 the difference was sometimes as much as 2%. Earlier still, through the era of industrial restructuring in the 1950s and 1960s, its preferential rate for the electric power, shipbuilding, coal mining, and steel sectors was $2\frac{1}{2}$% lower than the standard FILP interest rate, provoking the criticism that the JDB provided soft loans for industrial development. Some FILP agencies financing the provision of 'social capital' in the 1980s and 1990s charged rates of interest for their loans lower than those at which they borrowed from the Trust Fund Bureau Fund. Some of these loans were cross-subsidized from more profitable operations and, for some agencies, by subsidies from the central government through the General Account Budget.

EFFICIENCY AND EFFECTIVENESS

Government Subsidies to FILP Agencies

The change of emphasis, from one of mainly providing very long-term loans at preferential rates of interest for the creation of industrial capital, to the more broadly based functions described in previous chapters, meant that, not only was there greater uncertainty about the return on loans and investments, but some of the activities undertaken by some of the FILP agencies to implement national economic and social policies required continuous subsidization from the General Account Budget to cover their operating costs.

The Japanese government has partly subsidized some FILP agencies ever since the establishment of FILP in its modern form in 1953. In its early days, as much as a third of the total FILP Budget was financed by direct subsidy from the General Account, when the huge demand for investment capital from basic industries outstripped the supply from the Trust Fund Bureau Fund. Its contemporary significance, in the context of the criteria for investments and loans under the programme and their allocation to the FILP agencies, is the extent to which subsidization was essential to the continuing viability of FILP in conditions of deregulated interest rates. There are two issues.

First, some FILP agencies were increasingly dependent upon an annual subsidy in order to cover the costs of the spread between borrowing and lending. In the late 1980s and 1990s, FILP was unable to cover all the costs of its borrowed capital from (principally) the Trust Fund Bureau Fund at competitive market rates charged for its loans and investments. Central government was obliged to subsidize some of its financial activities in order to allow FILP agencies to continue to offer preferential rates of interest in some policy areas, such as housing, to which the government attached a high priority. Long-term, low-interest loans for house purchases were offered by the Government Housing Loan Corporation and the HUDC at rates lower than the Trust Fund Bureau Fund rate. The difference was made up by the central government as an explicit subsidy. For example, in 1994 the GHLC and HUDC borrowed from the Trust Fund Bureau Fund at 4.3%: the former provided home loans attracting a rate of interest of 4.0%; the HUDC charged 4.05% for its loans and investments. The central government subsidized their losses in order to reduce the costs of home ownership and rented apartments. As long-term interest rates fell with the progressive lowering of the official discount rate in the 1990s, the prime long-term rate fell below both the FILP interest rate and the subsidized rate charged by GHLC, HUDC, and other FILP agencies; in other words, such long-term loans from FILP agencies cost more than those available from the private sector. In 1993–4 the costs of borrowing from HUDC were higher than from the private sector, and many borrowers repaid their loans before maturity, financed by cheaper loans from city and commercial banks and financial institutions.

The second issue was the extent to which subsidization was an indication of the allocative 'inefficiency' of some of FILP's financial activities, and evidence of the inefficient use of public funds by some FILP agencies.

The concept of 'government subsidy' is vague, often ambiguous, and evidence of it is obscure or obfuscated. Here it is taken to mean the direct transfer or grant of funds from the General Account without the statutory requirement either to repay the principal and/or to pay interest. It excludes future discounted subsidy costs (discussed below), and indirect subsidies from the Trust Fund Bureau Fund in the form of continuing loans to some agencies where there was little prospect of repayment from earned profits, for example the JNR Debt Settlement Corporation from 1987 to 1997. Some agencies, such as the OECF, also received annual capital subscriptions from the General Account Budget, but were required to pay interest and repay the principal.

Many FILP agencies received, or had received, government interest rate subsidies from the General Account Budget, totalling between 1.1 and 1.9 trillion annually throughout the period 1977–96, the equivalent of between 3% and 10% of the FILP Budget (Table 28.1). After 1981 the amount of annual subsidy declined steadily until 1990. While that level of subsidization was not insignificant, neither did it claim an increasing amount of the General Account Budget; and, with the rapid growth of the overall FILP Budget, it represented a declining source of income for the FILP agencies as a whole. The deregulation of interest rates, and of some financial products in the 1980s, was not accompanied by an increase in subsidy, as conditions of negative spread were by now being experienced by some agencies, mainly the public banks and finance corporations, which were obliged to borrow at rates of interest from FILP higher than those that it charged clients for their loans and investments. Indeed, after 1987 there was a fall in the total amount of subsidy, and in its proportion of the overall FILP Budget.

Table 28.1 Direct subsidies to FILP agencies from the General Account Budget, FY1977–FY1996 (billion yen)

	Public banks and finance corporations								Other FILP agencies	Subsidies	
	GHLC		AFFFC		8 PBFCs		Total PBFCs				
	Total	%	Total	%	Total	%	Total	%	Total	Total	% of FILP Budget[a]
1996	427.4	32.3	99.3	7.5	745	5.6	601.2	45.4	721.6	1322.8	3.3
1995	410.9	30.9	100.7	7.6	761	5.7	587.7	44.1	743.3	1331.0	3.3
1994	404.5	30.0	100.8	7.5	681	5.0	573.4	42.6	772.0	1345.4	3.4
1993	404.5	31.8	108.1	8.5	434	3.4	556.0	43.7	715.0	1271.0	3.5
1992	394.0	31.5	118.3	9.5	416	3.3	553.9	44.3	696.2	1250.1	3.9
1991	374.0	30.7	120.9	9.9	468	3.8	541.7	44.5	675.9	1217.6	4.2
1990	354.0	30.0	119.8	10.2	658	5.6	539.6	45.9	636.6	1176.2	4.3
1989	354.0	28.8	141.8	11.5	806	6.6	576.4	46.9	652.3	1228.7	4.7
1988	344.0	27.8	144.1	11.6	831	6.7	571.2	46.1	667.6	1238.8	4.9
1987	343.3	27.7	143.7	11.6	845	6.8	571.5	46.1	667.5	1239.0	5.2
1986	344.3	24.8	143.4	10.3	714	5.1	559.1	40.3	827.7	1386.8	6.3
1985	341.3	20.6	139.8	8.5	516	3.1	532.7	32.3	1117.7	1650.4	7.9
1984	286.3	17.7	135.0	8.3	372	2.3	458.5	28.3	1163.5	1622.0	7.7
1983	281.5	16.8	130.2	7.8	326	1.9	444.3	26.5	1232.0	1676.3	8.1
1982	281.4	16.6	123.2	7.3	173	1.0	421.9	25.0	1266.6	1688.5	8.3
1981	217.4	11.0	91.0	4.6	165	0.8	324.9	16.5	1648.0	1972.9	10.1
1980	177.6	9.7	86.2	4.7	141	0.8	277.9	15.1	1555.7	1833.6	10.0
1979	132.5	8.3	78.7	4.9	130	0.8	224.2	14.0	1366.2	1590.4	9.4
1978	112.8	—	75.6	—	116	—	200.0	—	n/a	—	—
1977	107.1	—	66.2	—	94	—	182.7	—	n/a	—	—

[a] Subsidies were paid directly to FILP agencies, and were not included in the total of the FILP Budget.

Source: derived from data supplied by First Fund Division, Financial Bureau, MOF.

Subsidies were distributed unevenly among the FILP agencies. The share claimed by the 11 public banks and finance corporations increased annually from 14% in 1979 to nearly 47% of the total in 1989. As Table 28.1 shows, that increase was largely the result of the increasing subsidization of the GHLC, which increased fourfold between 1977 and 1996, to claim nearly a third of the total. In the latter year, its subsidy of 427 billion was equivalent to 4% of the amount it received in FILP finance. The other major beneficiary was the AFFFC, whose subsidy increased steadily from 1977 to 1988 to claim just under 12% of the total. Of the other public banks and finance corporations, five received small annual subsidies. Both the People's Finance Corporation and the Small Businesses Finance Corporation were subsidized regularly from 1983 onwards, but the amounts for each never exceeded 40 billion per year. Much smaller but regular annual subsidies were paid to the Japan Finance Corporation for Municipal Enterprises from 1967, 'as compensation for those costs incurred by [it] as a result of loans at below-market interest rates' (JFCME 1997*b*: 21); in FY1996 its subsidies totalled 5 billion. The Okinawa Development Public Corporation and the Environmental Sanitation Business Finance Corporation received smaller amounts. The JDB, the EXIM Bank, and the Hokkaido–Tōhoku Development Corporation received no subsidies until their reorganization in 1999. In FY2000 the new Japan Bank for International Cooperation received subsidies worth 306 billion for the overseas economic cooperation operations inherited from the OECF, and the Development Bank of Japan (incorporating the Hokkaido–Tōhoku Development Corporation), 84 billion. Of the non-financial FILP agencies, the Japan Highway Public Corporation and the Japan Private School Promotion Fund were the largest beneficiaries, each claiming more than a fifth of the annual total of FILP subsidies.

Another indicator of allocative inefficiency is the amount of carry-forward and unused FILP funds at the end of each fiscal year. In Chapter 24 I explained that only some 75%–85% of the funds allocated in the revised Budget were spent in the fiscal year. Carry-forward accounted for between 12% and 22% each year, with a further 3% or so remaining unused as projects were abandoned or cancelled. As FILP was used increasingly to finance countercyclical policies in the mid- and late-1990s, more funds remained unused or carried forward. In Table 28.2 central government borrowing and portfolio investment are netted out from the FILP Budget totals to obtain a more accurate picture of the amount of allocated funds actually used to finance the Investment and Loans Programme in each fiscal year for the period 1975–97.[1]

The conclusion to be drawn from the evidence presented there is that FILP was over-funded. In no year were the FILP agencies able to use more than 86% of the total amount allocated to them; in many years, especially in the 1990s, implementation fell well short of that figure. The rapid expansion of the FILP Budget in the 1990s was not

---

[1] Smaller values for carry-forward and unused FILP allocations are obtained from calculations based on the gross FILP Budget, including the funds allocated to portfolio investment and central government borrowing, both of which were almost always wholly used. Ishi (2000) presents his evidence in this way, and also includes the amount of carry-forward expenditure in budget totals. While his data show a larger proportion of FILP carried out than that above, there is nevertheless substantial carry-forward and 'disuse'. The conclusion is broadly similar, emphasizing over-funding and inefficiency.

Table 28.2 Over-funding the investment and loan programme, FY1975–FY1997[a] (trillion yen)

FY	Revised[b] plan	Carried out Total	Carried out % of revised plan	Carried forward Total	Carried forward % of revised plan	Unused Total	Unused % of revised plan
1997	39.237	28.031	71.4	7.330	18.7	3.876	9.9
1996	40.525	28.427	70.1	8.918	22	3.180	7.8
1995	44.174	24.652	55.8	9.661	21.8	9.861	22.3
1994	42.681	35.028	80.2	7.112	16.2	1.540	3.5
1993	45.373	36.012	79.4	7.290	16.0	2.066	4.5
1992	38.297	32.043	83.7	5.554	14.5	0.589	1.5
1991	31.314	26.493	84.6	3.965	12.6	0.8558	2.7
1990	29.090	25.013	85.9	3.851	13.2	0.2249	0.7
1989	27.547	23.312	84.6	3.790	13.7	0.4441	1.6
1988	25.915	20.595	81.5	3.999	15.8	0.6579	2.6
1987	24.903	19.273	77.3	4.989	20.0	0.6408	2.5
1986	22.227	17.438	78.5	4.143	18.6	0.6451	2.9
1985	20.871	16.663	79.8	3.836	18.4	0.3709	1.8
1984	20.951	16.049	76.6	3.570	17.0	1.3323	6.4
1983	20.924	17.324	82.8	3.394	16.2	0.2057	1.0
1982	20.836	17.265	82.9	3.354	16.1	0.2166	1.0
1981	19.623	16.204	82.6	3.219	16.4	0.2001	1.0
1980	18.256	14.990	82.1	3.119	17.1	0.1474	0.8
1979	16.885	13.234	78.4	2.945	17.4	0.7052	4.2
1978	15.541	10.802	69.5	3.241	20.9	1.4973	9.6
1977	13.926	10.814	77.7	2.649	19.0	0.4626	3.3
1976	11.389	9.400	82.5	1.886	16.6	0.1027	0.9
1975	10.285	8.475	82.4	1.705	16.6	0.1048	1.0

[a] General Account Revised and Settled Budgets.
[b] Net of central government borrowing and portfolio management.

Source: calculations derived from data supplied by the First Fund Division, Financial Bureau, MOF.

matched by the capacity of the FILP agencies, and their clients in the public and private sectors, to use all of the resources efficiently and effectively, especially where there was a surge of additional funds in large countercyclical packages. In 1995 FILP agencies could not use, or carried forward, nearly half of the revised Budget. From 1993 the amount of unused allocations increased sharply as projects were abandoned, cancelled, or deferred (see below).

Local governments were responsible for about 80% of the total carry-forward. For most, FILP funds were a source of last resort. Wherever possible, they financed capital projects from their tax receipts, local revenues, and other cheaper sources. The Financial Bureau's management of the FILP Budget enabled them to carry forward unspent allocations, and to draw upon them for a period of two months after the end of the fiscal year (Financial Bureau 1998a). Unused allocations were distributed evenly between FILP agencies and local governments in most years. Among the former, the JDB, the EXIM Bank, the Government Housing and Loan Corporation, and the Housing and Urban Development Corporation contributed most, but the individual amounts were normally less than 100 billion. However, in 1995, of the 9.8 trillion unused, the GHLC was responsible for more than 60% and the Small Businesses Finance Corporation for nearly 10%.

The absence of uniform objective criteria for measuring the performance of FILP agencies made it all but impossible to determine how efficiently the allocated FILP funds were used to achieve the broad objectives of 'policy-based finance', and the narrower objectives prescribed for each agency. In the first place, the fluctuating, unstable interest rate risks carried by each of them were not publicly disclosed; nor were the losses incurred in the management of assets and liabilities. Apart from those directly subsidized through the General Account Budget because they were unable to implement prescribed public policies without incurring operating losses, there were those public corporations and companies with inherited or accumulated debts, and for whom continuing FILP loans were used mainly to finance operating losses and to recycle those debts. As mentioned, the JNR Debt Settlement Corporation was the prime example, but there were also the semi-privatized rail companies and the Honshu–Shikoku Bridge Authority, whose debts had swollen to over 4 trillion by 2000.

Secondly, some FILP agencies took on more high-risk industrial/technological/ business projects, which the private sector would not or could not finance because the expectation of profit was very long-term, or the degree of risk unacceptable. The danger was that the Trust Fund Bureau Fund portfolio would become unbalanced, as those projects with greater potential for earning profits on medium and long-term loans were financed more through deregulated, competitive markets (after Tokyo's 'Big Bang' in 1998), while the less profitable were financed, if at all, through FILP supplemented with General Account Budget grants or interest rate subsidies.

Thirdly, the criterion of profitability became less significant in some funding decisions by some agencies, illustrated here by the lending practices of the Japan Development Bank. As was explained in Chapter 24, after the statutory change to its terms of reference in 1973, the JDB provided a much broader range of functions and services, in addition to the more traditional investment and loan programmes. Its 'risk-compensating' function provided funds for projects where obtaining private-sector finance was difficult because of technical or market risks, such as the commercial development of new technologies and funding for R&D. It also provided funds where there was a long lead-time for investment and recovery of that investment required a long period of time, such as projects for electricity supply, rail, and urban development; it supplied low interest-rate funds to supplement low earning capacity on projects where investment costs were heavily front-loaded, and where there was future public benefit, such as parking lots, conference halls, transport terminals; it supplied funds and supplemented the creditworthiness of projects carried out by organizations that had inadequate market strength, for example in joint ventures between the public and private sectors; finally, it supplemented and guided private financial institutions through the 'pump-priming' effects of soft industrial policies, and by inducing private investment into areas thought desirable in terms of the national economy. (This latter is the so-called 'cow-bell' effect, whereby private-sector financial institutions took their investment and loan cues from the lead of MOF and/or FILP agencies.)

A longer-term problem raised by the change from financing industrial development and new technologies, to financing housing, welfare, environmental, and energy projects was that such 'non-productive' projects contributed less directly to GDP than the returns from economically productive projects. In the short to medium-term, the potential losses to the growth of industrial capacity, output, and tax revenue added to the problems of the public-sector deficit. If the element of subsidization from the General Account increased, it added directly to the costs of government, and imposed a further burden of debt. Against that, it could be argued that the short-term financial costs were outweighed by the creation of conditions for economic growth in the longer term through the improvement of social capital and infrastructural services, and that the competitiveness of industrial sectors was enhanced through support for R&D of new products and processes. For example, MOC and GHLC estimated that ripple and multiplier effects of GHLC loans in FY1997 would be worth in future some 9 trillion in housing investment; would increase production by 17 trillion; and would increase demand for consumer durables and other goods by about 1 trillion (Fund Operation Council 1999*a*).

MANAGEMENT TENSIONS

The management of FILP from entry to exit was shared among three central ministries. The link between FILP and the investment of postal savings and postal life insurance premia on the one hand, and public pension funds on the other, raised issues of the role and function of MPT, responsible for the collection, management, and investment of postal savings, and of MHW in relation to the use of public pension funds. Here the main issues were the continuance of compulsory deposits with the Trust Fund Bureau Fund managed by MOF's Financial Bureau, and the extent of ministerial autonomy in the management of postal savings and pension funds. MPT's main concerns were the attractiveness of postal savings products and services to small investors, the security of those savings, and the maximization of the returns on their investment (and its continued control of a significant instrument of political influence). MHW shared a similar interest in security, but not in the accumulation of pension funds, contributions for which were mainly compulsory. It was however even more anxious than MPT to maximize the returns on their use, as those funds were progressively depleted with the pressures of an ageing population. From 1987, both MPT and MHW were allowed to invest a proportion of their statutory deposits with the Trust Fund Bureau Fund, independently of the Investment and Loan Programme. MPT's Financial Liberalization Fund absorbed annually about 12% of the gross FILP Budget, and had 10% of the total balance of outstanding loans. The capital market investments by the Pension Welfare Services Public Corporation were similar.

In the 1990s there was increasing tension between the interests and objectives of MPT and MHW, demanding ministerial discretion to manage their own funds, and those of MOF, in the management of their funds through compulsory deposits with the Trust Fund Bureau Fund, needing to cover the costs of borrowing and simultaneously to maintain a FILP interest rate competitive with the private sector. The flow of deposits into the Trust Fund Bureau Fund, the use of those funds to finance the FILP Budget, and its allocation among the agencies was managed by MOF's Financial and Budget Bureaux. Both were reluctant to see any diminution of the roles that FILP played as an integral element of the general public finance system. First, it provided a stable and reliable mechanism for the transfer of personal savings into priority or preferred policy areas of capital investment, with the direction, scope, and purpose steered by MOF. The weaker parliamentary accountability and control of the FILP relative to the General Account Budget, and the lack of transparency, provided MOF with an ideal bureaucratic instrument of budgetary control. The greater flexibility of FILP's operation enabled it to respond quickly to changes in the business cycle with additional public works spending. Secondly, FILP could and was used to relieve fiscal pressure on the General Account.

Thirdly, some of the FILP agencies, particularly the public banks and financial corporations, were controlled directly by MOF through sole or shared sponsorship; others were controlled indirectly, through the allocation of FILP funds to them through its Financial Bureau in concert with the Budget Bureau. Those long-established agencies such as the JDB and the EXIM Bank provided a fund of investment expertise and knowledge about industrial sectors, technologies, and individual companies available to MOF and other sponsors such as MITI, MOC, MOT, MAFF, and the Ministry of Home Affairs (responsible for local government), invaluable in the design and implementation of public policies. Finally, MOF and all other ministries with jurisdictional supervision and control of FILP agencies and Special Accounts, had a vested interest in their survival and in the continued expansion of FILP funds which provided the main source of income. The policy-based activities of the agencies, especially the public banks and finance corporations, coordinated with those of the relevant ministries and agencies, provided important complementary and supplementary mechanisms for the implementation of public policies. Equally important, FILP agencies provided 'resting homes' for bureaucrats on retirement, through *amakudari*, and career opportunities for serving officials, through secondment, as explained in Chapter 9.

FILP IN CRISIS

The spectacular growth of FILP from the early 1980s, the tensions in its management, operation, and control, and its exploitation as an instrument of general financial management and control created conditions of actual or impending crisis, inseparable from the wider crisis in the national public finances which deepened in the recession that followed the pricking of the economic bubble in 1990. The integration of the FILP

Budget into the general public finance system occurred largely as an instrumental consequence of MOF's pragmatic policies to alleviate the symptoms of central government deficit and debt in the period of fiscal reconstruction in the early 1980s. The principle that FILP was separate from the General Account Budget, both in the source of its funding and in the purposes for which its funds were allocated, became increasingly difficult to sustain in practice. As we have seen in Chapter 23, the use of FILP funds partly to finance new or expanded social, welfare, and environmental programmes of expenditure, and the substitution of FILP funds for some kinds of capital programmes normally financed through taxation in the General Account Budget, helped to relieve pressure on the main Budget throughout the period of fiscal reconstruction in the 1980s, and beyond. It enabled MOF both to constrain the growth of general government expenditure financed by the General Account Budget, and to make progress towards the achievement of objectives for the elimination of special deficit-financing bonds and the reduction of the bond dependency ratio, while simultaneously financing policies for more expenditure on housing, welfare, the environment, help for small businesses, and public works. At the same time, FILP also provided essential 'lubrication' for the whole debt-laden public finance system by underwriting the issue of bonds for both national and local governments, and by providing accommodation through cash-flow transfers between it, the General Account, and various Special Accounts. The amount of FILP funds allocated for the latter purposes increased from 18.5% of the total outstanding loans from the Trust Fund Bureau Fund in FY1991 to about 25% in FY1995. FILP became the largest holder of both central and local government bonds.

As a result of its integration into the general public finance system, and the multiple functions it performed, the FILP Budget had grown rapidly in the period 1975–99, absorbing nearly 10% of GDP annually, with the attendant risk of the misallocation of resources, and the 'crowding out' of private investment as economic growth slowed in the 1990s. FILP's multiple functions also added to the growing costs of maintenance, as the burden of debt-servicing increased, and the postponement of the repayment of principal became more common. To finance those costs simultaneously with the financing of loans for new projects, the Trust Fund Bureau Fund needed a constant supply of funds from its principal sources. That need was met partly by the supply of new deposits and premiums, but increasingly by the growing volume of redemption funds as the FILP system matured. However, with an increasingly elderly population, the volume of annual premium payments into the pension funds was expected to decline, and the balance of accumulated deposits to diminish, in the first quarter of the new millennium. Postal savings might be affected similarly, as the elderly liquidated savings to finance retirement, residential care, nursing, and ill health. In the shorter term, the continued attractiveness of postal savings to personal savers was threatened by increasing competition from financial institutions following the 'Big Bang' deregulation of financial services products and markets in 1998, adding to the difficulties experienced, since the deregulation of interest rates in 1987 and 1993, of using the accumulated funds profitably through the Trust Fund Bureau Fund and FILP. In FY2000 and FY2001 106 trillion of high-interest deposits in postal savings matured, about half of which was expected to be moved into higher yielding financial products offered by private financial institutions. As a result, the balance of accumulated deposits in the postal savings system was expected to decline for the first time since 1945 (*Nikkei Weekly*, 30 August 1999). The dilemma for MOF and MPT was that the logic of further financial deregulation threatened to erode still further the claim of postal savings to special status.

A further contributory factor to conditions of impending crisis was the continuing need of direct and indirect subsidy from the General Account Budget if FILP was to continue to be exploited for purposes of financing general government expenditure. Further increase in the amount of subsidy increased the pressure on the General Account Budget at a time (FY1997) when government was embarking upon policies of fiscal reform designed to limit the overall level of national and local government spending, and to reduce the fiscal deficit and the GDP–debt ratio.

THE CONTEXT OF REFORM

The context within which proposals for reform were discussed in 1996–7 was shaped by a number of politico-economic factors. First, Prime Minister Hashimoto was personally committed to the reform of the economy, and to the structure of the fiscal system. Secondly, the deterioration of the chronic crisis of public finance deficits and debts prompted radical measures to control the growth of the General Account Budget in the Fiscal Structural Reform Act of 1997. Thirdly, changes in the management and control of FILP funds at the 'entry' and 'intermediate' stages affected a multiplicity of different economic, political, and bureaucratic interests, with different values and objectives.

To take only the most obvious case of postal savings, MPT was opposed to privatization, or to any loss of its management and control of savings deposits. The link with FILP was crucial, providing the rationale and justification for the continued accumulation of postal savings, and hence MPT's role. It enabled it to claim that postal savings served a national purpose through their use as FILP funds to achieve agreed national economic and social objectives. In evidence it cited such factors as the correction of the externalities of industrial production (anti-pollution measures); the provision of greater economic competitiveness (aid for small businesses); and the provision of home ownership and cheap housing (housing loans and rent-subsidies). Support for the maintenance of the postal savings system was also provided, from different motives, by the Association of Postmasters and postal workers' unions, and by most members of the LDP's powerful postal *zoku*. On the other hand, banks and financial institutions, and their representative associations, had campaigned for some time to remove elements of so-called 'unfair competition' for the savings of small investors—for example MPT's time-deposit schemes, which they claimed they could not afford to match. At the same time, together with the Ministry of Health and Welfare, MPT was pressing for greater discretion in the management of its investments. MOF's Financial and Budget Bureaux were cross-pressured by those and other interests, and for the reasons given above had their own interests in the maintenance of the FILP system as an integral part of the general public finance system. On the other hand, they also had an interest in achieving a leaner and fitter FILP, driven more by a consideration of efficiency and need than by the size of accumulated savings and pensions funds.

Those factors provided the context for the discussion of the reform of FILP initiated by Prime Minister Hashimoto following the decision to deregulate financial services and markets in 1998. In so doing, he was also responding directly to the Minister of Health and Welfare, Koizumi Junichirō, who had accepted office in the new administration on the understanding that the issue of the reform of FILP, including the option of the privatization of postal savings, would be given urgent consideration.

REFORMING FILP

The immediate origin of the reform of the principles, practice, and management of FILP lies in two reports produced by a Subcommittee of the Fund Operation Council, the body that supervised the operation of FILP. This committee was set up in February 1997 as part of the broader initiative to reform the fiscal system, one of Prime Minister Hashimoto's six 'visions' outlined in the campaign for the general election to the Lower House in October 1996 (discussed in Chapter 4). Reform of FILP was also part of the broader initiative of the 'vision' for administrative reform, in particular of the proposals to reorganize the machinery of central government, one of which was to privatize the postal services, and another, to reduce the number of public corporations and rationalize their functions—57 of the (then) 92 public corporations were in receipt of FILP funds.

It was against that background of the interconnected strands of the widening agenda for the reform of Japan's politico-economy that the Committee began its review of the current tensions and longer-term problems and difficulties outlined earlier in the chapter. Charged with the 'promotion of reform', it was unusual in that it was not legally constituted as an advisory body, had no explicit terms of reference, and conducted its proceedings under the chairmanship of Professor Kaizuka Keimei, also chairman of MOF's Fiscal System Council, as a 'free-thinking group' (Kaizuka 1998). The membership, drawn from business and universities, also included the directors-general of the relevant bureaus in MOF, MPT, and MHW, and of the Bank of Japan. No options were foreclosed or precluded. However, its deliberations were not unconstrained. There were pressures from the then minister of posts and telecommunications, who had publicly canvassed the separation of postal savings from FILP, and argued for discretion to invest more or the whole of those funds in the private sector; and from the then minister of health and welfare, who wanted a similar discretion to manage the accumulated pension funds. An agreement at ministerial level obliged the Committee 'to consider the manner in which public pension funds may be managed', including the option of self-management through the market.

The prospect of a major review of public pensions in 1999 meant that decisions in principle had to be taken quite quickly. In fact, the Committee's first report, of 23 July

1997 (Chairman's Comments), indicated the direction the reform would take, but this was intended primarily to influence the formulation of the FILP budget plan for FY1998 in the light of the Cabinet's decision on 3 July to introduce budget caps on major spending programmes in the General Account Budget, and to cut general expenditures in real terms for the first time since 1982. Following the 3% cut in the total of the net FILP Budget in FY1997 (excluding the underwriting of central government borrowing and portfolio investment—both of which were subsequently increased), a further 6.8% reduction was planned for FY1998. That strategy, and the principles that underlayed it, were endorsed and elaborated in The Outline for Fundamental Reform of the Fiscal Investment and Loan Programme, the second report that the Committee produced in November 1997. As the two reports are consistent but overlap, they are dealt with here together (Fund Operation Council 1997). The general direction and substance of the proposed reforms were similar to those of the LDP's own Committee on the Promotion of Administrative Reform, which also reported in November 1997, although the latter took a more broadly favourable view of the argument for government-guaranteed bonds. Two PARC divisions, the Financial System Research Division and the Public Finance Division, were involved in the discussion of proposals for FILP reforms and influenced the context of the work of the Committee (Financial Bureau 1999).

In its general analysis of the current problems and difficulties with the operation of the FILP system, the Committee agreed with those who had long argued that the size and rapid growth of the annual Budget over the previous twenty years had been driven largely by the method of 'passive fund collection'. This was the first official acknowledgement that the size and expansion of the FILP Budget was determined largely by supply rather than demand—the need to invest the accumulated deposits in the postal savings and pension funds through the Trust Fund Bureau Fund. Secondly, the Committee acknowledged also that changes in monetary policy, and in the long-term and fixed interest rates that accompanied them, had created difficulties in the efficient and effective use of FILP funds, and in the management of assets and liabilities by the Trust Fund Bureau Fund and the FILP agencies. While affirming that the main objectives of the FILP system remained those of providing social infrastructure and other public goods, correcting externalities of the market, and supplementing the capital market by supplying long-term fixed rate funds, the Committee recommended that the allocation of funds should reflect more accurately and responsively changes in social and economic conditions. This meant a thoroughgoing and continuous review of the existing eight policy areas that absorbed the bulk of FILP funding, and (for example) responding to demographic changes, such as the needs of an increasingly elderly population for medical and welfare services, and the declining numbers of schoolchildren.

Nevertheless, the Committee provided only general guidelines for determining which policy areas and projects should be given priority. Priority among the eight categories was not prescribed in the allocation of the budget for FY1998, although priority areas, issues, and projects within them were identified (Financial Bureau 1998*b*). In practice, choice was determined not only by responsiveness to the short-term social and economic (and political) conditions urged by the Committee: there was also the broader context, provided by the reform and rationalization of the public corporations, of which most were eligible FILP agencies. Secondly, the range of policy areas funded by FILP was to be more restricted in future by stricter adherence to the principle that funds should be used to supplement the activities of private-sector financial institutions rather than as an alternative to them, and by greater concern with the probability of the redemption of principal, and the payment of interest in loan practices. A third factor determining the choice of policy areas and projects was the decision to separate FILP from the General Account Budget, and to avoid using the former as a means of relieving fiscal pressures on the latter.

Raising Funds

The future source of funds to finance FILP, even in the more limited and narrowly focused role envisaged, was the most contentious and intractable issue dealt with by the Committee. The historic link between FILP and both postal savings and pension reserves was broken, the government accepting the Committee's strong recommendation that compulsory deposits with the Trust Fund Bureau Fund should be abolished. Secondly, the size of the FILP Budget would in future be determined by need, and by the application of criteria of efficiency and effectiveness based on market principles.

The implication of those two decisions is far-reaching. How was FILP to be financed without the substantial funds provided traditionally through the compulsory and ample deposits of postal savings and pension funds? The Committee discussed three main alternatives. First, each FILP agency could issue its own bonds without government guarantees. Secondly, the government could issue collective FILP bonds to finance their activities as a whole, also without government guarantee. And thirdly, the government could issue government-guaranteed bonds. The argument for each turned on whether FILP was, or should be, seen as an explicit instrument of public policy, with the Budget and its allocation politically determined; or, alternatively, as a method of achieving certain public policy objectives mainly through the operation of the market. The move to a market-based system would oblige public corporations to raise capital through the issue of their own FILP agency bonds, but without government guarantees, the evaluation of the market providing an incentive for efficient financial management and a means of weeding out inefficient corporations. By contrast, the issue of 'FILP bonds' would give greater weight to public than market criteria, and to FILP as an explicit instrument of policy objectives determined politically. On that argument, if certain projects of public corporations were deemed necessary by government, then it should assume responsibility for their funding collectively by its credit, and be accountable to the Diet for their performance.

The Committee's final recommendation, accepted by the government, was a compromise. Those FILP agencies able to do so would issue their own FILP agency bonds but without even 'implicit' government guarantees. Such bonds could be either corporate bonds or asset-backed securities issued as bonds. The aim was to provide asset-backed bonds comparable to US revenue bonds, and to avoid 'implied-guarantee' bonds (Financial Bureau 1998b). Only in certain exceptional and temporary circumstances, for example where an agency was experiencing difficulty with the issue of its own bonds, would the government provide guarantees. To allow a proper market evaluation, it would become legally possible for those agencies to fail and go bankrupt; for subsidies to be ended; and for auditing and accounting practices to be brought into line with international standards and made more transparent. One unresolved issue was the degree of ministerial accountability for the performance of FILP agencies issuing their own bonds without government guarantee. In practice, if ministers approved their policies, it would be difficult for them to avoid responsibility if an agency failed or went bankrupt.

Those agencies unable to raise sufficient funds from the market to meet their needs, or where it was too expensive for them to do so, were to be provided with funds by the government through the issue of collective FILP bonds, provided their policies were approved and consistent with government objectives. To minimize the public burden, government would decide the total amount of FILP funds to be raised through the issue of bonds, and the terms of the loans. FILP bonds would be issued, and harmonized, with market principles and prevailing conditions.

In the transition period following the decoupling of postal savings and pension funds from the Trust Fund Bureau Fund and FILP, those savings and funds would be gradually phased into the market, and existing FILP debts phased out as loans matured. The necessary legislation to change the relationship between postal savings, pension funds, and the Trust Fund Bureau Fund on the one hand, and the legal status and responsibility of public corporations on the other, was enacted in 2000, and the new system was up and running by April 2001. The operation of FILP—the formulation of the Budget, the allocation of funds—was regulated largely by common law precedents and by MOF's rules and practices, and legislation was therefore unnecessary.

The Use and Management of FILP Funds

Two of the three basic principles of the FILP system—the integrated management and allocation of FILP funds, and the legal requirement of safe and secure management by the Trust Fund Bureau Fund—were changed as a result of the decision to break the link with postal savings and pension funds. Decisions about the size of the Budget, its allocation to FILP agencies, policy areas, and projects, and the use and management of funds by agencies were to be determined more by market principles and market-based criteria of the efficient use of capital, using techniques such as discounted cash flow and asset liability management, similar to those in use in the USA under the Federal Credit Reform Act. More weight was to be given to the assessment of the future consequences, intended and otherwise, of funding allocations: the probability of the 'certain redemption' of the principal and the repayment of interest on loans and investments, and the projection on a discounted cash flow basis of the future fiscal costs, such as interest rate subsidies. Evidence of the application of a more market-based approach was the tightening of the rules applying to the advanced repayment (to the Trust Fund Bureau) by FILP agencies of outstanding loans. In the mid-1990s some of them—HUDC for example—took advantage of low interest rates in the market to borrow from the private sector to repay (higher) fixed-rate loans in advance of maturity. The Trust Fund Bureau Fund suffered a loss because the discounted cash value of both interest payments and principal were not taken into account. From FY1997, rules of payment were changed to ensure that borrowers bore the full cost.

FILP Agencies

The number of FILP agencies financed in FY1998 was reduced from 55 to 48, and the functions of others merged, as part of the broader reform of central government's public corporations, details of which were given in Chapter 6. More significantly, responsibility for most but not all of the debts and financing of the JNR Debt Settlement Corporation and the Special Account for the National Forestry Service was transferred from FILP to the General Account Budget. In 1998, 15.8 trillion of JNR's accumulated debt of 27.8 trillion was transferred and subsumed in the costs of servicing the central government's overall debt, albeit by complex cash flow transactions between it and the Special Account for Postal Savings and the revenues from the tax on tobacco. Those costs of the National Forestry Service, such as the prevention of soil erosion, which could not be recouped by the sale of assets were also charged as a service on the General Account Budget. Of the accumulated debts of 3.8 trillion, 2.8 trillion were thereby transferred to the General Account.

The Independent Management of Postal Savings and Pension Funds

Both postal savings and the accumulated pension funds were to be managed independently of the Trust Fund Bureau Fund and the FILP system, after the legal end to compulsory deposits. There were some big issues and many practical difficulties to be overcome in the transition period. First, with nearly 20% of the total domestic savings, and with outstanding balances with the Trust Fund Bureau Fund of some 400 trillion, the potential influence on the market was huge. Secondly, independent management would have to balance market risk with prudence, to protect the savings of small savers who had traditionally sought the security of the government-backed Trust Fund Bureau Fund. Thirdly, the independent self-management of both postal savings and pension funds implied that the costs of any management failure would be borne by the organizations responsible, and would not be a burden on the public finances. However, any losses sustained by MPT or MHW would have to be covered by the Budget Bureau. Hence their investments would be regulated by Budget Bureau guidelines on the suitability of different types of investment instrument (Financial Bureau 1998*b*).

'NEW FILP'

Legislation was passed by the Diet in May 2000 to reconstruct the FILP system in accordance with the principles laid down by the Fund Operation Council's Subcommittee

FILP under Stress

in its two reports, details of which were worked out and agreed by its three working groups (Fund Operation Council 1999b). The new system began operation in April 2001, although the transitional period between it and the old is likely to stretch over several years to ensure that the financial markets are able to accommodate and adjust to the issue and use of new fiscal instruments, and are not distorted by the disposal of the outstanding and maturing FILP loans, or by the investment of huge postal savings deposits and pension reserves.

The structure of 'New FILP' is shown in outline in Figure 28.1. Postal savings and pensions fund reserves, now de-coupled from FILP, are independently managed and invested in the financial market. FILP agencies, some of which (e.g. the Japan Development Bank, EXIM Bank and the People's Finance Corporation) were merged with other public corporations and renamed, will now raise money to finance their capital investments and loans (to other public and private bodies) directly from the market, partly through the issue of their own FILP agency bonds, and partly through the framework of the reconstructed FILP (within the box in Figure 28.1) by the issue of government-guaranteed Bonds, and through loans obtained from the successor to the Trust Fund Bureau Fund, the Fiscal Loan Fund Special Account. The Industrial

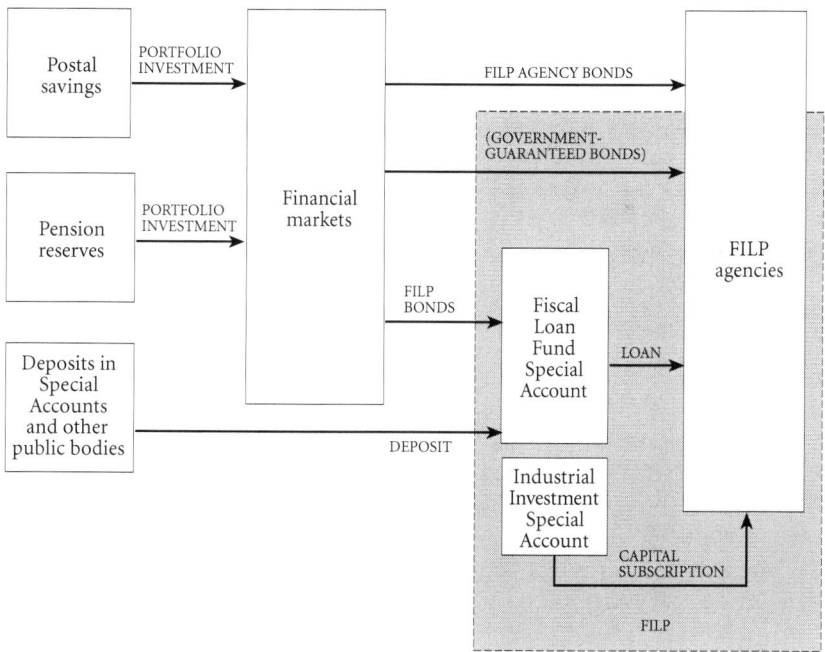

Figure 28.1 *The structure of FILP, April 2001*
Source: *FILP Report, 2000*, First Fund Division, Financial Bureau, MOF.

Investment Special Account will continue to provide a small amount of capital loans. The financing of FILP loans to FILP agencies will be through the issue of collective FILP bonds by the Fiscal Loan Fund Special Account, with those for the long term being purchased by the financial market on terms and conditions similar to those for long-term Japan government bonds. As before, there are some small deposits with the Trust Fund Bureau's successor from various Special Accounts.

The above paragraphs provide a sketch of the skeletal structure of the new system. I shall now put some flesh on it before briefly considering some of the possible effects and implications of the reformed system in conclusion.

'New FILP' is more narrowly defined as a credit extension scheme, a 'set of fiscal policies backed by capital subscription, loans, and guarantees' (Fund Operation Council 1999*b*: 1). The scope of its function is limited to the provision of interest-bearing funds to particular areas of fiscal policy as and when appropriate: first, for the creation and improvement of social infrastructure, and similar public services and goods; secondly, to encourage or guide investment in areas where the market cannot or will not provide funds; and thirdly, to continue to supplement the activities of financial markets by providing long-term, fixed-rate funds. There is a commitment in principle to the withdrawal of FILP from policy areas in which the need for public funds has declined, or is better provided by private finance through the market. The scope of its fiscal policies within those three areas will be defined after the completion of the review of the demands and needs of the traditional areas targeted by FILP—housing, environment, small businesses, and so on. In any case, their selection, and the allocation to them, will be determined more by discrimination and prioritization, the result of the use and application of quantitative analysis. While the outcome of those review processes, and the design and application of appropriate evaluative techniques, is uncertain, there is no doubt about the changes to the methods of financing the new FILP system.

The principle of passive fund collection (mainly through postal savings and pension reserves) has been abandoned. In future, the size and allocation of the FILP Budget will be driven by need and the demand of FILP agencies, and crucially by the supply of funds available in the market to finance them. Both loan rates and funding rates of the three new types of bond will be set by reference to market conditions and rates. The principle of 'harmonization with market principles' means the abandonment of the practice of setting the same rate for every loan regardless of maturity. In future, loan rates will vary with maturity based on the prevailing yield curve of Japan government bonds in the market. The deposit rates with the Trust Fund Bureau Fund will no longer be determined by the Cabinet, advised by the Fund Operation Council; borrowing through the issue of the new FILP bonds will be at rates determined in the market. The Trust Fund Bureau Fund is replaced by a new organization, the Fiscal Loan Fund.

The reform of the method of financing FILP agencies distinguishes those of their activities, projects, and policy areas that will continue to be supported by FILP funds in the new FILP framework from those that are to be financed independently of it through the issue of their own bonds in the market, without even an implied government guarantee. FILP agency bonds will be issued by each agency to finance the whole or a part of its activities and projects, under the supervision of, and subject to the approval of, the sponsoring ministry. The role of the latter will now include examination of the feasibility of the issue of the bonds, and the appropriateness of introducing other sources of private funds, for example through 'third-sector' joint public–private ventures, or through the medium of the new private financial initiative (PFI) legislation. FILP agency bonds will be issued normally without government guarantee to ensure a realistic market evaluation of their financial performance and prospects. If that is to happen, FILP agencies will have to make their decision-making processes more transparent (see below).

A framework for improved policy evaluation, essential for the clarification of the elements of public and private funding, is implicit in the reconstruction of the central executive, also implemented in 2001. Ministries and agencies will be obliged to conduct formal policy evaluations to determine need, priority, efficacy, and effectiveness, and to use outside experts and management consultants to do so. A Commission for the Evaluation of Policies and Administrative Agencies, set up in the new Ministry of Public Management, was charged with the review of the evaluation plans and procedures established in each ministry. Policy evaluations of a ministry's aims and objectives, policies, and financial performance will inescapably include the activities of those public corporations that fall within its jurisdiction and are currently in receipt of government grants, guarantees, and subsidies to finance a part or the whole of those activities designed to achieve public policy goals. This applies most obviously to the public finance corporations, such as the Development Bank of Japan and the National Life Finance Corporation.

FILP agencies will be allowed to issue bonds backed by the guarantee of the government in two limited circumstances. The first is unobjectionable. Few FILP agencies will be in a position in 2001 to raise capital in the market on their own initiative, while those with poor prospects of immediate profitability would be forced to pay cripplingly high rates of interest if they issued their own bonds. In such circumstances, the government will support issues by some agencies with explicit guarantees, and will provide temporary finance through the issue of government bills to avoid a credit crunch. The second circumstance is more problematic. FILP agencies are to be allowed to issue bonds with government guarantee as a method of supplementing their borrowing from government through the new FILP bonds. The risk is that the use of such means of financing projects and activities will loosen or weaken the financial discipline imposed by the market and increase the burden of taxation, because the costs of the guaranteed bonds will be higher than that of FILP bonds.

Reformed FILP will provide credit facilities for eligible FILP agencies to finance those activities that are consistent with public policy objectives. The financing of targeted areas and projects, for which the use of interest-bearing funds is appropriate and cost- effective, will be provided in the future by the issue of new FILP bonds offered to the public on terms and conditions similar to the risk- free Japan government bonds, and by making use of the existing market arrangements for the issue, sale, and redemption of those bonds. Funds raised in this way are low-cost and are loaned to eligible FILP agencies whose activities as a whole or in part fall within one of the three functional areas of public fiscal policy mentioned earlier. The size of the FILP Budget, and the allocation of funds raised in this way, is in principle to be determined by demand, need, and priority. Econometric techniques of quantitative analysis of costs and benefits will play a much larger role in determining them than in the past. In particular, given the history of open-ended subsidies to loss- making FILP agencies such as the JNR Debt Settlement Corporation, the National Forestry Service, the Japan Highway Corporation, and the Honshū–Shikoku Bridge Authority, and the institutionalized subsidization for explicit policy objectives of the activities of the Government Housing Loan Corporation and other public finance corporations, such analysis will be used to reveal the estimated discounted future costs of FILP subsidies of programmes and projects, and hence the future burden on taxation. Preliminary analysis by MOF in 2000 suggested that, to fill the gap created by the withdrawal of FILP funds, at least 5 trillion of subsidies would be needed annually over the next 40–50 years merely to make these and other FILP agencies solvent (MOF 2000*b*).

MOF's policy (subsidy) cost analysis (PCA) is similar in principle to discounted cash flow analysis and other such econometric techniques. It will be used to measure, weigh, and compare the flows of revenue and expenditures over the lifetime of capital projects, to help in assessments of estimated costs and benefits of competing projects, and to reveal the element of subsidy required. The Cost Analysis and Evaluation Working Group of the Subcommittee of the Fund Operation Council carried out pilot studies of five organizations to test the efficacy of the methods and the usefulness of the results. Combined, the five agencies accounted for one-third of the FILP Budget in FY1999. Their future liabilities on a discounted basis were estimated at 4.9 trillion over the lifetime of their projects, more than six times their annual operating subsidies in the FY1999 Budget (Fund Operation Council 1999*a*). The analysis was extended to a further 14 FILP agencies in 1999 based on their subsidy costs in the draft General Account Budget for FY2000, totalling 1.432 trillion. The future discounted costs of continuing those subsidies over the lifetime of the projects totalled 10.656 trillion, of which those of the Japan Highway PC contributed a half, and the GHLC a further 16% (FILP 2000).

Transparency

As in other areas of economic, financial, and administrative reform, the Hashimoto and Obuchi governments were committed in principle to the disclosure of more information, and to the transparency of the decision-making processes. All public corporations were required to observe new rules regulating the disclosure of information incorporated in legislation of June 1997. But if FILP is to operate more in harmony with the market, and the performance of FILP agencies is to be assessed by financial and management criteria commonly applied by financial institutions to private-sector firms, then the form, methods, and presentation of financial and management accounts will have to be radically revised, as recommended in the reports of the Subcommittee, and explicitly referred to in the Working Group's discussions subsequently. Public corporation accounting principles are to be harmonized with those of private-sector corporate accounting; the use of external audit adopted by some public corporations, and from 1998 by all local governments, is to be extended; and the balance sheet of assets and liabilities for FILP as a whole is to be drawn up on an accruals rather than a cash basis. To provide for financial loss and bankruptcy, the legal framework within which public corporations operate is being revised. Those are all necessary steps if the envisaged radical reform of FILP is to be brought about. The transitional period is likely to be protracted, not least because of those and other legal requirements, and the effects on the market.

Accountability

The FILP Plan will continue to be a part of the overall Budget submitted by MOF to the Diet after Cabinet approval. As explained in Chapter 19, the Plan comprised three tables (Zaitō-Sanpyō) and supporting references: the FILP financing Plan, which shows the budgetary allocations; the estimate of FILP funds required from the main sources—postal savings, pension reserves, and so on—to finance those allocations; and the functional allocation classified by policy areas, housing, environment, and so on. There was a legal requirement to obtain Diet approval for loans of five or more years from the Trust Fund Bureau Fund, and for the allocation to the public finance corporations. But in effect, the FILP Plan was a *de facto* representation. In future it will have a formal, legal basis, and the three tables will be revised and consolidated to classify FILP allocations by capital subscriptions, loans, and guarantees. FILP agency bonds are excluded from the Plan: only those explicitly guaranteed, with resource distribution functions, are counted. Loans to local government made voluntarily from (the decoupled) postal savings and postal life insurance reserves are counted as FILP, and are included in the Plan. The issue of the new FILP bonds are subject to limits approved by the Diet.

Effects

The effects of the changes will not be fully apparent for some time after the implementation of the legislation in April 2001. The transition period is likely to prove long, complex, and difficult, lasting perhaps as long as ten years. Until the change process has been completed, the consequences, intended and otherwise, of the abandonment of the passive collection of funds, and their integrated management and allocation through the Trust Fund Bureau Fund, are impossible to predict accurately. The effects on the financial markets of the borrowing of FILP agencies, and the investment of postal savings and pension funds, are equally uncertain. One anticipated difficulty arises from the maturity of large numbers of ten-year fixed-rate postal savings deposit accounts opened when interest rates were high in the early 1990s. Between 2000 and 2002, MPT estimated that some 31 trillion would be withdrawn; some independent analysts estimated perhaps as much as 106 trillion, or 40% of the total of postal savings. Most of the withdrawals will be re-deposited, despite the very low rates of interest, and the availability of alternative financial products in the deregulated financial markets, because of the security provided by government guarantees. However, both MOF and MPT felt that it was too risky for postal savings to continue to provide funds for FILP at the levels maintained throughout the 1990s. In consequence, the short-term borrowing requirements of prefectural and local governments, previously funded partly from the Trust Fund Bureau Fund and the Postal Life Insurance Fund at an annual average of some 8 trillion, were financed, exceptionally, by private banks.

The provision of long-term loans through the Trust Fund Bureau Fund will decline after 2001, as FILP agencies begin to issue their own bonds and the government begins to provide FILP bonds. Indeed, that process was already underway in the smaller Budget for FY2000, with the TFBF revenues cut by almost a quarter. For the first time since the creation of FILP, postal savings contributed no funds to them, while those from pension funds were reduced. Partly as a consequence, the amount of FILP funds available for investment and loans was cut from 39.3 trillion in FY1999 to 37.4. There was a still sharper fall in the reduction of funds allocated to portfolio management, from 13.5 to 6.2 trillion.

What happens in practice in the transition period will be shaped not only by the reactions of markets, but also by the attitudes of governments and MOF bureaucrats towards the use of the new system to achieve short- and medium-term political goals, as well as those economic and social objectives specified in policy areas and projects targeted for the fiscal policies in 'New FILP'. How the FILP agencies behave in the new envisaged regime of efficiency and cost effectiveness, with their performance subject to the discipline of financial markets, will depend on the interpretation and use (or exploitation) of the principles enshrined in the legislation. The unintended consequences of the changes to the system might prove difficult to control—for example the relationships between FILP agencies and their supervisory ministries, and with MOF. Encouraged to be more financially independent, even self-sufficient, FILP agencies might be less willing to accept ministerial direction, especially in those projects that are considered high risk; or to serve as an instrument of government fiscal policy without financial compensation for the costs of doing so. They might also be less willing to accept retirees from supervisory ministries and agencies.

The discipline of the market is intended to act as a spur to greater efficiency and cost effectiveness in the FILP agencies, as their performance comes to be subject to scrutiny in the market, and judged by criteria similar to those used in the evaluation and rating of comparable private-sector financial institutions. The risk of failure and bankruptcy is built into the reconstructed relationships between agencies and the government through revisions to the existing legislation. Just as the bankruptcy, nationalization, and disposal of the assets of the Long Term Credit Bank and Nippon Credit Bank signalled the formal end of the old and collapsing regulated and protected 'convoy system' in the banking sector, the failure of a FILP agency, if it is allowed to occur, will signal the formal end of the old, regulated FILP system. There are several candidates among the remaining FILP agencies. But the promised discipline of the market, a basic principle of the new system, was diluted even before the reforms were implemented. Both the Minister for Posts and Telecommunications and the Minister of Health and Welfare agreed with the Minister of Finance in December 1999 to give up some of their newly won market freedom. For seven years from April 2001, they have agreed to underwrite one-half of all those bonds issued by FILP agencies guaranteed by the government.

Much will turn on the extent to which MOF encourages the agencies to issue bonds without such guarantee. Some, such as the GHLC, have substantial asset-backed securities which could be used to raise capital in the money markets. The use of government-guaranteed bonds is intended as an exception to the issue of FILP agency bonds. The loophole could be exploited to protect and preserve a FILP agency from the adverse financial consequences of its performance, and market evaluation. Here the interests of the supervisory ministry or agency in sustaining an ailing or failed public corporation within its policy jurisdiction would be a material factor. As we have seen in earlier chapters, the campaign to 'rationalize and consolidate' the number and functions of the (then) 92 public corporations in the 1990s met with stiff opposition and obstruction from a variety of vested interests. It seems unlikely that those interests would not be mobilized to preserve a public corporation threatened with closure because of the judgement of the market about its financial viability, especially if its continued existence could be justified on the grounds of its public policy functions. Another critical test for the reformed FILP is the extent to which it continues to be used for the purpose of financing public works programmes and projects of local infrastructure, and providing loans and subsidies for small businesses, on the grounds of political expediency but for which there is little economic justification.

29

Coping with Fiscal Stress

Japan's main Budget exhibited three symptoms of fiscal stress throughout the whole of the 1975–2000 period: first, a recurring deficit, persisting throughout the business cycle, i.e. including years of both economic growth and decline; secondly, an increasing level of outstanding debt; and, thirdly, rising costs of servicing that debt, pre-empting an increasing share of the total Budget, and squeezing the amount of mandatory and discretionary programme expenditures. Those symptoms of acute fiscal stress first appeared in 1974–5, when MOF was forced to borrow to cover the costs of fast rising current expenditure in the 'welfare era' inaugurated in FY1973, and the slow-down in the economy following the first oil crisis. Its roots were, arguably, deeper still, stretching back to the end of the high-growth era in which the 'natural increase' of revenues generated annually by double-digit economic growth more than covered rising expenditure, and provided the means for the LDP to deliver annual tax reductions. In 1965 the Budget became unbalanced for the first time since the end of the Allied Occupation. It remained so for the rest of the century.

The growth of central government expenditure and falling tax revenues were the main causes of the deterioration in the national finances in the last quarter of the twentieth century. The persistence of large deficits on the General Account Budget, in conditions of low or stagnant economic growth, and negligible inflation produced an explosion of public debt. By the end of the century Japan's overall fiscal situation was the worst of any G7 country. By March 2000 the deficit on the General Government financial balance (excluding social security) was 10.7% of GDP, and for FY2000 was estimated at 10.1% (MOF 2000*a*). All but Japan had a trend from the beginning of the decade of improving financial balances. While gross debt continued to increase in all G7 countries, the rate slowed, levelling out in the early 1990s, and declining thereafter. Only in Japan was it rising.

In the first decade of the new millennium, Japan faced the prospect of a deficit and debt crisis of proportions unparalleled in the Western world, dwarfing that of the USA and the UK during the Second World War. MOF forecasted that by the end of FY2001 the accumulated debt of the central government alone would be more than 389 trillion. Combined with that of local government (283 trillion), the debt would be equivalent to more than 130% of forecasted GDP (MOF, 2000*b*). If unfunded pension liabilities and implicit and contingent liabilities of public finance and other corporations are included, it rises to more than 200%. There was the risk that debt of that magnitude would spiral out of control if fiscal policies remained unchanged. The OECD (1999*a*) estimated that the ratio of debt to GDP would rise slowly for about a decade, thereafter increasing rapidly to reach a level equivalent to almost three times GDP in 2026. Some analysts were much more pessimistic, predicting debt levels much greater, at 6.8 and 8.7 times GDP by that date (Ostrom 2000). If debt was allowed to reach such unprecedented levels, interest payments alone could consume more than a fifth of General Government outlays, and some 7% of GDP.

There are no quick fixes. Debt of such magnitude will not shrink of its own accord while conditions of both deflation and low economic growth persist; a growth miracle is unlikely without a radical restructuring of the economy. Nor will there be irresistible external pressures to liquidate the debt while Japan remains the world's largest creditor nation and more than 95% of government bonds remains in the hands of its own government institutions and domestic householders. Merely to stabilize the national debt by 2010 would require swingeing cuts in expenditure and massive increases in taxes, equivalent to almost 9% of GDP (OECD 1999c). There is no recent historical precedent for either in Japanese fiscal policy, and until the resumption of sustained, albeit modest, levels of economic growth there is little prospect that governments will commit time, energy, priority, and political will to reconstructing Japan's public finances.

The argument of the previous chapters is that the apparent improvement in Japan's overall fiscal situation in the 1980s, attributed by many analysts within Japan (e.g. Asako *et al.* 1991; Shibata 1993; Kawai and Onitsuka 1996; Ihori 1996) and outside (OECD *Japan Annual Survey, passim*) to the effectiveness of MOF's policies of fiscal reconstruction and consolidation, designed and implemented through the General Account Budget, fails adequately to distinguish the appearance and rhetoric of fiscal discipline and increasing control from the underlying reality. As I have shown, MOF was unable both to control the growth of central government's spending and to raise sufficient revenues from a 'decelerated' and then stagnant economy. More broadly, outlays grew uninterruptedly throughout the whole of the period 1975–2000. MOF was able to relieve temporarily some of the symptoms of fiscal stress by a variety of coping strategies providing short-term relief, but without remedying the underlying causes. It is true that cyclical factors exacerbated the condition of crisis—deficits, borrowing, and debt service costs all increased sharply in the recessionary years of the 1990s, as more than 100 trillion of additional public spending was planned (but not actually spent) between 1992 and 2000—and that the years of the bubble economy preceding them had encouraged expectations of yet more public spending, ratcheting up the base-lines of both the General Account and FILP Budgets. While those factors made the symptoms worse, they were not the cause of fiscal stress.

For most of the years 1975–2000, Japan had a stable, one-party, right-wing majority government and a centralized budgetary system. Crucially, it had an apparently 'strong' Ministry of Finance, with a formidable combination of formal constitutional and legal powers to raise taxes and control budget and off-budget expenditures, and (until 1997) responsibility for financial and monetary policies. It possessed hierarchical, organizational, and informational resources unmatched by any other ministry or agency; it was committed to a restoration of a balanced budget, and to the practice of those orthodox principles of 'sound financial management' described earlier in the book. It prescribed and progressively tightened guidelines for determining the size of the Budget and the relative priority of spending programmes, and it set budget ceilings for each ministry and agency. Yet, as we have seen in previous chapters, MOF was largely unsuccessful in reconstructing the fiscal system and achieving its main policy aims of reducing the deficit and the level of accumulated debt. Why was an apparently 'strong' ministry unable, unwilling, or frustrated in its attempts to implement agreed policies to constrain the growth of public spending and to raise more revenues by a radical restructuring of the tax system, the twin causes of the continuing fiscal crisis?

International events, pressures, and stimuli were contributory factors in the explanation of Japan's expansionary fiscal policies, on occasions decisively so, as in the U-turn of 1987. But the evidence presented in previous chapters does not support the contention that a 'reluctant Japan was pushed towards large fiscal deficits' as it bowed to the urgings of the US Treasury and the exhortations of G7, IMF, World Bank, OECD, and other international economic organizations (Tanzi 2000). Endogenous political, economic, and bureaucratic imperatives were more important drivers of fiscal policy-making through the last quarter of the twentieth century. Of course there was sometimes a coincidence of those domestic imperatives with 'foreign pressure', and it was often found politically expedient to explain and justify changes in fiscal or monetary policy as Japan's acceptance of its obligations as a leading member of the international economic community.

Maturity in Japan's public sector developed more slowly than in other G7 countries, partly because experience of welfare spending came much later, and partly because the tradition of high economic growth had generated substantial revenue surpluses. 'How to pay for it' questions were not a central concern of the budgetary process until the emergence of the fiscal crisis in the mid-1970s. The ageing of the population and the 'yoke of prior commitments'—factors that help to explain the failure of other industrialized countries to control long-term fiscal policy in the 1980s and early 1990s (Steurele and Kawai 1996)—undoubtedly contributed to the increasing pressures in the budgetary system for more public spending. But, while they made it more difficult for MOF to restrain the growth of demand-led programmes such as pensions, social security, and health and welfare programmes for the elderly, none of these was a major cause of MOF's failure to control the growth of public spending. Five other factors were more significant.

First, MOF's failure to win LDP politicians and business groups to its cause of radical tax reform until the late 1980s left it with an inadequate revenue base in an era in which a 'decelerated economy' generated insufficient 'natural increases' of revenues to accommodate the double burden of inescapable fixed costs and irresistible mandatory and discretionary expenditures without recourse to regular heavy borrowing. In the 1990s, tax revenues fell by 5.4% of GDP and accounted for two-thirds of the increase in budget deficits. The consequential costs of servicing the accumulating debt arising from the deficits exacerbated that difficulty.

Secondly, throughout the whole of the period 1975–2000, MOF was faced with the dilemma of trying to reconcile the contradictory aims of economic policy, which frequently dictated the need for increased public spending and tax cuts to stimulate the economy, and the narrower fiscal aims of reconstruction. The need to do so on several occasions meant that this spending imperative dominated much of the period. It helps to explain and justify why, faced with the conflicting policy aims, MOF resorted to temporary expedients and those budget stratagems and manipulations described in Chapter 25. While MOF was able to emerge from short bouts of countercyclical spending in the 1980s with its objectives for fiscal reconstruction still realistically attainable, even if progress towards them was deferred or delayed—as happened on three occasions for example with the target date set for the elimination of special deficit-financing bonds—it could not reconcile them with the rapid, huge expansion of the General Account Budget and FILP which the prolonged recession of the 1990s made inevitable.

The third factor inhibiting the effectiveness of its policies for fiscal reconstruction was the need to try to reconcile their implementation with the often conflicting politico-electoral strategic aims of the LDP, designed to sustain itself in power. In practice, spending programmes—especially those for public works, small businesses, and agriculture—financed through the General Account and 'off-budget' through Supplementary Budgets and FILP, implemented locally by local governments and both locally and regionally through the aegis of public banks and finance corporations, provided a source of patronage and clientelistic distributive politics for the LDP, helping to nourish and sustain Dietmen's personal electoral–constituency networks. These provided it with the means to continue to distribute substantial political favours and benefits in the outputs of expenditure programmes, and to frustrate policies for fiscal reconstruction.

The fourth factor was the nature of the budgetary processes through which the aggregate budget total was determined, and its distribution negotiated between the Spending Ministries and MOF's Budget Bureau. The aggregate or 'ceiling' for the General Account Budget (and for FILP) was set by MOF after discussion with senior LDP politicians and ministers. Throughout the whole of the period 1975–2000, even at times of acute crisis, the planned aggregate was always greater than that of the preceding fiscal year. The attempt at a planned cut, in FY1995, was made possible only by suspending the statutory payment of national debt redemption, a familiar short-term stratagem. Even so, the out-turn total was several trillion greater than that planned. The planned *statutory* cuts in FY1998 were abandoned in-year with Hashimoto's policy U-turn. Top-down limits were a necessary condition of effective control of spending, but, as Japan's experience shows, they were not sufficient. The 'ceiling' for each ministry's budget was negotiated with the Budget Bureau, together with the distribution of new money allocated to priority programmes. Although the prescription of budget guidelines nominally limited the amount of spending on each programme, their effectiveness was tempered in practice by the exploitation of spending loopholes provided by categories of 'exception' and 'exemption', and ad hoc dispensations for public works. Crucially, the budget guidelines did not apply to Supplementary Budgets or FILP, which provided further annual opportunities for Spending Ministries to argue for more public spending.

Once MOF had set the ceiling for the General Account Budget in June/July, it was almost always able to deliver the prescribed aggregate in the initial budget plan in

December, approved by Cabinet before submission to the Diet. The so-called 'revival negotiations' between the Budget Bureau and the Spending Ministries and Agencies were conducted not only within the general parameter set for the General Account Budget, but within the ceilings negotiated separately with each of them within which their budget requests were submitted. The effectiveness of MOF's control at the planning stage of the budget process was however qualified by its inability or unwillingness to restrain the pressures for more spending subsequently in-year, through Supplementary Budgets. Not subject to budget controls, the latter were inherently expansionary: the out-turn of both the General Account and FILP Budgets was almost invariably greater than the initial planned spending. Partly for that reason, MOF continued to insist on calculating, measuring, and comparing inter-year budget aggregates and programme totals on an annual plan–plan basis rather than on the more realistic plan–out-turn and out-turn–out-turn basis. In the management of the public presentation of its fiscal performance it was politically more expedient so to do, although this too was inherently expansionary.

In the 1990s many countries—among them the UK, Canada, and New Zealand—made major changes in their methods of planning, controlling, monitoring, and reporting on public spending to improve the quality of financial management in government. In both central and local government, multi-year resource budgeting and accruals accounting displaced annual cash-based systems. In Japan, however, MOF remained firmly wedded to single-year cash accounting and budgeting. Without medium-term expenditure plans, the single-year focus of both the General Account and FILP Budgets meant that the future costs of current and capital programmes were ill-considered, and invariably underestimated. This was especially true of public investment decisions, where sectoral plans were devised and implemented without analysis and evaluation of opportunity costs, costs and benefits, streams of discounted future revenues, and so on. Many of the subsidies to the FILP agencies were open-ended, and until MOF's pilot studies in 1998 little attempt was made to estimate the future costs of their continuance. While the annual budgeted subsidy for the Japan Highways PC was no more than 307 billion in FY2000, the estimated current discounted costs of continuing it over the lifetime of the construction of the road projects was 5.06 trillion, based on the interest rates for private-sector loans (Fund Operation Council 1997; FILP 2000).

To what extent was the lack of transparency of those budgetary processes a major factor in the explanation of the continuance of deficits and debt? They were undoubtedly opaque and labyrinthine, more so than in other G7 countries, but the underlying reality of Japan's fiscal situation was no secret. MOF did not conceal the details of its annual budget stratagems, or the manipulation of cash flows between the two budgets and 38 Special Accounts. The size and composition of the so-called 'hidden debt' of 47 trillion in the 1990s were public knowledge, and discussed in the media. More significantly, neither the LDP's own backbench supporters nor the main opposition parties in the Diet were disposed to argue consistently for less spending or more taxation to reduce the level of deficit and debt. Indeed, the wilder demands of the former were kept in check by the LDP leadership; while the (then) Japan Socialist Party used its position as the official opposition in the Lower House from time to time to obstruct the passage of budget bills as a means of extracting spending concessions from the government.

While there was some support among Diet parties for clean government, there was none of any significance for smaller government after Rinchō's dissolution in 1983, until the initiative of the Council on Fiscal Structural Reform in 1997. It was unlikely, therefore, that greater openness and accountability in the budget processes, for example by involving legislators in the determination of the size of the Budget(s) and its distribution, or in the prescription of budget guidelines and targets, would have checked the growth of public spending.

A fifth factor in the explanation of MOF's ineffectiveness in reconstructing the national finances was that it was very much less powerful in the budget processes than was commonly supposed, or was apparent from an inspection of *formal* budget institutions and structures. These provided the basis of the framework within which budget decisions were made, but why particular budget outcomes occurred was explained more by the *informal* politics of the budgetary processes, the interaction among the principal participants—the roles and strategies of ministers, party officials, bureaucrats, and special interest groups, the unwritten rules-of-the-game that regulated their behaviour, and their interaction in informal structures such as policy networks. Briefly, as we have seen, MOF's exercise of the formal discretionary authority vested in it by the constitution and by statute was constrained in practice by the exercise of countervailing discretionary power by other participants. It was locked into a system of mutually constrained power relationships, mainly with the LDP and the Spending Ministries, but also with some interest groups as well, and was rarely able to impose its constitutional and hierarchical authority on them and other participants, or to implement a directive strategy for determining the budget aggregate and its distribution. In the politics of public spending, it was obliged to negotiate discretionary authority to control, in a manner similar to that of the UK Treasury before the reforms of 1992 and 1998 (Thain and Wright 1995).

MOF's pragmatic and expedient response to continuous fiscal stress throughout the period of fiscal reconstruction and beyond was understandable and, from its perspective, *politically* rational. By exploiting the potential of FILP as a 'second budget'; by using it and several Special Accounts as alternative sources of finance to the General Account Budget; by cutting its contributions to local government's revenues and expenditures; by suspending statutory debt repayments, by temporary 'borrowings' and the manipulation of cash flows—by all of those short-term expedients, MOF was able to keep the fiscal ship afloat through the troubled waters of the early 1980s and the following decade, and to present an image and foster an illusion of public spending control consistent with apparent steady progress towards the achievement of its main policy objectives. It hoped and expected, not unreasonably, that a resumption of steady, if unspectacular, economic growth would enable it to repay its 'borrowings', and reduce both deficits and debts. It not only avoided (or at least postponed) the breakdown of the fiscal system: it reasserted, reiterated, and attempted to practise the principles of orthodox 'sound management'. Without the annual limits on the initial General Account Budget, and the negotiation of ceilings on ministerial budgets, public spending would have grown at a still faster rate. Guidelines for determining the relative priority of competing spending programmes at least obliged ministers, PARC officials, and even on occasion LDP backbenchers to talk the language of priority and discuss the allocation of scarce(r) resources, even if in practice the application of those guidelines was less rigorous than MOF intended. In a period in which the internal spending pressures that resulted from the expansion of welfare spending in the 1970s was fuelled by the expectations of LDP politicians, their clients, and aggrieved groups of still more public spending and lower taxes, this was no small achievement.

That said, any hopes that it had of making the surface appearance consistent with the underlying reality—in short, of making a reality of reconstructing the fiscal system according to its declared principles of 'sound management'—were destroyed by the fiscal effects of the bubble economy, which ratcheted up levels of public spending insupportable by the recent historic trends of GDP growth and contingent revenue yields, and by the plunge into deep and prolonged economic recession in the years that followed. Whatever progress had been made was slowed, then halted, and ultimately reversed as the fiscal imperative of the recession dictated massive amounts of borrowing to finance countercyclical spending, tax cuts, and concessions. Any gains that accrued from the implementation of the policies of reconstruction and consolidation evaporated. The *status quo ante* of 1975 was quickly restored. But this time round the fiscal crisis was much deeper and enveloped FILP, now swollen to two-thirds the size of the General Account Budget and experiencing its own crisis of identity and viability in an era of deregulated interest rates and liberalized capital markets. Fiscal reconstruction in the second half of the 1990s had a much broader connotation than the earlier concern with the tax structure, the budget system, and the growth of the General Account Budget: it touched all parts of the fiscal system. The crisis of the national finances was itself both a contributory cause and a symptom of a much broader crisis of the state, in which the latter's role and that of the political, bureaucratic, and economic institutions that sustained it were the subject of sustained critical debate.

The next chapter tests the explanation offered here against the evidence of comparative econometric analysis, and the hypothesis that the persistence of high fiscal deficits and debts in both mature and developing countries is associated with particular configurations of budget institutions.

30

Budget Institutions, Deficits, and Debts

THE 'COMMON POOL' PROBLEM

Economists seeking an explanation of the phenomenon of rising and persistent deficits and debts in both developed and developing countries, which occurred after the first oil crisis in the 1970s, have modelled the classic 'common pool' resource problem (Poterba and von Hagen 1999). Briefly, their argument is that competing groups vie for government expenditures, but their specific projects and programmes are financed not directly by specific (or hypothecated) revenues, but from a 'common pool' of broadly based taxation and other revenues. The costs of deficits that arise are broadly dispersed among those groups, while the benefits of higher spending on particular programmes are concentrated, resulting in higher deficits than those groups would choose for themselves if they internalized the costs of spending and consequential deficits. Modelling the common pool problem, 'electoral institutionalists' have interrelated budget outcomes to various 'political fundamentals'. Their conjectures that PR systems of representation and coalition governments have a greater bias towards deficits and debt than those of one-party majoritarian governments in pluralist systems are, however, not well supported by empirical evidence (von Hagen 1998).

The empirical work of 'fiscal institutionalists' is more robust, and more relevant to the present discussion. They argue that budget institutions affect fiscal outcomes. Budget institutions are 'all the rules and regulations according to which budgets were drafted, approved, and implemented' (Alesina and Perotti 1999: 14) There are three broad categories: rules that impose numerical constraints on the deficits, for example balanced-budget rules and explicit deficit–GDP ratios; procedural rules governing the preparation of the budget by the executive, and regulating the behaviour of the participants; and rules that determine the transparency of budgetary procedures and practices. Using the 'common pool' approach to budgeting, fiscal institutionalists hypothesize that budget institutions at the governmental (as opposed to parliamentary) level, which lead participants in the budget process to internalize the costs of budget deficits, result in smaller deficits. Internalization is more likely where budget institutions are centralized, hierarchical, and transparent. Conversely, the more fragmented, the less transparent, and the more collegial those institutions, the more likely are the occurrence and persistence of fiscal deficits and debts.

This chapter examines each of these elements in turn, and the UK's experience with a formal code of fiscal targets and rules. It then considers the extent to which proposals for the reform of the central executive, FILP, and the formal rules of the central budgetary system might contribute to a reconfiguration of budget institutions and processes more conducive to low or declining deficits in the twenty-first century. Here I compare the experience of Japan with some other G7 countries that have been more successful in controlling their public spending, eliminating deficits, and reducing the level of central/federal debt.

FRAGMENTATION

Fiscal institutionalists argue that the more fragmented is the budget process, the less individual groups of participants take account of externality in the costs and benefits of spending. The opposite of fragmentation is centralization of the budgetary process. 'A centralized budget process was one that strongly coordinates the spending decisions of individual decision-makers and forces them to take a comprehensive view of the budget' (von Hagen 1998: 5). There are two elements of fragmentation: the number of participants, and the diffusion of discretionary authority among them. As we have seen, Japan's central budgetary processes were highly fragmented, with a large number of statutory and non-statutory participants drawn from MOF, the Prime Minister's Office, Cabinet, and Secretariat, Spending Ministries and Agencies, 50–60 FILP agencies, a host of statutory and ad hoc advisory councils, formal and informal LDP organizations, and representative association of producer groups, besides prefectural and local governments. Resources of constitutional and statutory powers, information, expertise and organization were widely distributed among them. Discretionary authority to influence budget outcomes in both the General (and Supplementary) Account Budget and FILP was widely diffused.

Multiplicity and diffusion were partly a consequence of a collegial rather than hierarchical style of government, with MOF and the Spending Ministries comprising a federation of semi-autonomous states, as explained in Chapter 6. The diffusion of discretionary authority was also the result of the formal institutionalization of the LDP's policy-making apparatus in the budgetary processes, and the informal influence wielded top-down by the leadership and bottom-up (mainly through the Spending Ministries) by *zoku* and individual Dietmen, as explained in Chapter 20. Multiplicity and diffusion were also a consequence of the informal institutionalization over a long period of time of powerful producer groups within individual Spending Ministries and FILP agencies. There were, as a result, multiple decision- and veto-points.

TRANSPARENCY

By transparency, fiscal institutionalists mean not only the provision of clear information on all aspects of fiscal policy and its implementation to aid public understanding, control, and accountability, but also the existence of a single, comprehensive, and consolidated Budget covering all central government spending and revenues, with a single 'bottom line' for the accounts. Conversely, public finance systems with multiple budgets, 'off-budget' sources of expenditures and revenues, and special accounts lack transparency. On that criterion, Japan's central budgetary system was unusually opaque. There were two main budgets, 38 Special Accounts, some with hypothecated revenues and expenditures, regular institutionalized Supplementary Budgets excluded from formal budget controls, and the capital budgets of 50–60 public corporations and companies partly financed or subsidized through them. There was no one 'bottom line'.

These characteristics partly reflected the complexity of national budget-making, and the number of different types of budgets and accounts, that have resulted from their historical use for developmental purposes, and partly the closed nature of the policy processes in the Japanese political system. While the use of budgeting as a tool of economic growth and development is characteristic of most developed economies (more especially so in the Keynesian era) and all developing countries, Japan uniquely has been dubbed the first 'developmental state' (Johnson 1982). From the creation of the modern state after the Meiji Restoration, national budgets have been used explicitly as instruments of national economic and social policies to achieve national goals.

There is quite a good 'fit' between the explanation offered in the previous chapter of MOF's lack of effectiveness in reducing the levels of deficit and debt through policies of fiscal reconstruction and consolidation, and the hypothesis of the fiscal institutionalists. But before we can move to a discussion of their hypothesized reconfiguration of 'budget institutions' more conducive to lower deficits, there are some important qualifications to their analysis. First, as they themselves emphasize, in comparative analysis of deficits and debts there is the problem of the endogeneity of budget rules and regulations—that is, the extent to which they were inherent or imposed by the deliberate choice of voters or elected representatives (Poterba and von Hagen 1999). Briefly, favourable budget outcomes might occur because of changes to budget institutions to reflect society's aversion to past fiscal indiscipline. Secondly, fiscal instiutionalists also admit that budget outcomes might be influenced more by political factors, 'the political setting of the country', than by the modelling of the 'common pool' problem had thus far allowed for.

To which I here add a third qualification of my own. Their concept of 'budgetary institutions' is not well specified; the origins, substance, operation, and dynamics of budget rules and regulations, not well understood. From the perspective of public policy analysts, and that adopted in this book, too much weight is given to *formal* institutions, with the informal processes insufficiently articulated and incorporated. For example, whether a ministry of finance is 'strong' or 'weak' depends not only on the ascription of formal constitutional and statutory powers and status, but also on the particular circumstances in which it is able and willing to exercise discretionary authority relative to that possessed by others, regulated by the observance of informal policy rules (for example 'fair shares' in the allocation of the public works budget between MOC, MOT, and MAFF), and informal behavioural rules (whom to consult, when and how, and for what purpose). To take another example, the appearance of fiscal discipline and control through prescribed formal fiscal targets and controls might be belied by the reality of their interpretation and implementation. As we have seen, both MOF and Spending Ministries negotiated exemptions and exceptional treatment for particular spending programmes, and sought to exploit loopholes in apparently tightly drawn budget guidelines.

THE UK'S FISCAL CODE

Strategic institutional design to avoid or reduce deficits and debts would incorporate fiscal targets and rules, which fiscal institutionalists found were correlated with fiscal discipline and control. To achieve greater fiscal stability, several countries with comparable unitary and parliamentary systems of government to those of Japan have adopted fiscal codes, to which some have accorded constitutional status, providing a statutory framework for the design, conduct, monitoring, and evaluation of fiscal policy.

Drawing upon the experience of Australia and New Zealand, the Code for Fiscal Stability enacted by the UK in 1998 'describes what constitutes a disciplined and honest approach to managing the public finances', and sets out 'a process that ensures that Parliament and the wider public can monitor the Government's progress'. (HM Treasury 1998). Fiscal policy was henceforth to be conducted in accordance with five principles—transparency, stability, responsibility, fairness, and efficiency—enshrined in the Finance Act of 1998. *Transparency* was used here in the narrower conventional sense of openness in the setting of fiscal objectives, and the implementation of fiscal policy, to enable public monitoring and appraisal of performance. The aim was to provide a comprehensive description and assessment of the state of the public finances. *Stability* in the fiscal policy-making process implies the operation of fiscal policy predictably and consistently with the central economic objective of high and stable levels of growth and employment. *Responsibility* means that the government operates fiscal policy prudently, managing public assets, liabilities, and fiscal risks to ensure that the fiscal situation is sustainable over the long term. *Fairness* in the operation of fiscal policy takes account of the financial effects in future generations, as well as its distributional impact on the present generation. *Efficiency* in the use of resources ensures value for money, and that public assets were used efficiently.

'The [UK] budgetary process had far too long been shrouded in secrecy' (HM Treasury 1998: 17). From 1997 the UK Treasury was committed under the Code to the publication of a consultative *Pre-Budget Report*, including any proposals for significant changes in fiscal policy under consideration for introduction in the Budget, an economic and fiscal projection, and an analysis of the impact of the economic cycle on key fiscal aggregates. At the time of the Budget, the Treasury published (as it had done for some years) a *Financial Statement and Budget Report*, including economic and fiscal projections and an explanation of significant fiscal policy measures introduced in the Budget and their consistency with the achievement of fiscal objectives and operating rules.

In addition, the Code stipulated the publication of three new reports. *The Economic and Fiscal Strategy Reports*, published simultaneously, set out the long-term economic and fiscal strategy, including any long-term objectives for the key fiscal aggregates. The Code required each Report to present an analysis of the impact of the economic cycle

Budget Institutions, Deficits, and Debts

on the key fiscal aggregates, including estimates of the cyclically adjusted fiscal position, to ensure that the effects of the cycle were not ignored when policy decisions were made. It also provided illustrative projections of the outlook for the key fiscal aggregates for ten or more years ahead. The third document, *Economic and Fiscal Projections*, set out the key assumptions, forecasts, and conventions underpinning the projections of the key economic variables and the key fiscal aggregates: current spending and current revenue, the current balance, the Public Sector Borrowing Requirement, the General Government Financial Deficit, gross debt and net debt. Another innovation was the publication of a *Debt Management Report*, explaining the structure of borrowing, and the costs of government debt. These four reports were referred for scrutiny to a House of Commons select committee. The independent National Audit Office was given the new role under the Code of auditing any changes to the key assumptions and conventions underlying the fiscal projections, and reporting to Parliament.

The purpose of the Code, the five principles of fiscal management, and the key provisions of the published documents was intended to open up the budget processes and to provide for parliamentary scrutiny, for monitoring of the operation of fiscal policy, and for an independent assessment of changes to key assumptions and conventions underlying projections of the public finances. The Code did not however prescribe the government's fiscal objectives, targets, and rules: to do so would be 'unduly restrictive', and insufficiently flexible to respond to changing circumstances (HM Treasury 1998: 6). Further, it was for each elected government to choose and announce its objectives and rules, consistently with the principles set out in the Code. Those of the Labour government, which enacted the Code, were to ensure 'sound public finances' over the medium term, and to ensure that both spending and taxation impacted equitably within and across age generations. The objectives were reflected in the prescription of two fiscal rules.

FISCAL TARGETS AND RULES

Fiscal institutionalists hypothesize that the prescription of negotiated fiscal targets and constraints is more conducive to smaller deficits or reducing them. What those targets and constraints should be, how they should be operationalized and changed, and their effectiveness measured and evaluated, is however arguable. A balance has to be struck between on the one hand the need for rules that restrict profligate fiscal behaviour and provide, for example, for those principles of fiscal management outlined above in the UK Code, and on the other, a degree of flexibility in their operation to cope with changing circumstances. The major disadvantage of all fiscal targets and rules, especially where they are statutorily or constitutionally prescribed, is that they might be insufficiently flexible to meet changing circumstances, and might not allow for 'tax-smoothing' policies through the economic cycle. They also encourage creative accounting as programme managers and expenditure controllers seek to circumvent them.

Several G7 and other countries have set the fiscal objective of balancing the budget annually or over the medium term of the economic cycle, the latter allowing for fluctuations and expenditures that were cyclically (rather than structurally) determined and justified. The practical difficulties of monitoring and evaluating performance and progress towards a target over an indeterminate period of time are obvious enough. However, among others, the USA, UK, and Canada had achieved a balanced annual central/federal budget by 1999, and had estimated substantial cumulative surpluses in the first decade of the new millennium.

A narrower definition of the balanced budget is the 'primary balance', that is the balance on revenues and expenditures excluding the costs of borrowing and servicing debt. Other fiscal targets and rules restrict budget aggregates by types of expenditure and programmes. The so-called 'golden rule' restricts borrowing to capital spending, with current expenditures financed wholly by current revenues. The UK's Labour government adopted the 'golden rule' in 1997: 'over the economic cycle the government will only borrow to invest and not to fund current expenditures' (HM Treasury 1998: 16); in other words, current expenditures are balanced or in surplus over the cycle as a whole. The second fiscal rule—the sustainable investment rule—committed the government to hold public debt as a proportion of national income at 'a stable and prudent level' over the economic cycle. Thus, in the 1999 Budget the Chancellor announced that debt would be kept below 40% of national income throughout the cycle as a whole.

More common are fiscal rules that seek to control the trends of budgetary aggregates by the imposition of statutory top-down limits, such as those adopted in the USA in the 1990 and 1993 Omnibus Budget Reconciliation Acts, or by reference to criteria such as those prescribed as a condition of membership of the EMU. Targets may be set to control general government outlays as a proportion of GDP, or to reduce the deficit–GDP ratio and the gross debt–GDP ratio. Intermediate fiscal targets and controls include the 'golden rule' for the finance of current expenditure mentioned earlier, and spending 'caps' for budget totals and programmes, such as those statutorily implemented by Canada's federal government in 1991, and by the USA on discretionary spending programmes. Which types and combinations of fiscal targets and controls are more or most efficient and effective in achieving fiscal stability in the short term, over the medium term of the economic cycle, and in the longer term are impossible to say. Fiscal institutionalists hypothesize only that either delegation to a strong finance minister or 'commitment to negotiated budget targets can have a significant impact on the growth of the budget deficit' (Hallerberg and von Hagen 1999: 230).

Budget institutions do matter, but fiscal discipline and control are not only or mainly a consequence of 'top-down' aggregate fiscal rules and controls. 'Top-down' rather than 'bottom-up' budget processes are not necessarily conducive to smaller budgets.[1] Experience in Australia, New Zealand, and the UK points to the importance of the design of the budgetary system itself, in particular the processes of determining the composition of the budget, the processes of allocation and prioritization of programme expenditures, and the technical efficiency with which allocated resources are used. Besides published, binding commitments to aggregate fiscal discipline and

---

[1] For a theoretical and experimental demonstration, see Ehrhart *et al.* (2000).

control in fiscal codes, all three countries have altered the underlying incentives that govern the allocation and use of resources, achieving greater transparency in the budget processes in order to bind key players to particular fiscal outcomes, with penalties for transgression and failure. All three have devolved responsibility for budgets to line managers in Spending Ministries, and hold them to account for performance and outcomes. But their experience demonstrates as yet that there is no one way, no paradigm, that can be followed.

In the UK planning and controlling public expenditure in the new regime are implemented through contractual arrangements negotiated between the Treasury and the main ministries. They include three-year spending plans with departmental expenditure limits (DELs); public service agreements (PSAs) prescribing performance and efficiency targets for the delivery of public services; and departmental investment strategies to show how ministries manage capital effectively and how investment decisions are taken to maximize the benefits of extra investment. Monitoring and enforcement is overseen by the Cabinet's Public Spending Committee, chaired by the chancellor of the Exchequer.

A RECONFIGURATION OF JAPANESE BUDGET INSTITUTIONS?

Fiscal institutionalists suggest that, in order to avoid or reduce large deficits and debts, governments should design or reconfigure their budgetary institutions to centralize the budget processes, and to prescribe fiscal targets or controls agreed to collectively, with sanctions for their violation. Centralizing the budget processes in Japan's central government would mean reducing the level of fragmentation: cutting the number of participants and decision-points, increasing the coordinative powers of the central fiscal authorities—MOF, the Prime Minister and his Office, the Cabinet, and its committees—in order to specify policy objectives more clearly, and force consideration of the actual benefits and costs of spending and taxation policies to achieve them. MOF's illustrative medium-term simulations of the costs of continuing deficits on different economic growth and expenditure assumptions, published in FY1996–FY1998, provided some of the data necessary to that consideration, but it was in no sense a medium-term spending plan. It would also mean greater transparency in those budgetary processes, ideally one comprehensive and inclusive budget, and one bottom-line.

The design and introduction of an appropriate and effective set of budgetary institutions are affected by the 'political setting', by politico-economic, administrative, and bureaucratic factors such as those examined in the first part of this book, and by the historical origins and evolution of the fiscal system and budgetary organizations. In the Japanese case, for example, those include the particular weakness of the Cabinet and the collective responsibility of government, the institutionalization of the LDP in the budgetary processes, the fragmentation and lack of transparency in those processes, the growth and maintenance of the 'public works state', the embedded 'collective identities' of semi-autonomous Spending Ministries, and the dominant and dominating role historically played by MOF in national policy-making.

To what extent will the changes in the machinery of government implemented from January 2001 contribute to a set of budget institutions more conducive to lower or reducing deficits and debt? To what extent will there be a less fragmented and more transparent and accountable central budgetary system?

Less Fragmentation?

First, there is a reduction in the multiplicity of players, decision-points, and potential veto-points, as the number of Spending Ministries and agencies is cut from 22 to 13; the number of statutory advisory councils is reduced from 211 to 93; and, less certainly, the number of public corporations is further reduced and their functions consolidated. Secondly, the powers of the prime minister and Cabinet Office are purportedly strengthened to enable them to play a more strategic role in fiscal (and economic and other) policy-making. Against that evidence of a trend towards the further centralization of the budget process, the status and authority of the Ministry of Finance was weakened by the blame attached to it for perceived failures of economic, financial, and fiscal policy-making from the mid-1980s onwards, and the reputation of its bureaucrats for efficient and competent administration damaged by the evidence of improper and corrupt behaviour by several senior officials. As a result, it lost statutory functions, and the formal and informal powers that they conferred.

The reorganization of the central executive was a concerted attempt to further reduce MOF's dominant role at the heart of government. Its budget-making authority was directly threatened by the new Council of Economic and Fiscal Policy. Chaired by the prime minister, this was given formal responsibility for determining the budget strategy and compiling the budget. Besides the minister of finance, its members included the minister for economy, trade and industry, the minister for public management, home affairs and Posts and Telecommunications, the chief secretary to the Cabinet, the minister for economic, fiscal and IT policy, the governor of the Bank of Japan, and four private-sector members—two academics, and the chairmen of Toyota and Ushio Inc.

What role the Council will play in practice *vis à vis* the revamped Ministry of Finance is uncertain. It could perform more formally those functions previously discharged informally by the LDP leadership in the discussions preceding the June/July decision on the overall budget strategy. Alternatively, it could operate more independently of MOF, as the ad hoc Council on Fiscal Structural Reform acted in 1997, determining politically the size and distribution of the Budget, with the ministry providing advice and information, but with the initiative resting firmly with the politicians rather than Budget Bureau officials. In those circumstances, a weakened MOF would become weaker still, confronted in the implementation of a politically determined budget strategy by fewer but larger and potentially more powerful Spending Ministries. Where the lines of formal authority are drawn between politicians and Budget Bureau officials in the new arrangements will depend on the leadership of the prime minister, and his willingness to involve himself and his senior Cabinet and party colleagues in the detail of budget discussions, and upon the state of the economy. It will also be affected more generally by any reconfiguration of the relationships between bureaucrats and politicians, and by the formal and informal roles of each in the initiation and formulation of the annual budgetary strategy, the prescription of ministerial ceilings, and the allocation of shares of the Budget.

More certainly, changes in the formal functions, status, and powers of MOF, the Cabinet Office, and the Spending Ministries and agencies will not in the short term disturb their embedded 'collective identities', or change the rules-of-the-game that regulate the interaction of their members in the budgetary processes—the observance of those informal, unwritten behavioural rules conducive to widespread, inclusive, and continuous consultation; the sharing of information in relationships of reciprocity and trust; the disposition to seek consensual agreements, 'satisficing' rather than optimal solutions; and a negotiative rather than directive or impositional mode of interaction. The paradigm of the politics of public spending is likely to continue to be negotiated discretion.

More Transparent and Accountable?

Throughout the book, attention has been drawn to the scale, significance, and exploitation of 'off-budget' funds and accounts. Their assets, and implicit and contingent liabilities, are crucial in the calculation and assessment of the overall fiscal situation of central government and the public sector as a whole. Their exclusion from the calculations of General Government defined by the conventions of SNA provided an incomplete and misleading picture of the scale of government deficits and debts throughout the period 1975–2000. The deficits and debts of many bodies within the public sector—public corporations and special companies for example—were implicitly guaranteed by the central government, as was the case up to 1998 with the JR Debt Settlement Corporation and the National Forestry Service. While the central government was obliged to assume responsibility for their huge accumulated debts, their financial accounts were excluded from the financial balance of General Government. To what extent are budget institutions likely to become more transparent as a result of the administrative reforms enacted at the end of the twentieth century?

The agenda did not include proposals to make budgeting more comprehensive, for example by the abolition of the 'second budget', or its integration with the General Account Budget; nor were any major changes proposed in the number and financing of the 38 Special Accounts, other than those for the JR Debt Settlement Corporation and National Forestry. The principles of the reform of FILP set out by the Fund Operation Council began to be implemented in the Budgets of FY1997 and FY1998. The decision to sever the statutory link between FILP and postal savings and pension funds, and to compel the FILP agencies to compete for funds in the capital markets implemented in 2001, will have far-reaching consequences on those budget processes, and on the efficiency and effectiveness of the use of resources by the FILP agencies. FILP will become more independent of the General Account Budget, as the latter assumes responsibility for some of the debts of the FILP agencies, and subsidies to other agencies are phased out or subject to MOF's newly adopted analytic techniques of policy-cost evaluation. But the continuance of inter-budget transactions, and between both budgets and the Special Accounts, will continue to inhibit the preparation and publication of consolidated accounts incorporating all government revenues and expenditures.

Transparency and public accountability institutionalized in the fiscal frameworks of the UK, Australia, and New Zealand, and the adoption there and in many other G7 and OECD countries of resource budgeting, the principles and practice of accruals accounting, and the delegation of financial management and responsibility to line managers in Spending Ministries, had no counterpart in Japan's fiscal system. There was little evidence that any changes to budget rules and targets would alter that situation in the near future. The OECD (1997) noted that 'it was not possible to monitor progress towards the [then] fiscal objective [of a 3% deficit] using published documents', and repeated earlier pleas 'for a more analytical presentation of government accounts and consolidated statements, as well as returns based on existing legal and public accounting principles' (p. 75). Subsequently that and other fiscal objectives and targets prescribed in the Fiscal Structural Reform Act of 1997 were suspended to permit massive government borrowing in 1998 to finance some 40 trillion of nominal tax and spending measures to stimulate the economy. Suspension was accompanied by the abrupt halt to the 'period of intensive reform'. The short-lived experience with statutorily backed objectives, 'top-down' fiscal rules and targets, although briefly successfully implemented in the budget plans for FY1998, was unlikely to be repeated until the economy had resumed a profile of sustained growth. Even then, Hashimoto's successors will not wish to risk a repetition of the humiliating U-turn on fiscal policy that contributed to his downfall. Flexible budget guidelines subject to annual review and revision will seem preferable to the rigidity of statutorily backed controls in a multi-year budgetary system with the future costs of current and capital spending programmes planned over the medium term.

However, there were some encouraging signs towards the end of the twentieth century that MOF was becoming more responsive to criticisms of the lack of transparency in the budgetary processes. First, alarmed by the rapid rise in the level of the central government's accumulated debt, it announced in February 2000 its intention to prepare and publish a set of (more) consolidated national accounts to reveal the implicit and contingent liabilities in the fiscal system. Whether the preliminary national balance sheet published in October represented a real conversion to the principle of transparency, i.e. a first and necessarily crude attempt to measure, assess, and make public the scale of the liabilities and assets of both main budgets, pension funds, and public corporations and companies (but not those of local government), remains to be seen (MOF 2000*d*). Even where budgetary institutions, structures, and processes are more explicitly transparent than in Japan, as in the UK, attempts to use the concept of 'public sector net worth' have experienced 'difficulties in measuring accurately many government assets and liabilities' (HM Treasury 2000). Unravelling and calculating the assets and liabilities of many FILP agencies or pensions funds, for example, pose formidably complex accounting (and accountability) issues.

Secondly, there was growing awareness of the inadequacy of policy evaluation in Japanese central government. Special units for the purpose were set up in each ministry and agency, supervised and coordinated by the new Ministry of Public Management. As well, techniques of project appraisal and cost–benefit analysis were beginning to be used to assess the efficiency and effectiveness of public investment decisions; and, as mentioned earlier, MOF had begun to use policy-cost analysis to determine the real costs of the continued subsidization of FILP agencies. Measures such as these, if widely adopted, extended to other parts of the public sector, and employed systematically, would help to improve the efficiency and effectiveness of spending decisions. By focusing more attention on the objectives of policy, and comparing alternative ways of achieving them at least cost, the processes of making and carrying out budgets could become more transparent and comprehensible. For example, if the effects of countercyclical fiscal policies in the 1990s were mainly to redistribute income between prefectures, rather than to raise productivity and stimulate more economic growth, then cost–benefit analysis and related techniques of policy assessment and evaluation could help to define more clearly the objectives for both economic growth and income redistribution, establish target levels of income to be aimed at and cost alternative policies to achieve them.

References

Ahn, C. S. (1998). 'Interministry Co-ordination in Japan's Foreign Policy Making'. *Pacific Affairs*, 71/1: 41–60.
Akiyama, Masahiro (1994). Interview 11 April with Director-General, Finance Bureau, Defence Agency.
Alesina, A., and Perotti, R. (1999). 'Budget Deficits and Budget Institutions', chapter 1 in Poterba and von Hagen (1999).
Alexander, A. J. (1999a). *The Japanese Economy in Transition*. Report 44A, 19 November. Washington: Japan Economic Institute.
—— (1999b). *Is Japan Really an Outlier? An Examination of Economic and Government Variables*. Report 1A, 8 January. Washington: Japan Economic Institute.
—— (2000). *Prospects for the Japanese Economy*. Report 33A, 25 August. Washington: Japan Economic Institute.
Allison, G. D. (1993). 'Citizenship, Fragmentation and the Negotiation Polity', in Allison and Sone (1993).
—— and Sone, Y. (eds.) (1993). *Political Dynamics in Contemporary Japan*. Ithaca, NY: Cornell University Press.
AMA (1982). 'Staff Number Control', chapter 6 in IIAS Round Table, *Public Administration in Japan*. Tokyo: IIAS Tokyo Roundtable.
Anderson, S. J. (1993). *Welfare Policy and Politics in Japan*. New York: Paragon House.
Arai, Shokei (1994). Interview 25 November with Member of House of Representatives.
Arase, D. (1994). 'Public–Private Sector Interest Co-ordination in Japan's ODA'. *Pacific Affairs*, 67/2: 171–199.
—— (1995). *Buying Power: The Political Economy of Japan's Foreign Aid*. Boulder, Colo.: Lynne Reiner.
ARC (1997). *Final Report* of the Administrative Reform Council (Executive Summary), 3 December. Tokyo: MCA.
Asako, K., Itō, T., and Sakamato, K. (1991). 'The Rise and Fall of the Deficit in Japan'. *Journal of the Japanese and International Economies*, 5: 451–472.
Atoda, Naosumi (1994). 'Fiscal Deficits in Japan', unpublished mimeo, Institute of Fiscal and Monetary Policy, MOF, 30 March.
Bouissou, J.-M. (1998). 'Party Factions and the Theory of Coalitions: The Case of Japanese Politics under the Gojugonen Taisei'. Paper presented at ECPR/JPSA seminar, Kumamoto, November.
Brown, J. R. (1999). *The Ministry of Finance*. Westport, Conn.: Quorum Books.
Calder, K. E. (1988). *Crisis and Compensation: Public Policy and Political Stability in Japan*. Princeton: Princeton University Press.
—— (1989). 'Elites in an Equalising Role'. *Comparative Politics*, 21: 379–403.
—— (1990). 'Linking Welfare and the Developmental State: Postal Savings in Japan'. *Journal of Japanese Studies*, 16/1: 31–59.
—— (1993). *Strategic Capitalism*. Princeton: Princeton University Press.
Callon, Scott (1995). *Divided Sun: MITI and the Breakdown of Japanese High-Tech Industrial Policy, 1975–1993*. Stanford, Calif.: Stanford University Press.

Campbell, J. C. (1977). *Contemporary Japanese Budgeting.* Berkeley: University of California Press.

—— (1984). 'Policy Conflict and its Resolution within the Governmental System', in E. Krauss, T. Rholen, and P. Steinhoff (eds.), *Conflict in Japan.* Honolulu: University of Hawaii Press.

—— (1993). *How Policies Change: The Japanese Government and the Ageing Society.* Princeton: Princeton University Press.

—— (1996). 'Media and Policy Change in Japan', in S. Pharr and E. Krauss (eds.), *Media and Politics in Japan.* Honolulu: University of Hawaii Press.

—— (1999). 'Administrative Reform as Policy Change and Policy Non-Change'. *Social Science Japan Journal*, 2/2: 157–176.

Chinworth, M. (1992). *Inside Japan's Defense.* Washington: Brassey's.

Choy, J. (1999). *Japan's Banking Industry: The 'Convoy' Disperses in Stormy Seas.* Report No. 10A, 12 March. Washington: Japan Economic Institute.

Council on Fiscal Structural Reform (1997). *Final Report* of the Council on Fiscal Structural Reform, 3 June.

Cowhey, P. R., and McCubbins, M. D. (1995). *Structure and Policy in Japan and the United States.* Cambridge: Cambridge University Press.

Cox, G., and Thies, M. (1998). 'The Cost of Intra-Party Competition: The Single Non-Transferable Vote and Money Politics in Japan'. *Comparative Political Studies*, 31/3: 267–292.

Curtis, G. (1988). *The Japanese Way of Politics.* New York: Columbia University Press.

DA (1994). Interview 11 April with Director-General, Bureau of Finance, Defence Agency.

DBJ (2000). *Annual Report 1999.* Tokyo: Development Bank of Japan.

DeWit, A., and Steinmo, S. (2001). 'Policy vs Rhetoric: The Political Economy of Taxes and Redistribution in Japan', mimeo, Shimenoseki City University, Shimenoseki-shi, August.

Directory of the Finance Ministry (1986). *Shōwa 62-nenban Ōkurashō meikan* [MOF Directory 1987]. Tokyo: Jihyōsha.

Donnelly, M. W. (1984). 'Conflict over Government Authority and Markets: Japan's Rice Economy', in E. Krauss, T. Rohlen, and P. Steinhoff (eds.), *Conflict in Japan.* Honolulu: University of Hawaii Press.

Dore, R. (1999). 'Japan's Reform Debate: Patriotic Concern or Class Interest? Or Both?' *Journal of Japanese Studies*, 25/1: 65–89.

Economic Council (1996). *Examining the Public Finances and Social Security Issues towards the 21st Century*, English translation by EPA, 27 November. Tokyo: EPA.

—— (1999). *Ideal Socioeconomy and Policies for Economic Rebirth.* Report to the PM, 5 July.

Ehrhart, K.-M. et al. (2000). *Budget Processes: Theory and Experimental Evidence*, Working Paper B18. Bonn: Zentrum für Europäische Integrationsforschung, November.

Elliot, James (1983). 'The 1981 Administrative Reform in Japan'. *Asian Survey*, 23/6: 765–779.

Ensign, M. M. (1992). *Doing Good or Doing Well? Japan's Foreign Aid Programme.* New York: Columbia University Press.

EPA (1992). *The Five Year Economic Plan: Sharing a Better Quality of Life around the Globe.* Tokyo: Printing Bureau, MOF.

—— (1993). Interview 2 March with Deputy Vice-Minister, Minister's Secretariat.

—— (1994a). *Economic Survey of Japan: 1992–93.* Tokyo: EPA.

—— (1994b). 'Basic Plan for Public Investment', mimeo, unofficial translation, October. Tokyo: EPA.

—— (1995a). *Economic Survey of Japan, 1995.* Tokyo: EPA.

—— (1995b). *Monthly Report on the Economy.* Tokyo: EPA.

—— (1996a). *Social and Economic Plan for Structural Reforms towards a Vital Economy and Secure Life*. Tokyo: Printing Bureau, MOF.
EPA (1996b). *Economic Survey of Japan 1995–96*. Tokyo: EPA.
—— (1999). *Report on Deregulation*. Tokyo: EPA, 26 March.
ERI (1990). *A System of National Accounts: Framework and Concepts*, Economic Research Institute. Tokyo: EPA.
EXIM (1995). *Annual Report*, EXIM Bank. Tokyo: Chiyoda-ku.
FILP (1996). *FILP Report '96*, Financial Bureau, MOF, October. Tokyo: MOF.
—— (1997). *FILP Report '97*, Financial Bureau, MOF, October. Tokyo: MOF.
—— (1998). *FILP Report 1998*, Financial Bureau, MOF, October. Tokyo: MOF.
—— (1999). *FILP Report 1999*, Financial Bureau, MOF, November. Tokyo: MOF.
—— (2000). *FILP Report 2000*, Financial Bureau, MOF, February. Tokyo: MOF.
Financial Bureau (1998a). Interview 23 March with Morimoto Manabu, Director Local Fund Operation Division, Financial Bureau, MOF.
—— (1998b). Interview 7 November with Director of Fiscal Investment and Loan Department, Financial Bureau, MOF.
—— (1999). Interview 14 November with Director, Asset and Management Liability Office, Financial Bureau, MOF.
First Fund Division (1993). Interview 3 March with Nakagawa, M., Director; Nakajima, H., Deputy Director, Government Debt Division; Asakawa, J., Deputy Director, Second Fund Division, Financial Bureau, MOF.
—— (1994). Interview 18 April with Murao Nobutaka, Special Officer for Research and Planning, First Fund Division. Financial Bureau, MOF.
FSRC (1996). *Final Report on Restructuring the Fiscal System*, Fiscal System Research Council, Budget Bureau, MOF, 12 December.
Fukui, H. (1987). 'The Policy Research Council of Japan's LDP: Policy-Making Role and Practice'. *Asian Thought and Society*, 12/2: 3–31.
Funabashi, Yoichi (1988). *Managing the Dollar: From the Plaza to the Louvre*. Washington: Institute for International Economics.
Fund Operation Council (1997). First Report, *Chairman's Comments*, of Subcommittee on FILP Reform, 23 July; Second Report, *The Outline for Fundamental Reform of the FILP*, November. Tokyo: Financial Bureau, MOF.
—— (1999a). *Policy (Subsidy) Cost Analysis on FILP Projects: Summary of Report of the Working Group on Cost Analysis and Evaluation*. Tokyo: Financial Bureau, MOF, August.
—— (1999b). *Summary of the Discussion Concerning Fundamental Reform of FILP*. Tokyo: Financial Bureau, MOF, August.
Fushimi, Yasuharu (1994). Interview 7 April with Director of Salary Division, National Personnel Agency, formerly Deputy Director of the Coordination Division, Budget Bureau, MOF.
George, A. D. (1981). 'The Japanese Farm Lobby and Agricultural Policy-Making', *Pacific Affairs*, 54/3: 409–430.
—— (1988). 'Japanese Interest Group Behaviour: An Institutional Approach', in J. A. A. Stockwin et al. (eds.), *Dynamic and Immobilist Politics in Japan*. Honolulu: University of Hawaii Press.
Gwartney, J. D., Lawson, K., and Block, W. (1996). *Economic Freedom of the World*. Vancouver: Fraser Institute.
Haley, J. O. (1987). 'Governance by Negotiation: A Reappraisal of Bureaucratic Power in Japan', in K. B. Pyle (ed.), *The Trade Crisis: How Will Japan Respond?* Seattle: Society for Japanese Studies, University of Washington.
—— (1991). *Authority without Power*. New York: Oxford University Press.

Hall, P. A., and Taylor, C. R. (1996). 'Political Science and the Three New Institutionalisms'. *Political Studies*, 44: 936–958.
Hallerberg, M. and von Hagen, J. (1999). 'Electoral Institutions, Cabinet Negotiations, and Budget Deficits in the European Union', in Poterba and van Hagen (1999).
Hartcher, P. (1998). *The Ministry: The Inside Story of Japan's Ministry of Finance*. London: Harper-Collins.
Hatoyama, Kunio (1994). Interview 24 November with Member of House of Representatives.
Hayao, Kenji (1993). *The Japanese Prime Minister and Public Policy*. Pittsburgh, Pa: University of Pittsburgh Press.
Hayashi, Nobumitsu (1993). Interview 18 February with Deputy Budget Examiner, Budget Bureau, MOF.
Hirose, Haruku (1993). 'The Civil Service and Personnel Administration', chapter 2 in Masujima and O'uchi (1993).
Hirose, Michisada (1981). *Hojokin to Seikentō* [Subsidies and the Ruling Party]. Tokyo: Asahi Shinbun Sha.
H. M. Treasury (1998). *The Code for Fiscal Stability*, March. London: H. M. Treasury.
—— (2000). *Fiscal Statement and Budget Report*, March. London: H. M. Treasury.
Hood, C. (1991). 'A Public Management for all Seasons'. *Public Administration*, 69/1: 3–19.
Hori, Kasuke (1995). Interview 12 April with Acting Chairman, PARC.
Horié, Masahiro (1993). Interview 23 February with former Deputy Budget Examiner, Budget Bureau, MOF.
—— (1994). Interview 11 April with former Deputy Budget Examiner, Budget Bureau, MOF.
—— (1996). 'The Experience in Efforts to Keep the Civil Service Small: Systems and Practices of Manpower Control in Japan'. Paper presented to the International Colloquium on Civil Service and Economic Development: 'The Japanese Experience', 23 March 1994; revised 31 April 1996.
Horne, J. (1985). *Japan's Financial Markets: Conflict and Consensus in Policy-Making*. Sydney: Allen & Unwin.
Hrebenar, R. J. (1992). *The Japanese Party System*, 2nd edn. Boulder, Colo.: Westview Press.
—— (2000). *Japan's New Party System*. Boulder, Colo.: Westview Press.
IAM (1998). *Administrative Management and Reform in Japan*. Tokyo: Institute of Administrative Management.
—— (1999). *Administrative Management and Reform in Japan*. Summary of the 1998 Annual Report of the Management and Co-ordination Agency, March. Tokyo: Institute of Administrative Management.
Igarashi, Takayoshi (1999). 'Public Works at a Crossroads', *Social Science Japan*, 17 December: 3–5.
Ihori, Toshihiro (1996). 'Prior Commitments, Sustainability and Intergenerational Redistribution in Japan', in Steuerle and Kawai (1996).
IIAS (1982). *Public Administration in Japan*, edited by IIAS Tokyo Round Table Organising Committee. Tokyo: Institute of International Administrative Science.
Iio, J. (1993). *Min'eika no Seiji Katei: Rinchōgata Keikaku no Seika to Genkai* [The Political Process of Privatization: Results and Limitations of Rinchō-style Reform]. Tokyo: Tokyo Daikagu Shuppankai.
IMF (1999). *World Economic Outlook*. Washington: IMF, October.
Inoguchi, Takashi (1983). *Gendai Nihon seiji Keizai no kōzu: Seifu to shijō* [The Structure of Politics and Economy in Contemporary Japan: The Government and the Market]. Tokyo: Tōyō Keizai shinpōsha.
—— (1990). 'Conservative Resurgence Under Recession', in T. J. Pempel (ed.), *Uncommon Democracies*. Ithaca, NY: Cornell University Press.

Inoguchi, Takashi (1997). 'The Pragmatic Evolution of Japanese Democratic Politics', in M. Schmiegelow (ed.), *Democracy in Asia*. New York: St Martin's Press.
—— and Iwai, T. (1987). *Zoku giin no kenkyō: Jimintō seiken o gyūjiru shuyakutachi*. [A Study of Zoku-Giin Leaders of the LDP]. Tokyo: Nihon Keizai Shinbunsha.
Inoki, Takenori (1995). 'Japanese Bureaucrats at Retirement', in Kim *et al.* (1995).
Inose, N. (1997). *A Study of the State of Japan* (in Japanese). Tokyo: Bungei Shunjū.
Ishi, Hiromitsu (1989). *The Japanese Tax System* Oxford: Oxford University Press.
—— (1993). *The Japanese Tax System*. 2nd edn. Oxford: Oxford University Press.
—— (1995). 'Rigidity and Inefficiency in Public Works Appropriations: Controversy in Reforming the Budgeting Process in 1994'. *Journal of Japanese Studies*, 21/2: 404–411.
—— (2000). *Making Fiscal Policy in Japan: Economic Effects and Institutional Settings*. Oxford: Oxford University Press.
Ishiyama, Yoshihide (1994). 'The Macroeconomic Impact of Budget Deficits in the US and Japan', unpublished mimeo, Institute of Fiscal and Monetary Policy, MOF, 20 March.
Itagaki, H. (1987). *Zoku no Kenkyū*. [A Study of Zoku]. Tokyo: Keizaikai.
Itō, Dai-ichi (1988). 'Policy Implications of Administrative Reform', chapter 4 in J. A. Stockwin *et al.* (eds.), *Dynamic and Immobilist Politics in Japan*. London: Macmillan.
JDB (1995). *Annual Report*. Tokyo: Japan Development Bank.
JEI (1996). 'Hashimoto Administration Calculating Fiscal Figures'. Report 47B, 20 December. Washington: Japan Economic Institute.
—— (1997). 'Fiscal Reconstruction Plans Set'. Report 21B, June. Washington: Japan Economic Institute.
JFCME (1997*a*). 'Local Public Finances', Japan Finance Corporation for Municipal Enterprises paper to 29th Annual International Conference on Local Credit, September, Tokyo.
—— (1997*b*). *Annual Report 1997*. Tokyo: Japan Finance Corporation for Municipal Enterprises.
Jinji-in (annual). *Nenji Hōkokusho* [Annual Report]. Tokyo: Ōkurashō, Insatsukyoku.
Johnson, C. J. (1974). 'The Re-employment of Retired Government Bureaucrats in Japanese Big Business'. *Asian Survey*, 14: 953–965.
—— (1975). 'Japan: Who Governs? An Essay on Official Bureaucracy'. *Journal of Japanese Studies*, 2/1: 1–28.
—— (1978). *Japan's Public Policy Companies*. Washington: American Enterprise Institute.
—— (1980). 'Omote (Explicit) and Ura (Implicit): Translating Japanese Political Terms'. *Journal of Japanese Studies*, 6/1: 89/115.
—— (1982). *MITI and the Japanese Miracle: The Growth of Industrial Policy, 1925–1975*. Stanford, Calif.: Stanford University Press.
—— (1986). 'Tanaka Kakuei, Structural Corruption and the Advent of Machine Politics in Japan'. *Journal of Japanese Studies*, 12/1: 1–28.
—— (1989). 'MITI, MPT and the Telecom Wars: How Japan Makes Policy for High Technology', in Johnson *et al.* (1989).
—— (1990). 'Japan's Strategic Structures,' in S. N. Eisenstadt and Eyal Ben-Ari (eds.), *Japanese Models of Conflict Resolution*. New York: Kegan Paul International.
—— Tyson, L. D'A, and Zysman, J. (eds.) (1989). *Politics and Productivity: How Japan's Development Strategy Work*. New York: Harper Business.
Kaizuka, Keimai (1998). Interview 3 April with Chairman of the Fund Operation Council's Sub-Committee on FILP Reform.
Kamada, Kōichirō (1993). 'The Real Value of Postal Savings Certificates'. *Bank of Japan Monetary and Economic Studies*, 11/2: 59–96.

References

Kaneko, Yūko (1998). 'Japan's Bureaucracy: Its Realities and Future Direction of Transformation'. Paper by the Director of the Economic Statistics Clearance Division, Statistics Bureau, MCA, November.
Kase, Kazutoshi (1999). 'Economic Aspects of Public Works Projects in Japan'. *Social Science Japan*, 17: 16–19.
Kataoka, Hiromitsu (1996). *Kanryō no elite gaku* [Japan's Elite Bureaucrats]. Tokyo: Waseda University Press.
Katō, Hiroshi (1994). 'Thoughts on the Tax Reform Fiasco'. *Japan Echo*, 21/2: 33–39.
—— (1995). 'Preparing the Welfare System for the 21st Century'. *Economic Eye*, Spring: 26–29.
Katō, Junko (1994). *The Problem of Bureaucratic Rationality*. Princeton: Princeton University Press.
—— (1997). 'Withering Factionalism', in M. Schmieglow (ed.), *Democracy in Asia*. New York: St Martin's Press.
Katzenstein, P. J. (1996a). *Cultural Norms and National Security: Police and Military in Postwar Japan*. Ithaca, NY: Cornell University Press.
—— (1996b). *The Culture of National Security: Norms and Identity in World Politics*. New York: Columbia University Press.
—— and Okawara, N. (1993). *Japan's National Security*. Ithaca, NY: Cornell University Press.
Kawai Masahiro and Onitsuka Yūsuke (1996). 'Fiscal Policy, Global Savings and Investment, and Economic Growth', in Steuerle and Kawai (1996).
Kawakita, Takao (1991). 'The Ministry of Finance'. *Japanese Economic Studies*, Summer; trans. from chapter 4 of *Ōkurasho*. Tokyo: Kodansha, 1989.
Keddell, J. P. (1993). *Politics of Defence in Japan*. Armonk, NY: M. E. Sharpe.
Keehn, B. (1990). 'Managing Interests in the Japanese Bureaucracy'. *Asian Survey*, 30/11: 1021–1037.
Kemp, Peter (1999). *Guardian* (London), 29 October.
Kim, H.-K. et al. (1995). *The Japanese Civil Service and Economic Development*. Oxford: Clarendon Press.
Kishi, Nobuhito (1995). 'Japan's Invisible Unemployment Problem'. *Japan Echo*, 22/3: 38–43.
Kitaoka, Shin'ichi (1993). 'The Bureaucratisation of Japanese Politics'. *Japan Echo*, 20/2: 33–39.
Koga, Issei (1994). Interview 28 November with Member of House of Representatives.
Kogayū, Masami (1993). Interview 19 February with Chairman of Fair Trades Commission (Administrative Vice-Minister, MOF 1990–91; Director-General of the Budget Bureau, MOF, 1988–90).
Koh, B. C. (1989). *Japan's Administrative Elite*. Berkeley: University of California Press.
Kohno, Masaru (1992). 'Rational Foundations for the Organisation of the Liberal Democratic Party in Japan'. *World Politics*, 44: 369–397.
—— and Nishizawa, Y. (1990). 'A Study of Electoral Business Cycles in Japan: Elections and Government Spending on Construction'. *Comparative Politics*, 22: 151–166.
Komiya, Ryūtarō (1990). *The Japanese Economy: Trade, Industry and Government*. Tokyo: University of Tokyo Press.
—— (1999). 'Declining Population, The Size of the Government and the Burden on Public Debt', in C. Freedman (ed.), *Why Did Japan Stumble?* Cheltenham: Edward Elgar.
Komura, Takeshi (1993). Interview 2 March with Deputy Vice-Minister, Director-General's Secretariat, EPA (Director General, Budget Bureau 1996–97; Administrative Vice-Minister, MOF 1997–98).
Kondō, Tetsuo (1994). Interview 30 November with member of House of Representatives, formerly Chairman of PARC Division for Post and Telecommunications; Chairman of PARC's Banking Research Commission; Vice-Chairman of LDP's Tax System Research Council.

Koppell, B., and Orr, R. M. (eds.) (1993). *Japan's Foreign Aid: Power and Policy in a New Era*. Boulder, Colo.: Westview Press.

Kosai, Yutaka (1994). Interview 18 April with President, Japan Centre for Economic Research.

Kubono, Shizuharu (1993). Interview 16 February with Budget Examiner, Budget Bureau, MOF.

Kuribayashi, Yoshimitsu (1986). *Ōkurashō Shukeikyoku* [The Budget Bureau of the Finance Ministry]. Tokyo: Kodansha.

Kurimoto, Makoto (1993). 'The Tax Revenue Shortage and the Management of Government Finances'. *Japan Research Quarterly*, 24/4: 16–50.

Kuwayama, P. H. (1999). 'Postal Banking in the US and Japan: A Comparative Analysis'. Discussion Paper No. 99-E-18, Institute of Monetary and Economic Studies, Bank of Japan, June.

Laver, M., and Katō, J. (1998). 'Party Discipline and the Generic Instability of Decisive Structures', paper presented to ECPR/JPSA seminar, Kumamoto, November.

LDP (1993). *Liberal Democratic Party and its Central Office*. Tokyo: LDP, Nagata-cho, Chiyoda-ku.

Lincoln, E. J. (1988). *Japan: Facing Economic Maturity*. Washington: Brookings Institution.

—— (2000). *Change—Real and Apparent—in the Japanese Economy*. Report No. 13A, 31 March. Washington: Japan Economic Institute.

Local Fund Operations Division (1998). Interview 23 March with Morimoto Manabu, Director, Local Fund Operations Division, Financial Bureau, MOF.

Mabuchi, Masaru (1997). *Ōkurashō wa naze oitsumerareta no ka: Seikan kankei no henbō* [Why MOF Is in a Tight Corner: The Transformation of Politician–Bureaucrat Relations]. Tokyo: Chūō Shinpō Sha.

MAFF (1993). Interview 2 November with Director-General, Livestock Bureau, formerly Director of Budget and Accounts Division.

Maruyama, Junichi (1993). Interview 27 October with Maruyama Junichi, Special Officer for Planning and Research, Research Division, Minister's Secretariat, MOF.

Masujima, Toshiyuki (1993). 'The Rinchō Administrative Reform', chapter 8 in Masujima and O'uchi (1993).

—— (1998). 'Administrative Reform and Decentralisation in Japan: RINCHO and After'. Paper presented at the NIRA–NAPA Conference, 27–29 July, Tokyo.

—— and O'uchi Minoru (eds.) (1993). *The Management and Reform of Japanese Government*, Tokyo: Institute of Administrative Reform.

——————— (eds.) (1995). *The Management and Reform of Japanese Government*, 2nd edn. Tokyo: Institute of Administrative Reform.

MCA (1994). Interview 23 November with former Deputy Budget Examiner responsible for Science and Technology Policy, Budget Bureau, MOF.

—— (1997*a*). Interview 5 April with Director of Management for Administrative Reform, Administrative Management Bureau.

—— (1997*b*). *Secondment between Ministries, 1996* (in Japanese). Tokyo: MCA.

—— (1997*c*). *Organisation of the Government of Japan, 1997*. Tokyo: Prime Minister's Office.

—— (1997*d*). *Annual Report, 1997*. Tokyo: MCA.

—— (1998*a*). Interview 22 March with Director, General Affairs Division, Director-General's Secretariat.

—— (1998*b*). Interview 23 March with Director, General Affairs Division, Director-General's Secretariat.

—— (1998*c*). *Tokushu hōjin sōran* [Directory of Public Corporations]. Tokyo: MCA.

—— (1999). *Organisation of the Government of Japan, 1999*. Tokyo: Prime Minister's Office.

—— (2000). *White Paper on the De-Regulation Programme, 1998–2000*. Tokyo: MCA.

McCubbins, M. D., and Noble, G. W. (1995a). 'Perceptions and Realities of Japanese Budgeting', chapter 5 in Cowhey and McCubbins (1995).
—— ——(1995b). 'The Appearance of Power: Legislators, Bureaucrats and the Budget Process in the US and Japan', chapter 4 in Cowhey and McCubbins (1995).
Meyer, S., and Naka, S. (1998). 'Legislative Influences in Japanese Budgetary Politics'. *Public Choice*, 94/3–4: 267–288.
MHA (1994). Interview 19 April with Director, Local Finance Co-ordination Division, Local Finance Bureau.
MHW (1994). Interview 13 April with Director of Budget and Accounts Division.
MICHI (1998). *MICHI: Roads in Japan 1998*, Road Technology Research Board. Tokyo: Road Public Relations Center, September.
Mimura, Tōru (1993). Interview 17 February with former Deputy Budget Examiner, Budget Bureau, MOF.
MITI (1993). Interview 29 October with Director for Energy and Industrial Technology, Machine and Information Industries Bureau. Interview 4 November with Director-General, Economic Co-operation Bureau, formerly Director of Budget and Accounts Division.
—— (1994). Interview 1 December with Director of Quality of Life and Culture Division, Industries Bureau.
Miwa, Y. (1998). 'The Economics of Corporate Governance in Japan', in K. Hopt *et al.* (eds.), *Comparative Corporate Governance*. Oxford: Oxford University Press.
Miyajima, H. (1988). *Zaisei Saiken* [Fiscal Reconstruction]. Tokyo: Yūhikaku.
Miyawaki, A. (1993). 'The Fiscal Investment and Loans System towards the 21st Century'. *Japan Research Quarterly*, 2/2: 15–66.
MOC (1993a). Interview 5 November with Director and Deputy Director of Budget and Accounts Division.
—— (1993b). Interview 12 November with Director, Construction Contractors Division, Economic Affairs Bureau.
—— (1996). Interview 15 May with former Deputy Director, River Bureau.
—— (1997a). *White Paper on Construction in Japan 1997*. Research Institute of Construction and Economy. Tokyo: MOC.
—— (1997b). Interview 15 April with Director of Budget and Accounts Division.
MOE (1994). Interview 8 April with Deputy Director, Budget and Accounts Division.
MOF (1976). *The Japanese Budget in Brief*. Budget Bureau. Tokyo: MOF.
—— (1977). *The Japanese Budget in Brief*. Budget Bureau. Tokyo: MOF.
—— (1981). *The Japanese Budget in Brief*. Budget Bureau. Tokyo: MOF.
—— (1985). *The Japanese Budget in Brief*. Budget Bureau. Tokyo: MOF.
—— (1988). *The Japanese Budget in Brief*. Budget Bureau. Tokyo: MOF.
—— (1990). *The Japanese Budget in Brief*. Budget Bureau. Tokyo: MOF.
—— (1992a). 'Why a Discussion of Japanese Government Finance should not be Based on the General Government Financial Basis', unpublished mimeo, Budget Bureau. Tokyo: MOF.
—— (1992b). *The Japanese Budget in Brief*. Budget Bureau. Tokyo: MOF.
—— (1993a). Interview 27 October with Special Officer, Research and Planning Division, Minister's Secretariat.
—— (1993b). Interviews 17 February and 5 March with Director of Research Division, Budget Bureau.
—— (1993c). Interview 2 November with Deputy Director, Co-ordination Division, Budget Bureau.

—— (1993*d*). Interview 28 October with Special Officer for Planning and Research, First Fund Division, Financial Bureau.
—— (1994*a*). Interview 15 February with Deputy Budget Examiner, Budget Bureau.
—— (1994*b*). *The Japanese Budget in Brief 1994*. Budget Bureau. Tokyo: MOF.
—— (1994*c*). Interview 23 November with Budget Examiner, Budget Bureau.
—— (1994*d*). Interview 7 April with Deputy Budget Examiner, Public Works Division, Budget Bureau.
—— (1995). *The Japanese Budget in Brief*. Budget Bureau. Tokyo: MOF.
—— (1996*a*). *The Ministry of Finance: Organisation, Roles and Functions*. Institute of Fiscal and Monetary Policy. Tokyo: MOF, March.
—— (1996*b*). *The Japanese Budget in Brief*. Budget Bureau. Tokyo: MOF.
—— (1997*a*). 'Financial System Reform'. *Monthly Finance Review*, 16–26 August. Institute of Fiscal and Monetary Policy. Tokyo: MOF.
—— (1997*b*). *Highlights of the Draft Budget for FY1998*. Budget Bureau. Tokyo: MOF, December.
—— (1998*a*). Interview 17 March with Deputy Budget Examiner, Budget Bureau.
—— (1998*b*). Evidence to Finance Committee of House of Representatives, 18 February.
—— (1998*c*). *The Japanese Budget in Brief*. Budget Bureau. Tokyo: MOF.
—— (1998*d*). 'General Survey and Common Measures of the Three-Year Program for the Promotion of Deregulation'. *Monthly Finance Review*, May: 45–50. Institute of Fiscal and Monetary Policy. Tokyo: MOF.
—— (1998*e*). 'Outline of Financial System Reform Bill'. *Monthly Finance Review*, May: 4–19. Institute of Fiscal and Monetary Policy. Tokyo: MOF.
—— (1999). 'Highlights of the Fiscal Year 1999 Budget'. *Monthly Finance Review*, February: 76. Institute of Monetary and Fiscal Policy. Tokyo: MOF.
—— (2000*a*). *The Japanese Budget in Brief (1999)*. Budget Bureau. Tokyo: MOF.
—— (2000*b*). *The Japanese Budget in Brief (2000)*. Budget Bureau. Tokyo: MOF.
—— (2000*c*). Minister of Finance's Budget Speech to the Diet, 28 January. *Monthly Finance Review*, March: 6–8. Institute of Fiscal and Monetary Policy. Tokyo, MOF.
—— (2000*d*). 'Japanese Government Balance Sheet: Study Group Report', October. *Monthly Finance Review*, December: 6–10. Institute of Fiscal and Monetary Policy. Tokyo: MOF.
MOFA (1993). Interview 27 October with Director of Financial Affairs Division.
MOL (1994). Interview 14 April with Director of Budget and Accounts.
MOT (1994). Interviews 15 April and 24 November with Director of Budget and Accounts, Maritime Safety Agency.
Muhleisen, M. (1999). 'Too Much of a Good Thing? The Effectiveness of Fiscal Stimulus', in J. Bayoumi and C. Collins (eds.), *Post-Bubble Blues: How Japan Responded to Asset Price Collapse*. Washington: IMF.
Mulgan, A. G. (2000). *The Politics of Agriculture in Japan*. London: Routledge.
Murakami, Y. (1983). *Shin chūkan taishū no jidai* [The Era of the New Middle Class]. Tokyo: Chūō kōron Sha.
Murakawa, Ichirō (1994). *Nihon no kanryō* [Japanese Bureaucracy]. Tokyo: Maruzen Library.
Muramatsu, Michio (1991). 'The "Enhancement" of the Ministry of Posts and Telecommunications to Meet the Challenge of Telecommunications Innovation', in S. Wilks and M. Wright (eds.), *The Promotion and Regulation of Industry in Japan*. London: Macmillan.
—— (1993). 'Patterned Pluralism under Challenge', in Allison and Sone (1993).
—— and Krauss, E. S. (1987). 'The Conservative Policy Line and the Development of Patterned Pluralism' in K. Yamamura and Y. Yasuba (eds.), *The Political Economy of Japan, i, The Domestic Transformation*. Stanford, Calif: Stanford University Press.

Muramatsu, Michio and Mabuchi, M. (1991). 'Introducing a New Tax in Japan', in S. Kernell (ed.), *Parallel Politics: Economic Policy-Making in Japan and the United States*. Washington: Brookings Institution.

Nakagawa, Makoto (1994). Interview 8 April with Deputy Budget Examiner, Budget Bureau, MOF.

—— (1995). Interview 25 April with Deputy Budget Examiner, Budget Bureau, MOF.

Nakano, Kōichi (1998). 'Becoming a "Policy" Ministry: The Organisation and Amakudari of the Ministry of Posts and Telecommunications'. *Journal of Japanese Studies*, 24/1: 95–117.

Nakano, Minoru (1997a). 'The Changing Legislative Process in the Transition Period', in P. Jain and T. Inogochi (eds.), *Japanese Politics Today*. Melbourne: Macmillan Education.

—— (1997b). *The Policymaking Process*. London: Macmillan.

Nakazato, T. (1999). 'Social Capital and Economic Growth', *Financial Review*, December. Institute of Fiscal and Monetary Policy, MOF.

Nihon Keizai Shinbun Seijibu (1983). *Jimintō seichōkai* [The LDP Policy Affairs Research Council]. Tokyo: Nihon Keizai Shinbunsha.

Noguchi, Yukio (1994a). 'Closing the Books on the Bubble Years'. *Japan Echo*, 21: 8–18 (Special Issue).

—— (1994b). 'The Bubble and Economic Policies in the 1980s'. *Journal of Japanese Studies*, 20/2: 291–327.

—— (1995). *1940, taisei, saraba 'senji keizai'* [The 1940 Setup: Farewell to the Wartime Economy]. Tokyo: Tōyō Keizai.

North, D. (1990). *Institutions, Institutional Change and Economic Performance*. Cambridge: Cambridge University Press.

NPA (1995). *White Paper on Public Service Personnel*. The National Personnel Authority. Tokyo: Government Printing Office.

Obuchi, Keizō (1995). Interview 16 April with Vice-President of LDP.

OECD (1978). *Public Expenditure Trends: OECD Studies in Resource Allocation*. Paris: OECD.

—— (1980). *National Accounts of OECD Countries*. Paris: OECD.

—— (1993). *OECD Economic Surveys 1992–93: Japan*. Paris: OECD.

—— (1996). *OECD Economic Surveys 1995–96: Japan*. Paris: OECD.

—— (1997). *OECD Economic Surveys 1996–97: Japan*. Paris: OECD.

—— (1998). *OECD Economic Surveys: Japan 1998*. Paris: OECD.

—— (1999a). *Review of Regulatory Reform*. Paris: OECD.

—— (1999b). *OECD Economic Surveys: Japan*. Paris: OECD.

—— (1999c). *OECD Economic Outlook 65*. Paris: OECD.

—— (2000). *OECD Economic Surveys: Japan*. Paris: OECD.

Okimoto, D. (1989). *Between MITI and the Market*. Stanford, Calif.: Stanford University Press.

Olsen, J. P. (1988). 'Political Science and Organization Theory', paper to conference on 'Political Institutions and Interest Intermediation'. Konstanz, 20–21 April.

Ooms, H. (1985). *Tokugawa Ideology*. Princeton: Princeton University Press.

Orr, R. M. (1990). *The Emergence of Japan's Foreign Aid Power*. New York: Columbia University Press.

Osborne, D., and Gebler, T. (1992). *Reinventing Government*. Reading, Mass.: Addison-Wesley.

Ostrom, D. (1995). *Japan's Bad-Loan Problem: The Search For an Exit*. Report 1, December. Washington: Japan Economic Institute.

—— (1996). *Pork Barrel Politics and Productivity: Infrastructure Spending in Japan*. Report 4A, 2 February. Washington: Japan Economic Institute.

—— (1999). *Unemployment in Japan: How Serious is the Problem?* Report 2A, 15 January. Washington: Japan Economic Institute.

Ostrom, D. (2000). *Governments Deficits and Debts: Tokyo's Dilemma*. Report 2A, 14 January. Washington Japan Economic Institute.
Ōtake, Hideo (1993). 'The Rise and Retreat of Neoliberal Reform: Controversies Over Land-Use Policy', in Allinson and Sone (1993).
—— (1994). *Jiyūshugiteki Kaikaku no Jidai* [The Age of Liberal Reform]. Tokyo: Chūō Kōron.
—— (1996). 'Forces for Political Reform: The Liberal Democratic Party's Young Reformers and Ozawa Ichirō'. *Journal of Japanese Studies*, 22/2: 269–294.
Ozawa, Ichirō (1993). 'Turning Japan into a Self-Reliant Nation'. *Japan Record*, 20: 20–26.
—— (1994). *Blueprint for a New Japan*. Tokyo: Kōdansha International.
Pempel, T. J. (1987). 'The Unbundling of "Japan Inc.": The Changing Dynamics of Japanese Policy Formation', in K. B. Pyle (ed.), *The Trade Crisis: How Will Japan Respond?* Seattle: Society for Japanese Studies, University of Washington.
—— (1989). 'Japan's Creative Conservatism', in F. Castles (ed.), *The Comparative History of Public Policy*. Oxford: Polity Press.
—— (1997). 'Regime Shift: Japanese Politics in a Changing World Economy'. *Journal of Japanese Studies*, 23/2: 333–361.
—— (1998). *Regime Shift: Comparative Dynamics of the Japanese Political Economy*. Ithaca, NY: Cornell University Press.
—— and Muramatsu, M. (1995). 'The Japanese Bureaucracy and Economic Development', in Kim *et al.* (1995).
Posen, A. S. (1998). *Restoring Japan's Economic Growth*. Washington: Institute for Economic Affairs.
Poterba, J., and von Hagen, J. (eds.) (1999). *Fiscal Institutions and Fiscal Performance*. Chicago: University of Chicago Press.
Ramaswamy R., and Rendu, C. (1999). 'Identifying the Shocks: Japan's Economic Performance in the 1990s', in J. Bayoumi and C. Collins (eds.), *Post-Bubble Blues: How Japan Responded to Asset Price Collapse*. Washington: IMF.
Ramsayer, J. M., and Rosenbluth, F. M. (1993). *Japan's Political Marketplace*. Cambridge, Mass.: Harvard University Press.
Reed, S. (1986). *Japanese Prefectures and Policymaking*. Pittsburgh, Pa: Pittsburgh University Press.
Richardson, B. (1997). *Japanese Democracy*. New Haven: Yale University Press.
Rix, A. (1980). *Japan's Economic Aid*. London: Croom-Helm.
—— (1993). *Japan's Foreign Aid Challenge*. London: Routledge.
Rixtel, A. A. R. J. M. (1997). *Informality, Bureaucratic Control and Monetary Policy: The Case of Japan*, Tinbergen Institute Research Series No. 161. Amsterdam: Thesis Publishers.
Rosenbluth, F. M. (1989). *Financial Politics in Contemporary Japan*. Ithaca, NY: Cornell University Press.
—— (1993). 'Financial Deregulation and Interest Intermediation', in Allison and Sone (1993).
Sakaiya, T. (1994). *Bungei Shunjū*, February.
Sakakibara, Eisuke (1998). 'Moving Beyond the Public Works State'. *Japan Echo*, 25/1: 6–9.
Samuels, R. J. (1983). *The Politics of Regional Policy in Japan*. Princeton: Princeton University Press.
—— (1994). *Rich Nation, Strong Army*. Ithaca, NY: Cornell University Press.
Sasa, Atsuyuki (1995). *Chūō Kōron*, April : 62–73.
Satō, Seizaburō, and Matsuzaki, T. (1986). *Jimintō Seiken* [The LDP Administration]. Tokyo: Chūō Kōronsha.
Satō, S., Koyana, K., and Kumon, S. (1990). *Postwar Politician: The Life of Former Prime Minister Masayoshi Ōhira*. Tokyo: Kodansha International.
Schaede, Ulrike (1995). 'The "Old Boy" Network and Government–Business Relationships in Japan'. *Journal of Japanese Studies*, 21/2: 293–317.

Schaede, Ulrike (2000). *Co-operative Capitalism: Self-Regulation, Trade Associations and the Anti-Monopoly Law*. Oxford: Oxford University Press.

Schoppa, L. J. (1991*a*). *Education Reform in Japan*. London: Routledge.

—— (1991*b*). 'Zoku Power and LDP Power: A Case Study of the Zoku Role in Education Policy'. *Journal of Japanese Studies*, 17/1: 79–106.

Schwartz, F. (1993). 'Of Fairy Cloaks and Familiar Talks: The Politics of Consultation', chapter 9 in Allison and Sone (1993).

Seirōren (1993). *Amakudari hakusho* [White Paper on Amakudari]. Tokyo: Seirōren.

Seki, S. (1994). Interview 1 December with Director of Quality of Life and Culture Industries divisions, MITI.

Shibata, Tokue (ed.) (1993). *Japan's Public Sector*. Tokyo: University of Tokyo Press.

Shiga, Sakura (1993). Interview 24 February with Budget Examiner, Budget Bureau, MOF.

—— (1994). Interview 23 November with Budget Examiner, Budget Bureau, MOF.

—— (1995). 'Social and Economic Plan for Structural Reforms: Towards a Vigorous Economic and Secure Life'. Unpublished commentary on the National Economic Plan by the Director of the Planning Division, Planning Bureau, EPA, December.

Shinoda, Tomohito (1994). 'Struggle to Lead: The Japanese Prime Minister's Power and his Conduct of Economic Policy'. Unpublished Ph.D. thesis, Johns Hopkins University; published as *The Prime Minister's Power and Leadership* [Soridaijin no Kenryoku to Shidoryoku]. Tokyo: Toyo Keizai Shimposa.

—— (1998). 'Japan's Decision Making under the Coalition Governments'. *Asian Survey*, 38/7: 703–723.

Shōgenji, Shinichi (1999). 'Public Works in the Agricultural Sector'. *Social Science Japan*, 17 Dec.: 10–12.

Silberman, B. S. (1996). 'The Continuing Dilemma: Bureaucracy and Political Parties'. *Social Science Japan*, 7 Aug.: 3–5.

Smithers, Andrew (1995). *Japan: Growing Problems of the PKO*. London: Smithers and Col.

Sone, Yasunori (1985). *Shingikai no kiso kenkyū: kinō, taiō ni tsuite no bunseki* [Basic Research on Advisory Committees: An Analysis of their Function and Condition]. Tokyo: Keio University.

Steuerle, C. E., and Kawai, M. (eds.) (1996). *The New World Fiscal Order*. Aldershot: Avebury.

Stockwin, J. A. (1999). *Governing Japan*, 3rd edn. Oxford: Blackwell.

Sumi, Chikahisa (1994). Interview 20 April with Deputy Budget Examiner, Budget Bureau, MOF.

—— (1997). Interview 13 June with Deputy Director of First Fund Division, Finance Bureau, MOF.

Sumitaya, Shōji (1998). *Waste of Money By Japanese Officials* (in Japanese). Tokyo: Yomiura Shinbum-Sha.

Suzuki, T. (1999). 'Administrative Reform and the Politics of Budgetary Retrenchment in Japan'. *Social Science Japan Journal*, 2/2: 195–213.

Takahashi, Hideyuki (1988). 'Being a Department for Enterprise: A Case Study of the Ministry of Construction'. Paper delivered to the Anglo-Japanese conference on Government–Industry Relations, Tokyo, September.

Takayama, N., Kitamura, N., and Yoshida, H. (1998). 'General Accounting in Japan', in A.J. Auerback *et al.* (eds.), *Generational Accounting around the World*. Chicago: University of Chicago Press.

Takemura, M. (1997). 'Renritsu seikenka no an 'fukushizei' tekkai wa nani o monogataruka' [What the Withdrawal of the Welfare Tax under the Coalition Government Really Means]. *Bungei shunjū*, July: 336–338.

Takeshima, Kazuhiko (1993). Interview 24 February with Deputy Director-General, Budget Bureau, MOF.

Tanaka, Kakuei (1972). *Nihon Rettō Kaizōron* [A Plan For Remodelling the Japanese Archipelago]. Tokyo: Nikkan Kōgyō Shinbum-Sha.
—— (1973). *Building a New Japan* (English translation of Tanaka 1972). Tokyo: Simul Press.
Tanaka, Kazuaki, and Horié, Masahiro (1993). 'De-regulation', chapter 10 in Masujima and O'uchi (1993).
Tanaka, Masami (1991). 'Government Policy and Biotechnology Policy in Japan: The Pattern and Impact of Rivalry between Ministries', chapter 6 in Wilks and Wright (1991).
—— (1994). Interview 2 December with Director-General, Standards Bureau, MITI.
Tanaka Takashi (1994). Interview 21 April with President of the Bank of Yokahama, formerly Administrative Vice-Minister MOF, 1980–81, Director-General, Budget Bureau, MOF 1979–80.
Tanami, Kōji (1993). Interview 15 February with Deputy Director-General, Budget Bureau, MOF.
Tanzi, V. (2000). Letter to *Financial Times*, 19 December 2000.
—— and Shuknect, L. (2000). *Public Spending in the Twentieth Century*. Cambridge: Cambridge University Press.
Tase, Yasuhiro (1993). 'The Power-short Prime Minister'. *Japan Echo*, 20/2: 40–45.
Thain, C., and Wright, M. (1995). *The Treasury and Whitehall: The Planning and Control of Public Expenditure, 1976–1993*. Oxford: Oxford University Press.
Tilton, M. (1996). *Restrained Trade: Cartels in Japan's Basic Materials Industries*. Ithaca, NY: Cornell University Press
Ueno, Yoshiharu (1993). Interview 15 February with Deputy Budget Examiner for Economic Co-ordination, Budget Bureau, MOF.
Upham, F. K. (1987). *Law and Social Change in Post-War Japan*. Cambridge, Mass.: Harvard University Press.
—— (1993). 'Privatizing Regulation: The implementation of the Large-Scale Retail Stores Law', chapter 11 in Allison and Sone (1993).
Uriu, R. (1996). *Troubled Industries: The Political Economy of Industrial Adjustment in Japan*. Ithaca, NY: Cornell University Press.
Vestal, J. E. (1994). *Planning for Change: Industrial Policy and Japanese Economic Development, 1945–1990*. Oxford: Oxford University Press.
Vogel, S. (1994). 'The Bureaucratic Approach to the Financial Revolution: Japan's Ministry of Finance and Financial System Reform'. *Governance*, 7/2: 219–243.
—— (1996b). *Freer Markets, More Rules*. Ithaca, NY: Cornell University Press.
von Hagen, J. (1998). *Budgeting Institutions for Aggregate Fiscal Discipline*, ZEI Policy Paper B98-01, February. Bonn: Zentrum für Europäische Integrationsforschung.
Watanabe, Hiroyasu (1994). Interview 19 April with Director Co-ordination Division, Tax Bureau, formerly Budget Examiner and Deputy Budget Examiner, Budget Bureau, MOF.
Weinstein, D. E. (1995). 'Evaluating Administrative Guidance and Cartels in Japan (1957–1988)'. *Journal of the Japanese and International Economies*, 9/2: 200–223, June.
Wildavsky, A. (1988). *The New Politics of the Budgetary Process*. New York: Harper Collins.
Wilks, S., and Wright, M. (eds.) (1987). *Comparative Government–Industry Relations: Western Europe, the United States and Japan*. Oxford: Oxford University Press.
———— (eds.) (1991). *The Promotion and Regulation of Industry in Japan*. London: Macmillan.
Woodall, B. (1996). *Japan under Construction: Corruption, Politics and Public Works*. Berkeley: University of California Press.
Wright, M. (1988a). 'Policy Community, Policy Network and Comparative Industrial Policies'. *Political Studies*, 36/2: 593–612.
——(1988b). 'City Rules OK? Policy Community, Policy Network and Takeover Bids'. *Public Administration*, 66/4: 389–410.

Wright, M. (1991). 'The Comparative Analysis of Industrial Policies: Policies Networks and Sectoral Governance Structures in Britain and France'. *Staatswissenschaften und Staatspraxis*, 2/4: 503–533.

Wright, M. (1998a). *The Political Economy of Japan's Second Budget*. Comparative Budgetary Systems Working Paper Series, 9a, August, University of Manchester.

—— (1998b). *FILP in the Economy*. Comparative Budgetary Systems Working Paper Series, 9b, August, University of Manchester.

—— (1999a). *The Role and Significance of Public Works Expenditure in the Japanese Budget Process*. Comparative Budgetary Systems Working Paper Series, 20, October, University of Manchester.

—— (1999b). *The Effects and Effectiveness of MOF's Fiscal Reconstruction*. Comparative Budgetary Systems Working Paper Series, 23, October, University of Manchester.

—— (1999c). *Fiscal Reconstruction: The National Context and International Comparisons*. Comparative Budgetary Systems Working Paper Series, 39, December, University of Manchester.

—— (1999d). 'Who Governs Japan? Politicians and Bureaucrats in the Policy-Making Processes'. *Political Studies*, 47/4: 939–954.

—— (1999e). *The Outputs of the Budgetary System: Who Wins, Who Loses*. Comparative Budgetary Systems Working Paper Series, 24, October, University of Manchester.

Yamaguchi, Yutaka (1999). Paper to the Federal Reserve Bank Symposium on Monetary Policy, Jackson Hole, Wyoming.

Yamamura, Kōzō (1997). 'The Japanese Political Economy after the "Bubble": *Plus ça Change?*' *Journal of Japanese Studies*, 23/2: 291–331.

Yamazaki, M. (1986). *Jimintō to Kyōiku seisaku* [The LDP and Education Policy]. Tokyo: Iwanami shinsho.

Yasutomo, D. T. (1986). *The Manner of Giving*. Lexington, Mass.: Lexington Books.

—— (1995), *The New Multilateralism in Japan's Foreign Policy*. London: Macmillan.

Yonezawa, Junichi (1994a). Interview 8 April with Executive Director of the Bank of Japan, formerly Deputy Budget Examiner in Budget Bureau, and Director First Fund Division, Financial Bureau, MOF.

—— (1994b). Interview 29 November with Executive Director of the Bank of Japan.

—— (1995). Interview 24 April with Executive Director of the Bank of Japan.

Young, Michael K. (1984). 'Judicial Review of Administrative Guidance', *Columbian Law Review*, 84/4: 916–938.

Yusasa, H. (1986). *Kokkai 'zoku-giin'* [Zoku-Giin of the National Diet]. Tokyo: Kyōiku-Sha.

Zhao, Q. (1993). *Japanese Policy-Making*. Oxford: Oxford University Press.

Zysman, J. (1983). *Government, Markets and Growth: Financial Systems and the Politics of Industrial Change*. Ithaca, NY: Cornell University Press.

Glossary of Japanese Terms

Amakudari: 'descent from heaven' of bureaucrats into post-retirement public and private sector positions
Dangō: agreement by consultation, an institutionalized system of bid-rigging in construction and public works projects
Diet: National Assembly or Parliament
Endaka: strong yen
Erīto kōsu: elite course for career advancement of senior bureaucrats
Gaiatsu: foreign pressure (on Japanese government to adopt or change a policy)
Honshō: the home or Tokyo headquarters office of a ministry, the ministry proper
Jusen: (*jūtaku kinyū senmon gaisha*) housing loan associations
Kachō: director of a ministerial division
Kachō-hosa: deputy director of a ministerial division
Keidanren: Federation of Economic Organizations
Keiretsu: industrial groupings
Kōenkai: personal local electoral network
Kūdōka: hollowing out (of industry)
Nemawashi: literally, digging round the roots (i.e. behind the scenes manoeuvring)
Nikkeiren: *Ni*hon *kei*eisha *ren*mei (Japanese Federation of Employers' Association)
Nisei: second generation (politicians)
Ōkurashō: literally, the great treasure-store ministry, hence Ministry of Finance
Shingi-kai: advisory council
Shinkansen: 'bullet' railway train
Tokushu hōjin: public corporations (within the supervisory and controlling jurisdiction of ministries and agencies)
Zaimshō: Ministry of the Treasury (MOF's formal title after the reorganization of 2001)
Zoku-giin: policy tribe of LDP Dietmen with a shared interest in a particular area of public policy

Index

Administration programme:
  Budget outputs 393–4
Administrative guidance 175, 178, 200
  extra-legal processes 115–16
Administrative Management Agency (AMA):
  embedded loyalties of in MCA 112
  re-designated MCA 56–7 *see* separate entry
  reform 54–5
Administrative Reform 53–74
  after Rinchō 58–60
  aims of programme 70–2
  assessment of 71–4
  effects of in 1980s 57–9
  fiscal reconstruction 53–8
  Hashimoto's six 'visions' 67–72
  in the 1990s 60–74
  'new public management' 53, 58, 73
  see also Rinchō; de-regulation; decentralization
Administrative Reform Council (ARC):
  and reorganization of central government 109, 113
  Hashimoto sets up 121
Administrative Vice-Minister 36
  in ministries 103
  meetings of 119
  retirement posts 134
Advisory Councils:
  Nakasone and 121–2
  membership 113, 127
  new in 2001 110
  work 127–8
  functions 128–9
Agriculture, Forestry, and Fisheries Finance Corporation (AFFFC):
  function 478
  loans of 229
  MOF and MAFF control 154
  subsidies to 558–9
Alcohol Monopoly 100
Amakudari 173, 175–82
  as 'crisis management' 197
  Bank of Japan officials 181–2
  MOF's exploitation of 178, 563
  'management of regulation' model 175–6
  private banks, to 176–9
  private sector, in 175–9
  public sector boards 179
  securities and insurance industries, in 178
  'side-slip' of 1979
  see also MOF's elite bureaucrats

Bank of Japan (BOJ):
  bubble economy, and 28
  corruption in 181–2
  Governor's appointment in 181–2
  independent of MOF 68
  monetary policy and MOF 145, 157
  official discount rate 28
  resignation of Governor Matsushita 181–2
  Sumitomo, and 50–1
  supervision and regulation, 116
Banking Bureau (MOF) 167, 174, 179
  abolition 148
  convoy policy 156–7
  created 148
  functions 148
  see also MOF
Banking sector:
  bad debts and loans 32–3
  'Black November' 1997 32
  bank failures 32, 156–7
  convoy system 32–3, 156
  inspection and supervision by MOF 33, 50–1, 116
  public money and 32–3
  'regulatory forbearance' of 32–3
'Big Bang' 68, 71, 74, 561, 564
Board of Audit 211, 512
Budget Bureau 146–7
  bilateral ministerial negotiations 329
  'black list' of ministries 345
  budget control disputed by LDP 333–4
  budget examination 317–22
  budget hearings 313–17
  budget negotiations 322–5, 368–9
  budget requests submitted 312–13
  budget revival negotiations 334–9, 401–3
  budget strategy 277–8, 284–7
  coalition budgeting 330–3
  constructing political consensus 327–8, 373–4
  DBE hearings purpose and procedure 314–17
  DDG's role in budget scrutiny 316–17, 318–21
  defence budget 325–6
  deputy director-general (DDG) 287–8
  'dirty tricks' 345
  divisions in 146–7
  dominance in MOF policymaking 150
  failure to control spending 580–4
  functions 146
  hearings at four levels 313–14
  important items meeting 320

Budget Bureau (*Contd.*)
  LDP resolves conflict 329
  meetings 318–21
  minister of finance's meeting 321
  ministerial budget ceilings 287–90
  ODA 150
  officials' behavioural norms 340–5, 593
  PARC and draft budget 327–8
  policy coordinators 129–30
  real recovered bids 338–9
  research division's coordinating role 152–3, 290
  re-submitted bids 334
  revival margin allocated 338–9
  'revival negotiations' 334–9, 401–3
  'revival negotiations' origins 334
  revival stages 335–7
  revival stakes 337–8
  Rinchō 56
  ritual and ceremonial 334–5, 336, 337
  staff 146–7
  see also budget objectives; budget policies; revenue; budget guidelines; LDP; LDP and budget processes; PARC; *zoku*, Co-ordination division; director-general; budget examiner; deputy budget examiner; fiscal system research council
Budget Examiner (BE):
  ministerial ceiling 287–90, 301–5
  modus operandi 317
  norms of behaviour 340–3
  PARC and 328
  political player 373–4
  politicking 327–8
  rank 105
  reactive 340–1
  'revival negotiations' 336
  see also Budget Bureau; deputy budget examiner
Budget guidelines 57, 209, 249, 278–84
  annual review 278
  application of 283–4
  applied selectively 281, 283
  capital investment 282–3
  effects of tightening 408
  loosened 250–1
  ministerial ceilings 287–90, 301–5
  ministries exploit 303, 581–2
  priority programmes 281–2
  re-drawn in 1982 135
  spending freeze 248
  summary 279–80
  top-down limits insufficient 581
  see also General Account Budget; Budget Bureau
Budgeting:
  coalition 330–3

economic context 22–3
fiscal rules 590
for economic and social goals 587
formal process of co-ordination 129–130
'golden rule' 495, 590
ministerial autonomy 134–5
politico-economic context 21–52
see also General Account Budget; FILP; budget institutions
Budget institutions 585–95
  complexity 587
  consolidated national accounts 594
  fiscal codes 588–9
  fiscal institutionalists 585
  fiscal targets and rules 589–91
  formal 583
  'golden rule' 495, 590
  informal politics and 583
  informal structures 583
  less fragmented 592–3
  MOF's power threatened 592–3
  multiple and diffuse 586
  'off budget' 593
  'primary balance' 590
  reconfiguration of Japanese 591–5
  top-down limits 590
  transparency and accountability 594–5
Budget objectives 239–63
  achievement distant prospect 254–5
  assessment of achievement 503, 518–21, 535, 543–6, 578
  balanced budget 242, 245–6, 535
  Council on Fiscal Structural Reform 257–60
  dilemma 250, 580–1
  fiscal reconstruction, 1976–87 242–9, 487–521, 535, 578
  main 239, 246
  medium-term 247–9
  principles of reform programme 258
  quantitative targets 258
  reform act 1997 255
  reform of tax structure 240, 580
  restraining public expenditure 502–4, 505–6, 535
  revenue search 239–42
  'sound management' of finances 243–5, 518
  targets for bonds 247–9, 251, 253, 260, 497–8, 499–500, 502, 519
Budget outputs 377–409
  'balance' 389, 404–5
  central/local spending 385, 403–4, 506–11
  conclusions on 403–5
  current and capital 383–5
  gross/net 386
  LDP's role and influence on 408–9
  methodological issues 406–7

Index

ministerial shares 388–91
MOF delivery of spending total 378–81
MOF slows increase 381–3, 408
outcome of bilaterals 382–3
party political 401–3
planned and actual spending 378–81, 406–7, 504–6, 520
policy groups 391–6
principles of allocation 404
priority categories 384, 390, 408
programmes 396–401
quantitative analysis criticized 405–8
squaring fiscal circle 384
supplementary budgets 378–81, 407, 520–1
three ministerial profiles 387–8,
winners/losers in ministries 386–91, 403
winning/losing defined 386–7
winning/losing factors 389–91
zero/positive sum 387–8, 408
see also budget objectives; public works
Budget policies 239–63
austerity 249
budgetary stratagems 506–518
caps on spending 260–1
consolidation 249–52, 493–4
consumption tax 239
Council on Fiscal Structural Reform 257–60
crisis for 252–5
end of Tanaka's fiscal expansion 246–7
expansion 250–2
expenditure controls tightened 248–9
fiscal explosion 263
fiscal reconstruction 242–9, 487–521, 580–2
fiscal structural reform act 1997 255, 259–60, 262
'fiscally induced' inflation 243
medium-term strategy destroyed 254
Medium-term Fiscal Policy 1990 251
oil crisis effects on 248
priorities in spending 248–9, 281–2
reform initiative politicians and 257–8
reform origins 255–8
reform, rise and fall 255–63
rules-of-the-game 244–6, 496
'sound management' 243–5, 583
statutory controls of spending 260–1
'U turn' 262–3
see also budget guidelines; budget objectives; revenue
Budget processes 312–403, 586
fragmentation 586
lack of transparency 594
opaque 582–3, 587
reform 591–2
reform of elsewhere 590–1, 593
see also Budget Bureau
Budget strategy 275–90

bottom-up 277–8
Budget Bureau's role 276–8
FILP and General Account Budget 354
LDP influence 284–7
top-down factors 275–7
see also budget guidelines
Budget system 207–14
central 208
independent control of regained 216
Bureaucracy:
2001 reorganization and cuts 418
categories 410
central government 411–18
code of ethics 70–1
core policy-makers 418
corruption in 70, 134
cuts 411–12
cuts and squeezes 410–18
local cuts 417–18
new posts 413
numbers 416
reduction plans 411–12
see also bureaucrats; MOF's elite bureaucrats
Bureaucrats:
aim to weaken in 1998 113
behavioural rules-of-the-game 131–4
career norms 165
characteristics 159
councillor and counsellor 105
dominance challenged 79–81, 83–5
elite 159
hierarchy of 'career' 105
in networks 193, 333
key posts of 104–5
PARC divisions and 193
policy-making and 75–90, 131–4
policy-making in coalitions 201–2, 203–4
politicians and 75–90, 205
private schools 161–2
recruitment 159–61
retirees on boards 179
retirement 173–84
retirement into politics 182–4
role in 'developmental state' 75–6
socialization 161–5
Tokyo Law Faculty and 162–3, 172
university 160–1
women 161
see also MOF's elite bureaucrats; *amakudari*; bureaucracy

Cabinet 99–100
approves budget strategy 289
collective responsibility 1994–6 121
committees 124
co-ordinating function 118–19

Cabinet (*Contd.*)
  factions in 112–13
  ministers 99–100
  ODA initiatives 121–12
  re-shuffles 99–100
  role and functions after 2001 112–13
  size 99, 112–13
Cabinet Office:
  Council for Economic and Fiscal Policy in 158
  enlarged functions and authority in 2001 110–11
  staff 122
  staff numbers 416
Cabinet Secretariat:
  Cabinet Legislation Bureau 61, 123
  Cabinet Office and 110
  co-ordination by 122–5
  deputy chief secretary's role 122–3
  Office of 93–6
  offices in 123, 126–7
  reorganization in 1985 126
  staff 122–3
Campbell J.C. 6
Canada:
  balanced budget 550
  fiscal performance: *see* G7
  statutory 'caps' 590
Capitalism:
  'strategic' 80
  Japanese model 51–2
  resurgence of neo-classical economics 50
  western model 50
Central Bank of Commercial and Industrial Cooperation (*Shōkō Chūkin*) 154
Central government:
  aims of reform in 1998 108–9
  changes in organization of 108–13
  machinery 93–6, 592–3
  origins of changes in 109
  policy evaluation in 573, 595
  see also spending ministries and agencies
Central government debt:
  ad hoc bonds 253
  bond-dependency ratio 247, 249, 251, 253, 254, 258, 494–6, 498–9, 545
  bonds 17
  bonds outstanding 500–1, 546
  borrowing costs 18, 497–502
  compared with G7 545, 547–8, 578
  'hidden' 511, 515, 582
  liabilities in GG 534
  political implications of 245
  redemption 211, 512–13, 513–15
  reduction 68–9
  servicing 254, 501, 513, 546, 548
  size of 254, 578
  special deficit-financing bonds 54, 68, 209, 247–8, 251, 254, 260, 263, 495, 498, 502, 513
  see also GG; GGE; G7; General Government debt
Coalition Government:
  budgeting and 330–3
  consumption tax and 333
  led by LDP 44–6
  political turbulence and 1993–96 43–4
Commission on Industrial Competitiveness 121
'Common pool' problem 585–6
Consumption Tax:
  1988 legislation 241
  attitudes towards 240
  campaigns for 239–42
  effects of 491–3
  exploitation of principle 254
  failed attempts at 239–41
  increased 242, 333
  national welfare tax 43, 242
  need of 239–42
  unpopularity 241
  see also revenue
'Convoy policy' 156, 576
Coordination Division (MOF's Budget Bureau):
  budget ceilings 287–290
  budget examination 320–1
  budget guidelines 278
  budget negotiations 324–5
  budget preparation 151–2
  budget strategy 277–8, 285–7
  investment programme 256–7
  supplementary budgets 290
  see also Budget Bureau
Council for Economic and Fiscal Policy 158, 592–3
Council on Fiscal Structural Reform:
  composition 257
  objectives 257
  policies 257–60
  reconvened 262
  report 259–60
  set up 257
  work 258–90, 592
Countercyclical measures 254, 262, 263
  'clear water' 452–3
  effectiveness 452–4
  LDP initiative 334
  packages 427–9, 452
Customs and Tariff Bureau (MOF) 174
  functions 148

Daiwa Bank 156
Dangō 458

Index

Decentralization 64
Defence Agency:
  budget allocations to 386–91
  budget process 308–9
  budget request 325–6
  cabinet councillor 123
  corruption 134
  mobilizes support 307, 328
  programmes 259
  origins 93–6
  staff numbers 416, 417
  zoku influence 197–8
Defence Facilities Administration Agency 308, 401
Defence policy:
  1% ceiling 41
  budget allocation 325–6, 392, 393
  budget framework 41
  five-year plans 292
  organizational distribution of budget 401
  priority status conferred 281–2
Deputy Budget Examiner (DBE) 288
  budget requests 312–13
  Diet 339
  examines 317–18
  frustrations 344–5
  hearings 314–17
  in bureau meetings 318–21
  interacts 343–5
  ministerial ceilings 287–90, 301–5
  negotiated discretion 343, 373–4
  negotiates 322–5
  norms of behaviour 340–3
  political player 373–4
  reactive 340–1
  'revival negotiations' 336
  'ten commandments' 341–3
  see also Budget Bureau; budget examiner
Deregulation:
  implementation 61–3
  ministry regulations 62–3
  piecemeal and gradual 59–60
  pressures for 50
  programmes 60–1
  proposals for 59, 67–8
Development Bank of Japan 154, 477, 559
  see JDB
Diet 512
  checks on LDP 40–1
  'counter-measures' committee 40
  FILP Plan 362, 575
  HR budget committee 40–1
  role in budget 2, 339
  see also House of Representatives; House of Councillors

Director-general (Budget Bureau) 278
  budget strategy 285–6, 288
  bureau meetings 320
  coordinator 289–90
  Diet 339
  LDP leaders, and 326
  promotion 170–2
  see also Budget Bureau
Dodge, Joseph:
  'Dodge line' 9, 23, 65, 216, 244
Dokō Toshio 55

Earthquake:
  disaster relief 332–3
  Hanshin-Awaji 44, 124–5, 332
Economic Council 257
  National Economic Plans 265–7
  members 265
  ministries and agencies work with 265–6
Economic Forecasts 264–74
  annual 270–4
  conflicting pressures in 271–2
  context for budgeting 267
  National Economic Plan, in 267
  of GDP 271–4
  realpolitik of 271–4
  see also Economic Outlook
Economic Outlook 270, 271–2, 276, 324, 356, 496
Economic Strategy Council 267
  created 69
  tax reform 493
Economy:
  bubble economy 26–8, 32
  decelerated 24, 47–8
  growth in G7 538
  growth of to 1971 22
  high-growth era 23
  'locomotive theory' 24
  negative real growth 1974 23–4
  oil crises effects 23–4
  perceived insecurity 21
  recession 28–32, 51, 254, 262
  recovery as priority 263
  structural reform 65–7
  trade relations 48
  transition to slower growth 1965–73 13
  see also Economic Forecasts; deregulation
Economic Planning Agency (EPA)
  abolished 110, 158
  coordinating 125
  Economic Outlook 270–1, 272, 276, 324, 356, 496
  economic reform 66–7
  forecasting 125, 270–4
  ODA 117

Economic Planning Agency (*Contd.*)
  secondments in 67, 125
  staff 416
Education:
  'envisioned' reform of 71
  see also education and science programme
Education and Science programme:
  budget outputs 392, 393–4, 396
  budget unpacked 398–401
  revival negotiations 338, 403
  science and technology budget unpacked 399–401
  sub-programmes budget outputs 398–401
  'swings and roundabouts' 399
EMU:
  Maastricht criteria 548
Energy programme 281
  budget outputs 393
Environmental Agency 109
  public works 422–4, 435–6
  staff numbers 416
Environmental Sanitation Business Finance Corporation:
  functions 478
  MOF and MHW control 154–5
Export-Import Bank (EXIM):
  changed role 478
  merged with OECF 103
  MOF control of 154–5
  negotiations with FILP 357
  raising revenue 358
  title 103, 154–5
  unused FILP funds 561

Fair Trade Commission 437, 453
  chairman's post of, MOF monopoly 180
  collusive bidding 458
Farmers 451
  rice subsidies 260, 436
FILP *see* Fiscal Investment and Loan Programme
FILP agencies:
  allocative efficiency 561–2
  assets and liabilities 554
  bonds 568–9, 571, 572–3
  budget allocations 479, 567
  budget implementation 363–4
  budget outputs 467–8
  categories of 231–4
  debts 355
  differentiated by status and function 232–4
  high-risk projects 561
  interest rates for loans of 228–9, 364, 555–6
  methods of finance for 230
  'New FILP' and 572–3, 576–7
  number 230, 570

  outstanding balances 480, 481
  recipients of FILP funds 230–4, 467–8
  special accounts as 232
  special companies, banks as 232
  sponsoring ministries and agencies of 231–2, 563, 576–7
  subsidies 556–9, 574
  support industrial development 478–80
  'winners and losers' 469–70
  see also FILP; FILP outputs
(FILP) Fund Operation Council 228, 352–3, 566–72, 574
FILP outputs 461–84
  changing priorities 472–4, 474–5, 483–4, 567–8
  compared with General Account Budget 461–2
  defined 461, 483
  efficiency and effectiveness 480, 482–3, 567
  EXIM Bank's changed role 477
  functional classification 471
  gross budget 461–4, 483
  growth 461–7, 483
  investment and loans programme 464–7, 483, 559–60
  in-year changes 463–4, 465–6
  JDB allocations 476–7
  JDB changed role 475–7
  MOF's presentation 474
  MOF's presentation adjusted 474–5
  organizations 467–9, 479–80
  planned and real changes 466
  policy areas 469–74, 567–8
  policy areas winners and losers 470–3
  profiles 462–3
  roads and bridges 484, 468
  social and industrial investment 474–80, 483, 484, 567
  underspending 466–7, 559–61
  see also FILP; FILP agencies
Financial Bureau (MOF) 172, 174
  budget bureau and 356
  FILP divisions 353–4, 356–9
  FILP subsidies 358
  functions 148
  HUDC's budget-making 359
  local government finance 234, 360–1
  structure 148
  Trust Fund Bureau Fund management 224–8, 352–3, 562–3
  see also MOF; Budget Bureau
Financial Revitalization Commission (FRC) 33, 157–8
Financial Services Agency (FSA)
  created 158
Financial Supervision Agency
  bad debts and loans estimate 33

Index

created 33
within PM's Office 157
Financial System
  crisis in 32–3
  reform of 33, 68
  see also banking sector
Fiscal Crisis:
  in the 1990s 1
  origins of 1975 14–18
  problematique 18
  resurfaces 1991–96 252–5
Fiscal institutionalists 585
  analysis qualified 587–8
  fragmentation 586
  transparency 586–8
  see also 'common pool' problem
Fiscal Investment and Loan Programme (FILP) 215–35
  allocation to agencies 220–1, 356–60
  allocative inefficiency 557–9
  as alternative to main budget 222, 515–17, 536, 563, 563–4, 568
  assets of 230
  budget size 218, 219, 221, 222, 364, 567
  budget-making 346–64
  budget-making process 357–9, 574–5
  budget-size factors in 352–5, 364, 567
  cabinet approves budget 362–2
  capital market operations 224–8, 570
  carried forward funds 559–60
  characteristics 215–16, 218, 219–23, 551
  continuity of 215
  core value of policy community 349
  defined 215
  Diet and 362, 575
  efficiency and effectiveness 556–62, 567
  established 215
  evaluation 561–2
  expansion 554
  FILP agency bonds 568–9, 571–2, 572–3
  FILP bonds 569, 571–2, 573
  Financial and Budget Bureaux interaction 356–7, 360
  Financial Bureau's allocation, 356–9
  Financial Bureau's management and control 352–3, 562–3
  financial de-regulation effects on 553–4
  flexibility 362, 563
  fund operation council 228, 352–3, 566–72, 574
  GDP share 355
  General Account Budget 217
  implementation 363–4
  in crisis 563–5
  interest rates prescription 228–30, 555–6
  in-year budget changes 362–3
  issues in budget-making 347–8
  link with postal savings and pensions 71, 562, 568, 569–70
  local government funds and 234–5, 356–7, 360–1, 560–1
  local public enterprises and 234, 361
  'lubricant' for financial system 516, 552, 563–4
  management tensions 562–3
  market criteria adopted 569–570, 571
  MOF bureaux cross-pressured on 349–51
  MOF-MPT conflict 350–2, 562–3
  need for 551–2
  not counted in GG 536
  origins of 216
  over-funded 559–61
  policy community 346–8
  politics of postal savings 348–52
  Postal Life Insurance Fund and 223
  principles 219–21, 552, 569–70
  priorities 356, 567–8
  public-private ventures 217
  purposes 220, 551
  recipients of funds of 230–4
  reform alternatives 568–9
  reform of 68, 71, 565–77
  self-financing 221–2
  source of funds for 215–16, 221, 223–4, 225, 364, 552–4, 568–9
  subsidies 358, 556–9, 565, 574
  system 218–19
  tensions 552, 563
  'third sector projects' 358
  Trust Fund Bureau Fund law 216, 220
  under stress 552–7
  unused funds 559–60
  Zaitō sanpyō 362, 575
  see also 'New FILP; FILP agencies; FILP outputs; Trust Fund Bureau Fund; postal savings; Financial Bureau; local government finance; MPT; MHW
Fiscal Loan Fund Special Account 571–2
Fiscal policy:
  consolidation 249–52
  crisis declared 54
  expansionary 26, 250–1, 263
  reconstruction 242–9, 250
  reform of 30–1, 68–9, 255–63
  retrenchment abandoned 32, 69
  stimulus 26
  structural reform act 30, 69
  U-turn 31–2
  see also countercyclical; budget policies; budget objectives; fiscal reconstruction; revenue
Fiscal reconstruction 487–521, 580–2

Fiscal reconstruction (*Contd.*)
  1976–87 242–9
  abandoned 250
  appearance and reality 504–6, 518–21, 535, 578, 584
  borrowing 497–502
  budget deficit 494–9
  composition of tax revenues 491–2
  consumption tax 491–3
  declaration of 242, 257
  deferred debt redemption 513–15
  deficit bonds eliminated 247–9
  deficit bonds re-issued 254
  direct and indirect taxes 489–93
  fiscal gap 488–9
  'fiscal rigidification' 12, 17, 254, 500–2, 519–20
  hypothecated revenues 493
  initiative for 242–3
  local government spending cut 403–4, 506–11
  manipulation of cash flows 515–17
  manipulation of surpluses/shortfall 511–13
  measurement and budget base 503
  medium-term aim 247
  MOF's performance indicators 503–4, 518–21
  policy abandoned 250
  policy objectives 496, 501, 502
  restraining public expenditure 502–4
  revenue estimates 496–7
  revenue raising 488–94, 507
  spending plans and changes 504–5, 520–1
  tax burden 489, 494, 495
  transfer payments cut 508–9, 511
  transition to consolidation 493
Fiscal Structural Reform Act 30, 31, 69, 255, 259–60, 262, 268
Fiscal system 68–9
Fiscal System Research Council 152–3, 248, 258, 265, 269–70
  and fiscal reform 256, 270
  Budget Bureau and 269
  endorsement 290
  legitimizer 270
  Medium-term Fiscal Projection 269–70
  Medium-term Fiscal Policy 1990 251
  public works 330, 425, 445–6
  see also Budget Bureau
Food control programme:
  budget outputs 393, 396
France:
  policy coordination 136
Fuji, Hirohisa 184, 321
Furakawa Teijiro 122

GATT 531
General Account Budget:
  administrative context of in 1980s 53–8
  annual cash-based 207, 580
  balanced 9–11, 216
  base-line calculation 283–4
  bond-dependency ratio 12, 247, 249, 494–6, 519, 545
  bonds, deficit-financing in 54, 68, 209, 247–8, 251, 253, 263, 495, 498, 502, 513, 518–19
  bonds, construction in 209, 495
  borrowing for 17, 244, 497–502
  'caps' on spending 260–1, 280
  compilation 312–39
  creative accounting 518
  deficit-financing 13–14, 54, 247–9, 535
  deficits 16, 54, 68, 251, 252–3, 255–6, 263, 494–9
  deficits compared with G7 543–5
  defined 207, 209
  Diet procedures 339
  failure to control spending 580–4
  FILP as alternative to 407, 515–17, 564
  fiscal projections 54
  'fixed expenditures' in 209
  'general expenditures' in 209, 248, 279, 283
  local government finance and 209, 385, 403–4, 506–11
  main trends in 48–9
  MOF's performance indicators 503–4, 543–6, 582
  national debt redemption 513–15
  negative ceiling 55, 279–281
  objectives 9
  planning allocations 258
  pressures on relieved 407, 506–18, 564
  primary focus 407–8
  public sector role in 72
  public works in 424–32, 433–4
  rigidification 12, 17, 254, 500–2, 519–20
  rules-of-the-game 9–10, 244–5, 496
  settlement (outturn) of 210–11, 511–12
  settlement adjustment fund 211, 512, 513, 515
  spending freeze 248
  spending priorities 248, 281–2
  stress causes 578
  stress responses 583
  stress symptoms 578–9
  taxes in 209, 580
  unbalanced 11–13, 535
  zero ceiling 55–6, 279–281
  see also budget strategy; supplementary budget; budget outputs; Medium-term Fiscal Projection; Budget Bureau; revenue; budget guidelines; budget policies; budget objectives; fiscal reconstruction
General Government (GG):
  central government deficits 528–9
  defined 522

distribution of deficits 527–9
FILP finances excluded 536
fiscal balances 527–31, 578
G7 budget balances 540–1
G7 outlays composition 540
GG/GDP profiles 529–30
Japan and G7 537–50, 578
local government deficits 528–9
MOF's rejection 525–6
public corporations excluded 526
see also GGE; General Government debt; G7; central government debt
General Government debt 255–6
assets and liabilities 533
composition 534
consolidated gross 531–2
contingent FILP liabilities 536
defined and measured 531
G7 debt 541–3
gross and net profiles 532–3
Japan's spiralling 578–9
unconsolidated gross 531
underestimated net 532
see also GG; GGE; G7; central government debt
General Government Expenditure (GGE):
composition 523–5
G7 538–40
growth 522–3
see also GG, General Government debt; G7; central government debt
'Golden rule' 495, 590
Government Housing Loan Corporation (GHLC):
control of 154
FILP 'winner' 486–9
loans of 228, 358, 562
subsidies to 102, 557–9
unused FILP funds 561
Government enterprises 100
Government Printing Office 100, 415
Group of Seven Industrialized Countries (G7):
ageing population 549
balanced budgets 548, 549–50, 589–90
central/federal fiscal performance 543–6, 547, 549–50
EMU criteria 548
fiscal convergence 548–9
fiscal reconstruction 537, 546–50
GG gross/net debt 541–3, 548
GG trends analysed 540–1
GGE 538–40
GGE balances defined 540
GGE composition 540
investment 419
neo-liberalism 537
'new right' governments in 73
tax in 489, 495

see also GG; GGE; General Government debt; central government debt
Gyōten, Tōyō:
career profile in MOF 172
chairman of Bank of Tokyo 176

Hashimoto, Ryūtarō 171
and ARC 121
and jusen 156
and LDP factional fighting 42
and reform of central government 109
as welfare zoku 194–5
Council on Fiscal Structural Reform 257–60
credibility undermined 262–3
fiscal system reform 256–9
minister of admin. reform 45, 195
minister of finance 139, 140
party posts 190, 195
PM 44
policy-paralysis 30–1
six visions' 67–72, 109, 256
U-turn 31
Hata, Tsutomo:
and LDP de-alignment 42
minister of finance 139
PM 43
Hayami, Masaru 182
Hayashi, Yoshirō 321
Hokkaido Development Agency (HDA):
bureaux 113
cost/benefit 450
staff 413, 416, 417
Hiraiwa, Gaishi:
Chairman of Economic Council 266
Hiraiwa Report 266
Hokkaido-Tōhoku Development Finance Corporation:
control of 154
functions 478
Honshū-Shikoku Bridge Authority 516, 561
Hosokawa, Morihiro:
and administrative reform 60, 65
downfall 242
leader of Nihon Shintō 42
PM 42–3
policy-making in coalition 201–2
House of Councillors 182–3, 188, 190–1, 205, 241, 262, 339, 431, 455
House of Representatives 33–4, 37, 40, 78, 182–3, 188, 190–1, 205, 240, 256, 263
Budget Committee 41, 339
conduct of elections to 47
elections for 45, 436, 475
Housing and Urban Development Corporation (HUDC):
budget process 359–60

Index

Housing and Urban Development
    Corporation (*Contd.*)
  capital 359
  FILP and 561, 570
  subsidies 557–9
  title 103, 359
Hyōgō Regional Bank 179

Ikeda, Hayato 11–12
Industrial Investment Special Account
  set up 223
  funds for 223–4
Industry Competitiveness Council 69, 267
Institutionalism:
  historical 3, 87
  'rat choicers' 3, 83–5
  sociological 3
International Finance Bureau (MOF) 176
  created 149
  functions 149, 158
  retitled 149, 158
Ishi, Hiromitsu 445

Japan Bank for International Cooperation 103, 559
Japan Development Bank (JDB):
  allocates funds 363–4
  amakudari in 180
  'cow-bell' effect 562
  discretionary authority 363
  FILP funds unused 561
  FILP share declining 551
  lending rates 364, 556
  merged 103
  MOF control of 154–5
  negotiates FILP funds of 357
  planned budget 1994 476–7
  raising money 358
  role 475–7, 561–2
  title 103, 154
Japan Finance Corporation for Municipal
    Enterprises (JFCME):
  amakudari in 180
  control of 154
  functions 361
  local enterprises 361
  local government bonds and 234–5, 467
  subsidies 559
Japan Finance Corporation for Small
    Businesses:
  control of 154–5
  FILP funds unused 561
  functions 478
  merged 103
  subsidies 559
Japan Highway Corporation 360, 450
  subsidies 559, 574, 582

Japan International Cooperation Agency (JICA):
  created 117
  secondments to 133–4
Japan National Railways (JNR):
  debts 355, 515, 516, 517
  loans to 557
  sale of shares 58
Japan Socialist Party/Social Democratic Party
    (JSP/SDP):
  abandons socialism 43
  consumption tax *volte face* 242, 331, 333
  defence policy 41, 289, 308, 330
  in coalition 43–4
  obstructs budget 40–1, 582
  taxation 383
  see also Murayama
Japan Tobacco and Salt Co 179
  MOF control of 154
  sale of shares 58
Jiyūtō (Liberal Party) 158, 263
  coalition with LDP 45
  formed 44
JNR Debt Settlement Corporation:
  abolition of 103
  capital transfer 523
  debt transferred 570
  deficit of 102
  subsidies to 102, 557
Johnson, Chalmers:
  and 'development state' 76
Jusen:
  collapse 32, 436
  financing of 155, 156

Kachō:
  and policy-making 104–5, 132
Kaifu, Toshiki 37, 41–2, 108, 138, 139
Kaizuka, Keimei 566
Kajiyama Seiroku 31
  leadership of LDP 42
  party president candidate 44–5
Kanemaru Shin 42, 197
Katō, Hiroshi 127
Katō, Junko:
  taxation policies and politics 6
Katō, Kōichi 31, 160, 258
  attempted *putsch* 45
Keidanren:
  postal services 110
  reform and 55, 60
Kōenkai 458, 459
Koizumi, Junichirō:
  and privatization of postal services 110, 566
  Minister of Posts 351
  PM candidate 44–5
Kōmeito 38

Index

New Kōmeito and LDP coalition 45, 158
Komura, Takeshi:
  budget examiner 277
  deputy director-general EPA 67
  enforced resignation from MOF 123, 170
  reform of medical care 277
Kōno, Yōhei:
  President of LDP 43

Large-Scale Retail Law 59, 115–16
Liberal Democratic Party (LDP):
  and '1955 system' 51
  appointments in 185
  cabinets 37
  centralization of 35
  coalition with JSP 43
  coalition with Liberal Party 158
  coalition with New Kōmeitō 158
  constraints on power 40–2
  coordinator of policy making 130–1
  criticizes MOF 156, 205
  de-alignment 42–3
  distributes benefits and favours 98–9, 454–5, 457–8, 484
  domestic crises 22
  dominance of 21
  dominance of in Murayama coalition policy-making 202–4
  elections to Diet 37–8, 44, 241
  electoral preoccupation 34–5
  electoral strategy 39, 436, 454–5
  electoral system and 35, 84
  factional competition 21
  in government 1996–2000 44–5
  influence in policy-making 82–6, 194
  kōenkai 458, 559
  leadership of 185
  leadership's role in policy-making 282
  machinery of government and 108
  MOF links with 182, 184
  organizational structure 186–7
  policy networks 193
  policy-making control of 205–6
  policy-making in coalition governments 1993–96 201–5
  policy-making structures 185–206
  preferment in 99–100
  prime ministers and governments 38–9
  recruitment to 36
  relationships with bureaucrats in Hosokawa coalition 202
  rural interests in 458
  Tanaka-Takeshita-Obuchi faction 36, 41–2, 44, 46, 456
  see also PARC; LDP and budget processes; public works; *zoku*; policymaking

LDP and budget processes:
  appearance and reality 365–6, 409
  approves spending controls 408–9
  budget bureau's negotiations 368–9
  budget requests in ministries 305–8, 310–11, 367–8
  budget strategy 284–7, 289–90, 366–7
  'credit-claiming' 373, 403, 459
  indirect and implicit influence 371–3
  influence 334–4, 365–74, 581
  institutionalized consultation 370–1
  'knowing the LDP's mind' 372
  modes of influence 369–71
  monitors budget negotiations 325–9
  negotiated discretion 373–4
  outputs 369, 408–9
  public works 431, 438, 448, 454–5, 456
  resolves conflict in 329
  'revival negotiations' 334–9, 368–9, 401–3
  supplementary budgets 290
  symbolic influence 337, 369
  see also PARC; *zoku*; LDP
Liberal Party *see* Jiyūtō
Local Government Finance 213–14
  control of by MOF 213–14, 506–7
  FILP funds for 234–5, 356–7, 360–1, 560–1
  liabilities in GG 534
  loan permits 214, 234–5
  local allocation tax (LAT) 214, 491, 508
  local bonds 234–5, 356, 510
  local loans programme 214
  local public enterprises 234, 361
  local transfer tax (LTT) 214, 508, 509–10
  plan 213–14, 508, 510
  public investment 419–20
  revenues 507–9, 510
  transfer payments from budget to 214, 385, 508, 511
Louvre Accord 430, 525, 530

Maekawa Reports 26, 59, 60
Management and Coordination Agency (MCA):
  coordinating 125–6
  de-regulation 61–3
  embedded loyalties 112
  staff cuts plans 411–18
Market Oriented Sector Selective (MOSS) 50, 59
Matsushita, Yasuo 181
Medium-term Fiscal Projection 54, 256, 267, 268–9, 496
  alternative projections 268–9
  and fiscal aims 247–8
  inaugurated 242, 247
  Medium-term Fiscal Outlook 269
  preparation 152, 268–9
  purpose 247, 169

METI 109
Mieno, Yasushi 181
Minister of Finance 138-9
  budget conference 320
  former MOF official 139, 184
  policy-making 139
  staff 122, 139
  stepping stone 139
  Takemura as 139
  See also Budget Bureau
Minister's Secretariat (MOF) 141-5
  arranged marriages 164
  functions 141
  policy coordination 145, 150
  policy coordination division 141, 143
  research and planning division 144
  secretarial division 141, 143, 167
  senior staff 141
  see also MOF
Ministry of Agriculture, Food, and Fisheries (MAFF):
  2001 reorganization 109-12
  administrative vice-ministers in 103
  allocation in 304
  allocations to 386-91
  amakudari 101
  avoids cut-back 302-3
  biotech policy 117
  coordination division 119
  jurisdiction 115
  mobilizes support 307-8
  MOC and 444
  ODA 117
  origins 93-6
  plans 290
  priority programmes 302
  public corporations 101-3
  public works 422-4, 426, 435-6, 440, 441, 443, 444, 445, 450, 455, 457
  retirees 174
  staff 122, 413, 416
  zoku and 197, 308
Ministry of Construction (MOC):
  administrative vice-ministers 103
  allocations to 386-91
  amakudari 101
  budget strategy 293
  bureaux 113
  city bureau 440
  FILP agencies 357, 360
  globalization 126
  grand secretariat 107
  housing bureau 440
  HUDC's budget 359-60
  jurisdiction 115, 117

kensetsu zoku and 200
MAFF and 444
merged in 2001 109-12
mobilizes support 307
Nakasone and land-use reform 121
origins 93-6
plans 290
policy-making 293-4
public corporations 101-3
public works 422-4, 426, 435-6, 440-1, 445, 450, 453, 460
re-employment of retirees 174
river bureau 110, 294, 297, 440, 456
road bureau 440, 456
staff 413, 416
telecoms 117
zoku influentials 307
Ministry of Education (MOE) 71
  allocations to 386-91
  biotech policy 117
  budget and accounts division 300-1
  coordination division 120
  merged in 2001 109-12
  Nakasone and reform 121
  origins 93-6
  staff 416
  strategic aims 293
Ministry of Finance (MOF) 137-58
  advisory councils 74, 128, 153, 158
  appointments in BOJ 138
  banks and 33, 50-1, 155-6
  blame for policy failures 70, 155-6
  budgetary function 157
  budgets coordinated 216-17
  bureaux 140-2
  bureaux cross-pressured 349-50
  cabinet councillor post 123
  capital projects financed in two budgets 217, 563
  coordination in 145, 149-53
  coordinator 129-30
  corrupt behaviour 156
  crisis of confidence and authority 155
  declining power 1, 155-8, 333, 592
  economic role 138, 158
  establishment law 1949 137
  executive council 150-1
  FILP's fiscal role 563
  fiscal system research council 152-3, 248, 258, 265, 269-70
  functions 137-9, 157-8
  GDP forecasting role 125, 144
  hours of work 165
  interviews in 7-8
  junior ministers 139
  local bond plan 234-5

Index 623

local government finance 213–14, 234
monetary policy 145
origins of 93–6
patronage 101–2, 180–1
PM's secretary 120
public banks and corporations 101–3, 154–5
Rinchō and 54–8
small businesses 401–2
staff 140–1, 416
structural corruption in 134
target of reforms in 2001 110, 157, 592–3
'wining and dining' scandal 157, 333
see also Budget Bureau; Minister's Secretariat; minister of finance; MOF's elite bureaucrats; director-general
Ministry of Foreign Affairs (MOFA):
allocations 304, 386, 391
budget and accounts division 300
cabinet councillor post 123
globalization 126
grand secretariat 107
informal budget plans 295
key posts 104
ODA budget 117, 122, 323
origins 93–6
PM's secretary 120
reorganization of 2001 109–12
retirement posts in OECF and JICA 134
secondments 133
staff 416
see also ODA
Ministry of Health, Labour, and Welfare 109
Ministry of Health and Welfare (MHW) 124
and ODA 303
allocations to 386–91
biotech policy 117
merged in 2001 109–12
origins 93–6
Pension Welfare Services Corporation 349–52, 562
pensions funds 562–3, 565, 566, 570, 576–7
prestige 98
public works 422–4, 426, 435–6, 445
retirees 174
staff 122, 416
Ministry of Home Affairs (MHA) 124
allocations to 386–91
budget processes 309–10
decentralization 98
merged in 2001 109–12
origins 93–4
secondments 133
staff 416
Ministry of International Trade and Industry (MITI) 23
administrative vice-ministers 103
allocations to 386–91
amakudari 101
biotech policy 117
budget strategy coordination 298–300
coordination division 119
economic reform and 66
GDP forecasts 125
industrial policy regime 80–1
jurisdiction 115
Large-Scale Retail Stores Law 115–16
LDP 192
ODA 117
origins 93–5
PM's secretary 120
policy planning committee 293–4
public corporations 101–3
public works 422–4, 435–6
reorganization of 2001 109–12
rotation of officials 299–300
science and technology policy 281–2
secondments 132–4
'shadow cabinet' 293
small businesses 401–2
staff 416
telecoms 117
turf fights 116–17
'vision for the 1970s' 24
Ministry of Justice (MOJ):
and reorganization of 2001 109
origins 93–6
staff 416
Ministry of Labour (MOL):
allocations to 386–91
budget guidelines 295
budget hearings 305
bureau plans 292–3
coordination division 119
coordination in 298
merged in 2001 109
origins 93–6
plans 290
small businesses 401–2
staff 122, 413, 416
Ministry of Land, Transport, and Infrastructure 110, 113
Ministry of Posts and Telecommunications (MPT):
allocations to 386–91
amakudari 101
capital market operations 225–6, 348–52, 565, 570, 576–7
conflict with MOF 350–2, 562–3
globalization 126
grand secretariat 107

Ministry of Posts and Telecommunications (*Contd.*)
  merged in 2001 110–12
  origins 93–6
  postal life insurance fund 223
  postal savings 215–16, 350–1, 562–3, 565, 570
  postal savings privatization 565
  public corporations 101–3
  staff 416
  telecom wars 117
Ministry of Public Management 110–11
  policy evaluation 573, 595
Ministry of Transport (MOT):
  administrative vice-ministers in 103
  allocations to 386–91
  bureaux 113
  coordination division 119
  globalization 126
  merged in 2001 110–12
  origins 93–6
  public works 422–4, 426, 435–6, 440, 441–2, 445, 450
  staff 416
  telecom wars 117
Mint 100, 414–16
Mitsuzuka, Hiroshi 44
Miyazawa, Kiichi 41, 45, 108, 120, 138, 160, 184
MOF's elite bureaucrats 159–84
  administrative vice-minister 103, 170, 172
  administrative vice-ministers 'family' 180–2
  administrative vice-ministers retirement posts 176, 178
  amakudari practice questioned 173, 182
  as LDP Dietmen 182–4, 459
  career norms 165
  characteristics 159
  class cohorts 168
  core divisions 168, 169
  deputy director of division 166–7
  director of division 167
  en stage training 166
  erīto kōsu 167
  Governor of BOJ 181–2
  high-flyers 167–8, 169
  improper and corrupt behaviour 333
  induction 165–6
  influence on postings 167
  influence on retirement posts 173–4, 179–80
  LDP and 183–4
  monopoly of posts in some banks 176–7, 178
  norms of behaviour 340
  recruitment 159–61
  re-employment within 2 years 174
  retirement 134, 173–84
  retirement age 173
  retirement into PFCs 179–80
  retirement into politics 182–4
  retirement into private banking 176–9
  retirement into private sector 174–5
  retirement into public sector 179–82
  retirement options 175
  retirement to financial institutions 174
  rotation of posts 166–8
  secondments to ministries 132–3, 155, 168
  senior bureaucrats 169–70
  seniority rule 168–9
  small and medium-sized financial institutions influence in 178–9
  socialization 161–4
  strategic secondments in EPA 67, 125, 138
  succession to top posts 170–1
  Tokyo law faculty 160–1, 172
  women 161
  working conditions and norms 164–5
  see also amakudari; bureaucrats; MOF; minister's secretariat (MOF)
Mori, Yoshirō 45
Murayama, Tomiichi 330
  and admin. reform 60
  coalition and policy-making 202–4
  consumption tax rise 333
  PM 43
Muto, Toshirō 172

Nakao Eiichi 459
Nakasone, Yasuhiro 71, 108, 139, 198, 233, 257, 285
  consumption tax fails 40
  director-general of AMA 54
  president of LDP 37
  presidential style as PM 120–1
  rules out VAT 240
  strong-yen strategy 26
  use of advisory bodies 121–2, 129
National Debt Consolidation Fund Special Account 211, 511–12, 513, 515
  NTT scheme and 429, 431–2, 518
National Economic Plan 67, 69, 248–9, 252, 264–7, 356
  1970–73 23
  1979–85 252, 422
  1988–92 252, 422
  1992–96 265–6, 354
  1995–2000 266, 354
  1999–2010 267
  Economic Council and 265–7
National Forestry Service Special Account:
  capital transfer 523
  debts 516, 517, 570
  staff cuts 415

National Graduate School of Policy Studies 163
National Land Agency (NLA) 124
  bureaux 112
  coordination 125
  grand secretariat 107
  public works 450
  staff 416
National Life Finance Corporation 103
National Personnel Authority 71, 159, 163, 174, 176, 182
National Public Safety Commission
  and National Police Agency 93, 119, 120, 122, 123, 124
  in 2001 reorganization 109–10
  origins 93–6
  within PM's Office 97
'New FILP' 570–7
  accountability 575
  accounting principles 574–5
  behaviour of FILP agencies 576–7
  cost-benefit 574
  defined 572
  effects and implications 572–7
  FILP agency bonds 571–2, 572–3, 577
  FILP bonds 571–2, 573, 577
  financing FILP agencies 572–3
  Fiscal Loan Fund 571–2
  functions 572
  market-driven 572, 576–7
  policy evaluation 573
  structure 571–2
  subsidy cost analysis 574
  transition to 575–6
  transparency 574–5
  see also FILP
New Kōmeitō 45
Nikkeiren 60
Norio, Ohga 202
North, Douglas 2
NTT 197, 224, 515
  created 95
  sale of shares 58, 149, 429
  'telecom wars' 351
NTT Scheme 283, 429–32, 518
  continuation problems 431–2
  'cost deferred' 431
  distorts public works budget 432
  loan types 429
  origins 430
  redemption of loans 432
  relieves budget pressure 430–1
  underwritten 432
National Tax Administration Agency (NTTA) 153, 172, 179, 181
  bureaux 147–9
  director's status 148

functions 154
retirees from 175
staff 140

Obuchi, Keizō:
  and economic recovery 263
  and factions 42, 44
  and revival of economy 69
  death 45
  Minister of Foreign Affairs 44
  PM 44
  style of council politics as PM 121
'Off-budget' 404, 405, 409–34, 506
  exclusion from GG 593
  public works 425–34, 448, 455
  sources of 581
  supplementary budgets 209–10, 290
Ō'Hira, Masayoshi 121, 139, 239
  and fiscal crisis 242, 243
  minister of finance 54, 243
Okinawa Development Agency (OkDA):
  cost/benefit 450
  staff 416
Okinawa Development Finance Corporation:
  control of 154
  functions 478
Ōkurashō (MOF):
  great storehouse ministry 137
  title changed 155
  as Zaimshō 1
Olsen, J.P. 3
Overseas Development Aid (ODA):
  diplomatic tool 121–2
  growth 391, 393
  LDP and policymaking for 192, 194
  policymaking for 116, 133, 150, 194
  priority status conferred 281, 292
  programmes 259
Overseas Economic Cooperation Fund (OECF):
  capital loans to 557
  ODA 117
  secondments to 133–4
Oxbridge 163
Ozawa, Ichirō 156, 263
  and Ichi-Ichi line 202
  and LDP split 42
  as Secretary-General 42
  eminence grise 202
  national welfare tax 43

Parliamentary Vice-Ministers:
  Diet answers and 205
  number of 99, 205
Pension funds:
  FILP de-coupling 564, 566–7, 569–70, 571, 576
  subsidies suspended 515

Pension funds (*Contd.*)
  TFBF deposits 223–4, 225–6, 228, 352–3, 355
  see also TFBF
Pensions programme:
  budget outputs 393–4
  revival negotiations 403
Pension Welfare Services Public Corporation:
  capital market operations 225, 227, 228, 562
  control by MHW 349–52
  deposits in FILP 349
People's Finance Corporation:
  amakudari in 179–80
  FILP funds 483
  functions 478
  loans 482–3
  merged 103
  MOF control of 154–5, 563
  subsidies 559
  title 103
Plaza Accord 26, 28, 29, 121, 249–50
Policy Affairs Research Council (PARC)
  acting chairman's key role in 130–1, 190
  and LDP's policy-making structures 189
  budget requests and 305–7
  budget strategy role 285–6
  chairmanship of 190
  commerce and industry division 192
  commissions and committees 185
  division and ministry 193–4
  divisions 98–9, 185, 188, 190–1
  education division 192
  Executive Council of LDP and 188, 190
  FILP reform involvement 567
  integrated into policy-making processes 190
  Murayama coalition and 202–4
  ODA policy and 192, 194
  policy deliberation commission 185, 188, 322
  policymaking role 185–94
  politicians and bureaucrats 191–2, 193
  role 130–1, 185, 188, 322
  see also LDP; *zoku giin*
Policy coordination:
  agencies for 125–7
  biotechnology 117, 131
  formal processes of 129–31
  ill coordinated 124–5
  informal processes of 131–4
  inter-ministerial 118–36, 119
  organizational 118–29
  prerequisites of 118
  role of LDP in 130–1
  structures in coalitions 201, 202–4
  telecomms. 117
  UK and France 136
  zoku's role in 196–201

  see also policymaking; LDP and budgetary processes; rules-of-the-game; *zoku*; PARC
Policy Coordinating Council 331–2
Policy evaluation 573, 595
Policymaking:
  administrative guidance 115–16
  competition and conflict in 77–9, 114–36
  control of by politicians 205–6
  'counter revisionists' and 79–81
  extra-legal processes 115
  for ODA 116, 133, 150, 192, 194
  'governance by negotiation' 81–3
  in coalition governments 201–5
  in new policy areas 116–18
  industrial 80–1
  key posts in 104–7
  LDP influence in 78–9, 82–6
  minister of finance's role 139
  MITI's role in 80–1
  neo-pluralists and 77–9
  patterned pluralism in 77
  processes 75–90
  rational choice 83–5
  revisionists and 75–6
  'top down' 112–13
  see also policy coordination; LDP and budgetary processes; budget processes; rules-of-the-game
Politico-economy:
  '1940 system' 51
  '1955 system' 51
  changing 45–52
  context 21–52
  emergence of new order 51–2
  'regime shift' 46–50
Population:
  ageing of 18, 549
Postal Life Insurance Fund 223
  capital growth of 225–6
  interest rates on deposits of with TFBF 228–9
  profit and loss 480
  see also Trust Fund Bureau Fund; MPT
Postal savings 71
  assets and liabilities 554
  banks compete with 552, 565
  FILP source 215, 223–4, 225–6, 352–3, 355, 564, 566–7, 568, 569–70, 571, 576
  growth 553–4, 565
  interest rates control of 349–50
  politics of 348–52
  privatization 565–6
  special account 225–6, 562–3
  system set up 215–16
  TFBF deposits 228–9
  withdrawals 575–6

Index

see also MPT; TFBF
Postal Service 197
  and MPT 100
  privatization 110, 566
  staff cuts 415–16
Prefectures 457–8
Prime Minister:
  and Hanshin-Awaji earthquake 124
  as former MOF official 184
  budget strategy 288–9
  post created 93
  powers 120–1
  private secretaries 120
  role in budget strategy 285–6
  see also Hashimoto; Nakasone; Murayama; Obuchi; Takeshita
Prime Minister's Office:
  agencies within 96–7
  cabinet councillor post 123
  created 93–6
  reorganization 2001 110
  staff 416, 417
Privatization:
  postal service 110, 566
  sale of shares 58–9
Provisional Council for the Promotion of Administrative Reform (PCPAR) 246, 248, 258
  and inter-ministerial coordination 126–7
  and public corporations 65
  limited impact of 59–60
  succeeds Rinchō 58
  work in 1980s 58–60
Public corporations:
  accounting principles 574–5
  amakudari source 101–2
  coordinators 133–4
  defined 100
  FILP agencies as 101, 231–2, 233–4, 573, 577
  functions 65, 100–3
  ministries and 101–2, 573, 577
  MOF's PFCs 154–5
  policy evaluation 573
  reduction 58–9
  titular changes to 103
  see also PFCs
Public expenditure:
  encyclopaedia of 54, 56
  failure to control 580–4
  growth of 1965–74 14, 520–1
  restraint 502–6
  tax revenues and 1971–82 16
  see also General Account Budget; supplementary budgets; budget outputs; budget policies; fiscal reconstruction; budget guidelines

Public Finance Corporations (PFCs) 212–13
  Diet and 362
  FILP agencies as 101–2, 231, 232–3, 356
  FILP allocations 467–9
  functions 212–13
  in FILP system 233
  industrial development 478–80
  loans of 228–9, 556
  MOF control 154–5, 356
  numbers 102–3
  policy evaluation 573
  subsidies to 558–9
  'winners and losers' 468–9
  see also public corporations
Public Investment:
  ad hoc programmes 282
  Basic Plan for 252, 260, 287, 354, 422, 430, 446
  budget guidelines 279–81, 286–7
  budget programmes 282–3
  central government 419–20
  cuts in 260
  General Government 419
  gross domestic totals 419
  'public facilities' 420
  sectoral programmes 287
  see also public works; Structural Impediments Initiative
Public sector:
  change in 73–4
  compared in G7 72
  maturity in 580
  multi-layered 91
  role and size 47–8, 73, 410
Public works 281, 419–60
  ad hoc schemes 425
  agricultural-related 457
  allocation of budget for 434–47
  allocation within bureaux 442, 444
  allocation within ministries 437, 439–42, 443, 456
  appearance and reality 433–4, 447–50, 455
  'balance and fair shares' 434, 442, 444, 449, 456
  Budget Bureau and 286
  budget composition 437, 438, 439
  budget examiner for 286
  cancelled projects 451, 460
  capped 446
  categories 420–1
  characteristics 421
  contracts 458–9
  corruption 459
  countercyclical packages 427–9, 452
  'credit claiming' 459
  'crowding out' 453

Public works (*Contd.*)
  defined 420–2
  efficiency and effectiveness 450–4
  FILP finance for 432–3, 577
  General Account Budget outputs 393–3, 394, 424–5
  geo-electoral distribution 457–8
  guidelines 424–5
  inflexible allocation 434–5, 436–7, 449
  IT projects 303
  local government 420–1, 449, 451, 452–3
  local schemes 459
  NTT scheme 429–432
  'off budget' effects 433–4, 448, 455
  'off-budget' sources 425–434
  planned and real changes 426–7
  plans 422–4
  political expediency 431, 448
  political salience 454–5, 457
  prefectural distribution 457–8
  pressures for more 448
  prioritization 281, 436, 444–7, 457
  productivity effect 451
  project costs 453–4
  proposed reduction 453–4
  public criticism 460
  'public works state' 454–60
  rationale 421
  reform of 437
  rice-market opening and 260
  sectors 422–4
  Special Accounts 420, 449
  spending calculation 286–7
  Supplementary budgets 425–9
  under-spending 446–7, 450–1
  see also Public Investment; Supplementary Budgets; countercyclical; FILP; FILP outputs

Recruit-Cosmos 37, 41, 240, 431
Regulations 62–3 *see* deregulation
Revenue:
  burden 489, 491, 494, 495
  collapse of bubble economy on 252
  composition 489–92
  consumption tax 30, 239–42, 333, 491–3, 507
  direct/indirect tax ratio 489–93, 494
  estimates revised 276, 496
  falling 494
  fiscal reconstruction 488–94, 507
  'fiscal reconstruction without tax increase' 53–8, 240
  hypothecation 493
  national welfare tax 43, 156
  national welfare tax proposed and abandoned 242, 494
  'natural tax increases' 9–10, 211, 244–5, 512
  over-estimated yields 496–7
  rules-of-the-game 9–10, 244–5, 496
  shortages and surpluses 496–7
  shortfall issue dormant 241
  tax structure reform 239–42, 247, 249, 333, 518–19, 580
  tax/national income ratio 244, 489
  tax shortages and surpluses 497
  'windfall revenues' 529
  see also General Account Budget; Tax System Research Council; Tax Policy Research Committee; consumption tax
Rinchō 242–3, 413, 489
  agenda and work 55–57
  and MOF's budget dominance 55–58
  dissolved 58
  fiscal reconstruction 243
  launched 53
  membership 54
  proposes merger of agencies 135
  reports 56
  see also PCPAR
Road Improvement Special Account 213, 216
Road programme 217
  special account for 213
Rules-of-the-game 99–100, 135–6, 170, 258, 278, 297, 315–16, 324, 325, 329, 366, 373–4, 382, 496
  administrative guidance 115
  avoiding surprise 344–5
  bureaucratic behavioural 131–4, 366, 593
  capital and current spending 383–4
  Diet business 40
  implementing fiscal policy 244–6
  informal policy 344
  MOF and spending ministries 340–5
  negotiated discretion 373–4, 583, 593
  policy 366, 495
  revenue 9–10, 244–5, 496

Sagawa Kyūbin 437, 458–9
Saito, Jirō 181
  administrative vice-minister MOF 139
  and national welfare tax 156
  proto-typical MOF career 170
Sakaiya, Taichi 267
Sakakibara, Eisuke:
  'public works state' 454
  reprimanded 157
Sakigake (New Harbinger Party) 42–3, 44
Satō, Kōku 44
SCAP:
  reforms of 51, 93–6, 137
Science and technology:
  budget programme 281–2

Index

Second Budget see FILP
Securities and Exchange Surveillance Commission (MOF) 140
Securities Bureau (MOF) 140, 148, 156–7, 161, 174
Self-Defence Forces (SDF) 124–5, 308–9, 401, 410–11
  and earthquake 124–5
  see also Defence Agency
Settlement Adjustment Fund 512, 152
Shinkansen:
  political pressure for 338, 403, 447, 455
Shinozawa, Kyosuke 170
Shinseitō (Japan Renewal Party) 42, 444
Shinshintō (Japan New Party) 42, 44
Shōkō Chūkin 101
Shoup mission 14, 23
Small Business Credit Insurance Corporation
  control of 154
Small businesses programme:
  budget allocation 401–2
  budget outputs 393–4, 395, 396
Social Democratic Party (SDP) 242
  see also Japan Socialist Party
Social security:
  additional resources 281
  allocation to 282
  budget unpacked 396–8
  differential budget misery 397
  'envisioned' reform of 71–2
  exempt from cutback 281–2, 302
  funds 525–6
  growth 391, 393
  'partially funded system' 525–6
  pension costs in 549
  revival negotiations 388, 403
  special accounts 526
  sub-programmes budget outputs 396–8
  surplus on 524–5
  transfer payments 11
Special Accounts 211–12
  FILP funded 232, 234
  MOF manipulation 515–17
  public works 420, 449
  social security 526
Spending ministries and agencies, 91–113
  and public corporations 101–3
  'bottom line' 386
  budget and accounts division (BAD) 287–8, 291, 292, 294, 295–6, 300–1, 301–5, 314–15, 343–5
  budget ceilings 287–90, 301–5
  budget guidelines 295–6, 303
  budget negotiations 322–5
  budget process 291–311
  budget requests 100, 291

budget requests to MOF 312–13
budget winners/losers 386–91
bureaux and divisions in 104–7, 113, 292
continuity and change 93–6, 107–8
general affairs division in 119
hearings at Budget Bureau 313–17
in 1975–2000 92
in 2001 109–10
internal organization of 103–7
interviews in 7–8
jurisdictions and conflicts of 112, 114–16, 134–5
LDP influence on budget 305–8
lobby LDP 328
medium-term plans 292–3
minister's secretariat 106–7, 294
numbers 70, 109–10, 386
organizational types of 96–8
policy evaluation 573
posts in 104–7
reorganization of 107–13, 592–3
'revival budget negotiations' 334–9
'scrap and build' 65, 106, 297
secondments 132–4
secret covenants 132
staff numbers 410–18
status of 96–9
zoku, interest groups and 198, 201
  see also central government; policy coordination
Science and Technology Agency (STA) 116
  biotech policy 117
  policy coordination 125
  staff 416
Semiconductor Trade Agreement 50
Single Non-Transferable Vote (SNTV) 21, 43
Structural Impediments Initiative 28, 59, 252, 282, 354, 430, 530
Supplementary budgets 209–10
  counter cyclical 427–9
  difference from General Account Budget 210
  effects on spending plans 378–81, 406–7, 504–5, 520–1, 581–2
  FILP in-year changes 362–3
  institutionalized in budget process 209
  not subject to budget guidelines 210, 290
  number of in 1990s 209
  'off budget' public works 425–9
  preparation of 145, 290
  purpose of 209–10
  save MOF's face 290
  use of 210
  see also General Account Budget; fiscal reconstruction; public works
System of National Accounts (SNA) 522
Suzuki, Zenkō 54, 55, 57, 121, 139, 242

Takemura, Masayoshi 139, 156, 181, 321, 454
Takeshita, Noboru 108, 138, 185, 257, 285, 321, 329
  minister of finance 139
  Recruit-Cosmos scandal 41
  resignation as PM 42, 431
Tanaka, Kakuei 5, 76, 78, 170, 199, 233, 246, 518
  and 'building a new Japan' 23
  and political-bureaucratic network 36
  arrest 35
  conversion to big government 13
  private secretary 120
Tanaka-Takeshita faction 36, 41–2, 44, 46, 456
Tanami, Koiji 123, 170–1
Taxation *see* revenue
Tax Bureau (MOF) 153, 174, 276
  functions 147–8
  national welfare tax 150
Tax Policy Research Committee (LDP) 153, 191, 249, 269, 331
Tax System Research Council (of Government) 153, 239, 266, 270, 493
  land-tax rejected 28
  method of working 127
  proposes consumption tax 240
  recommends radical reform 241–2, 249, 493
  role 153, 270
  see also revenue
Taya, Hiroaki 172
Terasawa, Yoshio 274
Thain, C. and Wright, M. 2
Tōkai-mura:
  plutonium leak 125
Tokyo Law Faculty 160–1, 162, 163, 170, 172, 174
Tokyo University 159, 160, 161–2, 163, 172, 184
Treasury, H.M. (UK):
  behavioural norms 342, 345
  interviews in 7
  negotiated discretion 6
  planning and control of spending 2
  rules-of-the-game 316
Trust Fund Bureau Fund:
  advanced repayment to 569–70
  assets 364
  assets and liabilities mismatch 554–5, 567
  available for FILP 224, 352–3, 355, 364, 564, 566–7, 576
  capital market operations 224–8, 569, 570
  composition of 224
  deposits in 223, 564
  interest rate risk 555–6
  interest rates for deposits with 228, 364, 554, 555
  profit and loss 480
  purpose 223
  set up 216, 220
  size of 223, 570
  wound-up 571
  see also FILP; 'New FILP'; Financial Bureau; postal savings; pension funds; Postal Life Insurance Fund

UK:
  budget surplus 550
  civil service 168
  Executive Agencies 109, 113
  fiscal code 588–9
  fiscal performance: see G7
  fiscal rules 590
  'giant departments' 113
  new control regime 591
  policy coordination 136
Unemployment 28–9
Uno, Sōsuke 37, 41–2, 139, 431
Urban Development Corporation 103 *see* HUDC

USA:
  budget surplus 549–50
  fiscal performance: see G7
  policymaking 84–5
  top-down limits 590
Usui, Nobuaki 172

Wakui, Yoji 170, 171–2
Welfare Era:
  beginning of 13
Wildavsky Aaron:
  theory of government growth 1

Yamaichi Securities 32
'Yen bubble' 29, 50

Zenekon 458
Zoku-giin (Policy tribes) 36, 194–201
  agricultural 197, 204
  budget allocations 308, 459
  budget requests and 307–8
  case-studies of 200–1
  defence 197, 282
  defined 194
  dimensions of influence 198
  education 194, 198
  'guard dogs' 196–7, 198
  Hashimoto as 194–5
  'hunting dogs' 197, 198
  influence in coalitions 204
  Kensetsu 201
  mediator 197–8
  ministerial budget requests 307–8
  ministry bureaus and divisions and 201

MOC 307, 459
petition MOF 371
postal 565
'profit inspired' nexus and 198–201
reciprocal obligations 198–9

role and influence 194–7
size and influence 99
status attributed 194
typology of 200
see also LDP; LDP and budgetary processes